THE BILL GATES PROBLEM

The BILL GATES PROBLEM

RECKONING *with the* MYTH *of the* GOOD BILLIONAIRE

TIM SCHWAB

METROPOLITAN BOOKS
HENRY HOLT AND COMPANY
NEW YORK

Metropolitan Books
Henry Holt and Company
Publishers since 1866
120 Broadway
New York, New York 10271
www.henryholt.com

Metropolitan Books® and m® are registered trademarks of
Macmillan Publishing Group, LLC.

Image on page 224: *Bill and Melinda Gates*, Jon R. Friedman, 2010, Oil and collage on canvas attached
to wood panel. National Portrait Gallery, Smithsonian Institution; supported by a grant from the
Donald W. Reynolds Foundation and by the Marc Pachter Commissioning Fund.

Library of Congress Cataloging-in-Publication data is available.

ISBN: 9781250850096

Our books may be purchased in bulk for promotional, educational, or business use. Please contact
your local bookseller or the Macmillan Corporate and Premium Sales Department at (800) 221-7945,
extension 5442, or by e-mail at MacmillanSpecialMarkets@macmillan.com.

First Edition 2023

Designed by Kelly S. Too

Printed in the United States of America

1   3   5   7   9   10   8   6   4   2

For S.S. and S.S.

CONTENTS

Prologue

This is a difficult book to write because it is about a difficult man—one of the world's richest men and one of the most deeply secretive.

Bill Gates did not respond to multiple interview requests for this book, nor did anyone at the Gates Foundation ever agree to an interview at any point in my reporting on the foundation. Even before I published my first article on Gates in early 2020—or established myself as a journalist who would report on the Gates Foundation as a structure of power, not an unimpeachable charity—the foundation refused to sit for any interviews. As I published my investigations in the *Nation*, the *British Medical Journal*, and *Columbia Journalism Review*, the Gates Foundation always assumed a posture of nonengagement.

This silent treatment isn't unique to me. The foundation, as a rule, does not put itself or its leaders in a position where they might be pushed to explain contradictions in its work or forced to answer critical questions. Like any powerful organization, the $54 billion Gates Foundation engages with the media on its own terms.

At the same time, because so many people and institutions today depend on Gates's charitable dollars, many sources are reluctant to speak out for fear of professional consequences. You will find many unnamed sources in this book, and you should not doubt the reasons for their having requested anonymity. "It would be suicidal for someone who wants a grant to come out and publicly criticize the foundation," Mark Kane, a former head of Gates's vaccine work, noted in 2008. "The Gates Foundation is very sensitive to PR."

I also want to state up front why Melinda French Gates does not appear on an equal footing with Bill Gates in this book. It's because she is not an equal to Bill Gates at the Bill & Melinda Gates Foundation. I know this to be true because I've spoken to foundation staff who have made clear that Bill Gates is the alpha and the omega. And I know this because the foundation itself announced it in 2021. Following the Gateses' divorce, the foundation reported that Melinda, not Bill, would step down from the foundation after a two-year trial period if they could not agree to a power-sharing arrangement. It is Bill Gates's vast fortune from Microsoft that funds the foundation, and it is Bill Gates who ultimately is in charge of how the money is spent. This is not to say that Melinda doesn't have a very powerful voice or major impact on the foundation, and I do profile her work throughout the book.

Finally, one note on language: Technically speaking, the Gates Foundation is incorporated under tax rules as a private foundation. I use this term throughout the book, but I also refer to the Gates Foundation as a philanthropy and a charity.

THE BILL GATES PROBLEM

Introduction

You might not recognize the name "Paul Allen."

Allen was a vital spark plug who helped ignite the corporate engine of what became one of the most influential companies in the world, Microsoft. And, for a time, he was both the business partner and the best friend of one of the most powerful men ever to walk the earth.

The name "William Henry Gates III" you also may not immediately recognize. It's a grand name befitting a man who comes from generational wealth and privilege, a man born on third base. Bill Gates's mother came from a well-to-do banking family, and his father was a prominent lawyer in Seattle. As Gates described his upbringing, it was "Okay, this is the governor coming to dinner, or here is this political campaign, let's get involved in this." The family's network of influence afforded Gates unusual opportunities growing up—like serving as a page in both the Washington State legislature and the U.S. Congress.

Paul Allen, by contrast, was a middle-class son of a librarian—his family had to make sacrifices to get him into Seattle's most elite private school, Lakeside, where he befriended Bill Gates. "I was thrown into a forty-eight-member class of the city's elite: the sons of bankers and businessmen, lawyers and UW professors. With scattered exceptions, they were preppy kids who knew each other from private grammar schools or the Seattle Tennis Club," Allen, now deceased, wrote in his autobiography.

Lakeside's wealth meant students there had special privileges, like access to a computer—a rarity in the late 1960s. It was in the school's computer room that Allen formed an unlikely friendship with Gates, two years his junior. "You could tell three things about Bill Gates pretty quickly," Allen remembers. "He was really smart. He was really competitive; he wanted to *show* you how smart he was. And he was really, really persistent."

The boys' passion for computers quickly turned entrepreneurial as they recognized ways to monetize their burgeoning programming skills. The work also proved competitive. When Allen secured a gig working on a payroll program, he thought he could do it without Gates's help. Gates sent him an ominous message. "I said, 'I think you're underestimating how hard this is. If you ask me to come back, I am going to be totally in charge of this and anything you ever ask me to do again,'" Gates recalled. Allen, in fact, did end up needing help on the project, and as Gates explained, "It was just more natural for me to be in charge." With help from his father, Gates went on to legally incorporate their growing computer programming business, naming himself president and claiming a share in the company's earnings four times larger than the share he gave Allen.

After the two boys graduated, they remained close but went in different directions—Allen to the decidedly nonelite public school Washington State University, Gates to Harvard. Allen's unfocused academic career quickly fizzled, and he recounts Gates pushing him to move out East, where the two of them could turn their love of computers into something special. Allen dropped out of college and headed to Boston.

Allen describes himself as the "idea man"—he was constantly bouncing business plans off Gates, who played the role of the boss, and who usually shut Allen down. As Bill Gates remembers it, "We were always talking about, 'Could we stick a lot of microprocessors together to do something powerful? Could we do a 360 emulator using micro controllers? Could we do a time-sharing system where lots of people could dial-in and get consumer information?' A lot of different ideas."

After months of throwing the dart, Allen eventually hit upon a bull's-eye idea that Gates liked: writing a programming language for one of the world's first widely available home computers, the Altair. Gates cold-called the company's headquarters in New Mexico from his Harvard dorm room and, in classic Gates fashion, bluffed that he had new software for the Altair in development, nearly up and running. The company invited him to fly out to demonstrate the product. Gates and Allen spent a grueling eight weeks working to pull the program together. When it came time to meet with Altair, Paul Allen took the flight. Though he wasn't the dead-eyed bullshit artist Gates was, he at least looked like an adult. Gates, even well into adulthood, was renowned for his boyish appearance, which Microsoft later leaned into, promoting him as a whiz kid.

The business deal went through and brought enough success that Gates eventually dropped out of Harvard to focus on his new company. And it was *his* company, as Allen quickly learned. Even though Allen had played a vital and central role in the Altair deal—he also coined the name "Microsoft," a portmanteau of *microprocessor* and *software*—Gates immediately insisted on majority ownership, taking 60 percent of the company. Allen remembers being taken aback by his business partner's assertion of power, but he didn't argue.

Gates, apparently realizing how easy that deal had been, shamelessly brought Allen back into negotiations, where he claimed an even larger share. "I've done most of the work . . . and I gave up a lot to leave Harvard," he said. "I deserve more than 60 percent."

"How much more?"

"I was thinking 64–36."

Allen writes that he didn't have the heart to dicker with Gates, but the deeper truth, as I read it, was that he couldn't accept what was really happening: his best friend was screwing him. "Later, after our relationship changed, I wondered how Bill arrived at the numbers he'd proposed that day. I tried to put myself in his shoes and reconstruct his thinking, and I concluded that it was just this simple: *What's the most I can get?* . . . He might have argued that the numbers reflected our contributions, but they also exposed the differences between the son of a librarian and the son of a lawyer. I'd been taught that a deal was a deal and your word was your bond. Bill was more flexible."

As Microsoft grew, eventually relocating to Seattle, Allen continued to be an idea man. He recounts coming up with an important work-around that enabled Microsoft software to work on Apple computers, using a hardware device called the SoftCard. The product opened up a broad new market for Microsoft and drove millions of dollars in much-needed revenue in 1981. Allen, still wanting to believe that he and Gates were partners and peers, decided to use the success of SoftCard as leverage to press Gates for a larger share of the company. If Gates could renegotiate their percentages, why couldn't he?

"I don't ever want to talk about this again," Gates told him, shutting him down. "Do not bring it up."

"In that moment something died for me," Allen reflects. "I thought that our partnership was based on fairness, but now I saw that Bill's self-interest overrode all other considerations. My partner was out to grab as much of the pie as possible and hold on to it, and that was something I could not accept."

In a final ignominy, Allen, while recovering from treatment for the non-Hodgkin's lymphoma that eventually took his life, overheard Gates discussing a plan to dilute his shares, further diminishing his ownership stake in the company. After having strong-armed Allen to reduce his share in the company from 50 percent to 40 percent and then to 36 percent, Gates still wanted more.

"I replayed their dialogue in my mind while driving home," Allen said, "and it felt more and more heinous to me. I helped start the company and was still an active member of management, though limited by my illness, and now my partner and my colleague were scheming to rip me off. It was mercenary opportunism, plain and simple."

It's a devastating denouement in Allen's autobiography, which, though ostensibly an account of his unlikely path to becoming a multibillionaire, could also be read as a crushing reflection on his failed relationship with Bill Gates—a man he loved but who was himself incapable of true friendship because he saw himself as without equal. As Allen describes it, Gates's truest self is a man driven constantly to prove his superiority, "who wanted not only to beat you but to crush you if he could."

Dozens of books have been written about Gates, virtually all of them in the 1990s and early 2000s, and they widely describe his domineering spirit and his intensity. These accounts also profile his brash, belligerent, arrogant, and bullying behavior—seemingly toward everyone, whether friend or foe. Gates was not simply a passionate man but also a deeply emotional man, often described as childlike in his inability or unwillingness to control his temper. He seemed to relish dressing down subordinates at Microsoft. In the 1990s, *Playboy* described his style as "management by embarrassment—challenging employees and even leaving some in tears."

Paul Allen describes Gates's constant "tirades," "browbeating," and "personal verbal attacks" as not only acts of bullying but also a major suck on corporate productivity. With his focus on negative reinforcement, Gates became known for the famous catchphrase, "That's the stupidest fucking thing I've ever heard."

Some might argue that this kind of narcissism and intensity are required of an industry captain at the level Gates was operating in the global economy. Whatever the rationalization, Gates ruled his company with an iron fist—and also came to view the wider computer industry as his dominion. And the body count quickly piled up. "Bill would go to a very senior person at these other [computer companies] and yell at them or tell them it had to be this way, or if you don't do this we'll make sure our software doesn't run on your box. What do you do if you're one of these . . . guys? You're screwed. You can't have Microsoft not support your hardware so you better do what they say," recounts an early Microsoft employee, Scott McGregor. As another software executive noted in the 1990s, "It's part of Bill's strategy. You smash people. You either make them line up or you smash them."

Microsoft's biggest business coup came in the early 1980s, when IBM, then one of the world's most powerful companies, asked the comparatively tiny Seattle-based software upstart to write an operating system for its personal computers. Most news outlets reported this improbable deal as the product of nepotism. Gates's mother sat on the board of the United Way, one of the world's most prominent charities, alongside the head of IBM, a relationship that may have helped grease the wheels for her son. Gates's father had also been helping his son's software company over the years; his law firm's largest client eventually became Microsoft.

The problem with the IBM deal was that Microsoft didn't have an operating system. So, it found a firm that did and acquired the software. IBM's market power made the newly minted "MS-DOS" the industry standard, laying the groundwork for Microsoft's multibillion-dollar dominion over the computer industry. Decades later, most computers around the world still run on Microsoft's operating system, now called Windows. Bill Gates had turned his corporate mantra—"A computer on every desk and in every home running Microsoft software"—into a reality.

What this episode shows is that if there is a genius to Gates, it is not as an innovator or inventor or technologist. Rather, it's as a businessman; it's in his ability to understand the business dimensions of technology and innovation, to network and negotiate, and to stop at nothing until he controls the way it all works.

Over time, Bill Gates became one of the most feared industry captains. As Microsoft grew and grew, it began expanding beyond the narrow confines of computer software. It considered buying Ticketmaster, the monopolistic force selling tickets to concerts and sporting events. Then Gates made a high-profile appearance at a newspaper industry conference, sending shock waves around potential media acquisitions. (Microsoft went on to launch *Slate* magazine and MSNBC, from which it has since divested.) "Everybody in the communications business is paranoid about Microsoft, including me," media tycoon Rupert Murdoch said at the time.

At a point, Microsoft began to seem like less a monopoly and more an empire, viewed by businesses the way the U.S. military is by many governments. With the simple maneuvering of an aircraft carrier in one direction or the other, the Pentagon can quietly send a powerful message: *Your future is in our hands.*

"I've competed against Microsoft for years, but I never quite appreciated how big Microsoft has become, not just as a company, but as a brand and as part of the national consciousness," Eric Schmidt, then an executive at Novell (and later the CEO of Google), noted in 1998. "It's the products, the Microsoft marketing juggernaut, Bill Gates's wealth, all those magazine cover stories. It's everything."

The Microsoft juggernaut, however, was not impregnable. The company made a series of major missteps under Gates's leadership, failing to recognize the potential existential threat that the World Wide Web posed to Microsoft's market share. To play catch-up, Microsoft clumsily hatched a plan to bury the dial-up internet service provider America Online, in which Paul Allen personally had a large investment stake. Gates casually told an acquaintance of Allen's, "Why would Paul want to compete with us? I'm just going . . . to keep losing money every year until we have the number-one market share in online. How does it make sense to compete with that?" Allen saw the writing on the wall and divested.

Gates and Microsoft also aimed their attention at internet browsers, dominated by Netscape. Microsoft put the screws to computer manufacturers, pushing them to sell units preloaded with its own browser, Internet Explorer, alongside its operating system, Microsoft Windows.

This proved the beginning of the end for Gates at Microsoft. A high-profile antitrust court case followed, with the Department of Justice accusing the company in 1998 of exercising monopoly power. In an inexplicable act of hubris, Gates decided that he could personally outwit government prosecutors, agreeing to sit for a videotaped deposition—a deeply embarrassing performance that proved damaging to his company. For days, Gates played the role of an arrogant Mr. Know-It-All, tediously rearranging every question he was asked—he even debated the definition of the word *definition*—and constantly seeking to diminish the intelligence of the lawyers opposing him. (Videos of the deposition are available on YouTube.) It was a prime-time showcase of Bill Gates's capacity for evasion and unhinged god complex. Paul Allen—and the rest of the world—watched Gates's public dissembling with a mixture of fascination and horror.

"Anti-Microsoft sentiment became widespread and intense, and it cut Bill to the core," Allen noted. "He'd been the darling of the business press, the craft entrepreneur and technology genius. Now the media portrayed him as a bully who'd bent the rules and probably broken them."

The courts ruled against Microsoft in 1999, declaring it a monopoly that was stifling innovation, but many of the stiffest penalties, including a directive to break up the company, were overturned on appeal. Microsoft nevertheless continued to face high-profile legal challenges, from competitors and the European Union, that further cemented the company's toxic reputation.

Suddenly, people were throwing pies in Bill Gates's face. *The Simpsons* was ridiculing his monopoly-nerd overcompensation complex. Both Bill Gates and Microsoft needed a change. The Gates Foundation was born.

Bill Gates had already been dabbling in philanthropy throughout the 1990s, but as the antitrust legal activity escalated into a full-scale public relations crisis, he very rapidly scaled up his charitable giving by several orders of magnitude. By the end of 2000, he had plowed more than $20 billion into the newly formed Gates Foundation. Suddenly, Bill Gates was the most generous philanthropist on earth and, at the same time, the richest man in the world, with a $60 billion personal fortune. Paradoxically, he would enjoy these twin distinctions for decades to come. No matter how much money he gave away, he always seemed to remain the richest man in the world. (As I write this, though, he has slipped in the rankings to the sixth wealthiest person, with more than $100 billion to his name.)

Gates's sudden generosity in the midst of a public relations crisis was met with some well-founded skepticism initially. Yesteryear's robber barons and industry titans like John D. Rockefeller and Andrew Carnegie had used charity late in life to paper over the destructive business ventures that had made them so wealthy. And American philanthropy has always had a particularly rich tradition of scandal and controversy. In recent years, we've learned that convicted sex offender Jeffrey Epstein used charitable donations to build a network of influence that immunized him from public scrutiny. The Sackler family, whose profiteering from the sales of OxyContin helped drive an opioid epidemic in the United States, leaned hard into philanthropy to distract polite society from looking too closely into the source of their wealth. Lance Armstrong built a reputation as a humanitarian through his charitable work with the Livestrong foundation even as he faced accusations—later confirmed to be true—that his dominant cycling career had been fueled by performance-enhancing drugs. Hillary Clinton faced scrutiny when it was revealed that she, in her official capacity as U.S. secretary of state, met many times with donors to the Clinton Foundation, including Melinda French Gates (Clinton denied any undue influence). And the Trump Foundation announced that it would shut down in 2018 as the New York State attorney general accused it of "functioning as little more than a checkbook to serve Mr. Trump's business and political interests."

The ability of the global elite to use philanthropy to advance their private interests or reform their reputations was not lost on the news media in the early days of the Gates Foundation, and journalists at the turn of the millennium had the mettle to talk to Gates's critics and openly question his giving—such as his foundation's donating computers loaded with Microsoft software to public libraries. "This doesn't even qualify as philanthropy," one critic said at the time. "It's just seeding the market. You're simply lubricating future sales."

At the same time, another narrative began to emerge, one that gave Gates the benefit of the doubt. What might Gates, with his relentless attack dog spirit, accomplish if he set his sights on bullying sickness, hunger, and poverty into the corner, instead of burying his business competitors? In this telling, Gates became the great disrupter, someone whose upstart foundation in Seattle was bringing long-overdue accountability to the white-gloved world of philanthropy. "It means performing the research and hard-nosed analysis that Gates . . . had done for years in developing software products, but applying it instead to eradicating malaria or polio in developing countries," *Time* magazine reported in 2000.

If Gates began to find a soft landing in the news media, it may also be because his philanthropic efforts allowed us to indulge in our deep-seated fascination with wealth. Here was a man who had made obscene riches in business and now, it seemed, was giving it all away. He was a champion and a paradigm for how capitalism ultimately and invariably delivers on its promises to lift all boats. It also didn't hurt that the Gates Foundation began donating hundreds of millions of dollars to newsrooms (from the *Guardian* to *Der Spiegel* to *Le Monde* to ProPublica to NPR), nor that Melinda French Gates took a seat on the board of the *Washington Post* for a number of years.

Gates's philanthropic excursions also chimed with the prevailing neoliberal economic model of the day, which imagined that nimble, efficient private-sector actors could—and should—take over much of the work of our lumbering, bureaucratic government. From Big Agriculture to Big Education to Big Finance, Bill Gates became an important partner and invaluable front man for business interests, escorting corporate ideology into public life under the banner of charity. In the same way that Microsoft had rapidly advanced social progress by fomenting a computer revolution, Gates told us, his foundation would work with pharmaceutical and agrochemical companies to cure disease and feed the hungry.

U.S. president George W. Bush, in a 2007 White House Summit, celebrated this new model of philanthropy, calling it "a fantastic example of social entrepreneurship, using business acumen to address social problems." Gates went on to receive the Presidential Medal of Freedom from Barack Obama, an honorary knighthood from Queen Elizabeth II, and the Padma Bhushan Award for distinguished service from the Indian government. And his kudos seemed to build on one another. After he appeared on the cover of *Time* magazine as a Person of the Year for 2005, with Bono and Melinda pictured just behind him, the 109th U.S. Congress enshrined the moment with House Resolution 638, "congratulating Bill Gates, Melinda Gates, and Bono" on the honor. The legislation garnered 71 cosponsors.

"I don't think it's hyperbole to say that Bill Gates is singularly, I would argue, the most consequential individual of our generation. I mean that," journalist Andrew Ross Sorkin said at a *New York Times* event in 2019, sitting next to Gates. "What he did in the private sector in Microsoft changed the face of culture and how we live today. And what he is doing with his foundation is changing the world."

As the lore—or cult—around Gates's good deeds grew and grew, the world didn't so much forgive the extraordinary avarice and destructive monopoly power that had positioned him to be such a generous philanthropist as simply forget about Gates's first chapter. The sheer weight of the foundation's donations—around eighty billion dollars pledged through early 2023—shattered whatever suspicions remained around Bill Gates's intentions. However you look at it, his massive donations had clearly served a greater good than as a quick fix for his battered reputation. Gates really had committed himself to creating a long-lasting charitable institution—one that, as the foundation loves to broadcast, is saving lives.

At a 2006 event where multibillionaire Warren Buffett announced that he would be donating much of his personal fortune to the Gates Foundation, dramatically expanding its spending power, Gates announced that, within his own lifetime, "we would have vaccines and medicines to eliminate the disease burden" of the top twenty killers. Years later, in 2020, Gates doubled down on the foundation's commitment to "swing for the fences," trumpeting that "the goal isn't just incremental progress. It's to put the full force of our efforts and resources behind the big bets that, if successful, will save and improve lives."

Promises like this became the stock-in-trade of the foundation's identity. At every turn, Gates would draw our eyes to the shining city on the hill he was building, a place where "all lives have equal value." And, in a world desperate for heroes, most of us wanted to believe his utopian vision. Bill Gates became not only unimpeachable in his charitable crusade but also sacrosanct.

It is difficult to overstate how extraordinary, how complete, or how quick Gates's public transformation has been. He went from a greedy, coldhearted, tyrannical monopolist to a "soft-spoken philanthropist" and a "kind, compassionate and soft-spoken" leader, as ABC and CNBC, respectively, reported. Of course, Bill Gates has not actually changed. He did not have a brain transplant or experience a miraculous personality change. Gates remains the same domineering, brusque bully at the Gates Foundation that he had been at Microsoft, a cauldron of passions that freely erupts. "Bill was a complete and utter asshole to people seventy percent of the time, and thirty percent of the time, he was the harmless, fun, super-smart nerd," one former employee told me. "When you worked there," another former employee said, "one thing you appreciated about Bill was that he was unfiltered—for better or worse. It was exciting to hear Bill talk because it was like—what's he going to say today?"

Melinda Gates, by contrast, was exactly the same in private meetings as in public—polished, the source said, to the point of seeming scripted. And, of course, this meant that when the two showed up in meetings, "All eyes were on Bill. What's his body language like today? Is he swearing? Is he throwing things? Because Melinda wasn't going to do that."

Bill Gates has a way of putting himself at the center of attention, and he has never had much compunction about throwing elbows or temper tantrums. When the world doesn't turn his way, when he feels challenged or not in possession of the level of control he demands, all hell might break loose. Yes, human beings are complex, but Gates has never been "soft-spoken." If anything, his body of charitable work has been aimed at raising the volume of his voice. And he has very effectively used philanthropy to assert leadership over a wide array of topics, planting his flag and claiming dominion over the areas he pursued—from the so-called diseases of the poor to agriculture in sub-Saharan Africa to U.S. educational standards. Gates has ruled over these projects with a very clear ideology of how the world should work, devising solutions to social problems through innovation and technology, elevating the primacy of the private sector, promoting the importance of intellectual property, and, above all, reorganizing the world in a way that gave Bill Gates a seat at the decision-making table, often at the head.

The way Bill Gates practices charity is categorically different from the way you or I do. The Gates Foundation is not handing over money to poor people to spend as they wish. Nor is it assiduously going out into the field to talk to intended beneficiaries—to hear their concerns, consider their solutions, fund their ideas. Rather, Gates donates money from his private wealth to his private foundation. He then assembles a small group of consultants and experts at the foundation's half-billion-dollar corporate headquarters to decide what problems are worth his time, attention, and money—and what solutions should be pursued. Then the Gates Foundation floods money into universities, think tanks, newsrooms, and advocacy groups, giving them both a check and checklist of things to do. Suddenly, Gates has created an echo chamber of advocates pushing the political discourse toward his ideas. And the results have been stunning.

The Gates Foundation single-handedly bankrolled one of the most important, and controversial, changes in American education in recent years, called the Common Core State Standards, essentially a new operating system for U.S. education. Meanwhile, in many African nations, Bill Gates has become the loudest voice in agricultural policymaking, pushing dozens of new rules, regulations, laws, and public policies, always in line with his private-sector, corporate-led, patent-forward vision for how the global economy should work. And, during the Covid-19 pandemic, as our elected leaders fumbled to create a response plan, Gates parlayed his foundation's decades of experience with vaccines into a leadership role over the lives of billions of the poorest people on earth, essentially taking over the World Health Organization's response effort.

These bold interventions have been wildly successful in elevating Bill Gates on the world stage, but, in a practical sense, these efforts have all been major failures, both according to the foundation's own stated goals and according to any independent measure of success. It turns out that fixing complex problems, like public health and public education, is much more difficult than Bill Gates thought. And, as it also turns out, billionaire philanthropy is not the solution.

Yes, of course, the foundation's charitable giving has helped people at times, but its bullying approach has also created a vast body of collateral damage, which we have largely ignored. The dominant narrative guiding public understanding of the Gates Foundation has focused on its forward-looking goals, its massive donations, and the lives it claims to be saving. In this deeply unbalanced, one-sided discourse, there has been little room for serious public debate and little recognition around what the foundation is actually doing. Bill Gates is not simply donating money to fight disease and improve education and agriculture. He's using his vast wealth to acquire political influence, to remake the world according to his narrow worldview.

In short, we've been made to understand that Bill Gates is a philanthropist when he is, in fact, a power broker. And we've been made to see the Gates Foundation as a charity when it is, in fact, a political organization—a tool Bill Gates uses to put his hands on the levers of public policy. "He has immediate access to us because of his fame and reputation and what he's doing with his own money," Mitch McConnell, then Senate majority leader, noted in 2020. "In many of these countries, he's way more effective than the government is, and that's certainly value added for public health all over the world."

Gates uses this access—including meeting with everyone from Barack Obama to Donald Trump to Angela Merkel—to successfully pressure governments to direct billions of taxpayer dollars into his charitable projects. Our tax dollars richly subsidize Gates's charitable empire, yet all the glory goes to Bill Gates, who is subject to virtually no checks and balances around how he uses our money. *Forbes*, for years, has put Bill Gates on its annual list of the ten most powerful people in the world, yet because Gates exercises power through philanthropy, we don't scrutinize or challenge this power.

Perhaps the most impressive dimension of this influence is the chilling effect it creates. Though critics of the foundation are legion, many of the people who know it best are reluctant to speak up for fear of losing the foundation's patronage or incurring Bill Gates's wrath. This self-censorship is so widely understood that academics have even coined a term for it: *Bill chill*. It's one of many contradictions that define the Gates Foundation: the world's most visible humanitarian body is also one of the most feared organizations on earth.

This is not to say that Bill Gates does not have good intentions. And we should not doubt that he really believes he is helping the world. But we should understand that he's helping the world in the only way he knows how: by taking control. Bill Gates's flaw—perhaps his tragic flaw—across his career at both Microsoft and the Gates Foundation has always been his unyielding belief in himself, that he is both right and righteous in everything he does, the smartest guy in the room and a man born to lead.

In some respects, Gates's good intentions are precisely the problem. Take a survey of history's most odious leaders, and you'll find many true believers and pathological narcissists—men, or mostly men, who really believed they knew what was best for others. At some point, we have to be able to agree on how malevolent and undemocratic this model of power is. And we also have to agree that humanitarianism aimed at real human progress—equality, justice, freedom—requires us to challenge unaccountable power and illegitimate leaders.

And this means that Bill Gates is a problem, not a solution. He's taking power that he has not earned and does not deserve. No one elected or appointed him to lead the world—on any topic. Yet, here he is, thumping his chest, hogging the podium, and bleating into a megaphone his solutions on everything from climate change to contraceptive access to the Covid-19 pandemic.

Twenty years into Gates's grand experiment in philanthropy, we are long overdue for a reappraisal of the world's most powerful humanitarian, especially as a new generation of tech billionaires begins to follow in his footsteps. Jeff Bezos and his ex-spouse, MacKenzie Scott, have both pledged to give away most of their fortunes, more than $150 billion combined. Mark Zuckerberg has made similar claims, as have hundreds of other super-wealthy signatories to the "Giving Pledge" the Gates Foundation created to expand billionaire philanthropy. Counterintuitive as it sounds, the prospect of hundreds of billions—or even trillions—of dollars in philanthropic spending coming down the pike is cause not for celebration but, rather, for concern.

In the same way that the global elite use campaign contributions and lobbying to influence politics, philanthropy has become one more tool of influence in the billionaire's toolbox. The ability of the superrich to seamlessly turn their personal fortunes into political power is a clear signal of a failing democracy and a rise in oligarchy. And it's a clarion call for us to ask ourselves if this is the world we want to live in—one where the richest people have the loudest voices; where we applaud and exalt the hoarding of wealth by questionable business tycoons because they very publicly parcel it out in charitable projects that undemocratically advance their political worldviews.

Bill Gates is the ideal case study for interrogating this issue because, in many respects, he is the strongest example of the good deeds that billionaires can deliver, the very best example of what a well-intentioned global elite can achieve. As journalists spilled volumes of ink over the years interrogating the money-in-politics predations of the Koch brothers and Rupert Murdoch, they spilled even more ink praising Bill Gates as our "good billionaire," profiling his supposedly selfless charitable campaigns to save the world from itself. The news media, along with Gates's massive PR machinery, have created a world of simplistic narratives, if not fairy tales, sending a message that there are few criticisms of the foundation worth debating: Would you rather that Bill Gates spent his money on sports cars and mansions? Would the world really be better if we taxed Gates and let our dysfunctional government spend his vast fortune?

To answer these questions, and to really understand how Bill Gates turned his wealth into political power through philanthropy, we have to dig very deeply into a very dark, private institution. What we uncover is a charitable foundation whose activities are wholly unrecognizable under the common definition of charity and wholly unrecognizable from the foundation's rhetoric and stated mission.

We'll find a man who has managed to become richer, not poorer, during his tenure as the most generous person in the history of the world. We'll see how meaningless, or miserly, Bill Gates's donations are compared to his vast wealth—he gives away money he does not need and could never possibly spend. We'll see the Gates family generating untold personal benefits from their philanthropy, including billions of dollars in tax benefits, public applause, political power, and even the ability to enrich or empower organizations they are close to—as with the one hundred million dollars the foundation donated to the elite private high school Bill Gates and his children attended in Seattle.

We'll see tens of billions of dollars from taxpayers subsidizing Gates's charitable projects, yet very little taxpayer oversight of how he spends our money. We'll find that, in many places, we can't even follow the money, as the foundation trades in billions of dollars in dark money.

We'll find a charitable foundation that appears to be as much in the business of making money as in giving it away; that freely and broadly engages in commercial activities, handing out billions of dollars to private companies, collecting multibillion-dollar investment returns, and even launching and directing private enterprises. And we'll find whistleblowers from the private sector who allege that the foundation, like Microsoft before it, abuses its market power and acts in an anti-competitive manner.

We'll see the stunning network of influence the Gates Foundation has built, one that funds a vast constellation of surrogates and front groups to carry out the foundation's agenda. We'll watch as these organizations—created, funded, and run by the foundation—present themselves as independent bodies and give the appearance of robust support for its agenda. We'll explore how this surrogate power turns into political power, both at home and abroad, and we'll understand that Gates, at age sixty-eight, aims to expand his power in the decades ahead.

We'll find an organization that, by its own admission, is "driven by the interests and passions of the Gates family," not by the needs or desires of its intended beneficiaries. We'll find an organization enamored with itself—its experts, its answers, its strategies, and its founder—and that is eager to bulldoze anyone who gets in its way. We'll see a foundation with a retrograde colonial gaze that leans hard on high-paid technocrats in Geneva and Washington, DC, to solve the problems of poor people living in Kampala and Uttar Pradesh. And we'll find a man suffering from a bad case of main character syndrome, constantly asserting his leadership and expertise on issues in which he has no training, standing, or mandate.

We'll see an organization that ferociously brands itself as a champion of science, reason, and facts, but that openly trades in ideology. We'll see a philanthropy that spends large sums of money on evaluation and measurement of other organizations while going to extraordinary lengths to limit independent measurement and evaluation of its own work. We'll follow billions of dollars that flow from the foundation into universities and newsrooms that reliably avoid criticizing it. We'll find a "success cartel" of individuals and groups that are deeply afraid to voice criticism of Bill Gates, for fear of losing his patronage, but that are eager to point to his good deeds. And we'll hear accounts of the foundation's calculating, enterprising efforts to silence critics and stifle debate. But we'll also see the limits of these efforts to control and monopolize the discourse, as evident in the extraordinary criticism that has emerged around the foundation but has never received the attention it deserves.

We'll understand that Bill Gates is both a wolf in sheep's clothing and an emperor who has no clothes. We'll find a man who fights accountability with every fiber of his being and an institution whose activities never seem to measure up to its high-minded claims, whether it's the lives it purports to be saving or the human progress it is executing. We'll find a man who faces decades of personal allegations over workplace misconduct, both at Microsoft and the Gates Foundation, and who made the unthinkable decision to associate his charitable enterprise with convicted sex offender Jeffrey Epstein. We'll find that no matter how egregious Gates's missteps, and no matter how robust our so-called cancel culture, Bill Gates remains largely immune to checks and balances, even from Congress and the IRS.

We'll see a deeply ahistorical and unimaginative foundation that has chosen to resurrect failed charitable projects from decades ago, like the "Green Revolution" in African agriculture and a suite of activities in family planning that flirt with population control. We'll see an institution that for years has asked us to look to the horizon, to the game-changing technologies it would introduce and the groundbreaking interventions it would steward. And we'll see, in the specific and the general, how the foundation has failed to accomplish what it set out to do, whether it's eradicating polio, introducing breakthrough vaccines, revolutionizing agriculture and U.S. education, or leading the world on the Covid-19 response. We'll see an organization that continually fails forward by the sheer wealth it possesses.

We'll see an institution that thrives on the grotesque economic inequalities that govern the globe, that counts on the rest of us to be too poor or too stupid to say no to its largesse. We'll see that the more than $150 billion Bill Gates controls, through his personal wealth and his private foundation's endowment, are a totem and a driver of inequality, not a solution to it. We'll see that our world has not become a more equal or just place under Gates's world-making activities. We'll recognize that Gates's father-knows-best, drippings-from-my-table noblesse oblige is moving the needle in the wrong direction and, very often, doing more harm than good. We'll realize that the Gates Foundation's ambition is not so much to change the world but, rather, to keep it exactly as it is— aggressively pursuing a business-as-usual approach that obstructs the real social change needed to conquer inequality.

We'll find an organization that has reached its zenith and that is slowly sinking under the weight of its bureaucracy and hubris, one running on the fumes of a bygone era of neoliberal fantasies and desperately clinging to relevancy. And we'll find, at long last, a turn in the news media, which in 2021 went from cheerleaders to critics, publishing a spate of devastating headlines that show how ripe the cult of Gates is for reexamination: "Long Before Divorce, Bill Gates Had a Reputation for Questionable Behavior"; "Bill Gates Should Stop Telling Africans What Kind of Agriculture Africans Need"; "How Bill Gates Impeded Global Access to Covid Vaccines."

We'll recognize how vulnerable the Gates Foundation is and how responsible we all are for challenging it. We'll find ourselves looking in the mirror, asking why we have allowed Bill Gates to take so much power from us for so long. We will puzzle over our collective Stockholm syndrome, which has made us believe we should applaud Gates's usurpation of power, not challenge it. And we'll finally recognize that Bill Gates and the Gates Foundation are not just problems, but *our* problems.

1

Lives Saved

In a 2019 debate at the Oxford Union, the famed venue associated with Oxford University where fancy people formally argue, the proposition on the table was whether it is immoral to be a billionaire. Writer Anand Giridharadas argued in the affirmative, interrogating the sins of the superrich and the false promises of billionaire philanthropy.

"They find clever new ways to pay people as little as possible and as precariously as possible. They avoid taxes illegally and legally with trillions hiding offshore. . . . They lobby for public policies that don't benefit the public interest—in fact, [they] cost the public interest but enrich them. They form monopolies that asphyxiate competition. They cause social problems to make a profit . . . ," Giridharadas noted, hammering on the serial misdeeds of the the billionaire class. "And they use philanthropy, some of the spoils of dubiously gotten wealth, to whitewash not just their reputations but to actually create the ability to keep doing what they are doing. . . . These are knowing acts of immorality." Despite his oratorical talents and populist arguments, Giridharadas and his team lost the debate. They simply could not parry against Bill Gates.

This, essentially, was the counterargument of the opposing team, which drove home a good-billionaire narrative based on the Gates Foundation's good deeds. "You're saying that Bill and Melinda Gates are immoral despite the fact that they set up the Gates Foundation, operating in accordance with the belief . . . that all lives are equal," noted Princeton University philosopher Peter Singer. "The Gateses have given so far fifty billion dollars to endow that foundation, and there's going to be more to come. You're saying they're immoral although they have undoubtedly already saved . . . several million lives, perhaps more than any other living person today."

Variations on this winning argument have long played counterpoint to any criticism of the billionaire class. As high-profile political figures in U.S. politics—from Representative Alexandria Ocasio-Cortez to Senators Elizabeth Warren and Bernie Sanders—challenge the very existence of billionaires, they do so with considerable vulnerability. Because what they're arguing for is an end to the Gates Foundation and, by extension, the deaths of millions of children.

This talking point has become something of a conventional wisdom in the mainstream discourse on Gates, cited by so many people for so many years that it has become understood alongside the law of gravity and the certainty of death and taxes. If there are two things most people know about the Gates Foundation, it's the large sums of money it is giving away and the lives it is saving. "If you want to have a balanced, healthy, thoughtful perspective on Bill Gates, it has to start by understanding and processing the magnitude of what he has done, not by dismissing it," notes Vox writer Kelsey Piper, citing the "millions" of lives Gates has saved.

And when someone dares to put a critical lens on Bill Gates without kissing the ring, they will be notified: "Your article doesn't even mention that Gates has saved millions of lives of the poorest people in the world," the editor of *Inside Philanthropy*, David Callahan, noted in his criticism of the first piece I published on the foundation, a cover article in *The Nation* in early 2020.

As central as the lives-saved claim has become in the public discourse on Gates, it rests on a decidedly questionable foundation. It appears to have entered the public consciousness not through independent research and evaluation but, rather, through the rote recitation of the Gates Foundation and its vast PR machinery. "You know, there's over six million people alive today that wouldn't be alive if it wasn't for the vaccine coverage and new vaccine delivery that we've funded," Bill Gates noted at the American Enterprise Institute in 2014. "And so it's very measurable stuff."

A year earlier, however, Gates had said that his philanthropic funding had saved *ten* million lives. So, if saving lives is measurable, it's not an exact science. As Gates's numbers fluctuate year over year, one feature remains the same: the "lives saved" numbers always seem to come from the foundation or the groups it funds.

The foundation funded and appears to have provided editorial direction on a book titled *Millions Saved*, published by the Center for Global Development (whose largest funder—more than $90 million—is the Gates Foundation). The University of Washington's Institute for Health Metrics and Evaluation, the recipient of more than $600 million from Gates, published a "Lives Saved Scorecard" in *The Lancet*, examining the lives Gates had saved. There's also the "Lives Saved Tool" at Johns Hopkins University and another one from the Vaccine Impact Modelling Consortium. Both organizations are funded by Gates.

Though the foundation works on a wide array of topics—from U.S. education to African agriculture to family planning throughout poor nations—it devotes almost all its public relations firepower to promoting its work on global health and development because these are the areas where it can most forcefully point to success, to the lives it is saving.

Gates's lives-saved arms race reached its zenith in 2017, after Warren Buffett, one of the world's most renowned investors and richest men, asked Bill and Melinda Gates to reflect on what they had done with the thirty billion dollars he had given the foundation. "There are many who want to know where you've come from, where you're heading and why," Buffett's letter noted. "Your foundation will always be in the spotlight. It's important, therefore, that it be well understood."

In their public-facing response, Bill and Melinda thanked Buffett for "the biggest single gift anyone ever gave anybody for anything.

"We don't have sales and profits to show you," the letter to Buffett read. "There's no share price to report. But there are numbers we watch closely to guide our work and measure our progress. . . . We'll tell the story through the numbers that drive our work. Let's start with the most important one: 122 million, the number of children's lives saved since 1990."

As Bill Gates explained in the letter, "More children survived in 2015 than in 2014. More survived in 2014 than in 2013, and so on. If you add it all up, 122 million children under age five have been saved over the past 25 years. These are children who would have died if mortality rates had stayed where they were in 1990."

It was an eye-popping metric of success, one the foundation would later weave into its public presentations—and would pay the media outlet Fast Company to publicize. The *Guardian*, also funded by Gates, wrote its own glowing profile of the foundation having helped save 122 million lives, while the *New York Times* and countless other outlets piled on the praise. "It's hard, if not impossible, to put a figure on the number of lives saved," the *Dallas Morning News* editorial board noted when naming Melinda Gates "Texan of the Year" in 2020—an odd accolade given that she had lived in Seattle for decades. "A common figure on the internet is 122 million. What the exact number might be is anyone's guess, even as the foundation exhaustively tracks its efficacy in helping more people around the world lead healthy, productive lives."

There's something honest in the newspaper citing "the internet" as its source of information because it openly acknowledges that nobody really knows how many lives the foundation has saved. Yet there's also something deeply troubling when a major news outlet—whose job it is to scrutinize the powerful and cut through misinformation—puts the full weight of its editorial board behind a highly questionable public relations campaign.

So, where does the 122 million figure come from? In the the Gateses' original presentation of the number, they cite a graph from the *Economist,* showing childhood deaths falling over the decades. (The Gates Foundation, notably, appears to have a longstanding working relationship with the *Economist*'s sister organization, the Economist Intelligence Unit, though its not clear when that relationship began.) If you do the legwork to track down the untitled study from the *Economist*, you find that its graph is based on a study by the Brookings Institution. And if you track down the Brookings study, you find that the report is actually titled "Seven Million Lives Saved." Neither the *Economist* nor Brookings mentioned the number 122 million. The author of the Brookings study, John McArthur, said he didn't know how the foundation had arrived at that number, but he did offer context. "The result one gets depends on the question one is asking," he told me. "Different counterfactuals will give different answers—asking 'how much progress has the world made overall' will generate different answers than 'how much progress has been achieved relative to preceding trends,' and then there are a bunch of further measurement issues that fall under each strand."

This is an area where the Gates Foundation has unusual influence and power. By funding the studies and evaluations that tell the world what it is doing, the foundation can shape how the questions are asked or what data is used. This, in turn, shapes the studies' results and conclusions. The foundation also sometimes funds the news outlets that translate these research findings to the public. To a very large extent, this is the story of the Gates Foundation: much of what we know about its work, its methods, and its accomplishments comes from the foundation itself.

When we allow the foundation to define the metrics of its success—how many lives it has saved—and also to furnish the measurements, we give it a dangerous level of epistemic power, the ability to shape what we know and how we think about the world's most powerful private foundation. The result is that the Gates Foundation's self-constructed, self-aggrandizing marketing campaigns have become our starting point for understanding the foundation when they could just as easily be our starting point for challenging it.

The Gates Foundation did not respond to any press inquiries for this book, so it's unclear how it arrived at its much-publicized number. From Bill Gates's brief description, his analysis seems to be based on a do-nothing counterfactual—imagining that, without the Gates Foundation, the mortality trends from the 1990s would have continued unchanged through the 2000s and 2010s. That's not a particularly relevant or mean-ingful analysis, however—unless you believe that the world really would have come to a standstill had it not been for Bill Gates. Such an analysis also doesn't tell us how many of those 122 million lives were saved directly because of Gates and how many saved lives were related to countless other variables and interventions that had nothing to do with the foundation.

None of this is to say the Gates Foundation isn't helping save lives. It is. It's helping get vaccines into arms, for example, and vaccines save lives. But so do other interventions, like training doctors and nurses, building and staffing clinics, and investing in transportation infrastruc-ture to help patients reach those clinics. Where and how we spend our limited resources on public health, at a point, is a political question. And this is why the Gates Foundation generates criticism as an undemocratic force. It uses its wealth and bully pulpit to make sure its priorities are our priorities. It partners with wealthy nations, pushing them to direct foreign aid spending on the foundation's charitable projects, which diverts tax-payer dollars away from other interventions that might save even more lives or deliver other, more important benefits.

Upon close examination, many of Gates's claimed successes fall apart. A good case study is the foundation's work on rotavirus, which causes diarrhea and severe dehydration. In 2022, Bill Gates boasted, "We supported the creation of a new vaccine for rotavirus that has reduced the number of children who die of this disease every year by 75 percent, from 528,000 annually in 2000 to 128,500 in 2016."

Many, if not most, of these avoided deaths, however, have nothing to do with the foundation's work with vaccines. It is true that deaths from rotavirus are in decline, but that trend began years before the foundation started working on the disease, or before a vaccine was widely recommended for use in poor nations (in 2009). Improved sanitation and hand washing, clean drinking water, and the wider availability of oral rehydration therapy (and, more generally, the availability of health care) have all contributed to the mortality reductions. Also notable: a cruel irony of rotavirus vaccines is that they are not as effective in the poor nations where they are needed most as they are in wealthy nations. That doesn't mean they aren't an important tool. They just aren't the only tool—or the silver bullet solution the Gates Foundation wants them to be. Really improving public health requires us to address more fundamental issues related to poverty, like making sure people have access to a healthy diet, clean water, health care, income, and housing.

"Yes—biomedical technology (especially vaccines and antibiotics) has given us the ability to keep more and more people alive," David McCoy, a researcher at United Nations University, told me, "but this reliance on technology is fragile and [ignores the fact that] most premature mortality across the world is largely driven by poverty. Arguably, the heavy emphasis placed by the Gates Foundation on technology, and Gates's active neglect of the social determinants of health, mean the Gates Foundation is causing more harm than good."

McCoy authored one of the only independent analyses ever published into the proliferation of lives-saved claims, a 2013 academic study examining one of the Gates Foundation's biggest lifesaving partners, the Global Fund to Fight AIDS, Tuberculosis and Malaria. "The model to produce these [lives-saved] figures is highly suspect and incredibly biased as well," McCoy told me. "It involves all kinds of methodological imputations that are not really justified."

Even within Gates's narrow, pharma-focused approach to public health, we find major limitations. For example, nearly half of all children across the globe today are not vaccinated against rotavirus. Given that multiple rotavirus vaccines are available, and given that Bill Gates seems to have planted his flag and claimed ownership over the disease, doesn't he have to take some responsibility for these failures? If he's willing to take credit for the progress we've made, torturing or misrepresenting the data to inflate his foundation's accomplishments, does he not also have to own the shortcomings of his philanthropic work?

The really gaping bias in Gates's lives-saved narrative is that it fails to reckon with how many lives are being lost. Every year, around sixty million people die. It's a grim statistic underlined by a troubling reality: many of these people die from preventable or treatable diseases. This speaks to the paradox in modern medicine in which large numbers of people die because the cures are too expensive or because local health systems are not equipped to manage sickness. Again, it's a problem of poverty and of inequality. At times, it's also a problem of monopoly markets—of the way we've organized the political economy surrounding drugs, vaccines, and diagnostics.

In Bill Gates's view, patents and intellectual property protections reward companies for the enormous research and development costs they undertake to bring a new medicine to the marketplace. These companies took a risk and invested significant sums of money. So, as a reward, we give them legalized monopoly power in the form of patents as a way to recoup their costs. Monopoly patents lead to high prices, but if we changed our patent system, Gates argues, companies would have no incentive to develop new drugs, and lives would be lost.

Gates did not arrive at this position through independent research or dispassionate inquiry, however. His stance is informed by his career at Microsoft, whose revenues turn on the same patent (and copyright) considerations that drive the pharmaceutical industry. Without strong intellectual property rights, Microsoft could not have been successful, and Bill Gates would not be one of the richest men in the world. He also wouldn't be a philanthropist. Just as Gates believes that Microsoft's innovative technology ushered in the computer revolution, he sees pharmaceutical companies, and their patent-forward business model, as saving lives.

"The foundation at this point, we've saved about 10 million lives that otherwise wouldn't have been saved, and our goal for the next decade is 50 million. But we never would have been able to do that except for our partnership with the pharmaceutical companies," he noted in a 2013 presentation. "Thank god for patent laws that allow them to invent drugs that they get to sell, that then they get to hire researchers [to develop more patented drugs]. They are phenomenal at understanding the drug libraries, the assays, the things like that. And, in fact, none of their patents exist in any of these developing countries. We never run into IP [intellectual property] problems. Not a single time on a single thing. Because in the poor countries we work in, the poorest 90 countries . . . nobody files patents, nobody enforces patents. It's essentially a transfer of people buying drugs in [the] rich world who are now enabling these things to be done at marginal cost. All the vaccines we do, we understand the marginal cost—we make sure that's exactly what the pricing is for the [world's poorest people]."

In reality, millions of people have died and continue to die because of IP problems. Even if patents don't exist in poor nations, as Gates argues, that doesn't mean Pfizer's or Merck's monopoly patents don't shape prices—and access. Multinational pharmaceutical companies can't make money treating the poorest people on earth, so they often don't sell their drugs in those countries (at least not at a price people can afford). And as we saw with the Covid-19 pandemic, pharmaceutical companies also refuse to share their blueprints and recipes with generic manufacturers that could make drugs and vaccines cheaply for poor nations.

Many public health experts see Big Pharma and its monopoly patents as an obstacle to progress, not an engine of innovation. In her book *The Truth About the Drug Companies: How They Deceive Us and What to Do About It*, Marcia Angell, the former editor of the *New England Journal of Medicine*, skewers the idea that patents allow industry to recoup the costs of innovation. Industry's largest expense, by a wide margin, is on marketing, not research, as companies try to squeeze as much profit as possible from their monopoly patents. "The prices drug companies charge have little relationship to the costs of making drugs and could be cut dramatically without coming anywhere close to threatening R&D," Angell notes. "Now primarily a marketing machine to sell drugs of dubious benefit, this industry uses its wealth and power to co-opt every institution that might stand in its way, including the U.S. Congress, the Food and Drug Administration, academic medical centers, and the medical profession itself. . . . Only a handful of truly important drugs have been brought to market in recent years, and they were mostly based on taxpayer-funded research at academic institutions, small biotechnology companies, or the National Institutes of Health."

Whereas many medical experts and public health professionals see a need to reform the pharmaceutical industry and change (or challenge) our patent system, Bill Gates sees—and wants us to see—Big Pharma as a humanitarian partner, one that just needs the right incentives. His solution is to provide inducements to industry "to make markets work for the poor"—or to make monopoly medicine work for the poor. The most potent example of the foundation's "market-shaping" activities is its work with vaccines, which bring together Bill Gates's twin passions, commerce and innovation. "In the same way that during my Microsoft career I talked about the magic of software, I now spend my time talking about the magic of vaccines," Gates explained in 2011. "They are the most effective and cost-effective health tool ever invented. I like to say vaccines are a miracle. Just a few doses of vaccine can protect a child from debilitating and deadly diseases for a lifetime."

Gates's signature project with vaccines is an organization named Gavi (previously, the Global Alliance for Vaccines and Immunization), which the Gates Foundation founded with $750 million in seed money in 1999. The foundation would eventually plow more than $6 billion into the Geneva-based organization, making Gavi the single largest recipient of foundation funding by a significant margin. It is also a key source of Gates's lives-saved public relations.

The project boasts of having vaccinated nearly a billion children through routine immunizations, the net effect of which, it claims, has been the saving of 15 million lives. Bill Gates regularly cites Gavi as one of the projects he's most proud of in his philanthropic work. Melinda

French Gates also trumpets Gavi, which, she says, "has spurred a 40 percent decrease in the number of children in low- and middle-income nations who die before their fifth birthday." (These claims appear either uncited or cited to research funded by the foundation.)

Gavi, itself, doesn't develop new vaccines. Nor does it work with Big Pharma to transfer its vaccine technology to manufacturers in poor nations. Rather, Gavi pools large sums of money from donors—mostly from taxpayers—to purchase vaccines from the pharmaceutical industry. If Big Pharma didn't previously have an incentive to supply vaccines to poor nations, they do with Gavi, which puts up billions of dollars to move markets.

Gavi's single largest vaccine purchase over the years—of at least $4 billion—has been for pneumococcal vaccines, which protect against a common cause of pneumonia. At certain points, around half of Gavi's vaccine budget has gone toward pneumonia immunizations. This focus reflects the fact that pneumonia is the world's leading cause of vaccine-preventable deaths in children. Around four hundred thousand children die each year from infections that could be prevented if we had universal access to the pneumonia vaccine.

Gavi's approach to vaccine distribution, however, doesn't appear aimed at universal access. It works only in the poorest nations and, with pneumonia vaccines, covers only around half the children living there. And once nations become slightly less poor—at a point where people earn an average of five dollars a day—they "graduate" out of Gavi's program. One industry source cynically likened this to a drug dealer who hooks new customers with freebies—"the first high is on me"—and then expects them to start paying higher market prices going forward.

The marketplace for pneumonia vaccines over most of the last two decades has been governed by monopoly, or duopoly, power, controlled by Pfizer and GSK. The extreme market power of these two companies allows them to charge high prices—and they do. Hundreds of millions of people around the world go unvaccinated because they cannot afford immunizations and because Gates and Gavi don't reach them. Again, despite what Bill Gates asserts, patent monopolies have major impacts on the global poor.

"There are approximately 430 million children under the age of

15 living in countries with zero coverage of the PCV [pneumococcal conjugate vaccine]," according to Every Breath Counts, a coalition that notably includes the Gates Foundation. "The cost of this exposure is ultimately measured in children's lives lost due to pneumonia." The Gates Foundation's own funded research reports that the GSK-Pfizer "duopoly has limited supply and stifled competitive market forces that drive prices down," also noting that "price and supply barriers" leave millions of children without access to vaccines.

Even rich nations have struggled to negotiate access to pneumococcal vaccines. A 2014 *New York Times* investigation profiled how Pfizer's market power translated into difficulties for American pediatricians and families to get vaccines. In the United States, the price of Pfizer's pneumonia vaccine was, inscrutably, rising over time—not falling as one would expect because scaling up production should deliver efficiencies. The investigation also reported that after the government of Singapore, another wealthy nation, started mandating pneumonia vaccinations for all children, prices there inexplicably jumped 50 percent. The suggestion was that once Big Pharma had locked in a captive market, it could bilk consumers.

As Bill Gates describes it, monopoly medicine, left to its own devices, is governed by the law of trickle-down economics: "When you get this problem of these diseases—this sounds like an awful thing to say—but when diseases affect both rich and poor countries, trickle-down will eventually work for the poorest, because the high cost of development is recovered in the rich world and then, as they go off patent, they're sold for marginal cost to the poor, and everybody benefits."

Gates's utopian thinking hit some hard realities with pneumonia. Up until Pfizer's lucrative Covid-19 vaccine, pneumonia vaccines were the company's leading source of revenue, with annual sales at around six billion dollars. Pfizer has very likely recovered the money it put into developing its pneumonia vaccine many times over, but the golden moment Bill Gates describes—when the vaccine is suddenly "sold for marginal cost to the poor and everybody benefits"—never materialized.

Twenty years after the world's first pneumonia vaccine for children reached the market, it remains inaccessible to a huge swath of the globe. Millions of children have died, and continue to die, from a disease for which we have multiple highly effective vaccines. Cynically, we could say that Pfizer and GSK have made a killing off pneumonia. And one could argue that Bill Gates sat on his hands and watched it happen—or even encouraged it.

Instead of challenging the fundamental problem, the monopoly power of Pfizer and GSK, the Gates Foundation has nibbled around the edges, trying to create subsidies and incentives to coax monopolies to be more charitable—or, really, marginally less greedy. In one high-profile effort, Gates, Gavi, and other donors developed what was called an "advanced market commitment," putting up $1.5 billion to send a signal to the pharmaceutical industry that there was money on the table. The plan was aimed at "reducing the risk for vaccine manufacturers and incentivizing the creation of new, less expensive PCVs [pneumoccocal conjugate vaccines]."

While the fund promised to bring "new" competitor vaccines to the market, Gavi ended up handing out $1.5 billion pool of funds as bonus payments to GSK and Pfizer, essentially rewarding, if not entrenching, their monopoly power. Gavi always negotiates with pharmaceutical companies to secure lower prices than wealthy nations pay, but with the new bonus payments, Pfizer and GSK were receiving as much as $7 per dose. This is far less than rich nations pay but, nevertheless, several times higher than the cost of production, according to multiple estimates. "Certainly the whole notion was to create a sustainable model," Pfizer said in 2010, describing its work with Gavi. "It wasn't to make it into a money-losing proposition."

In reports to its investors, Pfizer trumpets the benefits of working with Gavi as both boosting corporate revenues and "earning greater respect from society." Bill Gates believes the global poor also benefit from this model of "creative capitalism." "So, for our foundation, where we're trying to help the poorest, our relationship with the pharmaceutical companies has been fantastic," he noted in 2014. "And it's great—every time they're successful, they come up with a new drug, they manage to keep profitable because of that. That's great for us because it means they're going to have a little bit more understanding to help us with our issues and a little bit more in the way of resources, all totally voluntary on their part to pitch in." At the time Gates made these remarks, his signature project in global health, Gavi, was paying more than half a billion dollars a year for pneumonia vaccines.

Gavi's monopoly-subsidy model found a high-profile critic in Doctors Without Borders, also called Médecins Sans Frontières (MSF), the Nobel Prize–winning humanitarian group that spends a billion dollars a year delivering medical help to poor nations. What makes MSF uniquely positioned to publicly criticize Gates and Gavi is that it is one of the only large international health organizations that has refused to take Gates funding, a principled step it took to maintain independence from the foundation.

MSF and other critics accuse Gavi of paying inflated prices for pneumonia vaccines, arguing that its negotiations have lacked transparency and accountability. Indeed, how does Gavi decide what is a fair price? If Pfizer and GSK can generate profits selling vaccines to Gavi, is this really charity? (Another point on transparency: Gavi refused multiple requests for an interview and did not provide responses to most questions sent by email.)

More important, the vast majority of Gavi's budget actually comes from taxpayers in Europe and the United States, which have pledged tens of billions of dollars to the project. Do we simply trust that the deals Gavi negotiates with Big Pharma are a good, just, and efficient use of taxpayer dollars?

One early adviser to the Gates Foundation, Donald Light, alleges that when he and other experts questioned Gavi's pricing, their names were removed from a report Gavi presented to rich donor nations, making it seem as though its pricing structure had been "unanimously endorsed, because no negative votes or minority opinions were allowed." Light cites industry sources to estimate that two thirds of the dollars Gavi planned to pay out for pneumonia vaccines would go as profits to Pfizer and GSK. (Pfizer did not respond to an interview request or questions I sent by email about its pneumonia vaccines. GSK also did not respond to specific questions sent by email, including if it generates a profit from its work with Gavi, but did offer a general response: "We reserve our lowest vaccine prices for Gavi.")

As MSF called for lower pricing, Bill Gates personally responded at one point, deploying the straw man argument—misrepresenting his opponent's claim in order to knock it down more easily. MSF has long argued that Pfizer and GSK should make their vaccines available to poor nations at $5 for the full three-dose regimen for children. Gavi pays between $9 and $21. Bill Gates portrayed MSF as arguing that vaccines should be free—zero dollars—and then denigrated the group's Communist-adjacent, utopian thinking. "I think there is an organization that's wonderful in every other respect, but every time we raise money to save poor children's lives, they put out a press release that says the price of these things should be zero. Every five years when we are raising billions [for Gavi]—that is the most effective foreign aid ever given, that saves millions of lives," Gates said. "All that does is that you have some pharma companies that choose never to do medicines for poor countries because they know that this always just becomes a source of criticism. So they don't do any R&D on any product that would help poor countries. Then they're not criticized at all because they don't have anything that these people are saying they should price at zero.

"To focus on 'why isn't everything free' is a misdirection that has to do with the fact that they don't actually know anything about the costs," Gates said.

It's an extraordinary expression of both entitlement and unaccountability. Gates and Gavi and its pharmaceutical partners keep cost information and pricing negotiations carefully hidden from public scrutiny and then expect the world to trust that they are operating in good faith with the billions of dollars in government donations they manage. Most extraordinary is Gates's attempt to shame his critics into silence, warning that if they complain too loudly, Big Pharma may simply walk away from the bargaining table—and lives will be lost.

Bill Gates claims that the pneumonia vaccine saves lives at a cost of about $1,000 per head, so it seems more than fair to apply the foundation's lives-saved analysis to his estimates. How many more lives could have been saved if a child could be vaccinated for $5 instead of the prices Gavi pays, between $9 and $21? If we multiply the price difference out across the billions of dollars Gates and Gavi have spent, the number of lives lost from Gavi's pricing structure becomes very large.

In one high-profile demonstration of resistance, MSF refused a donation of one million doses of pneumonia vaccines from Pfizer, arguing that honoring such a donation would legitimize Pfizer's monopoly power. "By giving the pneumonia vaccine away for free, pharmaceutical corporations can use this as justification for why prices remain high for others, including other humanitarian organizations and developing countries that also can't afford the vaccine," MSF's Jason Cone noted in 2016.

MSF had a counterproposal: It wanted to *buy* vaccines from Pfizer at the same price it sold them to Gavi. Pfizer refused at the time.

In some respects, the many criticisms around Gavi's lack of accountability speak to its status as a private institution that is not meaningfully beholden to the people it claims to serve. Gavi's board of directors, the people in charge of the organization, include veterans of and executives from the pharmaceutical and financial services industries, like GSK, Goldman Sachs, UBS, Temasek, RockCreek Group, and JPMorgan Chase. These corporate interests sit alongside the Gates Foundation at the decision-making table, plotting out how to spend Gavi's multibillion-dollar budget. Poor nations were not meaningfully involved in the creation of Gavi and have little decision-making power over it, holding only five seats on the group's twenty-eight-member governing board—even as Gavi is changing public health in these nations. A 2007 investigation by the *Los Angeles Times*, for example, reported that poor children in Lesotho were being shepherded to clinics to get vaccines made available through Gates and Gavi, but when they sought treatment for medical problems for which there are no vaccines, like malnutrition, there were no resources available. Staff even instructed vaccine recipients not to ask about medical care for other issues. As Queens College historian William Muraskin reported in the early years of Gavi, "Gavi was designed for the [poor] countries' good but not by the countries. It is vital to realize that the demand for this initiative did not emanate from the designated beneficiaries. Rather, the countries as a group have had to be wooed, 'educated,' and financially enticed to accept the Gavi's goals as their own. . . . Saving lives through immunization, not having countries set their own priorities, has always been the Gavi's supreme goal."

Gavi is also not accountable to the people who supply most of its funding: taxpayers in rich nations. Wealthy governments have consistently provided 80 to 90 percent of Gavi's funding over its five-year fundraising cycles—around thirty-five billion dollars—yet they too hold only five seats on Gavi's board, meaning they also have limited say over how their money is used. This model of governance, called a public-private partnership, is central to the Gates Foundation's charitable work, and we'll see it again and again in the pages ahead: the foundation creates new projects that claim to provide innovative and effective solutions, inserts itself (and often its allies and surrogates) on the board, then aggressively fund-raises most of the organization's budget from taxpayers. Organizations like Gavi move the locus of public health away from public institutions such as governments and intergovernmental (multilateral) institutions like the WHO and, increasingly, toward the private sector, which is not accountable to the public, nor required to operate in a transparent manner.

And in the deep-seated psychic influence of neoliberalism, many governments and public institutions have come to embrace this new model of governance, even as it clearly spells out their own marginalization. Diminishing and eroding the role of governments and public bodies is not so much a secret plot of the Gates Foundation as simply the water we have been swimming in over the last several decades. Relentless privatization—of schools, of health care, of the military, of space exploration, of prisons, of highways, of municipal water supplies—has been the acclaimed neoliberal solution to our supposedly lame and wasteful government bureaucracies. Democracy, the thinking goes, simply doesn't have the wherewithal to get the job done. It is this ethos that has made the Gates Foundation so powerful over the last two decades and has allowed it to become the most important voice in public health for the global poor.

ONE REASON BILL Gates has made health and medicine the central focus of his philanthropy is that this body of work allows him to draw so heavily on his experience at Microsoft. As he explained in a 2019 interview, 40 percent of the foundation's annual budget goes to research and development to bring new pharmaceuticals to market.

> When I say, "Okay, we're going to build a TB drug team, we're going to build a TB vaccine team, we're going to build a kill-all-the-mosquitoes-in-the-world gene drive CRISPR team [to fight malaria]," I get to, in terms of how we fund that, organize it—How many locations? Do we wait until they get this result before we scale it up? I get to use the same or 80 percent the same type of thinking that I exercised [at Microsoft]

in terms of "Okay, let's go do Windows, let's go do Excel." It's backing engineers. It's getting a sense of the team. What needs to be added to that team, are the IQs on that team adding up as opposed to subtracting from each other? . . . It is very, very similar.

When Bill Gates talks about "building teams" to tackle different diseases, he's being explicit about the hands-on role his foundation plays in pharmaceutical development. This includes working directly with Big Pharma and small pharma start-ups—for-profit, nonprofit, and academic developers of drugs, vaccines, and diagnostics. The foundation has even put five hundred million dollars into its own nonprofit pharmaceutical enterprise, the Gates Medical Research Institute (Gates MRI), which is developing new drugs and vaccines.

It's in this body of work that we see Bill Gates's greatest aspirations as a philanthropist: to be an innovator. Beyond creating complex procurement mechanisms that purchase medicine, like Gavi, Gates wants his foundation involved in the actual creation of new lifesaving pharmaceuticals. The Gates Foundation reports spending billions of dollars for projects related to pneumonia, for example, including funding directed at the development of new vaccines. Gates has given charitable grants to a stunning array of vaccine developers in this space, including GSK, Pfizer, SK bioscience, PnuVax, Genocea, Matrivax, the Serum Institute of India, and Inventprise.

"There were actually many, many more," Amit Srivastava, previously the Gates Foundation's global lead for pneumococcal vaccine development, told me. As examples, he pointed to the foundation's partnerships throughout China with companies like Sinopharm and Walvax. "Next to polio, that [pneumonia] was the highest priority for Bill." (We'll discuss Gates's quest to eradicate polio later in the book.)

In 2014, the foundation helped launch an entirely new, for-profit pneumonia vaccine company, Affinivax, providing $4 million in initial seed funding and taking two of the six board seats. In 2022, GSK acquired Affinivax for $2.1 billion. The deal likely delivered a financial windfall to the Gates Foundation, an investor in the company. In these and other ways, the fruits of Gates's charitable work often seem to fall into the hands of Big Pharma, which speaks to the foundation's deep-seated belief in the primacy of large multinational companies in the marketplace.

"You're just a tool to get an asset into another organization," one small developer who has worked with Gates told me, requesting anonymity. "That process of thinking of Big Pharma as partners [of the foundation] and thinking of little pharma as asset developers that need to go to Big Pharma is what creates problems for both innovation and for the little companies." Asked about this bias toward Big Pharma, Srivastava responded, "Is there any other truth? Does it happen in any other way? It's not that the Gates Foundation thinks this way, but this is the reality, isn't it?"

What he is describing is the business-as-usual model of pharmaceutical development. Small pharma and universities create innovative technology. Big Pharma acquires the tech and uses its global market presence to make sure medicines are profitable. It's the same model Microsoft used, and it's not surprising, and maybe not even controversial, that the foundation endorses this approach in its work on pharmaceuticals.

What is surprising, and controversial, is that the Gates Foundation, a nonprofit, tax-privileged charity, is so involved in the commercial marketplace around pharmaceutical development. Gates's expansive corporate partnerships have long raised questions about the blurring of the line between for-profit and nonprofit activities. Activists and scholars have produced a robust body of critical writing on this topic under the banner of *philanthrocapitalism*, a term coined by the *Economist* as a plaudit to describe Big Philanthropy's growing focus on the "triple bottom line"—financial, social, and environmental returns. Critics later co-opted the term and challenged its premise. How can capitalism, an economic system that depends on winners and losers, deliver equity? At what point should for-profit commercial enterprises be seen as partners to social progress, and at what point are they obstacles?

The Gates Foundation has drawn special attention from critics because it makes charitable gifts directly to for-profit companies. My own reporting previously uncovered that the foundation has even donated money—hundreds of millions of dollars—to companies in which the foundation's endowment reported holding stocks and bonds, like Merck,

Pfizer, and Novartis. This means the foundation is sometimes positioned to benefit financially from its charitable partnerships.

"It's been a quite unprecedented development, the amount that the Gates Foundation is gifting to corporations," Linsey McGoey, a professor of sociology at the University of Essex, who has written extensively about Gates's corporate ties, told me. "They've created one of the most problematic precedents in the history of foundation giving by essentially opening the door for corporations to see themselves as deserving charity claimants at a time when corporate profits are at an all-time high."

While critics often present the Gates Foundation as allied too closely with business interests, what I found in reporting this book is that the foundation itself is actually a competitor in the marketplace. It is launching and directing pharmaceutical enterprises like Affinivax and the Gates Medical Research Institute. At the same time, it is playing a hands-on role at companies producing competing products. As sources told me, the foundation today is not just a friend to Big Pharma; it *is* Big Pharma—and its engagement in the marketplace bears a striking resemblance to Microsoft's.

As the *New York Times* reported in 1998 of Microsoft:

> Its wealth and market power are such that no start-up software company can even consider opening its doors without first handicapping Microsoft's intentions. Create a promising new market niche, and Microsoft may soon follow with its armies of programmers and its marketing muscle to crush the fledgling company. Then again, it can just as easily be a benefactor. In truth, the goal of many start-ups is to get on the radar screen at Microsoft headquarters in Redmond, Wash., and get bought out, at a handsome profit. . . . Competitors may complain about Microsoft, but, like it or not, they must also cooperate with Microsoft because their programs must run on Windows.

Bill Gates has brought this same energy and acquisitiveness to his private foundation. With some of the diseases the Gates Foundation works on, it's difficult for smaller companies to operate or succeed without it. One industry source described the foundation as a kind of "kingmaker," deciding which companies move forward and which ones don't. Others see the foundation as a kingpin, acting as both a direct competitor in pharmaceutical markets and also a governor. By creating financial relationships with many, or even most, companies working on a given disease, the foundation can cultivate a level of influence over the entire landscape of pharmaceutical development.

The Gates Foundation, for example, serves as one of the world's largest funders of research and development on malaria, with most of this money going toward pharmaceutical development. According to one Gates-funded analysis, the foundation spends more money on malaria than the entire pharmaceutical industry combined—which speaks to the fact that this disease affects primarily poor people, from whom the pharmaceutical industry cannot profit.

We see something similar with tuberculosis. The foundation has spent more than three billion dollars on the disease and has even embarked on its own in-house drug development through the Gates Medical Research Institute, securing exclusive licenses for TB drug candidates from Merck and Scripps. Only the National Institutes of Health spends (slightly) more on TB drug development—and, notably, the Gates Foundation has helped underwrite the NIH's work with more than fifty million dollars in charitable grants. The foundation has "taken control of all money going into TB drugs," one industry source told me. "They have all the money to do the clinical trials. There's no opposition to that. You can't say no to the Bill and Melinda Gates Foundation. No one wants to point out that this is not just a monopoly, but this is inhibiting directly innovation."

Even with diseases that affect poor and rich alike, like Covid-19, the foundation can act as a potent market force. During the novel coronavirus pandemic, it developed close financial ties with a wide array of competing vaccine developers, and Bill Gates openly boasted of his close work with pharma companies. Most infamously, he let slip in a press conference that his foundation had even pushed one vaccine developer, the University of Oxford (which receives funding from the Gates Foundation), to partner with Big Pharma. The foundation later clarified that it had merely stressed to Oxford "the importance of aligning with a multinational company to ensure their researchers have the full range of capabilities and resources they need to bring their vaccine candidate to the world." Following Gates's advice, Oxford partnered with pharma giant AstraZeneca.

To really understand the Gates Foundation's market power, it's important to understand how the foundation works with the private sector. When it decides to give a charitable grant to a small start-up—or any other organization, for that matter—it's not just writing a check. It's usually coming on as a full partner. The foundation assigns one or more staff, called program officers, to manage the relationship. Gates may also bring in a battalion of professional consultants, usually McKinsey or Boston Consulting Group, to go over the business plan and look for efficiencies. There will be endless calls and meetings and check-ins and reporting requirements. The foundation might take an equity stake (a large shareholder position) in the company or even board seats—at times "observer" seats, as it did with Affinivax. At the same time, it may also create financial relationships with that company's closest competitors.

Through its hands-on role, the Gates Foundation treats its grantees as though they were commercial contractors, or even employees, giving them money, a list of instructions to follow, and a mandate to run decisions up the ladder at the foundation. If things go well, more money will flow. Again, as Bill Gates describes it, this is the innocent "team-building" work of creating new products, applying the foundation's vast in-house expertise—including the army of former pharma execs who populate the foundation's leadership. "Compared to most philanthropy where you think, 'Okay, I'll write this nice check to this organization,'" Gates said in 2019, "[our approach is] a very hands-on thing because I like using these skills that I'm addicted to."

Building a team means knowing its members inside and out, understanding their strengths and their weaknesses. So, the foundation will look under the hood at each company it funds, scrutinizing its technology, examining its batch records, looking at its chemistry manufacturing controls, and collecting detailed information about its commercial ambitions and capacity. The entire value of a company is wrapped up in this proprietary information—one source described it as the "crown jewels"—and the Gates Foundation will insist upon seeing it. "We had to disclose our step-by-step process. We had to give a ton of information," one former grantee told me. "And they said, 'We will not provide additional funding unless you provide this information.'" Another source told me that the foundation insisted on seeing extensive confidential information about their company's pharmaceutical development during the negotiation of a charitable grant. The foundation never came through with the money.

Buried on the Gates Foundation's website is a survey instrument that asks its vaccine development partners for detailed business information. "Any data received from a manufacturer or obtained during conversations with a manufacturer is treated as HIGHLY CONFIDENTIAL," the document notes. "No information provided by any one manufacturer will ever be shared with any other manufacturer or organization without explicit consent."

In the pages ahead, grantees are asked an exhaustive list of questions— the dose size of vaccines, batch equipment size, the company's estimated maximal capacity, the volume and price of the vaccine in each market where it will be sold, details of all expenses (research, labor, facilities, consumables, overhead), along with the registration costs and licensing fees. The questionnaire also probes for granular details about the company's other financing arrangements, like with which banks it has outstanding loans and for what amounts. "If any questions arise, please contact Robyn Iqbal," the document notes. According to LinkedIn, Iqbal later left the Gates Foundation to lead the "Competitive Intelligence team for global vaccine markets" at GSK. She did not respond to my press inquiry.

Is it appropriate for the Gates Foundation, as a nonprofit charity, to trade so freely in corporate intel and proprietary information? And what rules are in place to prevent the vast body of valuable confidential information the Gates Foundation collects from leaking to its close partners in Big Pharma, especially as Gates staff appear to revolve freely between the foundation and Big Pharma? Amit Srivastava, as another example, after playing a prominent role in pneumonia vaccine development at the Gates Foundation, including holding one of Gates's board seats at Affinivax, left the foundation to work for the world's leading seller of pneumonia vaccines, Pfizer. Can Srivastava really unsee the confidential business information he had access to from Pfizer's competitors while working at Gates?

Srivastava dismisses these concerns as "intellectually lazy." He said that in his career—which included positions at Gates and then Pfizer and then Orbital Therapeutics—confidentiality agreements were "standard practice," obviating worries about corporate intel being shared. (He would not provide copies of these confidentiality agreements.) He denied the characterization that the foundation was hoovering up trade secrets from partners. "There is no recipe, there is no information that, in aggregate, you could just take, like a file, and take it to a different company and say, 'Can you make this for me?'"

Srivastava did acknowledge, however, that the Gates Foundation regularly generates pushback from partners related to its collection of confidential business information, describing these discussions as normal business negotiations between an investor (in this case, the Gates Foundation) and a company. Sometimes, he said, issues arise when foundation staff take on a "self-reverential" posture, thinking "they're doing god's work and that they can run roughshod over grantees. I've seen this happen, and this can trigger some legitimate annoyances from grantees. . . . There is an art to asking for that information."

In his own previous work for the foundation on pneumonia vaccines, Srivastava describes a let-all-flowers-bloom strategy. The foundation invested in two kinds of companies: those that could bring a traditional vaccine to market and those working on disruptive new technologies. "At the end of the day, the foundation did not want to end up without a product . . . so we would often invest in two players for the same kind of thing—and that would also trigger a lot of emotion and a lot of discomfort" among grantees, he added. "The foundation wants to ensure that if we invest in something, then the population [of poor people] gets the product in the best case, or some kind of benefit. And so, part of gathering that information—about the health of the organization, the nature of technology—informs" the foundation's due diligence to make sure the work it funds goes to a charitable end.

While Srivastava again and again described the foundation's activities as "not unusual" and totally uncontroversial, the truth is that the foundation's far-reaching engagement in the commercial marketplace is unusual. The Gates Foundation is a nonprofit, tax-privileged charity that is acting like a private equity investor, venture capital fund, or a pharmaceutical company. It has positioned itself to see the confidential business information of competing companies, and it even asks charitable partners to sign "global access agreements" that give the foundation licensing claims to their technology (explored in more detail later in the book). And the foundation, of course, is run by Bill Gates, one of the world's most storied monopolists who stands widely accused of anti-competitive behavior.

This reputation has followed Gates from Microsoft to his philanthropic work. In perhaps the most famous public allegation, a leaked memo from the director of the World Health Organization's malaria program, Arata Kochi, complained in 2007 that the foundation had used its wealth to take over malaria research, which had become "locked up in a 'cartel.'" The foundation's monopolistic control over the research agenda then positioned it to influence WHO recommendations and priorities, which, Kochi warned, "could have implicitly dangerous consequences on the policy-making process in world health." And if anyone dared to challenge Gates's agenda, Kochi noted, the foundation and the army of surrogates it funds would mount "intense and aggressive opposition." The Gates Foundation later became the second-largest funder of the WHO, expanding its financial influence even farther.

While a number of stories like this have emerged over the years, with little apparent impact on the foundation, they have overwhelmingly examined the foundation's monopolistic power over research and policy. Sources I spoke to in private industry say that the Gates Foundation brings the same "cartel" mentality to its work in pharmaceutical development. The foundation's presumption of expertise and authority, its muscular use of money, and its seemingly unregulated ability to operate in commercial spaces, these sources say, have allowed it to exercise wholly inappropriate marketplace power. As one company describes it, "They're clearly ranking their horses—who is faster?"

And because it can take an ownership stake in every horse in the race— many different competing companies working on the same disease—the foundation also has some ability to influence the outcome of the race: who wins and who loses. The allegation isn't that Bill Gates is trying to hurt companies out of some pathological sadism but, rather, that he is unwittingly maiming his charitable partners out of pathological narcissism, that the foundation's father-knows-best ethos, a clear holdover from Gates's days at Microsoft, compels it to act in an anti-competitive manner. One company that formerly worked with the foundation brought up the fable of "The Scorpion and the Frog." As the story goes, the scorpion needs to cross the river, but it doesn't know how to swim. So, it asks the frog to carry it across. The frog reluctantly agrees. Halfway across the river, the scorpion stings the frog. As the two struggle in the water and begin to drown, the frog asks the scorpion why it would do such a thing. "Because it is my nature," the scorpion replies.

During my reporting for this book, I reached out to dozens of pharmaceutical developers and start-ups that have worked with the Gates Foundation. Most didn't respond, and most of the ones that did, did so anonymously. As one source told me, "I don't want to be highlighted in your book as someone who is sour on Gates. . . . He can come in and buy all of our stock and have me fired. You have to be careful." While pharmaceutical developers generally agree that the foundation's money is of great importance to the development of new drugs and vaccines for poor people, four small developers, each working on different diseases, offered consistent accounts of the foundation abusing its financial power. Two of them agreed to show me documentation supporting their claims.

Two developers said the foundation got involved in personnel issues, wanting to vet new hires to senior executive positions. "Gates was trying to tell me who I could and couldn't hire . . . in my own organization," one source told me.

Three developers described the foundation as playing an inappropriate matchmaker role either to advance or to obstruct business partnerships. One developer said the foundation had counseled one of its corporate partners against working with them. Another said the foundation had wanted to push them into a business relationship against their wishes. "To me, it was very obvious," the source told me. Gates's plan was, "How can we take this tech and give it to another company? How do we get you vetted so we can get you bought by another company?" This allegation seems to chime with the example we examined earlier, in which the foundation pressured the University of Oxford to partner with Big Pharma on its Covid-19 vaccine. It also appears in line with the foundation's clearly articulated belief that only the largest companies have the wherewithal to successfully market new products.

Another developer I interviewed alleged that the foundation thought one of its leading product candidates would be better served with a different developer, telling me the foundation sought to "acquire assets by any means." Two developers told me that the foundation's strong-arming and interference had effectively "killed" their products. Both these companies told me they had considered suing the foundation to recover damages, but had ultimately decided against it because of the time and expense it would have required. "I also recognized that the Gates Foundation had billions of dollars, and they could just stall forever," one source told me. "We need a class action suit, that's what we need."

These kinds of allegations present the worry that the Gates Foundation is preventing better, cheaper products from reaching the marketplace and that lifesaving drugs, diagnostics, and vaccines may be held up by the foundation's meddling, micromanaging, and malign influence. The foundation believes that its in-house expertise and its ability to scrutinize the technology of many competing technologies give it the unique ability to know what products will work and what won't. And it believes that its charitable mission justifies its extreme interventions in the marketplace because these efforts will bring new lifesaving pharmaceuticals to the global poor.

"To have the level of arrogance to believe that you actually know more than anyone else about everything," one source told me. "[Bill Gates] might know a lot more than someone about something, but he's not going to know more than everyone about everything. They have that level of arrogance [at the foundation]."

"They certainly think they have the best—the crème de la crème," another source noted.

What's beyond dispute is that the Gates Foundation has organized its charitable relationships in a way that gives it a great many levers to help or hurt the developers it funds, using sticks and carrots to compel a company's technology down the foundation's favored development path. It can give your company funding or stop funding you. It can decide to fund your competitor. It can make your project dependent on its money and then change the terms and conditions of the relationship in midstream.

If you get on the wrong side of the Gates Foundation—say, your company won't agree to a business partnership it wants—the foundation can make it very difficult for your company to court other funders. Two developers told me that the foundation had bad-mouthed their company to other investors, greatly damaging their ability to secure financing.

When the Gates Foundation talks and says that is has lost confidence in a company's technology, other investors generally listen.

One developer told me that another lever the foundation can pull to prod an unwilling partner is to place unreasonable demands on research and development activities, effectively delaying, or sabotaging, commercial progress. "They're deciding on the end points of trials, how, technically speaking, you're going to evaluate if a [drug, vaccine, or diagnostic] works or not. If you pick end points in a certain way, you can tank a whole product at great expense," another source noted. "With a little coercion, you could make it fifteen years instead of ten years. How do you slow it down? [The foundation can tell you] 'You should do another study.'

"These are people who have a lot of opinions and no expertise, and suddenly Gates is deciding how these products are developed. It's strange for a charity."

The nuclear option the foundation has at its disposal is suing, or threatening to sue, companies. And, on this point, we have a rich public record of documentary evidence to tell the tale. PnuVax, a small vaccine company in Canada, was, for a time, one of the foundation's biggest private-sector partners, if not also Gates's best hope for bringing a new pneumonia vaccine to market. Beginning in 2014, the foundation pledged close to forty million dollars in three different grants to the company. At some point, the relationship went sideways, and the foundation brought down the hammer. When Gates sued PnuVax, the legal complaint became public information—and it revealed a great deal. Filed by K&L Gates, the law firm bearing the name of Bill Gates's late father, the complaint includes a copy of the foundation's grant agreement with PnuVax. (These are usually hidden from public view.) The agreement shows a data table with the prices at which PnuVax was to sell its pneumonia vaccine—between forty-eight cents and one dollar per dose (depending on the volume). While Pfizer and GSK were taking many times that price via Gavi, the Gates Foundation had found, and invested tens of millions of dollars in, a company that it thought could make shots for a fraction of the price. The agreement showed that the foundation had insisted on creating a scientific advisory committee "to provide regular input and make recommendations" to the company—and the foundation declared its intention to play a role on this committee. Members of the committee, the agreement noted, could even attend the all-important meetings PnuVax held with the government regulators who would decide whether or not to green-light a new pharmaceutical product.

The documents offer a variety of indications that PnuVax was positioned for success. The company's CEO, in a previous role, had been "directly responsible for the launch and approval of Prevnar 7," the vaccine that launched Pfizer's pneumonia vaccine empire. PnuVax also had its own manufacturing facility, and it had already developed its pneumonia vaccine. In short, it didn't appear to be asking the foundation to fund early-stage research but, rather, was trying to get its vaccine across the finish line.

So why would Gates torpedo this deal? According to the complaint, from early 2019, the foundation accused PnuVax of "misused grant funds" and "unauthorized pre-grant expenditures." If you read through the eighty-five-page complaint (and accompanying exhibits), it becomes clear that PnuVax wasn't buying Ferraris with the foundation's money. Rather, Gates accused the company, among other allegations, of using a small portion of its grant money to make lease payments on its vaccine manufacturing facility. As the *National Post* reported before the lawsuit, PnuVax had fallen behind on its lease payments to the Canadian government, and the small start-up company decided to prioritize expenditures on developing its pneumonia vaccine. Gates alleged that the company had used foundation monies to pay off the lease and that this was a misuse of grant funds.

The question is, why would the foundation go nuclear over such a seemingly picayune transgression? If PnuVax had the kind of potential the foundation clearly believed it did—Gates had offered it three consecutive grants totaling almost forty million dollars—why go to the mat over such a minor issue? At the end of the day, wasn't PnuVax using Gates's money for expenses related to its vaccine development business?

The foundation's legal complaint made sweeping demands, asking for a money judgment to address PnuVax's alleged breach of contract and that the company pay for the foundation's attorney fees. Gates also asked the court to issue a judgment declaring that PnuVax had "failed to comply with the terms and conditions of the Grant Agreement."

The case ended eleven weeks later with a voluntary dismissal.

Global News reported that "the lawsuit by the Bill & Melinda Gates Foundation against PnuVax was voluntarily dismissed in May 2019 with no costs payable by either party." *Maclean's* wrote that the foundation's "inoffensive allegation was never proven." But, by that point, the damage had been done. A previous news cycle, led by an odd "exclusive" in the British tabloid the *Daily Mail*, had dragged the company's name through the mud.

Being sued by the most celebrated humanitarian organization in the world and branded as an untrustworthy actor, even if such claims are never substantiated, can have a long-term impact. Industry sources told me it can make a company radioactive to other investors. The *Globe and Mail* reported that, during the Covid-19 pandemic, PnuVax was extremely well positioned "to produce millions of doses of Covid-19 vaccine by the end of 2020," but that it had been enigmatically passed over by the Canadian government's funding program. PnuVax, notably, also never brought its pneumonia vaccine to market.

Just for perspective, it's worth reiterating the broader context. At the same time that the Gates Foundation was partnering with and then suing PnuVax, the foundation was partnering with many of PnuVax's competitors, like Affinivax. And the foundation has a board seat on Gavi, which was handing out billions of dollars to Pfizer and GSK for their pneumonia vaccines. (The Gates Foundation, itself, has also given more than $200 million—in charitable donations—to Pfizer and GSK for a variety of projects.) It's an extraordinary level of influence, at every level of the market—influence that looks and feels a great deal more like Microsoft than Mother Teresa. It clearly suggests that the same incorrigible lust for control that animated Bill Gates's leadership in software also energizes his work on pharmaceuticals at the Gates Foundation. And this shouldn't surprise us. As one industry source told me, quoting Maya Angelou, "When someone shows you who they are, believe them the first time."

It remains a mystery what exactly happened with PnuVax—the company would not agree to an interview for this book—but one industry source told me that its greatest advantage was in its capacity to produce the polysaccharides necessary for making pneumococcal conjugate vaccines. Other companies had their own advantages, the source said. "I understand why Gates cast a wide net—these guys had the saccharides, these guys had a neat sort of click technology, these guys kind of had the conjugation technology. No one had everything."

It's conjecture, but one can imagine the Gates Foundation wanting to play matchmaker, brokering a deal to pair up PnuVax's polysaccharide production with another company that the foundation, in all its wisdom, thought could put the technology to better use. And maybe PnuVax bucked, and things broke bad. It's just a guess, but it aligns with the allegations shared with me by other development partners of the foundation. And it seems to make as much sense as the claims found in Gates's lawsuit, which were voluntarily dismissed.

The big-picture question we have to ask is, at the end of the day, what has been the result of all Gates's meddling in the commercial marketplace? Can we chalk up all the strife and allegations of harm to the old saying "If you want to make an omelet, you've got to break a few eggs"? Do the ends justify the means?

Across most of the diseases the Gates Foundation works on, its track record of innovation is quite weak. Gates planted its flag as the leading voice on malaria, working with a number of different companies to develop a vaccine, eventually putting all its weight behind a GSK product. The GSK vaccine's efficacy was so weak that even the foundation distanced itself from the product. We see a similar story with TB, where the foundation put half a billion dollars into a nonprofit vaccine developer named Aeras, which shuttered in 2018. Gates also poured money into, and grandiosely promoted, its work on an AIDS vaccine and new TB drugs. Again and again and again, the game-changing innovations Gates promised never materialized. Yes, these failures speak to the complexity of these diseases, but many sources say they also speak to the foundation's bullying and micromanaging, which stifle innovation.

Several sources I interviewed cite the Gates Foundation's success in funding the development of MenAfriVac, a meningitis vaccine, but these sources were quick to note that this was an example of the best of what Gates could accomplish when it took its hands off the steering wheel. The foundation's funding for MenAfriVac began in 2001, when Bill Gates was still on full-time at Microsoft. (He didn't make the Gates Foundation his primary focus until 2008, and even then he continued to remain heavily involved at Microsoft.) His private foundation, at that time, had fewer than 100 people on staff—today it has close to 2000—and operated as a check-writing charity, organized around giving talented people money and trusting them to produce good work. It was a categorically different approach from the hands-on "team-building" mentality Bill Gates would later bring to his private foundation.

The other caveat on MenAfriVac is that the foundation, as always, dramatically overstates its success, claiming in 2021 that the vaccine "has effectively ended meningitis as a public health problem [in Africa]." In reality, since the introduction of MenAfriVac, which protects against only meningitis serotype A, outbreaks of the disease have continued along the so-called meningitis belt in Africa. Large pharmaceutical companies like Sanofi Pasteur and GSK sell vaccines that protect against four serotypes, but these vaccines have not reached the global poor the same way as MenAfri-Vac has, presumably because they are more expensive. And in a model of health care dependent on charity, beggars can't be choosers.

The real danger in the foundation's hyperbolic claims about solving meningitis is not just that such claims amount to misinformation but that they also breed complacency. If we believe that Gates has solved a disease burden, this draws attention away from a serious ongoing public health problem.

We see similar question marks attached to Gates's work on a pneumonia vaccine. What has been the effect of all the foundation's meddling? Two of the companies it worked with ended up being stopped by lawsuits—one by the foundation (PnuVax) and one by Pfizer (SK bioscience). Another company, Affinivax, ended up being acquired by GSK. And one of the foundation's lead staff on pneumonia went to work for Pfizer for a time. After all the foundation's moving of chess pieces, the inescapable truth is that Pfizer and GSK maintained their duopoly power, collecting billions of dollars along the way from Gates-funded Gavi.

The Gates Foundation didn't respond to any press inquiries for this book, but we can imagine that it would counter that its charitable ambitions are still being realized, that the diseases it works on are harder than it thought, and that its money will eventually deliver solutions. And it would point to its partnership with the Serum Institute of India, the largest vaccine manufacturer in the world.

Serum, run by multibillionaire Cyrus Poonawalla and his son, Adar, is perhaps the foundation's closest for-profit partner, the recipient of hundreds of millions of dollars in financial help from Gates for work on a variety of vaccines. Gates worked with Serum for more than a decade to develop a pneumonia vaccine, and at the end of 2020, it announced that the vaccine would be sold to Gavi for $2 per dose—significantly less than what Gavi had been paying Pfizer and GSK.

On the face of it, the Serum vaccine could be seen as a counterpoint to my sources who accuse Gates of acting in anti-competitive ways, of organizing its work to benefit large multinational companies, or of failing in its innovation agenda. The Serum vaccine shows that the foundation's expansive work with the private sector can, eventually, deliver results: a new, cheaper vaccine that, to boot, would be produced by a manufacturer located in India, a relatively low-income country of more than a billion people that has a very real need for expanded pneumonia vaccines. Gates's partners heralded the new vaccine as "a turning point that could lead to dramatic public health impact," putting pneumonia vaccines "within reach for children still without affordable access."

To date, however, the Gates-Serum vaccine has not clearly delivered on this promise. The vaccine appears to have limited distribution, which, to some extent, can be chalked up to the Covid-19 pandemic. But it's also true that the vast majority of the pneumonia vaccines Gavi plans on purchasing over the next decade, it reports, will come from Pfizer and GSK, not Serum. (Another caveat: while Gavi boasted a two-dollar price per dose with Serum, underlying documents show it will actually pay the company as much as seven dollars a dose with bonus payments, the same arrangement it has with Pfizer and GSK.)

Some sources also raise questions about how widely the Serum vaccine will be used, because other vaccines offer protection against more strains of pneumonia. Pfizer has long dominated the global marketplace with its Prevnar 13 shot, which protects against thirteen strains of pneumonia. Serum's new 10-valent PCV shot protects against only ten. If Gavi is picking up the tab, shouldn't we expect poor nations to select the most protective vaccines—from Pfizer? "This is an issue with the Gavi system," notes Kate Elder, a senior vaccines policy adviser at MSF. "Someone's like, 'Hey, do you want the Rolls-Royce, or do you want the VW?' They'll say, 'We'll take the Rolls-Royce.'"

And the market continues to move against Serum. Pfizer is rapidly advancing its new Prevnar 20 vaccine for children, which protects against twenty strains of pneumonia. Merck announced a new 15-valent vaccine, and GSK and Affinivax are advancing a 24-valent vaccine. In this valency arms race, one industry source told me, the Gates-Serum vaccine shouldn't be seen as a competitor or challenger to Big Pharma's market power. And this speaks, once again, to the Gates Foundation's reputation for organizing its charitable work in a way that does not directly challenge the largest multinational pharmaceutical companies. (Of course, we might also include Serum, the world's largest vaccine producer, as part and parcel of Big Pharma.)

It's not clear how successful the Serum vaccine has been to date—Gavi, PATH, Serum, and UNICEF would not provide any usage data. Gavi issue a press release in late 2021 boasting of its plan eventually to cover 90 percent of children in India. If it accomplishes this—and that remains to be seen—it will have a significant impact on global health because India is such a populous nation. At the same time, pneumonia affects children everywhere, not only in India.

The Gates Foundation has telegraphed its own message on the limitations of the Serum vaccine. In 2021, it announced a massive new project to advance a new 25-valent vaccine, working with a start-up company called Inventprise, notably run by a former top executive from Serum. Gates did not disclose the full scope of its engagement on the project, however.

Located in Gates's backyard in Redmond, Washington, Inventprise almost seems like a subsidiary of the foundation. Gates has pledged a total of $130 million to the company in charitable grants alongside an additional $90 million in "convertible debt" (usually designed to convert into an ownership stake). The company's articles of incorporation in the state of Washington show that five of Inventprise's seven "governors" (meaning, its corporate board) have ties to Bill Gates or the Gates Foundation. One of them, Niranjan Bose, is an employee of Gates Ventures, a private venture of Bill Gates that is separate from the foundation. It is difficult to understand this arrangement, unless Gates Ventures is also an investor in Inventprise—one of several places where Bill Gates's personal business affairs appear to overlap with the tax-privileged charitable activities of his foundation. Inventprise did not respond to an interview request or questions sent by email.

What's also notable about Inventprise is that records from the U.S. Patent and Trademark Office show the Gates Foundation has an ownership stake in the patent covering Inventprise's 25-valent pneumonia vaccine. This presents the appearance of a new level of commercial activity in the foundation's work, a kind of humanitarian vertical integration in which Gates gives out charitable grants to fund and develop a company's vaccine, takes an ownership stake in the underlying technology, and then, if the vaccine is successful, will direct Gavi to buy it with taxpayer dollars and distribute it to poor nations. If the foundation also takes an ownership stake in Inventprise, which seems to be the design of its financing arrangement, sales of the new vaccine could drive new revenue into the Gates Foundation.

It's difficult, then, to ignore the optics: The Gates Foundation is operating like a pharmaceutical company. One vaccine developer I interviewed believes that Bill Gates is actually trying to create the world's largest pharmaceutical company.

WHAT'S BEYOND DISPUTE is that the foundation enjoys unparalleled privileges in the marketplace. It is not taxed or regulated as a private company because all its deal making happens through charitable agreements. It is not scrutinized by the public or by journalists as part of Big Pharma because it wears the superhero cape of philanthropy. And, armed with its unimpeachable brand as a humanitarian body, the foundation can financially partner with competing developers in ways that Big Pharma probably couldn't.

It will be years before we know the outcome of the Gates-Inventprise deal, but we have two decades of history to look to for perspective. Nowhere in Gates's legacy do we see the manifestation of the disruptive, game-changing, silver-bullet solutions the Gates Foundation has promised—where a new drug or vaccine it develops suddenly revolutionizes public health.

Rather, history shows us that the foundation's tenure of work in global health, by and large, can be defined by its business-as-usual paradigm, including the slow and highly inefficient transfer of monopoly vaccines to the global poor. History also shows that its work is usually broadcast as a success, no matter the outcome and no matter the effects. The foundation and its surrogates put so much money and energy into lives-saved claims that it becomes virtually impossible to ask how many lives are being lost, how many pharmaceutical developers are being maimed, and how many better, cheaper products are being buried.

Or, how many more lives might have been saved if we had followed a different approach. Instead of partnering with Big Pharma, for example, why aren't we challenging its monopoly power, recognizing it as a root cause of low vaccination rates? Why aren't we demanding that these companies share their vaccine technology with manufacturers in poor nations so they can produce their own shots? And why aren't we conceptualizing public health in terms that go beyond pharmaceuticals? Just because Bill Gates says vaccines and drugs are the best way to fix public health, and the best use of our tax dollars, doesn't mean it is true.

The reason I focus the first chapter of this book on vaccines, pneumonia, and Gavi is that they represent some of the Gates Foundation's strongest claims: the lives the foundation says it is saving, the innovative pharmaceutical products it claims to be producing, and the work of which it is proudest. While Gates's entrepreneurial model of philanthropy can, truthfully, point to some important wins—the many children receiving vaccines through Gavi and the creation of the new Serum pneumonia vaccine—these accomplishments are hounded by caveats and beset with collateral damage.

The really troubling coda to this story concerns Gates's later work in the pandemic, where the foundation leaned on the same strategies and partners it had with pneumonia vaccines. As we'll explore later in the book, Gates and Gavi successfully sold their response effort as the "only truly global solution to this pandemic." Billions of taxpayer dollars flowed into the project, which promised to protect the global poor. The plan failed in ways that were both predictable and spectacular, as Gates's pharmaceutical partners directed vaccines to rich nations while poor nations went unvaccinated. The "lives lost" through Gates's hubris and mismanagement have never been tallied.

The Gates Foundation's assumed power over the Covid-19 pandemic was the ultimate referendum on its work in public health and should serve as the ultimate lesson in the dangers of giving unaccountable power to billionaires with big ideas. But had we paid attention, we could have learned this lesson years earlier.

2

Women

There are few real-life villains who compare to financier Jeffrey Epstein.

Epstein was found dead in his jail cell in 2019 while awaiting trial on charges of sex trafficking of minors. His day in court was meant to be a day of reckoning for a man accused of having caused incalculable harm to countless girls by abusing them and then enlisting them to have sex with the powerful, wealthy men with whom he surrounded himself. Epstein's trial was also meant as a corrective for the bizarre sweetheart plea deal he had made in 2008.

Epstein, who had been facing a potential life sentence, served only thirteen months in jail, spending much of it on work release. Prison, essentially, became a place where he slept at night. Though investigators—journalists, police, and the FBI—had located dozens of girls who said they had been sexually abused by Epstein—with allegations of a "sexual pyramid scheme" in which he paid girls to recruit other victims—in court, his crimes were mysteriously reduced to soliciting prostitution. In this version of events, Epstein was engaging in a financial transaction with a willing partner. "I'm not a sexual predator, I'm an 'offender,'" he told the press in 2011. "It's the difference between a murderer and a person who steals a bagel." He repeated the line to Gates Foundation employees he met that same year—a meeting organized by Bill Gates.

Gates was one of numerous wealthy and powerful men who made their way into Jeffrey Epstein's orbit—a kind of elite boys' club that also included public figures like Bill Clinton, Prince Andrew, and Donald

Trump. Epstein's death in 2019, which was ruled a suicide, meant that we may never get the full story of his relationship to these men, all of whom deny any involvement in illicit activities. Instead, we've been left with endless speculation, conspiracy theories, and journalists trying to understand how Epstein ingratiated himself into so many circles of power. With Bill Gates, one leading explanation is that Gates was the victim of a sociopathic con man.

"One of the questions that I hear repeatedly is: How on earth could someone like Gates ever have been exposed to Jeffrey Epstein *after* he was convicted as a sex offender," journalist Vicky Ward has asked, reporting her theories in *Rolling Stone* and *Town and Country* and on the podcast *Chasing Ghislaine*. "Difficult as this is to swallow, what I learned talking to people who worked with or around the financier is that part of Epstein's genius (I hate to use that word, but it's appropriate) was manipulation. In particular, he had a unique ability to use philanthropy as a tool to worm his way into circles where he otherwise might not have been invited."

Ward's analysis is in line with Gates's official explanation, in which he presents himself as a dupe. He met Epstein for one reason and one reason only: to discuss a philanthropic fund-raising effort that could "unleash hundreds of billions for global health–related work," Bill Gates's personal spokesperson told the media. The foundation did, in fact, meet with Epstein to discuss a funding vehicle he had proposed at JPMorgan Chase, but the health fund they brainstormed never materialized. "Over time," the spokesperson noted, "Gates and his team realized Epstein's capabilities and ideas were not legitimate and all contact with Epstein was discontinued."

Yet Gates's responses evolved significantly over time, as a number of journalists, in one of the most spirited looks ever at the world's most powerful philanthropist, turned up contradiction after contradiction. Most obviously: Why would one of the richest men in the world need help from Jeffrey Epstein to raise money? And how could Gates possibly have been duped into believing that Epstein was a good philanthropic partner?

Bill Gates has an army of people working to keep his reputation sterling and his person free from harm. By the time he met Jeffrey Epstein in the early 2010s, Epstein was a known felon and a registered sex offender—and someone whose misdeeds had also been widely profiled in the news media. It is not only unthinkable that Bill Gates did not know exactly what he was doing or who Epstein was, but it is also unreasonable. Melinda French Gates herself publicly stated that she immediately saw Epstein for who he was and made her feelings known to Bill. "I also met Jeffrey Epstein—exactly one time," she said in a 2022 interview. "Because I wanted to see who this man was. And I regretted it from the second I stepped in the door. He was abhorrent. He was evil personified. I had nightmares about it afterwards. So my heart breaks for these young women because that's how I felt, and here I'm an older woman. My god, I feel terrible for those young women. It was awful." Like Melinda French Gates, foundation staff also saw Epstein as a major threat to the foundation's reputation. It is also important to note that Bill and Melinda French Gates have three children, including two daughters—one of whom, at the time Gates was meeting with Epstein, was the same age as some of Epstein's victims.

After the news media extensively profiled his connection with Epstein, showing that the two had a much more significant relationship than Bill Gates had acknowledged, Gates went from a position of denying and downplaying allegations to issuing an apology—one rooted in a claim of ignorance: "I certainly made a huge mistake, not only meeting him in the first place, but I met with him a number of times. I had a goal of raising money for global health. I didn't realize that meeting with him almost downplayed the incredibly awful things he did. You know, I learned more about that over time."

Gates has never been forced to really respond to the many contradictions that continue to surround his relationship with Epstein, however. This means that the full story remains something of a mystery, one that may continue to unravel in the years or decades ahead as more sources come forward.

While it's easy to discount the Gates-Epstein relationship as gossip or as an unfair distraction from the important substance of Gates's philanthropy, it deserves close scrutiny for the simple reason that Gates invited Epstein to be a part of his philanthropic empire, an empire that has carefully cultivated an image as a champion of women. Gates recklessly chose to involve foundation staff, and the foundation's reputation, with Epstein—and did so for many years; Gates Foundation staff remained in contact with Epstein as late as 2017. His relationship with Epstein was also cited as having contributed to his divorce from Melinda French Gates, a split that may permanently change the direction of the Gates Foundation. The Gateses will continue to co-lead the foundation through mid-2023, at which point, Melinda French Gates may step down (or be asked to leave).

The Epstein story is also important because it shows how incapable Bill Gates is of taking responsibility for his actions—and how he's organized his life so that there is no mechanism to make him take responsibility. As a punishing news cycle reported his extensive relationship with the convicted sex offender, his foundation, incredibly, went silent. Virtually all Bill Gates's responses to allegations came from his personal spokesperson, not the foundation.

Even if we accept Gates's hard-to-believe explanation of his relationship with Epstein—that it was organized entirely around charity—this still leaves us to contend with a deeply troubling question: If Gates was willing to partner with a monster like Epstein to raise money for global health, what else is he willing to do to advance his agenda?

This troubling ends-justifies-the-means pathology appears throughout the work of the Gates Foundation, an institution that appears exceedingly comfortable, if not entitled, to use its power and influence to remake the world in ways that, at times, disempower others. This speaks to the idea of moral hazards—what people are capable of doing when they think no one is looking or when they imagine the rules don't apply to them—which could be seen as the ties that bind men like Epstein and Gates.

Jeffrey Epstein, like Bill Gates, was superrich. When he died, the financier's estate was valued at $577 million. He also left a legacy of philanthropic giving, directing money to scientific research and universities and participating with Bill Clinton on charitable activities in the early 2000s (before Epstein's first arrest). Also like Gates, Epstein was something of a power broker, building a rich Rolodex of contacts from the top echelons of science, finance, and politics. A now-famous picture of Gates and Epstein also includes Larry Summers, former U.S. treasury secretary, and James Staley, at the time a top executive at JPMorgan.

Many believe that Epstein's expansive connections to high-powered men helped him secure his plea deal in 2008, when he faced charges that could have locked him away for the rest of his life. He always behaved as if he were above the law—and, in certain practical respects, he was.

For decades, Epstein preyed on the weak and the vulnerable—young girls, many of whom had come from poverty or backgrounds involving abuse. And in his predation, a common accomplice was his wealth: he paid off his victims, offered to fund their schooling, or tried to buy their silence. Epstein also used his personal fortune to build goodwill, open doors, befriend other global elites, and, in the process, secure substantial immunity. And Bill Gates, for a time, would have been one of Epstein's most powerful allies in this regard; their association sent a signal to polite society that Epstein should be embraced as a potential philanthropic partner, not interrogated as a violent predator.

NEWS OF GATES and Epstein's relationship first broke in the summer of 2019, with reports that Epstein had "directed" a two-million-dollar donation from Bill Gates (not the Gates Foundation) to MIT's Media Lab in 2014. "For gift recording purposes, we will not be mentioning Jeffrey's name as the impetus for this gift," an internal Media Lab email noted.

Gates denied that Epstein had been involved in the gift, but the allegation nevertheless became a major story—because Epstein himself was a major story. He'd been arrested in July on sex trafficking charges, and journalists were busily excavating his network of VIPs. Of all the names that surfaced, the world's most visible humanitarian drew special scrutiny. After the first spate of stories broke, Gates began to publicly address his ties to Epstein. "I met him. I didn't have any business relationship or friendship with him. I didn't go to New Mexico or Florida or Palm Beach or any of that. There were people around him who were saying, hey, if you want to raise money for global health and get more philanthropy, he knows a lot of rich people. Every meeting where I was with him were meetings with men. I was never at any parties or anything like that. He never donated any money to anything that I know about," Gates said.

His denials, however, were contradicted by the findings of journalists. While Gates said he hadn't gone to "Palm Beach or any of that," flight records—which had already been reported in the news media— showed that Gates had, in fact, flown on Epstein's plane to Palm Beach. The news media went on to report that Gates had met with the convicted sex offender multiple times at Epstein's home in Manhattan, including at least one social event where women were present: Miss Sweden and her fifteen-year-old daughter. "A very attractive Swedish woman and her daughter dropped by and I ended up staying there quite late," Gates wrote in an email to colleagues the next day. So, why did Gates first tell the media, "Every meeting where I was with him were meetings with men. I was never at any parties or anything like that"?

New York Times writer James B. Stewart noted that Gates refused to specify the exact number of meetings he had with Epstein—yet another red flag. Based on his reporting, Stewart catalogued several: "This included visits to the [Epstein] mansion, seeing each other in Seattle, flying on Epstein's plane when we all know Bill Gates has his own forty-million-dollar plane. And then . . . why would Gates say, 'Oh, I had no relationship with him' when of course he knows what the facts are." Stewart's circumspection was informed by his own previous reporting on Epstein, which included a visit to Epstein's mansion in Manhattan a year earlier. "He's a registered sex offender, and after I rang the doorbell, it opens, and there is a beautiful young woman standing there who I didn't think was sixteen, but she could have been nineteen or something—and I thought, whoa, a sex offender has a beautiful young woman opening the door? So, I didn't have to go through the door before I realized there's something really weird going on here." Like Melinda French Gates, Stewart knew immediately who and what Epstein was.

Gates's less-than-forthcoming account sent a clear signal that there was more to the story, and journalists kept digging, reporting that Gates and Epstein had actually met dozens of times, that their relationship was personal in nature, and that the two men had even discussed Gates's failing marriage. Gates disputed all of these findings. News outlets also reported that Gates had been using Epstein as a conduit to get close to the Nobel Peace Prize.

There is some compelling evidence to support this allegation. Epstein had relationships with former Nobel winners like Frank Wilczek, Gerald Edelman, and Murray Gell-Mann. He also had a relationship with a think tank called the International Peace Institute (IPI), which had received donations from charitable foundations linked to Epstein.

In 2013, Epstein, Gates, and representatives of IPI met with Thorbjørn Jagland, the former prime minister of Norway and, at the time, the chair of the committee that awards the Nobel Peace Prize. Jagland later told journalists that the meeting, held in France, was related to his role as secretary-general of the Council of Europe, a human rights organization. The meeting, Jagland said, focused on a discussion of counterfeit medicines. He downplayed Epstein's involvement in the meeting, saying, "Bill Gates asked for it and explained why. He brought other people, including from IPI. I didn't have a routine of assessing the companions of the people I had meetings with."

This meeting raises a welter of questions. Gates had claimed that his relationship with Epstein was limited to brainstorming a fund-raising effort, so why were the two men taking a meeting together at a human rights group in Europe? Likewise, why would Bill Gates have sought out a meeting with someone on the Nobel Committee?

"While a Nobel Prize would certainly be a great honor, it is false to state that Bill Gates was 'obsessed' with the honor, set it as a goal, or campaigned for it in any way," Gates's spokesperson told one news outlet. "If Epstein had a plan or motivation to insert himself into any processes related to any awards or honors on behalf of Gates, neither Gates nor anyone he works with was aware of his intentions and they would have rejected any offers for assistance."

After Bill Gates met with Jagland and the International Peace Institute, the Gates Foundation began donating millions of dollars to the IPI. This raises obvious questions about a possible quid pro quo: that Gates was rewarding the IPI with charitable dollars for having facilitated an introduction to a Nobel jurist.

More notable, Epstein apparently was involved in coordinating the foundation's donation. Emails surfaced showing him, IPI, and one of Bill Gates's top deputies, Boris Nikolic, trading messages about the donation.

The finding presents Epstein as a direct intermediary in the Gates Foundation's charitable grant making, something the foundation denies: "The foundation has never had any financial dealings with Epstein. We work with the International Peace Institute, a grantee that supports our efforts to improve health in Pakistan and Afghanistan."

IN 1992, WHILE visiting New York City shortly after finishing her undergraduate degree at the University of Texas, Melanie Walker was having tea at the Plaza Hotel. Jeffrey Epstein also happened to be at the hotel, with Donald Trump, and the two men made a point of introducing themselves to Walker, half their age. Epstein discussed with her the idea of modeling—one news account said he dissuaded her, while another said he suggested an audition with Victoria's Secret. It was an offer Epstein might have felt comfortable suggesting because he was a financial adviser to the owner of the company, Leslie Wexner.

Thus began a relationship that appears to have lasted decades. *Rolling Stone* describes Epstein as having been a "mentor" to Walker, noting that as she went on to medical school in the 1990s, she maintained an address in a New York City apartment building owned by Epstein. The *New York Times* noted that when Walker graduated from medical school, Epstein hired her as his science adviser. It was a role she would also later play for Bill Gates.

According to her website, Walker made her way to Seattle in 2000 for clinical training at the University of Washington, and then, in 2006, joined the Gates Foundation as a senior program officer. There, she became acquainted with Boris Nikolic, who appears to play various roles in the Gates Foundation, Gates's personal wealth, and Gates's personal life. The two men reportedly travel and socialize together frequently. They were also professional collaborators, as Nikolic's name is attached to at least two patents on which Gates is listed as a co-inventor. When Gates made a major investment in the pharmaceutical company Schrödinger, the press release announced that Nikolic would be taking a seat on the board. In 2011, Nikolic and Gates met Epstein for the first time. After the meeting, Epstein emailed Melanie Walker to share the news of the meeting.

This backstory became a major headline in 2019, when a bombshell dropped. Just days before Epstein was found hanged in his jail cell, he amended his will, naming Boris Nikolic as one of his backup executors, putting him in a position of potential responsibility for managing his $577 million estate. The world naturally took an interest in who Nikolic was—and discovered that he was a longtime associate of, if not wingman to, Bill Gates. Nikolic told the press he was "shocked" to have been named an executor, saying he would not take on the role. He also described himself as a victim, saying, "Over the past few years, we have all learned that Epstein was a master deceiver. I now see that his philanthropic proposals were designed to ingratiate himself with my colleagues and me in an attempt to further his own social and financial ambitions. When he failed to achieve his goals, he started to retaliate."

As Vicky Ward reported this story in *Rolling Stone*, Epstein's naming Nikolic as an executor to his will was a final "fuck you" to Bill Gates, with Nikolic calling it "absolutely a retaliatory move." According to this version of the story, when Epstein put Nikolic's name in the will, he knew the news media would track the story back to Gates. Yet, in this telling, it has never been made clear what Epstein was retaliating against. Why did he feel so much enmity toward Bill Gates, who has repeatedly minimized his relationship with Epstein? Gates's account of his breakup with Epstein was that, as they continued to discuss a possible philanthropic partnership, the foundation lost confidence in him and walked away. There was never any account of the two men having a major falling-out. Gates has claimed that he barely knew Epstein and that their minor relationship was entirely professional in nature, not personal. Yet, we're also told that their failed philanthropic partnership stuck so deep in Epstein's craw that it was top of mind two days before his suicide, leading him to redraw his will to take Bill Gates down. It is a difficult narrative to follow, and it seems more than reasonable to ask whether there is more to this story.

One of the most important takeaways from the Gates-Epstein saga is the Gates Foundation's apparent inability to address the questionable behavior of its founder. As some large corporations took swift action to address allegations related to Epstein, the foundation sat on its hands.

Outside the foundation, a number of Epstein's associates faced some level of accountability. Top leaders vacated high-profile corporate positions—at Barclays, Apollo Global Management, and L Brands—under intense public pressure over their ties to the sex offender. Prince Andrew was stripped of his royal duties. President Donald Trump's secretary of labor, Alex Acosta, stepped down under criticism related to his role as a former prosecutor in Epstein's sweetheart plea deal in 2008. The optics present corporate America, the British monarchy, and the Trump administration as all having a stronger moral compass than the world's most celebrated humanitarian charity.

What made the foundation's silence especially troubling was the fact that, after the Epstein story broke, Bill Gates faced a number of allegations of personal misconduct from female employees at Microsoft and the Gates Foundation. He denied or downplayed the allegations as they emerged in rapid succession throughout 2021.

Gates did admit to one relationship with a Microsoft employee, claiming it had ended "amicably." Yet that admission came after Microsoft publicly stated that it had received a "concern" from the employee—who had specifically asked that Melinda French Gates be shown the letter she sent to Microsoft about her relationship to Bill Gates. "A committee of the Board reviewed the concern, aided by an outside law firm to conduct a thorough investigation," the company noted. "Throughout the investigation, Microsoft provided extensive support to the employee who raised the concern."

Microsoft later acknowledged another incident, in which Bill Gates emailed an "inappropriate" and "flirtatious" message to a midlevel employee, asking her to meet him outside the office. When the story broke, Gates's personal spokesperson responded, "These claims are false, recycled rumors from sources who have no direct knowledge, and in some cases have significant conflicts of interest."

As these and other allegations, spanning decades, came into public view, the public began to take a hard look at Microsoft itself. Hundreds of complaints of discrimination and harassment rolled in to Microsoft during Gates's leadership at the company (not all directed at Bill Gates), and Gates stepped down from the board of directors in 2020 as Microsoft probed misconduct allegations against him. (Gates denies stepping down because of any probe.)

In 2021, Natasha Lamb, managing partner of Arjuna Capital, spearheaded a successful shareholder resolution to force Microsoft to investigate the allegations of misconduct against Gates and make its findings public. "The case of Bill Gates is a classic example of money and power. Clearly, hitting on his employees was his move. That's how he met his wife. It's clear that kind of behavior continued," Lamb noted. "This leaves an open question as to how the board and leadership is addressing sexual harassment within the company. There was some change following MeToo in how the company was dealing with these issues internally. But clearly, you had this signal of bad behavior from the top, which sets the culture." The Gates Foundation, because it has no shareholders, is not subject to the same kinds of resolutions.

Throughout the allegations, Bill Gates has consistently denied that he mistreated anyone or behaved inappropriately toward women. Yet, to Natasha Lamb's point, the allegations against him weren't exactly news. Despite his public persona as a computer nerd or a soft-spoken philanthropist, Gates has always been a hard-driving alpha male. At Microsoft, he constantly tested the mettle of his subordinates with screaming matches, racked up speeding tickets driving his Porsche recklessly, and had long (allegedly) viewed the workplace as his sexual playground. Most of us, for example, have lost track of the fact that Melinda French Gates was once Gates's subordinate at Microsoft. And she wasn't the only employee with whom Gates reportedly had a relationship. In the early 1990s, the news media reported his having an "on-again, off-again romance with a product manager in Microsoft's marketing division" and several dates with a "low-level employee in Microsoft's information center."

Under Gates's leadership, Microsoft also developed a corporate reputation for questionable conduct toward women. According to the book *Hard Drive: Bill Gates and the Making of the Microsoft Empire*, in the company's earliest days, women were paid hourly wages—unlike men, who were salaried. When the women in the office asked for back pay for all the overtime hours Gates had pushed them to work, he refused. They filed a complaint with the state, prompting Gates to throw a tantrum; he screamed so violently that his face turned purple. And the company, allegedly, didn't hire its first female executives until it had to—to win a government contract that had affirmative action provisions requiring gender representation in the workforce. According to an anonymous Microsoft source quoted in *Hard Drive*, "They would say, 'Well, let's hire two women because we pay them half as much as we will have to pay a man, and we can give them all this other "crap" work to do because they are women.' That's directly out of Bill's mouth." The source added, "I thought it was surprising that he wasn't more sensitive to the issue."

In 2021, Maria Klawe went public about her service on Microsoft's board, between 2009 and 2015, saying Bill Gates was consistently hostile toward any suggestion of diversity, including the idea of opening up the company to women: "'Are you trying to effing destroy the company?'" she recounts him asking her. "They had launched a press release saying how I would help them bring more women . . . to help diversify Microsoft," Klawe told me. "And then when one actually suggested doing something [on the board], it was like absolutely zero openness from Bill."

Klawe sees the same contradictions in Gates's leadership at the Gates Foundation, describing him as "living a double life": "There's the person he projects as the leader he wants to be seen as, helping make the world a better place. And then in his day-to-day interactions, he treats women without respect." Klawe has said that "the work that the Gates Foundation has done in supporting poor women in Africa and many other parts of the world, it's obvious to me that that's not a priority for him, but he's willing to be videotaped saying it's a priority for him."

Misconduct allegations followed Gates into his philanthropic work. The *New York Times* reported an allegation that Gates had made an unwanted advance to a subordinate at the foundation who was uncomfortable with his overture. "Six current and former employees of Microsoft, the foundation and the firm that manages the Gates's fortune said those incidents, and others more recently, at times created an uncomfortable workplace environment," the *Times* reported. "Mr. Gates was known for making clumsy approaches to women in and out of the office. His behavior fueled widespread chatter among employees about his personal life." Gates denied the allegations of misconduct. The foundation publicly stated that it had never received any complaints or allegations against Bill Gates, so it had no reason to investigate him for misconduct— even as the news media very widely profiled the problem.

One former Gates Foundation employee told me a top foundation official had once asked that an attractive female staff member not attend meetings with Bill Gates because he would be distracted. "The place had a culture of excusing his behavior, I would say," the source said.

Reports also emerged that Gates's money manager, Michael Larson, who oversees both the foundation's endowment and most of Bill Gates's personal fortune, faced years of allegations of workplace misconduct, including inappropriate behavior toward women. Larson consistently denied or downplayed the allegations. After the major exposé, Larson kept his position managing the foundation's endowment.

The far-ranging allegations of sexism and sexual misconduct surrounding Bill Gates force us to reexamine his relationship with Jeffrey Epstein. While the leading explanations for his connection to Epstein are that it was innocently directed at philanthropy or self-servingly organized around a lobbying campaign to win a Nobel Prize, we also have to question other possibilities—that the relationship could have had something to do with Epstein's principal activities in life: sexual gratification and the exercise of power.

There's never been any direct allegation against Gates in this regard, and Gates, in his original explanation, went so far as to stress that his meetings with Epstein were with men, not women. Yet media reports show that Epstein surrounded himself with young, attractive women at these meetings with Gates. So, were women one attraction that drew Gates to Epstein?

Former victims of Epstein have said that he had pin-size cameras hidden all over his New York City mansion, the allegation being that Epstein's lifestyle of wealth and impunity was built on blackmail. He invited powerful men into his sexual pyramid scheme and collected compromising videos of them. (For what it's worth, a police raid of his Palm Beach mansion in 2005 found hidden cameras in two locations.)

Adam Davidson, cofounder of the NPR show *Planet Money* and a contributing writer to the *New Yorker*, looked deeply into these questions while producing the podcast *Broken: Seeking Justice*. On social media, Davidson reported that he had learned many things about Epstein during the course of his reporting that he couldn't publish, either because it could hurt one of Epstein's victims or draw a lawsuit from a rich and powerful man. He tweeted a thread on Twitter that went viral, arguing that we shouldn't give Epstein's cohorts, including Bill Gates, any benefit of the doubt.

> If someone spent any amount of time with Jeffrey Epstein, at a min-
> imum they saw him physically touching girls in provocative ways
> and rather gleefully showing off his ability to do so. More than likely,
> they were offered sex with whatever their preference was (Epstein did
> employ, abuse, and traffic women who weren't underage). . . . They
> knew. Yes, of course, many participated. But ALL knew . . . these men
> should not be invited into polite society. They should not be cele-
> brated on TV shows as experts on Covid or international relations or
> whatever.

In an interview, Davidson told me that Bill Gates deserves special scrutiny because, unlike many of the other men who made their way into Epstein's inner circle, Gates consorted with Epstein after his 2008 conviction, after he was a known felon. And, Davidson says, Gates's explanations for his relationship with Epstein are particularly implausible. As a fairly well-known and easily google-able convicted sex offender, Epstein would have been far more of a liability to Gates than an asset. Why in the world would Bill Gates have gotten so close to him for so long?

While revelations of Gates's relationship with Epstein, alongside allegations of misconduct with female subordinates, did somewhat diminish Gates's moral authority on the global stage, he remains very much welcome in polite society—and, presumably, will continue to as long as his checkbook remains open. The real irony is that the Gates Foundation has become one of the world's leading philanthropic funders of gender equity and women's empowerment. This giving could be seen as papering over the misconduct allegations that hound the foundation. And recipients of this money could be seen as laundering Bill Gates's reputation.

Philanthropic giving was also one of Jeffrey Epstein's most important accomplices and enablers. Davidson says Epstein's vast, decades-long grooming operation would not have been possible without his charitable giving. "One thing that philanthropy sells is a product called reputation management," Davidson notes. "It was part of the seduction. When you talk to the victims, they reference that [Epstein] was friends with all these powerful people. When you walk in [his mansion], there are photos of all these famous, powerful people. He has this connection to Harvard [through philanthropy]. He has this connection to MIT. . . . These women said part of the reason they didn't speak out against him was because he seems to know everyone. He seemed to be part of the powerful elite."

This same model of wealth, power, and impunity is also undeniably part and parcel of the cult of Gates. The endless PR broadcasting his good deeds and his big donations has helped drown out the allegations he has faced, or persuaded us to give him the benefit of the doubt. At the same time, an irresistible devil's bargain asks us to suspend moral judgment under the rationalization that a greater good may be served by his generous philanthropy—up to and including using the Gates Foundation's money to clean up the problems the foundation might itself be enabling or normalizing.

After a bruising news cycle in 2021, Bill and Melinda French Gates together announced that they were donating $15 billion to charity—that is, to their own private foundation—the largest sum they had donated by far since the massive donations they made at the height of their previous major PR crisis, the Microsoft antitrust trials. The *Washington Post* and other outlets rushed to report that the Gateses were the world's most generous givers in 2021. The foundation also appears to have elevated its work to "empower women and girls," reporting a billion dollars in charitable grants on this project. This includes a $500,000 donation to the Clooney Foundation for Justice, founded by actor George Clooney and his spouse, Amal Clooney, a human rights lawyer. The money supported the launch of an initiative called Waging Justice for Women. A quote from Amal Clooney notes on the group's website, "We can combat the injustice that women face by ensuring that unfair laws are overturned and that those who abuse women are held to account."

Will this noble fight for justice probe the misconduct allegations that surround their benefactor? What about the widespread allegations of harassment and discrimination from women working at Microsoft? What about the Gates Foundation's money manager, Michael Larson?

What about the Gates Foundation's yearslong, still-unclear relationship with Jeffrey Epstein? What about Epstein's countless victims? And what about the Gates Foundation's wholesale failure to address these issues internally? Should the foundation be a partner in the fight for accountability and justice—or should it be the target of the investigation? At what point does the world decide that the ends do not justify the means? The Clooney Foundation did not respond to multiple press inquiries.

To Adam Davidson's point, reputation management, undeniably, is a key function of philanthropy for men like Bill Gates. But there's more to the story than just reputation. When we embrace and applaud the Gates Foundation's philanthropic giving, we're doing more than burnishing Bill Gates's image. We're also handing over unaccountable power. If charity is a product too, there has to be a point at which we stop buying what Bill Gates is selling.

3

Taxes

Melinda French Gates's 2019 autobiography, *The Moment of Lift*, was an automatic bestseller, but it wasn't a critical hit. An NPR review—published online but not broadcast over the radio—called the book "more of a whisper than a call to action," describing it as "long on heart-warming anecdotes, short on argument." A week later, however, NPR broadcast a much higher-profile puff-piece interview with Melinda Gates on its *Goats and Soda* program, which is financially supported by the Gates Foundation.

We saw a similar flip-flop in the medical journal *The Lancet*, whose review of *The Moment of Lift* began with a damning critique and ended with ring-kissing conciliation. After examining the disconnect between Melinda French Gates's rhetoric on gender equity and the dearth of female leaders at the Gates Foundation, the journal landed on an odd non sequitur: "Gates's writing reveals her to be an exceptional person. She could have spent the family wealth on yachts, luxury holidays, and designer bags, but instead she has chosen to focus her career on improving global health. She comes across as someone who is thoughtful, a dedicated mother, and, overall, a compassionate person driven by faith, love, and connection."

What these book reviews show is how difficult it is to criticize the Gates Foundation without sandwiching that criticism between high praise that is often rooted in dangerous mythologies. Are we really to believe, for example, that Melinda French Gates doesn't go on luxury holidays or have designer bags? That she is sacrificing any personal indulgences through her philanthropic giving?

The Gates family spends truly obscene sums of money on themselves and lives categorically different lives from the rest of us. They have mansions, plural, filled with expensive things like original works by Leonardo da Vinci and Winslow Homer alongside expensive rare sports cars. The Gateses travel by private jet, even as this deeply pollutive activity stands at odds with Bill Gates's claimed leadership on climate change. Instead of owning a yacht, they prefer to rent one—the typical price is several million dollars *a week*. CNBC reports that the Gates family owns a private island in Belize, while the *New York Times* reports that Bill Gates rents out Frégate Island in the Seychelles by the week.

The Gates family also has an army of staff at their fingertips, ranging from private security to private schedulers. They spare no expense with their children, sending them to the most elite private schools. When the Gateses' son enrolled at the University of Chicago, he doesn't appear to have spent his first year in a cramped dorm room with a total stranger, as most American students do. Local news outlets reported that Bill Gates bought a $1.25 million house just off campus—boasting "3,000 square feet with four and a half bedrooms, sprawling deck space, a kitchen with quartz counter-tops, and built-in Viking appliances." Likewise, the Gates family bought their eldest daughter not just a horse, but a world-class horse-riding facility near San Diego, whose Dutch Olympiad "equestrian trainer," Harrie Smolders, is "formerly the top-ranked show jumper in the world," according to the website of Evergate Stables. (Gates also reportedly bought and sold a $26 million equestrian facility in Wellington, Florida.)

Also like other billionaires, the Gates family appears to take an ethically agnostic approach to financial investments, with little concern over harm to human health or well-being, including that of the poor people they claim to help. Though critical journalism of the foundation is rare, journalists have several times reported on the Gates Foundation's $54 billion endowment having investments in private prisons, weapons manufacturers, tobacco, fossil fuels, and even in chocolate and cocoa companies linked to child slavery. The investment income from this dirty money, the logic goes, can save lives through philanthropy.

The Gateses not only live like any other billionaire family, but they live among other billionaires, eagerly cloistering themselves off with other global elites at the World Economic Forum in Davos or the Sun Valley Conference in Idaho, where the superrich clap each other on the back and make business deals.

So, yes, Melinda French Gates is an "exceptional person"—an exceptionally *rich* person. Just because the Gateses and their private foundation are constantly reminding us of their generosity, of how they are going to give away all their money instead of spoiling themselves or their children, this does not make it true. It's a point that Melinda French Gates herself quietly began to acknowledge following her divorce—a legal transaction that made her a billionaire many times over in her own right. (As I write this in 2022, Bloomberg pegs her net worth at around $11 billion; *Forbes* puts it at closer to $7 billion.)

"It's important to acknowledge that giving away money your family will never need is not an especially noble act," Melinda French Gates wrote in an essay announcing her "Giving Pledge" to donate most of her wealth to charity. "There's no question in my mind that the real standard for generosity is set by the people who give even when it means going without."

There's honesty to this, but also false modesty. Melinda French Gates and her ex-husband have little compunction about wearing the noble crown, aggressively using their wealth to make their voice heard above others while gamely accepting high-profile awards and endless media adulation for their charitable acts. And they've never been particularly honest about the benefits they personally receive from their charitable giving—not just the political influence, the public relations, and the goodwill but also the billions of dollars in tax savings.

In the United States, the government rewards charitable giving with tax breaks, the idea being that charity unburdens governments (and taxpayers) of work it would otherwise fund—helping the poor, cleaning up the environment, fighting addiction, and so on. While most Americans make charitable contributions each year, the tax benefits from charity generally are reserved for rich donors. As former U.S. secretary of labor

Robert Reich notes, the U.S. Treasury loses out on tens of billions of dollars in tax revenue every year from these tax breaks, the large majority of which goes to wealthy charitable donors.

Ray Madoff, a law professor at Boston College, reports that the super-wealthy can reap tax benefits of up to 74 percent through philanthropy—from avoiding income tax, capital gains tax, and estate tax they would otherwise pay. In essence, every dollar a multibillionaire donates can generate up to seventy-four cents in personal benefits in the form of tax savings. Tax scholars widely describe this relationship as a tax subsidy: we, the taxpayers, are richly subsidizing the Gates Foundation. "I think people often confuse what wealthy people are doing on their own dime and what [they're] doing on our dime, and that's one of the big problems about this debate," Madoff told me. "People say, 'It's the rich person's money [to spend as they wish].' But when they get significant tax benefits, it's also our money. And, so, that's why we need to have rules about how they spend our money."

The problem is the current rules we have in place are too few, too weak, and too little enforced. Congress last substantively addressed the rules governing private foundations in 1969. While the practice of philanthropy has evolved substantially over the last fifty years, the law has not. As dull as it may sound, understanding taxation is important to understanding American philanthropy and the Gates Foundation. Again, if you pay taxes in the United States, then much of the money the Gates Foundation gives away is actually your money. And while Bill Gates is using your money (to remake the world in his vision), you don't get a say in how he's using it. Nor do you get credit for any of the Gates Foundation's work: all the glory goes to Bill and Melinda.

The Gates family rarely addresses the tax benefits they receive. The only reference that appears on the foundation's website was buried on its "Frequently Asked Questions" page:

> Do Bill and Melinda get tax breaks for their donations to the foundation?
>
> Many individuals enjoy tax benefits as a result of making charitable contributions. The amount of tax savings received depends on both the size of the charitable contributions and the person's annual income. Bill and Melinda have been exceptionally generous in making

contributions to the foundation, donating sums much larger than their
annual incomes. As a result, the tax savings they receive from these
contributions represent a very small percentage of the contributions.
From 1994 through 2020, Bill and Melinda gave the foundation more
than $36.8 billion. Those donations resulted in a tax savings of approx-
imately 11% of the contributions they made over that time.

The claimed tax savings—11 percent on $36.8 billion—amount to
around $4 billion in personal benefits to the Gates family for their dona-
tions.

Warren Buffett also publicly reports his tax savings, noting in 2021,
"In my own case, the $41 billion of Berkshire shares I have donated to
the five foundations [most of which has gone to Gates] has led to only
about 40¢ of tax savings per $1,000 given." That is, Buffett claims that his
personal tax savings are .04 percent—around $14 million on the $35.7
billion he's given to the Gates Foundation.

It's unclear how Gates and Buffett calculated these tax savings (11
percent and .04 percent, respectively), but we know that their self-serving
arithmetic is divorced from reality. Every dollar they donate is automatically spared from the 40 percent estate tax (that will be levied on their
wealth when they die) and other taxes, like capital gains tax on investment income (usually 20 percent).

A fairer, if conservative, assessment of the tax benefits that Buffett
and the Gateses personally receive is something on the order of 50 percent. So, of the $75 billion that Gates and Buffett have jointly donated
to the Gates Foundation through mid-2022, the U.S. Treasury has lost
something on the order of $37 billion in taxes. But this is only one part
of the tax revenue lost to Gates's charitable empire.

Consider the Gates Foundation's $54 billion endowment, a vast pile
of money invested in (as of late 2022) companies like Microsoft ($9.1
billion), Berkshire Hathaway ($7.9 billion), Canadian National Railway
($5.9 billion), Waste Management ($5.6 billion), John Deere ($1.3 bil-
lion), Caterpillar ($1.2 billion), Ecolab ($703 million), Walmart ($392
million), Coca-Cola FEMSA ($363 million), and Waste Connections
($290 million). (The foundation's money managers even hold board of
director seats at some companies; for example, at John Deere and Eco-

lab.) When these large corporations distribute profits to shareholders, or when shareholders cash out, we imagine that these monies will be subject to a 20-percent capital gains tax. If they flowed to Bill Gates's personal bank account, they would be. But because they're flowing to Bill Gates's nonprofit private foundation, they accumulate virtually tax free, subject to a nominal 1.39 percent tax rate. In this way, philanthropic foundations can function essentially as warehouses of wealth for multibillionaires, who can continue to exercise control over their money while benefitting from enormous tax savings.

Some years, the Gates Foundation actually generates more money from its investment activities than it gives away in charity. In 2013, the foundation reported $5.7 billion in investment income from its endowment, for example, while paying out only $3.3 billion in charitable grants. Between 2003 and 2020, its public-facing financial filings show that it paid out $59 billion in charitable grants while netting $48.5 billion in investment income. Given the foundation's extensive focus on wealth generation, why don't we tax it and regulate it the way we would an investment bank or a business?

Brian Galle, a law professor at Georgetown, offers a different take. He contrasts private foundations with government contractors, noting that both are private entities that receive taxpayer money to do work for the government. The difference between the billions of taxpayer dollars the government gives to a private contractor like Boeing, and the billions of taxpayer dollars it gives (in tax benefits) to prop up a private philanthropy, Galle told me, is that "government contractors are subject to several orders of magnitude more oversight and regulation than charities are. Given that they raise . . . similar concerns, it's kind of interesting that we've developed the law of public contracting so much but really haven't changed the law of charity at all in a hundred years," apart from that one overhaul by Congress in 1969.

Edgar Villanueva, author of *Decolonizing Wealth*, draws a different parallel, to what are called "federally qualified health centers," which provide health care for underserved communities. In order for these centers to qualify for taxpayer support, they must demonstrate their commitment to the communities they serve, creating boards of directors predominantly run by patients. Why aren't private foundations run by billionaires like Bill Gates subject to similar requirements? Insofar as Gates claims to be helping poor farmers in Africa and teachers in poor school districts in the United States, why don't any of these people sit on the governing board of the foundation? And what about taxpayers? If Gates is using our money, shouldn't we have a say in how it is used? Are we to simply trust that Bill Gates is spending our tax dollars in a prudent and responsible manner, delivering benefits to the public?

University of Pittsburgh law professor Philip Hackney notes that virtually anywhere we look across tax-exempt nonprofit institutions, private foundations can be seen as uniquely unaccountable to the tax-paying public. "Universities are typically more accountable to a larger audience. Even hospitals are typically accountable to a larger audience, in some sense at least," he notes. "Private foundations, though . . . We treat it like it's for the public benefit, but it's really just one wealthy person's conception of what things should be."

Hackney has called for an end to the tax benefits we give wealthy individuals like Bill Gates for charitable giving. "The enormous ability of that wealth to influence how we are all going to be governed—it's essentially going out and making democratic choices on our behalf through a nondemocratic means," he told me. "And that troubles me."

It should trouble all of us. We give Bill Gates generous tax breaks because his charitable work supposedly unburdens the U.S. government. But why would we want someone like Bill Gates taking on the work of our government—reorganizing public health and public education according to his narrow, ideological worldview? Insofar as philanthropy in the hands of someone like Bill Gates is clearly a tool of political influence, shaping all manner of public policy, why don't we scrutinize and regulate the Gates Foundation as a political organization just as we scrutinize and regulate lobbying or campaign contributions?

Even two former high-level foundation employees have cited a need for reforms at the Gates Foundation, writing in a 2021 op-ed, "Given that [the] founders receive a substantial tax benefit for their donations, the assets the [foundation] board oversees should be regarded as belonging to the public, with the board being held accountable to a fiduciary standard of care."

A more radical version of this call is to remove Bill and Melinda

French Gates from the foundation, installing independent board members who can make sure it is using public resources responsibly, not on pet projects or charitable endeavors that deliver private benefits. When the Gates Foundation donates $100 million to the elite private high school the Gates children attended in Seattle, Lakeside School, should Bill and Melinda French Gates get something on the order of $50 million in tax benefits from this gift? When the foundation plows incalculable sums of money into promoting Bill Gates's image as a do-good philanthropist, should we reward this with massive tax benefits? While the Gates Foundation claims that "the foundation's private inurement prohibition prohibits the foundation from being operated in a way that personally benefits Bill or Melinda," is anyone actually investigating this?

At the root of this issue are oversight and accountability—or, really, a lack of oversight and accountability—over how public resources (tax dollars) are being used. And across the political spectrum, writers, thinkers, and scholars widely cite a pressing need to rethink the current carte blanche that Big Philanthropy enjoys. Libertarian Stephen Moore (a former adviser to President Trump) has proposed that wealthy donors like Bill Gates should have to pay capital gains tax on money they donate; Moore has also proposed that Congress limit charitable deductions to $250,000 per household per year. "The question is whether a tax code that encourages dynastic family foundations is good for America," Moore wrote in the *Wall Street Journal* in 2017. "If Congress stopped letting billionaires pour money tax free into the foundation-industrial complex, it would go a long way toward lowering rates and making the tax code fairer for everyone. This would help the economy grow faster, which is the best way to help those in need."

On the political left, the late Sheldon Drobny, who worked for the IRS before founding the media company Air America, wrote in 2006:

> The Gates Foundation now has about $60 Billion under the control of the wealthiest people in America. They do not have to sell any of their positions in the stocks that they put under the tax-exempt umbrella. Furthermore, they can vote their stock holdings the same as if they did before and they can make the same investment decisions about

their considerable corporate holdings. Both Buffett and Gates exhibited the most predatory capitalistic practices as corporate executives and investors. Microsoft and Berkshire Hathaway are not models of socially responsible capitalism. That being said, this foundation will be in the long run richer than the Catholic Church, which has accumulated wealth and power for over 1500 years. However, the results will be exactly the same. They will never liquidate enough of their assets to do any real good for the most onerous problem we have as humans: the worldwide poverty that is caused by the great disparity between the haves and the have-nots.

Drobny proposed that Gates give away all of his money—except for $1 billion he could keep for himself. "He would still have a wonderful life," Drobny wrote.

If Drobny's view sounds extreme to you, it's worth remembering that philanthropy, as a tax-privileged entity, is not some immutable feature of the law. Congress had to create a pathway for the ultrarich to turn their personal fortunes into political power via tax-exempt philanthropy. And Congress can also dissolve this benefit. A hundred years ago, when American industrialists and monopolists sought to incorporate and institutionalize their charitable giving through the creation of the private foundation, Congress initially said no. That era's superrich robber barons, Andrew Carnegie and John D. Rockefeller, were vilified as greedy parasites, their charitable ambitions regarded as a power grab. "No amount of charities in spending such fortunes can compensate in any way for the misconduct in acquiring them," Theodore Roosevelt said at the time.

There was mainstream political animus against the superrich and their philanthropic ambitions at one point in the past, and there's no reason we cannot, or should not, resurrect this debate. There is a rich history of questionable charitable activities in American philanthropy to inform this interrogation. In the 1930s, automobile tycoon Henry Ford transferred much of his wealth, in the form of shares of the Ford Motor Company, to create the Ford Foundation, effectively shielding his wealth from the estate tax. During the 1950s, billionaire Howard Hughes transferred his stock in the Hughes Aircraft Company to the nonprofit Howard Hughes Medical Institute to avoid taxes, essentially incorporating a profit-seeking defense contractor under the auspices of a charitable medical research entity. Congress eventually scrutinized these activities. "The time has come, I think, to take a close look at the types of operations in which tax-exempt foundations are engaged. Already our survey indicates a number of apparent abuses or irregularities which would seem to conflict with the intent of Congress when it relieved certain institutions from the burden of taxation. An agonizing reappraisal is overdue," Texas representative Wright Patman reported to his fellow legislators in 1962.

In 1969, Congress passed new rules over private foundations, including forcing them to actually give away money—5 percent of their endowments a year. These new rules addressed some of the most egregious "abuses and irregularities." But the world of philanthropy and the nature of extreme wealth have both changed significantly over the last fifty years. Another agonizing reappraisal is in order. The divide between the superrich and the rest of us keeps growing, and billionaire philanthropy has little effect on the inequality all around us.

One obstacle to scrutinizing Big Philanthropy is the Internal Revenue Service. Though Congress has asked the IRS to play watchdog, it doesn't have the resources it needs to effectively monitor charitable activities, and it also doesn't have the incentive. Marcus Owens, a former director of the IRS's tax-exempt division who is now in private practice, explains that the fundamental mandate of the IRS is to bring in revenue to the U.S. Treasury. Private foundations operate on an essentially tax-free basis. So, from the IRS's dollars-and-cents perspective, there is little prospect of recouping missing tax revenue or discovering significant unpaid taxes from organizations that, generally speaking, don't pay taxes in the first place. "If you're the IRS commissioner and you're given a finite sum to spend on the agency, and your job is to make sure the U.S. Treasury has money in it, you are going to give a token nod to tax-exempt organizations," Owens told me. "One [IRS] agent looking at restaurants in Washington or New York City is going to generate a lot of money. . . . One agent looking at private foundations will probably pay their [own] salary, but it's not going to bring in tax dollars."

We can't know if the Gates Foundation has ever been audited by the

IRS because this isn't public information. But we do know that, when Congress passed its 1969 legislation creating new oversight of philanthropy, the IRS at the time envisioned auditing all large foundations every two years. Today, of the 100,000 foundations in existence, which warehouse close to a trillion dollars, the IRS conducts only around two hundred audits a year. One former employee at the Gates Foundation told me the foundation was not audited in the several years they had worked there. Phil Hackney, who worked in the Office of the Chief Counsel of the IRS between 2006 and 2011, said that during his years at the IRS, the service was willing to take on large private foundations, but he also acknowledged that the IRS had hemorrhaged staff over the last decade, losing significant capacity. "The lack of enforcement is palpable," Hackney said. Paul Streckfus, editor of the *EO Tax Journal* and previously with the IRS, said it's unimaginable that the IRS would have the staff available to fully audit the Gates Foundation—and he raised even more dire criticism: the lack of expertise within the IRS. What this suggests is a laissez-faire environment in which foundations are trusted to regulate themselves.

Generally speaking, it seems fair to believe that the IRS has to be strategic in taking on large, potentially adversarial actors like the Gates Foundation. An investigation by ProPublica and *Fortune* found that when the IRS dared to investigate Microsoft in the early 2010s—a time when Gates was still chairman of the board of directors—the company went on a counterattack. Microsoft helped create a front group, the Coalition for Effective and Efficient Tax Administration, which hired lobbyists and helped pushed Congress to eventually pass a bill that weakened IRS enforcement capacity. (Microsoft told the journalists that it "follows the law and has always fully paid the taxes it owes.")

The ProPublica story also reports that the IRS has internalized a cost-benefit analysis around "litigation hazards." The service's investigators eagerly work with companies to arrange compromises that can avoid time-consuming legal fights. Through legal appeal processes, large corporations are almost always able to reduce or avoid tax penalties. It's reasonable to think that such a cost-benefit calculation would factor into how the IRS approaches private foundations that essentially pay no taxes, especially one run by the former head of Microsoft.

It's worth noting the reason the IRS first pursued an investigation of Microsoft: its long history of tax avoidance. A 2012 Senate investigation into corporate tax avoidance in the United States profiled Microsoft as a case study of this widespread problem, detailing the billions of dollars in taxes it has avoided through the use of loopholes. Asked about these findings in a later interview, Bill Gates called them "hogwash."

According to the assessor's office for King County, Washington, which includes Seattle, Microsoft has even filed 402 appeals on its property taxes through 2019. This isn't particularly unusual: large corporations are always seeking to lower their tax burden.

Microsoft's ability to reduce its tax bill has invariably increased the value of the company for shareholders. This, in turn, has expanded the personal fortune of Bill Gates. Gates then donates his wealth to his private foundation, which slowly disburses the funds in the form of charitable grants.

Through a narrow, robbing-Peter-to-pay-Paul logic, we could say that, at the end of the day, Gates has indeed paid out billions of dollars through his philanthropic giving. But this ends-justifies-the-means arrangement misunderstands the fundamental inequity in letting large companies and superrich individuals play by different rules, and the fundamental irrationality in giving praise and power to a multibillionaire for giving away money he does not need. In a functioning democracy, everyone is supposed to pay their fair share of taxes and to have some basic, common claims to certain rights, opportunities, and privileges. If we lived in that world, there would be no obscenely rich people like Bill Gates, and there would be no need for philanthropic organizations like the Gates Foundation.

THOMAS PIKETTY'S 2013 book, *Capital in the 21st Century*—at nearly seven hundred pages, including economic equations and theory—did not seem like the kind of book that would be an international bestseller, but it was. It managed to strike a chord by explaining in detail that the rich are getting richer and that extreme wealth and inequality are bad for society. To combat the risks created by the growing specter of an aristocratic class of ultrarich oligarchs, Piketty has championed a new tax system that targets the wealth (capital) of the ultrarich.

Most people reading this book derive their income from actual work: the salaries, wages, commissions, and tips we earn from our labor. In contrast, the superrich take most of their money from watching their piles of money multiply through dividends, interest, and returns. In the United States, investment income is generally taxed at a lower rate than income from work. This system allows the richest Americans to pay some of the lowest taxes. It's also part of the reason the rich are getting richer than the rest of us.

One proposed fix is a wealth tax that would target the accumulated fortunes of the ultrarich—like each year taking a percentage of Bill Gates's entire personal fortune, currently estimated at more than one hundred billion dollars. If we had imposed a 3 percent wealth tax on Bill Gates every year since 2000, it would have generated thirty billion dollars in tax revenue. But, interestingly, it would have reduced his wealth by something like sixty billion dollars. By chipping away at Gates's assets, year over year, this would reduce the effects of compounding interest that create runaway fortunes.

Bill Gates, naturally, isn't a fan of the wealth tax, but he does fancy himself an intellectual, and he gamely waded into a critique of Piketty's book in 2014, penning a review on his personal blog, *GatesNotes*. "Yes, some level of inequality is built in to capitalism," Gates wrote, presenting himself as a moderate. "As Piketty argues, it is inherent to the system. The question is, what level of inequality is acceptable? And when does inequality start doing more harm than good? That's something we should have a public discussion about, and it's great that Piketty helped advance that discussion in such a serious way.

"Take a look at the Forbes 400 list of the wealthiest Americans," Gates continues, going full force into his rebuttal. "About half the people on the list are entrepreneurs whose companies did very well (thanks to hard work as well as a lot of luck). Contrary to Piketty's rentier hypothesis, I don't see anyone on the list whose ancestors bought a great parcel of land in 1780 and have been accumulating family wealth by collecting rents ever since. In America, that old money is long gone—through instability, inflation, taxes, philanthropy, and spending."

There is no room in the modern world for aristocrats and oligarchs, Gates argues, because our global economy is a dynamic, self-cleaning ecosystem. We should not pursue a wealth tax but, rather, Gates believes, a *luxury* tax. When a rich person purchases a yacht, they should have to pay a high tax. This would incentivize the superrich to spend less money on themselves and more on charity.

"Philanthropy also can be an important part of the solution set," Gates continued:

> It's too bad that Piketty devotes so little space to it. A century and a quarter ago, Andrew Carnegie was a lonely voice encouraging his wealthy peers to give back substantial portions of their wealth. Today, a growing number of very wealthy people are pledging to do just that. Philanthropy done well not only produces direct benefits for society, it also reduces dynastic wealth. Melinda and I are strong believers that dynastic wealth is bad for both society and the children involved. We want our children to make their own way in the world. They'll have all sorts of advantages, but it will be up to them to create their lives and careers.

Through a two-pronged approach of taxing the purchase of luxury items and pushing the superrich to give away their money voluntarily, Gates has a plan for wealth inequality. He actually arranged a call to speak directly with Piketty to share his views. It was a private call, but Piketty later said that Gates's position boiled down to "I don't want to pay more tax."

Not to be cowed, Gates took another bite at the apple in 2019:

> Although I mostly spend my time talking about the issues I'm really focused on—global health, education, and climate change—I get asked about taxes a lot. I understand why it comes up so often; I'm a natural focal point for this debate. The truth is, I've been pushing for a fairer tax system for years. It was nearly two decades ago that my dad and I started calling for an increase in the federal estate tax and for an estate tax in our home state of Washington, which has the most regressive tax system in the country. In 2010, he and I also backed a voter initiative that—had it

passed—would've created a state income tax. . . . It isn't always popular to stand up for higher taxes, so it's great that many Americans are having this conversation. I want to be as clear as possible about my views.

Gates's self-aggrandizing essay could be read as a long-winded way of avoiding, if not defaming, the wealth tax, which he never mentions. While it is true that Gates has offered generalized, rhetorical support for the idea of increasing taxes on the wealthy, what makes his claims as a tireless, courageous tax advocate especially hollow is that neither he nor his foundation appears to spend any meaningful resources pursuing tax policy changes. Bill Gates has no compunction about using his vast wealth to bend the world to his will, whether it's influencing vaccine policy or political decision-making on climate change. If he really were the passionate champion of a progressive tax system he claims to be, he could be a powerful voice. But this isn't how Gates operates. His philanthropic giving, to the extent that it overlaps with his personal wealth or privileges, tends to support, not challenge, his interests.

We see a similar disconnect in Warren Buffett, who, like Gates, has become a prominent public-facing champion of raising taxes on wealthy people. Yet the tens of billions of dollars he has donated to charitable causes do not appear to have been directed at tax reform.

It is also true that both Bill Gates and Warren Buffett have become phenomenally richer during their tenures as philanthropists. In 2000, *Forbes* pegged Gates's wealth at around $60 billion. By 2022, it had reached as high as $129 billion. For Buffett, his personal fortune grew from $26 billion to as high as $118 billion. This growth in wealth has been fueled in part by the extremely low tax rates the two men enjoy.

As MUCH OF the Western world sought a political response to Russia's invasion of Ukraine in early 2022, the United States made a big show of its economic sanctions against the so-called oligarchs who control Russia's wealth and who have outsize political influence. By freezing their assets or repossessing their yachts, the United States thought it could weaken Russia. "Treasury continues using the full range of our tools to expose and disrupt those who seek to evade our sanctions and hide their ill-gotten gains," U.S. treasury secretary Janet Yellen said in a 2022 statement. "Even as Russian elites hide behind proxies and complex legal arrangements, Treasury will use our broad enforcement authorities . . . to actively implement the multilaterally coordinated sanctions imposed on those who fund and benefit from Russia's war against Ukraine."

In the American political discourse, the news media took this narrative and ran with it, noting that Russian president Vladimir Putin might himself be personally vulnerable to economic sanctions. The *New York Times* leaned on unconfirmed rumors and "speculative news reports" to profile Putin's links to a billion-dollar palace on the Black Sea, a one-hundred-million-dollar yacht named *Graceful*, and luxurious properties in Monaco and France. "The problem for the United States and its allies is that none of these assets can be directly connected to the Russian president," the story noted. "Despite years of speculation and rumor, the extent of his wealth remains maddeningly opaque, even as billions of dollars have sluiced through the accounts of his close friends and luxury properties have been connected to family members."

In this telling of events, the super-wealthy in Russia hide their vast, ill-gotten wealth and avoid paying taxes—while also exercising undemocratic influence over Russian politics. It's a righteous narrative, but the damning moniker *oligarch* is one that most U.S. media outlets would never level at an American billionaire, even though men like Bill Gates appear richly deserving of such a title.

Gates, though he's never run for political office, is unambiguously one of the most powerful people in the world. His power comes entirely from his vast personal wealth, which comes from a monopoly that was widely regarded as destructive to the economy and from a company renowned for its tax avoidance. And as with Russian oligarchs, the details of Gates's personal wealth, which has been diversified beyond Microsoft, are guarded with extreme secrecy. "Few people know much about Mr. Gates's assets or [his money manager] Mr. Larson's tactics—and the two men want to keep it that way," the *Wall Street Journal* reported in 2014. "Real-estate investments, which range from the fancy Charles Hotel in Cambridge, Mass., to a 490-acre ranch in Wyoming once owned by William F. 'Buffalo Bill' Cody, are often cloaked in nondescript names to make it harder to trace the deals back to Mr. Gates." Gates's investment empire is run out of an "unmarked building in the Seattle suburb of Kirk-land," the outlet reported. "Mr. Larson is so protective of his boss that he used to be nicknamed 'the Gateskeeper,' says someone who worked with him. Employees who leave often sign confidentiality agreements barring them from talking about Cascade [the investment firm that manages Gates's wealth], people familiar with the matter say."

Not only is Gates's vast personal wealth kept from public view, but Gates, at one time, entrusted part of his personal fortune to convicted felons Andrew and Ann Llewellyn Evans, who had served time in prison for bank fraud. Only after journalists uncovered this in the 1990s did Gates move his money to a new investment group.

With the intense secrecy surrounding Gates's private wealth, the source of his vast fortune (from a monopoly), and the involvement of questionable money managers, is Bill Gates really that different from any Russian oligarch? He is according to the prevailing news narrative, which seems determined to highlight the generous impulse guiding Gates's wealth acquisition. As the *Wall Street Journal*'s 2014 profile explained, Gates's ever-expanding personal wealth was actually a public good: "That means more money can be plowed into the foundation's mission to fight disease and improve education in the developing world."

To be fair to Gates, we do know that he pays *some* taxes. We know this because the tax returns of the wealthiest Americans were leaked to ProPublica, which reported that Gates paid an average federal tax rate of 18.4 percent between 2013 and 2018 on the $17 billion in income he generated. As a point of comparison, a single worker who made $45,000 would pay income and payroll taxes at 21 percent. The news outlet also reported that the "true tax rate" of Warren Buffett in recent years has been one tenth of 1 percent. Buffett responded, classically, by pointing to his charitable giving: "I believe the money will be of more use to society if disbursed philanthropically than if it is used to slightly reduce an ever-increasing U.S. debt."

When criticized on the issue of taxes, Gates and Buffett can point to their extensive philanthropic giving, but making charitable dona-tions is no substitute for paying your taxes. When you and I pay taxes—unlike when Gates and Buffett make charitable grants—we can't directly control how that money is spent, and we get no credit or praise. Many readers probably are not happy to see their tax dollars go to government projects they don't support. Personally, I don't like that my tax dollars are being used to subsidize the Gates Foundation. But, unlike a multibillionaire, you and I can't opt out of up to 74 percent of our tax bill by becoming philanthropists. If we want to change our federal policymaking or budget decisions, we have to engage in the slow and messy process of democratic change. We have to pay our taxes, build political power, and make political arguments to push Congress to spend our tax dollars more responsibly.

Bill Gates's late father, Bill Gates Sr., presents an interesting footnote to the philanthropy-versus-taxes discourse. At the turn of the millennium, Gates Sr. became a leading political advocate in favor of preserving the estate tax—again, this is the tax levied on the assets of the superrich when they die. President George W. Bush, at the time, was leading a political campaign to end the so-called death tax, proposing a tax cut estimated to save the wealthiest 2 percent of Americans $236 billion.

According to interviews Gates Sr. gave at the time, he openly acknowledged that his counter campaign to tax the wealthy could, at times, inadvertently lead to tax avoidance. That is, when billionaires know that the estate tax will take a large percentage of any remaining assets when they die, this incentivizes them to give their money away. "A wealthy person has an absolute choice as to whether they pay the [estate] tax or whether they give their wealth to their university or their church or their foundation," he noted. Said another way: the superrich, unlike the rest of us, get to decide if they want to pay their full freight of taxes or become philanthropists.

"The richer you are, the more choice you have between those two," says Chuck Collins, an heir to the Oscar Mayer fortune who gave away much of his inheritance during his twenties and who worked closely with Bill Gates Sr. to promote the estate tax in the late 1990s. According to Collins, who continues to work on the issue of wealth inequality at the Institute for Policy Studies, Bill Gates Sr. believed that the estate tax could generate important tax revenues and also break up concentrated wealth—in addition to pushing the superrich into philanthropy. Gates Sr. even wanted to limit the tax benefits billionaires could take. "He said to me . . . it's a problem that his son is going to give—at the time, it was like eighty billion dollars—to the foundation and never have to pay taxes on any of that wealth," Collins recalls. "His view was that there should be a cap on the lifetime amount of wealth that could be given to charity where you get a deduction."

Gates Sr.'s writing and media interviews show that he had genuine concerns about the need to redistribute wealth through taxation—not simply because he thought social welfare was important but also because he thought the superrich owed it to the government. "If you have accumulated tens of millions, hundreds of millions or billions, you did *not* do it alone," Gates Sr. noted in one speech:

> You got help. Of course, this is not to take away anything from that person. Those of you in business know what it takes. These are probably hard-working and creative people who have made sacrifices. They deserve some reward for their leadership or entrepreneurship. But they didn't get there alone. Where would they be without this fantastic economic system that we have built together? Where would they be without public investments in infrastructure? Roads? Communication? Our system of property rights—and the legal system to enforce them. How much wealth would they have without the public investment in new technology? These advances have made us all more prosperous, whether we are software designers, restaurant owners, or neighborhood realtors. . . . Most of us benefit from society's investments. And those who have accumulated $10 million or $10 billion have *disproportionately* benefited from them. I believe it is fair to have an estate tax that captures a third of that wealth when it transfers to the next generation. It is a reasonable levy for the privilege of growing such wealth in our society. . . . The estate tax is an appropriate mechanism for a wealthy person to pay back society, a means of expressing gratitude for the amazing opportunities that we have. *Gratitude*—there's a word largely absent from our business publications. We live in a marvelous system with abundant commonwealth—yet we don't see it around us.

Gates Sr.'s calls on the superrich to pay taxes are actually an extremely modest political position—and it almost seems to conceptualize taxes as payment to the government for servicing the needs of private commerce and private billionaires. As economist Dean Baker describes it, there exists today a vast nanny state of government-created economic protections and benefits for the superrich, like the far-reaching intellectual property rights given to companies like Microsoft and Pfizer. Through copyrights and patents, these companies take advantage of government-supported monopolies, guaranteeing their dominance in the marketplace—in ways that can limit the ability of better or cheaper products to reach consumers. It's a mistake, then, to call on the rich to repay the government for these privileges. Rather, we need to eliminate the nanny state and also make the superrich pay their fair share. Nevertheless, Gates Sr.'s advocacy around the estate tax, as a form of gratitude for friendly government policies, shows how much berth there is for reforms against the growing appearance of oligarchy, in which the wealthiest industry captains pay the least in taxes and have the loudest voices in our democracy.

4

Fail Fast

"Failing fast" is *en vogue* as a mantra in corporate management, which means it has also become a way of life at the Gates Foundation, which pulls the best and brightest employees from Big Pharma, Big Tech, Big Consulting, and MBA programs.

"One of the great personal virtues of Bill and Melinda—and one of the key reasons I have devoted the bulk of my career to the Gates Foundation—is their willingness to change their minds," CEO Mark Suzman noted in the foundation's 2022 public-facing annual letter. "This is particularly true when compelling evidence reveals the potential for more effective ways to save and improve lives through our work. When we take risky bets, it is inevitable that some will fail. But rather than become more conservative, Bill and Melinda have chosen to fail fast, learn, and improve. From gender equality to K–12 education to climate adaptation investments as part of our agricultural development program, they have time and again approved new approaches and deprioritized older ones based on evidence."

The "fail fast" culture is particularly prevalent in the world of start-ups, where the foundation works extensively. The Gates Foundation has given more than $2 billion to private companies in charitable grants alongside a $2.5 billion charitable investment fund the foundation uses to push money into commercial enterprises. Some of this money has gone to pharma giants like GSK and Merck ($65 million and

$47 million in charitable donations, respectively), but much of it has gone to small start-ups whose names you wouldn't recognize.

When Gates's private-sector partners fail—or fail fast—it doesn't always mean the foundation walks away empty-handed. That's because it makes its partners sign "global access agreements" that give it a "world-wide, non-exclusive, perpetual, irrevocable, fully-paid up, royalty-free license to the Funded Developments and the background intellectual property." That's a long, legalistic way of saying the foundation can step in and license the company's intellectual property and technology— whatever vaccine, drug, or other product it helped fund—if the company isn't willing or able to direct it to charitable purposes. If a company goes out of business, or if the foundation views it as operating outside the bounds of their grant agreement, the foundation can exercise its license.

That the founder of Microsoft has organized his philanthropic giving around accessing technology from grantees might give us pause, but the Gates Foundation insists that its licensing claims are really designed to give the global poor access to lifesaving innovations—to promote "public goods" and "yield products that are safe, effective, affordable, and accessible for communities in low- and-middle-income countries." These agreements also offer a rationale to taxpayers and the IRS for Gates's counterintuitive model of charity, donating money to for-profit companies; the global access agreements, the foundation claims, guarantee that these charitable dollars go to charitable ends.

The problem is that there are far too many examples where Gates's access agreements aren't being enforced in a way that actually helps the intended beneficiaries. In 2015, the foundation announced a $55 million shareholder investment to assist in the "development of CureVac's platform technology and the construction of an industrial scale Good Manufacturing Practice (GMP) production facility." In the years thereafter, Gates gave a separate $5 million in grants to the German company for work on mRNA vaccine candidates, including "a vaccine that is able to elicit a broad protection against influenza viruses." The Gates Foundation, at one point in the company's history, was its second-largest shareholder and had the ability to nominate a member to CureVac's board.

Having put tens of millions of dollars into CureVac's production facility and vaccine development, the foundation seemed extremely well placed to exercise its global access agreements during the Covid-19 pandemic as CureVac was advancing its leading vaccine candidate. That is, the agreements should have given the foundation leverage to make sure that the global poor had access to CureVac's vaccine. A U.S. Securities and Exchange Commission filing I uncovered, however, showed that the Gates Foundation released CureVac from its global access agreements just at the time that CureVac was organizing a deal with GSK to advance its vaccine. The SEC document was highly redacted—large chunks were blacked out—but GSK told me the release was not related to Covid-19. This claim, of course, is not verifiable. Bigger picture: Why would the foundation release a grantee from any of its charitable obligations under any circumstances?

A few months after I published my findings on CureVac in 2021, the media outlet ImpactAlpha raised similar questions around the foundation's financial relationship with other Covid-19 vaccine producers, Moderna (a $20 million grant in 2016) and BioNTech ($55 million equity stake in 2019). These companies chose to direct their Covid-19 shots to the most profitable markets, shortchanging the global poor.

"When it came to providing global access to life-saving COVID vaccines, the Global Access Agreements appear to have failed their biggest real-world test," ImpactAlpha reported.

> For months, the foundation's inability or unwillingness to use the Global Access Agreements to help broker deals with vaccine suppliers to supply doses at affordable prices undermined the effectiveness of COVAX, the Gates-backed U.N. buyers' club that was meant to secure vaccine doses for the 91 low- and middle-income countries that qualify for foreign aid, or official development assistance. . . . Bill Gates, the Gates Foundation and others have cited voluntary agreements, including the Global Access Agreements, as part of their arguments against waivers of global intellectual-property protections for vaccine producers.

Similar failures surfaced around Covid-19 diagnostics. The Gates Foundation and other donors had for years put large sums of money into the company Cepheid, which had installed its diagnostic machines across Africa. During the pandemic, these devices proved practically useless because Cepheid was sending the cartridges the machines used, the actual diagnostic tests, to rich nations. MSF had calculated that Cepheid could make a profit selling its Covid-19 tests for as little as $5 per unit. Cepheid disputed this, but during the pandemic, the company found customers willing to pay as much as $50. More than $730 million in financial support—from taxpayers, the Gates Foundation, and others—has gone to Cepheid over the years. Where was the global access for poor people that Gates promised?

One final example concerns Merck's rotavirus vaccine. The Gates Foundation took a victory lap when Merck commercialized its RotaTeq vaccine, claiming, "Our investments helped support the development, licensure, and current rollout." Merck's vaccine, therefore, should have been covered by the foundation's global access agreements.

And it might have been—for a time. The Gates-funded Gavi had secured an agreement with Merck to deliver its rotavirus vaccine to West Africa. However, when Merck saw a more lucrative option—selling the vaccine in China at a price ten times greater than Gavi would pay—the company abandoned Gates and Gavi. The NPR program *Goats and Soda*, which gets funding from Gates, profiled this episode in detail. "This is deeply disappointing news and in the short term will mean that children are likely to miss out on this lifesaving vaccine, leaving them vulnerable to this horrific disease," Gavi's CEO, Seth Berkley, told NPR.

The NPR story amounts to a name-and-shame attack of Merck while avoiding the real story: Gates and Gavi don't seem to understand how pharmaceutical markets work. Of course Merck is going to follow the money—that's what for-profit pharma companies do.

These several examples show that the Gates Foundation's global access agreements are not functioning the way the foundation claims. They aren't guaranteeing access to the global poor, and they aren't reliably delivering public benefits or public goods. This raises questions about the charitable nature of the billions of dollars in support Gates gives to for-profit companies and whether we, taxpayers, should be on the hook to subsidize this work.

This also raises questions about whether the foundation's global access agreements serve another purpose for the foundation. As we saw in chapter 1, the Gates Foundation exercises far more leverage over the small pharmaceutical companies it works with than large enterprises like Merck. For small companies that describe working with the Gates Foundation as essentially a corporate takeover, Gates's global access agreements are one more lever the foundation can pull to exercise control. "Basically, for a tiny amount of money, the Gates Foundation gets to say, 'Give us all your trade secrets,'" one former grantee told me, describing the foundation's global access policies as intrinsically "susceptible to bad behavior," creating "perverse incentives" for the foundation to hurt its corporate partners, like pushing them into insolvency. If a company goes out of business, the Gates Foundation can step in and license the technology, assigning it to a different developer it finds more competent, for example.

This may sound hyperbolic but it's a real-world concern sources shared with me, and it is worth rereading the actual language of the Gates Foundation's global access agreements: a "worldwide, non-exclusive, perpetual, irrevocable, fully-paid up, royalty-free license to the Funded Developments and the background intellectual property."

"I was just horrified—well, not even horrified, but amused," another former grantee told me when they read this language in their grant agreement. "I genuinely thought this was a typo . . . a clerical error." This source chalked up the foundation's extraordinary licensing claims not to any malice but simply to the cutthroat business landscape in which Bill Gates's cognitive circuit board was forged—where "once you get to be a certain size, you either acquire your potential competitors or you bury them. Because, if you don't, your company is vulnerable. So, he [Gates] just sort of went with that mentality, and by the time he founded the Gates Foundation, he just brought everyone with him from Microsoft. So, everyone was just predisposed to that frame of mind."

This grantee recounts having sour conversations with other grantees, naïve academics, and young entrepreneurs who had not understood what they were giving away by signing up with Gates. Their attitude, the source said, was, "We're getting fucked but, whatever, it's our best opportunity [to get funding]."

As the Gates Foundation enrolls thousands of different grantees in its global access agreements, it gains licensing rights to a very large body of intellectual property and technology. In an interview, Rohit Malpani, a global health consultant and former board member of Unitaid, unpacked the real-world implications of the foundation's broad licensing claims: "Think of intellectual property as a bundle of sticks. Nobody owns the entire bundle of sticks. If there's ten sticks in the bundle, maybe the company owns seven, the NIH owns two sticks, and maybe the Gates Foundation owns one. And that one stick might be march-in rights [like licensing the patent to a third party] or a limited license to exploit the technology for these countries. So, for all of these investments the Gates Foundation has made over the years, they've acquired a lot of different forms of intellectual property. And all of that intellectual property provides them with a certain amount of, not only visibility as to what the technology domain looks like, but also to exert control and influence over how that intellectual property is exercised."

Malpani drew parallels to news reports of Bill Gates having become the single largest private farmland owner in the United States, saying that Gates and his private foundation may have quietly become one of the "most important owners of intellectual property for different therapeutics, diagnostics, and vaccines in the world today." He added, "That gives them enormous responsibility and influence over how these technologies develop and evolve. That means a waiver of intellectual property rights [as was widely endorsed around Covid-19 vaccines during the pandemic] . . . affects their own holdings of intellectual property. It also affects their ability to control how this intellectual property is developed and distributed around the world.

"In many ways, this mirrors very much the strategies that Microsoft had. The whole basis of the company was based on the accumulation of intellectual property, so, in some ways, it's not surprising that Gates has adopted this same approach—nominally, for philanthropic ends—but, ultimately, still, it's about having a certain level of control and influence. It's a recognition, before many others, that intellectual property was going to have a very central role in how global health is managed."

IN 2011, THE popular podcast and public radio program *This American Life* broadcast an extraordinary story about patent trolls—people who make money suing companies for infringing on their patents. Often these are frivolous lawsuits, based on overly broad patent claims. But patent trolls know that it's cheaper for companies to settle the cases with payments than to go to trial.

"Today, lots of investors and innovators in Silicon Valley, maybe the majority, would tell you the patent system is doing the exact opposite of what it's supposed to," host Ira Glass noted. "It's not promoting innovation, it's stifling it. Because patent lawsuits are on the rise. Patent trolls are on the move. Patent lawsuits are so common now that it's hard to find even one semi-successful startup in Silicon Valley that has not been hit with a suit. Which slows innovation, makes it harder for companies to prosper, hurts our global competitiveness . . . Costs us all more money when we buy the stuff these companies sell."

At the center of this story was a company named Intellectual Ventures, run by one of Bill Gates's longest-standing deputies, Nathan Myhrvold (though Gates isn't mentioned on the show). After leaving Microsoft in 1999, Myhrvold launched the company which, he said, "invests in invention." He continued: "I think you would find almost anyone who stands up for their patent rights has been called a patent troll."

This version of the story—the invention-forward narrative—had found a warm reception a few years earlier in the *New Yorker*. Writer Malcom Gladwell described Intellectual Ventures, or IV, as a kind of fizzing brain trust, a company where great minds pushed one another to new heights. Gladwell recounts how a single informal dinner involving eight of IV's big-idea men led to thirty-six different invention ideas that might be patented.

Though Gladwell didn't seem to recognize it, his profile of IV essentially described a boys' club of never-ending bull sessions, where self-styled polymaths came up with a lot of big ideas . . . but little more. Gladwell imagined that IV, in the decade ahead, would be a major disruptive, innovative, and revolutionary force driving social progress—the way, say, Alexander Graham Bell had been, changing the world with his telephone.

Today, IV claims to have launched more than fifteen companies, but, oddly, its website names only eleven—none of which appears particularly consequential to humanity or the economy. Most of them appear to be financially propped up by Bill Gates, including TerraPower, a nuclear power company that has yet to build a reactor or produce any energy. Bill Gates also appears to have, at one time, taken an investment stake in IV. According to a Securities and Exchange Commission filing from 2006, Bill Gates and Microsoft together had invested more than fifty million dollars in IV's Invention Science Fund.

Gates, apparently, was not a passive investor. He also made regular appearances at IV, either to throw around his intellectual weight in brainstorming sessions or to unwind from the politically correct demands of professional philanthropy.

Tom Paulson, a writer who once reported on Gates at the *Seattle Post-Intelligencer* and who later helped work on a cookbook with Nathan Myhrvold, said he remembers seeing Gates on occasion at IV's offices, usually disappearing into meetings. "Back then, it was already clear Gates was tired of the constraints put on him by operating at [the] Gates Foundation—the publicity constraints, the typical behavior expected of philanthropists. This was an outlet," Paulson told me. "Gates was creating this separate venture so he wouldn't have to run things by Melinda or the foundation."

Between 2009 and 2020, Gates and Myhrvold were listed as co-inventors on dozens of patents and patent applications. This includes a patent for a high-tech football helmet, designed to improve safety by protecting players against concussions. Other patents sound outright creepy, like one invention for "detecting and classifying people observing a person."

Through its production and acquisition of patents, IV forcefully presents itself as an engine of invention. It also describes itself as protecting small-time inventors from powerful companies that want to steal their ideas. When *This American Life* asked for real-world examples of IV looking out for the little guy, the company could not provide credible examples.

The reporters landed on a deeply troubling portrait of this very destructive new business model, as the patent litigation zeitgeist had unleashed a growing army of trolls challenging everything and everyone. When one group claimed to have a patent on podcasting, comedian and podcaster Marc Maron went public, calling the effort a "shakedown" for money. And IV became the public face of this expanding, invasive species, the patent troll.

"In other words, Intellectual Ventures goes around to companies and says, hey, you want to protect yourself from lawsuits? We own tons of patents," journalist Alex Blumberg reported in the story. "Make a deal with us. Our patents will not only cover everything you're doing in your business, [but] no one will dare sue you."

One Silicon Valley investor compared this model to a "Mafia-style shakedown, where somebody comes in the front door of your building and says, it'd be a shame if this place burned down. I know the neighborhood really well and I can make sure that doesn't happen. And saying, 'Pay us up.'"

After this high-profile investigation by an extremely popular podcast, a rational actor might have thought hard about the optics in partnering with IV. Not Bill Gates. Beyond whatever personal stake he may still have had in the company, Gates also wanted his foundation in business with IV. The result was a new project at IV called the Global Good Fund. The foundation had actually launched Global Good in 2010, the year before the *This American Life* investigation aired, but then broadly expanded the project in the years ahead. "Funded by Bill Gates and focused on a shared vision with Nathan Myhrvold, Global Good invents technology to solve some of humanity's most daunting problems," the website noted. The Gates Foundation describes Global Good as a "controlled subsidiary" in its tax filings. Through 2020, the foundation reports financial transfers—sometimes described as "capital contributions of cash and intellectual property"—of more than five hundred million dollars to the Global Good Fund.

Nathan Myhrvold, in early interviews, said the project was a for-profit business, though he didn't expect it to make profits. On paper, then, it appears the Gates Foundation controls a for-profit arm of one of the world's most notorious patent trolls.

As the Global Good project took on a higher profile at IV, it was seen as PR to humanize or redeem the company from its controversial business practices. As one critic told the press in the early 2010s, whoever runs Global Good "will be hard-pressed then to carry out enough good works to offset the colossal harm of his or her employer. Unless, of course, they choose to close the company and reform the patent system."

Myhrvold responded by pointing to his new humanitarian mission, asking his critics how much "god's work" they had done: "How big is their malaria research project? How much effort do they put into polio? I'm quite curious!" While companies like Facebook were creating "tools or toys for rich people," Myhrvold said, IV's Global Good partnership with the Gates Foundation was "solving the problems . . . for these poor people in Africa."

"I would hope that three to five years from now, we could point to a whole bunch of successful projects that were actually being deployed out in the field, where we would say, yeah, we invented a new technology," Myhrvold noted. "More kids got vaccinated. Malaria incidents went down. Researchers understood something they'd never understood before. That three to five years out, we would point to some really tangible ways that we had changed the world for the better. In ways that are really life or death issues for the people involved."

From its murky origins and with its uncertain mandate, the project shuttered a decade later with little indication of what it had accomplished. With the Gates Foundation's five-hundred-million-dollar funding, Global Good became one of its best-funded projects of all time. But where did the money go?

The webpage for Global Good boasts few achievements. There's a new wood-burning cookstove called the Jet-Flame that claims to reduce smoke—and, hence, smoke-caused respiratory problems. Jet-Flame's sparse website is only two pages, however, and there's very little public information about the product—or evidence of its adoption or use. Global Good also claims to have created new portable coolers, one for transporting bull semen and one for moving vaccines. Again, there's very little public information to stand up the impact of these products. There's also a report of Global Good's having teamed up with the company Element on an infant biometric project designed to keep track of children's health data.

If these accomplishments don't seem commensurate with the very large sum of money Gates gave the project, that may be because Global Good apparently served another purpose—as a repository for the foundation's own patents and intellectual property. And the reason we know this is a single passing reference in a 2016 research report the foundation commissioned at Stanford University, called "Making Markets Work for the Poor."

The report profiles a small start-up named Zyomyx, which was developing a potentially game-changing, cheap HIV diagnostic that could be used in places without electricity or trained medical professionals. With a single drop of blood, the diagnostic could figure out whether a patient needed antiretroviral therapy, the lifesaving treatment given to HIV-positive patients. But the company's technology was too undeveloped to get venture funding. For this reason, the Stanford report presented Zyomyx as a case study for the Gates Foundation's unique role in the marketplace, putting its money into high-risk, high-reward innovations that can help the global poor—and that otherwise might not get funding.

The foundation's first olive branch to the company was a ten-million-dollar loan. But there were terms on this money. Gates put a claim on Zyomyx's patents as collateral. "The simplest solution would have seemed to be to fund the . . . work with a traditional grant," the Stanford report noted. "But with the company so shaky, the Gates Foundation team felt that it was crucial to understand what would happen to the technology if the company went bust or, perhaps more likely, shifted its attention to more commercial products and markets. Grantees that violate their grant agreements can be made to repay the amount of the grant. The foundation wanted something more: a structure that would allow it to secure rights to the critical intellectual property."

Gates made the loan through a complex financial instrument described as "convertible notes that would convert to equity if Zyomyx found additional investors, was acquired, or went public in an IPO." Essentially, if the company turned out to be enormously profitable, the Gates Foundation would be positioned to share in the windfall. At the same time, Gates's financial deal was structured in a way that capped Zyomyx's potential profits from selling its product in poor nations—"potentially lowering the company's appeal to future investors," the report noted.

One might question why the Gates Foundation would make deals with companies that hurt their ability to secure other investors. Publicly, the foundation describes itself as mindful not to step on toes in this way. "How and where is the best use of philanthropic dollars, that's a challenge that we have to think about all the time because we don't want to displace or substitute government or private capital," Gates Foundation CEO Mark Suzman noted in 2022. Yet we could cynically observe that if the foundation made a start-up dependent on its funding by deterring other investors, it would have leverage to move the company in any direction it wished. "This is what happens: They give a big grant, then the foundation pulls out. . . . They got no business model left," one private developer told me. "If an organization becomes heavily dependent on a charitable foundation, and they let their research get guided by the priorities of that foundation, they have themselves to blame to some degree for the failures of that experience. It's just not good business."

Another source told me that the Gates Foundation structures deals that make it complicated to bring on other investors—who have to do significantly more due diligence, such as puzzling through the ramifications of Gates's licensing claims. "These [other] investors are going to go, 'No way, I'm not going to fund you!' So, essentially, Gates, what you're doing is you're undermining your own objective. These companies [that you're giving charitable grants to] will never be able to raise money. And you're not going to fund them—you're just giving them a grant. You're killing the very people you want to save." Another source I interviewed that had considered a partnership with Gates described the foundation as highly sensitive to these complications, not wanting to deter other investors from a project.

As it turns out, Zyomyx was still able to attract an outside investor. The multinational company Mylan realized that if Zyomyx could help diagnose more people with HIV, it would mean more sales of Mylan's HIV treatments. It didn't matter if Zyomyx lost money—because it would bring in new revenues to Mylan's other products.

Zyomyx's deal with Mylan triggered Gates's convertible investment, meaning the foundation's loan to the company turned into a massive ownership stake. Suddenly, the foundation owned a 48 percent stake in Zyomyx. The world's most visible nonprofit philanthropic entity was now running a for-profit business, in partnership with Big Pharma. The

Gates-funded Stanford report phrased it differently: "As Zyomyx's larg-est equity holder and an observer on its board [of directors], the Gates Foundation had the tools to protect its charitable objectives."

With the Gates Foundation at the helm, the project failed fast. Mylan eventually pulled out, and Gates began winding down Zyomyx, offering it a final $350,000 loan to keep the lights on so the foundation could gather up its technology. "The foundation has engaged Intellectual Ven-tures' Global Good division to maintain the Zyomyx patents and find a commercial partner who will be able to use the Zyomyx intellectual property to bring the product to market," the Stanford report explained. "Probability of success is low."

Following up on the Stanford study, I found patent records showing that the Gates Foundation appears to have acquired dozens of patents (and patent applications) from Zyomyx. The records show the foun-dation later reassigning some of this intellectual property in 2016 to a Canadian company called Stemcell Technologies, with the legal doc-ument noting that "obtaining and maintaining intellectual property protection for certain technology or information is an appropriate com-ponent of Global Access as a way to further the Foundation's program-matic and charitable objectives."

Gates never publicly announced or discussed this transfer of intel-lectual property that I can see. And the foundation's only reference to its work with Stemcell Technologies was a 2019 charitable grant for three million dollars that appears to have been related to a different project. Stemcell would not agree to an interview for this book, so it remains unclear what the company is doing with the patents.

Clearly the Gates Foundation and Stemcell believe the patents have value. Why else would they have gone to the trouble of acquiring them? So, Gates's acquisition and dispensation of IP once again raises questions about the fine line between the Gates Foundation's nonprofit, charitable activities and its commercial interests. How is it that the foundation's engagement, *charitable* engagement, with private companies is orga-nized in a way that allows it to acquire (or seize) valuable IP and then parcel it out to other companies? If these were commercial transactions of property between companies, there would likely be tax implications. Not so with the Gates Foundation, a nonprofit charity.

Through a search of public records held at the U.S. Patent and Trademark Office, I found thirteen different transactions in which the Gates Foundation acquired dozens of patents and patent applications, mostly related to pharmaceuticals. (Some of the patent records have redactions that limit what we can see, but none of them appears to mention Intellectual Ventures or Global Good by name.)

One notable example concerns Anacor Pharmaceuticals. In 2013, the Gates Foundation took a 2 percent stake in Anacor—and also gave the company an $18.3 million contract to work on a new drug discovery platform. Two and a half years later, Gates sold its equity stake for an $86.7 million profit—a seventeen-fold return on its investment. In 2016, Pfizer acquired Anacor for $5 billion, and patent records show a subsequent transfer of several batches of patents to the foundation. "Pfizer transferred patent rights for select assets to the Gates Foundation pursuant to a 2013 agreement Anacor had with the Gates Foundation," Pfizer told me by email. "As these assets were no longer under development at Pfizer, the Gates Foundation had an opportunity to take ownership and they elected to do so."

The foundation's acquisition of patents speaks to only one mechanism Gates uses to access intellectual property. It's important to remember that the Gates Foundation's global access agreements are normally directed at granting the foundation the ability to "license" the products and technology of its charitable partners, not to take exclusive ownership of their intellectual property and patents. It's also important to note that licensing technology usually won't carry the same public-facing paper trail as acquiring it. While we know the foundation's thousands of charitable grants (and global access agreements) give it access to an extraordinary body of intellectual property, we have little ability to see where and when the foundation exercises its licensing rights. This makes it difficult to understand the full scope of the foundation's interface with intellectual property. Or to understand who is benefiting or who might be injured.

In 2020, when IV shut down Global Good, it cryptically announced that it would split the project's spoils between two entities, the Gates Foundation and Gates Ventures. Gates Ventures is Bill Gates's "private office"—essentially, home base for many of his nonfoundation activities, including some private investments. Why would the work products of a philanthropy-funded project, Global Good, be handed over to Bill Gates's private office? Did Bill Gates have a personal financial stake in Global Good, in addition to the foundation's stake? This is one more place where we could raise questions about the appearance of Bill Gates mixing his private business interests with those of his foundation.

Who else might benefit? One industry source raised concerns about the Bill & Melinda Gates Medical Research Institute (often called Gates MRI). Organized as a subsidiary of the Gates Foundation, the institute is, for all intents and purposes, a pharmaceutical company. It's doing research and development on tuberculosis drugs and vaccines, Shigella vaccines, malaria antibodies, and infant probiotics. It's working under licenses with GSK and Merck. And it is run by Big Pharma alumni from Pfizer, Merck, Baxter, Takeda, and Novartis. The Gates Foundation has put more than five hundred million dollars into the project.

This means that, at the same time that the foundation has positioned itself to access the intellectual property of other developers, the foundation is essentially running its own pharmaceutical development enterprise, which has a very keen interest in intellectual property. The Zyomyx-Stemcell deal shows that the foundation is actively taking technology from the companies it works with and redistributing it. What's to stop it from handing over that technology to Gates MRI or to one of Gates MRI's partners?

Another obvious beneficiary of Gates's interest in intellectual property is Intellectual Ventures—and its investors, which, at least at one time, included Microsoft and Bill Gates (personally). Global Good created extremely valuable public relations to correct IV's image as the world's most notorious patent troll. It positioned Nathan Myhrvold to tell the world that IV was doing "god's work." That's great for IV, but what did taxpayers get out of this deal? "We do not have any info to share about Global Good beyond what is on IV's website," IV's press office told me, declining a request to interview Myhrvold.

One big-picture takeaway from the Global Good project concerns Bill Gates's dogmatic views about topics like intellectual property, and how Gates's philanthropic activities can be seen as doing more harm than good. As *This American Life* reported, the software industry very widely believes that our patent system is destroying innovation. Public health experts have long raised similar criticisms, arguing that intellectual property prevents cheaper, more accessible medicines from reaching patients.

While the Global Good project aimed to marshal a patent-forward response to these criticisms, its apparent failures only underline the problems that monopoly patents present.

IT'S EARLY MARCH 2022, and economist James Love is in his small office in Washington, DC, on the phone with a Senate staffer. He's talking about Xtandi. And he's talking about Bayh-Dole march-in provisions.

Through all the technical jargon and congressional shorthand, Love occasionally boiled down the argument in terms I could understand.

Xtandi is a prostate cancer drug that costs American consumers close to two hundred thousand dollars a year—five times more than elsewhere in the world. As Love explained on the call, Xtandi was developed with public resources at a public university, the University of California at Los Angeles, but the drug was now controlled by a Japanese pharmaceutical company that was bilking American consumers—cancer patients.

Insofar as the Democrats, led by President Joe Biden, talk a big game on drug pricing and taking on Big Pharma, Love argued, how could they avoid taking action on Xtandi? Going into the midterm elections, wouldn't this be a slam dunk?

It's unclear how closely the Senate staffer was listening—she didn't ask many questions during Love's lengthy explanations—but by the end of the call, Love thought he had secured an interest in a Senate sign-on letter. After hanging up the phone, he had a noticeable bounce in his step, pacing to work off some of his building energy.

The issue on Xtandi isn't one of substance, Love told me. The issue is politics. And Love knows the politics surrounding medicine patents, having seen firsthand how dogmatic and powerful Big Pharma is in this debate. He's also seen how Bill Gates has functioned as one of Big Pharma's most potent allies, a handmaiden, cheerleader, and champion wearing the veil of a well-meaning philanthropist. "Intellectual property rights that grant a monopoly are a bad fit for medical inventions because it leads to mass inequality, it's inefficient, it's morally repulsive—and [it] doesn't even really work that well in terms of the amount of resources that go in. And unexpectedly, the biggest opponent to [reforms] moving forward—it's not even the drug companies. It's one of the richest men in the world. It's Bill Gates, who bills himself as a friend of the poor," Love told me.

"Gates has probably been fine on a number of different issues," he continued, "but he's been an unbalanced and unhelpful voice when it comes to intellectual property rights. It's a blind side for him. It's almost like he doesn't know how to do math, like he doesn't know how to count. He's not objective at all. He's just ideological about this thing."

Love, who today runs a small NGO called Knowledge Ecology International, takes pains to present himself as an enemy to ideology, insisting he's not opposed to all patents. He offers energy-efficient technologies as an example. If companies want to use their patent protections to produce extremely high-priced, energy-saving appliances, consumers can relatively easily choose to buy a different product. With health and medicine, you don't always have that luxury. "My wife is a chemotherapy patient," Love says. "For the last ten years, if she didn't take the drug she was on, she'd probably die."

While Love's wife has been able to access the treatment she needs, millions of people have died from treatable or even curable diseases because the drugs they need are too expensive. And that's largely because such drugs are sold under monopoly patents that allow pharmaceutical companies to charge extremely high prices.

Love's advocacy presents an interesting counterpoint to Bill Gates. The two men are among the world's leading activists on intellectual property—James Love as a critic, and Bill Gates as a proponent. They are also close in age—Love is seventy-four, and Gates is sixty-eight—and they're both from the Seattle area. The home that Love was raised in is only about four miles from the 66,000-square-foot mansion Bill Gates built for himself on the shore of Lake Washington.

While Bill Gates went off to Harvard after high school, Love went to Alaska, working in canneries and commercial fisheries before starting several public interest NGOs. Eventually, he found his own way to Harvard, managing to get into a master's program at age thirty despite not having an undergraduate degree. He went on to work for famed consumer advocate Ralph Nader, helping lead a campaign to interrogate the greatest monopolist of the day. This included a 1997 conference called Appraising Microsoft, a two-day event that brought together leading critics of the software giant. Nader invited Gates, who declined to participate.

As Love and Nader were scrutinizing Microsoft's monopoly power over the computer revolution, Love's work was broadening into public health, where patents had become a flash point in the unfolding HIV/AIDS crisis. The virus spread across both rich nations and poor nations, creating a global activist movement. The attention this generated created an opening to challenge a leading cause of the epidemic: poor people could not afford the high-cost medicines, which were protected by monopoly patents.

This political contest was also the foreground for Love's first interaction with the Gates Foundation. At the 1999 World Health Assembly, where WHO member nations were meeting to discuss how to respond to the HIV/AIDS crisis, Love recounts seeing a drug industry representative handing out glossy pamphlets arguing that patents were not an obstacle to treatments. The pamphlets were stamped as having come from the William H. Gates Foundation, the predecessor to the Gates Foundation.

While Gates was carrying water for Big Pharma, Love was negotiating a deal with an Indian drug manufacturer named Cipla to begin producing a low-cost generic combination therapy that would allow millions of HIV/AIDS patients to access inexpensive, lifesaving treatment. Through a series of legal and political battles challenging the patent rights of Big Pharma, generic HIV/AIDS drugs began to flow into poor nations. Suddenly, for under a dollar a day—about one thirtieth of what the pharmaceutical industry had been charging—poor people could access a lifesaving treatment for HIV.

These efforts have not completely solved the HIV/AIDS crisis, but it would, nevertheless, be difficult to cite anything the Gates Foundation has done—over two decades of work, through eighty billion dollars in charitable pledges—that comes remotely close to the magnitude of this effort in terms of the effect it has had on human life. For all Bill Gates's talk about innovation and disruption and equity, his foundation works, hopelessly, within a paradigm that seeks to preserve existing power structures (and power imbalances), that insists that Big Pharma is part of the solution, not part of the problem. From HIV/AIDS to the Covid-19 pandemic, Bill Gates has consistently been on the wrong side of history, putting his ideological interest in monopoly patents ahead of the health of the poor people he claims to be saving.

The Gates Foundation became such an important obstacle to patent reforms over the years that Love, at one point, tried to delineate Gates's influence in a thirteen thousand–word time line. In places, Love's time line tracks the overlap between Microsoft and the Gates Foundation: as a company that depends on strong intellectual property rules, Microsoft has a great deal of shared business interests with Big Pharma and the Gates Foundation. Love's timeline, for example, cites Merck's CEO joining Microsoft's board of directors in 2001, the Gates Foundation hiring top Microsoft executive Jeff Raikes as its CEO in 2008, and the appearance of both Microsoft and the Gates Foundation in high-level intergovernmental meetings at the WHO related to intellectual property.

In Love's view, if you get rid of monopoly patents in the pharmaceutical industry, you have to replace them with something else—that is, there is a need to reward developers for their large research and development costs, especially because this R&D doesn't always translate into a successful new product. Love believes there's a critical role for pharmaceutical companies in the marketplace; they just need a different kind of incentive.

Love has offered a number of alternatives to patents that he says will create a more competitive, entrepreneurial marketplace, that will compel the pharmaceutical industry to focus on developing new drugs rather than marketing its patented medicines. One approach is to reward drug developers through prize money instead of monopolies. The prizes would be big—billions of dollars, for example, if a company brings a truly innovative product to market. And because the resulting drugs would not be governed by monopoly patents, generic producers would compete to bring the drugs to market as cheaply as possible. That would mean lower costs for medicine—and for national health care systems. In the United States, for example, we spend more than a half-trillion dollars each year on drugs.

Another proposal Love has backed is an international treaty in which nations commit a certain amount of money every year to research and development. This financial obligation could be met through national spending on purchases of patented pharmaceuticals because industry does put a small portion of its revenues back into R&D. But nations would get a far bigger bang for their buck through other financing mechanisms, like government grants, the full value of which would count against treaty obligations.

The proposed treaty, like most of the reforms Love endorses, was seen as a major challenge—and threat—to the pharmaceutical industry's patent-forward model. "Gates did everything he could to block discussions of this," Love told me. So did Big Pharma. In 2010, several Gates-funded groups worked with pharma giant Novartis to introduce a counterproposal to the treaty, raising funds to support nonprofit pharmaceutical development partnerships (most of which Gates funds). To date, no R&D treaty has been enacted, though public health experts and activists continue to push for one.

Sitting in Love's Capitol Hill office, we spoke late into the afternoon, Love rising from his seat every so often to make another cup of decaf in his Keurig and then launching back into stories about the malign influence of Bill Gates—a man he had never personally met, but who had long haunted his work.

As the winter day darkened the windows, Love gave me a time line of the ebb and flow of money to his own small nonprofit group, telling me that the more effective his political organizing was, the more freaked out his funders seemed to become. As the saying goes, the revolution will not be funded.

Love sees some of this, once again, as the Gates effect. The foundation has such a big voice—not just in fields like global health, but also as a leader in philanthropy itself—that it's hard to find anyone who wants to challenge its directives. The day after our interview, Love sent me a message saying more: "On the crowding out of donor money for global health, you could think of global health as a category that would attract billionaires, and we were unlucky enough to get stuck with Bill Gates, whose micromanagement and fetish for strong intellectual property and big drug companies has been a significant problem."

This sentiment yearns for a better billionaire, one who is less fascinated with, or dogmatic about, intellectual property, and less vested in

Big Pharma. Someone who was willing to turn the apple cart upside down and reorganize a major underpinning of the modern economy: the IP rights that govern the medicines we take.

But Love said something else in our interview, something that reframes his criticism and speaks to the limitations of philanthropy driving public health: "These . . . programs where [poor] people don't have skin in the game, where they don't kind of own them, where they don't kind of shape them themselves, they don't have a voice, they're not part of the conversation—I just don't know if that's helpful in the long run. When it's not your system, it's someone else's thing, some foreigner—people are just going to . . . have a different attitude to it."

Transparency

The Gates Foundation's gleaming glass-and-steel headquarters in Seattle is an expensive and impressive structure. It's actually two structures—each boomerang in shape—featuring 640,000 square feet of space and a LEED-certified platinum rating for energy efficiency. Built in downtown Seattle, across the street from the city's most famous landmark, the Space Needle, the half-billion-dollar buildings have a glass-heavy design that is meant to reflect, or transmit, the foundation's institutional values.

"We really wanted the foundation to feel transparent to people when they came here," Melinda French Gates remarked at the headquarters' opening in 2011. "The idea was to have a place where people could understand our work."

It's a message the foundation drives home to visitors. One source told me that on her first trip to the new headquarters, the foundation took great efforts during a tour to draw her attention to the architecture's openness. "I found that so telling," the source told me, "especially because you're in this compound which is absolutely in no way transparent. I just found the irony to be quite amazing. It's a marketing slogan almost."

It's more than a slogan, actually. It's an essential part of the foundation's brand. "It's not fair that we have so much wealth when billions of others have so little," Melinda French Gates wrote in a public-facing letter in 2018. "And it's not fair that our wealth opens doors that are closed to most people. World leaders tend to take our phone calls and seriously consider what we have to say. Cash-strapped school districts are more likely to divert money and talent toward ideas they think we will fund. But there is nothing secret about our objectives as a foundation. We are committed to being open about what we fund and what the results have been."

It's an odd rationalization, one that seems to argue that the foundation's professed transparency justifies its deeply unfair exercise of power. And it's based on a wholly false premise—that the foundation is open. "Surely you know this: employees sign agreements upon hire and upon separation," one former employee told me, declining an interview. "Speaking with you would likely violate the agreements those employees have signed." "Hi Tim," another former staffer noted, "I'm under legal restrictions and can't speak about the foundation on the record."

"It's very hard to know to what extent they would enforce [these legal restrictions]," yet another former staffer noted, "but there's obviously language in there that gives people pause for thought about saying something on the record that could be construed as being critical of the foundation. . . . And if you do that, you know the full force of the foundation will come down on you."

Employees and former employees are not the only ones who do not feel they can freely speak their minds. "I wouldn't feel comfortable discussing my work with the foundation without their express approval," one grant recipient told me. "That would've been part of any grant agreement we had in place with them."

Nondisclosure, nondisparagement, and confidentiality agreements appear to be a deeply institutionalized part of Bill and Melinda Gates's personal and professional lives. When outgoing employees of Cascade Investment, which manages the foundation's money and Bill Gates's personal wealth, receive severance pay, it is standard practice to require them to sign confidentiality agreements. At Bill and Melinda Gates's wedding in 1994, according to the *Seattle Times*, the hired help had to sign nondisclosure agreements (NDAs). The news outlet also interviewed one of Melinda's friends, a former vice president at Microsoft, who said that Melinda herself might have been subject to some kind of confidentiality rules: "That was part of her agreement with Bill. That she stays private."

Not all outgoing staff from the foundation sign NDAs. Even if they don't, current and former employees still have good reason to avoid criticizing the foundation. As one former staffer explained to me, "The foundation has its hands in everything. They fund everything. They give grants to everyone. They give contracts to everyone. If you are a person that works in the public sector, most anything you touch will be adjacent to the foundation. And many, many people that come to or leave from the foundation go to organizations that still have ties with the foundation. So, I think it's a fear for their future employment opportunities—that it would have an impact in some ways."

The upshot of the foundation's institutional culture of secrecy, of course, is that it makes it very difficult for anyone to investigate it or understand it on any terms other than those offered through its massive PR machinery. When Adam Fejerskov set out to research the Gates Foundation for his academic book *The Gates Foundation's Rise to Power: Private Authority in Global Politics*, he reached out directly to the Gates Foundation early in his project, hoping to set up interviews. Fejerskov was interested in how the foundation's work on gender equity had come into being and developed into such a large-scale funding effort. "Essentially, when I embarked on the project, I did what was most natural— which is to say, 'Can I approach this through public channels or official channels?' To me, as a scholar, that would be what I prefer: always to have official approval of the institution," he told me. The foundation declined his request, so Fejerskov had to find ways to get around its high walls.

So did Charles Piller, author of a 2007 investigative series on the Gates Foundation for the *Los Angeles Times*. "For the most part, they were unwilling to engage with me. They were unwilling to answer questions and pretty much refused to respond in any sort of way, except in the most minimal way, for most of my stories," Piller told me. "That's very, very typical of big companies, government agencies—to try to hope that whatever controversial issues have been raised in reporting will have [a] limited shelf life, and they'll be able to go back to business as usual."

If you look at the interviews Bill and Melinda French Gates give— which are legion—they virtually always go to forums and outlets where they know they won't be seriously challenged. At times, it is with outlets their foundation funds. The result is that Bill and Melinda French Gates can present themselves as open and engaged with outsiders—they're constantly doing interviews—when the very opposite is true.

In 2021, two former high-ranking employees wrote an op-ed calling for transparency reforms at the Gates Foundation, saying that it (and other foundations) "should be required to file detailed annual reports analogous to those filed by public companies. These reports should specify not only how the organization spent its money, but also why it made the choices it did, what results it has achieved (good or bad), and what risks it foresees. Over time, such transparent and comprehensive reporting could help to create a market-like mechanism of public accountability for a foundation's effectiveness."

This proposal was not particularly radical, but it does show that some former staff are willing to raise questions publicly about the foundation. As always, Gates's power is not absolute, but it is very, very substantial.

THE GATES FOUNDATION has long had an online database with a keyword search function that allows the public to search through the tens of thousands of charitable grants it has made. This certainly gives the impression of an open institution, one that allows you to follow the money. But anyone who has actually tried to use the database quickly learns how illusory that openness is.

If you wanted to look into the millions of dollars Gates has donated to a given project or organization, you have to scroll through page after page after page of results, which offer extremely vague phrases to describe how its grant money is used—"to develop sustainability models for savings-led financial services for the poor," "to support programmatic and evaluation efforts," "to inform our understanding of drivers and determinants of vaccine coverage and equity." These three grants went to CARE, Code .org, and Emory University, private institutions that are under no obligation to disclose the details of how the money was spent; nor is the Gates Foundation. These organizations are also not subject to public records requests or the Freedom of Information Act.

The foundation's grant database, I learned, is also missing very large sums of money. In my reporting, I would stumble across an organization whose website reported having received Gates Foundation funding, and then I'd realize that the foundation had reported no grants to that group. Or, vice versa: the foundation would have a record of giving grant money to a group, like the news outlet *Inside Higher Ed*, which would then publish a news article about Gates without disclosing to readers that it takes Gates Foundation funding. The Centre for Analytics and Behavioural Change (CABC), at one time, disclosed on its website its ties to the Gates Foundation, then removed the reference. No grants to this group appear in the foundation's database. When I asked the center about its relationship with Gates, I was told, "It's best that the Foundation deals with media queries about projects that they fund." The Gates Foundation refused all interview requests and inquiries I sent for this book.

The CABC brands itself as a kind of civic-minded James Bond operation—quietly entering into the political discourse and deploying potent "countermeasures" to redirect the conversation. "In the analysis of every [social media] conversation, we are able to identify people speaking on each side of the conversation ie: antagonists and protagonists," the center explains. "The protagonists are our allies, our citizen activists—those who are value aligned, and are already speaking in the conversation. Our dialogue facilitators . . . develop, nurture and curate our bank of citizen activists. They provide content, context and contacts, assist them to amplify and make their message more effective on social media. Closely aligned to this process is the development of strategy aligned content to amplify our message." But who is this "bank of citizen activists," and what messages are they covertly inserting into the public discourse? If this isn't a black ops propaganda campaign to manipulate public opinion, then why is it shrouded in so much secrecy?

After banging my head against the wall for months trying to make sense of the endless discrepancies in the Gates Foundation's financial records, I realized that its grant making is only one piece of its charitable expenditures. Under federal law, private foundations have to publicly disclose the details of their charitable grants, and Gates's records show around eighty billion dollars in awarded grants. This is the money that appears in its online database—with vague, one-line descriptions. But, I discovered, there is another large pool of money—six billion dollars in charitable contracts and "professional fees," the details of which the foundation zealously guards from public view.

According to its annual tax filings with the IRS, the foundation describes using this money for things like "grantee technical assistance," "communications," "outsourced services," and "strategy execution." This doesn't tell us where the money went, however. In 2013, the foundation reported in its annual tax filings having awarded 674 contracts valued at a total of $393,412,140. That was about 10 percent of the foundation's entire expenses for the year. The foundation, as required by the IRS, publicly reported the recipients of its five largest contracts: McKinsey, Boston Consulting Group, Slalom Consulting, Avanade, and McKinsey Nigeria—worth around $65 million. That leaves us with a black hole of $325 million in payments to unknown groups to advance the foundation's work. Over the years, the foundation has given out more than 9,000 contracts worth around $6 billion. Of that sum, nearly $5 billion went to undisclosed recipients. Where did this money go?

The *Chronicle of Higher Education*, a news organization, has publicly disclosed on its website receiving funding from the Gates Foundation in the form of a contract, not a charitable grant. As I discuss later in the book, I've stumbled upon a handful of other news outlets that report receiving funding from Gates that doesn't appear in their grant records—which, presumably, means the money came through a contract. What we can't see, and can't know, is how many different news outlets get Gates's money in this way. Could the foundation be spending billions of dollars buying influence over the news—in ways we can't see—in order to elevate its political agenda and push its favored public policies? Is that why so many news outlets report so favorably on Gates? It's a question that only the Gates Foundation and the IRS can answer. I've asked the foundation point-blank to provide me with a list of all contracts it has given to journalism outlets. It refused.

Where else could Gates's undisclosed billions of dollars in contracts and "professional fees" go? Anywhere and everywhere—to political advocacy groups, private companies, government agencies, private consultants, documentary filmmakers, and other groups to advance the foundation's political agenda in a wholly nontransparent manner. It is difficult to rationalize how it is that we allow a nonprofit charity to hide the basic details of its work from the taxpaying public, which richly subsidizes that work. Insofar as something like fifty cents of every dollar the foundation spends is public money, shouldn't we at least be able to know how Gates spends it? Why do we regulate, scrutinize, and debate other forms of political spending but don't give a second thought to the use of dark money by a private philanthropy?

The foundation's culture of opacity appears to have permeated the groups with which it partners, including the World Health Organization, where the foundation serves as the second-largest funder. A 2019 investigation by Vox, for example, profiled the foundation's less-than-transparent efforts to push private consultants from McKinsey into the WHO. "Though the WHO is a public institution," the reporters wrote, "the details of these engagements, and Gates's involvement, aren't available in the WHO's budgets or financial statements. . . . The information that is disclosed on the WHO's website is incomplete. The WHO has a portal with data on contracts the agency processes—but it excludes those paid for directly by donors like Gates. It's also missing information on what, exactly, consultants have been hired to do."

Such maneuvering violates the basic democratic principles that are supposed to govern the WHO, which is part of the United Nations. The lack of transparency, however, is of great benefit to the Gates Foundation, as it makes it harder to follow Gates's money or track its influence. We can't hold the foundation accountable if we don't know what it's doing.

One additional difficulty in following the money concerns the use of "sub-grants." The foundation publicly reports the primary recipient of its money, but these recipients then parcel the money out to other groups. As one specific example, the Poynter Institute told me that virtually all the money it had received from the Gates Foundation—"to improve the accuracy in worldwide media of claims related to global health and development"—was actually passed on to other groups. Likewise, Gates also gives billions of dollars to other foundations—like the Hewlett Foundation, the United Nations Foundation, and the Bill, Hillary and Chelsea Clinton Foundation—which then distribute the money to other groups. This means that the listed recipient of funding in Gates's grant records is not the only recipient and, at times, not actually the primary recipient. If we look across the more than thirty thousand charitable grants the foundation has given away, it is possible that the sheer number of individuals and institutions with financial ties to Gates could be an order of magnitude higher than what we can see in its records.

"The foundation works in partnership with many organizations, who in turn fund others," a foundation spokesperson noted when I asked about sub-grants years ago. "We don't post our sub-grants, but you're welcome to reach out to grantee organizations directly for more information." This was the classic kind of nonresponse I got from the foundation in the early days of my reporting (before it stopped responding to all inquiries). The Gates Foundation knows that no investigator can personally call or email the thousands of recipients of its funding. Nor is such an effort likely to yield results. Many Gates-funded groups I reached out to in my reporting for this book refused to respond to questions, for example—which is not surprising.

Gates's dark money also means it's very difficult to know who is really independent and who is in the foundation's pocket. Readers of this book might question whether your humble narrator himself picked up some undisclosed sub-grant, contract, or "professional fee" from the foundation along the way. I can tell you that I haven't—and I haven't—but I can't prove this, and neither can you. Equally troubling, if the foundation did open its books, it would only reveal another labyrinth of puzzles. Gates has created an endless array of "controlled entities" and independent organizations and financial instruments: grants, contracts, loans, endowment investments, program-related investments, purchase guarantees, and on and on. Additionally, Bill and Melinda French Gates sit atop a vast empire of diverse organizations that might fairly be described as a many-headed hydra. Here are the names of just a few: the Bill & Melinda Gates Foundation, the Bill & Melinda Gates Foundation Trust, the Bill & Melinda Gates Medical Research Institute, Gates Ag One, bgC3, Gates Ventures, Pivotal Ventures, Breakthrough Energy, Gates Policy Initiative, Exemplars in Global Health, the Giving Pledge, Global Grand Challenges, the Global Good Fund. Working at turns through their private wealth and through the foundation's endowment, the Gates family has a great number of vehicles at their disposal to advance their agenda. The size and complexity of the foundation and Bill Gates's broader empire is very much a part of the lack of transparency.

If Congress wanted to, it could consider making private foundations subject to public records requests the way government agencies are, compelling them to provide internal documents to anyone who asks.

Or, at the very least, why not require the Gates Foundation to publicly post every grant and contract it writes? That is, instead of allowing the foundation to post vague and often meaningless one-line descriptions of its charitable grants, why don't we insist on seeing the actual legal agreements the foundation writes with every grantee and contractor? This would not be a herculean task for an institution the size of the foundation. Why wouldn't we demand that this information be publicly available? Does the foundation have some legitimate claim to secrecy?

IN 2018, THE Associated Press published a rare critical investigation into how the Gates Foundation turns money into political power. "Gates's carefully curated web of influence is often invisible but allows his foundation to drive the conversation in support of its vision on how to reshape America's struggling school systems," Sally Ho reported. "The grants illustrate how strategic and immersive the Microsoft founder can be in pursuit of his education reform agenda, quietly wielding national influence over how schools operate."

The story profiled how the foundation's $44 million in donations "paid for research aligned with Gates' interests, led to friendly media coverage and had a role in helping write one state's new education system framework to influence the political debate surrounding the Every Student Succeeds Act." The investigation found that the largest recipient of Gates's political funding in this effort was New Venture Fund—but the news outlet didn't probe further into what this organization is.

The fund describes itself as a "fiscal sponsor" designed to "serve as the administrative host of [charitable] projects so that projects don't have to go to the trouble and expense of establishing themselves as independent nonprofit organizations." In practice, the fund could be seen as acting as a kind of middleman, or funnel, for wealthy donors. Instead of the Gates Foundation giving money directly to an organization, it gives money to New Venture Fund, which then administers and funds other groups—at times making it impossible to follow the money.

OpenSecrets has raised dark-money questions about the New Venture Fund and a sister nonprofit, reporting that they "have fiscally sponsored at least 80 of their own groups, bankrolling those entities in a way that leaves almost no paper trail." The *New York Times* has characterized New Venture Fund as part of an "opaque network" that has sought to advance liberal political causes in a nontransparent manner.

None of these reports mentioned the Gates Foundation, a major supporter of New Venture Fund. The foundation's $490 million in donations to the fund make it one of the single largest recipients of the foundation's giving. How this money is used, however, is often unclear and, at times, seemingly unknowable. Take, for example, a fifty-million-dollar grant Gates gave to New Venture Fund "to advance the work of the global development community by providing targeted funding to support global development policy, communications, and advocacy efforts." There are literally hundreds, if not thousands, of different places where this money could have gone—to newsrooms or think thanks or the WHO or private companies. This donation from Gates, for all intents and purposes, went into a black hole. And that may be the point.

New Venture Fund did not respond to multiple press inquiries.

Some of the Gates Foundation's funding to New Venture Fund is described with enough specificity to give us an idea of how it was spent. The Associated Press, for example, was able to track some of Gates's grants to New Venture Fund that were explicitly described as being used to "implement ESSA," the Every Student Succeeds Act—but even grants like these don't tell us to whom New Venture Fund gave the money or how, specifically, it was used. In short, we know that Gates is funding New Venture Fund for political purposes—to advance specific educational policies, in this case—but we can't actually see how the money is being spent.

Another Gates grant to New Venture Fund, for $50 million, does disclose its final destination—an organization called Co-Impact, which in turn gives out charitable grants to other groups. The Gates Foundation's current and former CEOs both sat on the group's board in mid-2022, holding two of five seats at that time. And the organization is run (and was founded) by Olivia Leland, who previously worked for the Gates Foundation. The organization's work appears indistinguishable from the foundation's: the biggest charitable grant Co-Impact gave through 2022, for example, was a $24 million donation to the Abdul Latif Jameel Poverty Action Lab at the Massachusetts Institute of Technology (a close partner of Gates), aimed at "reorienting national and state education systems" in Africa. These kinds of projects make Co-Impact seem, essentially, like an arm of the Gates Foundation (though it does boast other philanthropic sponsors, like MacKenzie Scott). Co-Impact did not respond to media inquiries.

At a certain point, it becomes difficult to know where the Gates Foundation ends and some of its grantees, or surrogates, begin—or if, indeed, there is any separation at all. The endless layers of obfuscation create a never-ending, Russian-nesting-doll effect in which the Gates Foundation appears able to fund, create, and direct new independent-seeming organizations through opaque clearinghouses like New Venture Fund, but to minimize the public appearance of its involvement. This allows it to build political power through creating a network of allies and the appearance of diverse and robust support for its agenda, an echo chamber of Gates-funded organizations.

One of the only federal rules governing large foundations is that they give away 5 percent of their assets every year. If Gates is making donations to groups over which it has decision-making power, this could be seen as the foundation's giving money to itself. There are many places where this appears to be happening—where Gates donates money to groups and then sits on their governing boards, which gives it influence over how its donated funds are spent. This includes the Global Fund to Fight AIDS, Tuberculosis and Malaria (recipient of $3 billion from Gates); Gavi ($6 billion); the Medicines for Malaria Venture ($727 million); the Alliance for a Green Revolution in Africa, or AGRA ($679 million); and the Coalition for Epidemic Preparedness Innovations ($271 million).

The foundation's internal "Board Service Policy" offers up other examples where Gates is "creating" or providing "significant" funding to organizations and then also sponsoring employees to play governance roles on those organizations' boards: AGRA, GAIN, FIND, Thrive by Five, 3ie, the Newark Charter School Fund, Aeras, the Global Fund, Gavi, iOWH, and the Gates Cambridge Trust. As organizations founded, funded, and governed by the foundation move their research and talking points into public, scientific, and political discourses, the Gates Foundation expands its influence in a nontransparent manner.

The Literacy Design Collaborative, or LDC, was originally an in-house project at the Gates Foundation, part of its embattled work to advance new "Common Core" educational standards in American schools (which we examine in detail later in the book). Gates then spun off this work into an independent nonprofit, LDC, putting more than thirty million dollars into the group through direct donations and support to school districts and nonprofit groups to work with it. Despite Gates's very significant role in LDC, the group's website includes only one passing reference to its origins at the Gates Foundation, buried in the bio of its founder, Chad Vignola. In a brief interview, Vignola downplayed Gates's involvement in LDC, describing the foundation as just one of many funders. But he did note a "soft reason" that his group might have originally decided to minimize its close ties to the foundation: "Not everyone, at least at that time, loved the Gates Foundation in the education world," he said. Vignola insists that LDC is wholly independent from the Gates Foundation.

Concerns about the foundation's surrogate power are not new. As far back as 2009, *The Lancet* highlighted Gates's close financial relationship with Seattle-based PATH, an NGO that has grown immensely with the help of three billion dollars in charitable grants from the foundation. That report questioned "whether some organisations might be better characterised as agents of the foundation rather than as independent grantees." PATH did not respond to my press inquiries.

The really stunning feature of Gates's use of surrogates, or agents, is that the people working in these organizations may not themselves realize the superstructure within which they are operating. In 2022, Katri Bertram, a consultant in global health, published a first-person essay describing this phenomenon: "At some point, I realised something that I at first found to be a coincidence, then amusing, then slightly uncomfortable, and later on worrying. No matter where I worked, whether NGO, consultant, or international organisation, *I was paid by one global health donor*. . . . Twenty years later, *I'm tired of being an astroturfer*. I'm tired of calling myself an independent consultant or claiming that I'm working for an independent NGO or organisation when I now know that's neither true, and increasingly also not the direction I think global health should take" (emphasis in original).

After publishing her piece, Bertram told me she got feedback from some readers that she was "feeding conspiracy theories."

THE FIRST EDITION of a new newsletter from Politico called *Global Pulse*, published in late 2020, offered remarkable and rare clarity about a vastly underreported story in the Covid-19 pandemic response: the Gates Foundation seemed to be in charge. "America may not be leading in global health anymore, but an American is," Politico reported. "Bill Gates is the architect of the global health infrastructure now at the forefront of the pandemic response."

From this revelation, it should have been a small, easy step to raise some obvious Civics 101 questions. Why was the world's then third-richest person, a software magnate with no medical training, serving as "the architect" of the response effort to the most pressing public health crisis in many generations?

Politico went in a different direction: "Everywhere you turn in this pandemic, the Gates Foundation is involved, which has fueled conspiracy theories amplified by anti-vaxxers that he caused the pandemic to vaccinate the world and get richer in the process or that he wants everyone in the world to be implanted with a microchip," the outlet reported.

It then looked to the Gates Foundation itself to explain the crazy making. "Conspiracy theories thrive on the notion that hidden secret things are happening," Mark Suzman, CEO of the Gates Foundation, explained. "And so one of the key things we do is to say we have no secrets, ask us questions and we will explain what we're doing and how we're doing it."

Versions of this victim narrative played out hundreds or maybe thousands of times during the pandemic as journalists spilled volumes of ink describing how the Gates Foundation, despite all its best intentions and good deeds, was being maligned by irrational criticism and attacked with misinformation. The foundation leaned hard into this reporting, using it as an opportunity to espouse its commitment to transparency. Bill Gates took endless questions from journalists about the conspiracy theories—in one instance, condemning them as "evil" and "crazy." The foundation also poured millions of dollars into charitable grants aimed at combating "misinformation" and "disinformation." The effect was to cement Gates's reputation as a champion of truth, reason, and transparency.

Some of the foundation's fiercest defenders were found in the "fact-checking" verticals that populate the news media today. PolitiFact and *USA Today* (run by the Poynter Institute and Gannett, respectively, both of which have received funds from the Gates Foundation) deployed their fact-checkers to defend Gates from "false conspiracy theories" and "misinformation," specifically the allegation that the foundation had financial investments in companies developing Covid-19 vaccines and therapies. In fact, the foundation's annual tax filings clearly showed hundreds of millions of dollars invested in companies working on the pandemic. That is, the foundation, while exercising significant decision-making power over the pandemic response, was positioned to benefit financially from the pandemic through its stock and bond investments, including in pharmaceutical companies like Pfizer and Gilead.

We can and should debate whether this is appropriate—but to have such a debate, we have to be able to agree on the basic facts. When journalists and fact-checkers make this impossible, when their "facts" steer us toward fiction, it means that these self-appointed truth seekers have become part and parcel of the very misinformation pathology they claim to be interrogating. It also highlights the almost cultlike status of Bill Gates during the pandemic, a leader whose adherents and followers zealously protected him from any scrutiny. The groupthink and herd mentality reached such a point during the Covid-19 crisis that any criticism of the foundation was apt to be branded as "conspiratorial" across news outlets and on social media.

After I discussed this phenomenon with writer Paris Marx on his podcast, *Tech Won't Save Us*, he posted a link to our talk—only to have Twitter suspend his account for "Covid misinformation." As fact-checkers and social media gatekeepers almost universally turned their focus in one direction, to defend and support Bill Gates, the Gates Foundation became the beneficiary of misinformation, not the victim.

It is true that unhinged conspiracy theories targeted the Gates Foundation during the pandemic—like the idea that Bill Gates had engineered the coronavirus—but one reason people are drawn to such ideas is that the foundation is so nontransparent and so undemocratic—and because the news media and the social media gatekeepers, instead of opening up a platform to interrogate Gates's arrogation of power, have chosen to applaud and defend it.

This is not normal, and people know this is not normal. And the failures of the news media lead to public distrust and create a marketplace for grifters, demagogues, and con artists to propose ridiculous theories and alternative "facts." The mainstream news media then take potshots at the stupidity of such theories. Lather, rinse, repeat—and what you end up with is two distinct piles of misinformed people: one group trading in absurd tales of Bill Gates implanting microchips in people and another one trading in equally far-fetched, equally dangerous mythologies about Gates's noble, selfless leadership in the pandemic.

What the emergence of conspiracy theories around Bill Gates also shows us is how polarizing a figure he is. This raises important concerns about his expansive role as a self-appointed spokesperson, or expert, on topics like vaccines and climate change. The simple fact is Bill Gates doesn't have expertise, training, or education in most of the topics where he asserts it. And, almost universally, he or his foundation has financial interests in the public policies he endorses. Gates is someone who often stands to gain financially—or his private foundation does—from the advice he gives. That fact alone makes him a terrible messenger on just about any subject.

For readers of this book concerned about vaccine hesitancy, are you not concerned that Bill Gates's interminable efforts to play expert might actually have the effect of driving such hesitancy? In a moment of public crisis like a pandemic, should it be a software geek whose foundation has far-reaching financial ties to vaccine companies giving prime-time advice on public health?

We can't blame Bill Gates as the sole driver of vaccine hesitancy, but he's not helping the situation. When the Gates Foundation aggressively uses its vast wealth to buy influence over the news media, the scientific discourse, and political debates—very often in opaque ways—it is begging the wider world simply to speculate and theorize as to what its real ambitions are, why this mega-foundation is so deeply secretive, and why in the world we would ever allow such a malevolent model of private power to take hold in a democratic state.

The reason the Gates Foundation cannot, constitutionally, be transparent is that doing so would reveal just how much power it has and how many levers it is pulling. The real solution to our Bill Gates problem is not simply for his foundation to be more transparent, however. It's for his foundation to lower its voice and unwind the unaccountable power structure it has built. Simply put, if Bill Gates wants to end the conspiracy theories surrounding his work, he should stop talking.

Lobbying

During my reporting for this book, a source sent me a document he had found years ago on an Amtrak train leaving Washington, DC. It was labeled as being Bill Gates's personal schedule from March 26, 2015. None of the people named on the schedule whom I reached out to would confirm or deny the schedule's authenticity, but the listed meetings line up with news reports of Gates's time in DC that day. The itinerary gives us insight into a day in the life of Gates, whose calendar is fastidiously organized, with precisely timed "car transfers" as well as details about who will accompany him on "ride-alongs" between meetings.

March 26 started with an 8 a.m. wake-up call from Chris Cole, whose name matches that on a LinkedIn profile for Watermark Estate Management Services, the company that manages Gates's work schedule. At 8:45 a.m., Gates's "security advance" whisked him from the Four Seasons hotel, the luxury chain Gates partially owns, to Capitol Hill, where a meeting with Sen. Lindsey Graham was followed by testimony at a hearing by the Senate Appropriations Subcommittee on State, Foreign Operations, and Related Programs.

In his testimony, Gates talked about the importance of marshaling taxpayer dollars to support Gates's effort to eradicate polio and Gates-led initiatives like Gavi. He also argued that the United States has a self-interest in expanding foreign-aid spending. "While the lives of people in poor countries will improve more than anyone else's over the next decade and a half, that improvement will have very positive consequences for the people of the United States," Gates told the committee. "Several countries that were once major aid recipients . . . have become U.S. allies and partners, as well as export markets for our farmers and manufacturers: Nigeria is the third-largest U.S. wheat market; Angola is the fourth-largest broiler-meat market; and Ghana ranks as one of the top 10 rice markets." It was an odd take from Gates, who often claims his foundation's focus is on helping African nations feed themselves. Here, on Capitol Hill, Gates read the room and offered a vision of Africa as a captive market for the U.S. economic empire: when Congress invests in Gates's health-related philanthropic efforts, the U.S. economy will grow.

Actor Ben Affleck was also at the hearing to offer testimony, drawing laughter with his opening quip—"Thanks for having me follow the greatest and most important philanthropist in the history of the world." In his testimony, Affleck echoed Gates: "This isn't charity or aid in the traditional sense. It's good business. With proper training and strategic investments, agriculture will become a driving force for Congo's economy." Affleck was there not just to add star power to the panel but also to promote his cause célèbre, a "social enterprise" he had founded called the Eastern Congo Initiative, which works with companies like Nespresso and Starbucks.

After the hearing, Gates's day began in earnest. According to his agenda, he had a private meeting with Senator Graham "and freshman Senators" and then a series of one-on-one meetings with Senators David Perdue, Patty Murray, Patrick Leahy, Roy Blunt, and Rand Paul.

After Gates's busy day on Capitol Hill, he went to the Gates Foundation's DC office, where he had fifteen minutes of "down time and media briefing" before a forty-five-minute interview with Vox journalist Ezra Klein, who later published a long, flattering story about Gates.

Gates then dined at the Four Seasons—his reservation was under a fake surname, "Bell"—with Ron Klain, a former chief of staff to two vice presidents (Al Gore and Joe Biden). Klain later became President Joe Biden's chief of staff.

By 9:00 that evening, Gates was off to the airport and on to other destinations. A busy day for a very important person.

This visit to Washington wasn't particularly unique for Gates, who, over the years, seems to have had unfettered access to virtually every elite power broker in DC. "I had a meeting with Trump in December and the appointees like secretary of state, or defense, OMB, a lot of jobs that affect us, until those people are confirmed we won't have meetings, but in the next month or two that opportunity will start," Gates casually noted in a 2017 interview. "So we'll engage, including myself personally, with all these key people just like we have in every administration."

In 2022, Gates told the media about his expansive, yearslong campaign to advance federal climate legislation, as another example. "Almost everyone on the energy committee came over and spent a few hours with me over dinner," he reported. Gates's interest in the legislation could be seen in terms beyond saving the planet—he has invested two billion dollars of his personal wealth in climate and energy technologies that could benefit from federal spending programs.

The prevailing reporting about Gates's political influence in Washington generally tends to describe his power rather than interrogate it, and it assumes that his access to Capitol Hill derives from his profile as a philanthropist. In reality, Gates's political influence comes the old-fashioned way: through money.

Bill and Melinda French Gates have put well over ten million dollars of their personal wealth into campaign contributions and political contests, including supporting a wide range of candidates like Mike Pence, Barack Obama, Katie Porter, Marco Rubio, Cory Booker, Lindsey Graham, Andrew Cuomo, Mitch McConnell, Rob Portman, and Nancy Pelosi.

Gates's financial influence can also be seen in its charitable giving to politically connected organizations, including the nearly $10 billion the Gates Foundation has donated to organizations based in the nation's capital—three thousand charitable grants, including donations to a never-ending stream of advocates who help put Gates's agenda in front of Congress and other political tastemakers. If we expand the geography slightly to the Beltway suburbs that comprise the DC metro area, Gates's giving crests to $12 billion. That's more than twice as much money as the foundation gives to the whole of Africa, a clear signal of where its real priorities lie.

The reason Washington is such a focus of the foundation is that the foundation's charitable empire is so heavily funded by tax dollars, which Congress controls. Gates's largest charitable projects are organized as public-private partnerships, where private philanthropies, private companies, and governments pool money (and supposedly leadership) to work on issues like vaccine distribution and agricultural development. Gates has given three billion dollars to the Global Fund to Fight AIDS, Tuberculosis and Malaria, for example, one of the foundation's best-funded initiatives. Yet governments have put more than sixty billion dollars into the project. Similarly, the Gates Foundation has awarded around six billion dollars to Gavi, while government donors have pledged thirty-five billion.

Putting pressure on elected leaders to keep the money flowing is a crucial part of all the foundation's work, essentially leaning on taxpayers to subsidize organizations that Gates has an outsize influence over. The foundation's annual reports once delineated a line item in its accounts for "donor government relations"—as much as forty million dollars a year—but stopped reporting this in 2021.

"Foreign aid budgets [from wealthy nations] . . . are about 130 billion a year. So, in terms of the bulk of money that helps the poorest . . . [it] is government aid money," Bill Gates noted in a 2013 speech. "And so our [the foundation's] 4 billion a year, although it's very big in the upstream— malaria vaccine, AIDS vaccine, diarrheal vaccines—when it comes to downstream delivery, we have to partner with these governments. And their tight budgets are making it so we have to go off and really make the case for this money that goes to other countries."

In that speech, Gates boasted that he had helped raise $5.5 billion for polio, more than half of which came from governments—funding he said would lead to the eradication of the disease by 2018. He missed his target, and as we'll examine later in the book, many experts describe the Gates-led eradication scheme as wrongheaded, if not a vanity project, arguing that this money could have helped far more people had it been used on other public health projects.

This gets to a core democratic question. An essential function of elected governments is deciding how to spend taxpayer dollars, making budgetary priorities through democratic decision-making. This is where monied interests can tilt the scales, using lobbying, campaign contributions and, yes, charity to push their priorities ahead of others.

This money-in-politics influence peddling, which gives the richest private actors the loudest voice, is obviously undemocratic, if not antidemocratic. And it's a game that Bill Gates plays expertly.

"Jetting in to Washington on Monday, Gates appeared with former President Bill Clinton at a public forum Tuesday morning and then went behind closed doors to speak to the Senate Republican luncheon," Politico reported in 2013:

> Throughout the day, there were face-to-face meetings with senior members of the Senate and House Appropriations committees important to Gates's health and agriculture agendas. And before flying out Wednesday, his schedule included time with Florida Sen. Marco Rubio, a rising young Republican star whose support could prove pivotal.
>
> "He's a character," said Sen. Rob Portman (R-Ohio). "Not your typical corporate CEO who comes in pounding the table."
>
> It's this side of Gates, the practical, unconventional Harvard dropout, that's most appealing for lawmakers caught in their own dysfunction.
>
> "I wish there were more like him around here," said Sen. Dan Coats (R-Ind.). "He's very results-oriented."
>
> "He is trying to get programs over the finish line that have stalled out," said Sen. Lindsey Graham (R-S.C.). "He is a guy with a real sense of detail. A great combination of a visionary who understands detail, and he is interesting to listen to because he can make a complicated issue understandable."

When asked by Politico to weigh in on a food aid program Congress was debating, Gates dodged the question: "We are not a lobbying organization," he said and then smiled. "But if you listen to our technical advice, you get a very positive feeling about this type of activity."

Gates evaded the question because philanthropies, generally speaking, are not allowed to engage in lobbying. As he hinted, however, that doesn't mean the foundation can't make its voice heard. Politico didn't report it, but the Gates Foundation has given $248 million to the ONE Campaign, whose sister organization, Data Action, later renamed One

Action, has spent tens of millions of dollars on lobbying, including on the Food Aid Reform Act that Politico had asked Gates about. A Gates Foundation employee even once sat on the board of directors for Data Action/One Action. Even if the foundation cannot always directly lobby Congress, it can count on its army of surrogates to make legislators see which way to vote.

Another Gates Foundation ally in this political contest was Rajiv Shah, a former high-level director at the foundation who had become the head of the U.S. Agency for International Development—and the face of the government food aid program Gates was pushing. Shah is one of a never-ending cast of characters who have moved through the perpetual-motion revolving door between the Gates Foundation and Capitol Hill (especially during Democratic administrations).

The only other place on earth where Gates has financial influence similar to that in Washington, DC, is Geneva, the other seat of power governing the foundation's sprawling empire. Switzerland houses some of Gates's most important global health public-private partnerships— Gavi; the Global Fund to Fight AIDS, Tuberculosis and Malaria; the Medicines for Malaria Venture (MMV); the Global Alliance for Improved Nutrition (GAIN); the Foundation for Innovative New Diagnostics (FIND); and the Drugs for Neglected Diseases Initiative (DNDi)—and it's home to the World Health Organization. These organizations have claimed nearly $13 billion from the foundation, making Geneva the number one destination for Gates's philanthropic giving, slightly ahead of DC.

Some of these Swiss organizations also have a presence in Washington. The Geneva-based Gavi keeps an office in DC, on Pennsylvania Avenue, and spends millions of dollars lobbying Congress, including on legislation that directly impacts Gavi's budget. For example, Gavi lobbied on the 2022 Consolidated Appropriations Act, which included a $3.9 billion pool of money to be made available for foreign aid projects aimed at public health. The legislation specifically cited Gavi's eligibility for the funds.

Many of Gates's closest charitable partners—MMV, AGRA, the International AIDS Vaccine Initiative (IAVI), GAIN, the TB Alliance, and Aeras—also lobby the U.S. Congress, spending millions of dollars in the hope of bringing billions of dollars in federal tax money into their pro-grams. The effect is to massively subsidize Gates's flagship projects.

Gates's political activities are not limited to the United States. In 2022, Politico and the German news outlet *Die Welt* examined how the Gates Foundation and its closest partners in the pandemic response, Gavi and CEPI, pressured U.S. and European governments to commit billions of dollars to support their work on Covid-19. This included a personal phone call between Bill and Melinda French Gates and German chancellor Angela Merkel in 2021. The outlet also reported, "In Germany, the Gates Foundation spent €5.7 million, about $5.73 million, in 2021 lobbying various agencies and officials in part to increase German support for the global vaccine effort. The foundation relied on 28 staff members registered to lobby in the German Parliament as well as specialists hired from the Brunswick Group, an advisory and consulting group." Politico, however, did not attempt to reconcile evidence of Gates's lobbying with the foundation's official position: "A spokesperson for the foundation said U.S. law prohibits private foundations from engaging in lobbying."

This is where federal regulations seem to dissolve into a gray area. The foundation has its own internal guidance that asserts its right to "influence regulations, administrative actions, or non-legislative policies" and "judicial decisions" in the United States and to "discuss legislative proposals or legislative actions with legislators and government officials regarding matters related to jointly-funded programs." Because so much of the foundation's work runs through projects jointly funded with governments—that is, public-private partnerships—this would appear to give the foundation carte blanche to effectively engage in lobbying across much of its portfolio, apparently both at home and abroad.

What we can't verify is how much money the foundation spends pressuring governments. Nor can we tally up the results of this intense fund-raising effort—the total taxpayer dollars, from nations around the globe, that have gone into subsidizing Gates's philanthropic projects. These questions are difficult to answer comprehensively because in the United States we do not regulate philanthropy as a political activity, like lobbying or campaign contributions. That means we don't require it to make public-facing disclosures about its political spending. And we usually pretend that the Gates Foundation's endless meetings with government officials are not aimed at influence peddling.

Many of the foundation's charitable grants are explicitly directed at efforts to "educate" and "inform" and "engage" policy makers, according to the brief grant descriptions the foundation publishes. For example, Gates has donated more than five million dollars to the Kyle House Group, including a grant "to educate policymakers on the impact of US foreign assistance programs on global health and development." Kyle House is a registered lobbying firm, but if it's using Gates's money to "educate" and "engage" policy makers—and not to push a specific legislative bill—this isn't considered lobbying. And, of course, Gates's donation was not specifically earmarked for lobbying.

Many organizations engage in this same kind of political advocacy—not lobbying on a specific piece of pending legislation but pushing elected leaders to be responsive to a certain platform. The reason the Gates Foundation is different is that we don't generally recognize that it is a political actor, or understand how much influence it has—shaping billions of dollars in aid spending and then positioning itself to manage how that money is spent. As taxpayer dollars flow into Gates's sprawling network of surrogates, who is evaluating and investigating whether this is a prudent, responsible, and effective use of public funds?

One prominent critic of the multibillion-dollar foreign aid complex that fuels Gates's work is Dambisa Moyo, a Zambian-born, Harvard-trained economist and author of the 2009 book *Dead Aid: Why Aid Is Not Working and How There Is a Better Way for Africa*. She argues that the feel-good, celebrity-driven calls for more aid and charity hurt Africa by creating a dependency on foreign donors. "Fundamentally, I don't think Africa needs more aid. I think it needs less aid," Moyo noted in a 2009 interview:

It needs governments to be made accountable to the domestic citizenry, and not accountable to donors. Africans stand in the hot African sun to elect their leaders, and it is those leaders who are charged with the responsibility of delivering social services and being accountable to their people. Clearly there was a vacuum that has allowed the celebrity culture to seep in, but it would seem to me that no society would appreciate their whole policy and the future of their children to be dependent on celebrities that actually don't live in these contexts.

I think the whole aid model emanates from a pity for Africa, a sense that Africa cannot do it, cannot achieve growth.

Moyo, who shares at least some dimensions of Bill Gates's pro-capitalist, pro-corporate worldview—she's held board positions at Barclays, 3M, Chevron, and Condé Nast—notably became Bill Gates's archenemy for a time. Though her book does not specifically interrogate, or even mention, the Gates Foundation, Gates took her arguments extremely personally. And in an apparently unscripted live Q&A at a public event in 2013, he struggled to maintain his composure while responding to an audience question about Moyo's writing.

"That book actually did damage generosity of rich world countries. You know, people have excused various cutbacks because of it," a visibly agitated Gates said. "Having children not die is not creating a dependency, having children not be so sick they can't go to school, not having enough nutrition so their brains don't develop. That is not a dependency. That's an evil thing and books like that—they're promoting evil!"

In 2016, the Gates Foundation put up funding for an all-expenses-paid weeklong trip, at $6,000 a head, for a group of U.S. congressional staffers to travel to Senegal. When they arrived, a member of the Gates Foundation staff was among the first points of contact, hosting a dinner that evening—after they first made an excursion to the Island of Gorée, a UNESCO World Heritage site. The agenda for the trip alerted the congressional staffers to how special this visit was: "President Obama visited the site in 2013; before him, high-profile figures like Pope John Paul II and Nelson Mandela did the same."

In the days ahead, the congressional travelers would tour Senegal's countryside, visiting a rice mill and a biogas energy facility, while also taking meetings with U.S. and Senegalese government officials. Staff dined in hotels and socialized into the night with Peace Corps volunteers, according to the itinerary.

The goal of the trip, organized by the Center for Strategic and International Studies, was to help Congress understand the importance of a U.S. government aid program called Feed the Future—how its "principles are applied, how the initiative's programs relate to other U.S. development investments, and how partners and beneficiaries perceive the impacts of those programs." And congressional staffers were told, in no uncertain terms, that this aid project was working: "Senegal's portfolio furnishes a snapshot of what Feed the Future programs seek to accomplish worldwide."

What congressional staffers may not have realized is that the funder of their trip had a keen financial interest in the continuation of Feed the Future, which was working on a $47 million partnership with Gates's most prominent agricultural initiative, the Alliance for a Green Revolution in Africa (AGRA). According to a federal database of grants and contracts, one year after the Gates-funded excursion, the federal government awarded an additional $60 million to AGRA.

This money didn't flow directly from this Gates-sponsored excursion, but by having the attention of congressional staffers for an entire week, and offering them a free trip, the Gates Foundation was, nevertheless, able to carefully present a narrative that helped advance its political goals. Though Gates's agricultural interventions in Africa have been widely criticized by academic researchers as ineffective and by African farmers as neocolonial (as we'll explore in detail later in the book), these perspectives cannot get the same visibility or traction with Congress as Gates's talking points. That's because there is no multibillionaire funding congressional trips to show their side of the story. The Gates Foundation can afford to send members of Congress on trips in ways that most organizations cannot—and it might even be one of the largest private funders of congressional travel. A search through public disclosures shows that the Gates Foundation has served as a sponsor for the following:

- a $14,000 trip for Arizona representative Kyrsten Sinema (now senator) to travel to Rwanda and the Democratic Republic of Congo in 2016 to learn about "maternal, newborn and child health issues," with Sinema and other travelers staying at the Serena Hotel in Kigali, which boasts of its "5-star comfort";

- a $14,000-per-head trip for Minnesota representative Erik Paulsen and his daughter to travel to Kenya in 2016 to get "direct insight on how U.S. investments are working to improve global health"; Maryland representative Andy Harris and his daughter also came on the trip, reporting that their trip cost only $7,500 per head;

- a $25,000 trip in 2014 to send Illinois representative Mike Quigley and his wife to Cambodia to learn about child and maternal health;

- an $18,000 trip to send Illinois representative Aaron Schock and his father to Ethiopia in 2010 on business class flights to learn about maternal and child health;

- $17,000 to send California representative John Garamendi and his spouse on business class flights to Tanzania in 2015 "to discuss security, terrorism, and international relations." According to the itinerary, Melinda French Gates presided over a roundtable on "putting women and girls at the center of development";

- a $9,000-a-head itinerary to send a fleet of Republican legislators—Ann Wagner, Susan Brooks, and Carol Miller and her spouse—to Guatemala in 2019, a trip that included chartered helicopters "to minimize transfer times between sites and maximize time for programming in-country"; and

- a $14,000-per-person trip for California representative Barbara Lee and her daughter-in-law to travel to Uganda in 2012 "to showcase the positive reach and scope of U.S. investments in programs that improve family health outcomes and save lives for women and girls in Uganda."

The examples go on and on—and all of this is legal.

It may surprise you—it certainly surprised me—but wealthy interests are allowed to sponsor educational trips for members of Congress and their staff. It's a clear exercise of money in politics, and, troublingly, it sometimes can be difficult to follow the money.

In 2008, a Washington, DC, think tank named the Center for Strategic and International Studies (CSIS) announced that it had received "the single largest foundation grant . . . in its history" from the Gates Foundation to start a new program called the Center for Global Health Policy. A few years later, the new project sent congressional staffers on business class flights for a weeklong learning tour about HIV/AIDS in South

Africa. The four staffers were joined on the trip by a senior program officer of the Gates Foundation, Tom Walsh, according to the itinerary. Another Gates staff member, Dr. David Allen, joined the group once they touched down in South Africa.

Though Gates was funding CSIS's Center for Global Health Policy at the time it organized this trip, though the topic and goals of the trip aligned with the Gates Foundation's agenda, and though Gates's representatives explicitly participated in the event, the public-facing ethics disclosure forms surrounding the trip do not report the Gates Foundation as a funder or sponsor. Throughout 2013 and 2014, the CSIS Center for Global Health Policy sponsored trips for congressional staffers to Zambia, Ethiopia, and Burma—trips that appear in line with the Gates Foundation's agenda and that included foundation staff. Yet the congressional disclosure forms CSIS filed did not name Gates as a sponsor.

It took repeated inquiries to CSIS over three months to get what was essentially a nonresponse to questions about why the Gates Foundation was not disclosed in ethical filings: "CSIS is a transparent institution," noted Andrew Schwartz, chief communications officer for the group. "Our funders are listed on our website and each project and funded work that we produce. It is against our policy to disclose itemized funding for our research."

Craig Holman, a government affairs lobbyist for Public Citizen, questions whether a loophole is being exploited. He said current disclosure rules require that Gates be listed as a sponsor in ethics filings only if the foundation explicitly earmarked charitable donations for Congressional travel and participated in planning the trip. "The congressional rules assume that a nonprofit foundation that has no role in planning the trip is not funding the trip for influence-peddling purposes and therefore need not be disclosed," Holman noted. "Clearly, this can be a false assumption in many cases and poses a loophole in the travel rules. If any entity is earmarking funds for congressional trips, whether or not they play a role in planning the trip, they should be . . . subject to disclosure, and let the public decide if there is any undue influence peddling going on."

What the questionable disclosures suggest is another problem at the heart of American politics: dark money. Monied interests not only have the loudest voice, but their financial influence is often hidden from the public. If the Gates Foundation's money is being used to pay for expensive trips for members of Congress and their family and staff, in ways that advance the foundation's agenda, shouldn't we have crystal-clear transparency about the details—the total money the Gates Foundation has spent on such projects, who is traveling on Gates's dime, what the travel entails, and how the trips advance the foundation's political agenda?

Some readers might question what harm could come from the foundation's efforts to get Congress interested in a topic like HIV/AIDS. This misunderstands the financial and political stakes at hand. The foundation has very specific, very narrow, and often very wrong ideas about what public health priorities should be. Do we focus on prevention or treatment? Do we spend our limited resources on building clinics or trying to create a new vaccine? Do we pursue aid programs that enrich Big Pharma, or that challenge Big Pharma? How do we decide? By funding congressional travel, alongside other activities, the foundation can help shape billions of dollars in aid spending, which affects the bottom lines of major pharmaceutical companies and the lives of millions, if not billions, of poor people. Yet the taxpaying public has few sight lines into Gates's political machinery.

One database of congressional travel disclosures, LegiStorm, cites the Gates Foundation as the fortieth-largest funder of congressional trips through mid-2022, having put up $467,269.54 to underwrite ninety-seven trips (mostly for Republicans). Yet Gates's actual funding of trips is almost certainly many times larger. For example, the foundation reports donating $11 million to CARE's "Learning Tours" program, which describes itself as taking "policymakers, government leaders and change-makers on short, intensive trips where they meet the people whose lives are being transformed through U.S. investments." CARE reports having taken more than 150 members of Congress and their staff on trips, along with dozens of journalists and government administrators. "CARE knows that when leaders witness the best U.S. foreign investments have to offer, up close and in person," the group's website notes, "they go home inspired, motivated and challenged to make change happen back in the U.S."

Another group that organizes trips with the foundation's money (alongside many other projects) is the Aspen Institute, a Washington, DC, think tank and recipient of more than $100 million from Gates. This includes a 2007 charitable grant for $664,000 "to inform an on-going group of senior committee staff on education policy issues and provide an opportunity to reflect and discuss in a neutral setting and build a collaborative working relationship." During the course of this grant, Aspen organized a trip for House and Senate staffers, described very similarly to Gates's grant: "a neutral forum to aid education policymakers in their efforts to improve student achievement."

The retreat's itinerary shows what appears to be a fast-paced walk-through of a variety of educational policies, including initiatives on teacher evaluation and performance-based pay that are central to the Gates Foundation's work. And the conference's first session was led by someone from a Gates-funded organization, Education Resource Strategies. While the language, timing, and goals of the Aspen trip appear to match up with Gates's funding and ambitions, once again, the disclosure forms do not list the Gates Foundation as a sponsor. They list only Aspen. Aspen did not respond to questions about why it did not list the Gates Foundation as a sponsor on disclosure forms. Senate and House Ethics Committees also did not respond to questions about discrepancies in disclosure forms. "No comment," said Tom Rust, staff director of the U.S. House of Representatives Committee on Ethics.

Strengthening oversight and disclosure rules presumably would help bring greater transparency to the Gates Foundation's money-in-politics efforts. It would help us understand how many millions of dollars—or maybe tens of millions of dollars—from the foundation are flowing into congressional travel. But transparency isn't a solution in and of itself. We should be asking how democracy is served by allowing private actors like Gates—or Microsoft, another large funder of congressional travel—to fund these trips. We shouldn't just be debating how to improve transparency but also why it is that Congress, under any circumstances, would accept paid travel from private actors.

We also have to understand that Gates's influence peddling goes far beyond the stated purposes of these trips. The foundation is not just buying goodwill or securing taxpayer support for its charitable agenda. It is also buying political cover for the foundation itself, if not also for the Gates family. Can we really expect legislators to bring new regulatory oversight to the Gates Foundation when those legislators are taking what look like family vacations to international destinations on the foundation's dime? Can we expect them to levy a new wealth tax on the Gates family?

WHILE CONGRESS HAS sought to limit the political activities of philanthropies, the Gates Foundation has many end-runs to circumvent these prohibitions, the most potent of which involves the Gates family's private wealth. That is, in the places where the foundation cannot freely engage in political spending, like campaign contributions or supporting ballot initiatives, Bill and Melinda French Gates simply fund this work through personal political donations. Searching for the precise sum total of this political spending is difficult because their disclosures list different names ("Bill Gates," "William H. Gates III") and various affiliations ("the Gates Foundation," "Gates Ventures," "Microsoft," "homemaker," and others), but we can nevertheless see hundreds of donations in excess of ten million dollars.

Bill Gates's largest-ever recorded political donation was two million dollars to the "Yes on 1240 Washington [State] Coalition for Public Charter Schools" ballot initiative in 2012. Pushing charter schools is a major agenda item for the Gates Foundation, but philanthropies can't directly fund ballot initiatives. So, Bill Gates simply made the contributions as a private citizen, using his massive wealth to effectively undermine the will of the people. Washington State voters had previously said no to charter schools in ballot initiatives in 1996, 2000, and 2004. With the help of Gates's political donations in 2012, the ballot passed by a razor-thin margin, with 50.69 percent of the vote. Even then, the fight was not over. Washington State courts ruled against charters in 2015. After the ruling, the Gates Foundation–funded Washington State Charter Schools Association "shepherded almost $5 million to keep the lights on at six charter schools and urged legislators to pass a new law," according to reporting by the Associated Press.

Gates and other education reformers, like the multibillionaire Walton Family Foundation (funded by the family behind Walmart), are passionate about charter schools because they represent a neoliberal innovation—privately managed publicly funded schools. As Bill Gates explained on *The Oprah Winfrey Show*, "They're allowed to not operate under the normal rules, whether it's the union rules or district rules." For all the energy and money that has gone into charter schools, decades of research show they do not outperform traditional public schools. Charters have also come under fire for driving segregation, as they proliferate in poor, urban environments.

The Gateses' ability to leverage their own personal wealth as private citizens in political campaigns—in ways that advance the interests of their private foundation—highlights the difficulty of trying to regulate the political power of billionaire philanthropy. Even if we could convince Congress to crack down on the Gates Foundation's political spending, what's to stop Bill and Melinda Gates from simply using their personal wealth to engage in adjacent political activities as private citizens? Nothing. Likewise, if the Gates Foundation can't legally lobby on a given issue, what's to stop Bill Gates from making a private donation to a nonprofit organization that can? Nothing.

In 2011, the Gates Foundation made a charitable contribution to the corporate-backed right-wing American Legislative Exchange Council (commonly known as ALEC), infamous for its efforts to introduce its own draft legislation into Congress. The foundation had given ALEC charitable funds "to educate and engage its members on efficient state budget approaches to drive greater student outcomes, as well as educate them on beneficial ways to recruit, retain, evaluate and compensate effective teaching based upon merit and achievement." After the donation drew public criticism, the foundation announced that it would no longer give grants to ALEC. But that doesn't mean Bill Gates couldn't simply use his private wealth to continue to support ALEC—something we cannot easily investigate.

Perhaps the most surprising money-in-politics activity we see in Gates's charitable work is the Gates Foundation donating money to governments, more than $1.3 billion in charity, in fact. In the United States, the Gates Foundation has donated money to the Centers for Disease Control and Prevention (CDC), the National Institutes of Health (NIH), the U.S. Department of Agriculture, the U.S. Agency for International Development, the Food and Drug Administration, and to state and county governments and school districts. The hundreds of grants are too numerous to catalogue in detail, but as an example, Gates gave $3 million to USAID "to provide a competitive granting fund that will be used to scale up a range of proven information and communication technologies to support the adoption of proven and appropriate agriculture technologies by smallholder farmers"—what sounds like coded language for promoting genetically modified organisms, or GMOs, a major agenda item for the Gates Foundation.

Gates also gives money to foreign government bodies—for example, $4.5 million to the city of Dakar "to successfully access capital markets to fund long-term investment that directly benefits the urban poor"; $1.5 million to the China CDC, "to evaluate the safety of oral polio vaccine"; $3.2 million to Public Health England, "to improve incidence measurement with improved biological assays and analytical methods"; and tens of millions more to government ministries in China, Burkina Faso, Liberia, Mali, Latvia, Ethiopia, Colombia, Rwanda, Zambia, Guinea, Cameroon, Niger, Uganda, Senegal, Lithuania, Bulgaria, Kenya, Vietnam, Nepal, Chad, Sierra Leone, and Sri Lanka. The largest portion of Gates's government funding that we can see—$700 million—actually has gone to two private foundations adjacent to the government, the CDC Foundation and the Foundation for the National Institutes of Health (FNIH). These foundations raise private-sector dollars to support the CDC and NIH, and to foster public-private partnerships. Funneling money to governments through adjacent private foundations shields some aspects of the donations from public records requests—and the NIH and CDC were not particularly cooperative or expedient in responding to Freedom of Information Act requests for this book.

Though Bill and Melinda French Gates are powerful political actors, we don't often recognize them as such, and that may be because they've gone to herculean efforts to disguise their political influence—as evident in a 2019 interview David Marchese of the *New York Times* did with Melinda French Gates:

David Marchese: To get back to philanthropy: What about the notion that the foundation's work on an issue like public education is inherently antidemocratic? You've spent money in that area in a way that maybe seems like it's crowding out people's actual wants in that area. What's your counter to that criticism?

Melinda Gates: Bill and I always go back to "What is philanthropy's role?" It is to be catalytic. It's to try and put new ideas forward and test them and see if they work. If you can convince government to scale up, that is how you have success. But philanthropic dollars are a tiny slice of the United States education budget. Even if we put a billion dollars in the State of California, that's not going to do that much. So we experiment with things. If we had been successful, David, you'd see a lot more charter schools. I'd love to see 20 percent charter schools in every state. But we haven't been successful. I'd love to say we had outsize influence. We don't.

David Marchese: Certainly you have more influence than, say, a group of parents.

Melinda Gates: Not necessarily. I went and met with a group of three dozen parents in Memphis. We thought we had a good idea for them. They were having none of it. So we didn't move forward. A group of parents, a group of teachers, they can have a very large influence.

The doublespeak from Bill and Melinda French Gates, in which they claim political leadership and decision-making power over issues like public health and public education and then eagerly disclaim it when it presents a liability, speaks to the foundation's "chameleon" nature. That's the word Adam Fejerskov, a researcher at the Danish Institute for International Studies, uses. "As a chameleon changes color to respond to different occasions and situations, the foundation is able to readily project shifting organizational identities, sometimes appearing as an NGO, sometimes as a multinational company, and sometimes even as a state actor," Fejerskov writes. "The Gates Foundation strategically practices a hybrid authority, allowing it to alternately expand and compress its organizational identity, sometimes assuming multiple organizational forms and at other times (particularly when faced with questions of legitimacy) reducing itself back to its initial shape as a private foundation, with limited accountability obligations."

This chameleonlike activity is at diametric odds with how a free and open democracy is supposed to work. We have all kinds of rules and regulations governing the flow of money into politics that are designed to help us see through the professional-grade camouflage that special interests deploy to darken their money or minimize the visibility of their political influence. The Gateses' ability to sidestep these rules speaks to the ways that extreme wealth is so destructive to democracy.

The problem is bigger than the Gates family, as the billionaire class today readily engages in a seamless mix of philanthropy and political coercion to advance its ideas, interests, and ideologies. In 2022, Politico profiled how Google billionaire Eric Schmidt was using his private philanthropy, Schmidt Futures, to help fund and staff the U.S. Office of Science and Technology Policy—charitable giving that positioned him to influence how the government organized the nation's spending on technology, potentially in ways that overlap with Google's interests.

In 2020, the *New York Times* profiled how presidential hopeful (and multibillionaire) Michael Bloomberg used his vast personal wealth to build "a national infrastructure of influence, image-making and unspoken suasion . . . propping up allies and co-opting opponents with a mix of political and charitable giving." The Koch brothers likewise famously put their personal fortunes to work engineering a decades-long effort to bend the American political discourse toward their right-wing agenda, including political donations and donating money to universities to shape how economic theory is taught.

At a point, it's easy to become fatalistic about how weak American democracy, or global democracy, has become and how easily elected leaders and government officials are co-opted by money and vested interests. But when we take a defeatist attitude, we cede even more power to men like Bill Gates, Charles Koch, and Michael Bloomberg. We must recognize at all times that billionaire philanthropists are not neutral charity workers or unimpeachable humanitarians, but, in fact, powerful political actors who seek to use their wealth to advance their own interests and reputations, often in ways that harm society and democracy. We also must recognize that our democracy is only as strong as we allow it to be and only as accountable as we force it to be.

Family Planning

60 Minutes is not only one of the most-watched news programs in the United States but one of the most-watched shows of any genre on television, drawing millions of viewers each Sunday evening to its journalistic investigations and human interest stories.

The show has also proven itself a reliable fan of Bill and Melinda French Gates, and in its coverage, we can see all the troubling tropes that play into the Gates Foundation story: the poverty porn depictions of helpless brown people who need saving, the wide-eyed journalist with his gee-whiz questions about the foundation's big ideas and audacious goals, and the incontrovertible goodness of "the most generous philanthropists in the world" who "intend to save millions of lives worldwide."

Another hallmark of this brand of news coverage, which has been fairly ubiquitous across the news media over much of the last decade, has been a laser focus on Bill Gates, the brilliant media tactician who seems to have an answer for every question and a confident solution to every problem. However, in *60 Minutes*'s first profile of the Gates Foundation, in 2010, the show flipped the script, turning its cameras on Melinda French Gates, noting that, though she seldom appears in the spotlight, she's been hard at work behind the scenes. "She travels often, probing for facts, analyzing needs, measuring the misery," presenter Scott Pelley explained, narrating over images of a poor, dusty unnamed village in the Indian province of Uttar Pradesh.

It was a big coming-out moment for Gates and long-overdue recognition of her work with the foundation. In Melinda French Gates's autobiography, *The Moment of Lift*, she writes that, for the first eight years of the foundation, she was actually doing more work there than Bill, who was still working full-time at Microsoft—even though Bill was getting all the credit.

It's also the case, however, that Melinda French Gates actively avoided the spotlight for years, and she enumerates the reasons for this: wanting to protect her personal privacy and spend more time with her three children—and also what sounds like insecurity, that deeply human trait that her spouse appears to be missing. As Gates describes it, she is a "perfectionist": "I've always felt I need to have an answer for every question, and I didn't feel I knew enough at that point to be a public voice for the foundation. So I made it clear I wouldn't make speeches or give interviews. That was Bill's job, at least at the start."

As the years went on, though, Melinda Gates has played a larger and larger public role at the foundation—still nowhere near the level of exposure of Bill, but her 2010 *60 Minutes* interview was a big step into the public eye. "I have to be here to see it and to feel it and to understand, you know, what motivates these people," she explained to Pelley. "And what is it that they're doing for their livelihood. Unless I can see it and feel it and touch it, I just don't feel like I do the foundation justice in terms of what we're trying to accomplish."

And the *60 Minutes* episode made crystal clear how desperately these poor villagers in India needed Melinda Gates. People there didn't know they needed to keep newborn babies warm or how to sterilize medical equipment, viewers were told, before the Gates Foundation intervened. Traveling to the Indian countryside with Gates, Pelley told viewers, is like going back in time to the "Middle Ages." With his multipocketed khaki cargo pants that seem to be the required costume for a newsman entering the bush, Pelley asked Gates whether her crusading efforts might create unintended problems for the world.

"We were at one of these meetings yesterday," Pelley probed, "and I remembered that a lady told you that she had eight children, and four of them had died in childbirth, or shortly thereafter. But if all of them had survived, she'd have eight children. And what the developing world does not need is more children."

Melinda Gates nodded vigorously and pounced: "I think that was the biggest a-ha to Bill and me. When we got into this work, we asked ourselves, of course, the same hard-nosed question you've asked—which is, if you get into this work and you start to save these children, will women just keep overpopulating the world? And thank goodness the converse is absolutely true. They don't do that. Because women say to themselves they want two children to survive into adulthood. If she knows that two will survive into adulthood, she will naturally bring down her population. So, as soon as she starts to see that getting them vaccinated or keeping them alive during the birth—she won't have as many children."

This "a-ha" moment and the virtuous circle Melinda French Gates described—the idea that improving public health translated not only into fewer deaths in the developing world but also fewer births—has become one of the foundation's most-cited talking points and a counterpoint to criticisms that its lifesaving work is leading to more mouths to feed. Fears of overpopulation run deep at the foundation, and improving public health is not the only tool it has deployed to reduce family sizes. In 2012, Melinda French Gates became the face of an ambitious $2.5 billion project to expand the use of contraceptives among poor women.

Yet, as is the case with most things at the Gates Foundation, this portfolio of work on family planning actually seems to track back to Bill Gates. When he was asked in 1993 whether he planned to give away any of his extraordinary wealth, he spoke about his interest in "population control." Two years later, he expanded his thoughts in his book *The Road Ahead*, writing, "Many of today's major social problems have arisen because the population has been crowded into urban areas. If the population of a city were reduced by even 10 percent, the result would be a major difference in property values and wear and tear on transportation and other urban systems."

A few years later, journalist Bill Moyers asked Gates about his fascination with overpopulation and contraception. "Did you come to reproductive issues as an intellectual, philosophical pursuit?" Moyers probed. "Or was there something that happened? Did you come upon—was there a revelation?"

Gates responded: "When I was growing up, my parents were always involved in various volunteer things. My dad was head of Planned Parenthood. And it was very controversial to be involved with that. And so, it's fascinating. At the dinner table my parents were very good at sharing the things that they were doing. And almost treating us like adults, talking about that."

Gates's father, a wealthy corporate lawyer and army veteran, might cut an odd figure as a leader of Planned Parenthood, but decades ago, the field we know today as "family planning" was organized less around women's rights or reproductive justice and more as a top-down effort to manage the world's growing population. Bill Gates Sr. later helped manage his son's first philanthropic efforts, which, as the younger Gates tells it, were organized around the idea that "population growth in poor countries is the biggest problem they face."

Overpopulation is actually a long-standing cause célèbre among many wealthy philanthropists. Billionaires like Ted Turner, Warren Buffett, and David Packard have all taken a very keen interest in the issue, for example. In 2009, Buffett, Turner, George Soros, Bill Gates, Oprah Winfrey, Michael Bloomberg, and other billionaires, made headlines when the news media discovered that they had organized a secret meeting in a private residence in Manhattan to discuss potential philanthropic partnerships, with Gates reportedly pushing the group to consider work on overpopulation.

Historically, the Gates Foundation has tracked this work to the social problems it believes overpopulation causes. In its early days, the foundation gave generously to the Population Resource Center to do outreach to "Congressional staff, state and local policymakers and key constituencies" about the negative impacts of population growth on public health and the environment. "The populations of most poor countries, which have the hardest time feeding and educating their citizens, will more than double between now and 2050," Bill Gates reported in 2012. "Melinda and I believe, though, that if the right steps are taken—not just helping women plan their families but also investing in reducing child mortality and increasing nutrition—populations in countries like Nigeria will grow significantly less than projected. Almost all the foundation's global programs focus on goals that will help with this."

The question we have to ask is, why is it Bill Gates's job, and goal, to reduce the population of Nigeria? Why do so many billionaires obsess over the procreative habits of the global poor? And why do the resulting family planning efforts so often seem to be organized around solving problems associated with crowding (climate change, poverty, hunger) rather than empowering women to take control of their fertility?

In Bill Gates's obsession with population growth, we get a glimpse into the troubled origins of the family planning movement. For the longest part of their history, contraceptives were not an emancipatory scrip for women but a tool of wealthy governments and philanthropists to limit the ability of poor people and people of color to reproduce. The foundation knows this story well because, in 2012, it invited a group of academics to share the history of eugenics in population control efforts with them—and because so many of the foundation's partners today are scarred by the legacy of eugenics.

For example, Gates has given more than fifty million dollars over the decades to EngenderHealth—once known as the Sterilization League for Human Betterment. Planned Parenthood, the recipient of close to a hundred million dollars from the Gates Foundation, is in the process of its own rebranding, publicly confronting the eugenicist sympathies of its founder, Margaret Sanger. As Planned Parenthood CEO Alexis McGill Johnson noted in a mea culpa published in 2021, "Up until now, Planned Parenthood has failed to own the impact of our founder's actions. We have defended Sanger as a protector of bodily autonomy and self-determination, while excusing her association with white supremacist groups and eugenics as an unfortunate 'product of her time.' Until recently, we have hidden behind the assertion that her beliefs were the norm for people of her class and era, always being sure to name her work alongside that of W.E.B. Dubois and other Black freedom fighters. But the facts are complicated."

Johnson describes how Sanger collaborated with the Ku Klux Klan, endorsed a Supreme Court decision that allowed tens of thousands of forced sterilizations, and supported deeply unethical experimentation on Puerto Rican women. "We must examine how we have perpetuated her harms over the last century—as an organization, an institution, and as individuals," Johnson noted, acknowledging the prejudice that continues to play out in Planned Parenthood's work. "We must take up less space, and lend more support."

This history of eugenics and population control is also inextricably tied to American philanthropy, which funded much of this work. In 2021, the Ford Foundation quietly issued a belated and extremely modest apology for its own historical population control efforts. "All of the great names of legacy philanthropy are implicated in this movement," Ford president Darren Walker said. That same year, the Rockefeller Foundation announced an effort to atone for its missteps: "This requires uncovering the facts and confronting uncomfortable truths, and this investigation is underway," Rockefeller president Rajiv Shah said.

It's critical to understand that the coercion, abuse, and violence that accompanied the population control movement were born of humanitarian intentions aimed at reducing poverty and suffering. These same good intentions are the reason these misdeeds should be a cautionary tale for the Gates Foundation, which must recognize that poor women remain vulnerable to the same exercise of coercive power, because family planning turns on the same power dynamics—of givers and takers, of rich donors and poor recipients. While the Gates Foundation clearly knows this history, it was eager to put it the rearview mirror as it expanded its work on family planning.

"Eugenics is morally nauseating, as well as discredited by science. Yet this history is being used to confuse the conversation on contraceptives today," Melinda French Gates writes in her one, brief mention of eugenics in her autobiography, which extensively covers the foundation's work in family planning. "Opponents of contraception try to discredit modern contraceptives by bringing up the history of eugenics, arguing that because contraceptives have been used for certain immoral purposes, they should not be used for *any* purpose, even allowing a mother to wait before having another child."

To Gates's point, it is true that some opponents, including a growing body of far-right political actors, seek to weaponize the eugenicist history of family planning, at times trading in misinformation.

Yet Melinda French Gates's eagerness to draw a bright white line between "modern contraceptives" and the history of eugenics, and to frame the conflict as being between people who support the use of contraceptives and those who don't, sidesteps the deeper conflict at hand—between the Gates Foundation's stated desire to empower women to plan their own families on their own terms and the practical effect of its work, which is to empower women in one direction: to have smaller families. This includes Melinda French Gates's targeted efforts to get 120 million poor women on contraceptives. It also includes charitable grants, like the six hundred thousand dollars the foundation gave to Populations Communications International "to promote small family norms and use of family planning through entertainment programs on radio and television."

Even so, Melinda French Gates insists that her foundation's work on family planning has no such agenda. "I have no interest in telling women what size families to have," she writes. "Our work in family planning leaves the initiative to the women we serve. That's why I believe in voluntary family planning."

This disconnect isn't particularly unique to Gates, as critics and scholars report that modern family planners widely seek to distance their work from that of the population controllers on which it is based. Leigh Senderowicz, professor of gender and women's studies at the University of Wisconsin, says that though we should expect to see coercion in modern family planning, few people study it. "Though virtually all family planning programs affirm a strong commitment to voluntarism and reproductive rights in their rhetoric, the regimes of measurement they employ to track progress are dominated by indicators of contraceptive uptake and fertility reduction," Senderowicz wrote in a 2019 academic study.

Matthew Connelly, a history professor at Columbia University who has studied the population control movement, made a related point in an interview: "To me, it's kind of an acid test: if you really want to walk the walk, why don't you put some money into treatment for infertility? The poorest countries of the world have extremely high rates of infertility—in many cases, it's from readily preventable or treatable causes. Yet, still, I challenge you to find a family planning program where they provide treatment for infertility. That's what you'd need to do. If you say it's about reproductive rights and health, that's what you would need to do."

Anne Hendrixson, a policy analyst at Collective Power for Reproductive Justice, offered a similar critique, telling me that family planning has to be understood in terms of offering women a full portfolio of services—not just a choice about whether or not to use contraceptives, but also *which* contraceptives to use, alongside access to abortion, fertility treatments, and a variety of reproductive health care like Pap smears, breast exams, and treatment for sexually transmitted diseases.

While the Gates Foundation clearly understands these perspectives and even parrots these points of view in its rhetoric, its philanthropic interventions, in practice, appear far more concerned with meeting numerical targets and managing corporate partnerships than supporting the rights of poor women to make their own decisions about their bodies.

As MELINDA FRENCH GATES tells it, FP2020 wasn't her idea.

Gates recounts being at a malaria meeting in Seattle when Andrew Mitchell, the United Kingdom's then secretary of state for international development, pitched her the idea of a summit on family planning. The word *summit*, however, hardly begins to describe what followed—a fund-raising campaign that would become "by far the largest sum of money ever pledged to support access to contraceptives," Gates writes in her autobiography. "Family planning had fallen off as a global health priority," she notes. "I knew that we would have to emphasize setting goals, improving data, and being more strategic. But I also knew that if we were going to set ambitious goals and reach them, we had to meet a much tougher challenge. We had to change the conversation around family planning . . . Advocates for family planning had to make it clear that we were not talking about population control."

And the foundation was highly effective at changing the conversation, quickly gathering allies and media support. It funded a study at Johns Hopkins University, for example, that the *New York Times* breathlessly profiled, reporting "that fulfilling unmet contraception demand by women in developing countries could reduce global maternal mortality by nearly a third." The *Times* also reported in detail the foundation's big upcoming summit in London, which aimed to do just that.

The summit raised more than $2.5 billion in new pledges to expand the availability of contraceptives, a project named Family Planning 2020.

Specifically, FP2020, as it is commonly called, sought to raise enough funds to enroll 120 million new women on contraceptives by the year 2020, focusing on the 69 poorest nations on earth, mostly in sub-Saharan Africa and South Asia. The Gates Foundation and UK taxpayers were the largest supporters, together pledging half of the initial money raised.

Because the project was supposed to be oriented around the voices and needs of poor women, Melinda French Gates knew she needed to do fieldwork. She recounts taking a trip just before the London summit to Niger, which she describes as "a patriarchal society with one of the highest poverty rates in the world, an extremely low use of contraceptives, an average of more than seven children per woman, marriage laws that allow men to take several wives, and inheritance laws that give half as much to daughters as to sons and nothing to widows who don't have children." Despite such problems, every woman Gates met on this journey seemed to have already found her way to contraceptives. She describes a forty-two-year-old woman named Adissa who, after giving birth to ten children, chose to get an intrauterine device, or IUD, which would allow her to take control over her fertility. "When you can't take care of your children, you're just training them to steal," Adissa told Gates.

This was the kind of voice and perspective that needed to be at the center of FP2020, Gates emphasizes, "to create a new conversation led by the women who'd been left out—women who wanted to make their own decisions about having children without the interference of policymakers, planners, or theologians whose voices would force women to have more, or fewer, children than they wanted."

Of course, the FP2020 launch summit was not held in Niger, but in London, at a glitzy event for wealthy donors. In fact, it's not exactly clear how much of a role anyone outside the Gates Foundation played in the launch. The lead UN agency working on family planning, the UN Population Fund, reports being excluded from initial plans—but had no choice but to jump on the train after it was moving. "Of course we did not want to play a second violin, but we also could[n't] not participate," its director of policy and strategy, Arthur Erken, told the news media. "This is the world we are living in." And it wasn't just the United Nations agency that was caught by surprise. "Countries such as Bangladesh and India were like 'Who the hell is FP2020?'" Erken later told the press.

One of FP2020's planning teams (led by the Gates Foundation) later explicitly reported that they had "constructed the FP2020 goal in early 2012 with little external input, driven by the pressure to formulate a goal in time for the July 2012 London Summit." As Melinda French Gates describes it, "We joined the UK government in a sprint to hold the summit in London in July of 2012, two weeks before everyone's attention turned to the opening of the London Olympics at the end of the month."

To some, the size, scope, and ultra-top-down rushed formation of FP2020 looked more like a power grab than a project of empowerment. There were also concerns with the project's numerical targets—getting 120 million on contraceptives by 2020—which smacked of past population control efforts. Once you start creating numerical targets, they quickly become quotas, and perverse incentives invariably appear to meet those quotas. Amnesty International, Human Rights Watch, the Center for Reproductive Rights, and hundreds of other organizations signed a petition expressing concern about potential coercion in the project: "The Family Planning Summit must ensure that the clocks are not put back on women's human rights: women's autonomy and agency to decide freely on matters related to sexual and reproductive health without any discrimination, coercion or violence must be protected under all circumstances," the petition read.

Before the London summit, Gates gave a TED Talk in which she briefly acknowledged how numerical targets play into the history of eugenics, yet she made no effort to reconcile the numerical goals at the heart of FP2020: "Some family planning programs resorted to unfortunate incentives and coercive policies. For instance, in the 1960s India developed very specific numeric targets and they paid women to accept having an IUD placed in their bodies."

Another question mark in her talk: Gates claimed that there were "hundreds of millions of families that don't have access to contraception today," saying that it would "change their lives if they did have access." How does the foundation know this? Because they've studied the "unmet need" of poor women. This sounds like a measure of how many women want access to contraceptives but it actually measures something different: fertile women who don't intend to have children in the near future and who are not using contraceptives.

"It's the most scientifically useless indicator in the world, but the most politically useful indicator," says Leigh Senderowicz of the University of Wisconsin. "It has nothing to do with contraceptive need or whether those needs are met. Its measurement has nothing to do with desire to use contraception or access to contraception. . . . You could live next to Planned Parenthood, decide you don't want contraception, and still be assigned as having an 'unmet need' by this indicator. The fundamental underlying assumption is every women needs to be on contraceptive every single moment of her life, except when she's actively and specifically looking to get pregnant."

That's a questionable place for a family planning project to find its premise. Given the history of coercion and eugenics in the philanthropic provision of contraceptives, why would the Gates Foundation frame its efforts around such a misleading metric, one that seems to prioritize enrollment in contraception over a woman's right to decide whether she wants to use contraception? Overstating, or at least overselling, the number of poor women who desire to be on contraceptives doesn't just misdiagnose the problem, but it begs donors to solve the problem.

Later in the chapter we'll examine two independent reports documenting the existence of coercion in family planning efforts as FP2020 moved to enroll millions of new women on contraceptives. But it's important, first, to introduce perhaps the most important perverse incentive driving the Gates Foundation's work in family planning—its prioritizing one specific kind of contraception: a hormone implant that goes in a woman's arm, providing contraception for three to five years. The foundation likes these implants because they are seen as a cost-effective contraceptive, a one-and-done implant that saves women many trips to the clinic that would be required with other kinds of contraceptives. As the foundation tells it, it independently came up with a financial scheme to coax Big Pharma to make its hormone implants more widely available in poor nations. Under the agreement, Bayer and Merck would agree to ramp up production of implants and make them available at a lower price in poor nations. If the contraceptives didn't sell, Gates and other donors would be on the hook to buy them.

Using its humanitarian platform, the Gates Foundation essentially was opening up new markets for Bayer and Merck, seeming to create a new profit center for their products: the global poor. In return, the foundation could trumpet having negotiated significant price reductions— Bayer, for example, dropped the price of its hormone implant, called Jadelle, by 53 percent. "Even with lower prices, higher volumes can drive bigger profits—a classic win-win for both consumers and producers," a Gates-commissioned report noted.

Implants are popular among contraceptive users, but also controversial. Unlike birth control pills or condoms, implants have to be both inserted and removed by professional health care providers—not an easy option for many of the poor rural women targeted by Gates's FP2020. As one of the longest-lasting contraceptives, short of sterilization, implants also have a history of use in population control efforts, as profiled in Dorothy Roberts's book *Killing the Black Body: Race, Reproduction, and the Meaning of Liberty*.

In her book, Roberts, a professor of law and sociology at the University of Pennsylvania, looks at a hormonal implant named Norplant, the predecessor to those subsidized by the Gates Foundation today. These implants were specifically designed by the Population Council for use in poor nations, Roberts reports, but were later embraced as a population control tool in the United States in the 1990s, as legislators widely considered mandates and incentives to expand their use in the Black community. States ended up driving demand for Norplant through targeted advertising, with some states making them free for poor women. While states aggressively steered women toward hormone implant insertions, clinics erected barriers to their removal—even when women experienced side effects that harmed their health. "The very features that enhance Norplant's convenience for women also allow for its coercive deployment. Unlike every other method of birth control except the IUD, a woman cannot simply stop using it when she wants to," Roberts writes.

The specter of eugenics that haunted Norplant in the United States should serve as a cautionary tale to the introduction of next-generation hormonal implants via FP2020. Joan Kilande, a program officer for the

NGO HEPS Uganda, which works on contraceptive access, told me in an interview that there are practical reasons to put women on a long-lasting contraceptive in Uganda. In some clinics, there may be a single midwife caring for dozens of pregnant women and also waiting on women seeking contraceptives. The midwife is simply not going to have time to explain all the choices to women. And clinics aren't necessarily going to have a wide array of different contraceptives in stock.

Of course, Kilande is clear that this isn't how the world is supposed to work. Women shouldn't be put in a position where they can't make an informed choice. The question, then, is, shouldn't the Gates Foundation use its muscle to make sure all contraceptive options are presented on an equal footing with implants in FP2020? Why not invest in making sure clinics have the resources they need to really empower women to take control over their bodies? Doesn't the foundation have a $54 billion endowment? Aren't autonomy and choice the ambitions of modern family planning and of Melinda French Gates?

"We can insist that all people have the opportunity to learn about contraceptives and have access to the full variety of methods," Gates said in 2012. "I think the goal here is really clear: universal access to birth control that women want. And for that to happen, it means that both rich and poor governments alike must make contraception a total priority."

The reality of the Gates Foundation's work on FP2020 appeared far different. In many places, the priority was around giving women access to hormone implants, not "the full variety of methods." The foundation at one point had $400 million on the line with its volume guarantee with Bayer and Merck—money it would have to pay out if FP2020 could not successfully move their implants into women's arms. "The Gates Foundation was guaranteeing sales volume almost three times the global demand before the price cuts," a Gates-funded study reported in 2016. That study also quoted Natalie Revelle, the foundation's lead on the project: "We were sweating . . . I was worried about having suitcases of excess implants and walking around trying to distribute them."

Gates's big bet on implants helped guarantee that the foundation's favored contraceptive would be widely available. And its decision to secure a volume that was three times larger than known demand created an obvious incentive to ramp up their use. As Anne Hendrixson notes, "Instead of simply meeting women's needs, the [project] also drives demand."

Demand creation should be seen as the third rail of family planning, according to one person I spoke to inside the Gates Foundation—who showed that at least some staff have digested the history of population control in the provision of contraceptives. That is, the work of family planning is supposed to turn on the needs, desires, concerns—and rights—of contraceptive users, not those of donors. Nevertheless, both FP2020 and the Gates Foundation have, in many ways, organized their work through creating demand for their own favored solutions.

The government of Malawi's 2015 strategy document under FP2020, for example, has an entire section related to "demand creation," including "revamping communications to promote more widespread usage" of contraceptives. The Gates Foundation's grant making over the years is littered with similar projects, like donations to a group called DKT "to develop and demonstrate a sustainable private sector model for increasing and sustaining demand for Sayana Press [a Pfizer injectable contraceptive] in key geographies."

With its massive investment in hormone implants for FP2020, the foundation could be seen as taking demand creation into a kind of *Field of Dreams* scenario—not so much "If you build it, they will come" but, rather, "If you flood the market, they'll have no other choice." While coercion is little studied in family planning, there are two independent reports documenting its appearance as FP2020 moved aggressively to enroll 120 million women onto contraceptives.

In 2019, Leigh Senderowicz published a study that found that clinics and providers were organizing their workloads around meeting quotas, overemphasizing the advantages of some kinds of contraceptives over others, and even using scare tactics to get women on contraceptives. Some women said they felt forced to use contraceptives, while others, in order to avoid the high-pressure, hard-sell tactics at clinics, avoided post-pregnancy checkups altogether. The study also found that clinics pushed women toward hormone contraceptives, including hormone implants, while some clinics would refuse to remove hormone implants before they ran through their full five-year course. These findings are a mirror image of those catalogued by Dorothy Roberts twenty-five years ago in the United States, as poor Black women were coerced into accepting Norplant devices and then had difficulty getting them removed.

A few months after Senderowicz's study emerged, a group of journalists working for the Dutch news outlet *De Correspondent* made similar findings. The reporters spent several days traveling with a mobile clinic in Uganda, where they documented demand creation in real time. In a matter of a few hours, the journalists found three women who came to the clinic seeking a contraceptive injection that lasted three months, but who, through the coaxing of the clinic staff, left with implants that would keep them infertile for three *years*. In another episode, they describe a woman who was having serious health issues that she believed to be side effects caused by her implant, which she wanted removed. Four times she asked the clinic to remove the implant, and four times they refused her. Instead they gave her ibuprofen and told her to be patient with the side effects. She ended up having to go to a private clinic, at significant cost to her, to have the implant removed. Her pain and bleeding immediately stopped. *De Correspondent*'s reports get some level of confirmation in macro-level data. According to FP2020's reporting, in 2015, only 16 percent of contraceptive users in Uganda used hormone implants; by 2020, that number had doubled. *De Correspondent* also documented, troublingly, that nurses and clinics in Uganda were financially incentivized to push implants. Under the auspices of a World Bank "result-based financing" mechanism, bonuses were given according to how many years of infertility the clinics delivered: sterilizing a woman delivers 12.5 euros; a multiyear contraceptive implant or IUD brings in 5 euros; and a short-duration hormone injection is rewarded with 0.60 euros.

The head of one of the leading contraceptive providers, Reproductive Health Uganda, ultimately acknowledged the problems with such inducements. "The donors are also mainly interested in index years [how many years of infertility they are sowing into local populations], this is how the impact is measured," Jackson Chekweko, director of the group, noted. "The problem is that is how we influence her choice. And that is wrong. And that mistake starts with the donors. But it is a two-way street. We as organizations also want to do well and promise to the donors that we will achieve those index years. As a result, you see that programs mainly emphasize permanent and long-acting contraception. This is not freedom of choice, it does not guarantee her rights."

FP2020 DOES NOT appear to have fully fulfilled Melinda French Gates's claimed rhetoric around women's empowerment and autonomy. And it also, notably, failed to meet its numeric targets. By 2020, the project had reached only 60 million women, not the 120 million targeted.

FP2020 didn't dwell on its shortcomings, however. It simply moved the goalpost, trumpeting, "In 2019 alone, these combined efforts prevented more than 121 million unintended pregnancies, 21 million unsafe abortions, and 125,000 maternal deaths."

The Gates Foundation was happy enough with the success that Melinda French Gates personally presided over the launch of the next iteration of FP2020—FP2030. (FP2030 refused an interview request and did not respond to my questions about FP2020.) As part of the announcement, the foundation boasted of a new $1.4 billion commitment "to develop new and improved contraceptive technologies, support family planning programs that reflect the preferences of local communities, and enable women and girls to be in control of their own contraceptive care—where, when, and how they want it." (In total, Gates reports putting more than $4 billion into all family planning projects over the life of the foundation.)

Not long after FP2030 got off the ground, women on the foundation's home soil faced new obstacles to their own family planning. When the U.S. Supreme Court overturned *Roe v. Wade* in 2022, allowing states to ban abortion, both Bill and Melinda French Gates were quick to publicly criticize the decision on Twitter—notable because the Gates Foundation has not historically supported abortion in its charitable work.

In a 2014 blog post, Melinda French Gates explained why, arguing that access to abortion and access to contraceptives should be seen as separate issues, noting, "the emotional and personal debate about abortion is threatening to get in the way of the lifesaving consensus regarding basic family planning. I understand why there is so much emotion, but conflating these issues will slow down progress for tens of millions of women. That is why when I get asked about my views on abortion, I say that, like everyone, I struggle with the issue, but I've decided not to engage on it publicly—and the Gates Foundation has decided not to fund abortion."

Many chalk up this position to Melinda French Gates's background as a Catholic. To the extent that this is true, it raises questions about the foundation's claimed identity as an institution guided by science and reason rather than religion and ideology.

The more important reason for the foundation's decision to avoid abortion may be political expediency and pragmatism. The Republican party in the United States opposes abortion and has long sought to forbid the use of tax dollars in funding abortion, including through the U.S. government's massive foreign aid giving. The so-called global gag rule, expanded under President Trump, for example, mandated that any family planning organization receiving U.S. foreign aid cannot work on abortion—even in work they do outside their U.S. government funding. (President Biden rescinded the global gag rule.)

The foundation, by sidestepping abortion, avoids a major hot-button issue for Congress, which directs billions of dollars to a wide variety of the foundation's charitable projects; USAID even served as a "core partner" on FP2020. But Gates's political positioning is not particularly principled or noble. It makes Bill and Melinda French Gates's comments about *Roe v. Wade* ring a bit hollow. How can they pretend to be champions and leaders on family planning while they've carefully avoided working on abortion for decades? Insofar as their work on family planning claims to support a woman's right to make her own decisions about her body, how can the Gates Foundation segment off abortion as a "separate" issue?

We could ask the same questions around the evidence of coercion in the Gates Foundation's family planning work—like demand creation and its clear focus on directing women to have smaller families. If the foundation wanted to be a leader and show its commitment to autonomy and choice, why wouldn't it at least acknowledge that coercion remains a part of modern family planning and then try to address it? Doing so would draw criticism to the foundation—and it would empower opponents of contraception and abortion, and could risk losing funding partnerships with the U.S. government. But what is the other option—to pretend that it doesn't exist? One haunting worry is that by not addressing the presence of coercion, family planners could even be seen as covering it up.

"I think a lot of people don't want to talk about this just because they don't want to give the anti-choice community anything to latch on to, which I'm very sympathetic to," Leigh Senderowicz told me. "But my other response is: we accuse the anti-choice community of being anti-science and cherry-picking the data they want to see and not caring about women's well-being. And we have to hold ourselves to a higher standard."

Senderowicz told me she actually met with the Gates Foundation to discuss her research and an indicator she developed called contraceptive autonomy, designed to measure dimensions of contraceptive choice and coercion. While Senderowicz put "contraceptive autonomy" on Gates's radar, she says that, to date, the foundation has not endorsed it.

What the foundation's work in family planning helps us understand is the bigger theme of coercion in all of the Gates Foundation's funding. A powerful funder like Gates doesn't have to hold someone down in order to force them to do something. The foundation can simply take over a field by flooding money in the direction they want that field to move. The foundation claims to measure what the "unmet need" is and then "creates demand" for its own narrow solutions. It's a model of power that allows the Gates Foundation to assert itself as a leader and that allows its multinational corporate partners to open new markets. But is it empowering to the people it claims to help? Is it building a world in which "all lives have equal value"?

None of this is to say that women have not benefited from the foundation's giving. Invariably, many have benefited from the availability of subsidized hormone implants in the FP2020 program, thanks to Gates. But we could say the same thing about the eugenics-minded population control efforts by philanthropists sixty years ago. Just because many users benefit does not obviate the need to interrogate the presence of coercion and abuse.

Honoring the principles of modern family planning requires us to create a strong public health system that can both implant and remove contraceptives, that can make a variety of contraception choices available, and that can offer a suite of other services. Meeting Melinda French

Gates's high-minded rhetoric of the family planning movement—around voluntary, autonomous decision-making—also requires that these services be affordable, even to poor women. The scope of this work clearly reaches far beyond the Gates Foundation's ambitions. More important, it reaches beyond its mandate.

We cannot and should not depend on the whims and predilections of billionaires to deliver contraceptive access—not only because this model is unaccountable but because it is unsustainable. What happens when the Gates Foundation decides that its work on family planning is too politically sensitive? Or what happens when Bill Gates dies? Or when Melinda French Gates decides to step down from the Gates Foundation? Do we look to another billionaire for answers, hoping that they are marginally more enlightened? In the here and now, millions of women may depend on the Gates Foundation for access to contraceptives, so it would be a mistake to terminate this work overnight. But it would also be a mistake to imagine that the Gates Foundation's work on this issue is a righteous social good deserving of our praise. If we want to build a family planning movement organized around self-determination and autonomy, it means doing the difficult, messy work of building political power, of committing to a world where reproductive health—and public health, more generally—is understood as a human right, not a privilege administered by the superrich.

Journalism

For a few brief years in the 1990s, Bill Gates hosted overnight retreats for elite business journalists at his family's property on the Hood Canal, outside Seattle. One account of these retreats, which became known as "pajama parties," describes a van of reporters who "chattered excitedly, like Scouts going to summer camp" on their way to Gates's compound, a sojourn that included a ride on a "Turbo Beaver" seaplane. After a sumptuous dinner, Gates led a bull session with the reporters, "holding court for nearly two hours."

It's difficult to read this account and avoid seeing the reporters of that era as being too close to their subject. If Elon Musk today were to hold annual "pajama parties" with top business reporters staying at his family home and feasting on caviar, leg of lamb, and copious amounts of wine, such a junket might be considered a scandal, with attending journalists ridiculed as sellouts or, at the very least, compromised.

But such was the magic of Bill Gates at that time, the Boy Wonder billionaire, the most powerful corporate executive in the most exciting industry in the world. It didn't hurt that Gates also had a crack PR team working for him, led by media guru Pamela Edstrom, who is credited with coming up with the idea for the pajama parties. Edstrom's daughter later wrote about the sophisticated media strategies her mother engineered— like leaking "exclusive Windows 95 puff stories to all the important newspapers and publications. The PR firm fed the *New York Times* a story with a marketing twist, the *Wall Street Journal* received a more technical angle, and *People* magazine got an exclusive revealing that NBC's *Friends* sitcom stars Jennifer Aniston and Matthew Perry would be doing a twenty-five-minute video, educating people on the wonders of Windows 95."

James Wallace, a former reporter at the *Seattle Post-Intelligencer*, says he also saw Microsoft trading favors with journalists, offering exclusive stories as a negotiating tool to keep negative reports about Bill Gates's personal life out of print. Wallace has also reported that Gates had a reputation for hitting on female reporters.

Writer William Zachmann came to know firsthand Microsoft's "stick-and-carrot" approach, which he said the company employed to torpedo his influential role as a columnist for *PC Magazine*. In 1990, *PC Magazine* drew media criticism when it was revealed that editor John Dickinson was also advising Microsoft on product development, an extraordinary conflict of interest. How can a Microsoft consultant oversee independent journalistic content about Microsoft? That cozy corporate relationship, Zachmann told me in 2021—sitting at a desk in front of a very large American flag, offering a disquisition that ranged from the Ancient Babylonians to William Burroughs—defenestrated him from the top echelons of computer journalism.

Zachmann says he actually was a fan of Microsoft, enjoying watching the upstart challenge stodgy, old-guard IBM. But he says he thought IBM could pull out one last commercial success with its OS/2 operating system. Microsoft, naturally, didn't like Zachmann's enthusiasm for a competing operating system, and it deployed both the stick and the carrot to move him, like a stubborn mule, down the right path. "They're offering to help me by telling me what I should write and basically implying that they could also help to enrich me, that I'll get a lot richer and famous if I get on board," Zachmann told me. "So that's the carrot. The stick is that they're leaning on my editors . . . and getting them to try to pressure me to write more favorably about Microsoft." Zachmann says the pressure from Microsoft forced him to leave the magazine, and he went public with his story. "They're in bed with Microsoft every which way from Sunday," he said of *PC Magazine* in 1994. (The magazine and Microsoft both denied any undue influence.)

When I interviewed Zachmann decades later, I asked him if he would be surprised to hear that the Gates Foundation was using the same stick-and-carrot strategy as Microsoft had.

"I would be dumbstruck to think they are doing anything else," he said. "That's the formula that's been used by these kinds of people for thousands of years. Literally for thousands of years," he repeated, rattling off stories of how a bygone era's elite power structures used some variety of public relations, subterfuge, and deception to create alternate realities and advance their agendas. "Manipulation of public opinion through the news is not a modern phenomenon."

ON LINKEDIN, ANDREW Estrada, a senior communications officer at the Gates Foundation (and my onetime press contact), defines his job as to "Maintain relationships with and regularly engage reporters from over 30 global top-tier outlets to advance the foundation's core advocacy objectives and strengthen the organization's reputation through positive media coverage."

That's not particularly surprising or controversial. PR offices inhabit all sorts of institutions and companies, trying to get their organizational names and wares in front of the public. What is unique about the Gates Foundation is the weapons-grade nuclear material it has in its arsenal to win influence. Gates can make charitable donations to newsrooms, directly underwriting their coverage. If Microsoft tried such a tactic—giving money to newsrooms—it would be vilified as bribery.

Not only is the foundation creating financial ties with newsrooms but it is also telling them how to use its money, for editorial coverage of specific topics or even through a specific editorial lens. And the world's most powerful and prestigious news outlets have opened their arms to Gates's generosity. The foundation's grant records show more than $325 million in giving to journalism through early 2023 to a stunning range of outlets: the *Guardian*, Al Jazeera, NPR, *Der Spiegel*, *Le Monde*, CNN, the *Atlantic*, *El País*, the *Financial Times*, the *Spectator*, the BBC, and myriad other newsrooms. Because Gates's funding flows through dark-money channels at times, the total sum the foundation gives to journalism is certainly higher, and likely significantly higher than what we can see. Media Impact Funders, which takes funding from Gates, reports that the foundation's total spending on all media since 2009—not just journalism—exceeds $2.5 billion.

As a point of comparison, when billionaire Jeff Bezos paid $250 million to purchase the *Washington Post*, he set off public concern and debates over how this might bias the newspaper toward Bezos's interests or Amazon's bottom line. By contrast, relatively little debate has emerged around Bill Gates's private foundation, even as it is funneling even larger sums of money into journalism.

While the full scope of the Gates Foundation's giving is unknowable, we can see that the foundation's money travels far and wide across the media landscape, funding print, digital, and documentary content alongside fellowships, conferences, and trainings. The foundation gave $1.9 million to Johns Hopkins University "to train U.S. journalists in covering global health and development issues by providing fellowships and reporting opportunities" and $165,000 to the Aspen Institute "to identify how journalism training can improve the quantity and quality of media coverage of health issues in the developing world." A more liberal analysis of Gates's funding would also include the more than $20 million given to the Alliance for Science, which gives out journalism grants and trains African reporters on agricultural policy, and the more than $35 million given to the New America Foundation, one of the only sources of fellowship funding for nonfiction book authors.

The foundation also funds organizations that have employed columnists from the *Washington Post* and the *New York Times*. *Washington Post* columnist Michael Gerson, for example, has repeatedly praised the Gates Foundation and Bill Gates in his columns over the last decade without disclosing to readers that he also worked for the ONE campaign, where the Gates Foundation serves as the largest funder and holds a seat on the board. Only after I contacted the *Post* did Gerson begin disclosing this conflict of interest to readers. Gates has even directed funding to the top journalism ethics body, the Poynter Institute for Media Studies, which is then put in the awkward position of publicly downplaying the potential biasing effects of Gates's funding.

The foundation has, over the years, also made a surprising number of donations to underwrite investigative journalism—the Mississippi

Center for Investigative Reporting, the Premium Times Centre for Investigative Journalism, the Bureau of Investigative Journalism, the Wole Soyinka Centre for Investigative Journalism, and ProPublica. You may have listened to the public radio show and podcast *Reveal*, produced by the Center for Investigative Reporting, which boasts its hard-hitting mission is to "hold people and institutions accountable for the problems they've caused or benefited from." *Reveal* did not respond to press inquiries about its Gates Foundation funding, and the outlet does not appear ever to have sought to hold Bill Gates or the Gates Foundation accountable. And how could it? The target of your investigation, generally speaking, cannot also be your funder.

Yet, in today's financially challenging media landscape—where news outlets continue to struggle to adapt to online news distribution—it is difficult to say no to Gates's money. Few news outlets are untouched by the foundation's funding, and it's also true that until a spate of misconduct scandals rocked the foundation in 2021, there have been few newsrooms willing to take a hard look at the world's most powerful philanthropy, to report on it as something other than an unimpeachable, well-meaning charity.

In 2010, the foundation made headlines with its $1.5 million partnership with ABC News for a reporting project called *Be the Change: Save a Life*. ABC's then president David Westin acknowledged at the time that the network had met with the head of Gates's global health program "to pick his brains" about story ideas. When the foundation was later asked about this obvious example of editorial influence—funding a news outlet and then pitching them story ideas—Gates's head of communications, Kate James, waved her hands at the allegation, saying, "We meet with news organizations and editorial boards all the time." If editorial boards are meeting "all the time" with the Gates Foundation, are they also meeting with Gates's critics? Of course not. Gates's critics, generally speaking, don't have the PR firepower to get past even the first gatekeeper at elite media outlets.

It's nevertheless true that journalists have at times directed a critical lens at the foundation's work, some of the reporting brilliant and some of it even focused on the foundation's biasing effects on journalism. A 2018 Associated Press investigation found that the Gates-funded news site

The 74 had published an "exclusive" story profiling a new study on education policy from two Gates Foundation grantees. The 74 did not initially disclose to readers its funding from Gates. By funding news outlets and also the expert sources these outlets cite, in ways that are often not transparent to news consumers, the foundation has an extraordinary ability to shape the public discourse, to change the very intellectual firmament around what we know about it and how we think about the topics it works on.

For every critical story published about the Gates Foundation, perhaps five thousand favorable or uncritical stories have emerged—a deeply unbalanced discourse that has presented a one-sided narrative that verges on misinformation, if not mythmaking. Over the last twenty years, and certainly over the last ten years, it would be difficult to name a more powerful, less scrutinized political actor than the Gates Foundation.

It may sound like high-minded moralizing, but news outlets are supposed to play a crucial role in strong democracies. They are even called the "fourth estate"—a fourth layer of public-minded checks and balances that goes beyond Congress, the president, and the courts. The role of journalism is to empower a small army of investigators to follow the money, to root out waste, fraud, and abuse, and to hold power to account. One old bromide defines the mission of journalism as to "afflict the comforted and comfort the afflicted."

Yet journalists, by and large, have been unwilling or unable to understand that the Gates Foundation is a structure of power, a political organization whose billions of dollars in charitable giving present exactly the kinds of conflicts of interest and money-in-politics problems that journalists are built to interrogate. Said another way, the Gates Foundation should be one of the most investigated institutions on earth. But it's not; it's one of the most admired.

There are many reasons for this beyond Gates's financial influence over newsrooms. The media turns on hero narratives, and Bill Gates has built a powerful halo effect around his philanthropic giving. His "good-billionaire" ethos—making heaps of money and then giving it away—is a particularly irresistible narrative because it allows us to indulge our deep-seated fascination with wealth and our love of money. It is also counterintuitive for journalists—for all of us, really—to look askance at someone who is donating money: With everything wrong in the world, are we really going to interrogate a rich guy giving away all his money? Notwithstanding these explanations, it also seems fair to say that the foundation's funding of journalism has been a crucial factor in breaking the brains of journalists and closing their eyes to the threat that Bill Gates presents to democracy and equality.

To be absolutely clear, Bill Gates is not plowing hundreds of millions of dollars into journalism because he believes in the democratic ideals of the free press or because he is a personal fan of watchdog reporting. His private foundation funds the media for the exact opposite reason—to defang his watchdogs and bring them to heel, to promote his agenda and embellish his brand, to create propaganda that builds his political power, and to control the narrative that guides public understanding of his work.

IN 2017, FREELANCE journalists Robert Fortner and Alex Park published a long investigation for *Huffington Post* titled "Bill Gates Won't Save You from the Next Ebola," which brilliantly foreshadowed Gates's later failure to manage the Covid-19 pandemic.

Using public records requests, the reporters uncovered emails from the Centers for Disease Control and Prevention practically begging the Gates Foundation to get off the sidelines, step up to the plate, and help out on Ebola. The email exchange would be humorous if the stakes of the conversation weren't so deadly. The Gates Foundation, arguably the world's most powerful actor in global health, was sitting on its hands, watching a deadly epidemic unfold in Liberia.

"We do not have a specific strategy or budget for emerging infections," Chris Elias, head of Gates's Global Development division, told then CDC director Tom Frieden. "But these are extraordinary times and I'd be willing to make the case internally if it makes sense."

Frieden responded, "Situation is incredibly dire. . . . I should brief you, Bill, and others next week. All of Africa is at risk. Support now is worth many times what support in a few weeks would be worth. Literally every day counts."

The foundation did eventually commit funds to ebola, pledging fifty million dollars and telling Frieden it wanted to focus its resources on an experimental treatment, hyperimmune globulin production (which ended up not working). Frieden pleaded with the foundation to be more practical—to invest not in high-tech commodities or uncertain interventions but, rather, in the unsexy on-the-ground work of stopping transmission. "Actually, our top ask of [the foundation] is to 'harden' or help make more 'fire-resistant' the countries to which this might spread," he wrote.

When Fortner and Park asked the foundation about the emails, they were not greeted by an open and transparent charity eager to discuss its work. They got the nuclear response. Bryan Callahan, deputy director of executive engagement at the Gates Foundation, went over their heads, reaching out to a *Huffington Post* editor by email. Callahan accused the writers of "harassment," and described them as "consistently biased against the foundation, prone to unsubstantiated assertions, and reliant on cherry-picked quotes and factual misrepresentations that can be easily disproved with desktop research."

Editor Kate Sheppard (who today teaches journalism at the University of North Carolina) was taken aback, but she told me in an interview that she tried a de-escalation approach. She personally offered to play intermediary with the foundation, taking over correspondence. If the Gates Foundation didn't trust her reporters, surely they could trust her. The foundation, apparently unsatisfied, went over Sheppard's head to reach another editor even higher up in the organization.

The foundation may have felt empowered to take such extraordinary steps because Gates had made a financial donation to *Huffington Post* for something called Project Zero, described as "a yearlong series to raise awareness of neglected tropical diseases and those working to eliminate them."

Sheppard didn't flinch when I asked if she thought the foundation was trying to get the story killed. "They were very intense," she said. "Certainly, it was above and beyond the kind of outreach I get from any entity, really—private, philanthropic, governmental. I've never had anything quite like that, where they were wanting to deal with the editor before the story even came out or [they] even answer[ed] basic questions by email."

The foundation's best and constant efforts did not kill the story, however. Sheppard, Fortner, and Park prevailed, publishing their excellent story—which was well reported, well substantiated, and independent. That doesn't mean Gates failed in its pushback, however. If the foundation is willing to go to the mat to challenge critical reporting in this way, up to and including what looks like attempted character assassination of individual journalists, this behavior will send a powerful message: If you target us, you will find yourself under uncommon pressure. And you will be foreclosing on potential funding from a billionaire foundation.

As Alex Park described it to me, the foundation sought to put "a wedge between us and the publication . . . if not to assert influence outright, [then] to give themselves a channel through which they could assert influence later. . . . They've dodged our questions and sought to undermine our coverage."

While the Gates Foundation clearly knows how to wield the stick, it also knows how to dangle a carrot. News outlets know implicitly that if they play nice with Gates, they are positioning themselves to receive (or sustain) charitable gifts. That's the message—or carrot—that visited Park and Fortner when they teamed up on a reporting project for the Dutch news outlet *De Correspondent* examining the Gates Foundation's work on polio. Incredibly, the Gates Foundation, once again, went over their heads.

Rachel Lonsdale, the head of Gates's polio communications team, contacted the outlet's editor, noting, "We typically like to have a phone conversation with the editor of a publication employing freelancers we are engaging with, both to fully understand how we can help you with the specific project and to form a longer term relationship that could transcend the freelance assignment."

This sounds an awful lot like an overture, like the Gates Foundation is proposing a financial relationship. To some, it might sound like a bribe. To all of us, it should sound like a power play. In journalism, this kind of communication is not normal or appropriate. There is no universe in which the target of a journalistic investigation should have private sidebars with editors to discuss coverage—or openly proposition them.

De Correspondent told me it rejected Gates's offer because of its potential to compromise the independence and integrity of its journalistic work. Park and Fortner once again managed to get their story out. When I reported this in *Columbia Journalism Review* in 2020, the foundation described the episode as "normal media relations." "As with many organizations, the foundation has an in-house media relations team that cultivates relationships with journalists and editors in order to serve as a resource for information gathering and to help facilitate thorough and accurate coverage of our issues."

From Park and Fortner's two episodes, we could say that there's no actual evidence of harm. The journalists were able to publish their stories. Gates didn't manage to kill the investigations. Yet it is unreasonable to think that every battle royale with the Gates Foundation always goes down this way. For every principled or stubborn editor or journalist, there are a hundred who will simply go with the flow and not make waves (in my experience as a journalist, at least).

The obverse story to Fortner and Park's comes from journalists who have taken funding from Gates and who shine light on other dimensions of editorial influence from donors.

In 2018, Bhekisisa, a media outlet based in South Africa and mostly funded by the Gates Foundation, published an essay about working with charitable donors, mentioning the Gates Foundation and the German government: "Bhekisisa's donor resources, and accompanying impact, has come at a great cost. It has radically changed staff members' job descriptions from being mere journalists or editors to spending significant time—often up to 30 percent for reporters and 40 percent for editors—as data collectors, fundraisers, event organizers, proposal writers, conference moderators, creators of information management systems and donor-report writers."

Adam Davidson, who cofounded the NPR show *Planet Money*, said he walked away from a funding deal with Gates because of the requirements it put on the journalism it funded. "When I was at *Planet Money*, I turned down a Gates Foundation grant because I felt their reporting requirements essentially violated journalist ethics. They wanted us to get permission for the kinds of stories we do based on their criteria,"

Davidson, who is no longer with NPR, told me. Specifically, he said the foundation wouldn't support a story on economic development in Haiti because it didn't work on that issue in Haiti.

One source who has worked for Gates-funded journalism projects, and who asked for anonymity, offered a similar story. "What's often happening with Gates's funding is people are getting it for things they wouldn't do otherwise and they don't necessarily want to do. But that's what the funding says they must. A couple times it's been like, 'We've just got to get this [project] out the door, because we've got the money, and we've spent the money and we need to show something for it.' Just to me that felt like a total inversion of the journalistic process; in both cases, it was something the [news] organizations didn't want to do," the source noted. "To me, we have so little time as journalists and so little funding. It just bothers me that we're running around on these box-ticking assignments for Gates. And this is the problem with so much foundation-funded journalism. The question I always have is: Would you do it [the journalism project Gates has assigned] anyway? And if the answer is no, then it's PR."

The source explained to me the specific mechanics of Gates's power, including the foundation's regular check-in calls. If you were to read a transcript of these calls, the source told me, you would be very hard-pressed to prove there was any effort at editorial control. But if you could listen in, you'd realize that you were actually part of a first-rate theatrical production. The foundation uses a variety of coded language and nonverbal signals to clearly telegraph its editorial desires. The foundation might offer an innocent-sounding question in passing—'Do you have work coming out about [Country X]?' And the newsroom would quickly learn to translate GatesSpeak: 'We're interested in seeing you do more reporting in [Country X].'"

If the Gates Foundation disapproved of a story idea, it would turn to stone, its silence conveying its disapproval. If the foundation liked your story idea, you might get an enthusiastic "Mm-hmmm." "They made their interests known without directing coverage explicitly, which is how this has worked from time immemorial," the source added. "I found it a bit confronting, to be honest. They were clear without being explicit."

This source, in 2020, described the foundation's editorial influence as a necessary evil because the dollars Gates gives are so important, allowing outlets to cover topics—essentially, reporting about poor people—that otherwise wouldn't appear in the news. When we spoke again in 2021, the source was less sure, telling me that Gates was effectively creating reporting ghettos for specialized topics, a media landscape where the only way to get reporting on topics like global health and development was to publish it through Gates-funded reporting projects. Such a system is not sustainable or independent, and it's not clear it's having an impact. Yes, the *Guardian*'s global development beat—funded by Gates—will publish reporting about the global poor, but the *Guardian* isn't creating an opening on its main news page or putting the stories in front of its biggest audience.

"Do I think it's bad that Bill Gates funds media?" the source said. "Probably not, but the way it's done is so nontransparent and so secretive, and with no accountability and no accounting for conflicts of interest, so it's hopeless. So, I don't know if there's a better way for Gates to be involved. For the moment, it's a hopelessly conflicted situation which nobody seems bothered about changing." The source added, "The sense that I get is that most people are just hugely grateful for the funding and don't really question it."

WHILE BILL GATES is widely celebrated as the most generous man on earth, during his tenure as the world's leading philanthropic donor, he has managed to nearly double his personal wealth. If journalists have failed to shed light on this contradiction, it may be because Bill Gates has been so effective at showing how widely economic gains have been shared, how everyone is getting richer.

"In 1990, more than a third of the global population lived in extreme poverty; today only about a tenth do," Gates wrote in *Time* magazine during his stint as a guest editor. (Bill Gates has also played guest editor at *Wired*, the Verge, *MIT Technology Review*, Japan's *Asahi Shimbun*, the *Times of India*, and *Fortune*.) "A century ago, it was legal to be gay in about 20 countries; today it's legal in over 100 countries. Women are gaining political power and now make up more than a fifth of members of national parliaments—and the world is finally starting to listen when women speak up about sexual assault. More than 90% of all children in the world attend primary school. In the U.S., you are far less likely to die on the job or in a car than your grandparents were."

Through Bill Gates's rose-colored lens, we see a world that is constantly becoming a better place. Creative capitalism, neoliberalism, and globalism are lifting all boats. Billionaires are giving back through philanthropy and saving millions of lives. Sure, there's room for improvement. No, the world isn't perfect, but we must not let the perfect be the enemy of the good. We must stay the course. The business-as-usual track we're on is working, more or less.

The Gates Foundation has leaned hard on its founder's positivism, even trademarking the term "impatient optimist." And when Bill Gates forcefully argues the case for optimism, or invites us to take a victory lap on the social progress that civilization has made, he makes it known that it's "backed by data."

Bill Gates likes to publish charts and graphs that he believes show radical improvements in the human condition. He boasts of data showing major drops in poverty, for example, defined as living on less than $1.90 a day. "The problem with this line is that, remarkably, it has no empirical grounding in actual human needs," Jason Hickel, an economic anthropologist at the University of Barcelona and the London School of Economics, told me. "Indeed, we now have very strong evidence to show that people living at this level, or even double this level, often cannot even access enough food, to say nothing of meeting other basic needs such as housing, health care, clean cooking fuel, et cetera."

Hickel cited data from the United Nations showing that the number of people who don't have enough food to eat is nearly three times higher than the number of people who supposedly live in poverty. "Food security is not a luxury; it should be central to any robust definition of poverty," Hickel said. "While incomes and consumption have been increasing at the bottom, the gains have been very small, very slow, and not enough to lift most people out of actual poverty. The daily incomes of the poorest half of the world's population have been increasing by only a few cents per year over the past four decades. And this despite extraordinary, unprecedented global economic growth."

If we took a fairer and more honest accounting of what poverty really looks like, Hickel told me, we would see that there are more people living in poverty today than ever before. His analysis raises damning, if not existential, questions for Bill Gates's worldview. It forces us to ask if the world is well served by an economic system in which men like Gates can acquire $100 billion fortunes while more than a billion people struggle to feed themselves. It requires us to interrogate whether Bill Gates's $54 billion private foundation can help deliver equity or should be seen as Exhibit A of the inequality that defines the world today.

Bill Gates has a different take. He insists that economic and social progress is real but is the victim of cynicism, which has seeped into journalism. "Why does it feel like the world is in decline?" he asks. "I think it is partly the nature of news coverage. Bad news arrives as drama, while good news is incremental—and not usually deemed newsworthy." And Gates's solution to the bias he sees has been flooding the media with funding to report out narratives of progress and stories of hope.

In 2009, the Gates Foundation launched the Living Proof Project, aimed at telling stories showing "the progress that is being made on the ground in the fight against extreme poverty" and the lives saved through interventions around HIV/AIDS. "By reporting success stories back to the people who funded them—American taxpayers and their representatives—we hope to reframe the current global health conversation," the foundation said, later adding more nuance to its mission: "It's not about saying everything is great; it's certainly not about saying all aid works. But it is about telling the stories that are too often ignored."

At some point, the foundation realized it didn't need to tell these stories through marketing campaigns. It could simply fund journalists. This included amplifying a burgeoning new brand of reporting called "solutions journalism," which challenges journalists to jettison their doom-and-gloom focus on waste, fraud, and abuse and to focus their reporting, instead, on what's working in the world, where we're seeing progress, and how we can bring about more change. The organizing hub for this new philanthro-journalism movement is a nonprofit group called the Solutions Journalism Network, run by David Bornstein and Tina Rosenberg. When I spoke to Bornstein and Rosenberg in 2020, the group's largest all-time funder was the Gates Foundation, which has given at least seven million dollars. The Gates Foundation also reports giving millions of dollars to other outlets for work on solutions journalism, including Grist and the Stichting European Journalism Centre.

As Bornstein explains it, "The main way that the news harms democracy is by providing a view of the world that is largely deficit framed. We are amply informed about what's going wrong, about what's ugly, about what's corrupt. But because we don't have a similar amount of information about what's growing, what are the new possibilities emerging, we have a very flawed, kind of one-sided view."

The Solutions Journalism Network bills its mission as to "legitimize and spread solutions journalism," and it claims to have trained and collaborated with more than five hundred news outlets and twenty thousand journalists. When SJN evangelizes its progress-forward worldview, it is inarguably changing the lens of journalism. It's creating an opening for reporting that sometimes exalts structures of power instead of challenging them. Gates-funded "solution journalists" at times profile the Gates Foundation's good deeds and innovative solutions, for example. In an interview, I asked Bornstein if he could provide examples of any critical reporting the Solutions Journalism Network had helped produce on the Gates Foundation. He took issue with the question. "Most of the stories that we fund are stories that look at efforts to solve problems, so they tend to be not as critical as traditional journalism," he said.

The group acknowledges on its website "that there are potential conflicts of interest inherent" in taking philanthropic funding to produce solutions journalism, which Bornstein elaborated on in our interview. "If you are covering global health or education and you are writing about interesting models [of change]," he said, "the chances that an organization [you are covering] is getting money from the Gates Foundation are very high because they basically blanket the whole world with their funding, and they're the major funder in those two areas." But if your journalism model, by design, takes funding from Gates and then elevates the voices and perspectives of Gates-funded groups, how do we differentiate it from public relations?

Bornstein and Rosenberg are not only the world's leading evangelizers of solutions journalism, but also its leading practitioners. For years, they wrote a column in the *New York Times* called Fixes, where they several times favorably profiled Gates-funded projects in education, agriculture, and global health. Twice in 2019, Rosenberg's columns exalted the World Mosquito Program, whose sponsor page on its website, at one point, landed on a picture of Bill Gates. In my nonexhaustive review of the six hundred Fixes articles published in the *Times* between 2010 and 2020, I found fifteen examples where Bornstein and Rosenberg wrote about Bill and Melinda French Gates, their foundation, or work their foundation funds. I wasn't the first person to notice this bias, or to bring it the attention of the *New York Times*.

In both 2013 and 2016, Tina Rosenberg wrote long, mostly favorable profiles of Bridge International Academies in her *Times* column. Bridge is a private school system in several African nations that Bill Gates personally invests in outside his work with the foundation. The schools have proven controversial not just because they seek to privatize education but also because of the questionable teaching model used in these for-profit institutions. Teachers receive little training, and their in-class instruction amounts to reciting word-for-word lesson scripts, delivered on such a tight schedule that there isn't always time for questions.

Leonie Haimson, a reader of the *Times* and head of the advocacy group Class Size Matters, was taken aback by Rosenberg's undisclosed conflict of interest—reporting on a Bill Gates–funded private school system without disclosing that she works for an organization funded by Bill Gates's private foundation. Haimson says this financial relationship introduced bias, and she cites, as an example, Rosenberg's editorial decision to cite Bridge's own self-published performance data as evidence that the academies' educational model "probably" works. Rosenberg also soft-pedaled the widespread criticism surrounding these schools to arrive at a conciliatory review: "The project should have been envisioned sooner, and the process should have been fairer. But if experimentation is justified anywhere, it's there," she wrote in 2016. "It's hard to look at Liberia's educational system and say: Do nothing new."

Haimson, realizing that Rosenberg had written other columns that seemed aligned with the Gates Foundation's education agenda, contacted the *Times* with her concerns, citing the newspaper's own ethical guidelines, which stress the importance of independence. "Having a NYT columnist who is funded by Gates who regularly hypes controversial Gates-funded projects ... without any disclosure of conflict of interest could be compared to running columns on the environment by someone who runs an organization funded by Exxon/Mobil," she wrote in one letter to the *Times* that she shared with me. She never got a response.

When I first reported on Bornstein and Rosenberg in 2020, the authors defended the independence of their work but acknowledged to me that they should have been publicly disclosing to readers their ties to the Gates Foundation in columns they wrote about foundation-funded projects. They asked their editors to belatedly add disclosures to several of their columns. It was more than a year later, after I repeatedly reached out to the *Times,* that the news outlet finally issued corrections to a few of their columns.

Similar ethical questions have followed solutions journalism to other corners of the media landscape. When the Gates Foundation and the Solutions Journalism Network partnered with the *Seattle Times* on a reporting project called EDLab, University of Washington professor Wayne Au criticized how the resulting reporting supported Gates's agenda. In an online forum in 2014, Au cited two "puff pieces" the *Seattle Times* had published about Teachers United, "a local Gates funded astro-turf group that is all aboard the corporate ed machine." "What is striking to me is the thin political range of the [*Seattle Times's*] Ed Lab. I see mainly 'safe' stories about mainstream stuff almost no one would question, and then I see stories like the two PR pieces about T[eachers] U[nited]. A lot of this has to do with what you and the *Times* count or value as 'what works' or as a 'solution.'"

Why wasn't the *Seattle Times* profiling parent activism against Gates's educational agenda? Au asked. Why not introduce readers to groups like the Badass Teachers Association, Social Equality Educators, and Northwest Teaching for Social Justice Conference, which offer solutions that challenge the Gates Foundation? "To me, all of these groups/programs are examples of solutions/what works," Au noted. "And all of them push back against the assumptive norms of what guides Gates's definition of solutions/what works, and these things generally don't appear in anything supported by the Times."

Au's criticism gets to the heart of the problem. The funders, promoters, and practitioners of this new brand of solutions journalism do not appear to be a very big tent of people. They proffer a narrow set of solutions that often chimes with the worldview, if not the actual work, of the philanthropies that fund them. To be sure, it is difficult to imagine a universe in which solutions journalism would see the Gates Foundation as a problem, or explore solutions—like saying no to its money.

For all the philanthropic money that has gone into "legitimizing" solutions journalism, this feel-good, progress-forward, impatiently optimistic brand of reporting appears to exist for one reason: large philanthropic donors. According to its two most recent tax filings, for 2020 and 2021, the Solutions Journalism Network reported revenues of around $20 million. Top staff like Bornstein and Rosenberg took home around $200,000 in compensation. These numbers would make many newsrooms swoon with envy.

But some journalists might also recoil in horror. Billionaire donors are fundamentally changing the practice of journalism. Through charity, the superrich can amplify an entirely new brand of reporting, one that elevates their worldview, their messages, and their brands. "I have not worked at a news org in the last ten years that has not had a big push toward solutions journalism," one journalist who has worked on several philanthropy-funded news projects told me. "People are doing it because they're chasing the money, not because it's a good thing. It's so nebulous, the definition. If you're applying for grant money [from a philanthropy], it often has to be under the solutions journalism framework. . . . Gates loved it. . . . Individual freelancers hate it. Editors just accept it; they see the benefit of it. It's so unexamined."

ONE OF THE single largest recipients of Gates's journalism funding has been NPR—at around $21.5 million. This is peanuts for the foundation but a very significant sum for a nonprofit newsroom, one that constantly seems to be shaking down listeners to donate $10 a month. Gates's generosity has presided over a wealth of reporting on the foundation's work—close to six hundred mentions of the Gates Foundation in NPR's reporting through 2019.

All of Gates's giving to NPR is earmarked for reporting on specific topics, elevating issues on which the foundation works, like education and global health. Normally, editors decide what topics, or "beats," get coverage, and this isn't an easy decision. Newsrooms can't cover every topic, and they always have to prioritize where they put resources. This is a crucial part of the editorial process: deciding which beats to cover and how many reporters to put on a given beat. The Gates Foundation can influence this editorial process by making funding available for its favored topics, and inducing news outlets to follow its lead.

Not so, says NPR. "Funding from corporate sponsors and philanthropic donors is separate from the editorial decision making process in NPR's newsroom," a spokesperson told me in an email. "Our editors make their own choices about what stories to cover and how to report them. NPR journalists have no role in selecting funders and sponsors. Our journalists are trained in the ethics and practices of journalism which prevent outside groups from influencing their objectivity, story selection, and reporting."

In 2019, NPR profiled an experimental housing program in Seattle funded in part by the Gates Foundation—yes, the foundation also funds housing—that pairs up trained "navigators" with poor families to help them find housing in wealthier neighborhoods with better schools and amenities. The project offered families an opportunity to "break the cycle of poverty," NPR reported, citing researchers who forecasted that participating children could see $183,000 greater earnings over their lifetimes. It was a strikingly specific and optimistic prediction for a housing program still in the experimental stage.

If you squint as you read the story, you'll notice that every quoted expert is connected to the Gates Foundation. But I doubt most readers or listeners really connected the dots: a Gates-funded news outlet promoted a Gates-funded project by citing Gates-funded experts.

According to reporter Pam Fessler, NPR's funding from Gates "was not a factor in why or how we did the story," adding that her reporting went beyond the voices quoted in her article. Nevertheless, this scenario often visits Gates-funded journalism. It's even possible that journalists working in a Gates-funded newsroom—reporting on topics that Gates funds—may not even realize that this is happening, that all the "expert" sources they're finding on their beats are tied to Gates. Or, if they do, they might not realize how much pressure Gates-funded experts are under to deliver the right message.

As previously noted, a former foundation staffer has described the foundation as "very sensitive" to criticism, pointing out that it would be "suicidal for someone who wants a grant to come out and publicly criticize the foundation." The official party line from the foundation, like most of its recipients, is that it has no influence over journalism. When I first raised questions in 2020, its response was, "Recipients of foundation journalism grants have been and continue to be some of the most respected journalism outlets in the world. . . . The line of questioning for this story implies that these organizations have compromised their integrity and independence by reporting on global health, development, and education with foundation funding. We strongly dispute this notion."

Over the years, a number of journalists have asked the foundation about its funding of journalism. The foundation sees no gray area. "It's driven by our recognition of the changing media landscape," it noted in 2010. "We've seen this big drop-off in the amount of coverage of global health and development issues. Even before that, there was a problem with a lack of quality, in-depth reporting on many of these issues so we don't see this as being internally driven by any agenda on our part. We're responding to a need."

In reality, the foundation isn't responding to a need. It's trying to create demand. It's using charity to bend editorial coverage toward Gates's favored topics, often in ways that lead back to Gates-funded expert sources, at times through Gates's preferred brand of solutions journalism. And the hundreds of millions of dollars it is giving to journalism erode the independence of newsrooms to put a hard, critical lens on the foundation's own work—though it does still sometimes happen.

In September 2019, NPR reported on a growing scandal around the foundation's decision to give a humanitarian award to Indian prime minister Narendra Modi, despite Modi's dismal record on human rights and freedom of expression. That story was widely covered by news outlets—a rare bad news cycle for Gates. We could argue this shows NPR does have the independence to put a critical lens on Gates. However, on the same day, the foundation appeared in another NPR headline: "Gates Foundation Says World Not on Track to Meet Goal of Ending Poverty by 2030." That story cites only two sources: the Gates Foundation and a representative from the Center for Global Development, whose largest funder is the Gates Foundation.

The lack of independent perspectives is hard to miss. Bill Gates is one of the richest men in the world and might reasonably be viewed as a totem of economic inequality, but NPR has transformed him into a moral authority on poverty. The limits of NPR's critical lens also came into focus in a February 2018 story headlined "Bill Gates Addresses 'Tough Questions' on Poverty and Power." The "tough questions" NPR posed in this Q&A came from a list curated by Bill Gates himself, which he previously answered in a public-facing letter. NPR reporter Ari Shapiro asked Gates about the foundation's funding influence and how this was making it difficult for would-be critics to raise their voices.

"We're fascinated to know what alternate priorities are being suggested because we want to make sure we're being very smart and just about which things we pick," Gates responded. "And if people have constructive criticism, boy, that's the way the world moves forward, is to listen to what they think we ought to be doing differently."

In journalism, this is the flash and siren that tells a journalist to probe further. *Mr. Gates, are you really unaware of any alternate priorities— other than those your private foundation has created? Mr. Gates, if you are so earnest and eager to solicit constructive criticism, why are there so many reports about your foundation bullying and steamrolling critics? Why is your foundation so secretive?*

NPR didn't go there—because it couldn't. Its years of funding from the Gates Foundation has created a level of reverence, or dependence, that had made the foundation, in some practical sense, sacrosanct for NPR—too important to criticize. Or, maybe it can be criticized, but only very carefully. The real risk in NPR's failure to ask actual "tough" questions is that it threatens to reduce the outlet's reporting to outright misinformation. It gives Bill Gates the last word and allows him to create an alternative narrative, if not an alternate reality.

It is tempting to argue that NPR should simply stop reporting on Gates to preserve its independence. But such a decision lets the Gates

Foundation off the hook. Again, journalism is supposed to challenge structures of power. It's NPR's job to turn a critical lens on the rich and powerful. If men like Bill Gates can just knock chess pieces off the board by throwing money at them, he automatically wins the game—because he has more money than anyone else (and could literally buy any newspaper or book publisher outright if he wanted).

NPR has to have the mettle and independence to challenge Gates, and that means it has to stop taking Gates's money. News outlets need to recognize that the currency of journalism is not money, but public trust. And they also need to appreciate that the masses are not asses. If we want people to support the news, and believe in democracy, we can't allow journalism to be one more tool of influence for the superrich.

BILL GATES IS a reader and fan of the *Economist*, and it's not hard to imagine why. The magazine's business-minded worldview chimes with his own and helps rationalize the market principles that guide virtually everything his foundation does.

So, it's not surprising that the Gates Foundation is giving money to the outlet—or, actually, to the *Economist*'s research and consulting arm, the Economist Intelligence Unit. This group is cited as having edited a 2011 Gates-funded report titled "Healthy Partnerships," which examines "how governments can engage the private sector to improve health in Africa." Likewise, when the Economist Intelligence Unit promotes its public policy consulting, it highlights its work with Gates "on several important initiatives. We contributed economic analysis and modelling to a project that sought to further three key foundation goals: lifting millions of subsistence African farmers above the poverty line, providing vaccines to children under one year of age, and improving access to clean water and sanitation for populations in selected developing countries. We also worked with the Gates and Clinton Foundations on a project to examine the global progress of women and girls and highlight key gaps."

It would appear that the Gates Foundation and the Economist Intelligence Unit have a robust relationship that goes back years, but, oddly, the foundation has no record of charitable donations to the Economist Group before 2022. Likewise, the *Economist* magazine reports on the Gates Foundation with some frequency, usually uncritically or favorably—without disclosing that its sister outlet works with Gates. (The *Economist* did not respond to a press inquiry about its financial relationship with the foundation.)

This kind of opacity makes it difficult to see the big picture of the Gates Foundation's influence—because news outlets don't reliably disclose Gates's money, or the foundation doesn't disclose its donations. Or both.

In my reporting, I've stumbled across myriad examples where news outlets (or parent media companies) reported having received Gates funding—*The Chronicle of Higher Education,* Vox, *Scientific American,* Fast Company, and *Huffington Post*—that doesn't appear in the foundation's grant records. In these cases, Gates's funding, presumably, came out of its multibillion-dollar pool of dark money, described earlier in the book.

In 2014, American Public Media, when asked about its failure to clearly disclose its financial ties to Gates, suggested that this was at the direction of the foundation, "as they want the focus to be on the program itself." Meanwhile, the prevailing and virtually universal ethical rules in journalism require newsrooms to disclose financial conflicts of interest to readers. In short, if you're reporting on the Gates Foundation, and you're funded by the Gates Foundation, readers must have this information. And failing to be transparent is a recipe for public distrust. If the foundation wanted to, it could require all newsrooms that receive its funding to clearly disclose this funding in every story they publish related to the foundation. But that doesn't appear to be a priority of the foundation.

Even when the foundation does report its journalism funding in its grant records, it can be difficult to really follow the money. In 2021, the foundation reported giving $720,000 to the Slate Group "to disseminate evidence and policy recommendations for a gender-intentional economic recovery from COVID-19." The money appears to have been used to launch a podcast at the Slate-owned media outlet *Foreign Policy,* called *The Hidden Economics of Remarkable Women,* which featured an interview with Melinda French Gates. Why not just clearly state the purpose and destination of its money in its grant records? Why make us work so hard to go from A to B to C?

As the foundation tells it, transparency is a core value of its work with newsrooms. "We follow a couple of really clear principles. The first is transparency: we always disclose openly that we have a partnership agreement and how much money is involved," a communications officer for the Gates Foundation said in 2016. "Another core principle is that all of our grantees maintain editorial and creative control. We very much value journalistic independence. And we are very clear that the content must be honest and accurate, regardless of whether it's positive or negative. Once the partnership is made, we step away from it."

Behind this hollow rhetoric, we have to understand how fundamentally disrespectful the foundation's engagement with newsrooms is. The foundation counts on journalists to be too poor or too unprincipled to say no to its money or directives. And journalists, after they take Gates's money, are in the awkward position of having to defend their financial relationship to their audience—which they usually do by parroting the foundation's bankrupt rhetoric about editorial independence.

My own view as a journalist is that Gates's funding is incompatible with journalism. The foundation is simply too powerful an organization, with too long a history of abuses in journalism and too little respect for the fundamental values of a free press—independence, integrity, and transparency—to have any role in news gathering.

I'm not entirely opposed to a charitable model for journalism, and I recognize the brutal economics that continue to maim modern news gathering—thousands of newsrooms have been shuttered in recent decades, for example. Charitable dollars seem to be a growing part of the funding stream that keeps journalism solvent, and in many places, these dollars are helping produce some important reporting. Some readers of this book probably make charitable donations to the media, like the growing array of donor-driven podcasts and newsletters that run on small individual donations. Likewise, my reporting on the Gates Foundation actually originated with a fellowship from the Alicia Patterson Foundation.

But not all charitable dollars are the same. Some donors fund journalism because they believe in supporting independent journalism. Other donors, like the Gates Foundation, fund journalism to advance their agenda, their brand, and their messages. And the foundation is a particularly malevolent actor in this regard because of the extreme wealth it controls. Its funding of journalism is introducing bias and distorting democratic debates, including public understanding of the Gates Foundation itself. And it's a key reason Bill Gates has become such a powerful and unaccountable figure in world affairs.

We can't easily prohibit the foundation from funding the news media, but newsrooms and journalists can start saying no to Bill Gates's money. And readers and listeners can start demanding transparency from newsrooms and calling out the endemic bias found in Gates-funded journalism. They can also unsubscribe.

Education

Ken Auletta is one of many writers who in the late 1990s and early 2000s tried to unravel Bill Gates's fidelity to monopoly power. "Gates was just enraged that the government would question his motives. He thought he was doing good. He thought he was creating an operating system that was almost universal. Wasn't that wonderful that everyone had the same system? You didn't have to build, like, two sets of railroad tracks around the country [for two different-size trains]," Auletta said in a press interview on C-SPAN, describing his book *World War 3.0: Microsoft and Its Enemies*. "What Gates couldn't understand was fear, that people would fear a monopoly, people would fear a concentration of power."

Decades later, after antitrust legal battles and widespread public criticism showed how gravely Bill Gates had miscalculated, he still has not processed this lesson. Gates maintains that Microsoft did nothing wrong—and as recently as 2019, he spoke publicly against the Department of Justice's contention that Microsoft was preventing better, cheaper products from entering the marketplace. "I can still explain to you why the government was completely wrong, but that's really old news at this point. For me personally, it did accelerate my move into that next phase, two to five years sooner, of shifting my focus over to the foundation."

In the same way that Gates sees standardized computer operating systems, like train tracks, as imperative to a functioning marketplace, he has set his foundation to creating a new modus operandi for U.S. education, deploying the same monopoly logic. "This is an area where if you do have commonality it's like an electrical plug you get more free market competition," he explained in 2014.

"If you have 50 different plug types, appliances wouldn't be available and would be very expensive," he said in another presentation.

This "commonality" Gates describes refers to a group of educational standards, called Common Core, that his foundation essentially willed into existence in the early 2010s. "When the tests are aligned to the common standards, the curriculum will line up as well—and that will unleash powerful market forces in the service of better teaching," Gates explained. And he made clear that he wasn't talking about the marketplace of ideas. He was talking about the commercial marketplace: "For the first time, there will be a large base of customers eager to buy products that can help every kid learn and every teacher get better. Imagine having the people who create electrifying video games applying their intelligence to online tools that pull kids in and make algebra fun."

Through aligning each state's educational standards, and relentlessly testing against those standards, the foundation promised that students across the country would all finally have access to the same high-quality education, no matter where they lived. The poor third-grader in Mississippi would have the same skills in reading and math as the wealthy third-grader in Washington State.

This messaging around equity allowed the foundation to create partnerships with all manner of stakeholders. Throughout the early 2010s, Bill Gates appeared in media outlets like Black Enterprise and *Ebony*, for example, describing his educational agenda as a civil rights issue: "Why isn't there outrage, absolute outrage over [disparity in the education system]? Why aren't there protests every day? I don't understand."

The foundation has also leaned heavily on the media to help drive its education reform agenda. Gates put four million dollars into underwriting a newslike NBC program called *Education Nation*, hosted by Tamron Hall and Brian Williams. Another two million dollars went into promoting the high-profile documentary film *Waiting for "Superman,"* which parrots Gates's educational reform agenda. The *Atlantic*, meanwhile, hosts Gates-funded summits on "the state of education" and publishes Gates-funded advertorials on "rebuilding the American dream."

The foundation's most potent ally and accomplice in the push for the Common Core state standards was probably the Obama administration. During Obama's first presidential run, the Gates Foundation, working with the Eli and Edythe Broad Foundation, spent sixty million dollars on a political advocacy campaign called Strong American Schools, which was designed to make educational standards a top issue in the presidential election. Analysts at the time said this kind of single-issue political spending was unprecedented.

After Obama took office in 2009, his education department immediately drew on the Gates Foundation for staff and ideas. Education secretary Arne Duncan had previously worked at the Chicago Public Schools, the recipient of tens of millions of dollars from the Gates Foundation. And Duncan went on to fill out his department with others who had worked with Gates. The foundation's presence was so ubiquitous that some began calling Bill Gates "the real secretary of education." Arguably, however, this wasn't Gates taking over federal policymaking on education as much as simply a mind meld around neoliberal reforms, part and parcel of a decades-old, corporate-conceived effort to overhaul American schools (as we'll explore in detail later in the chapter). This reform effort coalition included billionaire foundations, the federal government, and corporate supporters but had little room for teachers, parents, and students.

"Instead of actually working with teachers and listening to what teachers needed to make public education better," Randi Weingarten, head of the American Federation of Teachers, noted in 2014, Gates's team "would work around teachers, and that created tremendous distrust." That's one reason the AFT chose to stop accepting funds from the foundation.

Nicholas Tampio, a political science professor at Fordham University, describes the Gates Foundation as using the "McKinsey technique of making changes so fast that people can't respond in time to stop you." He told me, "The fact was it was just very, very difficult to try to explain to people what the issues were. Bill Gates—he never wanted to participate in a debate about the Common Core. Arne Duncan, John B. King Jr.— these were Obama's two secretaries of education—they wouldn't engage in debates about the Common Core. David Coleman, the architect of the Common Core, never engaged in a debate about Common Core."

Beyond the McKinsey playbook, the Gates Foundation also leaned on Big Tobacco's playbook, flooding money into advocacy groups, which gave the appearance of diverse and widespread support for Bill Gates's new educational standards—at times in ways that made it difficult to see Gates's funding role. The foundation's grant records, for example, show more than $11 million in grants for work related to the Campaign for High School Equity, with money going to the National Urban League, the NAACP Empowerment Programs, the Mexican American Legal Defense and Educational Fund, and others. However, these groups issued their political advocacy as "communities of color" and as a project of "Rockefeller Philanthropy Advisors," routinely failing to disclose their funding from the Gates Foundation. The foundation also found ways to elevate its message in front of Congress, like funding the Aspen Institute and the Postsecondary National Policy Institute to organize retreats for congressional staffers to learn about education policy.

Gates's multipronged political campaign worked—or seemed to work. States began adopting the standards before a final draft had been made public and despite the fact that there had been no pilot program or assessment to make sure Common Core was effective. The *Washington Post* called it one of "the swiftest and most remarkable shifts in education policy in U.S. history."

Alongside the *Post*'s investigation, the news outlet, unusually, published a video of its interview with Bill Gates. In the interview, journalist Lyndsey Layton pushed Gates to reconcile the many contradictions and address the many criticisms surrounding his foundation's work—not just asking him challenging questions, but repeating the questions when he didn't respond. It's extremely unusual for Bill Gates to find himself in a position where he is held accountable, and the *Post* interview shows plainly why: he does not have the constitution to engage in serious debate, or to be challenged. In short, he had a meltdown.

During the interview, Gates would go silent for long stretches, staring into the middle distance with stone-faced contempt to telegraph his fury, leaving Layton's questions hanging in the air. Then he would attack her questions as having no "substance." A transcript of part of the interview follows here, including Layton asking Gates about Microsoft's financial interests in Common Core, specifically in the creation of new educational software.

Gates: Do you think that passes, do you think that passes muster?

Layton: I, I don't know. I am not, I, this is the first time we've met . . . I'm not sure.

Gates: Okay, so give me the, give me the logic here.

Layton: The logic is . . .

Gates: What is it? You're saying that it's all out of self-interest? It's . . .

Layton: That, no, that that's, that that's one of the driving forces behind your embrace of the Common Core.

Gates: Meaning what?

Layton: Meaning Microsoft and Pearson just signed a deal to, to put the Common Core curriculum on the Surface [an electronic tablet device Microsoft sells]. So, you've got a product, Microsoft has a product now that it's, that it's selling . . .

Gates: Yeah, we had the old Pearson stuff. I, it, it, there's no connection to Common Core and any Microsoft thing.

Layton: Okay. Well I just, I want to understand this, but that's a, Bill, let me just tell you . . .

Gates: That's staying away from the substance, okay?

Layton: But it's a question when people know, when people learn that you are promoting the Common Core . . .

Gates: Do you seriously think that the reason I like the Common Core is for some self-interested reason? That's what you're saying.

Layton: No. I don't know that I believe that, and you don't seem . . .

Gates: You don't know. You don't know?

Layton: I don't think that I believe that.

At this point, an off-camera voice says they should move on to a different line of questioning. Elsewhere in the interview Layton asked Gates about his political influence and his reputation as "the unelected school superintendent of the country":

Layton: Well, let me tell you what, what I'm hearing when I talk to people in education policy. The running joke is sooner or later, everybody works for Gates because, when you look at how the breadth of, of your funding, and in terms of the advocacy work for the Common Core, you funded on the left of the spectrum, on the right of the spectrum: think tanks, you know, districts, unions, business groups. It's a wide variety. There, there are, it's harder to name groups, um, that are in education that haven't received funding that, from Gates, than it is to name all the groups that have. So, the suggestion is that because of that pervasive presence, that you set the agenda, that it's harder to get, to get contrasting views and to get real, honest debate because you are funding such a wide variety of actors in this field.

Gates: Boy, I, I, I guess we're not going to get to any substance, uh, here, I'm sorry. [Long pause] Our advocacy money is a rounding error, okay? The K–12 education [budget of the federal government] is six hundred billion dollars of money a year that is spent and try to compute the R and D percentage of trying out new things. . . . The, the Common Core, people will decide, and, no, we don't, we don't fund, if you know some right-wing group that we fund, if you know, some left-wing group. I don't know. I, I have no idea what you're talking about . . . we, we don't . . .

Layton: The American Enterprise Institute . . .

Gates: We don't fund political groups. We're not . . .

Layton: . . . think tanks . . .

Gates: . . . we don't fund Heritage, Cato, people like that. Uhh . . .

Layton: The American Enterprise Institute . . .

Gates: They had some experts on educational policy, that's true.

Layton: Fordham, the Fordham Institute, to do their writing . . .

Gates: These, these are not political things. These are things where people are trying to apply expertise to say, "Is this a way of making education better?" I mean at the end of the day, it's, I don't think wanting education to be better is a left-wing or a right-wing thing. And, so making sure there's as many experts—and, yes, some of them will have political . . . who are doing evaluations. So, all—we fund people to look into things. We don't fund people to say, "Okay, we'll pay you this if you say you like the Common Core." We've never done anything like that. We do evaluations of these things. And I think the amount of analysis that goes into how do we help teachers to do better, it's not enough. And yes, we are guilty of funding things where experts look at these things and say if they're good or not, and they may not get adopted, or the experts may decide that they don't like them. This one's come out pretty uniformly, no matter where you are politically. If you're into the substance of, should people learn the material they are going to take on a national test. Uhh, is it fair to a student not to have been exposed to that material? Did the high standards in Massachusetts allow Massachusetts students to do better than students in places where that curriculum was less ambitious in terms of what those students would learn? Uhh, and so, these are factual questions. They're not, you know, uhh . . . education can get better. That's uh, some people may not believe that education can change, we can do better. We're, we're not doomed to be worse than all these other countries at how we help our, our students get better. And, yes, we've engaged a lot of people. It's a rounding error. You know, education is a gigantic thing, and it, it deserves to have people of all political persuasions studying excellence.

Of course, the Gates Foundation's entire modus operandi is precisely what Gates disclaims: to carefully and selectively fund groups that will reliably support its agenda, flooding every possible influential actor with money to encourage them to support its work or at least to not publicly criticize it.

Academic researchers Sarah Reckhow and Megan Tompkins-Stange, from Michigan State and the University of Michigan, respectively, even spoke to foundation employees (anonymously) who acknowledged how Gates manufactures consent. "It's within [a] sort of fairly narrow orbit that you manufacture the [research] reports," one foundation official told the researchers. "You hire somebody to write a report. There's going to be a commission, there's going to be a lot of research, there's going to be a lot of vetting and so forth and so on, but you pretty much know what the report is going to say before you go through the exercise." Another foundation employee noted, "Anybody who cares to look would find very quickly that all of these organizations suddenly singing from the same hymnbook are all getting money from the same organization. . . . We fund almost everyone who does advocacy."

The *Washington Post*'s investigation offered a very specific example of how this happens. The foundation gave millions of dollars to the Hunt Institute, at that time affiliated with the University of North Carolina, to coordinate a network of political advocates—teachers' unions, La Raza, the Fordham Institute, and others. Though this coalition was nominally run by the Hunt Institute, the Gates Foundation's director of policy and advocacy, Stefanie Sanford, personally directed weekly conference calls with all the groups to decide "which states needed shoring up, the best person to respond to questions or criticisms, and who needed to travel to which state capital to testify . . . Later in the process, Gates and other foundations would pay for mock legislative hearings for classroom teachers, training educators on how to respond to questions from lawmakers."

Clearly, the Gates Foundation has chosen to work on educational policy through politics and political pressure—not simply through charity, research, and evaluation, as it claims. And this is precisely why Bill Gates became so emotional in the *Washington Post* interview: because he was being confronted with existential questions about the very nature of his philanthropy. Are you using your extreme wealth to undermine democracy?

While the Common Core State Standards were initially adopted in a large majority of states and seemed like a political coup, the project went on to draw critics from both the right and the left. By 2014, several states were already backtracking on the CCSS or jettisoning them entirely. Others kept the standards but rebranded them to defuse political pushback.

Diane Ravitch, a retired historian from New York University who previously served as Assistant Secretary of Education for Research under President George H. W. Bush, was one of many critical voices to emerge. In a blog post, she described how the foundation had "paid for the writing of the CCSS, the evaluation of the CCSS, the implementation of the CCSS, and the promotion of and advocacy for the CCSS." And then, on top of that, it had gone on to fund the creation of a new organization, EdReports.org, to make sure that textbooks were following the CCSS. "The idea that the richest man in America can purchase and—working closely with the U.S. Department of Education—impose new and untested academic standards on the nation's public schools is a national scandal," Ravitch said in 2014. "The revelation that education policy was shaped by one unelected man—who underwrote dozens of groups and was allied with the secretary of education, whose staff was laced with Gates' allies—is ample reason for congressional hearings."

Aside from the controversy Gates's political maneuvering drew, an independent evaluation went on to show that Common Core didn't actually do what Gates had said it would, improve education, a finding that even Gates-funded news outlets like Chalkbeat reported.

In the Gates Foundation's work on education, which goes beyond educational standards, we see that the foundation operates in very much the same way at home as it does abroad in poor nations—orchestrating controversial, undemocratic, top-down policy changes by working behind the scenes. And as we see elsewhere in Gates's work, the foundation's social engineering efforts in U.S. education haven't generally translated into improvements for the people it claims to help. By the foundation's own admission, its work on education has largely failed. Gates spent $650 million on an experiment to build smaller schools, for example, and then abandoned it when it failed to deliver results. The foundation also plowed hundreds of millions of dollars into new teacher evaluations and charter schools, controversial efforts that have failed to clearly improve education.

Even Bill and Melinda French Gates have publicly acknowledged how little they have accomplished. In a 2019 interview, Bill Gates compared his foundation's shortcomings in education to the great successes he believes he has had in global health. "We thought that because U.S. education is here [in the United States], and everybody is so rational and wants to do it so well, that we'd have big wins in U.S. education, like cut the dropout rate in half. The U.S. has the highest dropout rates both in high school and in college, higher than any country in the world," he noted. "Our success in terms of macro numbers, like high school drop-outs, math test scores, verbal test scores . . . Our success there is very small. We've poured a lot in. And, yes, I can point to charter schools that we've been involved in that—if you go and visit, it will be very uplifting. And that's great. That's close to a million kids a year. But there's fifty-two million kids in the U.S. in K–12, so if you help a million, you won't see it. It's in the rounding error."

If you read his words closely, you'll see that he's actually scapegoating his failures, claiming that his foundation doesn't have enough financial muscle to move the needle: "It's far more difficult partly because your money is tiny. Also, people are basically satisfied with the way it is. . . . This is one [area where] we underestimated how hard it is. And we're on sort of our third revision of the strategy. Still very committed to it. And, truthfully, we've probably helped more like four million out of fifty mil-lion [students]. So it's starting to show a little bit in the numbers."

Of course, Bill Gates's nebulous, halting claims about having "helped" students is a harder PR sell than his foundation's work in health, where it can claim to have "saved lives." And that's why it appears to spend so little of its PR marketing budget on promoting its work on U.S. educa-tion, a portfolio that has cost the Gates Foundation more than ten billion dollars—around 13 percent of its lifetime spending.

Gates's failures in education have to be seen in terms beyond wasteful spending because there are real-world consequences—for teachers, who are being told they don't know how to do their jobs; for students, who are treated as human guinea pigs in Gates's social experiments or made to believe they are unintelligent because they don't do well on the standard-ized tests Gates pushes; for parents, who have to puzzle through Gates's constant claims that U.S. education is in a state of crisis; and for tax-payers, who have contributed incalculable sums to supporting the Gates Foundation's educational reform agenda.

While the foundation has, to some degree, acknowledged its failures on education, it hasn't really owned them. It hasn't expressed any humility in the face of its serial mistakes or taken responsibility for the damage it has done. It has instead insisted that its wealth and privilege entitle it to keep throwing the dart, collateral damage be damned. "The fact that progress has been harder to achieve than we hoped is no reason to give up," Melinda French Gates noted in 2020. "Just the opposite. We believe the risk of not doing everything we can to help students reach their full potential is much, much greater. We certainly understand why many people are skeptical about the idea of billionaire philanthropists designing classroom innovations or setting education policy. Frankly, we are, too. Bill and I have always been clear that our role isn't to generate ideas ourselves; it's to support innovation driven by people who have spent their careers working in education: teachers, administrators, researchers, and community leaders."

BILL GATES'S PUBLIC persona is very much wrapped up in his identity as a businessman and then as a philanthropist. But underpinning his success, in Gates's own mind, is his superior intelligence. And one way that Gates knows he's one of the smartest people in the world is through his scores on aptitude tests. In the 1990s, journalists in Seattle tracked down a woman Gates briefly dated in college who said that when she first met him, he immediately wanted to know what her score on her college entrance exam had been—and he wanted her to know that he had gotten a perfect score. "It didn't strike me as being a great pickup line at the time," the woman said. "It's kind of amusing looking back on it, but at the time I really wasn't that amused. I thought maybe I hadn't heard him right. I thought it rather odd to say the least."

Most journalists, however, have embraced the Gates-as-genius narrative. In 2019, the three-part Netflix documentary series *Inside Bill's Brain*, as the name suggests, asked viewers to understand Gates through the lens of his computerlike cognition. Directed by Davis Guggenheim, who previously released the Gates-supported documentary *Waiting for "Superman,"* the film blurs the line between fiction and nonfiction in its deification of Gates. Guggenheim reports, for example, that Gates's score on a math test in middle school placed him as one of the most advanced students in the state, and then pivots to profiling the complex numbers-based problem solving Gates brings to his philanthropic work. *Inside Bill's Brain* also takes viewers along on one of Gates's famed "think weeks," profiled many times by the news media over the years, with Gates presented as a monklike intellectual who heads out to the countryside to spend a week in a spare cabin where he can be alone with his thoughts—and a huge bundle of thick books. "That's a gift, to read a hundred fifty pages an hour," Bernie Noe notes in the film. "I'm going to say it's ninety percent retention. Kind of extraordinary." Noe is presented to viewers as a friend of Gates. Unmentioned is the fact that, at the time, he was the principal of the private high school the Gates children attended—to which the foundation has given more than 100 million dollars.

Melinda French Gates, when asked in the film about Bill's big brain, almost had to stop the interview because she was laughing so uncontrollably: "It's chaos! . . . I wouldn't want to be in that brain. There is so much going on all the time. . . . It's unbelievable!"

In reality, it is these testimonies that are unbelievable—because they are built entirely upon the perspectives of people within Bill Gates's sphere of influence. The one-sided portrait misunderstands, and misinforms the public about, how Gates's brain always seems to short-circuit back to a faulty premise: "I'm right, and I know I'm right." It omits the countless critical voices who have seen Gates's intellect up close and who say it must be understood according to its limitations, not its expanses.

"One of the things about Bill Gates is he literally thinks he's one of the smartest people in the universe," notes Maria Klawe, who previously served with Gates on the board of Microsoft. "He's a highly intelligent and successful person, but he's definitely not one of the smartest people I've met. Partly because he doesn't know what he doesn't know. I mean, he really thinks he can go talk to somebody for a couple hours and he will understand deep things. One of my favorite arguments with Bill was when he told me that there was no real mathematical research being done in the last 20 years, that there were no real discoveries. First of all, I'm a research mathematician, but I'm also on the board of the Mathematical Sciences Research Institute at Berkeley, which is the top place in the world for convening mathematicians around the world to basically work on the hottest topics. I'm telling him about some of the recent discoveries in the last 20 years and how big this is, and he's like, 'No! No! I know. I've talked to somebody who really knew the field and they told me there were no recent discoveries.' And I'm saying, 'You're talking to somebody who really knows the field, and she's telling you that there are.' Just sort of crazy."

Gates brought the same know-it-all attitude to his private foundation, where he's organized his philanthropy according to the idea that he and his small team of experts—his brain trust of PhD staffers and McKinsey consultants—can sit in their war room in Seattle and engineer a solution to any problem.

In the foundation's conceptualization of American education, however, there isn't much consideration around the poverty and inequality that drive poor outcomes in education. Wealthy families in the United States tend to live in wealthy communities, where the high tax base funds excellent local public schools. Or, like the Gates family, they can pay out of pocket to send their kids to high-performing private schools. The opposite is true for poor families. Schools in poor districts have fewer resources, and students there have worse outcomes.

As Anthony Cody, a writer, former middle school teacher, and leading critic of the Gates Foundation, notes, academic success is predominantly guided by factors *outside* the school related to wealth and social class. That means Gates's classroom interventions—whether it's changing educational standards, supporting charter schools, evaluating teachers, or introducing new educational software—can't deliver the game-changing results the foundation claims. "We cannot solve the problem of educational inequity while we ignore the inequitable and inadequate resources available to low-income children in their homes and communities, as well as their schools," Cody writes.

This inequity includes the institutional racism found throughout our educational system. For example, getting a high score on standardized college entrance exams was, for decades, essential to getting into a competitive university. These are the same tests that Bill Gates looks to as validation of his own superior intelligence. In recent years, however, many have come to see these tests as a validation of privilege, not intelligence. The University of California school system, for example, which serves three hundred thousand students, no longer requires these entrance exams. Many other schools are also rethinking these tests, which have been shown to have racial and cultural biases. In the fall of 2023, more than eighteen hundred schools will not require test scores. Gates, meanwhile, has given around $35 million to the College Board and ACT, the vendors of college entrance exams, which, together, chart more than a billion dollars a year in revenue.

IQ tests have been largely abandoned for the same reasons, though it's not clear Bill Gates got the message. In 2005, *Forbes* reported that, after the U.S. Supreme Court issued a ruling against the use of aptitude tests in hiring practices (*Griggs v. Duke Power*), "Microsoft famously wiggled around Griggs by subjecting job applicants to verbal brain teasers." The author of the piece, Rich Karlgaard, wrote, "I spent five days traveling the country with Gates, and he must have talked about IQ a hundred times. Getting the brightest bulbs to work at Microsoft has always been his obsession."

Gates's blind spots around racial bias are particularly notable because he has specifically targeted his philanthropic interventions at poor students of color, with a stated mission "to significantly increase the number of Black and Latino students and students experiencing poverty who earn a diploma, enroll in a postsecondary institution, and are on track in their first year to obtain a credential with labor-market value."

It's worth considering Bill Gates's own education, which was not aimed at obtaining "a credential with labor-market value." Before his wealthy family sent him to Harvard, Gates attended the elite, private Lakeside School in Seattle. As he described it in one interview, "I was relieved from some classes, Math in particular, because I'd read ahead. So, I had quite a bit of free time.... I took my first job where I took off part of my senior year in high school . . . I was a page down in the State Capitol of Olympia, Washington. Then I went out and spent some time being a page back in Washington, DC."

The interviewer asked if all this self-direction was a model Gates believed should be widely adopted in education. Gates seemed to agree, saying, "Self-exploration is great, because you develop a sense of self-confidence and an identity of, 'Hey, I know this pretty well. I know this better than the teachers. Let me try and see if I can understand at the next level. Maybe I'm pretty good at this stuff.'"

Gates has given his own children the same rich educational experiences he had, but he has been far less charitable toward the poor children of color at the heart of his philanthropic efforts. For the masses and the commoners, education is not about enlightenment or critical thinking or creativity or dignity or self-discovery or even learning. It's about getting the necessary training to be useful contributors to the global economy.

"The Gates Foundation claims to know what will mitigate the problems within urban education, but its solutions do not include a critical analysis of power. Gates, a wealthy White man, purporting to have solutions to a problem that disproportionately impacts people of color reflects a colonizer relationship in and of itself." This is from the PhD dissertation of Alice Ragland, professor of race and ethnic studies at the Columbus College of Art and Design. In it, Ragland describes the Gates Foundation as "a colonizing, neutralizing, and supervising force in Black schools and communities." Her dissertation is one of the only published documents I found anywhere that dares to explicitly turn a racial lens on the Gates Foundation. The lack of attention to this issue is astonishing given how obvious the racial dynamics are in all the work the foundation does. "Just like the White philanthropists who influenced Black education during the 20th century, the new class of corporate philanthropists are supporting initiatives to ensure that Black students are getting their daily dose of docility through their schooling," Ragland writes.

This surveillance is achieved through standardized tests and the audit culture which determines what students are learning in poor urban schools, which teachers can stay and which are forced out, and sometimes what the school day entails down to the minute. These schools are placed on academic emergency and given Fs on state report cards based on their students' test scores, which justify their continued scrutiny and surveillance. This says to the public that these schools cannot function on their own, thus they need to be closely watched. Instead of placing any accountability measures on the systems that perpetuate educational inequality and racism in education, schools are held accountable for many issues that are out of their control.

Indeed, how did it become Bill Gates's job to fix schools for Black and Latino students? To measure how well they are doing? To implement solutions? What qualifies Gates as an expert or leader on this topic? As always, it boils down to brute force with a blunt instrument: money.

In an interview, Ragland explained that the Gates Foundation and other corporate reformers narrowly focus on "access"—on steering Black students into white corridors of power. Ragland said she doesn't discount the importance of expanding opportunities for underrepresented communities, but added that this can't be the whole story. "I focus on teaching about systems of oppression so that people can understand where they come from, where they fit into that system of oppression, so that when they see unequal power dynamics they can more easily recognize it, call it out, and do something about [it]," she told me. "In the absence of a critique of the entire system of oppression . . . we're going to be stuck on only making spaces steeped in white supremacy more accessible to people who have been excluded from those spaces."

Gates's conception of education might prepare students to one day work at a place like Microsoft, but is that the point of our educational system—"to obtain a credential with labor-market value"? In that paradigm, will students develop the critical thinking they need to question why a billionaire in Seattle has so much control over their lives?

"'The master's tools will never dismantle the master's house,'" Ragland told me, quoting the writer Audre Lorde.

When Oprah Winfrey invited Bill Gates on her show to talk about the crisis he sees in American education—and "how far will Bill Gates go to fix it"—she asked what would happen if we magically "eliminated our worst teachers."

"If you do that, then we [U.S. education] go from basically being at the bottom of the rich countries to being back at the top," Gates said.

Eliminating bad teachers was, for a time, a key part of the Gates Foundation's education reform agenda. And as with so many of its projects, the foundation leaned on taxpayers to provide much of the funding that went into this $575 million effort. "The most decisive factor in student achievement is the teacher," Gates said at the 2009 National Conference of State Legislatures. "You are the authorizers and [budget] appropriators of school reform in America. The president and the Congress can make recommendations—and they have passed a stimulus package with billions of dollars you can spend to advance school reform—but ultimately, you decide. I hope you decide to accelerate reform, because America is changing."

As Gates pushed state governments to align their budgets with his agenda and to think about improving education through improving teaching, he also advanced a new philanthropic effort to weed out low performers and reward the best teachers. The centerpiece of this effort was a pilot project in Florida. It was designed, as is always the case, as a public-private partnership. Gates promised to put up $100 million but also required the recipient, Hillsborough County (Tampa Bay), to come up with an equal sum of money. Over the years, the foundation aggressively promoted the pilot project as a vital intervention that was dramatically improving education. "We were blown away by how much energy people were putting into the new system—and by the results they we're already seeing in the classroom," Gates wrote in a 2012 *New York Times* op-ed. "Teachers told us that they appreciated getting feedback from a peer who understood the challenges of their job and from their principal, who had a vision of success for the entire school. Principals said the new system was encouraging them to spend more time in classrooms, which was making the culture in Tampa's schools more collaborative. For their part, the students we spoke to said they'd seen a difference, too, and liked the fact that peer observers asked for their input as part of the evaluation process."

As the foundation boasted of the project's success in the news media, the Hillsborough pilot was beginning to fall apart. Payroll costs for teachers ballooned by $65 million as financial incentives were paid out to better-performing teachers. Another $50 million was spent just on consultants.

The foundation's teacher evaluation program not only turned out to be financially damaging to the school district but there was little evidence that it actually improved education. "Measured against the state's

12 largest school districts, Hillsborough's rank has fallen from eighth to 10th," the *Tampa Bay Times* reported. "In its proposal to Gates, the district aimed to address the achievement gap affecting poor and black students, and to have 90 percent of its third-grade and eighth-grade students testing on grade level in reading and math. However, proficiency rates were between 53 and 59 percent on the 2014 Florida Comprehensive Assessment Test, and as low as 33 percent for black students."

Before its failure, the heavily promoted project had contributed to a nationwide zeitgeist of teacher accountability efforts—and a culture of blaming instructors for the poor performance of students. Some news outlets, for example, began publishing the names of low-performing teachers, evaluated according to their students' test scores. This name-and-shame exercise was demoralizing and humiliating to teachers and said very little about their actual ability or performance. But it apparently made for good headlines. One teacher in Los Angeles, after having been publicly named as a low-performing teacher by the *Los Angeles Times*, committed suicide, prompting hundreds of students, teachers, and parents to protest outside the newspaper's offices. (Teachers and parents, over the years, have also marched on the Gates Foundation's headquarters in Seattle, chanting in one protest, "Gates Foundation, you will fail! Education is not for sale!")

As the anti-teacher animus spiraled out of control, Bill Gates tried to reel back in the Frankenstein's monster he had helped create. And the *New York Times* gave him real estate to present himself as a champion of teachers, and an enlightened, compassionate partner in education reform. "Unfortunately, some education advocates in New York, Los Angeles and other cities are claiming that a good personnel system can be based on ranking teachers according to their 'value-added rating'—a measurement of their impact on students' test scores—and publicizing the names and rankings online and in the media," he wrote. "But shaming poorly performing teachers doesn't fix the problem because it doesn't give them specific feedback." Gates then argued for more nuance, noting that we need multiple, diverse measures of teacher effectiveness that go beyond student test scores. And to make his case, he pointed to his foundation's pilot program in Hillsborough County.

It would be three years before Hillsborough was exposed as a boon-doggle, but middle school teacher Anthony Cody had no problem see-ing through Gates's arguments. Cody's widely read blog at the time, in *Education Week* (a media outlet that, notably, receives funding from Gates), skewered Gates's preposterous good-cop routine. For all Bill Gates's rhetoric about using a variety of measurements in teacher evalu-ation, Cody noted, the Gates Foundation had carefully crafted its teacher evaluation metrics around student test scores.

Cody's blog post caught the attention of the then CEO of the Gates Foundation, Jeff Raikes, who invited him to discuss his criticism directly with the foundation. Cody was surprised to get the invitation and agreed to take a flight to the foundation's headquarters in Seattle. Yet, as Cody recounts it, Gates's invitation was not a good-faith effort to engage in dialogue, as Raikes had pitched it. It ended up being a one-way discourse.

"They worked very hard to convince me of their expertise in edu-cation, that they really did know what they were doing. I was hoping I would get more of a chance to convince them they were barking up the wrong tree. At the end of the day, we didn't really resolve anything. It wasn't really set up for that purpose in that effect," Cody told me. "Maybe [Raikes] thought that somehow, that if he could sway someone who was a vocal critic, then that would be a huge win."

Cody suggested to Raikes that the foundation set up a feedback mechanism that would allow teachers and students to provide thoughts and criticism to the foundation directly. Raikes didn't like that idea, but he did agree to an online dialogue, in which Cody and the foundation would exchange five essays. While Cody's essays were ostensibly in dia-logue with Gates, he said the foundation was not actually his primary audience. "I wanted to help teachers understand what was happening to their profession, what was happening to their professional organizations, what was happening to their working conditions, to their evaluation systems—to all these things that affected their ability to teach."

Cody wrote long, thoughtful essays about the real structural prob-lems in education, challenging the foundation's assertion that teachers didn't know how to do their jobs or that bad teachers were the biggest problem working against poor students. The foundation, in response, often reverted to talking points and forward-looking promises, including trumpeting early signs of success from the Hillsborough pilot project. At one point, the foundation also resorted to a cheap shot, essentially accusing Cody of "the soft bigotry of low expectations," arguing that his naysaying about Gates's educational reforms showed he didn't believe poor students of color could ever succeed. The responses, Cody said, "are pretty trite and on the order of 'We believe every student can learn' kind of pabulum that doesn't really respond substantively to the issues of how students are affected by the circumstances in which they live and how, as educators, we need to respond to that and not just wave textbooks at them in the hope that they climb out of their circumstances."

The exchanges proved embarrassing to the foundation. "Jeff Raikes and I had a phone conversation where he was not happy with the way things had gone," Cody told me. "I think somehow they hoped that they had found somebody that had found a middle ground with them or something. I don't know. I was very critical of the work they were doing. I was hoping that they would somehow respond to the substantive criticism that I was leveling at them instead of getting defensive." (Raikes did not respond to questions sent by email.)

When I interviewed Cody in 2022, he expressed astonishment at how little the Gates Foundation had accomplished given all the advantages it has. In Hillsborough, Gates had all the political chess pieces lined up—the money, the political actors, and even the teachers' union. The foundation also outspends everyone else in the advocacy space, including the news media. Yet, again and again, with every possible advantage on its side, it manages to fail.

"They are totally wrong about how people—how human beings—interact with the system that they're part of, whether it's students or teachers or administrators," Cody said. "They don't engage in a respectful way with those communities. They engage from the point of view of bringing expertise to bear and bringing resources to bear. And it's fundamentally flawed. Their experts have misled them, and I did my best to try to correct them, and they weren't interested."

In 2018, the Gates Foundation funded the RAND Corporation to study its teacher evaluation project. Its findings put a period (or an exclamation point) on a story that had already been widely written: Gates's teacher evaluation effort had failed. Even Gates-funded outlets like EdSurge reported this news.

We might give credit to the Gates Foundation for not doubling down on teacher evaluations and not strong-arming the RAND Corporation to produce a more favorable study. But if the foundation were really the organization it claims to be, working in partnership with teachers and communities, it would publicly apologize for its failures and offer compensation and reparations for all the harm it has caused, from the teacher-shaming culture it engendered to the tens of millions of taxpayer dollars that were spent, or wasted, on its failed pilot project in Hillsborough County.

AN IMPORTANT PART of the foundation's work in education, as in every other field where it operates, has been technology. As Bill Gates described in the lead-up to Common Core, more universal education standards would create a bigger market for educational software. And part and parcel of this burgeoning software market would be the collection of granular data from millions of students, which Gates believed would usher in a new era of personalized education.

A slick video produced by the foundation to promote its first big project in this space offered us a glimpse of this future, showing patient teachers coolly using digital tablets in classrooms, seamlessly assessing individual student comprehension in real time, and making finely tuned adjustments. Smiling, quiet, obedient students work independently to complete their assigned tasks, which are calibrated to give them just enough challenge to keep them interested and on task.

Of course, this is not how real classrooms work—where computers run out of batteries, where educational software crashes, where students have trouble understanding what they're doing or simply get bored, and where learning is a social exercise. The promotional video was advertising a one-hundred-million-dollar Gates project called inBloom, which described itself as the plumbing infrastructure through which student data would travel. The idea was that inBloom would be a trusted, independent data broker of sorts, streaming a rich river of student data that school districts and states would share with private companies and ed-tech entrepreneurs to create sophisticated software that improves education.

And this is one part of Gates's reform agenda where the federal government played a particularly important role. Even though the federal government could not, itself, force states to adopt inBloom or Common Core, the Obama administration did make a $4.35 billion pool of money available as an incentive for states to adopt the new educational standards. And one way that states could access the federal money was making a plan to create infrastructure to manage student data.

It's worth explaining this nuance in more detail: In the United States, education is largely funded and organized on the state and local level. This is why the Gates Foundation became such an important driver of the education reform movement, arguably acting as a proxy for the Obama administration. As a private foundation, Gates could freely engage in a very hands-on way with states without raising criticism of "federal overreach." In practice, the Gates Foundation was helping states write applications to secure a piece of the $4.35 billion in federal funding at the same time that the foundation was advancing Common Core educational standards—and at the same time that it was developing inBloom to handle all the data that would be coming down the pike.

Before inBloom really got up and running, however, a public furor erupted around data privacy. As Reuters reported:

> In operation just three months, the database already holds files on millions of children identified by name, address and sometimes social security number. Learning disabilities are documented, test scores recorded, attendance noted. In some cases, the database tracks student hobbies, career goals, attitudes toward school—even homework completion.
>
> Local education officials retain legal control over their students' information. But federal law allows them to share files in their portion of the database with private companies selling educational products and services. . . . While inBloom pledges to guard the data tightly, its own privacy policy states that it "cannot guarantee the security of the information stored . . . or that the information will not be intercepted when it is being transmitted."

Concerns about Big Brother in public schools heightened when inBloom made a fatal misstep, partnering with a subsidiary of Rupert Murdoch's media empire, just as Murdoch was in the midst of a major scandal involving data privacy. One of Murdoch's newspapers, *News of the World*, was shuttered upon news that it had been hacking into the voice mails of public figures—and into the phone of a schoolgirl who had been murdered. Activists seized on the scandal: How could multi-billionaires like Rupert Murdoch and Bill Gates be trusted to house the data of tens of millions of schoolchildren?

Like dominoes, states began pulling out of inBloom, quickly ending Gates's data surveillance program. "It's an important story because it's one of the few examples where parents alone—without any institutional support, really—fought against this huge effort by the Gates Foundation to collect and systematize all the personal student data," Class Size Matters executive director Leonie Haimson, a leading opponent of inBloom in New York, told me.

Haimson said that during the buildup of inBloom, she and others tried many times in many ways to engage with the Gates Foundation and its partners and surrogates in New York, but they were always met by silence or an imperious response—a tone set by the foundation. "They always act like, 'We get to do whatever we want, and nobody can tell us anything, and we have no interest in hearing from the people affected on the ground, and we won't even pretend to be interested in what people on the ground think or feel about what we're doing to their schools,'" Haimson told me. "'We don't even have the tiniest wish to make it appear as such . . .' even though they hired many, many different public relations companies. The arrogance of it is astonishing."

Parents and advocates stood up to Gates's arrogation of power and won, but the fight was not over. In 2017, the think tank Data and Society published a long autopsy of inBloom that, though it cites critical voices and presents as an independent appraisal, could be seen as aimed at helping the tech industry be more successful in future data surveillance efforts. "Any future U.S. edtech project will have to contend with the legacy of inBloom," the report noted, "and so this research begins to analyze exactly what that legacy is."

Data and Society has received funding from the Gates Foundation,

Microsoft, Microsoft Research, and Melinda French Gates's venture firm, Pivotal Ventures, and the overall takeaway of its report seems to be that parents and advocates are irrational, but were clever enough to capitalize upon inBloom's PR failures. "InBloom's ambition to be open and transparent actually left it vulnerable to public attack," the report concludes. "Unlike private companies whose discovery process is basically a black box, inBloom's processes were public, and thus open to scrutiny. . . . Large-scale, ambitious, public initiatives will continue to be slowed or meet a similar fate to inBloom if there is not a counter-narrative to the public's low tolerance for uncertainty and risk."

The report not only suggests that the Gates Foundation and its surrogates can rewrite history but also opens the door to a chilling suggestion—that the next data surveillance effort should be rolled out in schools with less transparency and openness and that proponents should spend even less energy on democratic engagement.

InBloom is only one part of the foundation's work on data collection and surveillance, which appears to be an ongoing ambition. This has included donating money to the private company ConnectEDU, which collected personal data from millions of students and then went bankrupt—which led to a major court battle over the company's planned sale of that data in bankruptcy proceedings. The Gates Foundation also funds Chiefs for Change and the Data Quality Campaign, which also work with student data.

Velislava Hillman, a researcher at the London School of Economics and Political Science, has tracked the ambitions of this burgeoning data surveillance apparatus, much of which is financially tied to Gates—"collecting granular data about children so they can profile children and identify all kinds of issues from the social to the emotional, what their conduct is in school, what their behavior, is, whether they're the child of an immigrant family, how they do in school academically and so on." All this data gets run through complex soothsaying algorithms, Hillman said in an interview, "supposedly telling the teacher which student is likely to cheat, which student is likely to be depressed at some point in time. I mean, we're talking about *Minority Report*," she added.

In this "techno-determined future," Hillman told me, kids could be tracked from a young age into a specific career and maybe even a specific company. In her research, she has found examples where schools embrace workforce development programs that explicitly partner with companies like Amazon and Cisco. Instead of learning art and music, students are learning technical skills these companies need. All this makes sense from a corporate perspective that sees the function of schools as churning out workers. "An engineer will immediately think, let's identify the data and see where the gaps are, and see how we can create a better fit between supply and demand," Hillman told me. "If you think, as a businessman, what is the most costly part of your organization? It is to retain and retrain your workforce."

IN THE MID-1990S, a number of state governors and a variety of business executives, including IBM's then CEO, Louis Gerstner Jr., held a series of meetings that discussed creating new, state-level educational standards—the kernel of what later became known as the Common Core. Out of these discussions was born Achieve, which claimed to be an educational nonprofit aimed at school reform, but which boasted a board of directors that included no schoolteachers or women. But Achieve did have the support of industry leaders, state governors, and the Gates Foundation. One of Gates's very first grants focused on public schools was a one-million-dollar gift to Achieve "to support comprehensive benchmarking and review of academic standards and assessments between states."

In the decades ahead, the nation's top industrialists became some of the most impassioned proponents of new educational standards. "If I'm looking for talent, why wouldn't I go to states that are using the Common Core State Standards, where I know what the performance of that education system is?" Rex Tillerson, the then CEO of Exxon, said in 2013. "Not only do I know its performance relative to other states, but I also know its performance relative to international work forces."

The then CEO of Time Warner, Glenn Britt, offered his own take in 2010, specifically citing his partnership with Gates: "Technological innovation requires the expertise of well-trained people, and the U.S. is falling behind in developing that talent. American students' performance in science, technology, engineering and math (STEM) is on the decline:

80% of 12th graders perform below proficiency levels in science, and U.S. students finished 19th in math and 14th in science among the 31 countries ranked by the Organisation for Economic Co-operation and Development."

For business interests, supporting education is also obviously good PR, allowing faceless companies to humanize themselves through devoted campaigns aimed at helping children. Likewise, we might also see a long-term strategy toward deregulation. As the private sector plays an ever-larger role in public institutions, like public education, it erodes the primacy of the state. Arguably, this has been Bill Gates's biggest effect on American education, opening spaces for more private-sector influence and challenging democratic control over schools. In promoting Common Core educational standards, for example, Gates demonized the alternative scenario—states democratically formulating their own standards—as "individual state regulatory capture."

Companies could also be seen as having a self-interest in redirecting taxpayer funding for education into what are, essentially, free training programs for their future employees. Indeed, Bill Gates's early philanthropic forays into education were criticized as a long-term (self-serving) business strategy to beef up the pool of computer programmers Microsoft could hire.

Microsoft might also have an interest in using education as a scapegoat for its questionable hiring practices. In 2012, it issued a research report claiming that the American education system wasn't producing enough qualified job candidates to fill the company's computer programmer jobs. The solution, as Microsoft saw it, was for Congress to undertake long-term investments to improve U.S. education—and, in the short term, to allow companies to more freely recruit foreign workers, who tend to be paid lower wages.

Neil Kraus, professor of political science at the University of Wisconsin–River Falls, sees this argument as at the heart of today's corporate-led education reform movement. "As they closed manufacturing facilities, targeted unions, created increasingly unstable work arrangements, and fought tooth and nail against raising the minimum wage, business interests began a campaign to blame poverty and declining economic opportunity solely on the schools," Kraus wrote in a 2021 op-ed. "The skills gap was invented out of whole cloth. The modern education reform movement was born."

Kraus tracks the "skills gap" narrative—the idea that there aren't enough qualified, educated American workers—to as far back as the 1980s, but he cites the Gates Foundation as one of its leading exponents over the last decade. Gates has plowed money into universities, think tanks, and the news media to create an echo chamber of research and data that has helped drive the skills gap narrative deeper into the public discourse.

A 2008 *New York Times* article about the foundation's "mission to help low-income students get the education required for steady employment in higher paying jobs," for example, cited a Gates-funded study from the National Center for Public Policy and Higher Education. In 2010, the *Times* profiled a report from the Gates-funded Center on Education and the Workforce at Georgetown University, which found that "the number of jobs requiring at least a two-year associate's degree will outpace the number of people qualified to fill those positions by at least three million in 2018." The center's report also predicted that "by 2018, about two-thirds of all employment will require some college education or better." This statistic—and the larger skills gap narrative—became a dominant trope in education policy circles. As the *Chronicle of Higher Education* (which has also received funding from Gates) reported in 2020, "Anyone who's been to a higher-ed conference or read a book on the topic in the past decade has no doubt heard some version of that prediction—some of us to the point of numbness."

As Neil Kraus told me, "They've been so successful on this [skills-gap narrative] that most people—including a lot of well-intentioned liberals—don't see it. They say, 'What's wrong with saying we're going to send all poor people to college?'" The answer, Kraus said, is that there is no skills gap. The Gates Foundation and its partners are creating false expectations and preparing kids for jobs that don't exist. Citing research from the U.S. Bureau of Labor Statistics, Kraus noted that most jobs in the American economy typically do not require advanced education—like the baristas at Starbucks and the packing jobs at Amazon. Federal labor data shows that the typical entry-level education required for 60 percent of all jobs across the U.S. economy is a high school equivalent or less.

Again, Gates-funded Georgetown researchers had predicted that, by 2018, the exact opposite would be true: that 66 percent of jobs would require "some college education or better." (Georgetown stands by its research, telling me its numbers are a more accurate and honest portrait.) Also notable, federal data shows that a third of college grads are actually underemployed. "When you look at data from the Departments of Labor and Education, as well as the Census Bureau and the Federal Reserve, and you look at scholarly research that's not funded by private industry or foundations, you find the actual story—which is the story of a labor force with the highest levels of educational attainment in history [working] in a low-wage, low-education economy, leaving large numbers of workers underemployed," Kraus told me. "Education generally cannot control the labor market. We cannot control the jobs that exist or the wages that are paid, yet we're blamed for both."

Though the Gates Foundation likes to publicize its efforts to push underprivileged students through college—and describes education as "the great equalizer"—one could see a certain cruelty in the foundation's setting children up to fail, pushing them into hugely expensive college degrees that frequently won't pay off as they've been promised. Millions of unemployed and underemployed college graduates will be made to feel as though they are losers because they're working at Target instead of finding their way to the cornucopia of jobs that Gates and its surrogates insist are available to college grads who make smart choices about their education.

What the Gates Foundation's work on "post-secondary success" also shows is the way the foundation has reduced education to a matter of economics and labor, not learning. Education reformers, for example, have begun to conceptualize education in terms of "cradle to career"; the Gates Foundation begins with its "early learning" program, continues through K–12 education, then college completion, extending into workforce development through Gates's program on "U.S. Economic Mobility & Opportunity." Also notable, Common Core education standards were actually reverse-engineered based on the knowledge and skills that companies thought high school grads should have.

"What journalists have missed is the systemic ambitions of the Gates Foundation," Nicholas Tampio of Fordham University told me. "[Bill

Gates's] dream is to create a system that takes people from being little kids into the workplace. The notion of systemic school reform is you take K–twelve, kindergarten through twelfth grade. All right, through the first years of college—then you're talking K–sixteen. But what about preschool? Okay, now you've got P–sixteen. All right, but what about the first four years after college graduation? P–twenty. Now, what if you're actually talking about prenatal. . . . Some people say prenatal all the way to, really, parts of your career."

And the foundation has found eager partners in Washington in these efforts. In 2014, Politico reported that the Gates Foundation had sponsored sixteen papers on "redesigning financial aid" for college, the authors of which had "become a fixture in Congressional hearings on reauthorizing the Higher Education Act." The story cited the Fordham Institute, calling Gates "one of the most influential forces in U.S. education policy, right up there with the Department of Education. Absolutely."

Gates has found bipartisan support too. In 2017, for example, Democratic senator Elizabeth Warren and Republican senator Orrin Hatch introduced the College Transparency Act. A press release from Warren's office noted, "Unfortunately, important information about whether or not a particular college or major pays off for students is currently incomplete. For example, despite the vast majority of students citing finding a good job as their primary reason for going to college, there is currently no easy way to evaluate the labor-market success of various programs or majors."

Nicole Smith, of the Gates-funded Center on Education and the Workforce at Georgetown, echoed this sentiment in an interview: "You have a lot of students graduating with these degrees and barely flailing, not understanding exactly what their career pathway is, and taking a long time to find themselves and figure out where they're going to work and exactly what they're going to do and how they're going to build a career on what they took at college."

The College Transparency Act, endorsed by the Gates Foundation, has raised well-founded privacy concerns related to its proposed data collection from students, but it should also raise questions about equity and justice. One has to ask if the new data made available in the College Transparency Act will be helpful in the ways that Congress (and the Gates Foundation) imagines; how many seventeen-year-old kids, as they consider applying for college, are going to make a purely economic decision about which coursework they pick and which college they attend—based on a careful review of newly available data on the relative "labor-market success" of a given university program? And why would we ask students, especially poor students, to think in these terms?

Throughout the foundation's work on education, we often find this kind of bootstrapping mentality, one that expects children to take personal responsibility for their own economic future instead of itself addressing the real obstacles in their way—the exorbitant price of higher education, the crushing debt that follows college, the abusive and asymmetrical labor market that awaits them (and that delivers outsize rewards to corporate investors), the long-standing efforts to weaken unions, the widespread appearance of corporate tax evasion, institutional racism and sexism, and on and on and on.

"Yes, of course, but that ain't in the cards, pal," notes Anthony Carnevale, director of Georgetown's Center on Education and the Workforce. "We don't have the votes [to address these kinds of issues], and we're not going to have the votes anytime soon." Presenting as the consummate Washington insider, Carnevale, a longtime Gates grantee, acknowledges that there are more vital policy reforms we could consider, but he argues that they are "politically irrelevant" because Congress will never move on those issues. "We have no other device that Americans will vote for [other than education reform] that provides opportunity."

At a point, however, what this political pragmatism really amounts to is fatalism, a deep-seated fear of real social change. It is a worldview that cannot imagine any political or economic reality other than the one in which we currently live—including the ability of superrich men like Bill Gates to put their hands on the levers of American education policy.

To be clear, this chapter is not meant to argue that people shouldn't go to college. They absolutely should, if they want to. But their participation in higher education should not be organized according to their station in life, and their choices shouldn't be dependent on the whims and predilections of billionaire philanthropists. They shouldn't be misled into believing that "education is the great equalizer," or that a college degree is necessarily going to deliver them middle-class status—or even an escape from poverty. Students should not be made to feel ashamed when they graduate and can't find a job. And they shouldn't be made to bear the burden of the structural problems driving inequality—like the ability of a very small percentage of the population to acquire obscene wealth, to avoid paying their fair share of taxes, and to turn their personal fortunes into political influence over our lives.

White Man's Burden

As the name suggests, the National Portrait Gallery in Washington, DC, part of the famed Smithsonian Institution, houses paintings and photography of notable Americans—which include a portrait of Bill and Melinda Gates. The work is stunningly lifelike, almost photographic, and if you look long enough, it's easy to get lost in the folds of their clothing. But it's also easy to discern the power dynamics at play.

The real focus of the portrait, of course, is Bill Gates, who is in the foreground, sitting on the arm of a chair in which Melinda is seated. This puts Bill in front, towering above her. The couple are in a glass house in front of Lake Washington in Seattle. Directly behind them is some kind of computer screen with a tableau of smiling, hopeful Black and brown faces—and the faint appearance of the Gates Foundation's motto, "All lives have equal value."

Taxpayers helped fund the creation of this painting, commissioned in 2008—the same year Gates Foundation CEO Patty Stonesifer became the chair of the Smithsonian's highest governing body, the Board of Regents. The Gateses' portrait appears to have been a smart decision for the Smithsonian. Though the Gates Foundation, generally speaking, does not fund art or museums, it would end up giving nearly sixty million dollars in donations to the Smithsonian in the years ahead.

The painter, Jon Friedman, would not agree to an interview, so it's unclear how intentional his imperial rendering of the power couple was. Yet it's difficult to avoid the "white savior" subtext in the work—Bill and

Melinda Gates looking regal, almost royal, in their fine clothes, sitting in their pristine glass house with their backs turned to a throng of smiling Black children.

Images of women and children of color inundate the foundation's website, and media reports commonly make similar depictions. Sometimes it's Bill bending over to administer an oral polio vaccine to a brown toddler; other times, it's Melinda holding a Black baby, looking almost triumphant. These are deeply humanizing portraits for the Gateses, but they could also be seen as dehumanizing to the nameless, dusty, disheveled children who appear almost as props in the photos. As Bill and Melinda French Gates tell it, however, these interactions are not mere photo opportunities. They are meaningful encounters that inspire the foundation's work.

"During the time we were engaged, we took our first trip to Africa,"

Melinda French Gates explained in 2016. "Neither of us had ever been to the continent of Africa. We went to see the animals and the savanna. We went on a safari. We took other couples with us. It was beautiful. We fell in love with everything we saw." On that trip, the Gateses apparently traveled in style, if not luxury—with Land Rovers, a private doctor, and even their own wine expert.

"But it's really not at all trite to say we really fell in love with the people. It started us on this series of questions, of sort of saying to ourselves, 'What is going on here? Why is it we can be in a Land Rover or jeep, but there aren't many great roads? And how is it that we see all these people walking along the road to an open-air market—men in flip-flops, women often with bare feet with a child in their belly and one on their back and something on their head? You know, what has gone on here that things haven't started?'"

Many would answer that question by pointing to the nature of our global economy, which depends on winners and losers; which has leveraged this power imbalance to purposefully and violently colonize and enslave poor nations; and which, today, continues to extract wealth or reorganize the economies of poor nations to serve the interests of the rich.

Melinda French Gates sees things differently. She believes that the economic system that made her family so wealthy can drive equality. "When I go to places like Malawi or Tanzania or Senegal, they say they all want to live in America," she noted in a later interview on CNBC. "We are lucky to live here. They want to live in these types of capitalistic societies."

In articulating the needs and wants of the global poor, as she often does, Melinda French Gates also trades freely in misery narratives that frequently paint a portrait of pitiful people in need of saving. "On a personal level, when you go in places in India, you know, you often see a mom with a baby strapped on her back, and maybe she's cooking over a boiling pot of water because she's selling what she's cooking. That's really unsafe for the baby; you get a lot of accidents," she said in a 2022 presentation announcing a new child care initiative with the World Bank and USAID. "You see a lot of adolescents, young adolescent girls with a baby on their hip during the day running around in unsafe places and in traffic with the baby's head kind of bobbling around. But think about what it means for the baby, the adolescent girl, and the mom. And on the converse side, you get them in safe, affordable child care, that baby can thrive, that adolescent girl can thrive and go to school, that mom can thrive in the work that she wants to do during the day."

On social media, women around the world took aim at Gates's colonial gaze. "You want to know how women and children are seen by the white world?" Themrise Khan, a global development researcher, wrote on Twitter. "Behold! @melindagates my mother straddled me on her hips many times while she was cooking etc. I turned out just fine. Maybe you should have tried it too before taking such ill informed perspectives." Geneva Health Files, the news outlet run by Priti Patnaik, added, "This is the clearest illustration of the distance not traveled. Global health elite are so far removed from local realities that it is embarrassing they have so much power to frame priorities."

Nowhere are the contradictions between the foundation's message of empowerment and practice of hegemony more apparent than in its finances. Though the foundation's mission is to help poor people, its model of aid is actually organized around helping the rich help the poor. Around 90 percent of the foundation's charitable dollars through early 2023—$71 billion of the nearly $80 billion it has pledged in charitable grants—goes to wealthy (and mostly white) nations. In fact, more than 80 percent of all of Gates's giving goes to just three nations: the United States, Switzerland, and the United Kingdom. More than 60 percent has gone to the United States alone.

While it makes sense that the Gates Foundation would look to U.S.-based groups for its work on U.S. education, this portfolio of work accounts for only a small portion of its spending. Across Gates's expansive body of work in poor nations, like its interventions on family planning, agricultural development, and diarrheal diseases, we see that the foundation's money predominantly lands in wealthy nations.

What this funding model suggests is that the foundation does not trust poor people to manage its money well. It also clearly shows that the foundation does not aim to build up the expertise and capacity of poor nations. It offers a long view of the world in which the poor will always be poor—and dependent on the goodwill of global elites.

Beyond the moral obliquities in this colonial mind-set, the Gates Foundation's giving should also raise dollars-and-cents questions. When Gates funds wealthy organizations in rich nations, this means an enormous percentage of its charitable dollars gets eaten up by administrative costs—high-paid white-collar workers in fancy office buildings in expensive cities like Washington, DC, and Geneva. Researchers describe this black hole of spending as "phantom aid." More perversely, the foundation's extravagant funding could be seen as disincentivizing success; Gates's charitable partners know that if they solve a problem, or effectively hand over solutions to the poor, they will lose out on big contracts from the foundation.

Even in places where the foundation is making donations to poor nations, there is often more to the story. The foundation's single largest investment in Africa has gone to the Alliance for a Green Revolution in Africa, or AGRA—the recipient of more than $675 million from Gates. This money represents close to 15 percent of all giving Gates reports going to the continent—yet, as described later in this book, AGRA is not an exclusively African organization. Gates and other Western donors conceived of, fund, and help manage the project.

As another example, EthioChicken has become one of the largest poultry companies in Ethiopia, thanks in part to millions of dollars in charitable giving from the Gates Foundation. The company was founded by an American businessman in partnership with a McKinsey consultant.

Gates's grant records show hundreds of millions of dollars in donations to groups with the word *Africa* in their name that are based outside the African continent—like the African Leaders Malaria Alliance (based in New York), the East African Center for the Empowerment of Women and Children (Virginia), the African Fertilizer and Agribusiness Partnership (New Jersey), and the Made in Africa Initiative (Hong Kong).

Philanthropist Peter Buffett (son of Warren) has described this model of charity as "philanthropic colonialism." "People (including me) who had very little knowledge of a particular place would think that they could solve a local problem," Buffett wrote in 2013.

> Whether it involved farming methods, education practices, job training or business development, over and over I would hear people discuss transplanting what worked in one setting directly into another with little regard for culture, geography or societal norms. Inside any

important philanthropy meeting, you witness heads of state meeting with investment managers and corporate leaders. All are searching for answers with their right hand to problems that others in the room have created with their left. There are plenty of statistics that tell us that inequality is continually rising.

Calling it "conscience cleansing," Buffett diagnoses the colonial lens embedded in philanthropy as destructive and manipulative: "The rich sleep better at night, while others get just enough to keep the pot from boiling over."

There's plenty of room to criticize Buffett's own colonial lens—critics say his philanthropy, the NoVo Foundation, has effectively colonized a small town in upstate New York, creating widespread dependence on his charitable grants, locally known as "Buffett Bucks." (A request for an interview with Peter Buffett generated no response.) But Buffett at least has some capacity to engage publicly with criticism, which is not something that can be said for the Gates Foundation. While we should not doubt that Bill Gates really believes he is helping the poor, we also cannot excuse or ignore the obviously colonial mind-set he brings to this work.

"When you go into a poor country, you want to fix health, you want to fix agriculture, you want to fix education, you want to fix governance," Gates explained in a 2013 keynote speech at Microsoft. "And it's the magic blend of those things, all of which reinforce each other."

"There's about a third of the world lives in countries where these things haven't come together," Gates continued. "It's clear that innovation, par- ticularly technical innovation—new vaccines, new seeds, monitoring things to make sure government workers do what they're supposed to do, including in education, that we can make much faster progress to get these people out these poverty traps now than ever before."

Here, Bill Gates seems to be owning his position in the world as a kind of extralegal overlord, a supra-governor engaged in nation build- ing, if not world making—shaping the policies, rules, and regulations that guide how poor people grow food, treat their sick, and educate their children and then carefully "monitoring" the nincompoop bureaucrats to make sure they complete the tasks Gates has assigned them.

"We've always wanted to have a robot that can go out in rural areas and help out in certain health care–type things . . . say, to help do a C-section in a rural area where that absolutely needs to be done," Gates said. "So, I don't think that's in the next ten years, but maybe in the next twenty or thirty. That kind of physical expertise can be made available very, very broadly."

It's a dim view of the future, one that speaks to the material limits of Gates's vision and of his "technology will save us" dogma. Gates cannot imagine a world in which poor nations have their own health professionals performing C-sections. And decades from now, he sees a world in which the poor *still* cannot care for themselves but in which they will have much improved lives via the patented bot surgeons he will import from Silicon Valley.

"They really epitomize a form of charity which is disempowering to the people that they claim to seek to benefit," David McCoy, a physician and researcher at United Nations University in Malaysia, told me. McCoy identified the foundation's funding bias toward rich nations as far back as 2009, and, in the decade since, he said, he's seen the foundation only solidify its position of privilege and expand the asymmetries of power that govern global health. "It comes back to this issue of power," he went on. "At the end of the day, a really good metric . . . to look at is: Has power been redistributed over the last twenty years since the Gates Foundation has been on the scene? And I think the evidence shows it hasn't. If anything, inequality, in terms of power, [has] actually gotten worse. There's been an even greater concentration of power and wealth in a few hands, even if lives have been saved during that time. By continuing to not address the more fundamental problems of structural inequality, and the injustice of that, they are able to maintain this position of being charitable and benevolent, which they are then able to translate, to turn into social power."

IT'S DIFFICULT TO examine the colonial mind-set driving the Gates Foundation's work without interrogating the racial dynamics embedded in it. Virtually everywhere the foundation works, whether in the United States or abroad, its focus is on poor people who look nothing like Bill and Melinda French Gates and who live categorically different lives.

Though institutional racism at the foundation remains virtually unexamined by researchers and reporters, in recent years, the foundation has nevertheless faced a growing body of public allegations.

Daniel Kamanga, cofounder of Africa Harvest Biotech Foundation International—one of the Gates Foundation's earliest and best-funded agricultural projects—penned an essay on LinkedIn about the murder of George Floyd by Minneapolis police officer Derek Chauvin, who knelt on Floyd's neck until the life was taken from him. For Kamanga, the atrocity brought to mind the racism he experienced working with Western donors. "I felt the full weight of the knee of racism engaging with donor organizations. I almost couldn't breathe during numerous engagements with the Bill and Melinda Gates Foundation. I have heard knee-on-neck stories from many African NGOs dependent on US, European and other donors. Some African NGOs mastered the game and bracketed the pain. Some became stooges of 'the Enemy.' Many of those who stood [up] to the donors are dead, killed by the weight of those pretending to support them."

In 2021, the Gates Foundation drew controversy upon revelations that its money manager faced accusations of racist behavior, alongside allegations of bullying and sexual misconduct. The money manager denied or downplayed the allegations, and the foundation allowed him to keep his job. A year earlier, the director of the Gates-funded Stop TB Partnership, Lucica Ditiu, faced high-profile accusations of racism. After the allegations became public, the Gates Foundation made a new, $2.5 million donation to support Stop TB's work, where Ditiu remains in charge. And the foundation continued to sit on the group's board of directors, represented by Gates Foundation staffer Erika Arthun.

"Gates sits on the Stop TB board and did nothing," one former employee, Colleen Daniels, told me, noting that she had directly emailed the Gates Foundation about internal problems. "Really what Gates showed me is they are willing to sacrifice people of color to maintain their own agenda.

"The biggest issue for me is Gates has really taken over global public health. They're defining the priorities, and they have done for at least fifteen years. I used to work at the World Health Organization and different UN agencies, and all of the agendas come out of what Gates wants them to focus on, because that's where the money comes from," Daniels notes. "The influence of Gates is too far-reaching. It's just another form of colonialism."

Julia Feliz recounts experiencing suffocating racism through their participation in a fellowship at the Alliance for Science, a Gates-funded, Gates-founded project designed to advance the foundation's agenda on GMOs. Feliz, who is Puerto Rican, called the fellowship a "lesson in Neocolonialism."

When Feliz challenged this racism, the program forced them out of the fellowship, sparking political activity across Cornell University, where the project was hosted at the time. A resolution issued by the school's student governance body condemned the Alliance's behavior. "Rather than 'science communication,' it was a training in sharing our deepest, most personal trauma, unrelated to GMOs—almost like poverty porn (filmed on video!) to pass around in an effort to convince people that looked like 'us' to accept GMOs while also showing white people 'See, we're Black, and we want this,'" Feliz told me via email.

"It was a training in exploiting our most private struggles to further neocolonialism regardless of the history, colonialism, and power over the Global South. The program was definitely not about honest and real conversations about GMOs and the issues around them. . . . In summary, I went to Cornell for intellectual discourse and instead, walked away realizing my skin color and private heart wrenching struggles were worth more than my individuality, abilities, achievements, or experience to a program furthering the exploitative system that only benefits those already in power."

The Gates Foundation appears to use this model widely, funding Black and brown "champions" and "storytellers" for the explicit purpose of amplifying its own agenda and creating the appearance of robust, diverse support for its work. The Gates-funded Generation Africa Voices project partners with the media giant Thomson Reuters to train African storytellers to "become champions for global development." The invited fellows each have their own webpage and "media pack," which includes a photo and a profile that appear ready-made to give journalists easy access to real, authentic African misery—whether it's having been a child soldier for the Lord's Resistance Army, or being set on fire by a stepmother, or having pursued an unsafe abortion through overdose of a chemical.

Many readers have probably heard episodes of the famed *Moth Radio Hour* broadcast over their local NPR station, but they probably don't know that the program has received $7.6 million from Gates "to help champions from the economically developing world craft first-person stories and share them with both decision-makers and a mass audience." A senior Gates Foundation executive sits on the Moth's board of directors, and the foundation reports collaborating with the group on polio eradication. "To change hearts and minds, we need good stories," the Gates Foundation reports. The Moth works hand in hand with the Gates-funded Aspen Institute's New Voices Fellowship, which seeks to elevate these voices in the news. The group boasts having produced nearly 2,000 public op-eds from its 189 fellows.

Another Gates-funded project, Speak Up Africa, claims to be organized, as its name suggests, around empowering and strengthening African democratic engagement. The Gates Foundation has given at least $45 million to the group, and the foundation holds a seat on its board. Gates's first charitable grants to the group didn't go to Africa, however. They went to New York City—to the twenty-fourth floor of the Trump Building in Manhattan, the location of the group's offices, according to Speak Up Africa's annual tax filing. (Later donations were reported as going to Senegal.) In practice, Speak Up Africa appears to use its voice to raise the volume of its benefactor's agenda, not local perspectives. The *Economist* highlighted the group's work in Dakar, for example, where the foundation has introduced a new, and apparently controversial, high-tech sewage treatment plant. "Shortly after the machine appeared, rumours that water extracted from sewage was being added to the city's drinking water caused uproar," the *Economist* reported. "Speak Up Africa, a Gates-funded policy-and-advocacy group, was called on to launch a public-information campaign. . . . The team says its monthly virtual meetings with Gates staff in Seattle offer a chance to discuss new ideas and meet international experts." (Questions emailed to Speak Up Africa's offices in New York and Senegal did not get a response.)

By elevating "champions" and "storytellers" and "fellows" who agree with and amplify Gates's agenda and worldview, or who won't challenge it, the foundation can give its work the appearance of great diversity, equity, and inclusion. But it is difficult to avoid seeing these efforts as deeply tokenistic and disrespectful. The simple fact is that the foundation spends far more resources trying to capture images of the global poor, capitalize on their stories, and co-opt their misery than it does actually listening to or working with them.

THE GATES FOUNDATION is not a particularly diverse workplace. Gates reported in 2021, for example, that only around 10 percent of its U.S.-based workforce is Black or Hispanic—compared to around 33 percent of the U.S. population.

Diversity at the Gates Foundation should probably be understood more broadly than in terms of race and ethnicity, however. How many people who work at the foundation have the lived experience of poverty or have grown up in the poor nations where so much of the foundation's work takes place? And how many staff grew up in wealthy families in rich nations—and attended Ivy League schools? How many staff have been schoolteachers or farmers—whose lives and livelihoods the foundation heavily influences through its charitable giving?

The foundation doesn't report this information, but we can see at least some level of diversity in its leadership. This includes Anita Zaidi, who appears to be the highest-ranking foundation official who is a person of color from a poor nation. A decorated physician from Pakistan, Zaidi has served as director of the foundation's vaccine development and surveillance, director of its work on enteric and diarrheal diseases, and also president of its work on gender equality. Project Syndicate calls her "one of the world's leading voices on issues affecting women and girls."

It's a questionable assertion from a dubious source—the Project Syndicate article does not disclose the news outlet takes funding from the Gates Foundation. There is, nevertheless, some truth to the idea that Zaidi plays several very high-profile roles at one of the most powerful political organizations in the world.

Though Zaidi works from the foundation's headquarters in Seattle, and is also a Harvard-trained scientist, her ties to Pakistan give her perspective on how the Gates Foundation works in poor nations, a topic she doesn't shy away from in interviews. Once asked about criticism that not enough foundation funding was going into "capacity development" in poor nations, Zaidi responded, "At the BMGF we look very carefully at how much of the grants that we are funding are going to low and middle income countries and how much to partnering US/western institutions." She went on to give several nonspecific examples, like "a program in India which was [in] clinical trial capacity development," but none from her home country of Pakistan. As it turns out, much of the foundation's funding to the country—five hundred million dollars in total—appears to have gone to organizations that Zaidi herself runs or to which she has close institutional ties.

Before joining the foundation, Zaidi served as chair of the pediatrics department at Aga Khan University. AKU today is the second-largest recipient of Gates's funding in Pakistan, taking in well over $100 million, much of it directed at child and maternal health. Zaidi continues to hold a part-time faculty position at the school and has continued to publish some of her scientific research under her AKU affiliation. She also personally makes high-profile donations to the school—something she can afford to do with her nearly $750,000 compensation package from the Gates Foundation. Sources say she remains a powerful institutional force inside Aga Khan through her work with one of the school's most potent external funders.

Another top recipient of Gates Foundation funding is Vital Pakistan Trust, which Zaidi founded and where she served as chair of the board of trustees as late as mid-2022. The group has received more than $33 million from the Gates Foundation for work related to child and maternal health. This appears to be virtually all of Vital Pakistan's funding, and some of this funding appears to have been spent on collaborative projects with AKU. Likewise, many members of Vital's board of trustees have historically come from AKU.

These relationships raise clear questions about financial conflicts of interest. Zaidi works for the Gates Foundation, which is donating tens of millions of dollars to an organization she was running, Vital Pakistan. At the same time, the Gates Foundation is also donating more than one hundred million dollars to a university where Zaidi plays a powerful institutional role. How can the foundation donate money to organizations that Gates Foundation staff help direct or where they play influential roles? At what point do we see this as charity, and at what point do we see the Gates Foundation, essentially, just giving money to itself?

"I have concerns about the way Gates operates anyway, but these particular connections are just so obvious," one source close to Aga Khan University told me. "When such high amounts of funding go to one institution or one set of institutions, you're building the research from one set of perspectives. . . . At a time when global health and development is moving toward decolonization and thinking more about equity, you need to be investing in a more diverse group of scientists and building the capacity of a more diverse set of institutions. If you are the largest, biggest philanthropic organization or funder, I feel that is an important role, which is not being fulfilled."

Another source described Zaidi as creating "a parallel value system" in the provision of health care that prioritizes "chasing Gates's money. . . . Money is power. Money allows you to hire people, promote people, and elevate them into leadership roles."

These two sources describe Zaidi as a kind of power broker in Pakistan, building powerful alliances that set the research agenda in public health. "She's politically savvy, politically astute, very strategic. Very, very ambitious," one source said. "I think she does care about things changing in Pakistan, but [at times] it's so difficult for me to see that, when I see so much of it is just is about wanting to be the leader in all of this. I think she can tell a good narrative."

Sources also described Zaidi's reputation for mentoring young researchers in ways that expand her own influence in global health. "They remain dependent on her for their careers," one source told me. "They are not in a position to say no."

"She never was the mentor that was going to let you be completely free," my other source said. "She was always going to have some control. You knew you were going to be fine [in your career] as long as you said yes to Anita Zaidi." But, the source added, this creates a culture where researchers at AKU become "great implementers of other people's ideas . . . just carrying on with her vision."

In many ways, this is the very colonial model that many scholars and researchers want to dismantle in order to build a new global health system that emphasizes self-determination and sovereignty—diagnosing, prioritizing, and solving problems locally, not seeing the world through the eyes of a billionaire foundation in Seattle.

Neither Zaidi nor AKU nor Vital Pakistan responded to press inquiries, so it remains unknown if or how Zaidi's financial conflicts of interest are managed. My sources were not surprised, saying that AKU would do everything in its power to protect Zaidi, the school's "golden goose"—the key link to Bill Gates's money. It is nevertheless notable that, after my multiple press inquiries, Zaidi appears to have taken a major step back from Vital. As of early 2023, she was no longer listed on the organization's board of trustees. And while her name used to inundate Vital's website, with references to her as a "renowned professor and a philanthropist," today it appears to have been almost entirely scrubbed out.

If Zaidi is AKU's conduit to Gates, she may also be Gates's conduit to Pakistan, a nation of vital geopolitical interest to the foundation. Globally, the foundation has devoted more than eight billion dollars toward polio eradication, and in recent years, much of Gates's focus has been in Pakistan, one of the last places on earth where "wild-type" polio still circulates. The foundation's grant records make it impossible to see how much of its polio budget has trickled into Pakistan, but the records do show that the largest recipient of Gates's funding in Pakistan is the local WHO office, which received $300 million from Gates, all of it for work on polio.

Some public health experts criticize Gates's crusade to eradicate polio as a pet project, one that distracts the world from far more important public health concerns. Polio is not a leading killer in Pakistan, for example; nor is it a major public health burden. In virtually every year since 1990, the country has had fewer than 1,000 cases of paralytic polio. By contrast, Our World in Data, which has received funding from Gates, shows that in recent years, there were 25 million people in Pakistan requiring interventions against neglected tropical disease and 28 million people who were undernourished. According to UNICEF, 38 percent of children in Pakistan experience stunting. One could name dozens of diseases and conditions more pressing in Pakistan than polio, and that's been the case for decades. The problem is that those diseases don't have a multibillionaire benefactor to make them a priority—or to pay the London-based advertising company M&C Saatchi "to engage the Pakistani diaspora as champions of polio eradication," as the Gates Foundation did.

One of Gates's biggest shows of force on polio in Pakistan came in the spring of 2022. As the Covid-19 pandemic took global attention away from his pet project, Bill Gates visited Pakistan—his first-ever personal visit there—to refocus the attention of its political leaders. It appears to have worked. "Polio eradication is a top priority for our government," said then prime minister Imran Khan, according to a Gates Foundation press release. "We are working at all levels to ensure that every child is protected with the polio vaccine and are grateful for the continued partnership and support from the Bill & Melinda Gates Foundation and our other polio partners."

Not long after Gates's visit, his polio campaign got another boost when academic researchers published an essay titled "When Will Pakistan Stand on Two Legs? A Polio Story." Coauthored by Fyezah Jehan—a physician at Aga Khan University, a mentee of Anita Zaidi's, a recipient of funding from the Gates Foundation, and someone who dined with Bill Gates during his visit to Pakistan—the piece reported, "The global health efforts towards vaccine procurement and delivery must continue. We have persevered through the unprecedented Covid-19 pandemic. We must not forget the terror of poliovirus."

The never-ending fight against polio, however, could be seen as emblematic of the ways that Pakistan is not standing on its own two legs but is, rather, leaning on a crutch of foreign aid and following the public health priorities of a billionaire in some distant land.

IN 2022, THE Gates Foundation funded and helped design a study that sought to boost the weight of newborns in Uganda and Guinea-Bissau with baby formula. While such a project sounds noncontroversial, if not righteous, it led to minor scandal because public health experts recommend breastfeeding exclusively, without the use of formula.

One group of international researchers condemned the study as offering "no benefit and large potential for harm" to participating families, saying the "trial violates basic ethical principles and human rights."

They described the study as being "in direct conflict with international public health breastfeeding recommendations," adding, "The benefits of the research accrue entirely to the scientists and potentially to Abbott Laboratories, the formula manufacturer."

This criticism speaks to the long-standing history of wealthy Western researchers using poor nations as a petri dish and poor people as guinea pigs. In the same way that large companies exploit poor nations for raw materials, wealthy research institutes have long engaged in the same extractive economies—taking data, labor, and credit.

The foundation's research agenda, in many places, has drawn criticism along these lines. The foundation, for example, instead of imagining a world where poor people have access to a diverse, healthy diet, puts money into silver bullet solutions of genetically engineering food crops with fortified vitamin content or working with Heinz, Kraft, Roche, or BASF to biofortify processed foods. The foundation has also funded research into giving healthy children in poor nations antibiotics because it believes this can reduce disease, a quick-win intervention that sidesteps the more important work of providing basic health care. In its work on vaccines, the foundation supports research to see if the global poor can manage with fewer doses than wealthy people receive, a cost-saving measure known as "dose sparing."

Throughout the foundation's charitable work, we see this same beggars-can't-be-choosers ethos. The blind spots and institutional racism speak to the historical underpinnings of "global health," a strange term for what, essentially, means public health for poor people—organized by researchers and policy makers from wealthy nations. Once called "tropical medicine," this field was developed not out of some humanitarian impulse to protect the poor but, rather, to keep colonists healthy as they plundered the tropics. Today, the public health of poor nations remains very much the province of powerful interests from the Global North, none more powerful than the Gates Foundation. The foundation wields a heavy hand in deciding which diseases, which approaches, and which researchers get money.

Such power dynamics have in recent years inspired an activist movement calling for a new era of social justice in science and health, trading under the hashtag DGH, or "Decolonize Global Health." In the same way that we can't talk about Big Oil without talking about climate change, it's difficult to talk about global health today without interrogating the power imbalances that define the field. The #DGH movement has rocked large humanitarian organizations like MSF, which stands accused of far-ranging institutional racism. The Gates Foundation, by contrast, does not appear to have received the same level of public criticism, likely because many do not want to bite the hand that feeds them.

The Gates Foundation, nevertheless, is clearly aware of this discourse and has even begun funding this space, for example making a three-hundred-thousand-dollar donation to the news outlet the New Humanitarian "to encourage action-oriented reflections and conversations within the media and humanitarian sector stakeholders about new and innovative ways of working and decolonizing aid." This funding speaks to the ways that powerful organizations, threatened by the decolonization movement, have sought to co-opt it.

"'Decolonizing' has become some sort of a buzzword that everyone wants to get out, oftentimes to prove your wokeness," Yadurshini Raveendran told me. Raveendran is founder of the Duke Decolonizing Global Health Working Group at Duke University, one of a growing number of campus activist groups working on this issue. "They want to participate in these conversations because it's the hot thing. It's the popular thing to be a part of, especially after the Black Lives Matter Movement," she said. "They're using this platform or conversation to prove that, 'Hey, we care about "diversity" or "representation," without really understanding what the movement is really standing for or trying to push for.'"

In our interview, Raveendran spoke at length about her own experience—she grew up in Sri Lanka, a former British colony, but completed a graduate degree at Duke University, a prestigious private school in the United States (where Melinda French Gates also attended). Her studies at Duke were even partially funded by a scholarship from the Gates Foundation. "I'm grateful that I had that scholarship, because otherwise I would not have been able to come here and do my work," Raveendran said, before adding a quick caveat: "Why did I have to leave my home country to get an education in public health here, in this part of the world, in order to help my people? It's just really ironic. I had to take a handout from a white organization when it was a white organization, the British Empire, that colonized my land."

When I interviewed her in 2021, Raveendran had just received her Covid-19 vaccination, which she cited as another non sequitur in global health. How was it that she, as a healthy, young person, could get vaccinated simply because she lived in the United States while her much more vulnerable parents in Sri Lanka had to wait in line, beholden to a chaotic, failing vaccine distribution effort the Gates Foundation had helped organize? (We'll explore that vaccine effort later in this book.) "It's just sad for me, that someone who made his billions from Microsoft or technology has so much say in the health care of the people who look like me and my family, who are so isolated from this man, who will never see the kind of money he has. But somehow, because he has this money, he has the agency over my health or my family's health."

Organizations that hold power in global health, like the Gates Foundation, tend to respond to the decolonization movement through incrementalist efforts, like opening up opportunities for researchers from poor nations to get access to expensive conferences and journals. But the premise of the decolonization movement, as Raveendran sees it, requires us to move beyond baby steps and instead take strides toward the "dismantling of oppressive systems that continue to hold power—white supremacy, capitalism, racism, sexism." And this means dismantling the Gates Foundation.

"They are the antithesis of the decolonial movement because they *are* the system. They perpetuate the system that is causing harm. If we were to decolonize, we would dismantle the system of aid where another [wealthy] country or another organization has to put in their money in order for us [in the Global South] to be healthy," she said. "I can't blame [Bill] Gates as being the sole perpetrator, because this is centuries of harm, but he is part and parcel of that conversation, for sure, because of how much power he is wielding."

The criticism around the foundation's colonial power speaks to the complex legacy of colonization and the wider context in which Gates operates today. As writers Caesar A. Atuire and Olivia U. Rutazibwa noted in 2021, "(Neo-) colonialism does not only produce a colonizer who exhibits paternalistic attitudes towards the colonized but also a colonized who develops a consistent lack of self-confidence; both feed on and perpetuate relations of dependency."

Olusoji Adeyi, former director of health and nutrition at the World Bank, directs his critical eye at what he calls "narcissistic charity." "The inconvenient truth is that contrary to popular assertions, the core problem is neo-dependency, not Neo-colonialism," Adeyi wrote in 2021. "It is ruinous for so many countries to be so dependent on, and strategically beholden to, the whims and kindness of strangers."

Calls to end financial dependency on foreign donors might suggest a bootstrapping ideology—that we need to end the welfare state, that poor people must take control over their own destinies. But this misunderstands the issue of justice. The centuries of economic harm wielded by colonizers must be redressed. And this can't happen through billionaire philanthropy, in which Bill Gates donates money in ways that advance his own agenda, funding organizations like Vital Pakistan, run by his close deputies.

As I write this, Pakistan is struggling to manage severe flooding, which has displaced millions of people. The growing severity of floods can be attributed to climate change, which is primarily driven by the emissions of wealthy nations. Should rich nations not be held financially responsible for cleaning up the mess they caused? We could bring that critique directly to the doorstep of Bill Gates, who, with his constant travel by private jet, is one of the largest individual carbon emitters in the world.

In my interview with Sikowis Nobiss, an enrolled member of the George Gordon Plains Cree/Saulteaux First Nation and the founder of the Indigenous-led Great Plains Action Society, she pointed to recent reports that Bill Gates has become the largest farmland owner in the United States, holding 242,000 acres—an area of land larger than Bahrain or Singapore or Barbados can claim. Nobiss told me this speaks to the Manifest Destiny mentality that has to be challenged in the political fight around climate change and decolonization. "Bill Gates is smart enough to understand—he's smart, he can do the math—that no one single person needs that amount of land," Nobiss said. "He's basically participating in the never-ending cycle of colonization."

Nobiss's solution? Gates should hand over his land as reparations. In the decolonization movement, it is the colonizers who have the most to lose—and are most threatened by the prospect of losing control, an issue that Muneera Rasheed explored in a commentary she published in *The Lancet Global Health*. "Historically, decolonisation has always been a violent process and global health might experience the same. Disrupting and calling out neo-colonial practices requires courage to bear the cost that comes with doing so," she wrote. "My message to those in leadership roles anywhere and who can spend their privilege of being in powerful roles: We must take sides."

This discourse around decolonization is not unique to global health, as even the field of philanthropy is grappling with questions about power and justice. "The process starts with asking the question, 'Where does the money come from?'" Edgar Villanueva, author of the book *Decolonizing Wealth: Indigenous Wisdom to Heal Divides and Restore Balance*, told me in an interview. "If you think about it through the place of truth and reconciliation, it begins with looking back and asking what harm has been done. I think for a lot of foundations . . . the work is very much looking forward, like, 'What do we do in the future?' without taking into account what happened in the past."

Of course, Bill Gates's wealth comes from Microsoft, a company he views as having been an engine of social progress, inspiring a computer revolution. Villanueva told me this view is fairly common among tech billionaires, the idea that "'We haven't harmed anyone.' Regardless, you have to take into account, when you look at folks who have been able to succeed in this country—especially if you're born white, if you're born into privilege—you're doing work inside of a construct that has created opportunities that others don't have in this country. So, you have to acknowledge that."

In some respects, this view—and this conception of charity—gets back to the root origin of the word *philanthropy*, which comes from Greek and translates as "lover of your fellow human." A charitable gift is meant to be an act of love, not an exercise of power. Giving away money is not supposed to magnify the asymmetries in power that govern society, but to collapse them. And this is precisely why, in many respects, Bill

Gates might be better described as a misanthrope—if he does not hate his fellow man, then he certainly views himself as superior. Gates's dead-eyed belief in himself and his powers, and his wholesale disregard for the wishes, needs, or rights of the poor people he claims to be serving, speaks to the fundamentally colonial lens through which he views his charitable giving. It highlights the existential limits of what he can accomplish, and it explains why the Gates Foundation has achieved so little.

Bloat

In 2014, the Gates Foundation was experiencing technical issues tracking and managing the charitable grants it made—a sad irony for an institution run by one of the world's most famed technologists. Worse, when the foundation embarked on a major, seventy-million-dollar project called Clarity, to fix the problems, it appeared to lead to even more confusion.

"Clarity was supposed to overhaul cross-program systems like investment management (e.g., grant management and tracking), for which IT resources played a significant part. The project was an utter failure," noted the findings of a 2017 lawsuit against the Gates Foundation. The lawsuit was brought by Todd Pierce, whom the foundation hired as its "chief digital officer" to help resolve its tech issues. Or, at least, that's what some senior staff thought Pierce had been hired to do. Others, including Bill Gates, had given Pierce the impression that he would be a "digital visionary," not simply an IT janitor.

Pierce filed a lawsuit, claiming he had been misled about his job description. He asked to be compensated for the income he would have made had he stayed in his previous job, as an executive at Salesforce. In 2018, courts ruled in favor of Pierce, awarding him almost five million dollars.

Bill Gates, the son of a corporate lawyer and someone extremely comfortable using the courts, wasn't about to accept defeat. The foundation proclaimed its own victory, citing Pierce's failure to demonstrate one

claim, negligent misrepresentation. "We continue to dispute the findings, characterizations of fact, and legal conclusions on the other claims,
which are not supported by the record and contradict well established
case law in Washington State," the foundation asserted. "A judgment has
not yet been entered and the amount of any judgment is still uncertain.
The foundation intends to appeal the decision."

And that's what the foundation did. In 2020, an appellate court ruled
that a new trial court would need to review what damages Pierce should
receive. Inside the foundation, staff say the litigious behavior sent a
chilling message. "I think that's when we realized, no, the foundation
will kind of come down on you," one former employee told me, explaining his reluctance to speak on the record. If Gates was willing to go to
the mat with Todd Pierce, what would it do, for example, if an employee
violated a nondisclosure or nondisparagement agreement?

Pierce's story illustrates more than the culture of fear that rules the
foundation. It also speaks to the bloated bureaucracy that has sapped
the foundation's energy, efficiency, and effectiveness. How could seventy
million dollars disappear into the foundation's morass of IT problems
with the Clarity initiative? How much more money vanishes into the
bloat of administrative costs to run the world's biggest philanthropy?
What does this mean for taxpayers who pony up something like fifty
cents of every dollar the foundation spends—or wastes?

And how do we reconcile this bloat with the image the foundation so
ferociously presents as a doggedly efficient, hyper-nimble private entity
that can do things that lumbering government agencies cannot? This
reputation is of great importance to Bill Gates, who has always imagined
himself as having a kind of principled workman mentality, bringing personal values of thrift and industriousness to all his work. "I'm very well
grounded because of my parents and my job and what I believe in. Some
people ask me why I don't own a plane, for instance. Why? Because you
can get used to that kind of stuff, and I think that's bad," he said in a 1994
interview with *Playboy*. "It takes you away from normal experiences in
a way that is probably debilitating. So I control that kind of thing inten-
tionally. It's one of those discipline things. If my discipline ever broke
down it would confuse me, too. So I try to prevent that."

In its early days, the Gates Foundation very much practiced the virtues that Bill Gates preached. At that time, it was extremely focused on actually giving money away. Of the foundation's $1.65 billion in expenses in 2000, $1.54 billion was money given away in charity. "The foundation is as spartan in structure and style as an Internet start-up," *Time* magazine reported that year. "There are just 25 employees, in contrast to 525 for the venerable Ford Foundation."

In 2007, the foundation's chief operating officer, Cheryl Scott, explained, "The most important thing a foundation does is choose a limited set of issues and develop expertise in them. Bill and Melinda have identified areas in which they think our grantmaking can help solve complex, entrenched problems that affect billions of people—like the AIDS and malaria epidemics, extreme poverty, and the poor state of American high schools."

By the end of 2021, the foundation's portfolio had ballooned to 41 program strategies managed by at least 1,843 employees. It was suddenly spending more than $1 billion a year—around 20 percent of its annual expenses—on administrative costs and "professional fees." Hundreds of millions—or maybe billions—of dollars from the foundation disappeared into the coffers of professional consultants, the nebulous, self-proclaimed experts-for-hire at outlets like McKinsey and Boston Consulting Group. And Bill Gates had begun traveling on his own private jet—the indulgence he once said would debilitate and confuse him.

As the foundation grew, its culture also changed. Perhaps the most common criticism I heard from grant recipients during my reporting was how difficult Gates had become to work with because of its intense bureaucracy and micromanagement. The foundation buries grantees with checklists and phone calls and paperwork. High turnover of foundation staff compounds the problem, forcing grantees to spend even more time bringing new foundation officers up to speed—and making them feel important and smart. Some organizations say they essentially have had to create a new full-time position to interface with the foundation's endless requests for information. One early grantee told me his first partnership with Gates took a month to finalize. His last grant, a decade later, took a year.

"It seems that a large number of staff got involved with every grant, and all their multitudinous questions had to be iteratively addressed," the source said, describing how grant applications were endlessly run up the ladder at the foundation, encouraging any and every meddlesome busybody to weigh in with questions, most of them irrelevant or simply foolish. "The people who wrote these questions have no idea what the field is about, who has done what, what has been done in the past." As this source sees it, the problems began when Bill Gates started spending less time at Microsoft and more time at the foundation. "We saw this day after day after day, the way in which he mismanaged the Gates Foundation. . . . When you're giving away money, it's pretty hard to detect that it's not being managed well. Recipients don't want to complain. Staff, I think, are under nondisclosure agreements."

Baylor University professor Peter Hotez, an early recipient of Gates funding for vaccine development, offers a more modest assessment, telling me the foundation "continues to be a net positive, but I do think they've gotten so big and so pervasive that there is diminishing returns on their productivity. I think they've gone past the point where they've maximized their productivity. . . . The solution, I think, is to roll things back a bit and become more of a foundation in the true sense, and less of either a company or an institute."

Bill Gates argues the exact opposite, claiming that the foundation's virtues today derive from its evolution from a check-writing charity into a powerhouse of experts who can organize entire fields of inquiry. "The Gates Foundation in an area like global disease is an institution," he said in 2013. "It's hiring scientists, researchers, deciding how to give the grants. And it's taken us ten years to get that institution to a level—sort of the level of excellence that, say, Microsoft had in 1995, where you really feel people are very analytical, on top of things. That's hard work. It's fun work."

Some sources I interviewed say that the foundation's bloat accelerated with the hiring of Trevor Mundel, who joined as its global health director in 2011 (coming from Novartis). Under his leadership, the foundation took a much more hands-on role over pharmaceutical development. Other sources question whether the foundation's bureaucratic excesses derive from rogue program officers and executives intoxicated by the power they wield. One scientist I interviewed recounted how his grant manager at the foundation would openly say, "I love this job because I can be in control of everyone's grant. . . . When I was in academia, I was the principal investigator of my own [grant] program. Now I'm the principal investigator of everyone's."

One of the biggest contributing factors to the bloat has probably been Warren Buffett—ironically, a renowned bloat hawk with a reputation for thrift. (News outlets routinely cite how Buffett has lived in the same relatively modest house in Omaha, Nebraska, since the 1960s.) When Buffett began making large donations to the foundation in 2006—at least a billion dollars every year—the foundation's swelling coffers created a cash-flow problem of sorts. Under IRS rules, the foundation has to give away 5 percent of its assets each year, so more money coming in means more money has to go out. Buffett also put additional rules on the foundation, saying his annual donations had to be given away the same year he donated them—this in addition to the annual 5 percent payout requirement.

Suddenly, the foundation had a huge spending burden, and it did not have enough trusted acolytes to soak up these vast sums of money. You could call it the *Brewster's Millions* effect. In the 1985 film version of the story, Monty Brewster, played by Richard Pryor, has a choice to receive a gift: accept one million dollars on the spot or take a chance at winning three hundred million. To do that, he has to undertake a challenge, spending thirty million dollars in thirty days. As Brewster quickly learns, spending very large sums of money quickly is quite difficult. In the real world of billionaire philanthropy, the Gates Foundation's embarrassment of riches had created the same challenge.

The solution for the foundation was what it internally called "forward funding"—creating new institutions and rapidly expanding funding to its largest grantees. This allowed it to get large sums of money out the door, even if, as it sometimes seemed, it was merely parking the money in the account of one of its surrogates. "We gave like a billion dollars at a time to them, knowing they wouldn't be able to spend it for ten years, or eight years," one former employee told me. "It didn't matter, because that billion was treated for us as meeting our payout requirements, and it was a place to park the money, basically. There's nothing wrong with it as long as the organization can responsibly grow into it."

The result has been that around 40 percent of Gates's charitable donations—more than $31 billion—have gone toward twenty megaorganizations, some of which function as surrogates for the foundation. Top recipients include Gavi; the WHO; PATH; the Global Fund to Fight AIDS, Tuberculosis and Malaria; UNICEF; the University of Washington;

the World Bank; the Rotary Foundation; the United Negro College Fund; Johns Hopkins University; the Medicines for Malaria Venture; Alliance for a Green Revolution in Africa; the Clinton Health Access Initiative (and other projects tied to Bill, Hillary, and Chelsea Clinton); the National Institutes of Health; Aeras; New Venture Fund; the Gates Medical Research Institute; TB Alliance; CARE; and the International AIDS Vaccine Initiative.

The foundation has also put billions of dollars into old-guard bureaucracies—including more than a billion dollars to a group of agricultural research stations set up by the Rockefeller Foundation and more than half a billion dollars to FHI 360, a K Street nonprofit development group with four thousand employees. Many of the foundation's closest partners and largest recipients are domiciled in expensive locales, like Geneva, Manhattan, and Washington, DC—meaning very large sums of money disappear into salaries of staff living in these high-priced cities. When the foundation built its own offices, it likewise spared no expense, pouring half a billion dollars into its ostentatious headquarters on prime real estate in downtown Seattle.

As always, we can go back to the foundation's superficial lives-saved logic and calculate how many lives are being *lost* through this excess. Every additional dollar that goes to extravagant buildings, expensive real estate, fringe benefits, bonuses, and consultants could be spent delivering vaccines and healing the poor. As Bill Gates himself has written on the subject of wasted public health spending, "Taxpayers have every right to be angry—I am furious—because when the goal is saving lives, any misspent money costs lives."

Gates wants us to think about lives in terms of dollars—he says saving a child's life costs less than a thousand dollars. If so, don't we have to understand that every billion dollars lost to bloat at the foundation translates into a million lives lost? The math is pure pabulum, of course, but this is the logic of the foundation. If journalists are going to lean on Gates's lives-saved mathematics to promote the foundation's good deeds, don't they also have to work out the other side of the equation?

Warren Buffett apparently was upset enough about the foundation's bloat in the mid-2010s that he directed a small reduction in the number of its staff, which in 2015 dropped from 1,460 to 1,449. The next year, however, the upward trend resumed, with staff size jumping to 1,579.

Inside the foundation, one former staffer told me, the human resources department had also put its head to accounting tricks to appease Buffett. To deflate its ballooning head count, for example, the foundation expanded the hiring of consultants and a growing army of what it calls "limited-term employees," essentially short-term contractors who serve alongside staff but get fewer benefits. The solution to bloat, then, was more bloat—and a two-tiered, unequal workforce.

Publicly, however, the foundation has always made a big show of its ruthless commitment to efficiency. Mark Suzman, after his appointment as the foundation's new CEO in 2020, wrote an internal email about a trip he took to Omaha to visit Buffett.

> He told me then that my most important job was to guard against the "ABC" risks of decay that all very large organizations face: arrogance, bureaucracy, and complacency. He has consistently pointed out that these risks are even greater for us as the country's largest philanthropy. He has urged us to "swing for the fences" and take risks that others cannot—always with the reminder that we should never be displacing private or public capital, but rather complementing it. Since we are not subject to the natural checks of market forces, he has reminded us to watch out for mission creep that takes us away from our core competencies—a caution that underpins my prioritization of robust internal and external checks on our budget and strategy processes to ensure we are always focused on our areas of greatest comparative advantage. And, most importantly, he has urged us to adhere to the highest standards of integrity and transparency.

Yet, what are these "standards of integrity and transparency" that Suzman and Buffett exalt? What do these standards say about the foundation's decision to build a sumptuous, half-billion-dollar headquarters?

There is reason to believe that the "ABCs" will continue to atrophy the foundation. In 2006, when Buffett first announced his partnership with Gates, he seemed to state that most of his money after death would go to the foundation. And the Gates Foundation has been working with McKinsey consultants to figure out how to manage what might be a fifty-billion-dollar or even one-hundred-billion-dollar inheritance from

Buffett. This would mean the foundation will be forced to spend ever larger sums of money, guaranteeing more mission creep and more bloat.

But it's also very possible that Buffett will change directions. He abruptly stepped down from the foundation's board of trustees in 2021 amid several high-profile scandals—Bill Gates's relationship with Jeffrey Epstein, allegations of misconduct with female employees, and the foundation's botched management of Covid-19. Does Buffett really want to continue to trust his legacy to such an embattled man? In 2022, the *Wall Street Journal* reported that Buffett might be planning to direct most of his wealth to the Susan Thompson Buffett Foundation, named after his late wife, rather than to Gates. If so, it would be a powerful statement about Buffett's loss of confidence in the effectiveness of the Gates Foundation.

Whatever Warren Buffett, born in 1930, decides to do, the Gates Foundation still has to contend with Bill Gates's personal wealth—more than $100 billion as of early 2023. Gates, born in 1955, could easily live until 2040 or later—his father died at age ninety-four—during which time his wealth will likely continue to grow. Gates has promised to donate virtually all his wealth to his foundation, which is supposed to shut down two decades after the deaths of Bill and Melinda.

This presents one more irony, or contradiction, in the Gates Foundation. For most of the last two decades, the foundation's endowment has been growing in size, not shrinking as you would expect of an institution in the business of giving away money. Between the billions of dollars in investment income the foundation generates each year, alongside yearly donations that Buffett and Gates make to the foundation, the foundation's coffers will continue to swell. With hundreds of billions of dollars potentially coming into the foundation in the decades ahead, it is very difficult to understand the endgame.

Internally, the foundation has reportedly brainstormed ideas to address its spending problem and the potential for a sudden windfall of cash, for example, if one of its benefactors died. One idea, apparently, is creating a massive savings account for poor children. Of course, it would be wholly un-Gatesian for the foundation simply to give poor people money to use as they wish—and that doesn't appear to be the plan. Rather, as described in media reports, the idea is to create a savings account on behalf of children. Presumably, beneficiaries will have to jump through hoops to access the funds and use the money in ways narrowly prescribed by Gates. Presumably too Gates will create a massive new surrogate to manage the money, with someone from the Gates family on the board in perpetuity.

The question marks surrounding the foundation's plans and the ultimate fate of the Gateses' massive wealth—and how the Gates children play into all this—speak not only to the foundation's lack of transparency but also to its sense of entitlement. Countless governments, NGOs, and poor people have come to depend on Bill Gates's wealth, but they have no idea how long this support will last or what comes next. And they're not allowed to ask. If we take the Gates model of philanthropy to its logical conclusion, we can imagine not only Bill Gates's private foundation growing in size, wealth, and power in the decades ahead but also the expanding role of other billionaires in world affairs. It presents us with a future in which a small group of super-rich global elites—Elon Musk, Jeff Bezos, Mark Zuckerberg, Michael Bloomberg, Charles Koch, Carlos Slim, MacKenzie Scott, Mukesh Ambani, Jack Ma—play an ever-larger role in global governance, organizing trillions of dollars to remake the world according to their own narrow interests, calling it philanthropy.

IN THE YEARS after the Great Recession, the political debate around the world's economic woes included endless references to "belt tightening" and "hair cutting." The simple, almost irresistible logic at the time was that, in a moment of economic crisis, we need to reduce spending. Many economists, however, argued that the government needed to keep spending to stimulate the economy—and to help poor people keep their heads above water.

In this debate, Bill Gates saw an opportunity to go on the attack and earn his wings as a powerful deficit hawk. He mounted a campaign to restructure the workforce in American education, speaking out in favor of a massive overhaul of teacher pay. "Pension generosity" and unjustified health care plans for teachers, he argued, translated into fiduciary irresponsibility that will mean "we will be laying off over a 100,000 teachers." As Gates saw it, funding teachers' inflated benefits packages was taking critical funds away from students and schools. "These budgets are way out of whack. . . . They've used accounting gimmicks and [a] lot things that are truly extreme," he said in 2011. "The default course—where the health care costs are squeezing out education—is quite bleak." Gates also took aim at salaries, arguing that teachers shouldn't necessarily be rewarded with higher pay for getting master's degrees or for remaining on the teacher workforce year after year. Rather, a merit-based pay system should reward truly effective and innovative teachers, or those who take on more work, larger classrooms, or difficult teaching environments.

Gates's campaigning, however, didn't work, and his dire predictions did not come to fruition. Schools haven't faced massive teacher layoffs, as Gates forecast. But they are struggling with a wave of teacher resignations, driven, in part, by funding cuts in education, which leave teachers overworked, under-resourced, and underpaid—a situation not helped by Gates's saber-rattling.

Bill Gates's attack on teachers' benefits showed not only how wrongheaded and dogmatic his policy positions are but also his stupendous hypocrisy. While Gates inveighed against teachers' supposedly inflated benefits, his private foundation, heavily subsidized by taxpayers, has forged what one former staffer called a "palladium" benefits package for its own high-paid employees. Current and former employees I interviewed spoke with some embarrassment about the business class flights, unlimited vacation days (paid), and fifty-two-week leave for new mothers and fathers offered by the foundation. (Parental leave was later pared down to six months.) "Very generous but totally unnecessary," one former employee noted. "People used to say, 'Come for the mission, stay for the benefits.'"

At the foundation's extravagant headquarters in Seattle, you'll find a private medical clinic and also a gym with free personal trainers. Staff have top-of-the-line insurance, access to backup child care, and, according to one document, up to $1,500 to support "employees in managing their work and personal life." Foundation staff are also highly remunerated. One employee told me that the only place to get comparable pay and compensation would be working in pharma. The foundation's most recent annual IRS tax filing reports that it had 1,843 employees and paid out close to $500 million in annual salaries and benefits—an average compensation package of around $250,000. Top staff make more than $1 million a year, including CEO Mark Suzman, who collects close to $1.5 million in total compensation.

OVER THE LAST decade, the Gates Foundation has created an almost cult-like image of its founder, organized around his generosity and also his supposedly autodidactic, polymath intellect—someone who spends his wealth freely on humanitarian endeavors and dispenses his personal time on heady self-enrichment. *Rolling Stone*'s 2014 profile of Bill Gates is illustrative, presenting him as consumed by knowledge and unconcerned with material wealth:

> Personally, Gates has very little Master of the Universe swagger and, given the scale of his wealth, his possessions are modest: three houses, one plane, no yachts. He wears loafers and khakis and V-neck sweaters. He often needs a haircut. His glasses haven't changed much in 40 years. For fun, he attends bridge tournaments.
>
> But if his social ambitions are modest, his intellectual scope is mind-boggling: climate, energy, agriculture, infectious diseases and education reform, to name a few. He has former nuclear physicists helping cook up nutritional cookies to feed the developing world. A polio SWAT team has already spent $1.5 billion (and is committed to another $1.8 billion through 2018) to eradicate the virus. He's engineering better toilets and funding research into condoms made of carbon nanotubes.

There is a great deal missing from this account, including some basic understanding that simply spending billions of dollars on diverse, high-minded endeavors doesn't translate into results. Nor does reading books make Bill Gates an expert or an intellectual. In many respects, Gates might best be seen as a dilettante, someone with many superficial interests. None of the things that *Rolling Stone* profiled him working on, for example, have materialized into real wins. His work on education reform has failed by his own admission. The revolution he promised in agriculture never arrived. His endlessly promoted efforts to engineer a new toilet have not fixed sanitation in poor nations. He has yet to eradicate polio and likely never will. Maybe the carbon nanotube condom has been a game-changer for Bill Gates's personal life, but it has had no real-world impact on sexually transmitted disease.

Gates's expertise mongering reached new heights in 2021, when he forcefully asserted himself as a leader on climate change, arguing that his own innovations—like a nuclear power company he started, TerraPower—would help deliver us from a climate disaster. He even secured nearly two billion dollars in support from taxpayers for the company, which has yet to build its first reactor and has already announced major delays.

In short, while Bill Gates may have a fertile mind and grand ambitions, there is also something decidedly undisciplined in his promiscuous desires and wandering eye. We could also draw a similar lesson from his leadership at Microsoft, which was constantly trying to stay ahead of the curve with new technologies—an interactive TV, an e-book reader, a portable media player, a smartphone, a personal digital assistant—that never quite panned out. Microsoft was always hugely profitable not because of its pathbreaking innovation under Gates but because of its monopoly power. "Their technique had always been to see who was winning, then set its sights to copy, overtake, and crush the competition," former Microsoft employee Marlin Eller and Jennifer Edstrom write in their book *Barbarians Led by Bill Gates: Microsoft from the Inside*.

Edstrom and Eller's book recounts Bill Gates's endless managerial snafus, failed strategic leadership, reorgs, and "monkey wrenches" that led to waste, duplication, and inefficiencies. One argument they make in the book is that Microsoft succeeded despite itself—despite its despotic and capricious chairman; despite its lumbering, labyrinthine bureaucracy; and often despite the existence of better products in the marketplace. "Some people like to use their talent and creativity to build things wonderful to behold," they write. "Others simply want to be in charge. Sadly, as organizations grow, they fill out their ranks with the latter, and Microsoft was no exception. There were too many chains of command to deal with, too many fiefdoms to placate."

Some insiders say the same chaos has taken hold at the Gates Foundation. After pouring billions of dollars into building up a new model of "product-development partnerships"—essentially nonprofit drug companies—the foundation reduced or eliminated support for many because they weren't moving fast enough. As multiple former grant recipients told me, Gates, instead of accepting how hard it is to create new drugs and vaccines, impulsively changed strategies, moving to in-house development. "Rather than say, 'It's the way it is,' they had to blame someone," one source said.

Foundation staff also widely criticize the foundation's culture of abrupt "reorgs" or "refreshes," suddenly, and seemingly irrationally, lurching from one strategy to another. "There's kind of a constant fear of, 'Will my job be eliminated because of a change in direction of strategy?'" one source told me. "Very arbitrary. Very chaotic."

As this former employee explained it, the foundation's corporate-style refreshes meant constantly bringing in new experts aligned with Gates's new strategies. And sending the old experts packing. "I think that goes back to the [Gates Foundation motto,] 'impatient optimism.' It's the impatient human capital strategy. There's no time to train people, there's only time to hire experts," the source said. The foundation impul-sively decides, "'There's no evidence of success. There's no impact. It's not working. Let's abandon this strategy and these people and go in a new direction. And let's have wins that we can measure fast.'"

On Glassdoor, a website where employees anonymously describe their workplaces, one Gates Foundation staff member described "per-formative layoffs" that kill institutional knowledge and grind the organi-zation to a halt: "New blood is not necessarily better and so much is lost and time wasted getting new people up to speed (especially since they're likely to get laid off 5 years later)." Another reviewer noted, "Higher level staff seem blind to the costs of this churn."

These criticisms are almost a mirror image of those levied by employ-ees of Microsoft. Journalist Kurt Eichenwald, in a long 2012 *Vanity Fair* profile, described the company's culture of routine, arbitrary mass lay-offs as destroying employee morale and productivity, and maiming the company's dynamism throughout the 2000s. While Eichenwald attri-butes this culture to Microsoft's then CEO Steve Ballmer, he could have directed it at the company's then board chairman, Bill Gates.

The Gates Foundation's impetuousness also manifests in its jettison-ing promising projects and doubling down on failed strategies. One for-mer employee told me that Bill Gates had become almost dogmatic about the virtues of a Pfizer contraceptive called Sayana Press, an injection that can be self-administered, saving women in rural areas from having to make long trips to distant clinics. Despite this advantage, foundation staff found that Sayana Press was not popular with users, even when heavily subsidized through charity. Nevertheless, Bill Gates continued to put resources into the project because he, personally, thought it was a good idea. It was a clear distillation of how much control Bill Gates has, and how top-down the organization really is, my source told me.

In 2018, University of Minnesota sociologist Rachel Schurman published an academic paper titled "Micro(soft) Managing a 'Green Revolution' for Africa," examining the business principles that Bill Gates had imported to his foundation's work on agriculture and also his domineering leadership style. Talking to former employees, examining their CVs, and reading publicly available employee reviews on Glassdoor, Schurman diagnosed a "managing up" culture in which staff organized their work toward one ultimate goal: pleasing Bill Gates.

"BMGF's professional staff have learned to focus on the man they consider the smartest in the world and to look to him for approval. This feature of the foundation's organizational culture inverts what *should* be the Gates Foundation's primary source of affirmation and accountability: those whose lives they seek to improve," Schurman wrote. "As a result, the intended beneficiaries of the Foundation's largesse are treated as passive objects of development rather than complex, knowledgeable social actors."

The same cult of Gates existed at Microsoft. The male-dominated corporate workforce, for example, would even ape Gates's iconic behavior of rocking in his chair in meetings. Melinda French Gates, in her autobiography, recalls another common behavior at Microsoft: the ego-driven, violent verbal clashes—"This wasn't just a spirited exchange; it was a brash, escalating face-off, almost a brawl, and I was thinking, 'Wow, is this how you have to be to do well here?!'" What she doesn't acknowledge is that it was her husband who drove this culture—and who was, himself, probably the biggest bully and fiercest antagonist in the office.

This big-man culture appears alive and well in at least some places at the Gates Foundation. One former foundation employee told Schurman, "You still have the need to show that you're the smartest. . . . So how do you display that? You display that by being very obnoxious, passive aggressive, by being critical of someone else's project—always with *the most intellectual of reasons*—always having a goal of having the bigger project or the one that Bill and Melinda like more, always being told by your grantees and the world how smart and wonderful you are, because they want your money."

One former staff member I interviewed told me they had a difficult transition out of the foundation, realizing how aggressive and supercilious their years at the foundation had made them. "I had a lot of bad behaviors I had to reset once I left Gates," the source noted. "Lots of type A personalities. The louder the voice, the more likely people recognized you. Lots of toxic male personalities that are not very good, but you kind of need to do them to get noticed by your leadership and your co-chairs. A lot of jockeying."

Other former employees I interviewed described simply suffering through the cult of Gates, guided by the belief that the foundation, for all its faults and despite Bill Gates, had the capacity to do good. Whatever their disposition, employees are unlikely to last long in an institution that roots its identify in efficiency, effectiveness, and equity building that constitutionally it cannot achieve.

Many of the problems with the Gates Foundation that I cite in this book track back to its size, like, for example, its ability to monopolize entire fields of inquiry or areas of public policy. What this chapter shows is that its size is also bad for the foundation itself. Its mission creep has atrophied the foundation's dynamism; its micromanaging has gravely diminished many charitable projects; its endless strategy refreshes have created internal chaos and hurt employee morale; and its profligate spending on its sumptuous headquarters and million-dollar salaries has created ever more distance between the foundation and its intended beneficiaries, people who live on only a few dollars a day.

The problem is that there is no earthly way to course-correct. Bill Gates has surrounded himself with a crew of well-wishers and sycophants, and has created an institutional culture that refuses to engage with criticism. Tens, possibly hundreds, of billions of dollars will continue to flow into the Gates Foundation's coffers in the decades ahead, further weighing it down. Unless Bill Gates is removed from the foundation, this money will be invested (or wasted) in creating an ever larger, ever more chaotic bureaucracy, one that is not only increasingly inefficient but also increasingly insensitive to the damage it is causing.

Science

Reetika Khera remembers when she got the email. The subject line read, "Eminent Panel, India Consensus, US$10,000." Khera, an economics professor at the Indian Institute of Technology, said she initially thought it was a scam. And after reading the email closely, she still wasn't sure.

The message came from the Copenhagen Consensus Center, a think tank in Denmark that boasted of its funding from the Gates Foundation in the first sentence of the invitation. Copenhagen wanted Khera to participate in a research conference where she and other eminent scholars would identify "the smartest solutions to some of India's most pressing development challenges, bringing economic evidence to inform state level policy decisions." The invitation made clear that this wasn't a purely academic exercise: the panel would interface directly with political leaders and the media to "spark a state-wide and potentially national debate on policy priorities."

Khera said she was astounded by the enormous sum of money she was being offered—a ten-thousand-dollar fee plus travel costs and other assistance—and by the brazenly transactional nature of the invitation. "What was distasteful about that was that the amount that they were offering was in the subject line of that email, a bait, almost—to make sure you click on it and read it," she told me by email after our phone interview. "I wonder if they were trying to enhance their own credibility and reputation, leaning on the credibility and reputation of academics like me." It didn't help that the email had come from Copenhagen

Consensus Center president Bjorn Lomborg, who has made a name for himself minimizing the threats of climate change. (Copenhagen did not respond to questions sent by email.)

For years, the Gates Foundation has leaned on Copenhagen, which helps recruit experts and drums up facts and figures that seem to support Bill Gates's worldview. In 2019, Gates wrote a long op-ed for the *Wall Street Journal* based on research from the center, which he described as "a think tank that uses sophisticated algorithms and the best available data to compare alternate poverty-fighting strategies." As he reported, Copenhagen had determined that his foundation's $10 billion in spending on vaccines, bed nets, and drugs had returned $200 billion in social and economic benefits. "What if we had invested $10 billion in energy projects in the developing world? In that case, the return would have been $150 billion. What about infrastructure? $170 billion. By investing in global health institutions, however, we exceeded all of those returns," Gates wrote. He did not mention that his private foundation funds the Copenhagen Consensus Center; nor was he crystal clear that his foundation had directly worked with the center to develop these estimates.

This arrangement in many ways defines the foundation's engagement with the scientific enterprise, an area where Gates has become one of most important private-sector funders in the world. The foundation has donated more than $12 billion to universities and helped underwrite more than thirty thousand scientific journal articles. This charitable giving allows the foundation to shape entire fields of research and to secure an astonishing level of epistemic power—influencing what we know about the foundation and how we think about it. "There is not a single organization working in global health that is not somehow related—most likely financially related—to the Gates Foundation," said Adam Fejerskov of the Danish Institute for International Studies. "And, of course, that is a huge problem, because it makes us ask who is setting the agenda in terms of what is being researched and what is not being researched."

According to the academic database Web of Science, the foundation, for example, is the second-largest private-sector funder of research appearing in the scientific journal *Vaccine* (after GlaxoSmithKline). Foundation employees also publish their own research extensively in the journal, having coauthored more than one hundred papers. Additionally, the head of the Gates Foundation's pneumonia program, Keith Klugman, sits on the editorial board of the journal. (He also sits on the board of the *Journal of Global Antimicrobial Resistance.*)

We see a variety of similar relationships throughout academic publishing, where the Gates Foundation acts as a funder, author, journal editor, and adviser. It has also built a wide network of influence through financial ties to top academic researchers and journal editors. The foundation, for example, funds commissions and high-profile leadership programs, like the Postsecondary Value Commission and WomenLift Health, that invite the participation of high-profile researchers.

Eric Rubin, the editor of the *New England Journal of Medicine*, has coauthored nineteen scientific papers that disclose funding from the Gates Foundation. At the same time, during his tenure as editor, the journal has published dozens of studies funded or authored by the Gates Foundation. "No foundation or nonprofit organization has any influence on my publications, and no funder has any influence on articles that the Journal publishes," Rubin told me by email.

Yet, a reasonable person could question this. At the beginning of the Covid-19 pandemic, Rubin's journal published a long commentary by Bill Gates in which he prescribed how governments should respond. Given that Bill Gates has no medical training, why was he given real estate in one of the most prestigious medical journals to play expert on the most important public health crisis in decades? Should we be surprised that Gates's commentary had many blind spots? He failed to mention Covid-19 testing or social distancing, for example—two early interventions that were essential to arresting transmission and preventing infections and death.

Gates, notably, also did not enumerate or detail his financial conflicts of interest for readers, as the journal requires authors to do. While the Gates Foundation had hundreds of millions of dollars invested in pharmaceutical companies, and while Bill Gates may also have personal investments in pharma, he did not provide the names or details of these financial ties, which would have alerted readers to the fact that he or his foundation was in a position to potentially benefit financially from the advice he was giving in the journal. Instead, Gates issued a vague, generalized disclosure that his financial conflicts were "numerous."

"Given the well-known extent of Mr. Gates's financial holdings, we felt comfortable characterizing them as 'numerous,'" Rubin told me in an email. "Readers can reasonably assume that any potential conflict is indeed possible for him." This sentiment seems to boil down to the all-too-common refrain: Bill Gates doesn't have to play by the same rules as everyone else.

As the pandemic wore on, the Gates Foundation eventually became the target of extensive criticism for its aggressive campaigning in support of patents, which were widely seen as limiting the production and distribution of vaccines. As this criticism of Gates spilled into the news media in the spring of 2021, Melissa Barber, a doctoral candidate at Harvard University, recounted on Twitter her own experience working with the Gates Foundation, on a research project related to intellectual property.

> Seattle micromanaged the methods so only a negative assessment was possible, even tho[ugh] the report would be published as independent/evidence based.
>
> At first I thought the Gates folks were just bad at methods. My colleagues were great, and we pushed back and tried to implement a rigorous/fair methodology.
>
> A funder has no business dictating the methods of an independent eval[uation], but we were told we had to do it their way.
>
> If you're wondering if maybe I just misunderstood what was happening, I got so frustrated one day I asked point blank if the entire point of the evaluation was to justify shutting down the initiative, and I guess they were so surprised they answered honestly and said yes.
>
> I left that job soon after and have been afraid to tell this story publicly b[e]c[ause] it's hard to find a job in health systems where Gates isn't at least indirectly involved.
>
> But this to say—even in the rare times Gates funds orgs pushing against the ip [intellectual property] status quo, be wary.

Barber's story describes not only the Gates Foundation's willingness to bend research to advance its agenda but also the complex avenues it has to do this. In science, the answer you get depends on the question you ask, the assumptions you make, and the data and methods you use. And this is where a researcher's, or a funder's, bias can change outcomes. As Barber explained it, the Gates Foundation "micromanaged" and "dictated" the methods, which forced the research down one path— toward the results and conclusion Gates wanted.

As reported earlier in this book, the head of the WHO's malaria program in 2007 alleged that the Gates Foundation's expansive funding of malaria research was hurting science by pushing the research community into "a cartel" where independent, critical viewpoints could not be raised. This too is an important dimension of Gates's funding influence. By using its money to amplify the voices of scientists who agree with its agenda, it can marginalize other perspectives.

The Gates Foundation's influence over research is well known, but many observers are reluctant to criticize the foundation publicly. As Melissa Barber noted, she had been afraid to tell her story publicly because so many jobs in the field of global health depended on Gates money. Simply put, many scientists are reluctant to bite the hand that feeds them, or that may one day feed them, a phenomenon that academic researchers call "the Bill chill."

Scholars I interviewed—who asked for anonymity—offered consistent, independent accounts of Gates's meddling in scientific research to make it line up with the foundation's agenda. One researcher working for a Gates-funded organization said it was normal to show drafts of studies to the foundation, giving them an opportunity to shape the research, which they did. Another source told me that when they applied for a job at the foundation, the interviewers made a point of describing how much influence the foundation had over the research it funded—both in the design of studies and in how the results were presented.

Such behavior speaks to the ways that monied interests seek to quietly influence science the same way they seek to influence politics. Securing favorable research advances bottom lines, gains regulatory approval, pushes legislators to adopt industry-friendly "science-based" policies, and inspires friendly media coverage. When powerful funders are involved in scientific research, the findings and results routinely support the funder's agenda. This well-documented bias, called the funding effect, appears across a wide range of research fields.

It's tempting to imagine the Gates Foundation having no "bottom line"—and no bias—as a humanitarian charity. And this is what makes its influence so malign. We imagine the foundation's role in science as an independent, neutral, check-writing charity, supporting science for the sake of advancing knowledge. In reality, the Gates Foundation, like Big Pharma and Big Tobacco, has deeply vested interests in the research it funds, which it calls on to deliver favorable results—whether it is tallying the millions of lives it is saving, studying the merits of its interventions, or publishing evaluations that support its ideological position on issues like intellectual property rights.

This doesn't mean that all Gates-funded researchers are hacks or sellouts. Many of the sources I leaned on to write this book are funded by the Gates Foundation and feel deeply conflicted about it—but they don't always feel there's another option. Likewise, among the tens of thousands of scientific papers the Gates Foundation has helped fund, we should expect to find important and valuable studies. This chapter isn't arguing that everything the foundation touches is always and at all times corrupted but, rather, it intends to show how the foundation's money can distort science. The threat Gates poses is in the aggregate, in the power it wields as a major funder to manipulate science when it wants to.

There are, of course, limits to Gates's influence. Researchers like Reetika Khera have said no to Bill Gates's funding. Melissa Barber bravely blew the whistle. And an impressive cadre of researchers in the social sciences (anthropology, geography, sociology, etc.), which Gates does not generally fund, have published a robust body of scholarship critical of the foundation. From its first days of operation, accomplished, high-profile scientists and researchers have raised questions about the aims and legitimacy of the Gates Foundation. So, it's not that critical research doesn't exist. It's that it doesn't have the same visibility in the scientific discourse, or the same influence in the public discourse, as the work Gates funds. To a very large extent, what we know about the Gates Foundation comes from the Gates Foundation itself.

CHRIS MURRAY IS a towering figure in the world of global health—and he enjoys a level of prestige and wealth like few others in academia. He's one of the highest-paid workers on the State of Washington's payroll, for example. In his position as director of the University of Washington's Institute for Health Metrics and Evaluation (IHME), he makes almost as much as the university president—around $800,000 in 2021. He's also one of the rare scientists about whom biographies are written while they are still alive.

In the 2015 book, *Epic Measures: One Doctor. Seven Billion Patients*, author Jeremy N. Smith describes Murray's pioneering work with health estimates as an extension of his medical training. Instead of treating individual patients, he's diagnosing the globe, using Big Data to solve a big problem: in a normal year on the planet, approximately sixty million people die, but most of them pass from this earth without an autopsy or medical records citing a cause.

Knowing why and where people are dying is crucial to improving global health, and this is what makes Murray's work with "health metrics" so important and influential. His scientific studies are among the most cited published research anywhere in science. Yet, with Murray's big ambitions also comes a massive ego, one that has made him a deeply polarizing figure in science. The field of global health is littered with war stories of researchers who have had run-ins and blowups with Murray, many of them beginning the same way: with a request that he show his work.

Colin Mathers, a private consultant, told me that, in his previous position managing health statistics at the World Health Organization, he served as a scientific adviser to the IHME, but he left because Murray would not share basic information about how he formulated his estimates. "We felt that without access to the data, we couldn't put our names to the results," Mathers said in an interview.

Sam Clark of Ohio State University said that when he asked the

IHME to provide the source code for a tool it used in its published estimates, the institute engaged in years of "obfuscation and blatant noncooperation" and later published a scientific paper attacking his work.

Another academic researcher asked to speak with me anonymously, saying he wanted to avoid provoking Murray, who turns "professional disagreements into personal accusations."

"Chris Murray has always had one of these kind of force-of-nature personalities," Andrew Noymer, a demographer at the University of California, Irvine, told me. "He does what he wants, when he wants—accountable to no one."

Smith's *Epic Measures*, more a hagiography than a biography, describes Murray as believing that "scientific progress relies on picking fights." The book recounts an incident in which Murray accused an academic researcher of inflating child mortality estimates 10 percent higher than his own. "He knows that deaths translate into money for child health programs. Deaths are money," Murray is quoted as saying. "Who's right? That's the only question. All that matters is being right."

Murray is not right, but he's also not wrong. Billions of dollars in spending—from health ministries, foreign aid offices, and philanthropists—lie in the balance of the health metrics enterprise. Inflating or deflating the incidence or prevalence of different diseases can affect funding decisions. Likewise, when health metrics show that a given intervention works—when we see infection or mortality numbers dropping—public policy can change. Getting health metrics right is important, which is why transparency, accountability, and independence are so essential. It is for this reason that scholars so widely question why Chris Murray—and Bill Gates—are in charge of this vital effort.

Bill Gates was a longtime fan of Murray's work leading up to the creation of the IHME, the foundation's highest-profile research project. Years before Gates provided seed money—and eventually more than six hundred million dollars—he had read a World Bank study Murray coauthored on the "global burden of disease," citing it as inspiring his decision to devote most of his philanthropic spending to fighting disease. "I saw . . . that 12 million children are dying every year," Gates told *Scientific American* in 2014. "Wow! It was mind-blowing to me that these preventable diseases—pneumonia, diarrhea, malaria and some other infections that infants get—had such a huge impact. That was the first time it dawned on me that it's not hundreds of different diseases causing most of the problem—it's a pretty finite number." Murray's research made Gates understand not only where to prioritize his spending but also the importance of health metrics more generally. If he was going to spend billions of dollars, he needed to measure and evaluate the effects of his spending.

When the Gates Foundation first got up and running, the World Health Organization had a robust health metrics program in place. Chris Murray had actually helped run it at one point. In the early 2000s, a change in leadership at the WHO—and Murray's brash managerial style—led to a falling-out, and Murray went on to become a vocal critic of the WHO, citing its "potential for manipulating the data." Could the WHO really be an impartial assessor of global disease when it was subject to political pressure from its member nations? The WHO, Murray reported, was simply "ill suited for the role of global monitoring and evaluation of health . . . We believe that the only viable solution will be to create a new, independent, health monitoring organisation."

What Murray did not clearly disclose was that he himself planned to run this new organization. He first secured a promise of $115 million from tech billionaire (and onetime Bill Gates adversary) Larry Ellison to start his new research institute at Harvard. For reasons that are not totally clear, Ellison abandoned the project before it got off the ground. The student newspaper at Harvard, the *Crimson*, citing an anonymous source, reported that "Ellison had expressed disenchantment with Murray in private meetings on his yacht."

His ambitions undimmed, Murray sought out another benefactor from the pleasure-craft class of American aristocracy. This took him to Seattle, where, with Bill Gates's money, he launched the IHME in 2007.

Gates undoubtedly liked Murray's Big Data approach to global health, but he may also have seen in Murray a man cut from the same cloth: a hard-driving personality with an entrepreneurial, combative spirit, someone with the rare combination of technical know-how and business acumen—and a desire to dominate. "Chris is super-good, but he likes controversy—and he doesn't back down," Gates said in an interview in 2014. "For the job of administering the normative database, he's not absolutely the perfect person."

While Gates uses the term *normative database*, others use *monopoly*. "In a relatively short period of time, the IHME has exerted a certain kind of hegemony or dominance on global health metrics production," Manjari Mahajan, a professor of international affairs at the New School, said in an interview. "It's a kind of monopoly of knowledge production, of how to know global health trends in the world. And that produces a concentration of epistemic power that should make anybody uncomfortable."

That hegemony meant overtaking the WHO as the leading purveyor of health metrics. One former official from the WHO, which Gates also heavily funds, told me, "We were told we had to work with IHME, and the people that IHME doesn't like were sidelined. . . . We were instructed to replace our statistics with IHME statistics. Now WHO is publishing documents with IHME statistics that have not been vetted by [member] countries." By controlling the data, or the estimates, that define the global burden of disease, Chris Murray and Bill Gates also have the power to control the narrative of the entire field of global health.

"What becomes problematic is when these numbers are imbued with authority. When those numbers actually . . . change the way institutions perceive health problems in certain countries, then it becomes a question of . . . will this country get funding to fight HIV depending on what the estimate of prevalence looks like?" noted Marlee Tichenor, an anthropologist at Durham University, in an interview. "In a lot of ways, these estimates shape what can and cannot be done." Tichenor sees a fundamental conflict of interest between the Gates Foundation being key "financiers of global health initiatives" while also controlling the "means by which we judge whether they succeed or not." Much of the "lives-saved" mongering that goes into Gates's public relations, for example, is based on numbers produced by the Gates-funded IHME.

Indeed, if Murray's criticism—or condemnation—of the WHO was that it was vulnerable to pressure from member nations, don't we also have to accept that the IHME is itself extremely vulnerable to outside pressure—from the Gates Foundation, which has its own interests in what the numbers show? Why does it make more sense for the IHME to exist in the private fiefdom of Bill Gates than in a democratically run institution like the WHO? Or, bigger picture, why should any institution have a monopoly? Why not create a vibrant scientific discourse with many competing bodies furnishing estimates?

Bill Gates believes the IHME "democratizes information" by bringing together 281,586 data sources from national health ministries, private insurers, and the scientific literature to a public-facing academic institute. The IHME then runs this vast data through complex analyses to present detailed portraits of the state of health, along with a growing body of other metrics, in virtually every corner of the globe. The institute's website offers interactive maps that allow users to drill down to virtually any village in sub-Saharan Africa, for example, to find out how many years of education people have; how incidences of malaria, HIV, and lower respiratory infections are changing over time; who has access to piped water; even how many men are circumcised.

Again, the numbers found in these maps aren't hard data but, rather, estimates—educated guesses, really—based on whatever data is available. The Gates Foundation, instead of focusing its money and energy on building up health records and infrastructure in poor nations to collect actual data about death and disease (the way rich nations do), has created a high-tech apparatus in Seattle to churn out good-enough estimates that flatten the Global South into best guesses. This has raised criticism that the IHME's work effectively amounts to a kind of "data imperialism."

"It creates an illusion of knowledge. It tells people in a lot of [poor nations] that they don't know what they know about themselves. That what you think you know, you don't know," Seye Abimbola, a senior lecturer at the University of Sydney, said. "That is the colonial experience."

A perhaps even more fundamental question concerns the quality of the IHME's work. Scholars widely describe the IHME as a "black box," a Wizard of Oz–like production that is carefully organized to disallow anyone from seeing behind the curtain. "It's quite impossible to criticize or, indeed, comment on their methods, since they are completely opaque," Max Parkin, of the International Network for Cancer Treatment and Research, told me.

Peter Byass, now-deceased professor of global health at Sweden's Umeå University, offered a similar critique. "From a scientific point of view, that makes it impossible for anyone to replicate or verify the estimates," he told me.

Ruth Etzioni, a professor of public health sciences at the Fred Hutchinson Cancer Research Center, echoed these criticisms. "It's impossible to do what they're trying to do rigorously. . . . The data is just not there to really quantify the impact of some of these diseases," she told me. "Instead of saying, 'You know what? That's not possible,' [the IHME says,] 'Here are some numbers.' You've naturally got yourself in an overpromising situation."

The IHME counters that "no estimate of a problem is interpreted as an estimate of no problem." And in an e-mail, it defended its estimates as transparent and published with statistical confidence intervals that inform users about the limitations of its work. Etzioni sees a pattern in its pushing its findings into the limelight while relegating "key caveats and uncertainties" to the fine print. She pointed out that even when the institute made a major mistake in its early Covid-19 projections—it had been using a bad model—it never issued a clear mea culpa.

And it was the high stakes of the pandemic that brought a new level of scrutiny—and competition—to the IHME. A number of researchers began publishing estimates, and began to see, in real time, what they had long suspected—that the IHME's complex estimates are not always particularly good or accurate. At times, they might even be hurting public health.

In the spring of 2020, U.S. president Donald Trump held a press conference in which his advisers pointed to IHME estimates as evidence that the pandemic would rapidly peak and then wind down in the weeks ahead. "Throughout April, millions of Americans were falsely led to believe that the epidemic would be over by June because of IHME's projections," data scientist Youyang Gu told me. "I think that a lot of states reopened [from lockdowns] based on their modeling."

Gu was one of many modelers who ended up competing with, and outperforming, the IHME during the Covid-19 pandemic, independently producing projections that appeared more accurate than Bill Gates's half-billion-dollar health metrics enterprise. Again and again during the pandemic, scholars pointed out major mistakes and errors in the IHME's research, openly lampooning the institute on social media. Yet, no matter how often the IHME's estimates proved wrong, or how loudly the wider research enterprise screamed, "The emperor has no clothes!" the message never quite got through.

"Many people do not understand how modeling works," Chris Murray wrote in a *Los Angeles Times* op-ed, brushing aside his critics before plowing ahead with more highly questionable, headline-grabbing projections. The IHME, for example, began charting the course for the pandemic many months in advance, while competing modelers more conservatively made projections only a few weeks into the future. This put the IHME's highly contested estimates in a position to guide policy-making ahead of other models, and draw more media attention.

"It seems to be a version of the playbook Trump follows," the demographer Sam Clark told me in 2020. "Absolutely nothing negative sticks, and the more exposure you get, the better—no matter what. It's really stunning, and I don't know any other scientific personality or organization that is able to pull it off quite like IHME."

When I first reached out to the institute in 2019 and asked about its controversial reputation in the academic community, an IHME spokesperson shot back, "Who is making such criticism, and where has the criticism been published or stated publicly?" Internally, however, the IHME was well aware of this criticism. In correspondence with the Gates Foundation years earlier, released through a public records request, the institute reported receiving criticism as a "black box," which it acknowledged was a potential "risk" to its future success. Similarly, the institute publicly pushes back on allegations that it has too much power, telling me that "for nearly all outcomes that we publish, there are alternative sources of estimates." Yet elsewhere, it has called itself the "gold standard in population health metrics" and "arguably the de facto source for global health accounting."

According to multiple sources, many Gates Foundation staff understand that there are serious problems, if not liabilities, with the IHME. But because Bill Gates personally likes the institute, Murray's project has become too big to fail—one more illustration of Bill Gates's top-down style of leadership.

Peter Byass noted in an interview that if the IHME were publicly funded, it would have to operate in a far more open and accountable manner. "If you've got enough billions, you can set up a foundation, and you can make the rules entirely as you wish," he said. The Gates Foundation "is both the rule maker and the rule keeper, in terms of how they choose to scrutinize grant holders. That's their privilege, because that's where they are in the marketplace."

However, the IHME is, technically, a public institution. It's part of the University of Washington and, theoretically, subject to its oversight. In practice, however, many scholars regard it as a private arm of the Gates Foundation. "IHME, by design, exists in this sort of this gray area," noted Andrew Noymer. "It's part of UW, but it's its own institution. It doesn't fully answer to them. It's public when it's fashionable to be public, but private when it suits them."

For most of its existence, the IHME was headquartered a few blocks from the Gates Foundation's offices in Seattle, not on the University of Washington campus. The institute's first temporary offices were actually located in the foundation's former headquarters. One former IHME employee told me the Gates Foundation freely calls in bespoke charts and graphs for Bill Gates's presentations, prompting entire teams of IHME researchers to drop everything else in service to their benefactor. "It really did feel like we were consultants for the Gates Foundation, and the scientific methods we used were often in service of getting the results we wanted . . . or the story he [Murray] thought the Gates Foundation wanted," the source told me. "There are thousands of hours cumulatively spent each year just on one-off requests from Bill Gates that trickle through from the Gates Foundation."

A public records request appeared to confirm this. The IHME, at one point, solicited an additional $1.5 million from the Gates Foundation to address "time-sensitive requests from BMGF leadership [that] often require repurposing IHME staff on the fly from other endeavors to meet analytic requests. Each request has had to be satisfied in addition to normal responsibilities, creating a ripple effect across projects."

Public records also show the IHME creating a dedicated team to service the foundation. The IHME's Foundation Response and Engagement Team, according to one grant proposal to the Gates Foundation, was led by Tamer Farag, whose LinkedIn résumé reports that he worked at the Gates Foundation before joining IHME and continued to serve as a "consultant advisor" to Gates while employed at the IHME. (At the same time, notably, Farag also reports serving as an adviser to Mali's Ministry of Health.)

Most revealing of all, Gates's original grant agreement with the IHME in 2007, released through a public records request, gave the foundation sweeping authority over the institute: approval rights over new hires for the institute's executive leadership, approval rights over institute board members, and approval rights over who does external evaluations of IHME and what criteria are used. (Such external evaluations are required by University of Washington bylaws.) Gates also requested "an opportunity to review and approve" press releases and reports related to the work it funds at IHME. The University of Washington signed off on this agreement.

When I first reported this in 2020, sources reached out to me with concern that UW would give such far-reaching influence to a private donor. The American Association of University Professors recommends that schools take steps to preserve "academic autonomy" from funders "by maintaining . . . exclusive academic control over core academic functions," including research evaluations and hiring. Some schools have found themselves in hot water for making the kind of concessions that UW has with Gates. After student activists at George Mason University, a public school in Virginia, uncovered that the Charles Koch Foundation had gained influence over university hiring through its charitable donations, an international scandal ensued. Headlines appeared everywhere from the *New York Times* to the *Guardian*, decrying billionaire industrialist Charles Koch's infringement on academic freedom.

"We're sort of the poster child for 'Don't let this happen to your institution,'" Bethany Letiecq, a former associate professor in the College of Education and Human Development at George Mason (now at the University of Maryland), told me. "And a lot of other universities look to us and say, 'What went wrong? How can we prevent this going forward?'"

I shared with Letiecq my findings about the Gates Foundation, including its purview of hiring, board appointments, evaluations, and press releases. "What we found at [George] Mason [University], similar to what you're finding with Gates, is they're given all kinds of benefits or access or oversight based on their funding. We think that's highly problematic when that comes to academic freedom," she said. "Once these relationships are established, I do think it is concerning, in the sense that they can change the whole mission of the university—to just be servicing their [private donor] interests. Public institutions of higher

education are sort of like the backstop of democracy. They're so important to the democratic function to critique, to demand transparency, to
seek truth and knowledge. I think that these big-money donors, while
they're important to universities . . . there's a serious cost, and I think
universities are super vulnerable." Letiecq said that Koch employed a
dark-money strategy at George Mason: instead of making donations to
the school, which would be subject to public records requests, it made
donations to a private foundation adjacent to the university. More than
80 percent of the Gates Foundation's giving to the University of Washington—$1.5 billion—followed a similar pathway, going to a university-
adjacent foundation.

When I asked the University of Washington Foundation about
these dark-money concerns, it did not respond. Instead, the university
responded on behalf of the foundation. "The same state ethics laws govern, regardless of whether a donation is made to UWF or UW directly,"
the school stated. UW also told me that the UW Foundation is currently
subject to public records requests, though it did not respond to follow-up
questions about whether this was always the case.

It's worth emphasizing that the Gates Foundation is not a typical donor
to UW. The Gates family name is emblazoned across UW's campus—the
William H. Gates Public Service Law Scholarship Program, Mary Gates
Research Scholarships, the Bill & Melinda Gates Chairs in computer
science, Mary Gates Hall. The Gates family—Bill's mother, father, and
two sisters—has over the decades held a variety of high-level positions
at UW, including sitting on its highest governing board, the Board of
Regents, and on the University of Washington Foundation's board.

The university disclaims that Gates has any untoward influence over
the school or that the Gates Foundation enjoys special privileges, for
example, in its funding of the IHME. "It's neither in the university nor the
Gates Foundation's best interests to have a relationship that is not based
on open science. That is what keeps our reputation as a top research university secure. And quite frankly the Gates Foundation wouldn't want to
be criticized for that either, I don't think," said Joe Giffels, senior associate vice provost for research administration and integrity. "The university wants any university activity, including the research that IHME

would do, to be free of undue influence and, in particular, bias from any source, quite frankly."

Giffels was unaware that the IHME had a controversial reputation, telling me, "I've not heard of any [ethical concerns]. And I would have heard of them if there were any." As he described it, the Gates Foundation does little more than write checks. "We would not consider the IHME to be an institute that was, you know, founded by the Gates Foundation. The Gates Foundation has provided a lot of financial support to the IHME—that's at the IHME's request. They [IHME] come up with individual projects, research questions they want to have answered and so on, and then they propose to the Gates Foundation—that the Gates Foundation provide funding for those things, as designed by the IHME. And then Gates either says yes or no," Giffels told me.

I also asked him about the foundation's role in approving new hires at the IHME. "Do we allow sponsors to approve hiring or possibly firing— that sort of thing? No, we don't—in the sense that the university is the employer, they are the employer of record, they are responsible for the employment, and they make final decisions over hiring and firing."

After the interview, I sent Giffels the grant agreement I had uncovered in which the university explicitly agreed to give the Gates Foundation approval rights over new hires for the institute's executive leadership. The university then appeared to reverse course. UW spokesperson Victor Balta sent me an email saying that this kind of influence was normative and routine for donors to UW. "The level of funder involvement outlined in the 2007 grant agreement is in line with the type of review and approval included in many research grant agreements with government funding agencies, institutes and other nonprofit organizations," Balta wrote me in an email. When asked for specific examples, he noted that when a university researcher abandons a government-sponsored research project, the sponsor will play a role in approving who takes over the grant. However, this seems categorically different from the broad influence UW has given Gates—not just in deciding who is in charge of its grant (Chris Murray), but also in holding approval rights over new hires across the institute's executive leadership alongside other rights and privileges.

After many email exchanges, the university began repeating the same answer: "UW would not sign a grant agreement that does not align with our mission and values." What I see in these rote responses, and in UW's failure to meaningfully reconcile the contradictions at hand, is an institution deeply committed to protecting its relationship with a valuable funder. It's a narrative that academics at other institutions know well. "It all sits under that bucket of undue donor influence and the university's willingness to sell academic freedom to the highest bidder," said Letiecq. "Whether it's the Gates Foundation or the Charles Koch Foundation . . . the threat to the academic freedom is the same."

If the Gates Foundation's generous donations have allowed it to play by a different set of rules at the University of Washington, there are other checks and balances in scientific enterprise that should come to bear on the IHME. The currency of science is, to a great extent, the studies that researchers publish in scientific journals. It's here where they describe, debate, and debunk findings. And, before publication, studies first undergo a gauntlet of scrutiny by editors and peer reviewers, who rigorously assess the merits of the researchers' work.

In this world of academic publishing, the IHME is a heavyweight champion, putting out some of the most widely cited studies in the world, many of which are published in *The Lancet*, one of the world's leading medical journals. While most scholars are lucky to publish one research article in *The Lancet* during a decades-long career, Chris Murray has published more than one hundred. He has made *The Lancet* home to most of the IHME's biggest studies, which lay out the "global burden of disease" that other researchers look to for health metrics. When scientists publish their own research on a given disease, they commonly cite IHME numbers on mortalities and infections. And each time a researcher cites IHME's studies in *The Lancet*, this increases the journal's "impact factor," a measure of its relative importance in the scientific literature. This can translate into prestige and influence for the journal, if not also raise subscription rates and advertising revenue for *The Lancet*'s for-profit owner, Elsevier.

Some scholars see perverse incentives driving this relationship, alleging that the benefits *The Lancet* derives from publishing IHME research have biased the journal's editorial oversight. Multiple sources I interviewed criticize *The Lancet*'s peer-review process, for example, which puts impossibly short deadlines on extremely complex IHME studies, leading to superficial reviews. "At the end of the day, [the peer-review process] pretends to be a validation of something it is not," Patrick Gerland, a demographer in the United Nations Population Division, told me.

"You can't go through the five thousand pages of tables and figures for *The Lancet* and say, 'I've noticed a mistake on page three thousand five hundred fifty-six, line twenty-five,'" said Peter Byass. "That's just not going to happen." Nevertheless, *The Lancet* publishes five-thousand-page appendices that are labeled as having been peer-reviewed. Scholars also question *The Lancet*'s editorial decision to allow the IHME to publish studies with hundreds of different authors. "You could sign on as a collaborator to IHME, and they'll send out draft papers to you," Colin Mathers explained. "You may or may not read them, you may or may not comment on them, but your name gets to be [included as] an author in the end, and IHME can then claim there are twelve hundred people from [various] countries who have reviewed all the results. I don't know how *The Lancet* squares that . . . with the standard scientific authorship requirements."

David Resnik, a bioethicist at the National Institutes of Health, elaborated on the importance of ethical rules around authorship for me: "When you have this many people, and their roles are ill-defined, you're losing the accountability and responsibility for it. It's not really telling [you] who did what or who did more."

Many feel that the IHME leans on so many authors as political gamesmanship. By offering international researchers the opportunity to coauthor a study in *The Lancet*—a feather in any researcher's cap—the IHME can present its research as far more robust and collaborative than it really is. The institute can also count on coauthors to serve as allies, apologists, and defenders—to deflect criticism of its "data imperialism" or challenge the allegation that the institute is a tightly run monopoly in Seattle.

The IHME insisted to me that it complies with proper authorship guidelines, but days before offering this defense—and shortly after I raised questions—it issued an internal memo announcing new guidelines around authorship and a strict new auditing process.

Perhaps the most striking irregularity in *The Lancet*'s relationship with the IHME concerns the institute's awarding a one-hundred-thousand-dollar prize to the journal's editor, Richard Horton, in 2019. Even inside the IHME, alarms went off. "I would like to understand what the long term thought process was in awarding Horton the prize," one IHME employee said in an internal email, "and how we are expected to defend that decision as staff when criticized for buying our way into the Lancet rather than being published based on the merit of our work?"

In a phone interview in 2019, Horton denied all allegations of impropriety, arguing—oddly—that because the award, called the Roux Prize, had come from the IHME's board of directors, it should be viewed as independent of the institute. "I see it as completely separate, personally," Horton said, noting that IHME board member Dave Roux, a cofounder of the private equity firm Silver Lake, funded the award.

The institute offered its own parsing, saying that the "IHME does not award the Roux Prize; it is the custodian of the prize. Moreover, it is quite implausible that there was any expectation of benefit to the Institute's Board—either collectively or to any individual member—by awarding Dr. Richard Horton the prize in 2019, given his terminal cancer diagnosis."

Years later, Horton continues to edit *The Lancet*—and continues to put the full weight of his journal into elevating the IHME's research. Horton does acknowledge the "very special relationship" his journal has with the IHME, but he defends it as good science. He notes that *The Lancet* publishes estimates from other research institutes, saying this helps create a robust debate that has historically been missing in global health, including during the WHO's reign as the leading purveyor of estimates. "The reason why it's very important to publish these papers in our journal is because it holds IHME accountable," he said in an interview. "If you publish a paper in *The Lancet* . . . scientists can look at that paper and say, 'Okay, do I think this is high-quality science? Do I agree with what they said? And do I agree with their interpretation?' And they can write letters to us, and they can say, 'Actually, we strongly disagree with X, Y, and Z,' and we will publish those letters, and that holds Chris Murray and IHME accountable for their work," Horton said.

"This is the way the science is done. It's self-corrective. . . . You publish the best work you can, then you see who, over time, falls out of view."

Horton's vision of a functioning, incrementalist system of knowledge creation, rich with debate and competition, however, is, in the eyes of many scholars, an alternate reality. What the IHME represents to the wider scientific community is a broken system of science that privileges wealth and power over independence and integrity. "It's a bit like the agenda in many developed countries over the last twenty, thirty years to privatize all sorts of functions that I had thought should properly be in the public domain with checks and balances and so on," Colin Mathers told me. "Gates, just because he charged us all too much for Windows for so long, is now in a position to decide—to change the global health landscape and the numbers, with little ability of others to push back."

Agriculture

Among the most storied corporate villains over the last thirty years, Monsanto ranks as perhaps even more notorious than Microsoft. To be sure, if Bill Gates had decided to put his energy into agriculture instead of computers, the company he would have made would look an awful lot like the seed and agrochemical giant from St. Louis. (Bayer acquired Monsanto in 2018.)

Monsanto's hard-earned reputation for controversy stems in part from the monopoly power it wields over our food system, seeking to control the genetic code of life itself. Over the last two decades, much of the corn and soy grown in the United States has contained genetic traits owned by Monsanto, the most well-known of which is being "Roundup Ready," which refers to the crops' immunity to the herbicide Roundup. That means farmers can spray their fields indiscriminately with weed-killing chemicals, eliminating weeds, while their crops survive thanks to their genetic modification. This presents a major benefit to farmers in terms of labor, as they are spared the hard work of pulling weeds by hand or trying to carefully spray individual weeds. Yet, the expanded use of agrochemicals has drawn concerns related to the environment and human health, which is one reason most nations, including much of Europe, don't grow GMOs (genetically modified organisms).

The GMO model is also expensive, and for it to make financial sense, it is generally used on the largest-scale farms. Growers plant vast acreages of monoculture corn or soy, apply synthetic fertilizer, and then hire crop dusters to blanket the fields with Roundup, the use of which has skyrocketed with the advent of GMOs. All this has been good business for Monsanto, which sells not only Roundup Ready GMO seeds but also the Roundup herbicides used with them.

Monsanto's market power has also reached onto farms in other ways. When farmers buy GMO seeds, they sign technology agreements that restrict how they can use them. And Monsanto isn't shy about verifying that farmers respect the terms and conditions of these agreements. As *Vanity Fair* reported in 2008:

> As interviews and reams of court documents reveal, Monsanto relies on a shadowy army of private investigators and agents in the American heartland to strike fear into farm country. They fan out into fields and farm towns, where they secretly videotape and photograph farmers, store owners, and co-ops; infiltrate community meetings; and gather information from informants about farming activities. Farmers say that some Monsanto agents pretend to be surveyors. Others confront farmers on their land and try to pressure them to sign papers giving Monsanto access to their private records. Farmers call them the "seed police" and use words such as "Gestapo" and "Mafia" to describe their tactics. When asked about these practices, Monsanto declined to comment specifically, other than to say that the company is simply protecting its patents. . . . Some compare Monsanto's hard-line approach to Microsoft's zealous efforts to protect its software from pirates. At least with Microsoft the buyer of a program can use it over and over again. But farmers who buy Monsanto's seeds can't even do that.

Monsanto has also generated controversy around its influence in the scientific enterprise. The University of California, San Francisco has an online library of documents detailing some of this influence, adjacent to its trove of documents examining Big Tobacco's industry playbook. As one of legion examples, in 2013 Monsanto contacted a number of academic scientists, suggesting that they produce policy papers based on talking points that the company furnished—which some professors did without disclosing Monsanto's role in the papers. One academic caught up in this scandal was Harvard economist Calestous Juma, who had also partnered on agricultural work with the Gates Foundation.

Gates funded some of Juma's academic research—and even created a fellowship to honor him after he died. And when Juma engaged in political advocacy activities, like a 2015 letter to the Food and Drug Administration in support of GMOs, he trumpeted his affiliation with the Gates Foundation but, naturally, made no disclosures about his close work with Monsanto. As with many of the areas where Gates works, the foundation has become a valuable front for industry ambitions, a charitable face for a corporate agenda.

The reason the Gates Foundation and Monsanto both worked so closely with Juma was what he represented for them: an African scholar—he was from Kenya—housed at a prestigious university in the West who could help promote Gates and Monsanto's shared goal of introducing GMOs to Africa. "The biggest area of arable land in the world that is underutilized at this point is in Africa," Monsanto executive Mark Edge noted in a 2016 news story that discussed the company's philanthropic partnership with the Gates Foundation. "There's a real business argument to be made. . . . Your choice is can you go in now, and you know that you're not going to make much money in it but can you lay those foundations for 10 or 15 years from now where it's going to be?"

Bill Gates spins the narrative differently, leaning on humanitarian arguments: "It's fine for people from rich, well-fed nations with productive farms to decline the use of GMOs. But they should not be allowed to impose their preferences on Africa."

At the same time, Gates doesn't appear to have much compunction about imposing his own preferences. As a self-described technologist, he is a true believer in GMOs, even as many experts question whether this technology can really benefit the smallholder farmers in sub-Saharan Africa whom the foundation targets. Asked in an interview with the Verge in 2015 whether poor nations had the necessary regulatory capacity to ensure that GMOs were safely tested and cultivated—and whether the foundation might step in to provide "quasi-regulatory oversight"—Bill Gates didn't blink:

We can fund training, so that they can have scientists who can staff their safety commission. We can make sure the [scientific] studies, they're done and done well. We can incent the companies that are making these great seeds for rich countries—we can work with them to make sure that it's at least available—actually at a lower price because that tiered price where poor countries get a better price has worked so well in medicines—that same type of thing we can make sure happens with these crops. But at the end of the day, they get to decide—which vaccines, which drugs, which seeds are okay. That's their country. But their expertise is developing, so I feel like they will make a good choice.

Gates's candor is remarkable as he, essentially, explains how his foundation seeks to control the entire approval process—except for the rubber stamp at the very end. He's training the African scientists who will regulate GMOs. He's creating the scientific studies they review. He's even intervening in private markets to make sure GMOs are available. And he isn't exaggerating.

Bill Gates has become one of the most powerful voices in African agriculture, a vastly underfunded sector where Gates Foundation donations have translated into far-reaching influence over public policy. The foundation has spent $6.5 billion on all agricultural projects, including lead funding to some of the most prominent agricultural organizations operating on the continent—organizations that look and feel African and often have the name "Africa" in their title. These surrogates—like the Alliance for a Green Revolution in Africa and the African Agricultural Technology Foundation, seem to function the same way Monsanto's corporate front groups once did: advancing their sponsor's agenda while claiming to be independent, or science-based, or farmer-forward, or African-led.

Gates's ambition to introduce GMOs is just one agenda item in a larger effort to industrialize African agriculture, making more productive, higher-yielding farms through expanded use of what are called "inputs"—chemicals, fertilizers, new seeds, and irrigation. It's a project that Gates has undertaken in close partnership with the multinational companies that sell these inputs, companies that have long eyed Africa as an untapped market. For the foundation, the goal is not profits but yields: "the need to find solutions so farmers—especially those in the poorest countries—have better tools and knowledge so they can grow enough food to feed their families."

Gates's interventions, however, have failed to deliver the "revolution" the foundation promised. Despite decades of political lobbying by vested interests, only one African nation grows any significant quantities of GMO food crops—South Africa. Likewise, we haven't seen the major decreases in hunger or increases in crop yields and farmers' incomes that Bill Gates promised his agricultural agenda would deliver.

The failures, however, don't mean the Gates Foundation isn't having an impact. "In so many ways, they are very much successful because they sold a narrative," Million Belay, head of the Alliance for Food Sovereignty in Africa, told me in an interview. "The narrative is African seeds are tired. The land of Africans is not fertile. The knowledge that Africans have is archaic. In order to produce more food, you need hybrid variety seeds. The soil is very tired, so you have to target it with lots of chemicals. Also, this is market-based agriculture, part of the neoliberal ideology."

The premise of the Gates Foundation's work is that African nations don't have the expertise or capacity or tools to manage their own food systems—that they need professionals and experts from the Global North to help them. The foundation does this by working with politicians and policy makers to change the governing laws in the African countries where it works, effectively acting as a lobbyist, placing its technical experts inside government agencies and even helping to create, fund, and staff entirely new agencies, like the Agricultural Transformation Agency (ATA) in Belay's home country of Ethiopia.

This new body—an "independent unit to support the Ministry of Agriculture to accelerate agricultural growth and augment the Ministry's work"—has benefited from at least $27 million from the Gates Foundation. In 2010, Ethiopian legislators codified the new agency, and a year later, a Gates Foundation senior program officer, Khalid Bomba, left the foundation to become the head of the ATA. A year after that, the foundation announced "the appointment of its first official representative in Ethiopia . . . [who] will serve as the foundation's liaison to the federal government of Ethiopia and the African Union." A rapid revolving door of staff between Gates and the Ethiopian agency followed in the years ahead. One group of researchers cited the ATA as being instrumental in fostering greater private-sector engagement in Ethiopian farming, including opening up new markets for seed and agrochemical giant DuPont.

As another example, the Gates-funded Alliance for a Green Revolution in Africa (AGRA) describes having worked on, over a recent four-year period, sixty-eight different policy reforms in Burkina Faso, Ethiopia, Ghana, Nigeria, Tanzania, Rwanda, and the East African Community (an intergovernmental body)—on everything from trade policy to seed laws to pesticides to regulations over fertilizer markets. "A combination of AGRA's policy and advocacy approach reduces the normal timetable to get agricultural policy reforms completed throughout the administrative and legislative processes," the group reports on its website. "All of this is aimed at strengthening effective and functional seed, fertilizer and market systems."

Gates's heavy hand also shapes national research agendas and training programs, according to Joeva Rock, an anthropologist at the University of Cambridge. "If it [Gates] were to disappear overnight, there would be immense repercussions for all types of institutions—anywhere from public breeding initiatives . . . to public educational institutions," Rock told me. "This isn't just shutting down these programs; it's shutting down training for scientists, for students."

This level of dependency and Bill Gates's top-down political maneuvering have proven controversial among the farmers Gates claims to help, and in 2021 and 2022, the pushback reached new levels of visibility, notably including a high-profile op-ed in *Scientific American* titled "Bill Gates Should Stop Telling Africans What Kind of Agriculture Africans Need." The piece was written by Million Belay and Bridget Mugambe of the Alliance for Food Sovereignty in Africa, the largest civil society organization in all of Africa, representing two hundred million farmers, fishers, pastoralists, and indigenous peoples across the continent.

We welcome investment in agriculture on our continent, but we seek it in a form that is *democratic and responsive* to the people at the heart of agriculture, not as a top-down force that ends up concentrating power and profit into the hands of a small number of multinational companies.

While describing how GM[O] seeds and other technology would solve hunger in African countries, Bill Gates *claimed* that "it's a sovereign decision. No one makes that for them." But the massive resources of the Gates Foundation, which he co-chairs, have had an outsized influence on African scientists and policymakers, with the result that food systems on our continent are becoming ever more market-oriented and corporate-controlled.

Belay told me in an interview that the Gates Foundation's charitable work on agriculture bears all the hallmarks of colonial power: seeking to modernize and civilize African nations while also advancing commercial interests, like pushing farmers to buy genetically modified seeds, fertilizers, chemicals, and other technology from multinational companies headquartered outside the continent. "When our agriculture is considered backward, and the only solution proffered is technology, then there is a civilization agenda," Belay said. "And that civilization agenda is not to civilize us but to bind us to the vagaries of this technology."

The Gates Foundation's intended beneficiaries have very widely and very explicitly asked Bill Gates to stop helping. A letter in 2021 with more than two hundred signatories called for the defunding of AGRA, Gates's flagship project in Africa. "Since the onset of AGRA's program in 2006, the number of undernourished people across these 13 countries [where AGRA works] has increased by 30 percent," the letter noted. "AGRA has unequivocally failed in its mission to increase productivity and incomes and reduce food insecurity, and has in fact harmed broader efforts to support African farmers."

Another protest emerged when the UN secretary-general announced that AGRA's president had been named Special Envoy to the 2021 UN Food Systems Summit. More than 150 organizations called on the United Nations to revoke the appointment, saying AGRA's presence "will result in another forum that advances the interests of agribusiness at the expense of farmers and our planet. . . . With 820 million people hungry and an escalating climate crisis, the need for significant global action is urgent."

Hundreds of religious groups and faith leaders also sent an open letter to Bill Gates, asking him to listen to African farmers rather than imposing his vision on them. "While we are grateful to the Bill and Melinda Gates Foundation . . . for its commitment to overcoming food insecurity, and acknowledging the humanitarian and infrastructural aid provided to the governments of our continent, we write out of grave concern that the Gates Foundation's support for the expansion of intensive industrial scale agriculture is deepening the humanitarian crisis."

The groups specifically asked the foundation for a dialogue, but it was months before they got even an initial response and then, finally, a meeting. Shortly after, the Gates Foundation appeared to announce in the news media that it was planning an additional two hundred million dollars in funding for AGRA.

"Truly this shows that no amount of input will dissuade them from supporting a system that is focused on short-term gains," Gabriel Manyangadze of the Southern African Faith Communities' Environment Institute told me. "Their engagement is therefore a public relations exercise as what we are requesting has found no space in their narrative."

If the foundation won't engage in good faith with the people it claims to be helping, that may be because it isn't trying to win hearts and minds. The goal, the overriding ambition, of the foundation is never to establish democratic legitimacy. It is to organize top-down policy changes, usually through antidemocratic means. The foundation believes it knows what is best for African farmers, who must get out of the way so that Gates can help them.

"They fund the researchers, they fund the research, they fund the drafting of laws, they fund projects, they funded agro-dealers, they got things off the ground. . . . It's a lot of money over time," Mariam Mayet of the African Centre for Biosafety told me. "It's just more neocolonialism dressed up in fancy language about empowerment and uplifting and so on. But it's just old-style colonial development and does not serve Africans, does not serve the continent."

Mayet pins Gates's growing influence on the failures of many African governments to step up and be accountable to their own people, saying the Gates Foundation has preyed on weak democratic institutions. "Another future could not be born because of the Gates's agenda and what it funded and stood in the way of—whatever transformation and transition that may have been possible, that could have resulted in less social exclusion, less inequities, less poverty, less marginalization of already vulnerable communities," Mayet said. She then ominously forecast what continuing down this path would bring: "a time bomb."

WHEN THE GATES Foundation creates new NGOs, it likes to use the term *alliance*: the Alliance for Science, the Global Alliance for Improved Nutrition, the Alliance for a Green Revolution in Africa. As the word suggests, these projects lean on allies working in common cause toward a shared goal. Rarely, however, do the targets of Gates's goodwill, the global poor or smallholder farmers, have a seat at the table. In the case of the Alliance for a Green Revolution in Africa, or AGRA, the allies include a bevy of corporate partners: Syngenta, Bayer (Monsanto), Corteva Agriscience, John Deere, Nestlé, and even Microsoft, which is "exploring the use of big data and AI in the digital transformation of AGRA."

AGRA claims that it also works with civil society groups and farmer organizations, but, notably, it does not name them. The group, to its credit, is currently led by someone from Africa—Agnes Kalibata, Rwanda's former agricultural minister. Yet AGRA's first president was Gary Toenniessen, food security director for the Rockefeller Foundation. And it's also true that the initiative would not exist without its white and mostly American funders.

AGRA was conceived of and launched by the Rockefeller and Gates Foundations, and the large majority of its funding comes from Gates—at least $675 million of AGRA's $1.1 billion in reported revenues. In the early years of its operation, most of AGRA's board members appeared to be non-African and/or based outside Africa, including multiple representatives from the Gates and Rockefeller Foundations. Even today, many top brass and board members are not based in Africa—like Rodger Voorhies of the Gates Foundation. Internal policy documents at the Gates Foundation describe AGRA as an example of where it is "creating a new entity and providing significant funding"—and also serving in a governance role over the group.

As late as 2016, a decade after AGRA's creation, a Gates-funded evaluation reported that "external stakeholders noted ambiguity over AGRA's identity, including its perception as an African institution." The evaluation cited a need to "re-fashion its institutional identity" as an "African-led, politically neutral entity that is distinct from BMGF." By 2020, a new Gates evaluation reported success: "AGRA, as a unique African body, is perceived to have more legitimacy to reach governments than other development partners, creating opportunity for effective advocacy. . . . It has the 'ear of government'—that is, highly regarded political access, the sort donors are not in a position to have."

AGRA is a takeoff from the original "green revolution" of the mid-twentieth century—an agricultural development project spearheaded by the Rockefeller and Ford Foundations and supported by the U.S. government. Yesteryear's green revolution, like today's, sought to industrialize agriculture around the world through the use of new seeds, agrochemicals, and irrigation. By increasing yields, the thought was, poor people could produce more food, end hunger, and become self-sufficient in agriculture. With massive investments from foundations and governments, the green revolution initially seemed to see major successes in countries like India, which charted substantial yield increases. Norman Borlaug, often referred to as the "father" of the green revolution, even won a Nobel Peace Prize for this work.

Yet many of the initial gains seemed to diminish or disappear over time. Applying large volumes of synthetic chemicals proved damaging to the soil. And the large funding required to pay for all the new inputs drove farmers into debt and then drove a decades-long wave of suicides. Another problem: input-intensive farming tended to be adopted by, and provide benefits to, the largest, wealthiest farms. Helping big farms get bigger generally means driving smallholder farmers off the land.

Virtually all scholars today acknowledge the green revolution's problems, and many (if not most) see it as a net failure whose harms outweighed its benefits. For Bill Gates, however, it was a black-and-white success. "In the 1960s, there was this thing called the Green Revolution, where new seeds and other improvements drove up agricultural productivity in Asia and Latin America," he said in a 2014 interview. "It saved millions of lives and lifted many people out of poverty. But it basically bypassed sub-Saharan Africa. Today, the average farmer there is only about a third as productive as an American farmer. If we can get that number up, and I think we can, it will help a lot."

Mark Dowie, in his 2001 book, *American Foundations: An Investigative History*, depicts the original green revolution as a cautionary tale: "New philanthropists wishing to learn about the pitfalls of large-scale grant making would be wise to study the fifty-year history of this project." Among other shortcomings Dowie cites, the original green revolution narrowly focused on scientific approaches to increasing yields, which were supposed to make food more widely available. There was little appreciation for the fact that, no matter how much yields were increased, the world's poorest people still wouldn't have enough money to buy food. That's true even today. Across the globe, there are now more than enough calories to feed everyone, even as a billion people around the world are food insecure. The problem with hunger is not our food supply—or not just the supply. It's also access. It's money.

Yet, in the narrow ambitions of philanthropy and international development, the goal is often to tackle the problems you think you can solve, that will rack up quick wins, rather than addressing root causes. For the original green revolutionaries, this meant a laser focus on increasing yields through research and development. "Science was something with which Rockefeller [Foundation] trustees felt completely comfortable," Dowie writes. "Economic justice, on the other hand, suggested socialism." And worries about socialism were a key driver of the original green revolution, which sought to foreclose on a possible red revolution. Hungry people, the green revolutionaries worried, translated into social unrest and an opportunity for Communist propaganda to take hold. "So for the first forty years of the Green Revolution, the growing surplus of food barely moved to where it was needed most—not because the government and nongovernmental international agencies weren't trying to improve the economic lot of the poor," Dowie writes. "They simply couldn't do so fast enough to compensate for the large numbers of subsistence farmers and their families who were being pushed off the land and impoverished by industrial agriculture. It was a political challenge that lay beyond the scope, interest, or ability of the foundations that had fomented the Green Revolution."

Either unaware of or unconcerned with this history, Gates helped launch AGRA in 2006 with the same premise, approach, and strategies as the original green revolution. The plan was to double yields and farmer income and to reduce food insecurity (hunger) by 50 percent by 2020. And the revolution was both televised and well funded.

While the Gates Foundation has been the largest funder by far, supplying around two thirds of AGRA's billion-dollar budget over the years, taxpayers have also contributed significant funds. The U.S. government has committed up to ninety million dollars, while British, Swedish, Dutch, German, Norwegian, Canadian, Danish, and Luxembourgian taxpayers have pledged tens of millions more. (The Rockefeller Foundation would not agree to an interview, but told me via email that it had donated $166 million to AGRA.)

Many African governments have also partnered with AGRA or organized their own agricultural budgets in ways that complement the alliance's green revolution approach. One study found that African nations put a billion dollars each year into subsidizing inputs like synthetic fertilizer and hybrid seeds, the same interventions AGRA prioritizes. Insofar as African governments are aligned with the foundation's agenda, and insofar as AGRA does have real African leaders, Gates can rightfully claim that it is working with the public sector, with governments, not against them. The new green revolution is, indeed, a public-private partnership.

But that doesn't mean it is a homegrown policy from African nations, born of a democratic process. With the Gates Foundation, donor governments, and major international agricultural research bodies all rowing in the same direction and putting hundreds of millions of dollars on the table, they create a powerful current that is difficult to row against. Additionally, AGRA has created institutional ties to governments, giving them grants, placing people inside agencies through secondments, and providing technical assistance. The message is loud, clear, and unyielding: *We have the money and the experts. Let us help you.*

The big question is: What have Gates and AGRA accomplished? Did AGRA meet its lofty goals to double yields and farmer incomes and to halve hunger by 2020? Has there been a revolution?

Tim Wise, a senior research fellow at Tufts University's Global Development and Environment Institute, sought to answer these questions, but when he reached out to AGRA requesting access to its data, the group refused. So, Wise relied instead on national-level agricultural data reported by the United Nations Food and Agriculture Organization. If AGRA was really having an impact in the thirteen nations where it has been working since 2006—Burkina Faso, Ethiopia, Ghana, Kenya, Malawi, Mali, Mozambique, Niger, Nigeria, Rwanda, Tanzania, Uganda, and Zambia—wouldn't that impact appear in national data? If there had been a revolution, wouldn't it be easily discernible?

What Wise found were marginal increases in yields across the different crops AGRA supports, but nowhere near the 100 percent gains AGRA had promised. Meanwhile, hunger had actually increased by 30 percent—not decreased by 50 percent, as AGRA had promised. A dearth of data on farmer incomes made it impossible for Wise to assess AGRA's goal of doubling incomes, but he reported that extreme poverty did not accelerate downward during AGRA's tenure.

Around the same time that Wise's analysis came out, a coalition of international groups from across Africa and from Germany published country-level case studies of AGRA's impacts, profiling a questionable loan scheme in Tanzania that could push farmers into debt and AGRA's prominent work with a non-African NGO in Zambia, CARE International. As these critical evaluations circulated, AGRA's first response was not to discuss or debate the findings but to attack them. This included sending a letter to the Tufts University Office of the Vice Provost for Research, challenging the integrity and ethics of Tim Wise's AGRA evaluation.

"AGRA is an African institution set up by [former UN secretary-general] Kofi Annan to try to transform African agriculture, not by BMGF/Rockefeller as has been falsely claimed," the letter, authored by Andrew Cox, the UK-educated chief of staff of AGRA, read. Cox complained that Wise didn't ask AGRA for a comment on his findings and noted that the study wasn't peer-reviewed. The letter acknowledged that Wise had reached out to access AGRA's data, but argued he wasn't "specific enough for us to help him, nor to explain what his purpose was."

"On the face of it," the letter continued, "it seems hard to see the most basic and reasonable professional and academic standards were applied."

Tufts confirmed with me that it had evaluated the complaint and deemed it without merit. What's particularly striking about AGRA's complaint was that it openly acknowledged that Wise had reached out, asking to access its data. The group had an opportunity to engage early on in the process, but it had refused. Then, when the research progressed without its participation, it cried foul.

AGRA's refusal to engage with Wise's independent evaluation speaks to a culture—a distinctly Gatesian culture—of nonaccountability and nontransparency. When the Al Jazeera podcast *The Take* reported on the growing criticism of AGRA in 2021, for example, neither AGRA nor Gates responded to inquiries from the journalists. My own efforts to reach AGRA also were not fruitful. During my reporting, I asked for copies of the alliance's most recent U.S. tax filing, which the IRS requires nonprofit organizations to make available. I received no response. In separate correspondence, I asked AGRA for details of its funding. Again, no response. I also asked for an interview. No response.

As criticism of AGRA mounted in 2021, the group did begin issuing a public defense—on its own terms and in its own time—often appearing to conjure up alternate realities. In one op-ed, AGRA board chair Hailemariam Dessalegn, the former prime minister of Ethiopia, asserted, "While there have always been detractors of our approach and success, these voices have become louder, deciding to campaign against our work through the media, despite being offered opportunities [to] engage directly." The op-ed went on to argue that AGRA was too small an actor to be blamed for growing hunger in the nations where it worked, attacking this criticism as "wrong and terribly misleading."

Yet, if AGRA and Gates do not believe they have the wherewithal to make a dent in hunger, why did they broadcast a goal of reducing it by 50 percent? And if AGRA is a champion of public engagement, why are there so many accounts of its operating in an unaccountable manner?

The group's nonresponses have only created more space for critics, who ramped up their campaigning to defund the alliance, including a petition aimed at USAID, the largest government funder of AGRA. Additionally, three members of Congress—Ilhan Omar, Sara Jacobs, and Tom Malinowski—sought to compel USAID to justify the millions of dollars it had spent supporting AGRA, citing concerns about the alliance's "potentially damaging effects on food security, the environment, and anti-poverty goals in the countries where it operates." Meanwhile, German activists put pressure on their government, with the German Ministry for Economic Cooperation and Development telling the news media in 2022 that it was reconsidering its ongoing participation with AGRA.

As this criticism grew louder, the Gates Foundation funded its own evaluation of AGRA, which acknowledged some of the findings of independent appraisals: "AGRA did not meet its headline goal of increased incomes and food security for 9 million smallholders." The Gates-funded evaluation also highlighted the alliance's successes—such as "accelerating policy reforms" and helping "incentivize private sector engagement." Still, critics pounced on some of the evaluation's underlying findings— for example, that AGRA's interventions appeared to offer the biggest benefits to wealthier, male farmers. The evaluation also showed that AGRA had failed to generate consistent yield increases and had not fully recognized the environmental impacts of its input-intensive model. These are some of the same criticisms that hounded the original green revolution. History appears to be repeating itself, as critics long predicted.

As some media outlets took an interest in the growing opposition to AGRA, the Gates Foundation responded by scapegoating climate change for the alliance's failures. No one should doubt that climate change affects farming, but we've known this for decades. If Gates pursued its agricultural strategy without climate change in mind, this once again raises questions about its claimed expertise and leadership.

Some readers at this point might be asking: Is there nothing the world can do for African farmers without being called colonial? Is there not, in fact, a major hunger problem in many parts of Africa? Couldn't many farmers, indeed, benefit from increased yields?

Of course, agriculture can and should be improved in many parts of the African continent. But it's not Bill Gates's place to organize how that happens. And we also have to widen the lens on what improvement looks like. With climate change bringing new challenges to our food system— increased temperatures, droughts, and volatile weather—we do, indeed, need a revolution in farming, but much of the work needs to happen in U.S. agriculture, the model toward which Gates is pushing African farmers.

In the United States today, farming is dominated by large-scale industrialized production. Small producers have been put out of business, their acres consolidated into larger and larger farms. Notably, if not astonishingly, Bill Gates has become the largest private farmland owner in the United States, a powerful emblem of how U.S. agriculture today has increasingly become the province of soft-palmed investors, not hardworking farmer families.

In U.S. agriculture—say, Gates's large acreage of corn and soy production in Nebraska—farmers typically spend large sums of money on expensive inputs (GMO seeds, agrochemicals, fertilizer) to churn out huge volumes of monoculture grain, much of which goes to industrial purposes, like making ethanol or corn syrup or feeding animals on factory farms. It's a high-yielding system, but it carries huge costs to the taxpayers who heavily subsidize it. Agriculture is a leading cause of carbon emissions too, with synthetic fertilizers (made from fossil fuels) accounting for much of the sector's emissions. (Expanding the use of synthetic fertilizers is a linchpin of AGRA's work and a favorite intervention of Bill Gates—arguably, a bigger passion for him than GMOs.)

This model has proven quite fragile, lacking the precise thing that food systems need: resiliency. The Covid-19 pandemic and Russia's invasion of Ukraine in 2022 both caused major disruptions in input markets, for example. African farmers who had followed Gates and AGRA's lead on the expanded use of synthetic fertilizer were suddenly faced with skyrocketing prices, while fertilizer manufacturers faced allegations of profiteering. Climate change will bring even more unpredictability to farming.

Many African farmer groups endorse a different model of agriculture, which trades under the academic-sounding name "agroecology." A complex, systems-based approach to farming, agroecology depends, for example, on local, low-impact solutions like using manure for fertilizer instead of buying synthetic chemicals from foreign manufacturers. Farmers can also improve soil nutrition through crop rotation and crop diversity. And instead of buying hybrid or GMO seeds before each growing season, farmers can save seeds and replant them year after year—as humans have been doing for millennia.

The Rodale Institute in Pennsylvania has been running side-by-side comparisons between agroecological farming and conventional, input-intensive farming for four decades, reporting similar yields between the two models, but major environmental and financial benefits to well-run agroecological farms. Schools like the University of Wisconsin and North

Carolina State University today offer degree programs in agroecology, teaching students "the science behind sustainable agriculture." In 2009, a major international assessment involving four hundred experts, jointly published by the World Bank and FAO, broadly emphasized the importance of agroecology—and cast doubt on the green revolution–style input-intensive model, including the role of GMOs, in poor nations. And a decade later, the UN Committee on World Food Security commissioned a study on agroecology that highlighted limitations in the green revolution approach, noting that environmental or social costs of these methods can offset the reported economic benefits.

Agroecology, of course, is a threat to corporate interests, which want farmers to buy their seeds and agrochemicals year after year. And this is why Tim Wise calls AGRA the "perfect neoliberal project": "It's not perfect in the sense that it relies on all these public funds and charitable funds—so it's not the free market in any meaningful way at all," he told me. "But it is all intended to open markets and create markets of multilateral investment and multinational investment and sales. . . . In other words, somehow, Monsanto needed to open up Africa to sell more of its seeds. Fertilizer companies needed new markets to sell more fertilizer. In all of that, Bill is very useful in that effort. How would it have happened without Bill? I don't think there would have been an AGRA without Gates."

In 2013, Mark Lynas took the foodie world by storm with his poster-boy good looks and coming-to-Jesus GMO conversion story. "For the record, here and upfront, I apologize for having spent several years ripping up GM[O] crops," he announced as a keynote speaker at the Oxford Farming Conference. "I am also sorry that I helped to start the anti-GM[O] movement back in the mid-nineties, and that I thereby assisted in demonizing an important technological option which can be used to benefit the environment. As an environmentalist, and someone who believes that everyone in this world has a right to a healthy and nutritious diet of their choosing, I could not have chosen a more counter-productive path. I now regret it completely."

Lynas's self-flagellation and crocodile tears made a splash with journalists around the world, who widely profiled his crisis of conscience—in outlets ranging from the *New Yorker* to *Slate*. Companies like Monsanto could not have bought better PR—which is why Lynas's story raised eyebrows for some.

To me, Lynas's story felt more than a bit manufactured. At the time, I was working as a researcher for an NGO called Food & Water Watch, investigating the corporate propaganda tactics that proliferated across the GMO debates. It seemed quite coincidental that Lynas, an unknown in the GMO world and also a relatively unknown writer, could generate so much attention from a rather staid speech at what appears to have been a corporate-funded agricultural conference.

The Guardian later uncovered leaked documents showing an industry effort to create new "ambassadors" to promote GMOs, including Lynas. The documents describe Lynas as "potentially" being involved in the effort. He denied being an ambassador—or even being asked. More questions appeared when his former peers in the activist movements came forward to say that Lynas had not helped "start" the anti-GMO movement, as he had claimed. "Lynas was a player, but not a very important player, and for a very short period of time. Maybe in his mind he was important, but I don't think anybody else saw him that way," Jim Thomas, a former Greenpeace organizer, said. "I feel saddened by the whole thing. He's built a very successful career on the back of portraying people who were his friends as unthinking."

Lynas's public brand became not just about promoting the use of GMOs but also attacking anyone who criticized the technology as being "anti-science"—the same talking point advanced by companies like Monsanto. This meant he was also singing from the same hymnal as Bill Gates. Gates praised Mark Lynas by name in an interview with Politico in 2013. A year later, the foundation launched a new project to promote GMOs at Cornell University, called the Cornell Alliance for Science, where Lynas was given a platform to expand his campaigning on GMOs.

The Alliance, to which the foundation would eventually give more than $20 million, promised to "add a stronger voice for science and depolarize the charged debate around agricultural biotechnology and genetically modified organisms." In practice, however, the Alliance for Science ended up becoming one of the most polarizing voices, even drawing criticism for distorting the scientific debate surrounding GMOs.

Lynas and the alliance ferociously pushed the notion of a "scientific consensus" on GMOs, for example, prompting a group of PhD researchers to issue a response in the scientific journal *Environmental Sciences Europe*: "The joint statement developed and signed by over 300 independent researchers, and reproduced and published below, does not assert that GMOs are unsafe or safe. Rather, the statement concludes that the scarcity and contradictory nature of the scientific evidence published to date prevents conclusive claims of safety, or of lack of safety, of GMOs. Claims of consensus on the safety of GMOs are not supported by an objective analysis of the refereed literature." (Lynas did not respond to my press inquiries, and the Alliance did not respond to specific questions.)

The Alliance for Science nevertheless appears to have been very effective at doing what Gates asked it to do: promote GMOs in poor nations. The alliance claims to have trained "796 science champions"—journalists, activists, and influencers who could spread the gospel of GMOs. Joeva Rock said that when she reads news about GMOs in Ghana, where she conducts much of her academic research, it often comes from journalists who have been trained by the Alliance for Science. Million Belay and Bridget Mugambe, writing in *Scientific American*, make a similar finding:

In Uganda, for example, the CAS [Cornell Alliance for Science] has recruited journalists and key government individuals working on agriculture, science and technology to the cause of promoting GM seeds. [Alliance] fellows write disparaging articles on agroecology, describing it as a "dead end," and promote biotechnology-based solutions in its stead. In Nigeria, Alliance fellows work closely with OFAB's [the Open Forum on Agricultural Biotechnology] Nigeria chapter, the National Biotechnology Development Agency, the Nigerian Institute of Public Relations and the Nigerian Institute of Management to advocate for biotechnology, often characterizing it as the only scientific option.

The net effect of the Alliance for Science and the Gates Foundation's broader ecosystem of influence, as these authors describe it, is "narrowing the democratic space for discussion of food systems in African countries. Opposing points of view are irrational, unscientific and harmful, they often insist."

In other words, the Gates Foundation and its surrogates don't want to win the debate on GMOs. They want to shut it down. And Bill Gates, personally, has played a significant role in this effort. In late 2022, when he traveled to Kenya to promote his work in agriculture (and to announce seven billion dollars in new funding for projects throughout Africa), he insisted that most advanced economies had already embraced GMOs: "Ninety-nine point nine (99.9) percent of crops in [the] West are GMO. Every piece of bread I have ever eaten is from GMO-modified wheat. Every piece of corn I have also eaten is GMO corn."

This is demonstrably false, however. There is no GMO wheat in commercial production anywhere in the world. And most nations on earth, including much of Europe, don't grow GMOs. Maybe Gates meant that most of the food we grow has had its genetics modified through one form of breeding or another—but that's true of virtually every crop everywhere in the world, not simply in the "West." Except for hunter-gatherer societies foraging wild edibles, most food has had its genes modified by human intervention—as when farmers, over the course of thousands of years, save seeds from the best-yielding or best-tasting crops year over year and replant them, slowly improving the genetic stock. But this is a categorically different breeding process from the genetic modifications Gates and Monsanto work on, like moving genetic constructs between unrelated species in the laboratory.

Readers of this book who are fans of GMOs or who think that poor nations could benefit from this technology should understand that the Gates Foundation, in many places, is actually contributing to polarization and sowing distrust. And they should understand that if GMO technology is going to be successful in poor nations, it should be local scientists producing the new seeds, according to local farmers' needs, following a robust public process that gets input from end consumers— without undue pressure from foreign philanthropists and multinational seed companies. They should also understand that whether or not a nation chooses to grow GMOs—or, for that matter, embrace or refuse any technology—is not a purely scientific decision.

In some respects, the large sums of money the Gates Foundation has put into promoting GMOs through efforts like the Alliance for Science could be seen as papering over the technical failures of GMO technology. For years, the foundation and other promoters have promised that GMOs would cure many of the world's food problems—solving hunger, correcting nutritional deficiencies, and lifting yields. And for years, the foundation has plowed money into a graveyard of mistrials for GMO crops that it believes Africans need.

One of the foundation's earliest bets was a $21 million project that began in the early 2000s, funding a group called Africa Harvest Biotech Foundation International, run by a former Monsanto associate, Florence Wambugu. The group—based in Washington, DC, according to the foundation's grant records—sought to engineer a new variety of sorghum with higher nutritional content. (Sorghum, a grain, is a staple crop in Nigeria, Ethiopia, Sudan, Niger, and other countries.) Gates's funding for the project appears to have ended in 2017, and there's very little public record of what the research effort accomplished. Wambugu's previous engineering effort, a GMO sweet potato at Monsanto, also appears to have failed. A competing sweet potato variety, created by Ugandan scientists without the use of GMOs, performed much better, according to media reports.

Gates also put money into a nutritionally fortified GMO banana that promised to fix vitamin A deficiencies, which can cause blindness and death. As of early 2023, the banana, after years of funding and promotion, has still not come to market. One researcher blamed the slow progress on the Ugandan people's "ignorance and misinformation" and also criticized the government's failure to enact necessary laws to advance the project.

The Gates Foundation also provided bandwagon funding for "golden rice," another GMO food crop that promoters said would deliver vitamin A and save lives. Despite basically bottomless investments since 2000 (by GMO seed companies, governments, and Gates) and endless hype by the news media, golden rice has failed to deliver these promised benefits. Only one nation, the Philippines, has begun commercial cultivation of the rice, and it remains to be seen whether this introduction, in 2022, will have major effects on human health, as has been so widely claimed.

Doug Gurian-Sherman, a former regulator of GMOs at the Environmental Protection Agency, is skeptical that the technology will deliver on its promises to revolutionize farming. "The reality is that ecosystems are highly networked and complex. So is the genome," he told me. Inserting new genetic traits into a crop to, say, improve yields is going to have a cascade of other effects on the plant. "It's kind of like when you see drugs advertised on TV. At the end, they'll have this list as long as your arm of side effects. Some may be rare or negligible; others more common and dramatic."

In 2009, Gurian-Sherman, who holds a doctorate in plant pathology and who later in his career worked for the Union of Concerned Scientists, published a series of studies showing that the claimed benefits of GMOs—things like increased yield and improved drought tolerance—have been widely overstated. The development of new genetic engineering technologies like CRISPR may offer "more potential to get smaller incremental changes that could collectively add up to some significance," he noted, "but how important that would be overall, especially compared to alternatives such as agroecology—I think it's very easy to overemphasize—it's too early days to know. The whole other piece of this is, how is this technology going to be used and developed? Who's going to control [it]? The power dynamics have not changed."

Bill Gates has a much less nuanced view. In an interview with the *Wall Street Journal*—titled "Bill Gates: GMOs Will End Starvation in Africa"—he said, "It's pretty incredible because it reduces the amount of pesticides you need, raises productivity, can help with malnutrition by getting vitamin fortification—so, for Africa, I think this is going to make a huge difference, particularly as they face climate change."

The "huge" benefits Gates promised for African farmers never arrived, yet Gates remains steadfastly committed to his high-tech agenda. And he has little patience for critics and naysayers. "If there's some non-innovation solution, you know, like singing 'Kumbaya,' I'll put money behind it," he said in a 2022 interview. "But if you don't have those seeds, the numbers just don't work. . . . If somebody says we're ignoring some solution, I don't think they're looking at what we're doing."

It would be much easier to take Gates seriously, or find his words less condescending, if he were actually rolling up his sleeves and doing the hard work to substantiate his grand promises. The foundation has been working on GMOs for close to two decades—what does it have to show for this, aside from all the interviews, marketing, promises, and PR?

Every fall, the Gates Foundation releases a big report called *Goalkeepers*, which claims to offer a broad survey of human progress, and Bill Gates's focus in 2022 was on agriculture, a clear signal of his plans to elevate its importance in the foundation's portfolio in the years ahead. Gates promoted the "magic seeds" his foundation was working on, and he stressed the need for other innovations, like using artificial intelligence and predictive modeling to create "a data-based vision of what farms will need to look like in the future."

Bill Gates's doubling down on agriculture in the face of growing calls to defund his agricultural projects speaks to the way this issue has become personal for him. Since the publication of his 2021 book, *How to Avoid a Climate Disaster*, he has aggressively sought to assert his expertise on climate change, a hard sell given that his private foundation has largely avoided the issue for the past twenty years. By expanding his work in agriculture, where he already has a foothold, Gates can claim leadership on climate change, focusing on technological solutions for our food system.

"I would also say that if temperature rise stopped today, you could say, 'Hey, you know, just take the best seeds we have now and adopt it for Africa,'" Gates said. "But temperature rise is not stopping. We do need the leguminous crops that make their own fertilizer. We do need the photosynthetic improvement. Those things [GMO crops] are 10 to 15 years away, but we need those because the temperature isn't leveling off." And just like that, Gates had bought himself a fresh fifteen-year time line.

There is absolutely no reason to believe that his innovation agenda will deliver. But we should also not doubt how committed Bill Gates is to his image as a champion for African farmers, whether they want him or not: "So on behalf of Africa—not just so they don't have malnutrition but so they develop their economies so they can fight climate change—getting their agricultural productivity up, for a ton of reasons, should be a top priority."

14

India

When Bill Gates's career as a philanthropist began in earnest, and he decided he wanted to focus on health, HIV/AIDS was an obvious place to begin. The high-profile disease had celebrity champions and even celebrity victims—from Magic Johnson to Freddie Mercury to Fela Kuti. But the real poster child for the disease was the continent of Africa, where large numbers of poor people were dying because they could not afford treatment. As the world turned its attention to the plight of Africa, so did Bill Gates. But he also directed his foundation to look to another corner of the globe, where there were growing worries about an approaching tsunami of infections—India.

India hadn't received the same level of support from the foreign aid funding complex, even as the nation had a larger population than the entire African continent. Bill Gates saw the market void and inserted himself in a big way, announcing a one-hundred-million-dollar program in 2002 to intervene where the Indian government was failing. "The recognition we came to, and one I think the government is also coming to, is that more needs to be done," he said.

Gates traveled to India personally to make the announcement. The visit ended up drawing controversy because, in tandem with his philanthropic donation, he also announced that Microsoft was making a four-hundred-million-dollar investment in India. The potential corporate benefits behind Gates's charitable gift weren't lost on journalists, who, in the early days of the foundation's work, had the mettle to challenge Gates.

The *New York Times* reported that Gates "deflected any suggestions that philanthropy could be good for business." *The Lancet* published a more pointed editorial, asking whether Bill Gates was a "philanthropist or commercial opportunist."

Gates's business-cum-philanthropy efforts in India came at a time when Microsoft was in an escalating conflict with the Indian government over whether that nation's vast public bureaucracy would embrace Microsoft's software or, instead, pursue free and open software alternatives, like Linux. By announcing a double whammy of investments from both Microsoft and his foundation, Bill Gates sent a clear signal to the Indian government about his value proposition. Using philanthropy to advance the corporate bottom line is a long-standing practice of Microsoft.

"We need to have great relationships with governments all over the world," Bill Gates said in 2008, speaking about Microsoft:

> And because we make a product whose marginal cost of production is very low—software—and because information empowerment is so directly what we're about, it's not a stretch in any way, the idea that we go into over one hundred countries and do these things where we donate massive amounts of software. We even give cash gifts, and we train teachers. And we make sure we get visibility for that and we make sure when we hire employees they know about that. When we're competing for government contracts, we remind people we're a good citizen in that country. I can't do the math for you in some hyper-rational way. I suppose you could go overboard on it, but versus not doing that, Microsoft is absolutely way better off.

In this interview, Gates went on to highlight a new Microsoft lab in India designed to help poor farmers and teachers. He noted that the project might get spun into the Gates Foundation. "If you figure out how to make governments love you by helping the poor people in that country," he said, "you get both the benefit of the government loving you and you get to say you helped the poor in that country."

Arguably, India could be seen as the jewel in the crown of Microsoft's software empire. In addition to the enormous market it offers for Microsoft products, it also boasts a workforce of highly trained programmers and engineers who have become an important part of Microsoft's bottom line—working for half of what the company pays employees in the United States.

It does seem more than a coincidence that India later became a major focus of the Gates Foundation. India today is the largest recipient of Gates money outside the United States or Europe, of more than six hundred charitable grants totaling close to $1.5 billion. The foundation's first-ever foreign office was in India, and its HIV/AIDS project, called Avahan, turned into a sprawling $300 million program, one of the foundation's biggest interventions of its kind at that time. In the years ahead, the foundation dramatically expanded its portfolio of charitable interventions in India to include maternal health, vaccines, financial systems, and other topics.

But it was a slow learning process. Figuring out how to work in India, and the need to work cooperatively with the government, began with some hard lessons in its early HIV/AIDS project. Manjari Mahajan was a graduate student at the time Avahan was getting off the ground in the early 2000s, and she found that foundation staff in India were open to discussing their work—a level of transparency and engagement that seems unthinkable today. Mahajan, an associate professor in international affairs at the New School, went on to publish her findings about Avahan's questionable legacy in academic journals. *Forbes India* reported a second, consistent account of the project.

According to these two reports, a defining feature of Avahan was its "go big or go home" ethos. Job interviews were held at some of the nation's fanciest hotels, and the very high salaries on offer attracted corporate talent from consulting companies like McKinsey. The director of Avahan, Ashok Alexander, a former senior partner with McKinsey, became the highest-paid employee at the foundation in 2007, taking home nearly five hundred thousand dollars in total compensation.

Asked about the five-star hotels, business class flights, and high-grade salaries, the foundation noted at the time, "We need the best talent to deal with an urgent problem on a war footing. If we need to get this talent from the corporate sector, we have to make it attractive for them." This meant hiring technical specialists at salaries three or four times higher than what government agencies were paying, setting the stage for a brain drain that attracted talented people who might otherwise have worked in the public sector. The foundation's rich spending also prompted a wide array of NGOs to line up behind its agenda. Mahajan's research profiles one group that changed its focus from adolescent health to follow Gates money—and priorities. By 2009, more than one hundred NGOs were working under the Gates Foundation's growing HIV/AIDS project.

Outside Avahan, the Indian government already had a robust HIV/AIDS program that other donors were working through, so, in some respects, the Gates Foundation was pursuing a parallel, independent strategy. And Gates was eager to contrast its approach with the Indian government's, trumpeting how its hard-nosed, business-minded strategy would move the needle. "If a NGO becomes a barrier between providing a service to society, then we will get another NGO. We will short circuit the power structure to get the service to the people. We focus on speed, on scale, and on sustainability," the director of Avahan said. "Our benchmarks are of the private sector. In the first year, we established our presence in 550 towns, with doctors, peer workers, and nurses. If we were a business organization, we would have been very proud of such rapid growth. We follow a business model with segmentation of the problem. Where in the social sector do you find such execution focus? Where do you find such structures of monitoring and evaluation?"

As the project got bigger and bigger, however, the Gates Foundation began to realize internally how minuscule its resources were in a nation of more than a billion people. And it realized that its silver bullet approach of devising succinct technical interventions wasn't as easy as the elegant flowcharts its army of consultants and MBAs had devised on paper.

"They go in and they think distributing condoms and information is going to bring about behavioral change in the high-risk groups, especially sex workers," Mahajan told me in an interview. "They find that it doesn't work. So, they go back and try some other intervention, and that doesn't work. They are partnering with all these NGOs, and so, they start listening more carefully to what these NGOs are saying, which is, 'What good is it for a sex worker to have a condom if she is going to be beaten up by a customer if she tries to use it?' So, they realize they have to understand the broader social and cultural dynamic."

Mahajan said the Gates Foundation deserves credit for demonstrating its capacity to learn and pivot. Yet the lesson went only so far. While the foundation's leadership came to realize its targeted interventions were too narrow, it also realized it didn't want to take on the difficult, messy work of public health—building up the infrastructure and capacity of the nation to deliver the full scope of interventions needed against disease. "This type of broad-ranging structural work is not what we set out to do," the foundation acknowledged.

Gates began formulating an exit plan, imagining it would hand off Avahan to the Indian government. As part of this plan, it issued press releases and grants that fundamentally changed the program from one that worked outside government to one that was now working closely with it. Mahajan reports that when she asked about the changing strategy, the foundation insisted that its plan had always been to hand the project off to the government.

Bill Gates had his own version of events. "One of the first programs we worked on in India was called Avahan, an HIV prevention program that's now reaching millions of the people most at-risk for contracting and spreading the virus. With many international partners, we helped launch the project, refining it and measuring its impact along the way. After the first 10 years, the government of India has decided to take it over," Gates said in 2012. "This is a great example of what collaboration between funders and governments can achieve. Avahan is saving lives, and it would not exist if we hadn't provided funding and technical assistance to test out a promising new idea. However, the Indian government is scaling and sustaining the effort over the long-term. This pattern has been repeated across the country over the past several decades, and aid has steadily become a smaller and smaller portion of the national economy."

The reality was nothing like the success story Bill Gates described. The Indian government deemed Avahan to be hugely expensive in terms of the benefits it delivered—and totally unsustainable. "We told them you can't create a huge number of assets and then just leave and expect the government to take over everything," the head of the Indian government's HIV response effort told the news media. "We can never offer a replicable model. And if we are unable to sustain the programme, all of their effort will be for naught."

"Avahan's approach is too resource-intensive," another Indian official noted. "This is not a model that can be replicated or scaled up by the state."

One HIV activist from that era whom I interviewed echoed these sentiments, recounting to me having conversations with midlevel government employees along the lines of, "How does BMGF think they can just hand over such a huge thing, and they think we will want to take it up and run it? Where do we have the capacity to run it? Where do we have the people?"

Forbes India was unsparing in its final analysis of Avahan, headlining its story, "How Bill Gates Blew $258 Million in India's HIV Corridor." For all the foundation's chest-thumping about its private-sector dynamism and hard-nosed business approach, from a dollars-and-cents perspective, Gates's project seemed better defined by its wasteful spending and weak outputs. Avahan simply had not achieved what it had set out to do.

And as with all Gates Foundation interventions, when Gates abruptly changes its mind and abandons a project, there is collateral damage. The foundation's profligate spending on Avahan had created a significant cottage industry of grantees who were left scrambling to rejigger their missions and priorities to find new funding. *Forbes India* profiled a former sex worker who had found gainful employment as a "peer educator" under Avahan. Now that the Gates project was shutting down, the woman worried about whether she would have to return to sex work—at age forty-five.

The other question *Forbes* raised was, "In a country where a branded condom sells for just 10 cents, what did Avahan spend on? It's difficult to say because Avahan's finances are largely opaque."

One public health professional I interviewed, who has spent much of his career working on Gates Foundation grants, insisted that Avahan was enormously successful, telling me that if Gates hadn't done this early work, there would, indeed, have been a major HIV/AIDS crisis in the nation. Asked if there was any independent research or scholarship supporting this claim, the source said they did not know. The Gates Foundation, likewise, trumpets that its work prevented six hundred thousand HIV infections, a claim based on academic research the foundation itself funded, not an independent evaluation. It is true that the predicted "tsunami" of HIV/AIDS in India never came to pass, but this is widely considered to be due to faulty projections, not because of the Gates Foundation's interventions.

One clear lesson the foundation learned from Avahan was the importance of partnering closely with governments on the front end and not simply creating projects and expecting governments to take them over. It's a lesson that echoes throughout the foundation's work today, a kind of axiom on which its entire charitable enterprise exists and a marketing dance that helps manage public opinion. By bringing government partners and taxpayer dollars into public-private partnerships, the foundation gets political buy-in, public-facing legitimacy, and huge sums of money that it wouldn't otherwise have. And it allows the foundation to argue that it's not some puppet master pulling strings but simply one of many collaborative partners.

When pressed about its influence, the Gates Foundation often points to the fact that its annual charitable funding pales in comparison to government spending, whether on U.S. education or public health abroad. Gates also likes to describe itself, when convenient, as merely playing a "catalytic" role—to innovate new interventions that, if they work, governments can take and scale up. The idea is that the foundation comes up with the big ideas, does the pilot projects, plows money into measurement and evaluation, and then calls on governments to do the tedious, difficult work of "scaling up"—trying to turn Gates's big ideas into real change.

It's a model the foundation continued in its second chapter of work in India, focused on the states of Uttar Pradesh and Bihar, where it has funded a small army of "technical support units" that engage in a far-ranging array of public health interventions. As the former head of the foundation's India office, Nachiket Mor, described it in an interview in 2016:

The big focus has been maternal and child health. . . . One of the big challenges is women delivering at home in settings that are not entirely safe. We spent a lot of time thinking how frontline workers coordinate better. . . . We are starting to think about larger challenges, what about financing? We need surgeons—UP [Uttar Pradesh] has C-section rates of 1 per cent, Kerala at 35 per cent is too high, but 1 per cent is too low. You need surgeons, we are starting to engage with that conversation, trying to understand the issue. Is it that we have surgeons, is it just about transferring them to the right location, or is it that we don't have enough surgeons? Can . . . doctors be reskilled? We are starting to engage with medicine supply chains, electronic health records, etc.

As this quote shows, the foundation has extremely broad ambitions in its work, coordinating health care workers, organizing health financing, dramatically increasing C-sections, and even organizing medical doctors to perform the procedures.

Early on in my reporting on the foundation, sources in India began reaching out to me with stories of Gates's inappropriate overreach into the state's public health. Some pointed me to the fact that the foundation had chosen the University of Manitoba in Canada and the Atlanta-based CARE to lead its projects in India—one more example of the ways the foundation leans on wealthy Western institutions to carry out its work in poor nations. Gates has given around $800 million to these two entities, but vague grant descriptions make it difficult to know exactly how much is going to their work in India versus other projects. (I also searched Gates's grant database for references to Bihar and Uttar Pradesh, finding around $750 million for projects there—only 10 percent of which actually went to organizations based in India.)

One source who previously worked with the state government health department in Bihar described the Gates Foundation as inserting its people into the state bureaucracy, where they then assert their superior technical expertise and insist that they must vet all decisions. "They are working as bottleneck for many health care programs. They aren't letting other organizers work. They have a monopolistic influence," the source told me. "This guy is sitting in every policy health meeting of Bihar health department and even accompany with top most bureaucrat during his field supervision visits. He's a nonstate actor. How come he is sitting in every meeting?"

A promotional video about Gates Foundation work in Bihar describes the project as strengthening, not weakening, the government. The video reports that the state's mostly poor and rural population did not use the government-run hospital system until Gates and its partner CARE got involved. "The challenge for us was to augment trust in the public health system," a narrator explains over grave music and a montage of fading facilities. After the government of Bihar partnered with Gates and CARE, the video tells us, everything changed. Visits to public health clinics soared, as did immunization rates. And, of course, the project is saving lives, with maternal and infant mortality rates dropping by more than 30 percent.

But where do these numbers come from? How much credit does the Gates Foundation really deserve for this work? Why do the Gates Foundation and CARE benchmark their success based on data from 2005—years before the foundation's interventions began? (CARE did not respond to questions about its work with the Gates Foundation in India.)

"My honest take is that, yes, health indicators have improved. But that the true driver is overall improvements in standards of living," one source who previously worked on a Gates Foundation grant in India told me. "The social determinants of health are a much more significant driver of changes in health indicators than anything else. Health indicators will likely improve in spite of this type of intervention rather than because of [it]."

To be fair to the Gates Foundation, it can't be accused of hijacking public health in India because, as it tells it, it was invited to do this work. The foundation has signed formal agreements with state and federal governments—and it appears to believe it will one day hand off its programs to government agencies, just as it sought to do with Avahan. Sources who have worked closely with the Gates Foundation in India told me there's virtually no chance this transition will work.

One source described the foundation's project as an "unsustainable, top-heavy operation," drawing comparisons to Gates's previous work on HIV/AIDS with Avahan. "The government of Bihar is already asking, 'How do we afford this? How do we take on this program that you have poured hundreds of millions of dollars into?'" the source noted. "If you think about Avahan, it kind of was set up as technical support unit. That's the entire model of India, using technical support units. What they end up doing is funding largely North American orgs. . . . [Then] there's this mad scramble to figure out sustainability, to figure out transition—and it fails time and time again."

The real problem, this source said, is that the Gates Foundation is doing work that governments are supposed to do, creating "a parallel system"—a term that another source also used—that undermines the public sector. When governments see Gates taking on a portfolio of work, resource-constrained public agencies aren't going to spend their time, energy, or money trying to learn how to take over the foundation's sprawling and expensive plan. Instead, my source explained, their point of view is, "Those guys are doing it, so why should I do it?" At the same time, the organizations currently managing Gates's projects in India (and elsewhere) also have no interest in seeing their work transition to the government; doing so would mean their groups would lose out on lucrative grants and contracts from the foundation. This kind of perverse incentive speaks to a fundamental paradox in humanitarian aid, a multibillion-dollar industry whose survival depends on the perpetuity of poverty.

Across the foundation's portfolio of work, there is always a worry that the foundation, under the auspices of helping the public sector, is actually replacing or displacing the government. When Bill Gates changes his mind about these projects, as he did with Avahan, or when he dies, which he certainly will one day, will governments simply take over the work he started? And what happens to all the groups, workers, and clinics that have organized their work around Gates's agenda when the funding suddenly stops?

Manjari Mahajan believes it's a mistake to overstate the Gates Foundation's influence in India. "Talking about Gates's role in India has to be couched within the larger scale of doing work on health in India. Gates's funds are a small drop in that massive enterprise," Mahajan told me. "Bihar and UP are massive states—the population of Bihar exceeds that of Germany; Uttar Pradesh is even bigger. So, achieving any significant impact in these two states is not an easy undertaking. The Gates-funded initiatives in these two states have had mixed and sometimes limited impact. So, one has to be careful in giving them too much credit in transforming health systems. The foundation's stories have had an outsize role in the media, but the picture on the ground is more complex."

What Mahajan is saying is not that the Gates Foundation isn't a powerful player in India, but just that it doesn't have the same level of influence as it might in, say, a smaller, poorer nation—or even in a powerful institution like the World Bank or the World Health Organization. As Mahajan sees it, Gates's power is "less in outright privatization or marginalization of the state, and more in attempts to enroll the state into new logics of corporate managerialism and data-driven programming."

Aashish Gupta, a demographer at Oxford, made the same point about the relatively small scale of the foundation's work in India compared to the government's, but he argued that the foundation's size has to be understood in terms of its access to power and also its tendency to lean into the class divisions that define Indian society. To Gupta's point, the foundation hired a board member of the Reserve Bank of India to direct its work in India for a time and has also developed close ties to the nation's elite corps of bureaucrats, the Indian Administrative Service, who are extremely well positioned to help fast-track the foundation's programs. By drawing on the elite sector in India, and by importing technical experts from the United States and Canada, the foundation is able to punch far above its weight class.

"From an Indian democracy perspective, this sort of story is really useful, because a large part of how inequality in India is created is through these upper-class networks—who gets hired where and what do they do with it. . . . None of the global organizations are thinking very carefully about equality within developing countries," Gupta told me. "I think it's helpful to understand how organizations like Gates are sort of hand in glove with the elites, with the wealth in these countries."

Whereas Gupta said the Gates Foundation "reproduces that hierarchy in the public health world," the Indian government's work is subject to certain affirmative action–like hiring rules that encourage some level of socioeconomic diversity—for example, related to caste—that can chip away at elite privilege.

· · ·

FOR BILL GATES, few public health interventions have the impact, the lifesaving impact, of vaccines. So, in the mid-2000s, when a new vaccine was approved for the human papillomavirus (HPV), which can cause cervical cancer, the Gates Foundation immediately endorsed it in a big way—even though the foundation doesn't generally work on cancer. As Gates saw it, the HPV vaccine was a perfect case study for why the foundation exists—to correct market failures.

The foundation's work in health is aimed mostly at diseases that affect poor people—which Big Pharma avoids because such diseases don't offer attractive profit margins. The reason the pharmaceutical industry (Merck and GSK) tackled the HPV vaccine was that it would be a major profit maker in rich nations. But, as Bill Gates saw it, the real value of these vaccines is in poor nations. Women in wealthy nations with access to good health care can get regular screenings to look for abnormalities that suggest cancer risks and then treat them as needed. Poor women will never get these screenings. They're the ones who need the one-and-done vaccine. "In rich countries you can usually spot it [the virus] and take care of it. But in fact, if you get this HPV—the virus—in a developing country, the chance that it will be stopped is almost zero. And so you'll get cervical cancer and a lot of those women will die," Bill Gates said. "So [the] HPV [vaccine] really belongs in the developing countries. And so now the work is being done to get the price down, to get the volume up."

Of course, it's not up to Bill Gates to decide if the HPV vaccine "belongs in developing countries." It's up to local policy makers and legislators—and the constituents to whom they are accountable. Gates, nevertheless, can have financial influence over the decision-making process. This includes donating money to help establish and expand immunization technical advisory committees in countries across Africa and Asia. These groups generally provide scientific and technical advice to governments, which informs national vaccine policy. In India, the Gates Foundation has served as the funder of India's Immunization Technical Support Unit, which provides "techno-managerial" assistance. The Indian government defines the unit's roles as "evidence based planning, program operations, monitoring and evaluation, strategic communication, cold chain and vaccine logistics management and support for Adverse Event Following Immunization."

One person who previously worked directly with the unit told me that the Gates Foundation positioned itself in this role to review draft reports and provide feedback, saying the foundation once asked that changes be made to a report to make it seem more favorable, apparently to push government endorsement of a vaccine. The source said Gates's requested change may not have altered the government's final decision, but it was an example of the influence the foundation had.

Srinath Reddy, the former head of Public Health Foundation of India (PHFI), which Gates funded to manage the technical support unit, said he had no knowledge of any such influence and stressed that the unit wasn't a decision-making body, that it simply provides technical information and scientific advice. He did acknowledge, however, that there are well-founded questions to be raised about Gates Foundation funding of this work. "If you ask me, in retrospect, should this have been done different? I believe so. But did PHFI play the role of influencing the decisions on behalf of the funding agency, the Gates Foundation? I believe the answer is no," he said. "Let me put it this way, if the government had set up ITSU [the Immunization Technical Support Unit] with its own funding, it would have been the ideal arrangement." Reddy made this point several times in the interview, describing the Gates Foundation's expanding work in India as the product of weak government support for public health. His own organization, founded in part with Gates money, was born out of this problem, he said. "There were no institutions for multidisciplinary training in public health. We needed very effective institutions. Thailand has it. Bangladesh has it. But India neglected public health education for a number of decades, since independence."

Reddy was reluctant to criticize the Gates Foundation directly, but he did speak many times generally about the need for foreign entities to play a smaller role in Indian society. "I believe the priorities for [the] Indian health system, the priorities for Indian science, should be set by Indian technical experts and Indian health system managers," he said. Foreign donors and experts should be allowed to sit at the table, he said, only after these priorities have been "fully justified in [the] India context."

Reddy also made a point to distance PHFI from the Gates Foundation's early work on HPV vaccines in India, noting that his organization was concerned about ethical issues, which later drew widespread controversy. That scandal began with a $28 million donation Gates awarded to the Seattle-based PATH "to strengthen the capability of developing countries to reduce cervical cancer incidence and deaths." This description obfuscates how the money was actually spent: on an international trial, or "demonstration project," of HPV vaccines in Peru, Uganda, India, and Vietnam.

As Gates sought to demonstrate the merits of the HPV vaccine, medical ethicists and feminist groups in India raised concerns. The women's health organization Sama organized a letter with more than fifty signatories opposing the Gates-PATH demonstration project, citing concerns related to the vaccine's questionable efficacy, its high cost, potential side effects, and Merck's aggressive marketing efforts. The letter specifically questioned whether vaccines would be seen as substitutes for cervical cancer screenings, taking attention away from basic preventative care. Again, Bill Gates, personally, had specifically described the HPV vaccine as a substitute for routine screenings. Instead of doing the complex work of building up public health capacity, the Gates Foundation seemed to want to blanket poor nations with the vaccine.

Around the world, scientific questions and an ethical debate around HPV vaccines emerged, including among researchers in Bangladesh, who raised a number of ethical concerns about an HPV demonstration project done in partnership with the Gates-funded Gavi. The eleven-year-old girls enrolled in the study were told about the importance of the vaccine, for example, but not about the importance of cervical cancer screenings. "In Bangladesh, the immunization program still holds the public's trust and is regarded as the most successful public health program in the country," the authors wrote. "Hence, to preserve ethical standards, adding any new vaccine to the existing program requires thorough investigation of its compatibility, necessity, and fit-for-purpose."

While the contemporary discourse around vaccines often seeks to shut down any criticism of vaccines as "anti-vax," a more sober, rational conversation would acknowledge the complexities in the decision-making process governments undertake around new vaccines. The Gates Foundation actually offers good perspective on this issue, told through the story of India's decision to adopt a pneumonia vaccine. In a post on its website, the foundation reports, "Such a decision is not simple for any country. First, it involves determining whether the vaccine addresses an actual problem: How many children are sickened by pneumococcus? How does that compare with other causes of childhood death or illness? Also, what are the costs? What *won't* get funded if we add this vaccine? For India, gathering this information would take time."

The foundation described this fact-finding mission as a public process organized by "an expert committee of the Indian government." What it didn't disclose was the Gates Foundation's long-standing role in funding the body that provides techno-managerial support to this expert committee. Not only that, but the foundation underwrote the creation of the pneumonia vaccine and had a keen desire to see the vaccine used. Should the fate of this vaccine be determined through a process that, at least at one time, involved input from a Gates-funded body?

At the very least, shouldn't the foundation be open, honest, and forthcoming about playing so many roles? Failing to do so opens the door for the public to believe that something is being hidden—which, of course, is a recipe for vaccine hesitancy.

It's a concern that the Gates Foundation should know well. During the course of the Gates-funded HPV demonstration project in India, seven school-age girls died, prompting the government to shut down the trial. A government investigation found that the study had failed to get proper consent from the parents of underage schoolgirls. The researchers had also not set up an adequate reporting mechanism for potential harmful side effects related to the vaccine. The government stated that the deaths were not related to the vaccine, but questions continued to surface when it was reported that no autopsies had been conducted.

The alleged ethical missteps in the Gates-funded study unleashed a major backlash, with public health professionals accusing Gates's partner, PATH, of using Indians as "guinea pigs." A parliamentary inquiry condemned the study as a "blatant violation by PATH of all regulatory and ethical norms." It also cited the appearance of financial conflicts of interest. "Had PATH been successful in getting the HPV vaccine included in the universal immunization programme of the concerned countries, this would have generated windfall profit for the manufacturer(s) by way of automatic sale, year after year, without any promotional or marketing expenses. It is well known that once introduced into the immunization programme, it becomes politically impossible to stop any vaccination."

Noting the "monopolistic nature" of the HPV vaccine—controlled by Merck and GSK, which donated six million dollars' worth of vaccines to the Gates-PATH study—the parliamentary report described a "well planned scheme to commercially exploit a situation" through "subterfuge."

The criticism landed back on the Gates Foundation, which, with its endless partnerships with Big Pharma, was in no position to defend itself as an independent charity. In a rare moment of clarity—the likes of which we have never had in the United States—Indian legislators, policy makers, and journalists began very publicly interrogating the phenomenal financial conflicts of interest underpinning the Gates Foundation's charitable enterprise.

The foundation makes charitable donations and engages in a wide variety of other financing mechanisms that help Big Pharma grow their businesses. At the same time, the foundation is positioned to benefit financially from some of these corporate partnerships because its $54 billion endowment includes stocks and bonds in pharmaceutical companies. Bill Gates may also hold investments in pharmaceutical companies through his private $100 billion fortune, the details of which are not public.

PATH called the charge of ethical misconduct "inaccurate in many details," saying it "incorrectly implies violations of approved practices." The Gates Foundation, meanwhile, called the allegations of wrongdoing "misinformation." PATH is one of the single-largest recipients of funding from the Gates Foundation—more than three billion dollars reported in grant records, though the full number could be significantly higher—and at times seems to function almost as a subsidiary of Gates. The organization did not respond to my request for an interview about its relationship with the Gates Foundation.

The fallout from the scandal may have created public distrust in Indian medical regulators. Public health experts noted at the time that the HPV uproar would make it harder to do clinical trials in India. This, in turn, could make it harder to bring new lifesaving drugs to market. To date, the HPV vaccine has not been included in India's national immunization program, though the Gates Foundation and the Serum Institute have developed a new HPV vaccine that may change this in the years ahead.

Even if we take the charitable view that Gates and PATH did nothing wrong in the HPV trial in India, we at least have to acknowledge that it is a bad idea for the foundation to play so many roles in India's vaccine policy. Can you imagine if, say, the richest man in India decided to host and fund a key technical advisory unit that helped inform national vaccine policy in *your* home country while also funding the development and testing of new vaccines, brokering deals with major pharmaceutical companies, and helping direct Gavi, one of the world's leading vaccine distribution mechanisms?

Readers living in wealthy nations probably can't imagine this level of foreign influence. If such a thing happened in my home country, the United States, there would be congressional investigations. Legislators would pass new laws to clamp down on foreign influence. The news media would scream vaguely xenophobic headlines about foreign oligarchs meddling in domestic affairs. And public distrust in vaccines would likely rapidly expand.

The HPV scandal appears to have provided a long-overdue vent for well-founded frustrations around Bill Gates's imperial excursions, which some in India may place in the context of the country's history as a British colony. "One man deciding what is good for the entire world is highly problematic," one source in India who worked on a Gates-funded vaccine project told me. "It is the same philosophy which dictators around the world have used—and still use. How does one man know what is good for everybody?"

• • •

IN THE AFTERMATH of the HPV scandal, the government of India imposed a series of changes that altered the foundation's work there. Officials in the Ministry of Home Affairs raised sharp questions about the Gates Foundation's outsize influence over civic life—and also scrutinized whether the foundation was exploiting a loophole in the law that allowed it to operate in India without the level of government oversight normally imposed on international groups. Specifically, India asks foreign-based organizations to register with the Foreign Contribution (Regulation) Act (FCRA), which the Gates Foundation didn't do.

"Since it is not registered under the FCRA, the funding of NGOs doesn't come under the government's watch list. It is not clear where and what they are funding. It is a loophole and it can open gates for other NGOs as well to use this route to escape scrutiny," an anonymous government official told the news media. "No inspections can take place and thus no taxes are paid. The BMGF works as a marketing office for U.S. pharmaceutical vaccines."

Indian media reported that the Gates Foundation, instead of registering under the FCRA, found a different modus operandi—as a "liaison office" under the jurisdiction of the Reserve Bank of India. Reporting at that time, as far as I can tell, didn't mention the fact that the director of Gates's India office, Nachiket Mor, according to Mor's LinkedIn profile, sat on the board of the Reserve Bank of India between 2013 and 2018, a period that overlapped with his work at the Gates Foundation between 2015 and 2019. This conflict of interest did surface later and prompted a lobbying effort to remove him from the bank's board. Mor ended up stepping down from the bank before his term was completed. He declined a request to be interviewed for this book.

It's not clear that the Gates Foundation did anything wrong in its registration, and it appears that other international foundations, like the Ford Foundation, also operate through the Reserve Bank. But the high-profile criticism from Indian government officials, nevertheless, shows how deeply anti-Gates sentiment had circulated.

In 2017, government scrutiny also came to bear on Gates's close ally, if not surrogate, Public Health Foundation of India, to which the

Gates Foundation has given at least $82 million. Ministry officials told journalists that they were concerned about Gates's financial influence over Public Health Foundation, and the government went on to place new restrictions on its ability to receive foreign funds. (These restrictions were lifted in 2022.)

The Indian government also announced a plan that seemed designed to reduce Gates's role in India's Immunization Technical Support Unit, moving the project from the Gates-funded PHFI into a government ministry. Srinath Reddy of PHFI noted that Gates actually continued to fund the program, simply moving it from PHFI to JSI, a private consultancy. At the end of 2021, the foundation gave a two-year, $1.75 million grant to JSI to support the transition of the unit to the government. This suggests that the earliest that the government might take it over would be late 2023, many years after public criticism of Gates's role first emerged. In short, whatever efforts the Indian government took to rein in the foundation went only so far.

One reason for this may be Gates's cunning political response to all the negative attention it was receiving. As public sentiment against the foundation gathered steam, the foundation did not sit on its hands. In 2019, it stunned the world by giving Indian prime minister Narendra Modi a high-profile humanitarian award—at the same time that Modi was in the midst of an international PR crisis related to human rights abuses in Kashmir, India's only Muslim-majority region. So many news outlets covered the controversy that even NPR, funded by Gates, was compelled to tell the story, reporting that three Nobel Peace Prize winners had condemned the Modi award. The issue escalated further when a communications officer in the Gates Foundation's India office resigned in protest, publishing a long essay about her decision in the *New York Times*.

"I had joined the Bill & Melinda Gates Foundation because I truly believed in its mission—that every life has equal value and all people deserve healthy lives. I resigned from it for the exact same reason. By presenting Mr. Modi with this award, the Gates Foundation is going against its own core belief," Sabah Hamid wrote. "The Gates Foundation has crossed the wide gulf between working with a regime and endorsing it. That is not the pragmatic agnosticism of an organization working with the government of the day, but a choice of siding with power. I will choose to walk a different path."

It's difficult to believe that the Gates Foundation, with its army of PR flacks, did not foresee the major fallout from this award. We can presume that the foundation made a calculation, believing that the political benefits of honoring Modi outweighed the costs. Under public scrutiny around its political influence in India, the foundation perhaps saw that its future in the country appeared to be in jeopardy. But it had too much invested in India, and too much of its legacy in global health depended on its projects working there. Some of the foundation's most important partners, including the for-profit Serum Institute, the largest vaccine manufacturer in the world, are located in India. And, again, India is the largest destination for Gates funding outside the United States and Europe. If the foundation were blackballed in India, its entire global health portfolio would be significantly diminished—and, who knows, it might even create a domino effect, with other nations questioning the foundation's outsize influence.

We might also ask what the Gates Foundation's waning influence in India might have meant for Microsoft. In the same way that Bill Gates's philanthropic endeavors seem to create a halo that shines brightly on Microsoft, we could argue that the Gates Foundation's significantly reduced role in India might have diminished Microsoft's influence. Manjari Mahajan's research notes that when the Indian government gave Bill Gates the Padma Bhushan Award for distinguished service—ostensibly for his philanthropic work—many government sources saw it as a recognition of his work with Microsoft. When Gates returned the favor, offering Prime Minister Modi a humanitarian award, it seems fair to ask whether such an award, at such a precarious time for Modi, might also have won favor for Microsoft.

However we view the award, it is very difficult to understand the logic of this decision outside the idea that, for Bill Gates, the ends justify the means. Getting Modi's blessing means moving obstacles out of the foundation's way, clearing a path to allow the foundation to seek new avenues of influence.

In 2022, the headhunter Flexing It announced that it was recruiting two "strategy consultants" for an unnamed "American private foundation" to assist the Indian government with its upcoming duties leading the G20, a meeting of political leaders from twenty powerful countries to discuss the global economy. The job description suggests that the unnamed foundation would work directly with the Indian government:

- Specialist will be attached to dedicated G20 working groups, and would develop concept notes/issue notes/background documents, themes and key priorities in respective areas for India's G20 forthcoming presidency.

- Would need to prepare draft outcome documents for the G20 meetings, and to help with negotiation process and negotiation strategy, including live drafting of document during negotiations.

- Develop knowledge on the state of play on issues discussed in G20 Working Group and to work towards proposals that would garner consensus in G20.

- Responsible to cover meetings and perform liaison duties with various Line Ministries/Departments of GoI, Think Tanks, International Organisations and G20 member & invitee countries etc.

A source with direct knowledge confirmed that the unnamed "American private foundation" was the Gates Foundation.

Covid-19

Years before the word *Covid* burned itself into public consciousness, researchers at the University of Oxford's Jenner Institute had been developing a new way to make vaccines and had even begun work on an earlier strain of the coronavirus.

Throughout the early days of Covid-19, news reports profiled Oxford's promising vaccine and the possibility that it would be academic researchers, not Big Pharma, who would deliver us from the unfolding global crisis. In those early media profiles, the Oxford lab acknowledged one weakness: it didn't have the full confidence of the marketplace. "What we struggle against all the time is the perception from funders that we can't do this," Adrian Hill, director of the Jenner Institute, said.

As the pandemic marched on, however, many naysayers seemed to have come around to the university's vaccine's enormous potential. A big feature in the *New York Times* cited the institute's early and broad efforts to line up agreements with foreign manufacturers to produce the vaccine—if and when it got regulatory approval. Looming in the background of the *Times* story was the Gates Foundation, the only expert source cited. "It is a very, very fast clinical program," said Emilio Emini, then a top vaccine executive at the Gates Foundation. The *Times* noted in passing that Gates was "providing financial support to many competing efforts."

It would be months before Gates's full role at Oxford became public knowledge, but the foundation's appearance in the article was a clear signal of its growing role in the wider response effort, where it was flexing the muscles it had developed after decades of work on vaccines. The foundation was expanding its ties to competing vaccine companies and also positioning itself at the center of a loosely organized WHO effort that promised to deliver vaccines to the global poor.

Gates's leadership role gave it influence over the direction of billions of dollars in taxpayer funds that flowed into the pandemic response. As one example, nearly 90 percent of the $3.2 billion lifetime budget (through December 2022) of the Coalition for Epidemic Preparedness Innovations has come from taxpayers, most of which is then used to subsidize pharmaceutical industry research and development. In 2022, CEPI confirmed via email that the Gates Foundation sits on all four of its internal committees that control how that money is spent.

Both behind the scenes and in the public spotlight, Bill Gates emerged as one of the most influential actors in the pandemic, and the media welcomed him with open arms, viewing him as a potent counterpoint to U.S. president Donald Trump, who had sought to downplay the novel coronavirus's severity. "We know how to work with governments, we know how to work with pharma, we've thought about this scenario," Gates said in 2020. "We need—at least in terms of expertise and rela-tionships—to play a very, very key role here."

Neither the World Health Organization nor wealthy nations were prepared for Covid-19, Gates said, and the pandemic couldn't realisti-cally be solved through governments. It needed to be a public-private partnership—and Gates needed to be at the head of the table. "We're always talking with WHO," he said, "but a lot of the work here to stop this epidemic has to do with innovation in diagnostics, therapeutics and vaccines, which isn't really [the WHO's] bailiwick."

Arguably, one reason that the WHO didn't have the expertise or capacity to manage the pandemic is that its authority had been eroded by the rise of the Gates Foundation. Gates has far more money than the WHO and has taken over key functions of its work. The foundation had also become the second-largest funder of the WHO, which allowed it to shape what the organization worked on and what it didn't. As the *New York Times* reported, the WHO had "wanted to take more of a leadership role in the vaccine deal making [during the pandemic], but the Gates Foundation and global nonprofits said they worried that drugmakers would not cooperate. They worked to focus the agency's role on regulating products and advising countries on distributing them, among other responsibilities."

Bill Gates doesn't particularly respect the WHO—in one public appearance during the pandemic, he casually noted, "If you're not very good, you'll stay working there for a long time"—but he appears to treat it as a necessary evil. By funding the WHO, the Gates Foundation can buy its blessing (or silence), gain the imprimatur of legitimacy, and, to a significant extent, control its work.

What all this meant is that, when the Covid-19 pandemic arrived, the fate of the global poor, and their ability to access vaccines, was not in the hands of governments or an intergovernmental multilateral body like the WHO. It was in the hands of Bill Gates. "He had enough money and enough presence in the area for a long enough period of time to be positioned as the first mover and the most influential mover. So, people just relied upon his people and his institutions," James Love, director of the NGO Knowledge Ecology International, told me. "In a pandemic, when there is a vacuum of leadership, people that move fast and seem to know what they're doing, they just acquire a lot of power. And [Bill Gates] did that in this case."

What Love is describing is not leadership, of course. It's a coup. And, as usual, the Gates Foundation locked down its power by erecting walls to prevent others from meaningfully participating in the response effort or even understanding what was happening. "You have an enormous amount of power that affects everyone around the globe, and there should be some accountability, some transparency. People are not asking unreasonable things," Love told me in 2020. "Can you explain what you're doing, for example? Can you show us what these contracts look like? Particularly since [Gates is] using their money to influence policies that involve our money."

Kate Elder, a vaccine policy adviser at Médecins Sans Frontières, echoed these same concerns in a 2020 interview: "Increasingly, I see less information coming from the Gates Foundation. They don't answer most of our questions. They don't make their technical staff available for discussions with us when we're trying to learn more about their technical strategy [on Covid-19] and how they're prioritizing certain things. . . .

They have blocked many discussions we've proposed with technical experts, instead putting us through to a PR person."

While public health experts raised concerns about the foundation's takeover of the Covid-19 pandemic response and about its patent-forward, Big Pharma–friendly strategy, the news media clung to a hero narrative that portrayed Bill Gates as a visionary leader and generous philanthropist. Journalists widely cited a TED Talk he gave in 2015 about pandemics, bombastically reporting that Bill Gates had "predicted" the novel coronavirus outbreak. As the pandemic became a reality, few outlets had the presence of mind to ask the really obvious question: Should an unelected billionaire be given this much influence over a major global public health crisis?

As the initial weeks of the pandemic became months, Bill Gates reached the absolute zenith of his philanthropic career, becoming one of the most sought-after talking heads in the world's most urgent crisis. Not since his golden-boy days at Microsoft, before his antitrust trials, had Gates been such a vitally important public figure. The crush of media attention was so great, and the hero worshipping so nearly universal, that Gates, perhaps inebriated with his newfound influence, often wandered off script.

In an interview on Trevor Noah's *The Daily Show*, Gates said his foundation was providing funding—what sounded like billions of dollars—to construct manufacturing facilities for seven different vaccine candidates so that production capacity would be in place when the vaccines were approved. The *Wall Street Journal* and others rushed to report Gates's announcement, part of an endless stream of stories profiling how the billionaire was rolling up his sleeves and getting the job done. After the manufacturing facilities story had circulated widely, the foundation clarified that it wasn't actually building factories.

Gates also became unusually open-throated about his influence over the commercial marketplace, letting slip in a press conference that his foundation had pushed the University of Oxford to change its business model as it rapidly advanced its Covid-19 vaccine. "We went to Oxford and said, you are doing brilliant work . . . [but y]ou really need to team up, and we told them a list of people to go and talk to," Gates recounted.

Trevor Mundel, president of Gates's global health program, later clarified, "We discussed with the University of Oxford the importance of aligning with a multinational company to ensure their researchers have the full range of capabilities and resources they need to bring their vaccine candidate to the world."

Oxford ended up partnering with AstraZeneca, and Bill Gates's loose-lipped comments, in this case, drew criticism. Oxford had previously publicized its intention to make its vaccine widely available to the global poor through an open license—as opposed to an exclusive license with Big Pharma. An open license would allow any capable manufacturer in the world to access the vaccine technology and, with the right funding and help, start scaling up production. For many, this business model would be key to combating the Covid-19 pandemic, getting as many facilities churning out vaccines as fast as possible.

"I personally don't believe that in a time of pandemic there should be exclusive licenses," Oxford's Adrian Hill had told the media at the start of the pandemic. In that brief statement, Hill was leaning on the fulcrum issue that held in the balance how the pandemic would play out. In a marketplace where virtually every human on earth is going to need multiple doses of a new vaccine, the pandemic was either going to be one of the most potent and lucrative monopoly markets ever devised or it was going to be a game-changing moment in modern medicine where we pushed aside Big Pharma's business-as-usual approach in favor of open, equitable distribution. It would be the biggest test of the pharmaceutical industry's political muscle since the HIV/AIDS crisis, when poor nations and activists around the globe fought to gain access to lifesaving drugs by successfully challenging the monopoly patents that had previously made the cure too expensive.

Many public health experts and activists had coalesced around a rallying cry for a "people's vaccine" during the pandemic, one that would not be governed by Big Pharma's intellectual property rights, patent claims, or exclusive licenses. Proponents of a people's vaccine brought to the table an undeniable dollars-and-cents argument. The Covid-19 vaccines proceeded from research funded by government agencies. Taxpayers were also pouring money into helping companies speed up vaccine development efforts. Given the public research and public funding that went into the creation of these vaccines, shouldn't the public have a say in how they are distributed? As the economic costs of the pandemic reached into the trillions of dollars, were we going to let Big Pharma's exclusive licenses and patent rights hold the world hostage? Literally millions of people were dying. Why wouldn't we work cooperatively to get every capable manufacturing facility up and running at full speed, patents and licenses be damned?

When Oxford, following its meeting with Gates, gave AstraZeneca an exclusive license, it dashed one leading hope for such a "people's vaccine." "It basically means that the concentration of power and decision making continues to rest squarely in the field of corporations, where pharmaceutical companies get to decide at what scale, at what volume, and what prices they are setting and who they are selling to first," Kate Elder told me.

The Gates Foundation, as always, insisted that Big Pharma was a trusted partner. "I think the pharmaceutical companies are going to make good on what they promised, I really do, because the whole world is watching," Melinda French Gates said in late 2020. "So as soon as this vaccine is available, it will run straight through this system."

The Gates Foundation had this confidence because it had its hands on the levers of "this system." The reason the foundation was positioned to lean on Oxford, for example, is the hundreds of millions of dollars it had given to the university through charitable grants. This included previous funding directly to the Jenner Institute, which developed Oxford's Covid-19 vaccine.

Oxford had also received funding from CEPI, founded and funded by Gates. In March 2020, CEPI announced that it was backing Oxford's vaccine with a relatively small donation. After Gates pushed Oxford to partner with a multinational, and after Oxford and AstraZeneca announced their partnership in April, CEPI almost immediately came through with a promise of up to $384 million. By June, CEPI and Gavi had announced a $750 million deal with AstraZeneca "to support the manufacturing, procurement and distribution of 300 million doses of the vaccine." And as Bill Gates tells it, he and his foundation remained integrally involved with the vaccine's development. "Every week we're talking with AstraZeneca about, okay, what's going on in India, what's going on in China, and . . . assuming that the Phase Two [clinical] data and eventually the Phase Three data is promising, that we're ready to go with that," Bill Gates noted in a press briefing.

> Our foundation has a lot of vaccine expertise and deep relationships with the manufacturers, and so, we've taken our staff and now are looking at each of these [potential vaccine] constructs and the data and [are] making sure that for the ones that are the most promising, there is a plan to have multiple factories in Asia, multiple factories in the Americas, multiple factories in Europe. . . . We understand which of these vaccines we can scale up the production, and I'm hopeful that it will be at that large number, because the cooperation from the pharma companies, of saying, "Yes, you can use my factory to make someone else's vaccine," we're getting a very good response to that, and that's really unprecedented.

Throughout the pandemic, Bill Gates got a lot of mileage promoting his matchmaking work on these "second-source agreements"—pairing up "vaccine companies in rich countries with counterparts in developing countries that specialize in producing safe, high-quality, and affordable doses at a very high volume." As Bill Gates explained it, "It's hard to overstate how unusual these second-source agreements are. Imagine Ford offering up one of its factories for Honda to build Accords. But given the scale of the problem and the urgency of solving it, many pharmaceutical companies are seeing the benefit of working together in new ways like this."

In Gates's mind, the solution to vaccine access was not jettisoning monopoly patent rights or exclusive licenses, or pursuing a "people's vaccine." The solution was torturing monopoly markets to make them work for the poor. And Gates had the daring and the hubris to believe that his foundation had the expertise, capacity, network, and negotiating skills to organize the marketplace and the pandemic response in a way that would protect poor nations.

The foundation's second-sourcing efforts focused heavily on the Serum Institute of India, a private company and the largest vaccine manufacturer in the world. Under an agreement with Gates, Serum became a second-source producer of the AstraZeneca and Novavax vaccines—because the foundation put up a three-hundred-million-dollar subsidy. "Our foundation took on some of the financial risk, so if it [AstraZeneca] doesn't get approved [by regulators], Serum won't have to take a full loss," Bill Gates said.

The foundation's total pledges to Serum appear to be the same amount of money Serum itself was putting into the project—in some respects, making Gates and Serum equal partners, if not also a dynamic duo: the world's most powerful actor in global health teaming up with the world's largest vaccine manufacturer. Yes, the Gates Foundation would have to put up large sums of its own money to induce Big Pharma to go where it wanted, but that's always been the foundation's win-win model of charity and profit.

Almost immediately, Gates's plan faltered. Serum drew criticism in January 2021 when it made a deal that charged the South African government 250 percent more than European governments were paying for the Oxford-AstraZeneca vaccine. Again, the explicit goal of the Gates Foundation's complex interventions in private markets is always "global access," making products accessible to people in poor nations. How was it that this massive charitable exercise, from the very first steps, presided over a business model that charged the poor more than the rich? The South African government was quoted as saying, "The explanation we were given for why other high-income countries have a lower price is that they have invested in the [research and development], hence the discount on the price."

At the same time, Serum continually struggled to deliver the doses it had promised. A major fire at its facilities killed five people, which the company initially claimed had no impact on vaccine production, but later said had dramatically delayed production. Critics then cried foul when Serum invested hundreds of millions of dollars in a financial services company while also claiming it needed more financial support from the government for vaccine production.

As a major wave of Covid-19 infections spread across India, the government effectively issued an export ban, directing Serum's shots into the arms of Indian citizens. This brought Gates's grand plan for vaccinating poor people across Africa to a grinding halt for a time. A special envoy of the African Union, Strive Masiyiwa, told the press that he had warned Gates's vaccine distribution program "not to put all its eggs in one basket." (Notably, Masiyiwa later joined the board of the Gates Foundation.)

The Oxford-AstraZeneca vaccine faced other hurdles in the marketplace. While the vaccine initially seemed well suited for poor nations because it didn't need to be stored in subzero temperatures—some nations do not have reliable access to electricity to run freezers—its lower efficacy made it less attractive. News outlets also reported that poor nations began avoiding the AstraZeneca vaccine because its short shelf life meant many doses expired before they could be used. Serum, at one point, halted vaccine production because it was sitting on an unused stockpile that risked expiring. Also notable, the development of the AstraZeneca vaccine was so "plagued by missteps," as journalists widely reported, that it was never approved by the FDA for use in the United States, even as U.S. taxpayers put more than a billion dollars into the project. Oxford nevertheless claims that its vaccine, created in partnership with AstraZeneca, saved more lives than competing vaccines during the first year vaccines were in use. But how many more lives could have been saved through a people's vaccine? The poorest nations in Africa, comprising one-fifth of the world's population, received less than 3 percent of the total number of Covid-19 vaccines distributed (from all manufacturers) in 2021.

Gates's other big vaccine bet, Novavax, faced even more serious problems as it struggled to get its vaccine across the finish line. Industry experts had cast doubt on the company from the beginning of the pandemic, noting that it had never brought a vaccine to market. The U.S. government awarded Novavax $1.6 billion for its vaccine, and the Gates-funded CEPI had chipped in another $400 million. Despite this financial support, Novavax's vaccine didn't end up getting its first regulatory approval, in Indonesia, until late 2021, and it didn't get the green light from the FDA until July 2022.

While Gates had created financial relationships with a wide variety of Covid-19 vaccine companies, through either direct charitable donations or by overseeing large donations from CEPI, it had placed its biggest bets on AstraZeneca, Novavax, and Serum. One important takeaway from the limited success of these efforts concerns Gates's claimed authority in pharmaceutical development—and whether Gates's far-reaching influence over private markets can be rationalized through the foundation's supposedly unique expertise.

· · ·

BEYOND THE FOUNDATION'S far-reaching work with vaccine developers and manufacturers during the pandemic, Gates also initiated and took control over a loosely organized structure at the WHO, called COVAX, to buy vaccines for the global poor. The idea was that wealthy nations would pool money and partner with poor nations, creating a massive fund that could be used to negotiate deals with Big Pharma.

More than a dozen Gates Foundation staff sat on various boards and working groups of COVAX, and Gates had similar influence on adjacent charitable projects aimed at delivering diagnostics and treatments. One news account described COVAX as a "Gates operation, top to bottom. It is designed, managed, and staffed largely by Gates organization employees."

While the foundation had its hands on the levers, it had put its surrogates CEPI and Gavi in charge, allowing Gates to disclaim any influence (or responsibility) when convenient. "The PR person at the Gates Foundation will often say, 'Oh, you know, the Gates Foundation is not on that body, I really suggest you direct your questions to Gavi or CEPI,'" Kate Elder of MSF told me. "It's sometimes frustratingly laughable . . . I don't take that as particularly honest." Elder also raised questions about Gates, Gavi, and CEPI running the WHO response effort because these are private organizations, not government bodies or multilateral institutions driven by governments. "We have certainly heard some concerns from governments that don't know Gavi, that haven't had a relationship with Gavi before and have challenges with the thought of giving a large sum of money to Gavi—and giving Gavi the power to negotiate on their behalf for future Covid-19 vaccine access," she told me in 2020.

As a private enterprise, COVAX had no public mandate and little legitimacy on the global stage, and criticism around transparency and accountability hounded the project. "They are pushing us, cornering us, in order to make us pay," Juan Carlos Zevallos, Ecuador's then health minister, told the press. "We don't have a choice about which vaccine we would like to use. It is whatever they impose on us. . . . They say, 'You don't get to choose, but you pay.'"

The biggest factor working against COVAX was the global marketplace. Wealthy nations began making one-off deals with pharmaceutical companies to secure vaccine doses for their citizens. This every-man-for-himself approach, however selfish, was not surprising. Of course elected leaders in wealthy nations were going to move aggressively to protect their constituents. What's surprising—astonishing, really—was that the Gates Foundation and its partners didn't plan for this.

As wealthy nations ordered enough doses to immunize their citizens many times over, the news media began to wring its hands over vaccine hoarding—and over the growing realization that the pandemic response would be defined by a divide between the haves and have nots, the rich and the poor, the winners and losers. This reality became known as vaccine apartheid.

This, of course, was all good business for Big Pharma, which prioritized sales to the richest nations that could pay the highest prices. Some pharmaceutical companies made unverifiable promises to sell their vaccines on a nonprofit basis during the pandemic, but that commitment didn't alter the logic of the market. Against the buying power of rich nations willing to pay high prices, Gates's underfunded buyers' club could not secure doses.

A year after the first vaccines were available in rich nations, the poorest people in the world were almost entirely without access to them. Even more poignantly, in June 2021, COVAX sent twice as many vaccines to the United Kingdom as it did to the entire continent of Africa. "The result is that poorer countries have landed in exactly the predicament COVAX was supposed to avoid: dependent on the whims and politics of rich countries for donations, just as they have been so often in the past," the Associated Press reported. This analysis, like most of the critical reporting that came out about COVAX, failed to mention that it was a Gates Foundation project.

As the global poor went unvaccinated, more than a hundred national governments signed on to petition the World Trade Organization to suspend Covid-19 vaccine patents, the first step in a process that could allow additional manufacturers to begin production, expanding the availability of vaccines to the poor. Waiving patents, in and of itself, wouldn't solve the problem—Big Pharma would still need to share the know-how and help manufacturers scale up production—but it was a first, crucial step.

In response, Bill Gates declared that the poor nations calling for waivers—the same poor nations his foundation claims to serve—didn't understand how the world worked. "Supply has been limited not because of IP rules, but because there aren't enough factories capable of handling the more complicated process of making vaccines," he wrote.

Throughout 2021, Bill Gates became the most visible public apologist for Big Pharma's patent rights, repeatedly giving media interviews in which he argued that patents didn't matter. "The thing that's holding things back in this case is not intellectual property. There's not, like, some idle vaccine factory with regulatory approval that makes magically safe vaccines," he told Sky News. "There's only so many vaccine factories in the world, and people are very serious about the safety of vaccines. And so, moving something that had never been done—moving a vaccine, say, from a J and J [Johnson and Johnson] factory into a factory in India—it's novel—it's only because of our grants and expertise that that can happen at all." Showing just how far removed he was from reality, Gates even went so far as to assert that his pandemic response effort was succeeding, saying it "doesn't get a perfect grade, but it does get a very high grade. . . . We're going to get to the point of equity."

As Gates conjured up the image of a well-functioning response effort led by his foundation, one in which every capable manufacturer was already up and running at maximum capacity, companies began going public almost as whistleblowers, saying that they, in fact, were being boxed out of production. "We have the facilities and equipment, bioreactors, we have fill-and-finish capability. Depending on how much help we get with technology transfer, we could be ready in a few months," the Canadian company Biolyse told the press. "I don't understand pharma's stance on this. Everyone needs to make money, sure. But this is a very serious situation and there's no reason to be this harsh."

The Associated Press and then the *New York Times* and then the Intercept began profiling manufacturing facilities around the world that appeared capable of producing vaccines, some of them explicitly saying they were ready, willing, and able. Human Rights Watch, MSF, and others pulled together another list of one hundred facilities around the globe that could potentially be put into production. Nobel-winning economist Joseph Stiglitz, citing evidence of spare capacity, wrote, "Any delay in ensuring the greatest availability of vaccines and therapeutics is morally wrong and foolish—both in terms of public health and the economy. The [patent] waiver is a critical first step."

Even Chelsea Clinton jumped into the fray. With her coauthor, Achal Prabhala, of AccessIBSA, Clinton argued that, to help production, President Biden should force U.S. companies to share their vaccine technology with companies that have manufacturing capacity. The piece profiled how Russia had worked with India to rapidly and cheaply retrofit a manufacturing facility that had not previously made vaccines.

Against the growing evidence that patents were, in fact, a major bottleneck, Bill Gates doubled down, recklessly burning through all the political capital he'd built during the first year of the pandemic. Again and again, Gates put himself in front of news reporters to campaign for the preservation of patents, at times becoming emotional. In one interview, he drew on his most famous put-down from his days at Microsoft to attack calls for a patent waiver: "That's the stupidest thing I've ever heard."

Gates's position seemed to boil down to the borderline racist idea that poor nations were not sophisticated enough to produce vaccines and that if we opened up manufacturing too broadly, it might lead to safety issues that could hurt people and increase vaccine hesitancy. As one former Gates Foundation employee told me, even if we accepted the foundation's argument that there was no spare manufacturing capacity to produce vaccines safely, why hadn't the Gates Foundation, as a self-professed leading expert and visionary on pandemics, foreseen this problem and addressed it? The foundation had been working on vaccines for two decades. It was sitting on a $54 billion endowment. And Bill Gates, we'd been told again and again, had "predicted" the pandemic. Did it really never occur to the Gates Foundation to help build advanced, sophisticated manufacturing facilities in poor nations?

In May 2021, the United States, under pressure to respond to the growing appearance of vaccine apartheid, publicly announced it would join the growing number of countries calling for a patent waiver. This shifted the political balance for the Gates Foundation, which, a day later, cravenly announced it now supported a "narrow" waiver—an astonishing reversal for a foundation that had zealously claimed that patents didn't matter.

The failures of the foundation and the visuals of insincerity—or incompetence—became so apparent that, at some point, even the news media began stating the obvious: the emperor has no clothes. While journalists in 2020 had viewed the Gates Foundation as too important to criticize—I personally had enormous difficulty getting editors to publish my work—something broke loose in 2021. The *New Republic* published a six-thousand-word story—featuring a cartoon portrait of Bill Gates wearing devil's horns—looking at Gates's history of destructive and obstructive advocacy around intellectual property in public health. Critical stories also appeared in places like the Intercept, the *Observer*, and the *Seattle Times*. For the first time in more than a decade, journalists were building a news cycle that put the Gates Foundation under real scrutiny. Critical voices that had long been on the margins of the news media began to find a place in more mainstream outlets. And Twitter became a hotbed of viral threads about Gates's driving role in vaccine apartheid. The message was as clear as it was common: Bill Gates was on the wrong side of history.

"What we're seeing [in the Gates Foundation's role in the pandemic] is the accumulation of twenty years of very careful expansion into every aspect in global health—all of the institutions, all of the different companies that often have these early-stage technologies, as well as all of the advocacy groups that speak to these issue, and all of the research institutions," said Rohit Malpani, a global health consultant and, at the time I interviewed him, a board member of the global health initiative Unitaid. "It also therefore reflects the failure of the Gates Foundation. The fact that they exert so much influence and even control over so many aspects of the [pandemic] response . . . and the fact that we are seeing so much inequity speaks to the influence that they have and [suggests that] the strategies that they've set out have not worked. And they have to own that failure."

But the Gates Foundation never did have to own that failure. As quickly as critical reporting about its work in the pandemic appeared, a far bigger story broke: the Gateses' divorce. The news media's short attention span quickly pivoted from Bill Gates's failed philanthropic leadership to his so-called wandering eye and allegations of sexual misconduct.

Journalists went on to widely pen autopsies of the faceless COVAX, but they virtually never put a hard critical lens on the Gates Foundation. In early 2023, for example, the *New York Times* reported that COVAX had paid out $1.4 billion to pharmaceutical companies for vaccine orders that were never delivered, Exhibit Z of the dysfunction and waste in the Gates-led effort. But the story mentioned the Gates Foundation only once, in passing.

One of the longest and highest-profile stories came from the Bureau of Investigative Journalism. Co-published with *El País*, STAT, and Ojo Público, the story had the potential to reach millions of readers, to shape public understanding about the failures of COVAX, and to point to policy solutions. The editors and journalists, however, made the editorial decision to completely bury the foundation's leading role in COVAX in the eighty-third paragraph of the story.

By minimizing Gates's role, the journalists misinformed the public—and failed to hold the Gates Foundation to account. (Full disclosure: I had been invited to co-report this story, but I declined because I knew Gates's funding would make it virtually impossible for me to independently report on the foundation's role in COVAX.) The bureau, like virtually every outlet, claims that its funders have no editorial influence over the work it publishes.

It wasn't long before the foundation was funding scientific research boasting of the millions of lives COVAX had saved; Gavi, which in 2020 had called COVAX the "only truly global solution to this pandemic," amplified the lives-saved PR. And Bill Gates announced that he would remain the leading authority on pandemics with the publication of his book *How to Prevent the Next Pandemic*. Naturally, there was never any accounting of how many lives could have been saved had we had a people's vaccine—nor how many lives were lost under the deeply inequitable vaccine distribution plan Bill Gates designed.

If we wanted to be exceedingly generous to the Gates Foundation, we could argue that it deserves some credit for having spent years prior to the Covid-19 pandemic shoring up the vaccine industry, which could be seen as giving the world a head start against the novel coronavirus. This was the argument Melinda French Gates tacitly made at the beginning of the pandemic: "Thank goodness we're not starting from where we were 20 years ago, with a crumbling vaccine system [and having] to rebuild it."

It is worth asking how the world might have fared in the Covid-19 pandemic without the Gates Foundation. If Gates hadn't intervened at the University of Oxford, might Oxford's Jenner Institute, in fact, have pursued an open license? Would that plan have worked? If Gates didn't exist, would Big Pharma still have had sufficient PR firepower to bend the knee of the global economy to its monopoly patents? If Gates hadn't inserted itself so forcefully in the pandemic response, might we have been able to imagine an alternative pathway to producing and distributing vaccines? Before the next pandemic comes, don't we owe it to ourselves to run out these counterfactuals? Shouldn't we accept that Bill Gates's master plan didn't work with Covid-19, and shouldn't we bet that his plan won't work in the next pandemic?

While the Gates Foundation created financial ties to many competing Covid-19 vaccine developers, we can nevertheless point to examples of vaccines that succeeded without Gates's help. Throughout the pandemic, the international media looked to the success of Cuba, where young children were vaccinated before those in the United States, for example. The Gates Foundation has never funded work in Cuba—its grant agreements explicitly state that the U.S. embargo prohibits it from doing so. It is this same embargo that has, for decades, cut off Cuba's access to much of global commerce, which is why the state had to develop its own public biotech sector, including homegrown research and development capabilities. After producing its own Covid-19 vaccine, Cuba exported doses to Vietnam, Venezuela, Syria, and Nicaragua. If Cuba can do this—without Bill Gates's help—can't other poor nations also build their own capacity, not just in manufacturing vaccines but also in doing the research and development to innovate new ones?

Peter Hotez, dean of the National School of Tropical Medicine at Baylor College of Medicine, in Houston, Texas, said building up this capacity is part and parcel of his lab's efforts, including its Covid-19 vaccine, Corbevax. Produced in partnership with the Indian company Biological E Limited, Corbevax was a late-arriving vaccine, but nevertheless boasted delivering more than 75 million shots through the fall of 2022. With a per-dose price of $1.90, Corbevax appears to be less expensive than other vaccines, including the Gates-Oxford-AstraZeneca-Serum shot. To boot, Hotez's effort focused on making the vaccine available to manufacturers in poor nations. For example, the Indonesian company Bio Farma announced that it would produce the vaccine under the name IndoVac.

Hotez's team accomplished all this despite having been largely boxed out of most major funding streams. Corbevax secured only five million dollars from CEPI and four hundred thousand dollars from the NIH, Hotez told me. By comparison, Gates, CEPI, and taxpayers pledged two billion dollars to Bill Gates's top-pick vaccine manufacturer, Novavax. Despite this massive help, Novavax told me it had delivered only around 73 million doses through early August 2022, about the same level of distribution as Corbevax.

"We could have gone much further and faster had we had a higher level of support from Gates and CEPI," Hotez told me. "The impression that Gates gives is that they think only the multinational vaccine companies have the chops to get the job done, and therefore that's where the focus is . . . , and to which I say, Look, it's also equally wrong to demonize the multinational pharma companies. They do a lot of good, and they provide a lot of access to the Gavi alliance. The mistake, I think, is not recognizing the role of low- and middle-income country vaccine producers."

Hotez said all his work on vaccines is organized around partnerships with poor nations. Corbevax, for example, boasts using a relatively easy technology that can be quickly scaled up. The idea is to move beyond the simplistic model of charity, not just donating doses to poor nations but empowering those nations to produce their own. "We've provided a different model, and now there's proof of concept that it works through Corbevax. There's a need to balance the portfolio more. It's not only the Gates Foundation, it's also Operation Warp Speed [the U.S. federal funding program for Covid-19 vaccines]. . . . The mistake was it's all about speed and innovation, it's all about incentivizing pharma companies. The mistake was an upstream science policy failure," Hotez said, "not recognizing that the LMIC [low- and middle-income country] producers had an important role."

Helping poor nations produce their own Covid-19 vaccines, Hotez notes, puts them on the pathway to develop other vaccines—for other diseases. Some diseases affect only a few poor nations. There will never be a major incentive for pharmaceutical companies to work on these projects. If vaccines are to be an integral part of solving these diseases, shouldn't poor nations be able to make their own, in response to local needs and according to local decision-making? Or do we ask poor nations to sit on their hands awaiting the goodwill of foreign philanthropists and pharmaceutical companies, expecting them to slowly take action?

"The whole point is balancing that vaccine ecosystem. That includes the multinational pharma companies—they'll also have an important role—but also embracing other types of organizations," Hotez said. "We do something that Gates and others have not been interested in, which is training and doing that capacity building, which I think is probably as important as the actual products."

What's particularly notable about Peter Hotez is that, years ago, he was a rising star in the Gates Foundation's orbit, someone who had received tens of millions of dollars in foundation funding. Throughout the early 2000s, Hotez and Bill Gates almost appeared to be part of a mutual admiration society. "In fact, I'd like to acknowledge Professor Peter Hotez," Gates said in a 2008 speech at George Washington University, "who's doing inspiring work on tropical diseases here at GW and is an important partner of our foundation." Two years earlier, Hotez told the news media, "The great thing about the Gateses is they are funding the diseases no one else will fund."

For reasons that are not clear, the foundation stopped funding his work a decade ago. Hotez insists there was no falling-out, saying the foundation simply decided to go in a different direction. Leading up to the big win with Corbevax, Hotez said, morale dropped as his lab struggled to advance their work. But he still credits the foundation for much of his success, and in our interview, he was always careful to sandwich any criticism of the foundation with praise. "If it wasn't for the Gates Foundation, Peter Hotez wouldn't be Peter Hotez. What that did for us was not only support the hookworm vaccine, but supported us with the infrastructure to make vaccines in the first place—with the quality control, quality assurance, and also the methods of how you get a vaccine through regulatory authorities. All of that infrastructure was supported by Gates for the purposes of hookworm, but we've been able to repurpose it to all of our other vaccines as well. If you were to say to me, 'What's the first thing you would do if you saw Bill Gates right now?' I would say, 'I would just thank him for making all that possible' [laughing]. Then I'd tell him how some things need to get fixed."

On social media, where Hotez counts hundreds of thousands of followers, critics sometimes attack him as a kept man of Bill Gates, citing his previous funding from the Gates Foundation and his eagerness to publicly praise Gates's work. The reality of their relationship seems quite different. While Hotez's and Gates's passions and work do seem to be in lockstep—they are perhaps the world's two leading public champions for vaccines, both focused on diseases affecting poor nations—Bill Gates and the Gates Foundation, to my eye, almost seem to be competing with Hotez.

One year after Hotez published his book *Preventing the Next Pandemic*, for example, Bill Gates published an almost identically titled book, *How to Prevent the Next Pandemic*. Similarly, the Gates Foundation is funding the development of a schistosomiasis vaccine at Texas Tech University in the same state as Hotez's lab, which also has a leading schistosomiasis vaccine candidate. I asked Hotez about this.

"I guess the frustration I have is they miss opportunities to partner with fellow travelers, almost like they're going into competition," he said. "The schistosomiasis vaccine is a great example. It'd be easy for them to add on our vaccine candidate to what they're doing. Instead, we have to go off on our own and seek funding. And, let's face it, when Gates gets involved, there's no one who can put up that level of support like Gates. With the Gates Foundation, you're dealing with ten to the seven dollars. [10^7 translates to 10,000,000.] Having to go out after to grants for ten to the five and ten to the six dollars [$100,000 and $1,000,000], you've got to get a lot of those make up the difference. It's not easy. It would be so much more straightforward if they would just add on our antigen [to the trials they're currently funding], and test them in combination or separately," he said, explaining that he has specifically asked the foundation to support his vaccine. "We're not interested in competing, by any means. It's ridiculous. We would love to partner with them. I was very grateful when we were funded by the Gates Foundation because they can do a lot of good."

Gates's reluctance to fund Hotez might relate to their differing conceptualization of public health and the role of vaccines. A good example of this is the new malaria vaccine that the pharma giant GSK rolled out in 2021. The vaccine was widely criticized for its low efficacy and for the large sums of time and money that went into its development. Even the Gates Foundation, which funded the vaccine, publicly distanced itself, telling the news media that it was going in a different direction.

Hotez has a different take: "For these more complicated targets like malaria, like schistosomes [the parasites that cause schistosomiasis], like hookworm, it's unlikely you're going to get a vaccine that is as effective as a measles vaccine or a polio vaccine. They're going to be partially protective. And what I've said to the Gates Foundation and the WHO and others is we have to think about those types of vaccines in a new way, that they're not going to be replacement technologies. They're going to be companion technologies. Even though we'll have a malaria vaccine, we're still going to need bed nets and antimalaria drugs. But this [vaccine] will be an important ally. And the world hasn't really understood how to think about vaccines in that context."

This is a real-world assessment of vaccines from a medical doctor and vaccine developer. Bill Gates, a college dropout with no medical training, has a very different take. He calls vaccines "magic" and markets them as "miracles." From that mind-set, a "partially protective companion technology" isn't going to get Gates where he wants to go—achieving the goal he set to eradicate malaria.

In a 2003 interview, Gates expressed great confidence that his foundation could develop a highly effective malaria vaccine: "Absolutely. No doubt. . . . You know, I'd say, quite certainly within the next 20 years and ideally in the next 10 we'll have a good vaccine for malaria. . . . But because of computer technology now, medical advances will move at an incredible pace. The next 20 or 30 years will be the time to be in medicine. Many of the top problems, I'd say most of the top problems, we'll make huge advances against." In 2009, Gates expanded these forward-looking claims: "We're on the verge of some big advances—malaria, diarrhea, AIDS prevention. Each one of these things in the next two or three years—we're going to achieve some very big milestones: getting some new vaccines out, discovering new approaches."

In 2010, then CEO of the Gates Foundation Jeff Raikes elaborated on this: "We're not really the organisation that's involved in bed-nets for malaria. We're much more involved in finding a vaccine."

As it turns out, bed nets appear to have been the single most important intervention against malaria—and the Gates Foundation has, in fact, given billions of dollars to the Global Fund, which distributes them. But it is also true that, under the foundation's leadership, progress against malaria has leveled off, even before the pandemic. Though we have many tools to treat and prevent malaria, we continue to see hundreds of millions of cases each year and hundreds of thousands of deaths, mostly of children. Gates's "huge advances" and "big solutions" and innovation agenda, which the news media have endlessly, uncritically hyped, have not delivered.

As Hotez's lab continues to advance several vaccine candidates—against hookworm, schistosomiasis, and Chagas disease—he struggles, he told me, not only to find funding but also to imagine what will happen if the vaccines are successful. Without Gates Foundation support, how will he negotiate a marketplace that is essentially governed by the Gates Foundation? The foundation and its surrogates, in many ways, *own* the infrastructure in which Hotez's vaccines will succeed or fail. And, of course, there's an extremely large body of evidence demonstrating that Bill Gates does not like competition.

"I'm confident there will be evidence of effectiveness [of our vaccines], but whether they get to market depends on unknown forces," Hotez told me. "What's exhilarating about what we're doing is that, without the Gates Foundation, there's no road map for these vaccines. That's what's exhilarating but also what's terrifying, what keeps me up at night."

Conclusion

In the same way that Captain Ahab's dogged pursuit of the mighty whale Moby Dick led him into increasingly irrational and self-destructive behavior, polio has become something of a white whale for Bill Gates, an obsession that has clouded his common sense and good reason. "I've sort of, in a sense, put the foundation's reputation on the line that we're to going to get smart and do whatever it takes [to eradicate polio]," he says in the Netflix docuseries *Inside Bill's Brain*. "If you try to eradicate and fail, that's very bad because you tarnish the entire reputation and credibility of the whole global health effort."

That's actually not true. Failing to eradicate polio would tarnish Bill Gates's reputation, not that of the "whole global health effort." Leading voices in global health have long questioned Gates's crusade to eliminate polio from the earth. As Donald A. Henderson, credited with leading the world's only successful eradication (a WHO effort against smallpox), noted in 2011, "Fighting polio has always had an emotional factor—the children in [leg] braces, the March of Dimes posters. . . . But it doesn't kill as many as measles. It's not in the top 20." Henderson, now deceased, said in another interview, "When you're doing polio, you're not doing other things. Through 2011, in several countries—Nigeria, India and Pakistan—they were giving polio vaccines but they were not, for example, giving the DPT [diphtheria-tetanus-pertussis] vaccine or the measles vaccines."

In the decade ahead, medical experts would continue to question whether the money and energy going into polio eradication may actually have hurt broader aims of public health, citing, for example, refrigerators at medical clinics in poor nations so fully stocked with polio vaccines that there was no physical space for measles doses. "Would there have been other ways to spend that money which would have saved even more children from really nasty diseases?" Oliver Razum, an epidemiologist at Bielefeld University, asked in 2021.

What this criticism speaks to are "opportunity costs"—what potential successes we miss out on when we choose to follow Gates's priorities; what work doesn't get funded when taxpayers' money is directed to Gates's public-private partnerships; how many more people might benefit, or even how many more lives might be saved, if we pursued a different pathway. With polio, few would argue that we shouldn't vaccinate children, but many public health professionals endorse a strategy aimed at controlling polio, not the ends-of-the-earth eradication strategy the Gates Foundation has pursued, which takes an order of magnitude more resources. Instead of funding armies of vaccinators to go door-to-door to administer polio vaccines, why not put that money into funding clinics where people can receive the polio vaccine alongside other medical treatment?

The Gates Foundation has put more than eight billion dollars into polio, and by the early 2010s, Bill Gates was telling the media that eradicating polio "is the single thing I work on the most." Nevertheless, taxpayers in rich nations, and in poor nations, have put more money into polio— billions of taxpayer dollars have flowed into the project at the urging (or de facto lobbying) of the Gates Foundation. The foundation has also pushed the WHO to keep polio as one of its very top priorities, which has diminished its capacity to work on far more consequential public health problems, like pandemic preparedness, TB, malaria, and HIV/AIDS.

The global polio eradication campaign, which preceded Bill Gates but which likely would not have continued without his foundation's support, has driven down cases of wild-type polio into the double digits— fewer than a hundred people around the globe carry the virus that causes paralysis. And this progress has given Gates the momentum he needs to keep the donor money flowing into his pet project. "Polio is at a very magical point where we have so few cases that if we really intensify our efforts we'll completely eradicate the disease, making it only the second time that's been done," he said in 2013. "And that means you'll save all the costs of vaccination in the future and nobody's at risk of ever being paralyzed again. We're orchestrating a lot of donors and new science to get this thing finished in the next three to five years."

Gates missed his target, and in recent years his campaign has presided over a rise in polio—and its sudden reappearance in wealthy nations. That's because the eradication effort has depended on oral immunization—the media sometimes publishes images of Bill Gates squeezing drops of the vaccine into the mouths of children—that includes a weakened strain of the polio virus. The idea is to give the immune system a small taste of polio and build up an ability to fight it. The problem is that the weakened virus found in the oral vaccine can mutate and be passed on to others, infecting those who are not immunized. Rarely but reliably, the oral polio vaccine will actually *cause* paralysis—and outbreaks that lead to more cases. (Wealthy nations, like the United States, use a different polio vaccine that does not contain a live virus and cannot cause vaccine-derived paralysis.) According to reporting in the *British Medical Journal* by writer Robert Fortner, more than one thousand people throughout Africa were paralyzed in 2020 by vaccine-derived polio.

"The eradication initiative was aware at some point, as they moved toward eradication," Fortner told me in an interview, "that vaccine-derived cases were going to be greater in all likelihood than cases from the wild virus." The problem, he said, was that Gates and other partners didn't move quickly enough, and they still don't seem to have a solution. When I interviewed Fortner in July 2022, it was one day after the news media reported that a man in New York had been paralyzed by vaccine-derived polio.

In some respects, the eradication campaign might have been doomed to fail from the beginning because it operated in such a top-down fashion, proceeding from ideology, or vanity, rather than science and democracy. Historian William Muraskin of Queens College quotes Gates Foundation employees openly explaining their "blame-and-shame" strategies to pressure local leaders to get in line with Gates's eradication agenda, while also using inducements—or, as they condescendingly call them, "goodies." Even before the foundation became the leading voice on polio, the eradication effort, Muraskin reports, "worked to deter research, distort publications, silence and banish critics, all in the name of achieving the public good." Muraskin writes:

> No matter how much goodwill global health people may have . . . they take upon themselves the right to judge which local, regional and national leaders are "illegitimate," and then work to bypass, co-opt, "educate," manipulate or otherwise circumvent these stumbling blocks to achieve their noble goals. Who made them judges over develop-ing world leaders? Who appointed them, who elected them, who are they accountable to? They seem blind to the similarities between their claims to beneficent interventions today and the similar claims of the Western colonial powers in the past. The basic attitude is the same: we know what is best for these people, their rulers are oppressive, incom-petent and corrupt. In the past, the "wise men" of the West simply took the countries over. Today, they just work to "guide" them in the right direction. In the past, it was Christianity and Civilization that gave them the right. Now it is Universal Values, Humanitarians, and Global Public Goods.

In Bill Gates's determination to eradicate polio, we see how blurred the line becomes between his good intentions and his enormous ego. Every big man wants to point to something big he's done. U.S. president Donald Trump tried (and failed) to build a continuous border wall with Mexico. Industrialist and philanthropist Andrew Carnegie built thou-sands of libraries, many of which still stand today and carry his legacy. The bridges, parkways, and parks Robert Moses built indelibly changed New York, and some still bear his name.

So, where is Bill Gates's big accomplishment? Microsoft Windows? A collection of exaggerated claims around the lives he has saved, under-girded by research he funded? The "Giving Pledge," his bullying effort to push more of his billionaire peers into philanthropy? Gavi, his complex procurement mechanism that, essentially, fund-raises money from gov-ernments to buy vaccines from Pfizer?

Gates needs to eradicate polio to rationalize all the wind and swagger he's brought to his charitable work, to substantiate the endless claims and promises he's made about curing disease. And he will, apparently, go to extreme lengths to accomplish this, no matter the opportunity costs, no matter the experts' criticism, and no matter the damage it causes.

In reporting this book, I often asked sources to name what they thought Bill Gates's biggest accomplishments were. Virtually everyone struggled to come up with specific examples, instead pointing in the general direction of the billions of dollars he has given away. "I was there when the Gates Foundation was born," one grantee told me. "Can you imagine all of us nerdy scientists looking at this pot of money as a way to now make our lives more meaningful? Not just easier, but more meaningful—taking our lab and staff and developing it into a product. It was transformational. You can't overlook the importance of a champion for the poorest of the poor who nobody gives a shit about." The source added, "We need champions and need advocates. . . . It's better to have a flawed champion than no champion at all."

This narrative speaks to Gates's good intentions, and it frames the merits of his work around the spectacle he created. He made the world pay attention. He is well-meaning, even if imperfect. But what's missing from this assessment is the fact that Bill Gates hasn't been a champion of the poor as much as of himself. He's asked us to direct our gaze not to the plight of the global poor but, rather, to his own philanthropic efforts to save them. Whether it is taking the podium at the World Health Organization or the World Economic Forum, posing for photos with poor children in some unnamed province or state, or sitting for interviews with *60 Minutes* or CNN, the focus of the Gates Foundation is not on global poverty. It's on Bill Gates. Between the media attention, the tax benefits, the awards, the political power, and the PR, the biggest beneficiary of the Gates Foundation, then, is Bill Gates himself.

More important, the poorest of the poor never asked Bill Gates to be their champion. They didn't review his candidacy or his policy positions and then elect him to any office. There was never any public debate over his leadership, priorities, or agenda. The same is true in wealthy nations, where taxpayers have put billions of dollars into Gates's public-private partnerships with very little public debate or scrutiny over these expenditures. Gates simply assumed power by claiming leadership over unpopular and difficult areas—how to feed, medicate, and educate poor people.

It's tempting to ask, at this point in the book, well, how *should* someone like Bill Gates spend his philanthropic dollars? This framing, however, elides more fundamental questions about power. When we allow one person—any person, no matter how benevolent or well intentioned—to acquire extreme wealth, we're giving that person extreme power. The question, then, is not how Gates's money could be better spent, but why we allow anyone to have this much money and power in the first place.

As a practical matter, we should also ask whether Gates's vast wealth is really his to control. His fortune comes from one of the most widely criticized monopolies in the history of the world, which used its extreme market power to push its extremely mediocre and often infuriatingly glitchy software into our lives. Microsoft is also very widely criticized for tax avoidance. From this questionable business, can we say that Gates *earned* his vast wealth? That he *deserves* it? That it is his to use freely as a tool to advance his political worldview? That society benefits from this arrangement?

We must also consider existential questions about the ability of a billionaire—any billionaire—to drive social progress through philanthropy. The success of Gates's giving seems to turn on the myth of the benevolent tyrant, our belief that handing over undemocratic power to one man is the price we have to pay to, say, vaccinate the poor. As we've seen, Gates's outputs aren't particularly impressive, effective, or efficient; nor are his efforts delivering the "equity" he claims is the central focus of his work. The Gates approach puts poor nations in competition for limited donor dollars in order to deliver public health to their citizens. It conceives of health care as a privilege, or a gift, rather than a human right. And it spends untold sums of money on pomp, circumstance, and public relations to make the world believe that this is the best, if not the only, solution.

All that being said, it is beyond dispute that the wealth Bill Gates controls—his $100 billion private fortune and the $54 billion endowment of his private foundation—could be of enormous benefit to society. Yes, the world needs Bill Gates's money. But it doesn't need Bill Gates.

Fixing our Bill Gates problem, then, means separating Gates from his money. The soft approach is to consider reforms to the Gates Foundation, finding ways to make it actually function as a charity that gives away money rather than as a political tool, tax break, and PR machine for Bill Gates. Though the Gates Foundation essentially self-regulates today, that privilege comes from Congress, which could just as easily impose new, strict regulations that force it to act in a more charitable manner. Ultimately, it's up to our elected legislators, and to us, the people who elect members of Congress, to decide how, or if, we regulate philanthropy.

Just as Congress undertook an "agonizing reappraisal" of philanthropy in the 1960s, we are very long overdue for new rules and regulations governing billionaire philanthropists. We could also look to the IRS and the Washington State attorney general, who both have direct oversight of the Gates Foundation but have chosen not to exercise those powers, either because of a lack of resources or of political will. We could also ask the Department of Justice to investigate the anti-competitive allegations the foundation faces in pharmaceutical development.

Reformers have already proposed a number of modest new rules for private foundations that could rein in the Gates Foundation. Tax scholars want foundations to give away a larger percentage of their endowments every year instead of the currently mandated 5 percent. Making foundations pay out larger sums will accelerate their time line to bankruptcy, limiting the long-term political influence that an institution like the Gates Foundation can have.

We might also insist that the payout requirement apply to *money actually given away to others*. As Linsey McGoey notes in her book *No Such Thing as a Free Gift*, "If a gift is to be actually given—that is, if it's actually meant to be surrendered by a donor, preventing him or her from further claims on that gift—that donor has no right to involvement." If the Gates Foundation wants to pour billions of dollars into underwriting groups it controls—that is, the money it gives to its surrogates and agents—this should not be considered as charity or count toward its payout requirements. Nor should the extraordinary sums the foundation spends on its own bloated bureaucracy—like the billion dollars a year it spends on McKinsey consultants, administrative costs, and maintaining its grandiose headquarters in Seattle.

The charitable nature of Gates's gifts must also be questioned because the Gates family can so often be seen as deriving a benefit, whether it is the one hundred million dollars the foundation has donated to the elite private school the Gates children attended or the foundation's generous giving to journalism, which has burnished the reputation of the Gates

Foundation and the Gates family. Gates's giving to newsrooms, like its gifts to private companies, should be viewed as commercial contracts, not charitable gifts, and should not be subject to any tax benefits.

Reformers of Big Philanthropy have also proposed a new era of transparency, which would require the Gates Foundation to explain its work. This should include a clear distillation of its financial flows and an end to its culture of dark money. It could also mandate that the foundation be subject to public records requests and that it make public all grants and contracts it signs.

We could also consider a different governance structure at the foundation, bringing in a strong, independent board to make sure that Bill Gates cannot single-handedly control how the foundation's money is spent. My own belief is that, if the foundation is to continue, Bill Gates should not be allowed to play *any* institutional role in it. When Gates moves his private wealth into his private foundation, which he controls, this is not charity, and we should create rules that make this clear.

If not Bill Gates, then who should run the Gates Foundation? A group of puppets whom Bill Gates appoints? Of course not. The people who should have control over the foundation's wealth should be drawn from the intended beneficiaries of the foundation—teachers, students, farmers, doctors, and patients from the poor locales the foundation serves. They could take control over the foundation and purposefully spend very large sums of money each year to rapidly draw down its endowment. Arguably, the most just way to accomplish this would be to make onetime cash payments from the foundation's bank account to the poorest people in the world. This act of charity would actually entrust and empower the poor to make their own decisions over how to spend Gates's money. It's not going to change the world, but it would accomplish far more than Bill Gates's father-knows-best philanthropy.

Some readers might be incredulous at these solutions, asking how exactly this is going to happen. Do we really believe that Bill Gates will go quietly into the night, relinquishing power over the philanthropic empire he has built? Of course not. The Gates Foundation has spent very large sums of money, through charitable donations, to build up a massive special interest group to defend Bill Gates's unregulated "freedom to give," as the Gates-funded Philanthropy Roundtable describes it. The foundation has given around five hundred million dollars in donations into what could be called the philanthropy-industrial complex, underwriting the professional class of white-collar philanthropy defenders, apologists, and practitioners who present a formidable obstacle to reform efforts.

Corporate interests like Big Pharma, Big Ag, and Big Ed, if not also the U.S. State Department, have a very keen interest in the perpetuity of Bill Gates's philanthropic career—because he presents as a powerful statesman who, while claiming to help the global poor, is very actively engaged in helping the rich and advancing U.S. economic interests (and corporate interests, more generally). In the same way that the U.S. government seeks to create export markets for American technology and other commodities, so too does the Gates Foundation, whether it is Pfizer vaccines or Monsanto (now Bayer) GMOs.

Against this political opposition, can we work through current political channels to challenge Bill Gates? More to the point, if we did build the necessary political power to create new regulations over the Gates Foundation, wouldn't Gates simply shut down his foundation and start giving away his wealth as a private citizen?

This is the innovative spirit that Meta (Facebook) founder Mark Zuckerberg and his spouse, Priscilla Chan, brought to their philanthropic giving, legally organizing their philanthropy as a limited liability company instead of a nonprofit private foundation. This means they forgo some tax benefits but gain a significant measure of opacity, shielding the details of their philanthropy from public scrutiny. As weak as current regulations around private foundations are, they at least give us some sight line into the Gates Foundation's work—like its annual tax filings, which allow us to see how some of the money flows.

In some respects, Bill and Melinda French Gates already appear to be following Zuckerberg's lead, spending more and more time and money on side projects like Breakthrough Energy, Pivotal Ventures, Gates Ventures, and other quasi-philanthropic efforts organized as companies, not private foundations.

This is where it becomes clear that really fixing our Bill Gates problem has to go beyond congressional reforms to the Gates Foundation. As long as Bill Gates maintains his extreme wealth, he will remain a canker on democracy. He will find ways to use his vast fortune to acquire and wield undemocratic power—if not through his private foundation, then through other means.

Finding a solution also requires us to widen the lens on the problems at hand. The foundation describes its work as "guided by the belief that every life has equal value" and as helping "all people lead healthy, productive lives." This mission and vision have great merit, but they necessarily require us to imagine a world where everyone has basic rights and privileges and can fulfill their most basic needs—a decent place to live, basic health care, clean water and enough food to eat, educational opportunities, the ability to find gainful employment, legal protections from discrimination, and other basic democratic rights.

Can we confidently state that the Gates Foundation moves us in this direction? Under Gates's model, the global poor will never have clean water, but *some* will have access to rotavirus and polio vaccines that offer some protection against sickness caused by dirty water and poor sanitation. The poor will never have access to basic health care systems that provide routine cancer screenings, but *some* will have access to HPV vaccines that allow some protection against cervical cancer. Poor women will never have full autonomy over their reproductive health, but *some* will have access to the limited contraceptive choices Gates subsidizes. Farmers in many African nations will have access to the foundation's favored solutions, synthetic fertilizer and, maybe, eventually, GMO seeds, but they may be asked to take on devastating debt or watch their soils degrade from the chemical inputs. The poorest school districts in the United States, likewise, will be subject to new tests and surveillance mechanisms that Gates believes they need to succeed, but the students there will never have the encouragement or freedom that Gates's own children have had to develop and explore their intellectual interests.

Bill Gates and the Gates Foundation cannot be expected to fix all the world's problems or single-handedly resolve global poverty, but that's not really the issue. The question we have to ask is whether Gates's model of charitable giving is moving us in the right direction or, in fact, setting up distractions and roadblocks to the real, systemic changes we need. Can we truly achieve equality in the face, or by the hand, of billionaire oligarchs? On some basic level, can't we see that the Gates model boils down to empowering the wealthiest people on earth to make decisions for the poorest?

These questions will become increasingly important in the years ahead, as Bill Gates has coaxed close to 250 of the world's richest people to sign a "Giving Pledge" in which they promise to give away the majority of their wealth. We are asked to celebrate these acts of generosity and marvel at the life-changing potential in the hundreds of billions—or maybe even trillions—of dollars in philanthropy coming down the pike. But a more sober analysis would consider the hundreds of billions of dollars in lost tax revenue this charitable giving will produce. It would also question whether philanthropy can offset the very significant societal harms involved in the creation of most of these vast fortunes.

Philanthropist Mark Zuckerberg's wealth comes from a company beset by allegations of harm—from corporate tax avoidance to the Cambridge Analytica scandal to invasion of privacy to the distribution of misinformation. Jeff Bezos made headlines in late 2022, when he announced that he would devote most of his wealth to philanthropy—but on the same day, Amazon, the company that made him so wealthy, announced that it would be laying off ten thousand workers. Bezos's ex-wife, MacKenzie Scott, likewise has received much praise and glory for her disruptive approach to philanthropy, making massive, no-strings-attached donations to support underrepresented communities—yet we must also consider the ongoing harm embedded in her wealth from Amazon, which wields monopoly power in the marketplace, pays very little in taxes, and fights unionization efforts aimed at correcting widely reported labor abuses. Billionaire Chuck Feeney deserves credit for reportedly making good on his promise to give away almost all his fortune, much of it anonymously, yet he carefully organized his wealth creation around tax avoidance—and the sale of products damaging to human health, like the cigarettes and booze sold in his duty-free shops.

Sam Bankman-Fried, the cryptocurrency billionaire facing federal fraud charges (as of early 2023), asked the world to celebrate his rapid acquisition of wealth, promising that he would donate 99 percent of it to charity. In late 2022, Bankman-Fried's crypto empire came crashing down, and a teachers' pension plan in Ontario was among the big losers, seeing losses of nearly one hundred million dollars. Staff from Bankman-Fried's charitable arm, the FTX Future Fund, resigned, issuing a statement saying, "To the extent that the leadership of FTX may have engaged in deception or dishonesty, we condemn that behavior in the strongest possible terms."

Even with our best billionaire philanthropists, we have to reckon with the damage, greed, or tax avoidance that fuels their charitable giving. And we have to consider the idea that if we really care about equity and want the world to be a more equitable place, we should reorganize our economy and society in a way that doesn't allow the accumulation of such extreme wealth by a very small group of people.

There are many ways to do this, but the most obvious corrective is a new era of taxation. This means putting an end to the tax avoidance strategies of multibillionaires and multibillionaire corporations, making Bill Gates (and Big Pharma and Big Tech and everyone else) pay their fair share. My own view is that with the richest people on earth, like Bill Gates, the currently proposed wealth tax—even Bernie Sanders's proposal to take eight percent a year from the very richest people—doesn't go far enough. A wealth tax would limit Bill Gates's ability to become richer, but it would not change the fact that he is obscenely rich. Addressing our Bill Gates problem requires us to consider far more aggressive taxation measures, either a much higher wealth tax or a different mechanism. Some readers might balk at the idea of asking our current brain trust of elected officials in Washington, DC, to redistribute Bill Gates's vast wealth, questioning whether these crooks, cronies, and reprobates are better stewards of his money than his philanthropy is. It is true that much of the money would be poorly used and misspent, but isn't the Gates Foundation already misspending the money? Look at its serial failed philanthropic endeavors, its bureaucratic mire and bloat, it's crony-style surrogate power, its wasteful spending on its half-a-billion-dollar headquarters, and it's endless expenditures on self-promotional, self-serving PR. If some amount of money is going to be misused regardless, why not put it into a democratic body, where we would have some control over it, where it would be subject to at least some checks and balances? And as a basic matter of principle, why not ask Bill Gates to play by the same rules as the rest of us, to pay his fair share in taxes?

How we manage Bill Gates's wealth really boils down to what kind of world we want to live in and how much we care about equity, justice, freedom, and democracy. It's easy to feel cynical or skeptical about changing the world, but it's important to recognize that we don't really have a choice. The fight has already begun. And the world is already turning against men like Bill Gates.

Look at popular culture and the proliferation of movies and episodic shows—*Silicon Valley, Succession, Billions, Ozark, Loot, Don't Look Up, Glass Onion*, and on and on and on—where billionaires are presented as amoral villains and billionaire philanthropy as a self-serving vanity project or political tool. Look at our political discourse, where mainstream candidates are being asked questions about the one-percenters and whether billionaires should even exist. All around us, the signs are clearly pointing to gathering distrust in and distaste for oligarchy and the false promises of tech billionaire philanthropists.

Look at the Covid-19 pandemic, which exposed how grotesquely inefficient and inequitable our economic system is, prioritizing the needs of the rich over those of the poor and prioritizing the patent rights of Big Pharma over the public health and economic well-being of the planet. Look at political and social movements like Occupy Wall Street and Black Lives Matter—on which the Gates Foundation remained deadly silent—which call for reorganizing our society in ways that directly challenge the excess wealth and "white savior" mentality that drives Bill Gates's philanthropic work. And look at climate change, where Bill Gates's shameless efforts to assert his leadership—preposterously proposing that his own new, untested technologies will one day save the planet—have been fairly widely panned, even in mainstream publications. Climate change will bring unthinkable destruction to all our lives in the years ahead, and it will show us again and again how wrongheaded and illegitimate Bill Gates's claimed role in public life is.

At the Gates Foundation's annual "Goalkeepers" gala in late 2022, the foundation invited climate activist Mikaela Loach as one of the speakers. She used her brief time at the microphone to skewer the foundation's model of change, arguing that an economic system based on a few big winners and many more losers can't deliver equity as the foundation claims. "I think billionaires shouldn't exist," Loach said.

> We can't just talk about redistributing wealth, if we're not redistribut-ing power as well as that. . . . And so when we interrogate power, we have to then ask: Who holds the power in this room? Who holds the power in the world? Who's deciding what solutions are being chosen—like whose name is on the foundation? Who's making these decisions, and then therefore who's creating the narratives and who's in control of those narratives? And how does this maybe limit the solutions that we're pursuing? Maybe we're not actually transforming the world; maybe we're just continuing the world as it is now but making it look a little bit different. How can we demand more?

What this statement of protest shows is that the Gates Foundation, even at its own highly scripted, carefully curated VIP events, can't paper over its crisis of legitimacy. Bill Gates can no longer hide from his critics, who are coming to his doorstep, stepping over the threshold, sitting at his dinner table, asking for third helpings—and cracking jokes about the fact that the emperor has no clothes.

In every corner of Gates's empire, we see his claimed subjects in revolt. We've seen parents, teachers, and activists challenge Gates's Common Core educational standards, successfully kill off the foundation's hundred-million-dollar data surveillance project in public schools, and march on the Gates Foundation's headquarters in Seattle. We're seeing a growing movement to "decolonize global health," one that presents an existential challenge to how the foundation does business in health and medicine. We're seeing farmers and farmer groups across Africa openly challenging Gates's agricultural interventions and calling for the defunding of the Alliance for a Green Revolution in Africa. We're even seeing a growing number of Gates's super-wealthy peers form coali-tions, like TaxMeNow and Patriotic Millionaires, call for higher taxes on the rich.

We have also seen a very significant turn in journalism, as the news media took off the blinders in 2021, finally seeing that Bill Gates was not the messiah they had described him as for most of the last decade. That's a welcome sign, because if we don't have strong, independent newsrooms, we will have great difficulty building the democratic power we need to challenge illegitimate power structures like the Gates Foundation. To create strong journalism, we have to hold the institution of journalism itself accountable. My own view is that if journalists cannot gather the news without Bill Gates's money, they should be put out of business. And I believe we need to think more broadly, if not universally, about saying no to Gates's money.

The only reason anyone listens to Bill Gates, about anything, is his vast wealth. His money is his power. If we start saying no to Gates's money, we diminish his power. Should our elected leaders and staffers in Congress (and their family members) accept expensive international trips on the Gates Foundation's dime? No. Should our public universities accept billions of dollars from the foundation and then allow it to influence the research conducted at these schools? No. Should we take seriously NPR's fund-raising drives while the news outlet eagerly solicits millions of dollars from Bill Gates's private foundation? No.

We also need to start saying no to Bill Gates when he asks us to put our tax dollars into subsidizing the public-private partnerships he creates. Reducing public support of the foundation will rapidly diminish its undemocratic power, cutting down both its funding and its moral authority.

As we work to unwind the Gates Foundation, however, this must happen in a deliberate and thoughtful way. Too many people today depend on Gates—entire public systems have been organized around its funding and priorities—to dismantle the foundation overnight. Readers should also remember that many of the key sources who helped me write this book were grantees and employees of the Gates Foundation. Challenging the foundation cannot be a witch hunt that automatically attacks everyone in Gates's financial sphere of influence as hacks or sellouts. There are many thoughtful people laboring in Gates's charitable empire who want to see changes, but who may face legal action or career suicide if they publicly criticize the foundation.

My hope is that we can create spaces for these people to raise their voices, to speak up and speak out about the problems they see. And when they do, my hope is that journalists and the public receive these stories with open ears, eyes, and hearts. We are extraordinarily long overdue for an open, honest debate about the Gates Foundation, and there are simply too many questions surrounding the nature of its charitable work—questions that demand answers.

Is it appropriate for the foundation to engage so freely in commercial activities, funding and even suing companies? Acquiring intellectual property from grantees? Launching its own pharmaceutical enterprises? Can we really chalk up the several consistent allegations of anti-competitive behavior as a few sour grapes? Can we ignore how similar the allegations against the foundation are to those against Microsoft's monopoly power? Can we ignore the ways in which the Gates Foundation's vigorous support for patent rights benefits Microsoft? Why is no one investigating these activities?

Should the foundation be allowed to trade in billions of dollars of dark money—unspecified expenses for consultants, professional fees, and fiscal sponsors? Shouldn't we be able to see the actual grants and contracts? Shouldn't we be able to clearly map out Gates's network of influence—seeing, for example, every governing board on which the Gates Foundation sits? If the foundation is using our money, don't you agree that we should be able to easily follow the money?

As a taxpayer, do you believe that Bill Gates is a good steward of your dollars? Are you convinced that the tens of billions of dollars governments donate to his public-private partnerships constitute a fair, just, and efficient use of public funds? Is it not obvious that the extraordinary sums of money that taxpayers are putting into Gates's projects could easily save millions of lives without Bill Gates? Is Gates actually bringing added value, or is he just extracting credit? What about the billions of dollars in tax breaks we give to Bill Gates, Melinda French Gates, and Warren Buffett for their charitable donations? Why have we organized our tax system in a way that allows the wealthiest people to avoid the most taxes? Is billionaire philanthropy really an acceptable substitute for taxation?

Are you comfortable with the current governance of the Gates Foundation, which sits on its hands as its founder faces an extraordinary range of allegations of misconduct, including a yearslong still-unexplained relationship with Jeffrey Epstein? Is it appropriate for this man's foundation to be one of the world's leading funders of work on women's empowerment?

Should Bill Gates be meeting constantly with members of Congress? Should his foundation be funding congressional travel? Should the foundation be inserting itself into official roles in foreign nations to provide technical advice to inform vaccine policy in India and agricultural development in Ethiopia? Should the foundation be allowed to donate hundreds of millions of dollars to government agencies? Under what definition of charity do we place these activities? If philanthropy is a money-in-politics tool, why don't we regulate it as we do lobbying or campaign contributions?

Do you disagree that the public discourse on the Gates Foundation over the last decade has been deeply unbalanced? Do you believe that Gates's funding of the news media has played no role in this pack journalism? At what point do we acknowledge that the foundation's paying the news media to evangelize its narratives of human progress amounts to misinformation—and a distraction from the abundant evidence of inequity and poverty all around us?

Is it healthy for Bill Gates's private foundation to have so much control over the scientific enterprise, dominating if not monopolizing entire fields of research? Are you not disturbed by the many allegations of Gates willfully using its funding to distort science? Is it good for society to have an institution with this much epistemic power—over universities, over think tanks, and over the media?

Is billionaire philanthropy the solution to inequality, or is it an emblem of inequity? Is Bill Gates even a philanthropist? Are his charitable gifts organized as an expression of love or as an exercise of power? Is he deserving of the endless uncritical praise for giving away small sums of money he does not need? Or should we, instead, interrogate why Gates hoards a one-hundred-billion-dollar fortune while so many people on earth struggle to make ends meet? Is Gates generous or greedy?

How can we see the foundation as a humanitarian body when it actively invests its endowment in companies and industries that harm the poor people it claims to serve? Can we really condone this dirty money under an "ends justify the means" rationalization, that the investment returns may one day help the poor through philanthropy? How can we see the Gates Foundation as a charitable organization when it generates billions of dollars a year in investment income, at times more money than it gives away in charitable grants? And what is the endgame for the Gates Foundation—to become an ever larger, ever wealthier, ever more powerful institution? Is that good for society?

If you are a religious person, can you point to any scripture, doctrine, or holy book that rationalizes or endorses this model of wealth and power? Or, if you understand the world through politics, what theory or ideology can you point to that makes sense of Bill Gates and the Gates Foundation, outside the idea of oligarchy?

Can you look across Bill Gates's philanthropic empire and clearly, confidently state that he is doing more good than harm? Are you unconvinced that another world is possible? Do you believe the human race is doomed to massive inequality and that the very best we can do is hope that our oligarchs are good oligarchs and that our billionaires are good billionaires—that they use their vast wealth in ways that help the world and do not hurt it? Can you read the words of Martin Luther King Jr.—"True compassion is more than flinging a coin to a beggar; it comes to see that an edifice which produces beggars needs restructuring"—and not hear a deep and troubling echo that quakes the foundation Bill Gates has built?

I don't think that any serious-minded person can look at Bill Gates and the Gates Foundation today and say that changes are not necessary. My hope is that readers understand that their opinion counts—that it should count every bit as much as Bill Gates's opinion, that we should aspire to a world in which the richest guy doesn't have the loudest voice. Adding your voice to the public debate builds the democratic power we need to confront Gates's undemocratic arrogation of power.

Challenging the Gates Foundation is only one small battle in a much larger war—against wealth inequality; against colonialism; against injustice; against racism, sexism, intolerance, and prejudice; against all these antidemocratic forces—but it's an important fight because Gates is such a powerful oligarch and such an important totem. Billionaire philanthropy, as practiced by someone like Gates, preys on our cultural biases to disguise its influence. It makes us believe that a billionaire's giving away his vast fortune is an unimpeachable act of charity that must be exalted, rather than a tool of power and control that must be challenged.

NOTES

PROLOGUE

ix **"It would be suicidal for someone"**: Sandi Doughton, "Not Many Speak Their Mind to Gates Foundation," *Seattle Times*, August 2, 2008, https://www.seattletimes.com /seattle-news/not-many-speak-their-mind-to-gates-foundation/.

x **Melinda, not Bill, would step down**: "Bill & Melinda Gates Foundation CEO Mark Suzman Announces Initial Plans to Evolve Governance as Bill Gates and Melinda French Gates Commit $15 Billion in New Resources to Deepen and Accelerate the Foundation's Efforts to Address Inequity," Bill & Melinda Gates Foundation, July 7, 2021, https://www.gatesfoundation.org/ideas/media-center/press-releases/2021/07 /bill-melinda-gates-foundation-mark-suzman-plans-evolve-governance.

INTRODUCTION

1 **like serving as a page**: David Allison, "Transcript of a Video History Interview with Mr. William 'Bill' Gates," National Museum of American History, Smithsonian Institution, 1993, https://americanhistory.si.edu/comphist/gates.htm.

1 **"I was thrown into a forty-eight-member class"**: Paul Allen, *Idea Man: A Memoir by the Cofounder of Microsoft* (New York: Portfolio, 2011).

2 **"If you ask me to come back"**: *Inside Bill's Brain: Decoding Bill Gates*, episode 2, at 9:30, directed by Davis Guggenheim, aired September 20, 2019, on Netflix.

2 **four times larger than the share**: Walter Isaacson, *The Innovators: How a Group of Hackers, Geniuses, and Geeks Created the Digital Revolution* (New York: Simon and Schuster, 2015).

2 **Gates pushing him to move out East**: Allen, *Idea Man*.

2 **"360 emulator using micro controllers"**: Allison, "Transcript of a Video History Interview with Mr. William 'Bill' Gates."

2 **Gates cold-called the company's headquarters**: Allen, *Idea Man*.

3 **Allen spent a grueling eight weeks**: Allen, *Idea Man*.

3 **Allen remembers being taken aback**: Allen, *Idea Man*.

3   the deeper truth, as I read it: Allen, *Idea Man*.

3   "Bill was more flexible": Allen, *Idea Man*.

3   a hardware device called the SoftCard: Allen, *Idea Man*.

4   "I don't ever want to talk about this again": Allen, *Idea Man*.

4   After having strong-armed Allen: Allen, *Idea Man*.

4   "to crush you if he could": Allen, *Idea Man*. Allen tells a story about watching the NBA team he owned, the Portland Trailblazers, face off in a championship game against Michael Jordan and the Chicago Bulls. Jordan's ability, and desire, not just to win but to dominate astonished Allen—and it made him think of someone else he knew.

5   "management by embarrassment": David Rensin, "The Bill Gates Interview: A Candid Conversation with the Sultan of Software About Outsmarting His Rivals," *Playboy*, July 1994.

5   "personal verbal attacks": Allen, *Idea Man*.

5   "That's the stupidest fucking thing I've ever heard": John Seabrook, "E-mail from Bill," *New Yorker*, December 26, 1993, https://www.newyorker.com/magazine/1994 /01/10/e-mail-from-bill-gates.

5   "You're screwed": Jennifer Edstrom and Marlin Eller, *Barbarians Led by Bill Gates* (New York: Henry Holt, 1998), 30.

5   "You smash people": James Wallace and Jim Erickson, *Hard Drive: Bill Gates and the Making of Microsoft* (New York: John Wiley and Sons, 1992), 212.

5   helped grease the wheels for her son: Associated Press, "Mary Gates, 64; Helped Her Son Start Microsoft," *New York Times*, June 11, 1994, https://www.nytimes.com/1994 /06/11/obituaries/mary-gates-64-helped-her-son-start-microsoft.html; Wallace and Erickson, *Hard Drive*, 189.

5   his law firm's largest client: Rob Guth, "Raising Bill Gates," *Wall Street Journal*, April 25, 2009, https://www.wsj.com/articles/SB124061372413054653.

5   found a firm that did and acquired the software: Allen, *Idea Man*; Wallace and Erickson, *Hard Drive*, 185.

5   newly minted "MS-DOS": Wallace and Erickson, *Hard Drive*, 202–4.

6   his corporate mantra: Todd Bishop, "Microsoft at 40: How the Company Has Changed, and Stayed the Same," GeekWire, April 4, 2015, https://www.geekwire.com /2015/microsoft-at-40-how-the-companys-goal-has-changed-and-stayed-the-same/.

6   It considered buying Ticketmaster: Allen, *Idea Man*.

6   went on to launch *Slate* magazine and MSNBC: Josh Halliday, "Microsoft Sells MSNBC.com Stake," *Guardian*, July 16, 2012, https://www.theguardian.com/media /2012/jul/16/microsoft-msnbc; Michael Kinsley, "My History of Slate," *Slate*, June 18, 2006, https://slate.com/news-and-politics/2006/06/michael-kinsley-s-history-of -slate.html.

6   "paranoid about Microsoft": David Bank, *Breaking Windows: How Bill Gates Fumbled the Future of Microsoft* (New York: Free Press, 2001), 14–15.

6   "It's everything": Steve Lohr, "Where Microsoft Wants to Go Today: Further Moves into Home and Office for the Software Giant," *New York Times*, January 5, 1998, https://www.nytimes.com/1998/01/05/business/outlook-98-media-technology -where-microsoft-wants-to-go-today.html.

6 **"Why would Paul want to compete with us"**: Allen, *Idea Man*.

7 **Department of Justice accusing the company**: "Justice Department Files Antitrust Suit Against Microsoft for Unlawfully Monopolizing Computer Software Markets," Press Release, May 18, 1998, U.S. Department of Justice, Washington, DC, https://www.justice.gov/archive/atr/public/press_releases/1998/1764.htm.

7 **many of the stiffest penalties**: Ted Bridis, "Judge Rules Microsoft Is a Monopoly," AP News, November 5, 1999, https://apnews.com/article/fffc2a3a5757f38b9e f47c1e862e80a2. Amy Harmon, "U.S. vs. Microsoft: The Overview: Judge Backs Terms of U.S. Settlement in Microsoft Case." *New York Times*, November 2, 2002, https://www.nytimes.com/2002/11/02/business/us-vs-microsoft-overview-judge -backs-terms-us-settlement-microsoft-case.html.

7 **face high-profile legal challenges**: Charles Arthur, "Microsoft Loses EU Antitrust Fine Appeal," *Guardian*, June 27, 2012, https://www.theguardian.com/technology /2012/jun/27/microsoft-loses-eu-antitrust-fine-appeal; Steve Lohr and David D. Kirkpatrick, "Microsoft and AOL Time Warner Settle Antitrust Suit," *New York Times*, May 29, 2003, https://www.nytimes.com/2003/05/29/technology/microsoft -and-aol-time-warner-settle-antitrust-suit.html.

8 **plowed more than $20 billion**: Katie Hafner, "Bill Gates and His Wife Give Away $3.3 Billion," *New York Times*, February 6, 1999, https://www.nytimes.com/1999/02 /06/us/bill-gates-and-his-wife-give-away-3.3-billion.html.

8 **the richest man in the world**: Lisa Singhania, "Gates Stays Atop Billionaires Club," *Washington Post*, June 16, 2000, https://www.washingtonpost.com/archive /business/2000/06/16/gates-stays-atop-billionaires-club/453c7e6b-804b-4e90-acdf -8629a11f33e6/.

8 **he has slipped in the rankings**: "The World's Real-Time Billionaires," *Forbes*, n.d., https://www.forbes.com/real-time-billionaires/.

8 **Sackler family**: Tim Schwab, "US Opioid Prescribing: The Federal Government Advisers with Recent Ties to Big Pharma," *BMJ* 366 (August 22, 2019): l5167, https://doi.org/10.1136/bmj.l5167.

8 **fueled by performance-enhancing drugs**: Corrie MacLaggan, "Exclusive: Live-strong Cancer Charity Drops Lance Armstrong Name from Title," Reuters, November 15, 2012, https://www.reuters.com/article/us-cycling-armstrong-livestrong -idUSBRE8AE00020121115.

8 **Hillary Clinton faced scrutiny**: Hannah Fraser-Chanpong, "Hillary Clinton Denies Donors Influenced Her as Secretary of State," CBS News, August 24, 2016, https://www .cbsnews.com/news/hillary-clinton-denies-donors-influenced-her-as-secretary-of -state/.

8 **Trump Foundation**: Brian Naylor, "Trump Foundation to Dissolve Amid New York Attorney General's Investigation," NPR, December 18, 2018, https://www.npr .org/2018/12/18/677778958/trump-foundation-to-dissolve-amid-new-york-ags -investigation.

9 **"lubricating future sales"**: Katie Hafner, "Gates's Library Gifts Arrive, but with Windows Attached," *New York Times*, February 2, 1999, https://www.nytimes.com /1999/02/21/us/gates-s-library-gifts-arrive-but-with-windows-attached.html.

9 **"hard-nosed analysis"**: Karl Taro Greenfeld, "Giving Billions Isn't Easy: Bill and Melinda Gates," *Time*, July 24, 2000, https://content.time.com/time/subscriber/article /0,33009,997529,00.html.

9 **the board of the *Washington Post***: "Melinda Gates Joins Washington Post Co. as Director," *Washington Post*, September 10, 2004, https://www.washingtonpost.com /archive/business/2004/09/10/melinda-gates-joins-washington-post-co-as-director /1de38078-e749-4bb1-a4ce-430469a25070/.

10 **George W. Bush**: Bill Shore, "Bush Recognizes Social Entrepreneurship," *Seattle Post-Intelligencer*, January 16, 2007, https://www.seattlepi.com/local/opinion/article /Bush-recognizes-social-entrepreneurship-1225470.php.

10 **Presidential Medal of Freedom**: "The Presidential Medal of Freedom," The White House, 2016, https://obamawhitehouse.archives.gov/campaign/medal-of-freedom; Chris Young, "Bill Gates Receives Honorary Knighthood," March 2, 2005, https:// www.nbcnews.com/id/wbna7065790; Shanoor Seervai, "Bill and Melinda Gates Receive Indian Civilian Award," *Wall Street Journal*, January 28, 2015, http://blogs .wsj.com/indiarealtime/2015/01/28/bill-and-melinda-gates-receive-indian-civilian -award/.

10 **Congress enshrined**: "H. Res. 638, 109th Congress (2005–2006), Congratulating Bill Gates, Melinda Gates and Bono for Being Named Time Magazine's 2005 Person of the Year," Congress.gov, December 18, 2005, https://www.congress.gov/bill/109th -congress/house-resolution/638?s=1&r=80.

10 **"changing the world"**: "Bill Gates Talks Philanthropy, Microsoft and Taxes," *New York Times*, DealBook event, November 6, 2019.

10 **shattered whatever suspicions**: The foundation has pledged to give away eighty billion dollars, but most of its gifts are awarded over a period of years, so the full eighty billion will not leave the foundation's coffers for several years.

11 **top twenty killers**: Dawn Fratangelo, "How Gates Changes Global Public Health," NBC News, June 27, 2006, https://www.nbcnews.com/id/wbna13580687.

11 **"isn't just incremental progress"**: Bill and Melinda Gates, "Why We Swing for the Fences," *GatesNotes*, February 10, 2020, https://www.gatesnotes.com/2020-Annual -Letter.

11 **"soft-spoken"**: Ron Claiborne and Ben Forer, "Bill Gates Criticizes Long-Held Norms in America's Education System," ABC News, March 3, 2011, https://abcnews .go.com/US/bill-gates-education-microsoft-founder-schools-teaching-teachers /story?id=13051251; Rainer Zitelmann, "Bill Gates Was an Angry, Difficult Boss in Early Microsoft Days—Here's Why Employees Still Liked Him," CNBC, February 24, 2020, https://www.cnbc.com/2020/02/24/bill-gates-was-difficult-boss-in-early -microsoft-days-but-employees-still-liked-him.html.

13 **"He has immediate access to us"**: Megan Twohey and Nicholas Kulish, "Bill Gates, the Virus and the Quest to Vaccinate the World," *New York Times,* November 23, 2020, https://www.nytimes.com/2020/11/23/world/bill-gates-vaccine-coronavirus .html.

17 **"success cartel"**: This term is taken from Yogesh Rajkotia, "Beware of the Success Cartel: A Plea for Rational Progress in Global Health," *BMJ Global Health* 3, no. 6 (November 1, 2018): e001197, https://doi.org/10.1136/bmjgh-2018-001197.

CHAPTER 1: LIVES SAVED

21   **"clever new ways"**: "Anand Giridharadas: It Is Immoral to Be a Billionaire," Oxford Union Debate, September 5, 2019, YouTube, 3:25, https://www.youtube.com/watch?v=axN8ppre-mU.

22   **"already saved"**: "Peter Singer: It Is NOT Immoral to Be a Billionaire," Oxford Union Debate, September 5, 2019, YouTube, 4:00, https://www.youtube.com/watch?v=SYgMtZODcVQ.

22   **"If you want to have a balanced, healthy"**: Kelsey Piper, "Bill Gates's Efforts to Fight Coronavirus, Explained," Vox, April 14, 2020, https://www.vox.com/future-perfect/2020/4/14/21215592/bill-gates-coronavirus-vaccines-treatments-billionaires; Kelsey Piper, Twitter, May 29, 2019, https://twitter.com/KelseyTuoc/status/1133761319646089217.

22   **"Your article doesn't even mention"**: David Callahan, Twitter, March 17, 2020, https://twitter.com/DavidCallahanIP/status/1240101039837032448. Note: My article did explicitly cite Gates's claims of having saved millions of lives; Tim Schwab, "Bill Gates Gives to the Rich (Including Himself)," *Nation*, March 17, 2020, https://www.thenation.com/article/society/bill-gates-foundation-philanthropy/.

22   **"over six million people alive today"**: "From Poverty to Prosperity: A Conversation with Bill Gates," Interview by Arthur C. Brooks, American Enterprise Institute, March 13, 2014, https://www.aei.org/wp-content/uploads/2014/03/-bill-gates-event-transcript_082217994272.pdf?x91208.

22   **had saved *ten* million lives**: Bill Gates, "Watch the Full Bill Gates Keynote from Microsoft Research Faculty Summit 2013," *Official Microsoft Blog*, July 15, 2013, https://web.archive.org/web/20210120012355/https://blogs.microsoft.com/blog/2013/07/15/watch-the-full-bill-gates-keynote-from-microsoft-research-faculty-summit-2013/.

23   *Millions Saved*: Center for Global Development, "Millions Saved—FAQ," final question, http://millionssaved.cgdev.org/frequently-asked-questions; The Center for Global Development describes its work as being independent of its funders, but also describes the Gates Foundation as integrally involved in the *Millions Saved* book: "Gates Foundation staff played a role in the book's production by participating in the review of evidence around a short-list of cases put together by the CGD team and by providing advice and feedback on the overall project."

23   **"Lives Saved Scorecard"**: Tim Schwab, "Are Bill Gates's Billions Distorting Public Health Data?," *Nation*, December 3, 2020, https://www.thenation.com/article/society/gates-covid-data-ihme/; Christopher Murray and Ray Chambers, "Keeping Score: Fostering Accountability for Children's Lives," *The Lancet* 386, no. 9988 (July 4, 2015): 3–5, https://www.thelancet.com/journals/lancet/article/PIIS0140-6736(15)61171-0/fulltext.

23   **"Lives Saved Tool"**: Bloomberg School of Public Health, "Lives Saved Tool (LiST)," Johns Hopkins, n.d., https://www.jhsph.edu/research/centers-and-institutes/institute-for-international-programs/current-projects/lives-saved-tool/; Jaspreet Toor et al., "Lives Saved with Vaccination for 10 Pathogens Across 112 Countries in a Pre-Covid-19 World," *eLife* 10 (July 13, 2021): e67635, https://doi.org/10.7554/eLife.67635.

23   **lives-saved arms race reached its zenith**: Bill Gates and Melinda Gates, "War-ren Buffett's Best Investment," *GatesNotes*, n.d., https://www.gatesnotes.com/2017 -annual-letter.

24   **later weave into its public presentations**: Karen Makar, "An Overview of the Bill and Melinda Gates Foundation," Presentation at the Fourteenth H3Africa Consortium Meeting, Accra, Ghana, September 25, 2019, https://h3africa.org/index.php/forteenth -meeting/#1569927279633–30d6cced-5af7; FastCo Works, "Five Renowned Design-ers Illustrate Global Health Stories You Should Know About," Fast Company, February 15, 2017, https://www.fastcompany.com/3068156/five-renowned-designers -illustrate-global-health-stories-you-should-know-ab.

24   **glowing profile of the foundation**: Sarah Boseley, "How Bill and Melinda Gates Helped Save 122M Lives—and What They Want to Solve Next," *Guardian*, February 14, 2017, https://www.theguardian.com/world/2017/feb/14/bill-gates-philanthropy -warren-buffett-vaccines-infant-mortality; Timothy Egan, "Bill Gates Is the Most Interesting Man in the World," *New York Times*, May 22, 2020, https://www.nytimes .com/2020/05/22/opinion/bill-gates-coronavirus.html.

24   *Dallas Morning News*: "Melinda Gates: The Dallas Morning News Texan of the Year 2020," *Dallas Morning News*, January 2, 2021, https://www.dallasnews.com /opinion/editorials/2021/01/02/the-dallas-morning-news-texan-of-the-year-2020 -melinda-gates/. Gates's original post announcing the 122 million lives saved tele-graphed a message to many, apparently including the *Dallas Morning News*, that Gates, alone, is responsible for saving 122 million lives. If you squint as you read the original announcement, Bill and Melinda French Gates do gesture to other partners: "Our goals are shared by many other organizations working to save and improve lives."

24   **the *Economist***: "The Causes of a Welcome Trend," *Economist*, September 27, 2014, https://www.economist.com/international/2014/09/27/the-causes-of-a-welcome -trend.

24   **Economist Intelligence Unit**: The Economist Intelligence Unit, "Solutions, Public Policy," https://web.archive.org/web/20210329121552/https://www.eiu.com/n/solu tions/public-policy-consultancy/; "Healthy Partnerships: How Governments Can Engage the Private Sector to Improve Health in Africa," World Bank and Interna-tional Finance Corporation, 2011, v, accessed at http://graphics.eiu.com/upload/eb /Healthy-Patnerships_ExecSummary_StandAlone.pdf.

24   **"Seven Million Lives Saved"**: John W. McArthur, "Seven Million Lives Saved: Under-5 Mortality Since the Launch of the Millennium Development Goals," *Brook-ings* (blog), Brookings Institution, September 25, 2014, https://www.brookings.edu /research/seven-million-lives-saved-under-5-mortality-since-the-launch-of-the -millennium-development-goals/.

26   **"the creation of a new vaccine for rotavirus"**: Bill Gates, "By 2026, the Gates Foun-dation Aims to Spend $9 Billion a Year," *GatesNotes*, July 13, 2022, https://www .gatesnotes.com/About-Bill-Gates/Commitment-to-the-Gates-Foundation?WT.mc _id=2022071380100_Commitment_BG-TW_&WT.tsrc=BGTW.

26   **deaths from rotavirus are in decline**: Bernadeta Dadonaite, Hannah Ritchie, and Max Roser, "Diarrheal Diseases," Our World in Data, n.d., https://ourworldindata.org

/diarrheal-diseases#rotavirus-vaccine-protects-children-from-diarrheal-disease; "WHO Recommends Rotavirus Vaccine for All Children," Reuters, June 5, 2009, https://www.reuters.com/article/health-us-vaccines-rotavirus/who-recommends -rotavirus-vaccine-for-all-children-idUKTRE5541U620090605.

26 **not as effective in the poor nations**: Victoria Jiang et al., "Performance of Rotavirus Vaccines in Developed and Developing Countries," *Human Vaccines* 6, no. 7 (2010): 532–42, doi:10.4161/hv.6.7.11278.

26 **McCoy authored**: David McCoy et al., "Methodological and Policy Limitations of Quantifying the Saving of Lives: A Case Study of the Global Fund's Approach," *PLOS Medicine* 10, no. 10 (October 1, 2013): e1001522, https://doi.org/10.1371/journal .pmed.1001522.

27 **nearly half of all children**: "The Epidemiology and Disease Burden of Rotavirus," RotaCouncil, 2019, https://preventrotavirus.org/wp-content/uploads/2019/05/ROTA -Brief3-Burden-SP-1.pdf.

27 **sixty million**: "Number of Deaths per Year, World," Our World in Data, n.d., https:// ourworldindata.org/grapher/number-of-deaths-per-year.

28 **"nobody files patents, nobody enforces patents"**: Gates, "Watch the Full Bill Gates Keynote," 26:20.

29 **"to sell drugs of dubious benefit"**: Marcia Angell, *The Truth About the Drug Companies: How They Deceive Us and What to Do About It* (New York: Random House, 2004). Note: Beyond marketing expenses, pharmaceutical companies also spend large sums of money on lobbying and legal costs to protect or advance their bottom lines, including preserving favorable rules and regulations around patents.

29 **"make markets work for the poor"**: "Bill & Melinda Gates Foundation Hosts Panel Discussion on 'Making Markets Work for the Poor,'" BusinessWireIndia, June 21, 2018, https://www.businesswireindia.com/bill-melinda-gates-foundation-hosts -panel-discussion-on-making-markets-work-for-the-poor-58748.html.

29 **the foundation's "market-shaping" activities**: "Le Monde Philanthropy Event," Paris, France, October 24, 2016, Transcript, Bill & Melinda Gates Foundation, https://www.gatesfoundation.org/ideas/speeches/2016/10/bill-gates-le-monde -philanthropy-event.

29 **"magic of vaccines"**: Bill Gates, "My Annual Letter: Vaccine Miracles," *GatesNotes*, February 16, 2011, https://www.gatesnotes.com/health/bills-annual-letter-vaccine -miracles.

29 **vaccinated nearly a billion children**: Gavi, Annual Progress Report, 2020, https:// www.gavi.org/sites/default/files/programmes-impact/our-impact/apr/Gavi -Progress-Report-2020.pdf. Note: Gavi uses the awkward metric "future deaths prevented."

29 **projects he's most proud of**: Sharon Lougher and Joel Taylor, "Bill Gates on Conquering Malaria, Curing Sick Kids . . . and Buying a Jet," *Metro News*, June 25, 2015, https://metro.co.uk/2015/06/25/bill-gates-conquering-malaria-curing-sick-kids -and-buying-a-jet-5266360/; Bill Gates, Interview by Walter Isaacson, CNN, February 22, 2021, http://edition.cnn.com/TRANSCRIPTS/2102/22/ampr.01.html.

30 **"their fifth birthday"**: Melinda French Gates, "The Daunting, Damning Number That Should Spur Us to Action," Pivotal Ventures, June 19, 2019, https://www

.pivotalventures.org/articles/the-daunting-damning-number-that-should-spur-us
-to-action.

30   **of at least $4 billion**: Gavi, "Disbursements and Commitments," n.d., https://www
.gavi.org/programmes-impact/our-impact/disbursements-and-commitments.
Note: By late 2022, Gavi had its disbursement data updated only through 2018.

30   **around half of Gavi's vaccine budget**: Gail Rodgers, "Time Well Spent: The Complex Journey of a Life-Saving Vaccine," Bill & Melinda Gates Foundation, April
22, 2022, https://www.gatesfoundation.org/ideas/articles/creating-life-saving-pcv
-vaccine-for-pneumonia-india. Note: Gavi boasts of having introduced pneumonia
vaccines into sixty of the seventy-three nations where it has worked, reaching 255
million children. PCV is a multidose immunization. It's unclear whether 255 million
refers to doses delivered or children fully immunized.

30   **leading cause of vaccine-preventable deaths**: Gail Rodgers, "Pneumococcal Vaccine Update," Presentation to International Congress on Infectious Diseases, 2018,
https://isid.org/wp-content/uploads/2019/04/18thICID_Rodgers.pdf.

30   **from infections that could be prevented**: Gail Rodgers, "Creating a Life-Saving PCV
Vaccine for Pneumonia in India," Bill & Melinda Gates Foundation, n.d., https://www
.gatesfoundation.org/ideas/articles/creating-life-saving-pcv-vaccine-for-pneumonia
-india?utm_source=to&utm_medium=em&utm_campaign=wc&utm_term=lgc.
Note: The vaccine discussed throughout this chapter is the pneumococcal conjugate
vaccine, which is approved for use in children. This vaccine protects against a leading cause of pneumonia, *Streptococcus pneumoniae* bacteria.

30   **covers only around half the children**: Gavi, "Pneumococcal Vaccine Support,"
January 2023, https://www.gavi.org/types-support/vaccine-support/pneumococcal.
Note: Médecins Sans Frontières (MSF, aka Doctors Without Borders) reported that
supply shortages in Gavi's pneumonia vaccination program resulted in "an estimated
26 million children born without access to PCV," the pneumococcal conjugate
vaccine.

30   **"graduate" out of Gavi's program**: Gavi, "Eligibility," n.d., https://www.gavi.org
/types-support/sustainability/eligibility. Note: Specifically, Gavi's eligibility threshold, according to World Bank data, is $1,730 in gross national income (GNI) per
capita.

31   **"lives lost due to pneumonia"**: Androulla Kyrillou, "Zero Dose PCV Children Dan-
gerously Exposed to Pneumonia," *Stop Pneumonia / Every Breath Counts* (blog),
April 23, 2020, https://stoppneumonia.org/zero-dose-pcv-children-dangerously
-exposed-to-pneumonia; "Every Breath Counts Coalition Members," *Stop Pneumonia / Every Breath Counts* (blog), n.d., https://stoppneumonia.org/about-us/.

31   **"duopoly has limited supply"**: Mark R. Alderson et al., "Development Strategy and
Lessons Learned for a 10-Valent Pneumococcal Conjugate Vaccine (PNEUMO-
SIL®)," *Human Vaccines & Immunotherapeutics* 17, no. 8 (August 3, 2021): 2670–77,
https://doi.org/10.1080/21645515.2021.1874219.

31   **it could bilk consumers**: Elisabeth Rosenthal, "The Price of Prevention: Vaccine
Costs Are Soaring," *New York Times*, July 3, 2014, https://www.nytimes.com/2014/07
/03/health/Vaccine-Costs-Soaring-Paying-Till-It-Hurts.html.

31   **"trickle-down"**: Michael Kinsley, *Creative Capitalism: A Conversation with Bill*

Gates, Warren Buffett, and Other Economic Leaders (New York: Simon and Schuster, 2008).

31 **sales at around six billion dollars**: Pfizer's 10-K Form for Year Ending December 31, 2021, U.S. Securities and Exchange Commission, PDF, 103, https://www.sec.gov /Archives/edgar/data/78003/000007800322000027/pfe-20211231.htm.

32 **"advanced market commitment"**: Gavi, Annual Progress Report, 2020. Note: Gates contributed $50 million of the $1.5 billion. Taxpayers from Italy, the United Kingdom, and Canada provided most of the funds.

32 **"incentivizing the creation"**: Rodgers, "Time Well Spent."

32 **$7 per dose**: Gavi, "The Pneumococcal AMC: The Process," https://www.gavi.org /sites/default/files/document/amc/AMC_ProcessSheet2009.pdf; Gavi, "How the Pneumococcal AMC Works," n.d., https://www.gavi.org/investing-gavi/innovative -financing/pneumococcal-amc/how-it-works; and Pfizer, "Proxy Statement for 2018 Annual Meeting of Shareholders: 2017 Financial Report," n.d., https://www.sec.gov /Archives/edgar/data/78003/000093041318000973/c90444_def14a.pdf. Note: Gavi's bonus payments applied to the first 20 percent of doses delivered. The base price Gavi pays for pneumonia vaccines is around three dollars.

32 **several times higher than the cost**: Andrew Pollack, "Deal Provides Vaccines to Poor Nations at Lower Cost," *New York Times*, March 23, 2010, https://www.nytimes .com/2010/03/24/business/global/24vaccine.html; Donald Light, "Saving the Pneumococcal AMC and Gavi," *Human Vaccines* 7, no. 2 (February 1, 2011), https://doi .org/10.4161/hv.7.2.14919.

32 **"a money-losing proposition"**: Pollack, "Deal Provides Vaccines to Poor Nations at Lower Cost."

32 **boosting corporate revenues**: Pfizer, Forms 8-K, Ex-99, July 28, 2015, and DEF 14-A, March 15, 2018, U.S. Securities and Exchange Commission, https://www.sec.gov /Archives/edgar/data/78003/000007800315000031/pfe-06282015xex99.htm; Pfizer, "Proxy Statement for 2018 Annual Meeting of Shareholders."

32 **"has been fantastic"**: Bill Gates, "From Poverty to Prosperity: A Conversation with Bill Gates."

32 **his signature project in global health**: Gavi, "Disbursements and Commitments."

33 **principled step**: That's not to say that MSF is entirely free of Gates's influence. When it created the Drugs for Neglected Diseases Initiative, it accepted funding from the Gates Foundation. While perhaps the highest-profile actor in global health that is independent of Gates, MSF does not often directly antagonize the Gates Foundation. "DNDi Receives $25.7M from the Bill & Melinda Gates Foundation to Develop New Medicines for Neglected Diseases," DNDi, December 11, 2007, https:// dndi.org/press-releases/2007/dndi-receives-257m-from-the-bill-a-melinda-gates -foundation-to-develop-new-medicines-for-neglected-diseases/.

33 **lacked transparency**: Daniel Berman and Rohit Malpani, "High Time for GAVI to Push for Lower Prices," *Human Vaccines* 7, no. 3 (March 2011): 290, https://doi.org /10.4161/hv.7.3.15218; Global Health Watch, *Global Health Watch 5: An Alternative World Health Report* (London: Zed Books, 2017), 302.

33 **Gavi's budget actually comes from taxpayers**: Gavi, "Funding," n.d., https:// www .gavi.org/investing-gavi/funding.

33 **names were removed from a report**: Ann Danaiya Usher, "Dispute over Pneumo-coccal Vaccine Initiative," *The Lancet* 374, no. 9705 (December 5, 2009): 1879–80, https://doi.org/10.1016/S0140-6736(09)62078-X.

33 **profits to Pfizer and GSK**: Light, "Saving the Pneumococcal AMC and Gavi."

34 **"organization that's wonderful"**: Sarah Boseley, "Bill Gates Dismisses Criticism of High Prices for Vaccines," *Guardian*, January 27, 2015, https://www.theguardian.com/global-development/2015/jan/27/bill-gates-dismisses-criticism-of-high-prices-for-vaccines.

34 **$1,000 per head**: Boseley, "Bill Gates Dismisses Criticism of High Prices for Vaccines."

34 **"why prices remain high"**: James Hamblin, "Doctors Refused a Million Free Vac-cines—to Make a Statement About the Pharmaceutical Industry," *Atlantic*, October 14, 2016, https://www.theatlantic.com/health/archive/2016/10/doctors-with-borders/503786/.

35 **veterans of and executives**: Gavi, "Board Members," n.d., https://www.gavi.org/governance/gavi-board/members. Note: Several sources told me that the Gates Foundation exercises uniquely strong influence over Gavi, even though it techni-cally only holds one board seat. Additionally, research from Katerini Storeng at the University of Oslo offers a specific example of Gates's long shadow. Storeng inter-viewed a former Gavi employee who recounts that staff would take down certain posters at Gavi's headquarters just before Bill Gates arrived for meetings because staff knew the posters' message—promoting "health systems strengthening"—would infuriate Gates (who wants Gavi to target its spending on distributing vaccines, not the diffuse and often immeasurable work of building up public health infrastruc-ture). Storeng's research, nevertheless, shows that there can be differences of opin-ion within Gavi about how to best use its resources. One former Gates Foundation staffer told me that Bill Gates was so infuriated with Gavi's growing focus on health systems at one point that he seemed to be orchestrating a "coup" to refocus Gavi on vaccines; Katerini T. Storeng, "The GAVI Alliance and the 'Gates Approach' to Health System Strengthening," *Global Public Health* 9, no. 8 (September 14, 2014): 865–79, https://doi.org/10.1080/17441692.2014.940362.

35 **"Gavi's supreme goal"**: William Muraskin, "The Global Alliance for Vaccines and Immunization: Is It a New Model for Effective Public–Private Cooperation in Inter-national Public Health?," *American Journal of Public Health* 94, no. 11 (November 2004): 1922–25.

35 **hold only five seats**: Gavi, "Funding"; Gavi, "Gavi Board," n.d., https://www.gavi.org/our-alliance/governance/gavi-board; Gavi, "Annual Contributions and Pro-ceeds 30 June 2022," n.d., https://www.gavi.org/investing-gavi/funding. Note: Both donor countries and recipient countries have five board seats. The $35 billion figure comes from pledged donations to Gavi through 2025. Gavi would not respond to detailed questions sent by email about its funding. My calculation tallied up the "grand total" of "Donor governments and the European Commission" for periods 2000–2010, 2022–2015, 2016–2020, and 2021–2025.

36 **40 percent**: Village Global, "Bill Gates on Startups, Investing and Solving the World's Hardest Problems," Interview by Julia Hartz, 2019, YouTube, 24:00, https://www.youtube.com/watch?v=W5g4sPi1wd4.

37 **billions of dollars for projects related to pneumonia**: The Gates Foundation's public reporting of its charitable grants makes it difficult to pinpoint its precise spending on specific topics. Grants totaling close to $5 billion have gone toward projects that the foundation has categorized as related to pneumonia, though many of these projects are also coded as being directed at other diseases or topics.

37 **stunning array of vaccine developers**: Gates's donations to Genocea, Pfizer, and GSK are not specifically earmarked for work on pneumococcal conjugate vaccines but they nonetheless create financial ties that give the foundation potential avenues of influence. Likewise, the foundation also has provided co-funding, with the U.S. Biomedical Advanced Research and Development Authority, to a project called CARB-X to support other companies that work on pneumonia vaccines, like Vaxcyte and SutroVax, though Gates's money was not directed at work on pneumonia. "Vaxcyte Announces Expanded CARB-X Award to Advance Development of VAX-A1, a Vaccine to Prevent Group A Streptococcus Infections—Vaxcyte, Inc.," Press Release, August 5, 2021, https://investors.vaxcyte.com/news-releases/news -release-details/vaxcyte-announces-expanded-carb-x-award-advance-development -vax/; "CARB-X Funds SutroVax to Develop a New Vaccine to Prevent Group A Streptococcal Infections," News, CARB-X, September 3, 2019, https://carb-x.org /carb-x-news/carb-x-funds-sutrovax-to-develop-a-new-vaccine-to-prevent-group -a-streptococcal-infections/.

37 **"many, many more"**: Notably, the Gates Foundation has not publicly disclosed giving money to these companies for work on pneumonia.

37 **seed funding**: GSK/Affinivax, "Affinivax Launches Novel Vaccine for Global Impact on Infectious Diseases—Affinivax," Press Release, October 30, 2014, https:// web.archive.org/web/20210921135547/https://affinivax.com/affinivax-launches -novel-vaccine-for-global-impact-on-infectious-diseases/; Affinivax, "Board of Directors—Affinivax," Affinivax, n.d., https://web.archive.org/web/20150201121843 /http://affinivax.com/about/board-of-directors/. Note: The deal actually included milestone payments that could increase the payout to more than $3 billion.

37 **acquired Affinivax**: "GSK to Acquire Clinical-Stage Biopharmaceutical Company Affinivax, Inc.," Press Release, Affinivax, May 31, 2022, https://web.archive .org/web/20221002223521/https://affinivax.com/gsk-to-acquire-clinical-stage -biopharmaceutical-company-affinivax-inc/.

37 **financial windfall**: Bill & Melinda Gates Foundation, IRS 990 Filing, Addendum to Part VI-B, Line 5d, Expenditure Responsibility Statement.

38 *philanthrocapitalism*: "The Birth of Philanthrocapitalism," *Economist*, February 25, 2006, https://www.economist.com/special-report/2006/02/25/the-birth-of -philanthrocapitalism.

38 **My own reporting**: Schwab, "Bill Gates Gives to the Rich (Including Himself)."

39 **"deserving charity claimants"**: See also Linsey McGoey, *No Such Thing as a Free Gift: The Gates Foundation and the Price of Philanthropy* (New York: Verso, 2015).

39 **"Its wealth and market power are such"**: Lohr, "Where Microsoft Wants to Go Today." Note: An accompanying chart to the article enumerated a long list of companies Microsoft had invested in or acquired over the previous three years: Hotmail, DreamWorks, NBC, Vermeer Technologies, and dozens more.

40 **spends more money on malaria**: PATH, "Bridging the Gaps in Malaria R&D: An Analysis of Funding—From Basic Research and Product Development to Research for Implementation," PATH, 2018, 8–9, https://www.malariavaccine.org/resources /reports/investigating-second-valley-of-death-malaria-rd.

40 **securing exclusive licenses**: "Calibr and Bill & Melinda Gates Medical Research Institute Announce Licensing Agreement for Novel Candidate Tuberculosis Treat- ment Compound," Yahoo! Finance, February 15, 2023, https://finance.yahoo.com /news/calibr-bill-melinda-gates-medical-130000099.html; "Merck and the Bill & Melinda Gates Medical Research Institute Announce Licensing Agreement for Novel Tuberculosis Antibiotic Candidates," BusinessWire, October 18, 2022, https://www .businesswire.com/news/home/20221018005485/en/Merck-and-the-Bill-Melinda -Gates-Medical-Research-Institute-Announce-Licensing-Agreement-for-Novel -Tuberculosis-Antibiotic-Candidates.

40 **spends (slightly) more**: "Tuberculosis Research Funding Trends," Treatment Action Group, December 2022, Figure 10, https://www.treatmentactiongroup.org/resources /tbrd-report/tbrd-report-2022/. Note: The Gates Foundation grant records show $10 million in donations to the NIH and the National Institute of Allergy and Infectious Diseases and $44 million to the Foundation for the NIH, all earmarked for work on tuberculosis.

40 **let slip in a press conference**: Tim Schwab, "While the Poor Get Sick, Bill Gates Just Gets Richer," Nation, October 5, 2020, https://www.thenation.com/article /economy/bill-gates-investments-covid/.

41 **Oxford partnered with pharma giant**: Erin Banco, Ashleigh Furlong, and Len- nart Pfahler, "How Bill Gates and Partners Used Their Clout to Control the Global Covid Response—with Little Oversight," Politico, September 14, 2022, https: //www .politico.com/news/2022/09/14/global-covid-pandemic-response-bill-gates -partners-00053969.

41 **"hands-on thing"**: Village Global, "Bill Gates on Startups, Investing and Solving the World's Hardest Problems," 26:55.

42 **survey instrument**: Bill & Melinda Gates Foundation, "Production Economics for Vaccines," 2016, https://docs.gatesfoundation.org/Documents/PE_Vaccines_Appendix _2016.xlsm.

42 **Iqbal later left the Gates Foundation**: Robyn Iqbal, LinkedIn profile, https://www .linkedin.com/in/robyniqbal/.

44 **"locked up"**: "WHO Official Criticizes Gates Foundation 'Cartel' on Malaria Research," New York Times, February 18, 2008, https://www.nytimes.com/2008/02 /18/health/18iht-gates.1.10134837.html.

44 **second-largest funder**: WHO Programme Budget Web Portal, n.d., https://open .who.int/2020–21/contributors/contributor.

47 **forty million dollars**: Bill & Melinda Gates Foundation v. PnuVax, United States District Court, Western District of Washington at Seattle, March 12, 2019, IV, A.14 and B.15. Note: While the foundation pledged close to $40 million to Pnuvax, the foundation's grant records show it only delivered around $12 million.

47 **K&L Gates**: Bill & Melinda Gates Foundation v. PnuVax; "K&L Gates Mourns Passing of Longtime Partner and Humanitarian William H. Gates, Sr.," K&L

Gates, September 15, 2020, https://www.klgates.com/KL-Gates-Mourns-Passing-of-Longtime-Partner-and-Humanitarian-William-H-Gates-Sr-9-15-2020.

47   **forty-eight cents**: Bill & Melinda Gates Foundation v. PnuVax, Exhibit 2, page 9.

47   **scientific advisory committee**: Bill & Melinda Gates Foundation v. PnuVax, Exhibit 2, page 9.

48   *National Post*: John Ivison, "Federal Agency Nearly Shut Down Single Largest Canadian Recipient of Gates Funding," *National Post*, November 28, 2017, https://nationalpost.com/news/politics/john-ivison-despite-gates-funding-canadian-startup-nearly-bankrupted-after-nrc-ignored-rent-leniency-pleas.

48   **"failed to comply with the terms"**: Bill & Melinda Gates Foundation v. PnuVax, VII.

48   *Global News*: Andrew Russell, "Gates Foundation Sues Canadian Company over 'Misuse' of $30M Grant to Develop Pneumonia Vaccine," *Global News*, November 28, 2017, https://globalnews.ca/news/5035009/gates-foundation-sues-canadian-company-over-misuse-of-30m-grant-to-develop-pneumonia-vaccine/.

49   *Maclean's*: Justin Ling, "Where Did Canada's Vaccine Effort Actually Go Wrong?," *Maclean's* (blog), May 31, 2021, https://www.macleans.ca/news/canada/where-did-canadas-vaccine-effort-actually-go-wrong/.

49   *Daily Mail*: Boer Deng, "Bill Gates Charity Sues Drug Firm," *Times*, March 8, 2019, https://www.thetimes.co.uk/article/bill-gates-charity-sues-drug-firm-rf8gnfxq3; Kayla Brantley, "Bill and Melinda Gates Sue Company That Was Awarded a Grant of Up to $30 Million to Develop a Pneumonia Vaccine for Children—But Allegedly Used the Money to Pay Off Its Back Rent and Other Debts It Racked Up," *Daily Mail Online,* March 7, 2019, https://www.dailymail.co.uk/news/article-6777959/Bills-Melinda-Gates-sue-company-paid-30million-develop-pneumonia-vaccine.html.

49   **passed over by the Canadian government's**: Marieke Walsh, "Ottawa Passed Over Private Sector Plans to Produce a Covid-19 Vaccine Domestically," *Globe and Mail*, December 7, 2020, https://www.theglobeandmail.com/canada/article-feds-passed-over-private-option-with-plans-to-produce-covid-19-vaccine/. Note: Public records show the foundation filing relatively few lawsuits, so there's no evidence that legal action is a systematic part of how it works with grantees. But we also have to accept that the large majority of companies and other grantees would never get to that point with the foundation; just the threat of a lawsuit would be an extremely powerful motivator to get a partner in line.

50   **working with a number of different companies**: The foundation reports extensive grant funding for work on malaria vaccines, including money to companies, universities, and nonprofits: Agenus, Antigen Discovery, Inc., the Broad Institute, CureVac, Duke University, Fraunhofer USA, Inc., GatesMRI, Infectious Disease Research Institute, Kymab Limited, National Institute of Allergy and Infectious Diseases, Sanaria, Seattle Biomedical Research Institute, Stanford University, Tetragenetics, and others. Gates's financial support for GSK's malaria vaccine apparently went through PATH; "PATH Welcomes Landmark Financing Agreement for GSK's Malaria Vaccine," PATH, August 4, 2021, https://www.path.org/media-center/path-welcomes-landmark-financing-agreement-for-gsks-malaria-vaccine/.

50   **The vaccine's efficacy was so weak**: Jennifer Rigby, Natalie Grover, and Maggie Fick, "Why World's First Malaria Shot Won't Reach Millions of Children Who

Need It," Reuters, July 13, 2022, https://www.reuters.com/business/healthcare -pharmaceuticals/why-worlds-first-malaria-shot-wont-reach-millions-children -who-need-it-2022-07-13/.

50 **vaccine developer named Aeras**: "IAVI Acquires Aeras TB Vaccine Clinical Programs and Assets," Press Release, IAVI, October 1, 2018, https://www.iavi.org/news -resources/press-releases/2018/iavi-acquires-aeras-tb-vaccine-clinical-programs -and-assets. Note: Technically, all of Aeras's work output appeared to be folded into another Gates-funded product developer, IAVI, which, oddly, focuses on HIV/ AIDS.

50 **funding for MenAfriVac began**: PATH, "Lining Up for Hope—and a Meningitis Vaccine," PATH, June 15, 2018, https://www.path.org/articles/lining-up-for-hopeand -a-meningitis-vaccine/; PATH, "The Meningitis Vaccine Project: A Groundbreaking Partnership," June 15, 2015, https://www.path.org/articles/about-meningitis-vac cine-project/.

50 **he continued to remain heavily involved at Microsoft**: "Bill Gates Steps Down from Microsoft Board," Reuters, March 13, 2020, https://www.reuters.com/article/us -microsoft-bill-gates/bill-gates-steps-down-from-microsoft-board-idUSKBN2103BH; Daisuke Wakabayashi, "Bill Gates Bids a Teary Farewell to Microsoft," Reuters, June 27, 2008, https://www.reuters.com/article/us-microsoft-gates/bill-gates-bids-a-teary -farewell-to-microsoft-idUSN2630130120080628.

51 **"has effectively ended meningitis"**: Anita Zaidi, "Geographically Distributed Manufacturing Capacity Is Needed for Improved Global Health Security," Bill & Melinda Gates Foundation, July 28, 2021, https://www.gatesfoundation.org/ideas/articles /covid19-vaccine-geographic-distribution.

51 **protects against only meningitis serotype A**: Katya Fernandez et al., "Meningococcal Meningitis Outbreaks in the African Meningitis Belt After Meningococcal Serogroup A Conjugate Vaccine Introduction, 2011–2017," *Journal of Infectious Diseases* 220, no. S4 (October 31, 2019): S225–32, https://doi.org/10.1093/infdis/jiz355.

51 **presumably because they are more expensive:** CDC, "About Meningococcal Vaccines," Centers for Disease Control and Prevention, October 18, 2022, https://www .cdc.gov/vaccines/vpd/mening/hcp/about-vaccine.html. Note: Gavi reports having shipped 22 million doses of the A, C, W, and Y meningococcal vaccines through 2020, compared with 332 million doses of MenAfriVac; Gavi, Annual Progress Report, 2020.

51 **stopped by lawsuits**: "Pfizer's Patent Barrier Foils Korea's 1st Pneumococcal Conjugate Vaccine," *Korea Biomedical Review*, February 20, 2019, https://www.koreabiomed .com/news/articleView.html?idxno=5168.

51 **Cyrus Poonawalla**: "About Us," Serum Institute of India Pvt. Ltd., n.d., https://www .seruminstitute.com/about_us.php; Gavi Staff, "New Collaboration Makes Further 100 Million Doses of Covid-19 Vaccine Available to Low- and Middle-Income Countries," Gavi, September 29, 2020, https://www.gavi.org/news/media-room/new -collaboration-makes-further-100-million-doses-covid-19-vaccine-available-low.

52 **Gavi for $2**: PATH, "Developing a More Affordable Pneumococcal Vaccine," PATH Case Study, n.d., https://www.path.org/case-studies/developing-more-affordable -pneumococcal-vaccine/.

52   **"a turning point"**: Alderson et al., "Development Strategy and Lessons Learned for a 10-Valent Pneumococcal Conjugate Vaccine (PNEUMOSIL®)," 2670–77.

52   **vast majority of the pneumonia vaccines**: Gavi, "Supply Agreements," n.d., https://www.gavi.org/investing-gavi/innovative-financing/pneumococcal-amc /manufacturers/supply-agreements.

52   **seven dollars a dose with bonus payments**: UNICEF, "Pneumococcal Conjugate Vaccine (PCV) Price Data," https://www.unicef.org/supply/documents/pneumococcal -conjugate-vaccine-pcv-price-data.

52   **protects against only ten**: Note: Pfizer's Prevnar 13 covers all ten serotypes covered by Serum's Pneumosil, including 1, 5, 6A, 6B, 7F, 9V, 14, 19A, 19F, and 23F. See https:// pneumosil.com/ and https://prevnar20.pfizerpro.com/.

52   **protects against twenty strains**: "Pfizer Announces Positive Top-Line Results from Phase 3 Study of 20-Valent Pneumococcal Conjugate Vaccine in Infants," Press Release, Pfizer, August 12, 2022, https://www.pfizer.com/news/press-release/press -release-detail/pfizer-announces-positive-top-line-results-phase-3-study-20.

53   **24-valent vaccine**: Merck, "U.S. FDA Approves Merck's VAXNEUVANCE™ (Pneumococcal 15-Valent Conjugate Vaccine) for the Prevention of Invasive Pneumococcal Disease in Infants and Children," Merck.com, https://www.merck.com/news/u -s-fda-approves-mercks-vaxneuvance-pneumococcal-15-valent-conjugate-vaccine -for-the-prevention-of-invasive-pneumococcal-disease-in-infants-and-children/; Affinivax, "GSK to Acquire Clinical-Stage Biopharmaceutical Company Affinivax, Inc."

53   **cover 90 percent of children**: "India Completes National Introduction of Pneumococcal Conjugate Vaccine," Press Release, Gavi, November 12, 2021, https://www .gavi.org/news/media-room/india-completes-national-introduction-pneumococcal -conjugate-vaccine.

53   **significant impact on global health**: WHO and UNICEF estimates show that only 25 percent of Indian children were fully vaccinated in 2021, and it is not clear what portion of the vaccines came from Serum: "Pneumococcal Vaccination Coverage," World Health Organization, n.d., https://immunizationdata.who.int/pages/coverage /pcv.html?CODE=IND&ANTIGEN=&YEAR=.

53   **announced a massive new project**: "Inventprise Announces Investment of up to $90 Million to Advance Its 25 Valent Pneumococcal Conjugate Vaccine Candidate into Proof-of-Concept Clinical Trials," BusinessWire, November 10, 2021, https:// www.businesswire.com/news/home/20211110005245/en/Inventprise-Announces -Investment-of-up-to-90-Million-to-Advance-its-25-Valent-Pneumococcal -Conjugate-Vaccine-Candidate-into-Proof-of-Concept-Clinical-Trials; "Meet Our Leadership Team," Inventprise, n.d., https://inventprise.com/?page_id=1576.

53   **"convertible debt"**: The foundation's Strategic Investment Fund online database classifies its financing of Inventprise as "convertible debt," which normally means the debt converts to equity. Gates previously had a convertible debt financing arrangement with Zyomyx, for example, which ended up giving the foundation a 48 percent stake in the company. Bill & Melinda Gates Foundation, "Portfolio," SIF.gates, n.d., https:// sif.gatesfoundation.org/portfolio/; "Inventprise Receives $30M, Appoints New CEO and Expands Corporate Board, "Inventprise," April 27, 2022, https://webcache

.googleusercontent.com/search?q=cache:j_e9JCOLzfIJ:https://inventprise.com /%3Fpage_id%3D19092&cd=1&hl=en&ct=clnk&gl=us&client=firefox-b-1-d; Dennis Price, "Eyes Wide Open: Good Reasons for a Bad Investment in a Low-Cost HIV Test," in Stanford University with ImpactAlpha, *Making Markets Work for the Poor*, Supplement, *Stanford Social Innovation Review* (Summer 2016): 35.

53 **seven "governors"**: Query of Washington State Corporations and Charities Filing System, January 31, 2023, https://ccfs.sos.wa.gov/#/. Note: Board members include Donna Ambrosino, a consultant who reports serving on advisory positions at the Gates Foundation and the Gates-founded CEPI (LinkedIn, https://www.linkedin .com/in/donna-ambrosino-m-d-a37b6037/details/experience/); Niranjan Bose, a director at Gates Ventures (LinkedIn, https://www.linkedin.com/in/niranjanbose /details/experience/); Andrew Farnum, who previously held high-profile positions at the foundation and at the Bill & Melinda Gates Medical Research Institute (LinkedIn, https://www.linkedin.com/in/andrew-farnum-4b180a1); Ralf Clemens, a scientific adviser to the Gates Foundation (LinkedIn, https://www.linkedin.com/in/ralf -clemens-75578513/details/organizations/); and Stewart Parker, a Seattle-based consultant who previously ran the Gates-funded Infectious Disease Research Institute (IDRI) (LinkedIn, https://www.linkedin.com/in/stewart-parker-4819975/details /experience/); Julie Emory, "Tech Moves: USAFacts Picks Microsoft and Amazon Vet as CTO; Zillow CMO Departs; and More," GeekWire, April 8, 2022, https:// www.geekwire.com/2022/tech-moves-usafacts-picks-microsoft-and-amazon-vet -as-cto-inventprise-names-ceo-realnetworks-appoints-kontxt-president/.

53 **Gates Ventures**: Gates Ventures, for example, makes investments in other companies, like Beyond Meat. U.S. Securities and Exchange Commission, Form S-1, 2018, Exhibit 4.2, https://www.sec.gov/Archives/edgar/data/1655210/000162828018014471 /exhibit42bynd.htm.

53 **the Gates Foundation has an ownership stake**: U.S. Patent and Trademark Office, Patent application 17151445, January 18, 2021, https://assignment.uspto.gov/patent /index.html#/patent/search/resultAbstract?id=20210220461&type=publNum and https://legacy-assignments.uspto.gov/assignments/assignment-pat-55975-160.pdf. Note: The patent appears, as of early 2023, to still be a patent application, not yet a granted patent.

55 **"only truly global solution"**: Seth Berkley, "COVAX Explained," Gavi, September 3, 2020, https://www.gavi.org/vaccineswork/covax-explained; Katerini Tagmatarchi Storeng, Antoine de Bengy Puyvallée, and Felix Stein, "COVAX and the Rise of the 'Super Public Private Partnership' for Global Health," *Global Public Health*, October 22, 2021: 1–17, https://doi.org/10.1080/17441692.2021.1987502.

CHAPTER 2: WOMEN

56 **Epstein was found dead**: "Jeffrey Epstein: Financier Found Dead in New York Prison Cell," BBC News, August 10, 2019, https://www.bbc.com/news/world-us-canada -49306032.

56 **facing a potential life sentence**: David Klepper and Jim Mustian, "Epstein: How He Died and What It Means for His Accusers," AP News, August 11, 2019, https://

apnews.com/article/jeffrey-epstein-ap-top-news-florida-new-york-fl-state-wire-b7 6666895e674991a6782d77b726d085.

56   **soliciting prostitution**: Julie K. Brown, "How a Future Trump Cabinet Member Gave a Serial Sex Abuser the Deal of a Lifetime," *Miami Herald*, July 2, 2020, https://www.miamiherald.com/news/local/article220097825.html.

56   **"a person who steals a bagel"**: Andrea Peyser, "Wait, He's Allowed to Have Kids?," *New York Post*, March 3, 2011, https://nypost.com/2011/03/03/wait-hes-allowed-to-have-kids/.

56   **He repeated the line**: Emily Flitter and James B. Stewart, "Bill Gates Met with Jeffrey Epstein Many Times, Despite His Past," *New York Times*, October 12, 2019, https://www.nytimes.com/2019/10/12/business/jeffrey-epstein-bill-gates.html.

56   **Bill Clinton**: Bevan Hurley, "From Trump to Prince Andrew: All the Biggest Names Embroiled in the Maxwell Trial," *Independent*, January 23, 2023, https://www.independent.co.uk/news/world/americas/crime/ghislaine-maxwell-epstein-prince-andrew-prison-b2267523.html.

57   **"philanthropy as a tool to worm his way"**: Vicky Ward, "How Jeffrey Epstein Used Philanthropy to Worm His Way into Powerful Circles," *Town and Country*, July 15, 2021, https://www.townandcountrymag.com/society/money-and-power/a37025814/chasing-ghislaine-maxwell-jeffrey-epstein-vicky-ward-new-podcast/.

57   **JPMorgan Chase**: Flitter and Stewart, "Bill Gates Met with Jeffrey Epstein Many Times, Despite His Past."

58   **someone whose misdeeds**: Brown, "How a Future Trump Cabinet Member Gave a Serial Sex Abuser the Deal of a Lifetime"; Paul Harris, "Prince Andrew's Link to Sex Offender Jeffrey Epstein Taints Royalty in US," *Observer*, March 13, 2011, https://www.theguardian.com/uk/2011/mar/13/prince-andrew-jeffrey-epstein; Conchita Sarnoff and Aitken Lee, "Jeffrey Epstein: How the Hedge Fund Mogul Pedophile Got Off Easy," *Daily Beast*, March 25, 2011, https://www.thedailybeast.com/articles/2011/03/25/jeffrey-epstein-how-the-billionaire-pedophile-got-off-easy; Landon Thomas Jr., "Financier Starts Sentence in Prostitution Case," *New York Times*, July 1, 2008, https://www.nytimes.com/2008/07/01/business/01epstein.html?_r=3&oref=slogin&dbk=&pagewanted=all.

58   **"my heart breaks for these young women"**: Analisa Novak, "Melinda French Gates on Painful Divorce, Current Relationship with Bill Gates and Taking a 'Different Path,'" Interview by Gayle King, *CBS Mornings*, March 3, 2022, at 2:30, https://www.cbsnews.com/news/melinda-french-gates-bill-gates/.

58   **foundation staff also saw Epstein**: Flitter and Stewart, "Bill Gates Met with Jeffrey Epstein Many Times, Despite His Past."

58   **the same age as some of Epstein's victims**: Gates's eldest daughter was born in 1996, making her a teenager during much of the time Gates was meeting with Epstein, between 2011 and 2014; Maria Pasquini, "Bill and Melinda Gates Celebrate Daughter Jennifer's 26th Birthday: 'Incredibly Proud,'" April 27, 2022, https://people.com/human-interest/bill-gates-melinda-french-gates-celebrate-daughter-jennifer-gates-26th-birthday/.

58   **"I certainly made a huge mistake"**: "Bill Gates Opens Up About Divorce and Infidelity

Accusations," Interview by Savannah Guthrie, NBC News, 1:45, https://www
.youtube.com/watch?v=7T87-aGadwM.

59   **as late as 2017**: Flitter and Stewart, "Bill Gates Met with Jeffrey Epstein Many Times,
Despite His Past."

59   **may permanently change the direction**: "Melinda French Gates on Painful Divorce,
Current Relationship with Bill Gates and Taking a 'Different Path.'"

59   **The Gateses will continue to co-lead the foundation**: Nicholas Kulish, "Bill Gates
Can Remove Melinda French Gates from Foundation in Two Years," *New York Times*,
July 7, 2021, https://www.nytimes.com/2021/07/07/business/bill-gates-melinda-gates
-divorce-foundation.html.

59   **When he died**: Edward Helmore, "Jeffrey Epstein Signed New Will to Shield $577M
Fortune Days Before Death," *Guardian*, August 22, 2019, https://www.theguardian
.com/us-news/2019/aug/22/jeffrey-epstein-trust-fund-will-damages.

59   **in the early 2000s**: Michael Gold, "Bill Clinton and Jeffrey Epstein: How Are They
Connected?," *New York Times*, July 9, 2019, https://www.nytimes.com/2019/07/09
/nyregion/bill-clinton-jeffrey-epstein.html; Jack Crowe, "Epstein's Lawyer Claimed the
Alleged Pedophile Helped Devise the Clinton Global Initiative," Yahoo! Finance, July 8,
2019, https://finance.yahoo.com/news/epstein-lawyer-claimed-alleged-pedophile
-223701676.html.

59   **includes Larry Summers**: Flitter and Stewart, "Bill Gates Met with Jeffrey Epstein
Many Times, Despite His Past."

60   **"impetus for this gift"**: Ronan Farrow, "How an Élite University Research Center
Concealed Its Relationship with Jeffrey Epstein," *New Yorker*, September 6, 2019,
https://www.newyorker.com/news/news-desk/how-an-elite-university-research
-center-concealed-its-relationship-with-jeffrey-epstein.

60   **his network of VIPs**: "A Timeline of the Jeffrey Epstein, Ghislaine Maxwell Scandal,"
AP News, June 28, 2022, https://apnews.com/article/epstein-maxwell-timeline-b9f1
5710fabb72e8581c71e94acf513e.

60   **"I was never at any parties"**: John Jurgensen, "In Bill Gates's Mind, a Life of Processing," *Wall Street Journal*, September 10, 2019, https://www.wsj.com/articles/the
-mind-of-bill-gates-revealed-on-netflix-11568107801.

61   **Epstein's plane to Palm Beach**: Chris Sparo, "Bill Gates Flew with Jeffrey Epstein on
the Lolita Express in 2013," *Daily Mail Online*, August 12, 2019, https://www.dailymail
.co.uk/news/article-7350469/Bill-Gates-flew-Jeffrey-Epstein-Loliota-Express-2013
-years-pedophile-prison-stay.html.

61   **"This included visits"**: James Stewart, "NYT: Bill Gates Repeatedly Met with Jeffrey
Epstein / Velshi & Ruhle / MSNBC," Interview by Stephanie Ruhle, MSNBC, You-
Tube, October 15, 2019, 0:50, https://www.youtube.com/watch?v=WnKQ4tzg7ow.

61   **"beautiful young woman"**: Stewart, "NYT: Bill Gates Repeatedly Met with Jeffrey
Epstein," 2:25.

61   **Gates's failing marriage**: Lachlan Cartwright and Kate Briquelet, "Jeffrey Epstein
Gave Bill Gates Advice on How to End 'Toxic' Marriage, Sources Say," *Daily Beast*,
May 16, 2021, https://www.thedailybeast.com/jeffrey-epstein-gave-bill-gates-advice-on
-how-to-end-toxic-marriage-sources-say.

62   **relationships with former Nobel winners**: Kate Briquelet and Lachlan Cartwright,

"Bill Gates Thought Jeffrey Epstein Was His Ticket to a Nobel Prize, Ex-Staffer Says," *Daily Beast*, May 18, 2021, https://www.thedailybeast.com/bill-gates-thought-jeffrey -epstein-was-his-ticket-to-a-nobel-ex-staffer-says.

62 **International Peace Institute**: Tore Gjerstad and Gard Oterholm, "Bill Gates and Jeffrey Epstein Met with Nobel Committee Chair," *DN Magasinet*, October 2, 2020, https://www.dn.no/magasinet/dokumentar/jeffrey-epstein/thorbjorn-jagland/terje -rod-larsen/bill-gates-and-jeffrey-epstein-met-with-nobel-committee-chair/2-1- 885834.

62 **"assessing the companions"**: Gjerstad and Oterholm, "Bill Gates and Jeffrey Epstein Met with Nobel Committee Chair."

62 **"or campaigned for it"**: Gjerstad and Oterholm, "Bill Gates and Jeffrey Epstein Met with Nobel Committee Chair."

62 **Boris Nikolic**: Tore Gjerstad and Gard Oterholm, "Behind the Scenes: How Jeffrey Epstein Helped Billionaire Bill Gates Fund UN-Affiliated Think Tank Projects," *DN Magasinet*, October 4, 2020, https://www.dn.no/politikk/terje-rod-larsen/bill-gates /jeffrey-epstein/behind-the-scenes-how-jeffrey-epstein-helped-billionaire-bill-gates -fund-un-affiliated-think-tank-projects/2-1-885697.

63 **"Pakistan and Afghanistan"**: Gjerstad and Oterholm, "Behind the Scenes."

63 **University of Texas**: Vicky Ward, "What Was the Real Relationship Between Jeffrey Epstein and Bill Gates?," *Rolling Stone* (blog), August 3, 2021, https://www.rollingstone .com/culture/culture-features/jeffrey-epstein-bill-gates-connection-1206453/; Flitter and Stewart, "Bill Gates Met with Jeffrey Epstein Many Times, Despite His Past."

63 **Victoria's Secret**: Ward, "What Was the Real Relationship Between Jeffrey Epstein and Bill Gates?"

63 **It was an offer Epstein might**: Gabriel Sherman, "The Mogul and the Monster: Inside Jeffrey Epstein's Decades-Long Relationship with His Biggest Client," *Vanity Fair*, June 8, 2021, https://www.vanityfair.com/news/2021/06/inside-jeffrey-epsteins -decades-long-relationship-with-his-biggest-client.

63 **Epstein hired her as his science adviser**: Ward, "What Was the Real Relationship Between Jeffrey Epstein and Bill Gates?"; Flitter and Stewart, "Bill Gates Met with Jeffrey Epstein Many Times, Despite His Past."

63 **senior program officer**: Melanie Walker, personal website, Wayback Machine, https:// web.archive.org/web/20210713221706/https://www.melaniewalkermd.com/copy-of -connecting-information; Flitter and Stewart, "Bill Gates Met with Jeffrey Epstein Many Times, Despite His Past."

63 **Nikolic, who appears to play**: Flitter and Stewart, ""Bill Gates Met with Jeffrey Epstein Many Times, Despite His Past."

63 **a co-inventor**: "Micromolded or 3-D Printed Pulsatile Release Vaccine Formula- tions," U.S. Patent US-20210205444-A1, July 8, 2021; "Fortified Micronutrient Salt Formulations," US-11541017-B2, January 3, 2023. In SEC documents, Nikolic has described himself as having served as "Chief Advisor for Science and Technology to Bill Gates" at bgC3 from April 2009 to April 2014. In his bio at Biomatics, Nikolic describes himself as having helped lead "select . . . for-profit and not-for-profit invest- ment activities" for Bill Gates. The *New York Times* and another source reported that he worked as a science adviser to the Gates Foundation. See Editas, Form S-1, U.S.

Securities and Exchange Commission, January 4, 2016, https://www.sec.gov/Archives/edgar/data/1650664/000104746916009534/a2226902zs-1.htm; "Team," Biomatics Capital, https://biomaticscapital.com/team/; Flitter and Stewart, "Bill Gates Met with Jeffrey Epstein Many Times, Despite His Past"; "Bill & Melinda Gates Foundation, Crossovers Dump $120 Million into Editas Medicine to Advance Genome Editing," BioSpace, August 10, 2015, https://www.biospace.com/article/bill-and-melinda-gates-foundation-crossovers-dump-120-million-into-editas-medicine-to-advance-genome-editing-/.

63 **pharmaceutical company Schrödinger**: "Schrödinger Receives Additional Equity Investment from Bill Gates," PRWeb, December 13, 2012, https://www.prweb.com/releases/2012/12/prweb10229213.htm.

63 **met Epstein for the first time**: Flitter and Stewart, "Bill Gates Met with Jeffrey Epstein Many Times, Despite His Past."

63 **After the meeting**: Tara Palmeri, "The Women Who Enabled Jeffrey Epstein," *Politico Magazine*, May 14, 2021, https://www.politico.com/news/magazine/2021/05/14/jeffrey-epstein-investigation-women-487157.

64 **"shocked" to have been named an executor**: Neil Weinberg, "Jeffrey Epstein's Executor Is Ex-Science Adviser to Bill Gates," Bloomberg, August 19, 2019, https://www.bloomberg.com/news/articles/2019-08-19/epstein-s-11th-hour-executor-is-ex-science-adviser-to-bill-gates.

64 **"he started to retaliate"**: Ward, "What Was the Real Relationship Between Jeffrey Epstein and Bill Gates?"; Flitter and Stewart, "Bill Gates Met with Jeffrey Epstein Many Times, Despite His Past."

64 **foundation lost confidence in him and walked away**: Flitter and Stewart, "Bill Gates Met with Jeffrey Epstein Many Times, Despite His Past."

64 **The simpler and more reasonable explanation**: Bloomberg reported that Nikolic and Epstein were both high-level clients of JPMorgan Chase, where Epstein was known as a "center of influence" because he brought in so many wealthy clients. The outlet reported an unnamed source saying that "Nikolic waxed enthusiastic about Epstein's financial advice," though Nikolic told Bloomberg that he had no business ties with Epstein. Weinberg, "Jeffrey Epstein's Executor Is Ex-Science Adviser to Bill Gates."

65 **Apollo Global Management**: Tim Schwab, "Will the Gates Foundation's Board Ever Hold Bill Accountable?," *Nation,* February 2, 2022, https://www.thenation.com/article/society/gates-foundation-board-accountability/.

65 **sweetheart plea deal**: Annie Karni, Eileen Sullivan, and Noam Scheiber, "Acosta to Resign as Labor Secretary over Jeffrey Epstein Plea Deal," *New York Times*, July 12, 2019, https://www.nytimes.com/2019/07/12/us/politics/acosta-resigns-trump.html. Note: Donald Trump had to explain his own relationship with Epstein after an interview from 2002 surfaced that quoted him as saying, "I've known Jeff for fifteen years. Terrific guy . . . He's a lot of fun to be with. It is even said that he likes beautiful women as much as I do, and many of them are on the younger side." Trump later downplayed his relationship with Epstein, noting in 2019, "I had a falling out with him a long time ago. I don't think I have spoken with him for 15 years. I was not a

fan." Natalie Colarossi, "20 People Who Trump Has Personally Known and Then Claimed He Didn't," *Business Insider*, January 28, 2020, https://www.businessinsider .com/people-trump-said-he-didnt-know-but-did-photos.

65 **"support to the employee who raised the concern"**: Emily Glazer, Justin Baer, Khadeeja Safdar, and Aaron Tilley, "Bill Gates Left Microsoft Board amid Probe into Prior Relationship with Staffer," *Wall Street Journal*, May 16, 2021, https:// www.wsj.com/articles/microsoft-directors-decided-bill-gates-needed-to-leave -board-due-to-prior-relationship-with-staffer-11621205803.

65 **midlevel employee**: Emily Glazer, "Microsoft Executives Told Bill Gates to Stop Emailing a Female Staffer Years Ago," *Wall Street Journal*, October 18, 2021, https:// www.wsj.com/articles/microsoft-executives-told-bill-gates-to-stop-emailing-a -female-staffer-years-ago-11634559950.

65 **discrimination and harassment**: Dan Levine, "Microsoft Women Filed 238 Discrimination and Harassment Complaints," Reuters, March 13, 2018, https://www .reuters.com/article/us-microsoft-women-idUSKCN1GP077.

65 **Gates stepped down**: Glazer et al., "Bill Gates Left Microsoft Board amid Probe into Prior Relationship with Staffer."

66 **"bad behavior"**: Sally Ho and Matt O'Brien, "Bill Gates' Leadership Roles Stay Intact Despite Allegations," AP News, May 18, 2021, https://apnews.com/article /bill-gates-philanthropy-business-208b2d1139e55517643e47a9edbce266. Note: The subsequent Microsoft investigation, by law firm ArentFox Schiff, proved to be something of a whitewash, briefly addressing only one allegation against Gates, in which an employee claimed he "had subjected her to inappropriate communications and conduct." The employee's complaint "made references to sexual harassment and the me too movement." Bill Gates claimed the interactions were consensual; ArentFox Schiff, Memorandum to Microsoft Board of Directors, "Transparency Report on Shareholder Resolution Project," November 11, 2022, https://blogs.microsoft.com /wp-content/uploads/prod/2022/11/Final-Microsoft-Transparency-Report.pdf.

66 **speeding tickets driving his Porsche**: Wallace and Erickson, *Hard Drive*, 240–41.

66 **"on-again, off-again romance"**: Wallace and Erickson, *Hard Drive*, 415–16.

66 **his face turned purple**: Wallace and Erickson, *Hard Drive*, 162–63.

66 **affirmative action provisions**: Wallace and Erickson, *Hard Drive*, 291.

67 **opening up the company to women**: Melkorka Licea, Ashley Stewart, Rob Price, and Becky Peterson, "Insiders Say Bill Gates Was an Office Bully Who Pursued Sexual Affairs, and That His Squeaky-Clean Image Was Merely Good PR," *Business Insider*, June 21, 2021, https://www.businessinsider.com/bill-gates-melinda-divorce -affairs-bully-womanizer-2021-6?r=AU&IR=T.

67 **same contradictions**: *The Billionaires Who Made Our World*, season 1, episode 2, directed by Storm Theunissen, aired February 14, 2023, on Channel 4, 25:50, https:// www.channel4.com/programmes/the-billionaires-who-made-our-world.

67 **"the work that the Gates Foundation has done"**: *The Billionaires Who Made Our World*, 4:00.

67 **Gates had made an unwanted advance**: Emily Flitter and Matthew Goldstein, "Long Before Divorce, Bill Gates Had Reputation for Questionable Behavior," *New York*

Times, May 16, 2021, https://www.nytimes.com/2021/05/16/business/bill-melinda -gates-divorce-epstein.html.

67 **it had no reason to investigate**: Schwab, "Will the Gates Foundation's Board Ever Hold Bill Accountable?"

68 **Larson kept his position**: Anupreeta Das, Emily Flitter, and Nicholas Kulish, "A Culture of Fear at the Firm That Manages Bill Gates's Fortune," *New York Times*, May 26, 2021, https://www.nytimes.com/2021/05/26/business/bill-gates-cascade-michael -larson.html.

68 **with men, not women**: Flitter and Goldstein, "Long Before Divorce, Bill Gates Had Reputation for Questionable Behavior."

68 **impunity was built on blackmail**: Daniel Bates, "EXCLUSIVE: Jeffrey Epstein Had Surveillance Cameras Hidden Throughout His Properties Worldwide in a 'Blackmail Scheme' to Extort His Powerful Friends, Victims Tell New Netflix Doc About the Pedophile," *Daily Mail*, May 27, 2020, https://www.dailymail.co.uk/news /article-8361607/Jeffrey-Epsteins-surveillance-cameras-blackmail-scheme-extort -powerful-friends.html.

68 **found hidden cameras in two locations**: Andrew Marra, "The Man Who Had Everything: Jeffrey Epstein Craved Big Homes, Elite Friends and, Investigators Say, Underage Girls," *Palm Beach Post*, July 11, 2019, https://www.palmbeachpost.com /story/news/2006/08/14/had-everything-jeffrey-epstein-craved-big-homes-elite -friends-and-investigators-say-underage-girls/4712721007/.

68 **He tweeted a thread on Twitter**: Adam Davidson's Twitter thread, available at https:// web.archive.org/web/20220605234021/https://twitter.com/adamdavidson/status /1533082314321842179.

70 **world's most generous givers**: Maria Di Mento, "$15B from Gates, French Gates Tops 2021 Biggest Gift List," *Chronicle of Philanthropy*, republished in *Washington Post* and *Economic Times*, December 31, 2021, https://web.archive.org/web/2022 0101164421/https://www.washingtonpost.com/business/15b-from-gates-french-gates -tops-2021-biggest-gift-list/2021/12/31/b7e13146-6a64-11ec-9390-eae241f4c8b1 _story.html and https://economictimes.indiatimes.com/magazines/panache/bill-gates -melinda-french-top-2021-biggest-gift-list-with-15-billion-donation-to-foundation /articleshow/88629051.cms?from=mdr. Note: The foundation at some point quietly edited the press release on which the article had been based, adding an asterisk leading to a fine-print disclosure that Bill Gates actually had not donated fifteen billion dollars in 2021, but that he planned to donate the money over an undefined period in the future. The next year, Bill Gates executed the same PR ploy, announcing that he was making a twenty-billion-dollar donation to the Gates Foundation. See Gates's press release before and after the correction; Mark Suzman, "Moving Forward," Bill & Melinda Gates Foundation, n.d., https://web.archive.org/web/20210707150517/https: //www.gatesfoundation.org/ideas/articles/gates-foundation-trustees-commitment and https://web.archive.org/web/20220111192720/https://www.gatesfoundation.org /ideas/articles/gates-foundation-trustees-commitment.

70 **"combat the injustice"**: "Waging Justice for Women," Clooney Foundation for Justice, https://cfj.org/project/waging-justice-for-women/.

CHAPTER 3: TAXES

72 **2019 autobiography**: *New York Times* Best Seller List, May 26, 2019, https://www
.nytimes.com/books/best-sellers/2019/05/26/.

72 **"long on heartwarming anecdotes"**: Lily Meyer, "'The Moment of Lift' Is More of a
Whisper than a Call to Action," NPR, April 23, 2019, https://www.npr.org/2019/04
/23/716066240/the-moment-of-lift-is-more-of-a-whisper-than-a-call-to-action.

72 *Goats and Soda*: Michel Martin, "Melinda Gates on Marriage, Parenting, and Why
She Made Bill Drive the Kids to School," *Goats and Soda* (blog), NPR, April 28,
2019, https://www.npr.org/sections/goatsandsoda/2019/04/28/717438397/melinda
-gates-on-marriage-parenting-and-why-she-made-bill-drive-the-kids-to-scho; Tim
Schwab, "Journalism's Gates Keepers," *Columbia Journalism Review*, August 21,
2020, https://www.cjr.org/criticism/gates-foundation-journalism-funding.php.

72 **ring-kissing conciliation**: Devi Sridhar, "Holding a Mirror Up to Global Health,"
The Lancet 394, no. 10204 (September 28, 2019): 1136, https://doi.org/10.1016
/S0140-6736(19)32170-1.

73 **original works by Leonardo da Vinci**: Mark David, "Inside Bill and Melinda Gates's
Bonkers Portfolio of American Real Estate," *Robb Report* (blog), May 7, 2021,
https://robbreport.com/shelter/celebrity-homes/bill-and-melinda-gates-houses
-real-estate-1234611739/; "The Fabulous Life of Bill Gates, the Richest Man in the
World," *Business Insider India*, July 26, 2021, https://www.businessinsider.in/tech
/the-fabulous-life-of-bill-gates-the-richest-man-in-the-world/slidelist/.37361017
.cms#slideid=37361018.

73 **private jet**: Tim Schwab, "Bill Gates, Climate Warrior. And Super Emitter," *Nation*,
February 16, 2021, https://www.thenation.com/article/environment/bill-gates-
climate-book/.

73 **Instead of owning a yacht**: Isabel Vincent, "Bill Gates Shops for Climate-Saving
Farm Aboard Polluting Yacht," *New York Post*, November 3, 2021, https://nypost
.com/2021/11/02/bill-gates-shops-for-climate-saving-farm-aboard-polluting-yacht/;
Danielle Haynes, "Bill Gates Renting Yacht for $5 Million," UPI, August 10, 2014,
https://www.upi.com/Top_News/US/2014/08/10/Bill-Gates-takes-vacation-on
-330M-yacht/8141407687450/.

73 **Fregate Island in the Seychelles**: Taylor Locke, "Bill and Melinda Gates Just
Announced Their Divorce—Here's a Breakdown of the Billionaire's Wealth," CNBC,
May 4, 2021, https://www.cnbc.com/2021/05/04/next-comes-the-divorce-settlement
-breakdown-of-bill-gates-wealth.html; Kerry Hannon, "The Draw of a Spit of Land
Surrounded by Blue," *New York Times*, February 10, 2015, https://www.nytimes.com
/2015/02/10/business/the-draw-of-a-spit-of-land-surrounded-by-blue.html.

73 **cramped dorm room**: "Bill Gates Buys $1.25 Million Home Near University of Chi-
cago," April 30, 2018, CBS Chicago, https://www.cbsnews.com/chicago/news/bill
-gates-buys-home-near-university-of-chicago/.

73 **Evergate Stables**: Evergate Stables, https://evergatestables.com; "Our Team Index,"
Evergate Stables, https://evergatestables.com/our-team; Brian Bandell, "Bill Gates,
Jennifer Gates' Trust Sells Wellington Equestrian Property," *South Florida Business*

Journal, March 24, 2022, https://www.bizjournals.com/southflorida/news/2022/03
/24/bill-gates-jennifer-gates-21w1-trust.html.

73   **equestrian facility in Wellington, Florida**: Bandell, "Bill Gates, Jennifer Gates'
      Trust Sells Wellington Equestrian Property."

74   **chocolate and cocoa companies**: Alex Park, "Is the Gates Foundation Still Invest-
      ing in Private Prisons?," *Mother Jones* (blog), December 8, 2014, https://www
      .motherjones.com/politics/2014/12/gates-foundation-still-investing-private
      -prisons; Laura Starita and Timothy Ogden, "A Conflict of Interests: When Foun-
      dations Invest in Arms and Tobacco," *Alliance Magazine* (blog), November 21, 2017,
      https://www.alliancemagazine.org/analysis/conflict-interests-foundations-invest
      -arms-tobacco/; Reed Abelson, "Charities' Investing: Left Hand, Meet Right," *New
      York Times*, June 11, 2000, https://www.nytimes.com/2000/06/11/business/charities
      -investing-left-hand-meet-right.html; Alan Rusbridger, "Dear Bill Gates: 'Will You
      Lead the Fight Against Climate Change?,'" *Guardian*, April 30, 2015, https://www
      .theguardian.com/environment/2015/apr/30/dear-bill-gates-will-you-lead-the-fight
      -against-climate-change; Charles Piller, "Money Clashes with Mission," *Los Angeles
      Times*, January 8, 2007, https://www.latimes.com/business/la-na-gates8jan8-story
      .html.

74   **Conference in Idaho**: Sydney P. Freedberg, Nicole Sadek, and Brenda Medina,
      "How Uber Won Access to World Leaders, Deceived Investigators and Exploited
      Violence Against Its Drivers in Battle for Global Dominance," *ICIJ*, July 10, 2022,
      https://www.icij.org/investigations/uber-files/uber-global-rise-lobbying-violence
      -technology; Theo Wayt and Lydia Moynihan, "Scandal-Ridden Bill Gates Spotted
      at Sun Valley," *New York Post*, July 8, 2021, https://nypost.com/2021/07/08/scandal
      -ridden-bill-gates-spotted-at-sun-valley/.

74   **exceptionally *rich* person**: Bloomberg Billionaire Index, Bloomberg, n.d., https://www
      .bloomberg.com/billionaires/profiles/melinda-f-gates/; *Forbes* real-time net worth,
      Forbes, https://www.forbes.com/profile/melinda-french-gates/?sh=75c3eedc2fcc.

74   **"Giving Pledge"**: Melinda French Gates, "The Giving Pledge," https://www.giving
      pledge.org/pledger?pledgerId=428.

74   **charity unburdens governments**: Gallup, "Percentage of Americans Donating
      to Charity at New Low," Gallup.com, May 14, 2020, https://news.gallup.com/poll
      /310880/percentage-americans-donating-charity-new-low.aspx; Kelsey Piper, "The
      Charitable Deduction Is Mostly for the Rich. A New Study Argues That's by Design,"
      Vox, September 3, 2019, https://www.vox.com/future-perfect/2019/9/3/20840955
      /charitable-deduction-tax-rich-billionaire-philanthropy.

75   **Robert Reich notes**: Robert Reich, "Philanthropy of Wealthy Not Always Chari-
      table," *SFGate*, December 20, 2013, https://www.sfgate.com/opinion/reich/article
      /Philanthropy-of-wealthy-not-always-charitable-5082580.ph.

75   **up to 74 percent**: Roger Colinvaux and Ray Madoff, "Charitable Tax Reform for
      the 21st Century," *Tax Notes*, September 16, 2019, https://scholarship.law.edu/cgi
      /viewcontent.cgi?article=2017&context=scholar.

76   **"more than $36.8 billion"**: "Foundation FAQ," Bill & Melinda Gates Foundation,
      Web archive found at https://web.archive.org/web/20221215081139/https://www
      .gatesfoundation.org/about/foundation-faq.

76 **"Berkshire shares"**: "Comments by Warren E. Buffett in Conjunction with His Annual Contribution of Berkshire Hathaway Shares to Five Foundations," News Release, Berkshire Hathaway, June 23, 2021, https://www.berkshirehathaway.com /news/jun2321.pdf.

76 **$75 billion**: Gates, "By 2026, the Gates Foundation Aims to Spend $9 Billion a Year." Note: Bill Gates announced in July 2022 that he intended to donate an additional $20 billion to the foundation in 2022. These figures won't be verifiable in Gates's tax records until after this book is submitted for publication.

76 **Canadian National Railway**: Bill & Melinda Gates Foundation Trust, U.S. Securities and Exchange Commission, Form 13-F, November 14, 2022. Note: Bill & Melinda Gates Foundation Trust, IRS 990 filing for period ending December 2021.

76 **John Deere and Ecolab**: Alan C. Heuberger, in "Our Leadership Team," John Deere, https://www.deere.com/en/our-company/leadership; "Board of Directors," Ecolab, https://investor.ecolab.com/corporate-governance/board-of-directors/default.aspx.

77 **actually generates more money**: It's quite complicated to find and tabulate these numbers because the foundation's financial reporting is complex and constantly changing. In the early years of the foundation, it did not publish financial audits, only its annual tax returns. And some of its URLs, or links, to audits are dead or missing. Later, the foundation put its endowment into a separate entity, the Gates Foundation Trust, which reports its own financials. To find the Gates Foundation's investment income, I used "investment income, net" as reported in its annual financial audits, which were not published until 2003. I used the Gates Foundation's annual 990 IRS filings (Part I, Column D) to tabulate its charitable grant making, because audits do not appear to separate out charitable grants from other administrative expenses. Some readers may notice that elsewhere in the book I have reported Gates pledging $80 billion in charitable grants, not $58 billion, as I do here. The discrepancy stems from two places. One, my analysis here only spans 2003 to 2020. Two, I'm looking at money that the foundation has actually paid out, not money it has promised to pay out in the future. Many foundation grants are paid out over several years, so, for example, a large $100 million award in 2020 might be paid out in yearly increments over the next decade.

77 **Edgar Villanueva**: "Health Center Program Award Recipients," Health Resources and Services Administration, n.d., https://www.hrsa.gov/opa/eligibility-and-registration /health-centers/fqhc and https://bphc.hrsa.gov/compliance/compliance-manual /chapter20.

78 **shouldn't we have a say**: In the chaos surrounding Bill and Melinda French Gates's divorce, Warren Buffett resigned from the board, and the foundation rushed to add new board members, all of whom had institutional or financial ties to the Gates Foundation, meaning they were not independent, and not likely to challenge Bill Gates: Tom Tierney came to Gates's board from the nonprofit consulting firm Bridgespan, which has received at least $32 million from the Gates Foundation. Baroness Minouche Shafik is director of the London School of Economics, which has received $13 million from the foundation. Strive Masiyiwa, the Zimbabwean telecom billionaire, also based in London, previously served as chair of the board for Alliance for a Green Revolution in Africa (AGRA), an organization founded and funded by Gates. Later, the foundation added Dr. Helene D. Gayle, president of Spelman College, and

Ashish Dhawan, founder and CEO of the Convergence Foundation, to its board of trustees, noting that "both new board members have worked with foundation grantees." Schwab, "Will the Gates Foundation's Board Ever Hold Bill Accountable?"; "Bill & Melinda Gates Foundation Appoints Two New Members to Board of Trustees," Bill & Melinda Gates Foundation, August 18, 2022, https://www.gatesfoundation .org/ideas/media-center/press-releases/2022/08/gates-foundation-appoints-new -board-members-helene-gayle-ashish-dhawan.

78 **"fiduciary standard of care"**: Alex Friedman and Julie Sunderland, "How to Fix the Gates Foundation," Project Syndicate, May 28, 2021, https://www.project-syndicate .org/commentary/gates-foundation-future-after-divorce-reform-by-alex-friedman -1-and-julie-sunderland-2021-05?barrier=accesspaylog.

79 **elite private high school**: Tanza Loudenback, "Bill Gates' Kids May Not Inherit His Fortune, but He Is Setting Them Up for Success in Other Ways," *Business Insider*, November 28, 2017, https://www.businessinsider.com/bill-gates-private-high-school -lakeside-seattle-2017-11.

79 **Gates's image as a do-good philanthropist**: "Foundation FAQ," Bill & Melinda Gates Foundation, https://www.gatesfoundation.org/about/foundation-faq.

79 **carte blanche that Big Philanthropy enjoys**: Stephen Moore, "George Soros's $18 Billion Tax Shelter," *Wall Street Journal*, November 23, 2017, https://www.wsj.com /articles/george-soross-18-billion-tax-shelter-1511465095?elqTrackId=2ccfb43f ab6548bc84638c42d730c12c&elq=cfbcb0ddbe3d4f77827bd44cdd1f7fd8&elqaid =16835&elqat=1&elqCampaignId=7289.

79 **"Gates Foundation now has about $60 Billion"**: This is inaccurate. The foundation in 2006 had $33 billion in its endowment. Press releases at the time had announced that Warren Buffett was donating $30 billion to the Gates Foundation, but that was the value of Buffett's planned donations, which were actually parceled out into small yearly donations, not one lump sum.

80 **except for $1 billion**: Sheldon Drobny, "The Gates and Buffett Foundation Shell Game," *HuffPost*, August 22, 2006, https://www.huffpost.com/entry/the-gates-and -buffett-fou_b_27780.

80 **Theodore Roosevelt said**: Robert Reich, "A Look Inside Just Giving," *Princeton Press* (blog), July 24, 2020, https://press.princeton.edu/ideas/a-look-inside-just-giving.

80 **In the 1930s**: Eric John Abrahamson, "Control Stock: Corporate Power and the Tax Reform Act of 1969," *HistPhil* (blog), February 11, 2020, https://histphil.org/2020/02 /11/control-stock-corporate-power-and-the-tax-reform-act-of-1969/.

81 **Howard Hughes Medical**: Mark Potts, "New Trustees Weighing Fate of Hughes Aircraft," *Washington Post*, May 13, 1984, https://www.washingtonpost.com/archive /business/1984/05/13/new-trustees-weighing-fate-of-hughes-aircraft/ae2a094a -8a5f-496b-b77d-0c6e322328e9/; Richard L. Berke, "Hughes Institute Settles Tax Case," *New York Times*, March 3, 1987, https://www.nytimes.com/1987/03/03/us /hughes-institute-settles-tax-case.html.

81 **"agonizing reappraisal is overdue"**: *Congressional Record* 16999 (1962) (statement of Rep. Wright Patman).

81 **In 1969, Congress passed**: Ray D. Madoff, "The Five Percent Fig Leaf," *Pittsburgh Tax Review* 17, no. 2 (2020): 341.

82 **the IRS at the time**: Marcus S. Owens, "Charity Oversight: An Alternative Approach," Working Paper No. 33.4 (note 1), Hauser Center for Nonprofit Organizations, Harvard University, October 2006, https://cpl.hks.harvard.edu/files/cpl/files/workingpaper _33.4.pdf.

82 **the 100,000 foundations**: IRS, Statistics of Income, Returns of Tax-Exempt Organizations, Employee Retirement Plans, Government Entities, and Tax-Exempt Bonds Examined by Type of Return (Table 21) and Type of Foundation and Size of End-of-Year Fair Market Value of Total Assets, 2018 (most recent data available), https://www.irs.gov /statistics/soi-tax-stats-domestic-private-foundation-and-charitable-trust-statistics.

82 **around two hundred audits a year**: This number refers to audits of tax returns, not organizations. If the IRS audits a foundation's tax filings over the previous three years, the IRS tallies this as three audits. So, the actual number of unique foundations the IRS audits is likely far fewer than two hundred.

82 **IRS had hemorrhaged**: The Institute for Policy Studies has proposed shifting oversight of philanthropy out of the IRS and creating a new office, the Office of Charity Oversight, to be funded through a tax on investment income of private foundations. Chuck Collins and Helen Flannery, "Gilded Giving 2022," Institute for Policy Studies, July 2022, https://ips-dc.org/wp-content/uploads/2022/07/Report-Gilded-Giving -2022.pdf.

82 **laissez-faire environment**: The Gates Foundation's location in Seattle also gives the state of Washington purview over its charitable work. The Washington State Attorney General's (AG) Office told me that it did not have full-time staff dedicated to investigating charitable activities until 2014, a decade after the Gates Foundation became the largest philanthropy in the world. "We generally do not comment on pending investigations, including confirming whether or not they exist," the office noted. "If we receive a complaint regarding a private foundation, we would investigate and bring an enforcement action if we find one is warranted." Through a public records request, I discovered that the AG's office does receive complaints about the Gates Foundation, including a flurry of complaints about financial conflicts of interest in 2020. But I also uncovered internal correspondence stating explicitly in 2019 that the office had never investigated Gates. "We've never had any reason to look at Gates," David Horn, senior counsel in the Office of the Attorney General, noted in an internal email.

A separate entity in Washington State, the Office of the Secretary of State, also has some minor oversight role over the Gates Foundation. Notably, the foundation has donated more than two million dollars to the Office of the Secretary of State to support a library it manages. The office did not respond to questions about this gift. Washington state attorney general Bob Ferguson also would not agree to an interview. From everything we can see, Washington State, like Washington, DC, isn't paying attention to the activities of the Gates Foundation.

82 **weakened IRS enforcement capacity**: Paul Kiel, "The IRS Decided to Get Tough Against Microsoft. Microsoft Got Tougher," ProPublica, January 22, 2020, https:// www.propublica.org/article/the-irs-decided-to-get-tough-against-microsoft -microsoft-got-tougher; Jacob Kastrenakes, "Bill Gates to 'Substantially Increase Time' at Microsoft After Stepping Down as Chairman," The Verge, February 4, 2014,

https://www.theverge.com/2014/2/4/5377226/bill-gates-steps-down-microsoft
-chairman-named-tech-advisor.

82 **internalized a cost-benefit**: There's also a question of whether the Gates Foundation
is too close to the IRS. A Gates Foundation attorney served on the IRS's Advisory
Committee on Tax Exempt and Government Entities between 2015 and 2018, which
should have given the foundation an open forum to discuss its concerns and to brain-
storm the "development of innovative and cooperative problem solving strategies"—
the stated purpose of the advisory committee. During the time the foundation had a
representative on this committee, the IRS finalized new rules that helped the Gates
Foundation and other large philanthropies expand their financial engagements with
the private sector through a program called Program-Related Investments.

The IRS, generally speaking, was not particularly helpful during my reporting.
It would not agree to interviews, and it denied my FOIA seeking any complaints
it had received about the Gates Foundation—on the grounds that such complaints
were "confidential." Federal Advisory Committee Database, Advisory Committee on
Tax Exempt and Government Entities, Committee Detail, https://www.facadatabase
.gov/FACA/apex/FACAPublicCommittee?id=a10t0000002ondOAAQ; "Steps to
Catalyze Private Foundation Impact Investing," The White House, April 21, 2016,
https://obamawhitehouse.archives.gov/blog/2016/04/21/steps-catalyze-private
-foundation-impact-investing.

83 **investigation of corporate tax avoidance**: Jennifer Liberto, "Offshore Tax Havens
Saved Microsoft $7 Billion in Taxes—Senate Panel," CNN Business, September 20,
2012, https://money.cnn.com/2012/09/20/technology/offshore-tax-havens/index
.html; "Subcommittee Hearing to Examine Billions of Dollars in U.S. Tax Avoidance by Multinational Corporations," Press Release, website of Senator Carl Levin,
September 20, 2012, https://web.archive.org/web/20121212035753/http://www
.levin.senate.gov/newsroom/press/release/subcommittee-hearing-to-examine
-billions-of-dollars-in-us-tax-avoidance-by-multinational-corporations/.

83 **Bill Gates called them "hogwash"**: Bill Gates, Interview by Jeremy Paxman, *BBC
Newsnight*, January 23, 2014, https://www.youtube.com/watch?v=baUmdtrZp90.

83 **402 appeals on its property taxes**: Schwab, "Bill Gates Gives to the Rich (Including
Himself)."

83 **slowly disburses the funds**: Mark Curtis, "Gated Development: Is the Gates Foundation Always a Force for Good?" Global Justice Now, June 2016, https://www
.globaljustice.org.uk/sites/default/files/files/resources/gjn_gates_report_june_2016
_web_final_version_2.pdf.

84 **target the accumulated fortunes**: The Institute for Policy Studies has proposed a
2 percent wealth tax on the assets of large charitable foundations "that are closely
controlled by donors." That is, the Gates Foundation could be seen as part and parcel of Bill Gates's personal wealth because he, effectively, controls how it is used, so
there is an argument to be made that the foundation's endowment should be subject
to a wealth tax. Some economists have also said that a tightly controlled billionaire
philanthropy like the Gates Foundation might be subject to a wealth tax. Collins
and Flannery, "Gilded Giving 2022"; Emmanuel Saez and Gabriel Zucman, "Progressive Wealth Taxation," BPEA Conference Drafts, September 5, 2019, https://

www.brookings.edu/wp-content/uploads/2019/09/Saez-Zucman_conference
-draft.pdf.

84   **chipping away at Gates's assets**: To explain the math: If Gates earns a 10 percent
      return on his investments of $100 billion this year, his wealth would increase by $10
      billion, to a total of $110 billion. But if Congress levied a 3 percent wealth tax on his
      original $100 billion at the beginning of the year, he'd be working with only $97 billion.
      Under this scenario, his 10 percent investment return ($9.7 billion) would bring his
      net worth up to $106.7 billion. So, the 3 percent wealth tax would generate $3 billion
      in revenue for Treasury, but it would reduce Gates's personal wealth by an even larger
      number, $3.3 billion—from $110 billion to $106.7 billion. Over the last twenty years, a
      consistently levied 3 percent wealth tax would have magnified these effects—generating
      $30 billion in tax revenue, but reducing Gates's wealth by $60 billion. I did this calcula-
      tion using Gates's estimated yearly wealth according to the *Forbes* billionaires list.

      I ran my calculations by University of California economist Gabriel Zucman,
      who pointed me to the website taxjusticenow.com, which models how different
      wealth tax proposals would have changed the personal wealth of the superrich—
      had the tax been in place as far back as 1982. According to these models, Senator
      Elizabeth Warren's wealth tax would have reduced Bill Gates's wealth, as it stood in
      2020, from $117 billion to $21 billion. Bernie Sanders's plan would have reduced it
      to $15 billion.

84   **critique of Piketty's book**: Bill Gates, "Why Inequality Matters," *GatesNotes*, Octo-
      ber 13, 2014, https://www.gatesnotes.com/Books/Why-Inequality-Matters-Capital
      -in-21st-Century-Review.

85   **"We want our children to make their own way"**: The Gateses' children enjoy ultra-
      wealthy lifestyles, and each will almost certainly inherit a large sum of money. It is
      preposterous to claim that they will have to "make their own way in the world."

85   **It was a private call**: Aimee Picchi, "Thomas Piketty: Bill Gates Doesn't Want to
      Pay More Tax," CBS News, January 5, 2015, https://www.cbsnews.com/news/thomas
      -piketty-bill-gates-doesnt-want-to-pay-more-tax/.

86   **"It isn't always popular"**: Bill Gates, "What I'm Thinking About This New Year's
      Eve," *GatesNotes*, December 30, 2019, https://www.gatesnotes.com/About-Bill-Gates
      /Year-in-Review-2019.

86   **meaningful resources pursuing tax policy:** The only record I could find of Gates
      putting money into tax reform was a $250,000 donation in 2006 to oppose a ballot
      initiative aimed at repealing Washington state's estate tax.

86   **We see a similar disconnect in Warren Buffett**: The Obama White House at one
      point even proposed the so-called Buffett Rule, aimed at taxing the wealthy. The
      plan went nowhere, and even if it had, it's not clear if or to what degree it would
      have increased taxes on Buffett's wealth. The White House had emphasized that
      the Buffett Rule would tax the superrich in a manner that was "equitable, including
      not disadvantaging individuals who make large charitable contributions." Office of
      the President, Fiscal Year 2013, Budget of the U.S. Government, Office of Manage-
      ment and Budget, 39, https://obamawhitehouse.archives.gov/sites/default/files/omb
      /budget/fy2013/assets/budget.pdf.

87   **Janet L. Yellen said**: "U.S. Treasury Blocks over $1 Billion in Suleiman Kerimov

Trust," U.S. Department of the Treasury, June 30, 2022, https://home.treasury.gov /news/press-releases/jy0841.

87   **one-hundred-million-dollar yacht named *Graceful*:** Mike McIntire and Michael Forsythe, "Putin Faces Sanctions, but His Assets Remain an Enigma," *New York Times*, February 26, 2022, https://www.nytimes.com/2022/02/26/world/europe /putin-sanctions-money-assets.html?campaign_id=249&emc=edit_ruwb_20220406 &instance_id=57801&nl=russia-ukraine-war-briefing&regi_id=94181639&segment _id=87708&te=1&user_id=5affd5c339e726b5205a2a069c754d1b.

87   **damning moniker:** "Episode 138: Thought-Terminating Enemy Epithets (Part II)," Citations Needed, June 9, 2021; https://citationsneeded.medium.com/episode-138 -thought-terminating-enemy-epithets-part-ii-dea4bfcda8c7.

87   **"harder to trace the deals":** Anupretta Das and Craig Karmin, "This Man's Job: Make Bill Gates Richer," *Wall Street Journal*, September 19, 2014, https://www.wsj .com/articles/this-mans-job-make-bill-gates-richer-1411093811.

88   **served time in prison for bank fraud:** Craig Torres, "Convicted Felons Handle Gates Fortune," *Wall Street Journal*, March 7, 1993, https://archive.seattletimes.com /archive/?date=19930307&slug=1689167.

88   **uncovered this in the 1990s:** Das, Flitter, and Kulish, "A Culture of Fear at the Firm That Manages Bill Gates's Fortune."

88   **with the intense secrecy:** At times, the secrecy surrounding Gates's personal wealth borders on an alternate reality. Following Bill and Melinda's divorce in 2021, the *New York Post* and other outlets reported that Bill had razed a mansion he recently bought in San Diego, a massively wasteful, climate-destructive decision that created a deeply annoying construction zone for neighbors and beachgoers. Though the article quotes neighbors saying they had personally seen Gates at the construction site where a new mansion was being built, and though the *Wall Street Journal* had previously reported on his purchase of the property, Bill Gates's PR people told the *New York Post* that Gates did not, in fact, own it. So, how do we prove or disprove this? Property records in San Diego County don't tell us who owns the house. They tell us *what* owns the house: a financial vehicle called "2808 of Trust," in care of the Northern Trust Company in Seattle. Neither the county nor Northern Trust could say who the actual owner was. See Mary K. Jacob, "Bill Gates Turns $43M Mansion into 'Bachelor Pad' Nuisance," *New York Post*, March 23, 2022, https://nypost.com /2022/03/23/bill-gates-is-turning-43m-mansion-into-bachelor-pad-nuisance; Katherine Clarke, "Bill and Melinda Gates Buy Oceanfront Home Near San Diego for $43 Million," *Wall Street Journal*, April 21, 2020, https://www.wsj.com/articles /bill-and-melinda-gates-buy-oceanfront-home-near-san-diego-for-43-million -11587509127.

88   **average federal tax rate of 18.4 percent:** "America's Top 15 Earners and What They Reveal About the U.S. Tax System," ProPublica, April 13, 2022, https://www.propublica .org/article/americas-top-15-earners-and-what-they-reveal-about-the-us-tax -system. Note: ProPublica reported that on his average yearly income of $2.85 billion, Gates was able to deduct 22 percent of it from taxes—presumably due in part (or in whole) to his charitable giving. As ProPublica describes it, the IRS has "a generous pro-

vision of the tax code [that] allows [billionaires] to deduct the full value of the stock at its current price—without having to sell it and pay capital gains tax." ProPublica would not share Bill Gates's tax documents with me; see Paul Kiel, Ash Ngu, Jesse Eisinger, and Jeff Ernsthausen, "America's Highest Earners and Their Taxes Revealed," ProPublica, April 13, 2022, https://projects.propublica.org/americas-highest-incomes-and -taxes-revealed/.

88 **"slightly reduce an ever-increasing U.S. debt"**: Jesse Eisinger, Jeff Ernsthausen, and Paul Kiel, "The Secret IRS Files: Trove of Never-Before-Seen Records Reveal How the Wealthiest Avoid Income Tax," ProPublica, June 8, 2021, https://www.propublica .org/article/the-secret-irs-files-trove-of-never-before-seen-records-reveal-how-the -wealthiest-avoid-income-tax.

89 **end the so-called death tax**: David Cay Johnston, "Questions Raised on New Bush Plan to End Estate Tax," *New York Times*, January 29, 2001, https://www.nytimes .com/2001/01/29/business/questions-raised-on-new-bush-plan-to-end-estate-tax .html.

89 **"absolute choice"**: "Bill Moyers Interviews Bill Gates, Sr. and Chuck Collins," PBS NOW, January 17, 2003, https://billmoyers.com/content/toolbooths-digital-higway -bill-gates-sr-chuck-collins-inheritance-tax-scientist-devra-davis-killer-smog-jump started-clean-air-act/#inheritance-tax.

90 **"marvelous system"**: "Remembering Bill Gates Sr.," *Inequality.org* (blog), https:// inequality.org/great-divide/remembering-bill-gates-sr/.

91 **a vast nanny state**: Dean Baker, "The Conservative Nanny State," Center for Economic and Policy Research, 2006, https://web.archive.org/web/20061002021111/http://www .conservativenannystate.org/cnswebbook.pdf.

CHAPTER 4: FAIL FAST

92 **"take risky bets"**: Mark Suzman, "2022 Gates Foundation Annual Letter: Board of Trustees, What's Next," Bill & Melinda Gates Foundation, n.d., https://www .gatesfoundation.org/ideas/articles/2022-gates-foundation-annual-letter-trustees.

92 **$2 billion to private companies**: "Strategic Investment FAQs," Gates Strategic Investment Fund, n.d., https://sif.gatesfoundation.org/faq/.

92 **pharma giants like GSK**: Note: The foundation's tax records show charitable grants to GlaxoSmithKline I+D, S.L., and GlaxoSmithKline Biologicals.

93 **"global access agreements"**: CureVac, Draft Registration Statement, Ex. 10.7, U.S. Securities and Exchange Commission, June 22, 2020. Note: As the foundation describes it, "Global Access requires that (a) the knowledge and information gained from a Programmatic Investment be promptly and broadly disseminated, and (b) the Funded Developments be made available and accessible at an affordable price to our intended beneficiaries. Within the Global Health and Global Development pro- grams our beneficiaries are the people most in need living in developing countries and within U.S. Programs they include low income students, students of color and first-generation college students, and the educational systems serving these commu- nities." "Global Access Statement," Bill & Melinda Gates Foundation, n.d., https:// www.gatesfoundation.org/about/policies-and-resources/global-access-statement.

93 **access agreements aren't being enforced**: "CureVac Collaboration," Bill & Melinda
    Gates Foundation, n.d., https://www.gatesfoundation.org/ideas/media-center/press
    -releases/2015/03/curevac-collaboration.

93 **CureVac's board**: Tim Schwab, "Is the Shine Starting to Come Off Bill Gates's
    Halo?," *Nation*, May 7, 2021, https://www.thenation.com/article/society/bill-gates
    -foundation-covid-vaccines/.

94 **Why would the foundation release**: Note: As it turns out, CureVac's vaccine
    ended up being a bust, so we never got to see how the company's access com-
    mitment to the Gates Foundation fully played out. From outward appearances,
    however, the company planned its business model around serving wealthy nations,
    not the global poor. This included an agreement to supply 405 million doses to the
    European Commission; Schwab, "Is the Shine Starting to Come Off Bill Gates's
    Halo?"; Jon Cohen, "What Went Wrong with CureVac's Highly Anticipated New
    MRNA Vaccine for COVID-19?," *Science*, June 18, 2021, https://www.science.org
    /content/article/what-went-wrong-curevac-s-highly-anticipated-new-mrna
    -vaccine-covid-19.

94 **relationship with other Covid-19 vaccine producers**: David Bank and Dennis
    Price, "Linchpin of Gates Foundation's Health Strategies, 'Global Access Agreements'
    Fail Their Covid-19 Test," ImpactAlpha, June 10, 2021, https://impactalpha.com
    /the-linchpin-of-gates-foundations-health-strategies-global-access-agreements-fail
    -their-covid-19-test/; "BioNTech Announces New Collaboration to Develop HIV
    and Tuberculosis Programs," Press Release, BioNTech, September 4, 2019, https://
    investors.biontech.de/news-releases/news-release-details/biontech-announces-new
    -collaboration-develop-hiv-and/.

94 **Similar failures surfaced**: Cepheid's failure to deliver global access during the pan-
    demic followed criticism around the company's alleged profiteering from its TB
    diagnostic, which it boasts of having developed with Gates Foundation support. In
    2017, a report sponsored by Unitaid, a global health agency, cited the "potentially
    monopolistic arrangement" in Cepheid's dominant market position in tuberculosis
    diagnosis, which could affect prices. The foundation's global access agreements, once
    again, did not appear to be making the corporate products it funded available to the
    poor at a fair, accessible price; Cepheid, Form 8-K, Ex. 99.01, U.S. Securities and
    Exchange Commission, 2006; David Lewis and Allison Martell, "Donors Bet on a
    US Firm to Fix Testing in Africa. Then Covid-19 Hit," Reuters, March 1, 2021, https:
    //www.reuters.com/investigates/special-report/health-coronavirus-africa-cepheid/.

95 **gone to Cepheid**: Lewis and Martell, "Donors Bet on a US Firm to Fix Testing in
    Africa. Then Covid-19 Hit."

95 **Merck's rotavirus vaccine**: "Enteric and Diarrheal Diseases," Gates Foundation
    Strategic Overview, November 2009, https://docs.gatesfoundation.org/Documents
    /enteric-and-diarrheal-diseases-strategy.pdf. Note: It's unclear what these "invest-
    ments" were or how significant a role the Gates Foundation played because there is
    no record of charitable grants to Merck for work on the rotavirus.

95 **profiled this episode in detail**: Robert Fortner, "Why you might think like Bill Gates
    about global health," (blog), February 13, 2016, https://robertfortner.posthaven.com
    /why-you-might-think-like-bill-gates-about-global-health.

95   **"miss out on this lifesaving vaccine"**: Michaeleen Doucleff, "Merck Pulls Out of Agreement to Supply Life-Saving Vaccine to Millions of Kids," *Goats and Soda* (blog), NPR, November 1, 2018, https://www.npr.org/sections/goatsandsoda/2018 /11/01/655844287/merck-pulls-out-of-agreement-to-supply-life-saving-vaccine-to -millions-of-kids.

95   **name-and-shame attack of Merck**: NPR later published another big feature, again vilifying Merck, but this time also praising GSK for filling the rotavirus vaccine gap Merck had left. This kind of coverage feels like very lightly filtered public relations from Gates, slapping Merck on the wrist while richly rewarding GSK. Michaeleen Doucleff, "It Looked as Though Millions of Babies Would Miss Out on a Lifesaving Vaccine," NPR, May 31, 2019, https://www.npr.org/sections/goatsandsoda/2019 /05/31/726863111/it-looked-as-though-millions-of-babies-would-miss-out-on-a -lifesaving-vaccine.

96   **"worldwide, non-exclusive, perpetual"**: Grantees have the ability to negotiate or push back on the terms and conditions of the global access agreements, but it is impossible to know how often this happens or what form the negotiations take because Gates's grant agreements are usually hidden from public view.

97   **popular podcast and public radio program**: Ira Glass, Alex Blumberg, and Laura Sydell, "When Patents Attack!" Episode 441, *This American Life*, NPR, July 22, 2011, https://www.thisamericanlife.org/441/transcript.

98   **Writer Malcolm Gladwell**: Malcolm Gladwell, "In the Air," *New Yorker*, May 5, 2008, https://www.newyorker.com/magazine/2008/05/12/in-the-air.

98   **names only eleven**: "Spinouts," Intellectual Ventures, n.d., https://www .intellectualventures.com/spinouts.

99   **including TerraPower**: Catherine Clifford, "Bill Gates-Backed Nuclear Demonstration Project in Wyoming Delayed Because Russia Was the Only Fuel Source," CNBC, December 16, 2022, https://www.cnbc.com/2022/12/16/bill-gates-backed -nuclear-demonstration-delayed-by-at-least-2-years.html; Alan Boyle, "Echodyne Radar Venture Flies Higher with $135M Funding Round Led by Bill Gates and Baillie Gifford," GeekWire, June 13, 2022, https://www.geekwire.com/2022/echo dyne-radar-venture-flies-higher-with-135m-funding-round-led-by-bill-gates-and -baillie-gifford/; Alan Boyle, "Bill Gates leads $84M Funding Round to Boost Kymeta Antenna Venture's Push into New Markets," GeekWire, March 15, 2022, https:// www.geekwire.com/2022/bill-gates-leads-84m-funding-round-to-boost-kymeta -antenna-ventures-push-into-new-markets/; Paul La Monica, "Crowd-Safety Firm Backed by Bill Gates and Peyton Manning Makes Wall Street Debut," CNN, July 19, 2021; Lisa Stiffler, "Intellectual Ventures Spinoff Modern Electron Raising Cash for Heat-to-Electricity tech," GeekWire, December 27, 2021, https://www.geekwire .com/2021/intellectual-ventures-spinoff-modern-electron-raising-cash-for-heat-to -electricity-tech/; Alan Boyle, "With Backing from Bill Gates, Pivotal Commware Raises $50M for 5G products," GeekWire, February 11, 2021; Devin Coldewey, "Gates-Backed Lumotive Upends Lidar Conventions Using Metamaterials," *TechCrunch*, March 22, 2019, https://techcrunch.com/2019/03/22/gates-backed-lumotive -upends-lidar-conventions-using-metamaterials/.

99   **more than fifty million dollars**: Microsoft, DEF 14A, U.S. Securities and Exchange

Commission, October 4, 2006. Note: SEC documents report that Microsoft "owns 44.9% of ISF's outstanding Class A Units and Mr. Gates' investment company owns 18.7% of ISF's outstanding Class A Units and one ISF Class D Unit." It's possible that Bill Gates and Microsoft both have other investments in IV. *Forbes* reported in 2018 that a Microsoft subsidiary in Ireland wrote down a more than $130 million investment in a fund associated with IV. Nathan Vardi, "After 10 Years, Nathan Myhrvold's $3 Billion of Private Equity Funds Show Big Losses," *Forbes*, June 1, 2018, https://www.forbes.com/sites/nathanvardi/2018/06/01/after-10-years-nathan-myhrvolds-3-billion-of-private-equity-funds-show-big-losses/.

99 **throw around his intellectual weight**: Note: In 2013, *60 Minutes* briefly reported on Bill Gates's work with IV, "where he is both an investor and an inventor," according to the program; "Bill Gates, 2.0," *60 Minutes*, CBS, aired July 28, 2013, 4:00, https://www.youtube.com/watch?v=cPy0nWYYCFg.

99 **protecting players against concussions**: Taylor Soper, "Bill Gates and Intellectual Ventures Attempt to Patent a High-Tech Football Helmet," GeekWire, January 11, 2017, https://www.geekwire.com/2017/bill-gates-intellectual-ventures-attempt-patent-high-tech-football-helmet/.

99 **"detecting and classifying people"**: Bill Gates's name is attached to a wide array of patents, many of them owned by Microsoft and apparently aimed at harvesting data from people's digital identities—"personal data mining," "determining influencers," and "rewarding independent influencers." Another one, straight out of *Minority Report*, is described as "sensors for collecting information about a customer or group of customers as they move through" a store, along with "face recognition, pose recognition, transaction recognition, and biometric sensing," with the goal of creating "advertisements in realtime in retail establishments." U.S. Patents 20170053190-A1, 7930197-B2, 8290973-B2, 9135657-B2, and 20080004950-A1.

99 **looking out for the little guy**: Ira Glass and Zoe Chace, "When Patents Attack . . . Part Two!" Episode 496, *This American Life*, NPR, May 31, 2013, https://www.thisamericanlife.org/496/when-patents-attack-part-two.

99 **patent litigation zeitgeist had unleashed**: Glass and Chace, "When Patents Attack . . . Part Two!"

100 **"We own tons of patents"**: Glass, Blumberg, and Sydell, "When Patents Attack!"

100 **the website noted**: Intellectual Ventures, "What We Do," https://web.archive.org/web/20190605202401/https://www.intellectualventures.com/what-we-do/global-good-fund/our-work.

100 **"controlled subsidiary"**: This $500 million, notably, did not come through charitable grants from the Gates Foundation, but rather through transfers from the Gates Foundation's endowment. Bill & Melinda Gates Foundation Trust, 990-PF, Statement 12, Transfers to Controlled Entities, 2010–2020. Note: In 2010, the annual tax filing of the Bill & Melinda Gates Foundation Trust reports receiving a donation of intellectual property valued at $11,084,733, apparently a gift from Bill Gates. It also reports transferring to Global Good "capital contributions of cash and intellectual property" worth more than $16 million. It's not clear if these two transactions of intellectual property are related.

100 **the project was a for-profit business**: Todd Bishop, "A Feisty Nathan Myhrvold

Defends His Quest for 'Global Good,'" GeekWire, August 10, 2012, https://www
.geekwire.com/2012/feisty-nathan-myhrvold-defends-quest-global-good/.

100 **whoever runs Global Good**: Bishop, "A Feisty Nathan Myhrvold."

101 **From its murky origins**: "IV's Global Good Fund: A Legacy of Impact Invention,"
September 2, 2020, https://www.intellectualventures.com/buzz/insights/ivs-global
-good-fund-a-legacy-of-impact-invention.

101 **claims to reduce smoke**: "Cleaner, More Efficient Cooking: Global Good Embeds
Technology into Jet Flame Cookstove," Intellectual Ventures, October 30, 2019,
https://www.intellectualventures.com/buzz/insights/helping-families-with-cleaner
-efficient-cooking; "Jet-Flame—Turn Your Fire into a Jet!" Jet-Flame, n.d., https://
www.jet-flame.com/.

101 **transporting bull semen**: "IV's Global Good Fund: A Legacy of Impact Invention."

101 **infant biometric project**: "Global Good Fund, Element to Develop Biometric ID Tool
for Infants and Children—Biometric Update," n.d., https://www.biometricupdate.com
/201711/global-good-fund-element-to-develop-biometric-id-tool-for-infants-and
-children. Note: The Gates Foundation has funded other similar projects, like an infant
biometric program by the University of California San Diego; see "Researchers Receive
$2.4 Million from Gates Foundation for Infant Vaccination Identification," *UC San
Diego Today*, November 8, 2016, https://today.ucsd.edu/story/researchers_receive_2.4
_million_from_gates_foundation_for_infant_vaccinatio.

102 **"Making Markets Work for the Poor"**: Price, "Eyes Wide Open," 35.

102 **"critical intellectual property"**: Price, "Eyes Wide Open," 32.

102 **"convertible notes"**: Price, "Eyes Wide Open," 33.

102 **"lowering the company's appeal"**: Price, "Eyes Wide Open," 33.

103 **"displace or substitute"**: "Reflecting on the Evolution of the Foundation: A Q&A with
Mark Suzman," Bill & Melinda Gates Foundation, February 4, 2022, https://www
.gatesfoundation.org/ideas/articles/evolution-of-the-foundation-qa-mark-suzman.

104 **"As Zyomyx's largest equity holder"**: Price, "Eyes Wide Open," 34.

104 **"Probability of success is low"**: Price, "Eyes Wide Open," 34.

104 **acquired dozens of patents (and patent applications)**: U.S. Patent Reel, Frame
040775/0094, December 30, 2015, Assignment of Patents from Zyomyx to Bill and
Melinda Gates Foundation.

104 **Stemcell Technologies**: U.S. Patents 7998696, 8304203, and 8765391, Assignment of
Patents from Bill and Melinda Gates Foundation to Stemcell Technologies Canada,
Reel/Frame 040405/0749, May 31, 2016.

104 **a 2019 charitable grant**: The Gates Foundation's grant records show a $2.9 million
donation to Stemcell Technologies "to develop optimized methods for the generation of antibody producing B-cells from stem cells to be used to protect against
infectious diseases in the developing world."

105 **drug discovery platform**: David Bank and Dennis Price, "Returns on Investment:
How a Broad Bet on a Biotech Company Paid Off in Promising Drugs for Neglected
Diseases," *Making Markets Work for the Poor*, Supplement, *Stanford Social Innova-
tion Review* (Summer 2016): 35–36.

105 **patent records show**: Amrutha Penumudi, "Pfizer to Buy Anacor in $5.2 Billion
Deal for Access to Eczema Gel," Reuters, May 16, 2016, https://www.reuters.com

/article/us-anacor-pharma-m-a-pfizer-analysis-idUSKCN0Y7143; U.S. Patents, Reel /Frame 050856/0936, 050867/0447, 050856/0921, 050863/0578, 052454/0630, 052454 /0582, 052456/0805, and 052456/0761, Assignment of Patents from Anacor to Bill & Melinda Gates Foundation.

105 **ability to "license" the products**: Tracking ownership of patents is difficult because patent holders notoriously use shell and holding companies to reduce transparency about ownership. This was an important part of the *This American Life* story, which reported on the layers of obfuscation surrounding IV's financial interest in patents.

105 **Gates Ventures**: SEC filings show that Gates Ventures has taken stakes in companies like Exicure; see Exicure, Inc., Schedule 13G, U.S. Securities and Exchange Commission, October 5, 2017, https://www.sec.gov/Archives/edgar/data/1580115 /000110465917061162/a17-22926_1sc13g.htm.

106 **Who else might benefit?**: "Research Priorities," Bill & Melinda Gates Medical Research Institute, n.d., https://www.gatesmri.org/research-priorities/.

106 **licenses with GSK and Merck**: Charles Wells, "What Does the Future Look Like for TB Care?," Interview by Emily Henderson, News-Medical.net, August 5, 2022, https:// www.news-medical.net/news/20220805/What-does-the-future-look-like-for-TB -care.aspx; "Merck and the Bill & Melinda Gates Medical Research Institute Announce Licensing Agreement for Novel Tuberculosis Antibiotic Candidates," Merck.

106 **Big Pharma alumni**: "About Us," Bill & Melinda Gates Medical Research Institute, https://www.gatesmri.org/about-us/. See profiles of Emilio Emini, Manfred Lauchart, and Taryn Rogalski-Salter.

106 **taking technology from grantees**: In one case that we can see, the Bill & Melinda Gates Medical Research Institute took over development of a malaria drug in what began as a charitable partnership between the Gates Foundation and a private company, Atreca. Under the agreement, detailed in SEC filings, Gates MRI acquired "commercial rights in Gavi-eligible countries located in malaria-endemic regions of the world, while Atreca will retain commercial rights in the U.S., Europe and parts of Asia." It's not clear that this is an example of Gates exercising its global access agreement. See Atreca, Form 8-K, Ex.99.1, U.S. Securities and Exchange Commission, November 2, 2021, https://www.sec.gov/Archives/edgar/data/1532346 /000117184321007383/exh_991.htm.

107 **bilking American consumers**: "DeFazio, Doggett Lead Members in Urging HHS to Lower Cost of Prostate Cancer Drug," Press Release, February 8, 2022, website of United States Congressman Peter DeFazio, https://web.archive.org/web /20220211152659/https://defazio.house.gov/media-center/press-releases/defazio -doggett-lead-members-in-urging-hhs-to-lower-cost-of-prostate.

108 **shore of Lake Washington**: Madeline Stone and Matt Weinberger, "19 Crazy Facts About Bill Gates' $127 Million Mansion," *Business Insider*, December 7, 2018, https:// www.businessinsider.com/crazy-facts-about-bill-gates-house-2016-11.

109 **consumer advocate Ralph Nader**: "Appraising Microsoft I: Real Audio of the November 13–14 1997 Appraising Microsoft Presentations," November 13–14, 1997, http://www.appraising-microsoft.org/1st.html; "Nader Responds to Microsoft Letter," November 13, 1997, http://www.appraising-microsoft.org/rnstatemt.html.

109 **manufacturer named Cipla**: Brian Till, "How Drug Companies Keep Medicine out

of Reach," *Atlantic*, May 15, 2013, https://www.theatlantic.com/health/archive/2013
/05/how-drug-companies-keep-medicine-out-of-reach/275853/.

109   **treatment for HIV**: Katherine Eban, "How an Indian Tycoon Fought Big Pharma to
Sell AIDS Drugs for $1 a Day," Quartz, July 15, 2019, https://qz.com/india/1666032
/how-indian-pharma-giant-cipla-made-aids-drugs-affordable/.

110   **thirteen thousand–word time line**: "Microsoft, Gates Foundation Timeline," *Knowledge Ecology International* (blog), November 29, 2010, https://www.keionline.org
/microsoft-timeline.

110   **High-level intergovernmental meetings**: World Health Organization, Intergov-
ernmental Working Group on Public Health, Innovation and Intellectual Property,
List of Participants, April 28, 2008, https://apps.who.int/gb/PHI/pdf/igwg2/PHI
_IGWG2_DIV2_REV2.pdf.

110   **A half-trillion dollars each year**: David Muoio, "Nationwide Drug Spending Grew
7.7% in 2021, Will Increase Another 4%-6% in 2022," FierceHealthcare, April 12,
2022, https://www.fiercehealthcare.com/finance/nationwide-drug-spending-grew
-77-2021-will-increase-another-4-6-2022.

111   **worked with pharma giant Novartis**: Martin Enserink, "Another Global Health
Fund? Here's Why," *Science*, May 19, 2010, https://www.science.org/content/article
/another-global-health-fund-heres-why.

111   **No R&D treaty has been enacted**: Soumya Swaminathan et al., "Reboot Biomedical
R&D in the Global Public Interest," *Nature* 602, no. 7896 (February 2022): 207–10,
https://doi.org/10.1038/d41586-022-00324-y.

CHAPTER 5: TRANSPARENCY

113   **glass-heavy design**: "Bill and Melinda Gates Foundation," NBBJ, https://www.nbbj
.com/work/bill-and-melinda-gates-foundation.

113   **headquarters' opening in 2011**: Kristi Helm, "The New Gates Foundation Headquarters Reflects Charity's Roots—and Reach," *Seattle Times*, May 21, 2011.

113   **the architecture's openness**: Note: Curiously, the *New York Times* review of the
building noted that the foundation had also banned whispering inside the headquarters. Lawrence W. Cheek, "New Office Designs Offer Room to Roam and to Think,"
New York Times, March 17, 2012, https://www.nytimes.com/2012/03/18/business
/new-office-designs-offer-room-to-roam-and-to-think.html?ref=business.

114   **"committed to being open"**: Bill and Melinda Gates, "10 Tough Questions We Get
Asked," *GatesNotes*, n.d., https://www.gatesnotes.com/2018-Annual-Letter.

114   **"part of any grant agreement"**: David Bank, who runs the media site ImpactAlpha,
reports having signed a nondisclosure agreement (NDA) when he worked with the
foundation on a reporting project. David Bank, "What Went Wrong in Gates Foundation Investment in $1 Billion Healthcare Fund for 21st-Century Megacities?,"
Medium (blog), June 16, 2018, https://medium.com/@davidmbank/abraaj-group
-liquidation-tests-champions-of-sustainable-development-goal-3-73ea53728669.

114   **confidentiality agreements**: Gabriel Sherman, Nick Bilton, and Emily Jane Fox, "Bill
and Melinda Gates's Epic Divorce Saga Enters Its Next Phase," *Vanity Fair*, June 7, 2021,
https://www.vanityfair.com/news/2021/06/bill-and-melinda-gates-divorce-saga-next
-phase.

114 **standard practice to require them to sign**: Das, Flitter, and Kulish, "A Culture of Fear at the Firm That Manages Bill Gates's Fortune."

114 **"she stays private"**: O. Casey Corr, "Melinda French Gates: A Microsoft Mystery—She Married High-Profile Bill Gates, but Wants Her Life Kept Private," *Seattle Times*, June 4, 1995, https://archive.seattletimes.com/archive/?date=19950604&slug=2124492. Note: The state of Washington, in 2022, issued new rules limiting the use of nondisclosure agreements in the workplace to protect whistleblowers and the ability of employees to speak out about waste, fraud, and abuse. Several former foundation employees directed me to the rules, unsure what they meant for the NDAs the foundation uses. Amy Rolph, "Most NDAs Are Now Outlawed in Washington State. Will Whistleblowers Speak Up?," GeekWire, July 19, 2022, https://www.geekwire.com/2022/most-ndas-are-now-outlawed-in-washington-state-will-whistleblowers-speak-up/.

116 **"mechanism of public accountability"**: Friedman and Sunderland, "How to Fix the Gates Foundation."

116 **scroll through page after page**: Before I began my first investigation into the Gates Foundation, I contacted them to see if they would give me an Excel spreadsheet containing all their charitable grants—as an alternative to using their poorly designed online grant database. Having all the grants in one spreadsheet would have allowed me to do sophisticated analyses—such as ranking top donors, top destinations of funding, and so on. I pestered the foundation for months, making it absolutely clear that if they didn't give me the spreadsheet, I would create my own from available records. The foundation finally relented and sent the spreadsheet by email—with orders that I not share it with anybody. After I began publishing my investigations, the foundation made the spreadsheet publicly available for all users on their website. The foundation also stopped communicating with me.

116 **record of giving grant money**: Scott Jaschik, "A Tool to Compare Colleges," *Inside Higher Ed*, November 4, 2021. Note: After I contacted the author, the outlet corrected the article, adding a financial disclosure about its ties to Gates. See Web archive at https://web.archive.org/web/20211104085628/https://www.insidehighered.com/news/2021/11/04/gates-foundation-effort-releases-new-tool-compare-colleges.

117 **James Bond operation**: "Our Process," *Centre for Analytics and Behavioural Change* (blog), n.d., https://cabc.org.za/our-process/.

117 **shrouded in so much secrecy**: The Gates-funded project, during the time it was disclosed on CABC's website, was briefly described as working on "neutralising strategies to win over those who are vaccine hesitant." This may sound noncontroversial, but without more details, it is not possible to understand the scope, meaning, impact, or consequences of the project. Perhaps more importantly, the lack of transparency means there is no way to verify Gates's money was really used for this purpose, or whether it might have also been used on other topics to advance the foundation's agenda.

117 **"grantee technical assistance"**: Bill & Melinda Gates Foundation, Statement 5, 706, IRS 990 filing for period ending December 2019.

118 **674 contracts**: Bill & Melinda Gates Foundation, Line 16c, column d, Part I; also Part VII, IRS 990, 2013.

118 **10 percent of the foundation's entire expenses**: Bill & Melinda Gates Foundation, Line 26, column d, Part I, IRS 990, 2013.

118   **five largest contracts**: Bill & Melinda Gates Foundation, Part VII, IRS 990, 2013.

118   **not a charitable grant**: "The Chronicle of Higher Education and the Gates Foundation," *Chronicle of Higher Education*, July 14, 2013, https://www.chronicle.com /article/the-chronicle-of-higher-education-and-the-gates-foundation/.

119   **"WHO's website is incomplete"**: Julia Belluz and Marine Buissonniere, "McKinsey Infiltrated the World of Global Public Health. Here's How," Vox, December 13, 2019, https://www.vox.com/science-and-health/2019/12/13/21004456/bill-gates -mckinsey-global-public-health-bcg. Note: One specific Gates-funded McKinsey effort sought to evaluate a fund-raising scheme for Unitaid—asking airline passengers to make small donations when purchasing tickets. McKinsey projected $1 billion in new annual revenues from the project. Unitaid set aside tens of millions of dollars to get the program up and running. The project returned only $14,000.

119   **to other foundations**: Gates, for example, is the second-largest all-time funder of the United Nations Foundation, having awarded it $380 million. UNF then donates money to a variety of groups. It publishes an annual tax filing showing some of the recipients—but not all and not in a way that allows us to see which funds came from the Gates Foundation. In total, the Gates Foundation has donated close to $7 billion to organizations with the word *foundation* in their name.

120   **"who in turn fund others"**: Again, in the early days of my reporting, the foundation occasionally provided email responses to some questions.

121   **a rare critical investigation**: Sally Ho, "AP Analysis Shows How Bill Gates Influences Education Policy," AP News, May 16, 2018, https://apnews.com/article/melinda -gates-north-america-bill-and-melinda-gates-foundation-us-news-ap-top-news-a4 042e82ffaa4a34b50ceac464761957.

121   **"fiscal sponsor"**: "How We Work," New Venture Fund, n.d., https://newventurefund .org/how-we-work/.

121   **dark-money questions:** Anna Massoglia and Karl Evers-Hillstrom, "Liberal 'Dark Money' Operation Behind Ads Urging Republicans to Support Impeachment," OpenSecrets News, November 20, 2019, https://www.opensecrets.org/news/2019/11 /liberal-dark-money-op-impeachment/.

122   **advance liberal political causes:** Kenneth P. Vogel and Katie Robertson, "Top Bidder for Tribune Newspapers Is an Influential Liberal Donor," *New York Times*, April 13, 2021, https://www.nytimes.com/2021/04/13/business/media/wyss-tribune-company -buyer.html.

122   **two of five seats**: "Our Governance," Co-Impact, Web archive from May 6, 2022, https://web.archive.org/web/20220506211132/https://co-impact.org/our-governance. Note: By 2023, Co-Impact had reported that current and former Gates employees held three of seven board seats. See https://co-impact.org/our-governance/.

122   **is run (and was founded) by Olivia Leland**: "Olivia Leland," Co-Impact, n.d., https:// www.co-impact.org/our-team/olivia-leland/.

123   **Poverty Action Lab**: "What We Fund," Co-Impact, n.d., https://www.co-impact .org/gender-fund-what-we-fund/; Madeline Brancel, Margaret Andersen, Samuel Wolf, and Demitria Wack, "The Next Generation of Rigorous Education Research: J-PAL Launches the Learning for All Initiative," Abdul Latif Jameel Poverty Action Lab (J-PAL), January 25, 2023, https://www.povertyactionlab.org/blog/1

-25-23/next-generation-rigorous-education-research-j-pal-launches-learning-all
-initiative.

123   **Co-Impact did not respond**: In another example, a Gates Foundation executive
boasted of having helped create a group named WomenLift Health. WomenLift
Health's global advisory board includes a Gates Foundation executive, and the organization's mission—"to expand the power and influence of women in global health
and catalyze systemic change to achieve gender equality in leadership"—is indistinguishable from the Gates Foundation's own high-profile work on gender equality. Its
website cites the Gates Foundation and New Venture Fund as partners, but the foundation has no record of donations to the group. It may be that Gates funds WomenLift
through donations to New Venture Fund. WomenLift did not respond to my press
inquiry. "Poverty Is Sexist: A Q&A with New Gender Equality Division President
Anita Zaidi," Bill & Melinda Gates Foundation, n.d., https://www.gatesfoundation
.org/ideas/articles/gender-equality-president-anita-zaidi; "Global Advisory Board,"
WomenLift Health (blog), n.d., https://www.womenlifthealth.org/global-advisory
-board/; "Partners and Collaborators," *WomenLift Health* (blog), n.d., https://www
.womenlifthealth.org/partners-affiliates/; "About Us," *WomenLift Health*, https://web
.archive.org/web/20201117075245/https://www.womenlifthealth.org/our-mission.

123   **opaque clearinghouses**: Other "fiscal sponsors" Gates funds include Rockefeller
Philanthropy Advisors, the Global Fund for Women, NEO Philanthropy, and the
ThinkWell Institute. These organizations are under no obligation to disclose what
they do with Gates's money—even as they create projects, hubs, initiatives, and
campaigns that can advance the foundation's agenda. When I asked Rockefeller
Philanthropy Advisors to help me understand what specifically they'd done with
Gates's funding, the group would not provide this information, telling me their
organization "prioritizes reporting to our funders."

123   **Global Fund**: "Members," Global Fund, n.d., https://www.theglobalfund.org/en/board
/members/; "Board of Directors," Medicines for Malaria Venture, n.d., https://www
.mmv.org/about-us/people-governance/board-directors; "Rodger Voorhies," *AGRA*
(blog), March 2, 2021, https://agra.org/ourpeople/rodger-voorhies/; "Leadership,"
CEPI, https://cepi.net/about/whoweare/.

123   **sponsoring employees to play governance roles**: The Bill & Melinda Gates Foundation, Board Service Policy and Guidelines, https://docs.gatesfoundation.org
/documents/board-service-policy.docx. Note: It is virtually impossible to track the
full extent of Gates's governance roles at the organizations it funds because this
may not always be disclosed, because the foundation does not publicly disclose
all recipients of its funding, and because the foundation funds thousands of organizations. In a cursory search, I found many examples: Dan Green, global content
and campaigns director at Gates, sits on the board of Global Citizen, part of the
Global Poverty Project—to which the foundation has given $54 million ("Board
of Directors," Global Citizen, n.d., https://www.globalcitizen.org/en/about/who
-we-are/board-directors/); Ankur Voram, chief strategy officer at the Gates Foundation, serves on the board of Innovations for Poverty Action, to which Gates has
given more than $45 million ("Board of Directors—IPA," n.d., https://www.poverty
-action.org/people/directors); Philip Welkhoff, malaria program director at the Bill

& Melinda Gates Foundation, is on the board of the Hertz Foundation, to which Gates has given $5 million ("Our People," Fannie and John Hertz Foundation, n.d., https://www.hertzfoundation.org/about-us/our-people/); AVAC, to which Gates has given more than $90 million, reports board members and advisers loaded with current and former Gates Foundation staff ("Board," AVAC, July 24, 2013, https://www.avac.org/board).

124 **nonprofit, LDC**: Gwen Walden, Lauren Marra, and Katrina Briddell, "Going Beyond Grantmaking: Using External Help to Extend a Foundation's Core Competencies and Increase Its Impact," *Foundation Review* 7, no. 1 (March 31, 2015): 116.

124 **PATH did not respond**: David McCoy, Gayatri Kembhavi, Jinesh Patel, and Akish Luintel, "The Bill & Melinda Gates Foundation's Grant-Making Programme for Global Health," *The Lancet* 373, no. 9675 (May 9, 2009): 1645–53, https://doi.org/10.1016/S0140-6736(09)60571-7.

124 **"being an astroturfer"**: Katri Bertram, "Astroturfing in Global Health—Why This Is a Serious Problem (for Me)," *Katri Bertram* (blog), September 16, 2022, https://katribertram.wordpress.com/2022/09/16/astroturfing-in-global-health-why-this-is-a-serious-problem-for-me/.

125 **"Bill Gates is the architect"**: Carmen Paun, "A World Without America," Politico, August 4, 2022, https://www.politico.com/newsletters/global-pulse/2020/10/22/a-world-without-america-490668.

125 **"implanted with a microchip"**: Full disclosure: One of the articles Politico linked to was my own.

125 **attacked with misinformation**: This included a sympathetic Reuters article by Kate Kelland in 2021: Kate Kelland, "'Crazy and Evil': Bill Gates Surprised by Pandemic Conspiracies," Reuters, January 27, 2021, https://www.reuters.com/article/us-health-coronavirus-gates-conspiracies-idUSKBN29W0Q3. Later that year, Kelland became the chief scientific writer for the Gates-founded Coalition for Epidemic Preparedness Innovations (https://www.linkedin.com/in/kate-kelland-b5995618/); Kate Kelland, LinkedIn, n.d., https://www.linkedin.com/in/kate-kelland-b5995618/?originalSubdomain=uk.

126 **combating "misinformation"**: Examples include $100,000 to the International Center for Journalists, $960,000 to BBC Media Action, and $1.5 million to Media Ecosystems Analysis Group.

126 **power over the pandemic**: Schwab, "While the Poor Get Sick, Bill Gates Just Gets Richer."

126 **Paris Marx**: Other Twitter users have told me that they have also been suspended for sharing information about the Gates Foundation. I also use Twitter, and I've never been deplatformed or suspended.

CHAPTER 6: LOBBYING

129 **Chris Cole**: Chris Cole, LinkedIn," n.d., https://www.linkedin.com/in/chris-cole-1158ba96/; Licea et al., "Insiders Say Bill Gates Was an Office Bully Who Pursued Sexual Affairs."

129 **Sen. Lindsey Graham**: James Fontanella-Khan, Mark Vandevelde, and Simeon Kerr, "Bill Gates Vehicle Buys $2.2Bn Stake in Four Seasons from Saudi Royal," *Financial*

Times, September 8, 2021; "Ben Affleck, Bill Gates Urge Foreign Aid for Congo," *Washington Post*, March 26, 2015, https://www.washingtonpost.com/video/politics/ben-affleck-bill-gates-urge-foreign-aid-for-congo/2015/03/26/dcf4f7b0-d3df-11e4-8b1e-274d670aa9c9_video.html.

129   **marshaling taxpayer dollars**: Bill Gates, Written Testimony Presented Before the Appropriations Committee of the United States Senate, Subcommittee on State, Foreign Operations, and Related Programs, March 26, 2015, https://www.appropriations.senate.gov/imo/media/doc/hearings/032615%20Gates%20Testimony%20-%20SFOPS.pdf.

130   **Affleck was there**: "Partnerships" and "About," Eastern Congo Initiative, n.d., https://www.easterncongo.org/about/partners/ and https://www.easterncongo.org/about-drc/.

130   **and Rand Paul**: Note: Gates's handler in many of his meetings, according to the itinerary, was Michael Deich, a Washington insider who has his own "revolving door" profile at OpenSecrets. Before working for Gates, Deich was employed at the lobbying firm Van Scoyoc and in the federal government, at the Office of Management and Budget and the Council of Economic Advisers; "Revolving Door: Michael Deich Employment Summary," OpenSecrets, n.d., https://www.opensecrets.org/revolving/rev_summary.php?id=26121.

130   **journalist Ezra Klein**: Ezra Klein, "The Most Predictable Disaster in the History of the Human Race," Vox, May 27, 2015, https://www.vox.com/2015/5/27/8660249/bill-gates-spanish-flu-pandemic.

130   **Gates then dined at the Four Seasons**: Ron Klain, biography at Harvard Law School, n.d., https://web.archive.org/web/20190109011819/https://hls.harvard.edu/faculty/directory/11755/Klain; Oliver Milman, "Ron Klain to Reportedly Step Down as Biden Chief of Staff," *Guardian*, January 21, 2023, https://www.theguardian.com/us-news/2023/jan/21/ron-klain-biden-chief-of-staff-white-house.

131   **"Trump in December"**: Anna Palmer, "The Playbook Interview: Bill Gates," Politico, February 14, 2017, https://www.politico.com/story/2017/02/bill-gates-playbook-interview-234987.

131   **campaign to advance federal climate legislation**: Akshat Rathi and Jennifer A Dlouhy, "Bill Gates and the Secret Push to Save Biden's Climate Bill," Bloomberg, August 16, 2022, https://www.bloomberg.com/news/features/2022-08-16/how-bill-gates-lobbied-to-save-the-climate-tax-bill-biden-just-signed#xj4y7vzkg.

131   **Gates's interest in the legislation**: Katy Daigle, "Bill Gates Upbeat on Climate Innovation Even if 1.5C Goal Out of Reach," Reuters, December 20, 2022, https://www.reuters.com/business/environment/bill-gates-upbeat-climate-innovation-even-if-15c-goal-out-reach-2022-12-20/.

131   **wealth into campaign contributions**: Analysis of campaign contribution records at opensecrets.org and followthemoney.org.

132   **Global Fund to Fight AIDS, Tuberculosis and Malaria**: "Bill & Melinda Gates Foundation" and "Government and Public Donors," n.d., https://www.theglobalfund.org/en/private-ngo-partners/resource-mobilization/bill-melinda-gates-foundation/ and https://www.theglobalfund.org/en/government/.

132   **government donors have pledged**: "Annual Contributions and Proceeds 30 June 2022," Gavi, the Vaccine Alliance, n.d., https://www.gavi.org/news/document -library/annual-contributions-and-proceeds-30-june-2022.

132   **"donor government relations"**: Bill & Melinda Gates Foundation, Annual Report 2020, https://www.gatesfoundation.org/about/financials/annual-reports/annual-report -2020.

132   **"downstream delivery"**: Gates, "Watch the Full Bill Gates Keynote," 39:00.

133   **"Jetting in to Washington on Monday"**: David Rogers, "Bill Gates, Time Traveler," Politico, May 8, 2013, https://www.politico.com/story/2013/05/bill-gates-congress -091090.

134   **Food Aid Reform Act**: "Client Profile: One Action," 2013 lobby spending, Open-Secrets, n.d., https://www.opensecrets.org/federal-lobbying/clients/summary?cycle =2013&id=D000055001; Mark Tran, "US Congress Votes Down Bill to Unshackle 'Tied' Food Aid," *Guardian*, June 20, 2013, https://www.theguardian.com/global -development/2013/jun/20/us-congress-bill-food-aid.

134   **Data Action/One Action**: Data Action, IRS 990 tax filing, 2004; "David Lane to Head ONE Campaign," Bill & Melinda Gates Foundation, n.d., https://www.gatesfoundation .org/ideas/media-center/press-releases/2007/10/david-lane-to-head-one-campaign. Note: Data Action changed its name to One Action in 2008. See IRS 900 tax filing, 2008, 29.

134   **Agency for International Development**: David Rogers, "A Food Fight over Aid Program," Politico, April 24, 2013, https://www.politico.com/story/2013/04/a-food-fight -over-aid-program-090607; "Statement on Dr. Rajiv Shah, USAID Administrator-Designate," Bill & Melinda Gates Foundation, n.d., https://www.gatesfoundation .org/ideas/media-center/press-releases/2009/11/statement-on-dr-rajiv-shah-usaid -administratordesignate.

134   **revolving door**: Note: LegiStorm reports twenty-eight current and former Gates Foundation employees who have also held positions working in government or as lobbyists.

134   **Swiss organizations**: "Contact Gavi," Gavi, n.d., https://www.gavi.org/contact-us; "Client Profile: Gavi Alliance," OpenSecrets, n.d., https://www.opensecrets.org/federal -lobbying/clients/summary?id=D000051207; "Bill Profile: H.R.2471," OpenSecrets, n.d., https://www.opensecrets.org/federal-lobbying/bills/summary?id=hr2471-117.

134   **Gates's closest charitable partners**: Analysis of Open Secrets database.

135   **"German Parliament"**: Banco, Furlong, and Pfahler, "How Bill Gates and Partners Used Their Clout to Control the Global Covid Response—with Little Oversight."

135   **"jointly-funded programs"**: Bill & Melinda Gates Foundation, "U.S. Private Foundation Funds and Advocacy," n.d., https://docs.gatesfoundation.org/documents /advocacy-guidelines.pdf.

135   **public-facing disclosures**: We can make crude guesses at Gates's spending. A search of the foundation's grant database for words like *legislator*, *Congress*, *policy*, and *Parliament* turned up more than three billion dollars in donations. One example is a ten-million-dollar gift to the Global Poverty Project "to cultivate political will and citizen engagement to drive public policy and build the political, parliamentary and congressional champions needed to achieve global health and development priorities."

136   **not specifically earmarked**: Kyle House, nevertheless, does explicitly lobby for myr-
       iad groups in Gates's charitable empire, including CEPI, PATH, and Gavi. See "Lob-
       bying Firm Profile: Kyle House," OpenSecrets, n.d., https://www.opensecrets.org
       /federal-lobbying/firms/summary?id=D000074887.

136   **"celebrity culture"**: "Is Aid Killing Africa? Dambisa Moyo Talks About Dead Aid
       on ABC," Interview by Australian Broadcasting Corporation News, March 17, 2009,
       YouTube, 1:25, https://www.youtube.com/watch?v=HIPvlQOCfAQ.

137   **Gates's archenemy**: "About Dambisa," Dambisa Moyo, n.d., https://dambisamoyo
       .com/about/.

137   **"That is not a dependency"**: "Bill Gates' Shocking Personal Attacks on Dr. Dambisa
       Moya and Dead Aid," video of Q&A session at the University of New South Wales,
       May 28, 2013, YouTube, 1:00, https://www.youtube.com/watch?v=5utDdxveaJc.

137   **$6,000 a head**: Jordan Dickinson, employee post-travel disclosure form, U.S. House
       of Representatives Committee on Ethics, September 8, 2016.

137   **"Nelson Mandela"**: Jordan Dickinson, employee post-travel disclosure form.

138   **Alliance for a Green Revolution**: "Scaling Seeds and Technologies Partnership Will
       Accelerate Progress to Reduce Hunger, Poverty in Africa," U.S. Agency for Inter-
       national Development, n.d., https://2012–2017.usaid.gov/news-information/press
       -releases/scaling-seeds-and-technologies-partnership-will-accelerate-progress.
       AGRA at some point dropped Senegal from its list of focus countries, but during the
       time of this trip, it had a partnership with Feed the Future in Senegal; USAID, Feed
       the Future, "Mid-term Performance Evaluation of the Scaling Seeds and Technolo-
       gies Partnership (SSTP) in Africa: Wave Two Survey Report Smallholder Farmers'
       Adoption of Improved Seeds in Program Areas," July 2, 2019, i, https://agra.org/wp
       -content/uploads/2020/07/SSTP-WAVE-2-mid-term-evaluation-USAID.

138   **$60 million to AGRA**: Analysis of USAspending.gov, Cooperative Agreement FAIN
       AIDOAAA1700029, September 30, 2017, https://www.usaspending.gov/award/ASST
       _NON_AIDOAAA1700029_7200.

138   **Arizona representative Kyrsten Sinema**: Kyrsten Sinema, employee post-travel
       disclosure form, U.S. House of Representatives Committee on Ethics, March 17,
       2016.

139   **Minnesota representative Erik Paulsen**: Erik Paulsen and Andy Harris, employee
       post-travel disclosure form, U.S. House of Representatives Committee on Ethics,
       March 17, 2016. Note: WorldVision did not respond to a press inquiry asking about
       the discrepancy between Paulsen and Harris's reported trip costs.

139   **Illinois representative Mike Quigley**: Mike Quigley, employee post-travel disclo-
       sure form, U.S. House of Representatives Committee on Ethics, December 8, 2014.

139   **Rep. Aaron Schock**: Aaron Schock, employee post-travel disclosure form, U.S.
       House of Representatives Committee on Ethics, September 24, 2010.

139   **California representative John Garamendi**: John Garamendi, employee post-travel
       disclosure form, U.S. House of Representatives Committee on Ethics, August 21,
       2015.

139   **fleet of Republican legislators**: Ann Wagner, Susan Brooks, and Carol Miller,
       employee post-travel disclosure forms, U.S. House of Representatives Committee on
       Ethics, May 14, 2019.

139 **$14,000-per-person**: Barbara Lee, employee post-travel disclosure form, U.S. House of Representatives Committee on Ethics, April 18, 2012.

139 **examples go on**: The foundation also appears to freely engage in similar travel activities with state legislators. Public records from the state of New York show that the Gates Foundation, working with the Aspen Institute, proposed to the state's education department that it send "up to seven" people to Washington, DC, to discuss one of the foundation's educational initiatives. "The foundation will cover all travel and lodging costs associated with the convening," Gates staffer Adam Tucker noted in the invitation. It is virtually impossible to track the foundation's money going into fifty different states—which could be larger than its spending at the federal level. It's also possible that Gates funds travel for legislators from foreign governments. This question went beyond the scope of my reporting.

139 **Center for Global Health Policy**: "CSIS to Launch Center for Global Health Policy," Press Release, CSIS, August 18, 2008, https://www.csis.org/news/csis-launch-center -global-health-policy.

140 **new project sent congressional staffers**: Heidi Ross, employee post-travel disclosure form, U.S. House of Representatives Committee on Ethics, January 31, 2013.

140 **did not name Gates as a sponsor**: Theresa Vawter, employee post-travel disclosure form, U.S. House of Representatives Committee on Ethics, April 9, 2013; Kristin Dini Hernandez, employee post-travel disclosure form, U.S. House of Representatives Committee on Ethics, March 7, 2014; Janice Kaguyutan, employee post-travel disclosure form, U.S. House of Representatives Committee on Ethics, September 4, 2014.

141 **"Learning Tours" program**: "Learning Tours," CARE, n.d., https://www.care.org/our -work/advocacy/learning-tours/.

141 **150 members of Congress**: "CARE Learning Tours Alumni," CARE, n.d., https:// www.care.org/our-work/advocacy/learning-tours/alumni/.

142 **Aspen organized a trip**: Jess Gross and Lindsay A. L. Hunsicker, employee post-travel disclosure forms, U.S. House of Representatives Committee on Ethics, October 24, 2008.

142 **sponsor on disclosure forms**: Note: The ethics filings from some but not all congressional staffers include the original invitation letter they received from Aspen, which reports, "Attendance is by invitation only, with no outside observers or lobbyists. Funding is provided solely by grants from established foundations—no government, individual, foreign, corporate or special interest money is accepted. Foundations supporting this project are the Bill and Melinda Gates Foundation and the Carnegie Corporation of New York." However, in the actual ethics disclosure forms, Gates and Carnegie are not listed as sponsors. See Catherine Brown, employee post-travel disclosure form, U.S. House of Representatives, Committee on Ethics, October 30, 2008.

143 **excess of ten million dollars**: Analysis of campaign contribution data at opense crets.org.

143 **largest-ever recorded political donation**: Bill & Melinda Gates Foundation, "U.S. Private Foundation Funds and Advocacy."

143 **Pushing charter schools is a major agenda item**: "Washington Charter School

Initiative, Initiative 1240 (2012)," Ballotpedia, n.d., https://ballotpedia.org/Washington_Charter_School_Initiative,_Initiative_1240_(2012).

143   **no to charter schools**: Washington Charter School Initiative, Initiative 1240, 2012.

143   **the ballot passed by a razor-thin margin**: Washington Charter School Initiative, Initiative 1240, 2012.

143   **courts ruled against charters**: Sally Ho, "Bill Gates Among Billionaires Fueling Charter-School Movement Across U.S. and Here in Washington," Union-Bulletin .com, July 15, 2018, https://www.union-bulletin.com/news/local/education/bill-gates -among-billionaires-fueling-charter-school-movement-across-u-s-and-here-in -washington/article_48d1a97c-f6c2-593e-81f9-904b40bb416b.html.

144   **Bill Gates explained on *The Oprah Winfrey Show***: "Bill Gates Interview on Oprah Farewell 2010.09.20," YouTube, 6:00, https://www.youtube.com/watch?v =Z5lmBCnVALQ.

144   **do not outperform traditional public schools**: Lyndsey Layton, "Charters Not Outperforming Nation's Traditional Public Schools, Report Says," *Washington Post*, June 25, 2013, https://www.washingtonpost.com/local/education/charters -not-outperforming-nations-traditional-public-schools-report-says/2013/06/24 /23f19bb8-dd0c-11e2-bd83-e99e43c336ed_story.html; Eve L. Ewing, "Can We Stop Fighting About Charter Schools?," *New York Times*, February 22, 2021, https://www .nytimes.com/2021/02/22/opinion/charter-schools-democrats.html.

144   **under fire for driving segregation**: Kate Zernike, "Condemnation of Charter Schools Exposes a Rift over Black Students," *New York Times*, August 21, 2016, https:// www.nytimes.com/2016/08/21/us/blacks-charter-schools.html.

144   **American Legislative Exchange Council**: Yvonne Wingett Sanchez and Rob O'Dell, "What Is ALEC? 'The Most Effective Organization' for Conservatives, Says Newt Gingrich," *USA Today*, April 3, 2019, https://www.usatoday.com/story/news /investigations/2019/04/03/alec-american-legislative-exchange-council-model -bills-republican-conservative-devos-gingrich/3162357002/.

144   **no longer give grants to ALEC**: "Gates Won't Pull ALEC Grant," BuzzFeed News, April 10, 2012, https://www.buzzfeednews.com/article/buzzfeedpolitics/gates-wont -pull-alec-grant.

144   **simply use his private wealth**: In 2019, Bill and Melinda French Gates actually started a new lobbying arm adjacent to the foundation, called the Gates Policy Initiative. After initial news reports raised questions, the foundation appears to have largely abandoned the project, perhaps realizing what a political liability it was—and how many other channels it had to influence politics behind closed doors. Rosalie Chan, "Bill and Melinda Gates Are Launching a Lobbying Group," *Business Insider*, June 13, 2019, https://www.businessinsider.com/bill-gates-melinda-gates-lobbying -group-2019-6.

146   **"three dozen parents in Memphis"**: David Marchese, "Melinda Gates on Tech Innovation, Global Health and Her Own Privilege," *New York Times Magazine*, April 15, 2019, https://www.nytimes.com/interactive/2019/04/15/magazine/melinda -gates-foundation-interview.html.

146   **foundation's "chameleon" nature**: Adam Moe Fejerskov, *The Gates Foundation's Rise to Power: Private Authority in Global Politics* (New York: Routledge, 2018), 20–21.

147   **overlap with Google's interests**: Alex Thompson, "A Google Billionaire's Fingerprints
       Are All Over Biden's Science Office," *Politico*, March 28, 2022, https://www.politico
       .com/news/2022/03/28/google-billionaire-joe-biden-science-office-00020712. Note:
       Gates Foundation staff have served as advisors on dozens of federal committees,
       according to the General Services Administration, Federal Advisory Committee Act
       (FACA) Database, https://www.facadatabase.gov/FACA/apex/FACAPublicSearch#.

147   **Michael Bloomberg**: Alexander Burns and Nicholas Kulish, "Bloomberg's Billions:
       How the Candidate Built an Empire of Influence," *New York Times*, February 15, 2020,
       https://www.nytimes.com/interactive/2020/02/15/us/politics/michael-bloomberg
       -spending.html. Note: The story profiled specific allegations of censorship (or self-
       censorship) by recipients of Bloomberg's philanthropic giving that are uncannily
       similar to those that engulf the Gates Foundation: "In interviews with The Times,
       no one described being threatened or coerced by Mr. Bloomberg or his money. But
       many said his wealth was an inescapable consideration—a gravitational force pow-
       erful enough to make coercion unnecessary."

147   **Koch brothers**: Jane Mayer, *Dark Money: The Hidden History of the Billionaires
       Behind the Rise of the Radical Right* (New York: Anchor, 2016); Center for Public
       Integrity, "Why the Koch Brothers Find Higher Education Worth Their Money,"
       Center for Public Integrity, May 3, 2018, http://publicintegrity.org/politics/why-the
       -koch-brothers-find-higher-education-worth-their-money/.

CHAPTER 7: FAMILY PLANNING

148   *60 Minutes*: "The Gates Foundation: Giving Away a Fortune," *60 Minutes*, CBS, aired
       September 30, 2010, https://www.cbsnews.com/news/the-gates-foundation-giving
       -away-a-fortune/. Note: *60 Minutes* appears to have reported on the Gates Foun-
       dation five times, always favorably; Charlie Rose, "Bill Gates 2.0," *60 Minutes*, CBS,
       May 21, 2013, https://www.cbsnews.com/news/bill-gates-climate-change-disaster-60
       -minutes-2021-02-14/; Charlie Rose, "The Giving Pledge," *60 Minutes*, CBS, March
       27, 2016, https://www.cbsnews.com/news/60-minutes-giving-pledge/; Scott Pelley,
       "Why Bill and Melinda Gates Put 20,000 Students Through College," *60 Minutes*,
       CBS, September 2, 2018; Anderson Cooper, "Bill Gates: How the World Can Avoid
       a Climate Disaster," *60 Minutes*, CBS, February 15, 2021, https://www.cbsnews.com
       /news/bill-gates-climate-change-disaster-60-minutes-2021-02-14/.

148   **gee-whiz questions**: "The Gates Foundation: Giving Away a Fortune," 0:10.

148   **province of Uttar Pradesh**: "The Gates Foundation: Giving Away a Fortune," 2:20.

149   **Bill was getting all the credit**: Melinda Gates, *The Moment of Lift: How Empower-
       ing Women Changes the World* (New York: Flatiron Books, 2019). Note: This is not
       entirely supported by the foundation's public-facing tax records, which report the
       number of hours worked by certain employees. In the early years of the foundation,
       Bill and Melinda both reported working the same number of hours—between five
       and eight per week. Notably, Bill had the title of "trustee," while Melinda had the
       lesser-sounding title of "manager." See Bill & Melinda Gates Foundation, Part VII,
       IRS 990 filing, 2001.

149   **"what motivates these people"**: "The Gates Foundation: Giving Away a Fortune,"
       2:30.

149   **poor villagers in India**: "The Gates Foundation: Giving Away a Fortune," 3:25.

149   **Traveling to the Indian countryside**: "The Gates Foundation: Giving Away a Fortune," 0:55.

149   **"she'd have eight children"**: "Extra: Gates on Population Rates," from "The Gates Foundation: Giving Away a Fortune," https://web.archive.org/web/20200531121459 /https://www.youtube.com/watch?v=7_xEn5mudP8.

150   **"survive into adulthood"**: Note: Some users of contraceptives do not identify as women, but the Gates Foundation appears to focus its family planning efforts narrowly on women—which is why this chapter follows this focus. Generally speaking, the foundation does not appear concerned with how its work on "gender equality," or any other issue, intersects with nonbinary or transgender communities. Of the nearly $80 billion the Gates Foundation has pledged in charitable gifts, only two donations (around $350,000) mentioned transgender communities.

150   **expand the use of contraceptives**: Candid, "Gates Foundation Announces $2.6 Billion in 'Family Planning' Commitments," *Philanthropy News Digest*, July 12, 2012, https://philanthropynewsdigest.org/news/gates-foundation-announces-2.6-billion -in-family-planning-commitments.

150   **"population control"**: Seabrook, "E-Mail from Bill."

150   **"population has been crowded into urban areas"**: Bill Gates, Excerpt from *The Road Ahead*, published in *Newsweek*, November 26, 1995, https://www.newsweek .com/road-ahead-181290.

150   **fascination with overpopulation**: Bill Moyers, "A Conversation with Bill Gates: Making a Healthier World for Children and Future Generations," Transcript, Bill Moyers.com, May 9, 2003, https://billmoyers.com/content/conversation-bill-gates -making-healthier-world-children-future-generations-transcript/. Note: It appears this softball interview—with renowned reporter Bill Moyers—may have been sponsored by the Gates Foundation, whose grant records show a $500,000 grant in 2003 "to support a forum and broadcast production of a global health dialogue between Bill Gates and Bill Moyers at Columbia University's Mailman School of Public Health."

151   **odd figure as a leader of Planned Parenthood**: Bill Gates Sr. is deceased, so he could not be interviewed about his interest in family planning. News outlets have reported that Gates Sr. served on both local and national boards of Planned Parenthood. The national Planned Parenthood organization would not confirm or deny this. See Lisa Stiffler and Todd Bishop, "Bill Gates Sr., 1925–2020: Microsoft Co-Founder's Father Made His Own Mark on Seattle and the World," GeekWire, September 15, 2020, https://www.geekwire.com/2020/bill-gates-sr-1925-2020-microsoft-co-founders -father-made-mark-seattle-world/.

151   **manage his son's**: "Bill Gates' Q&A with Chris Anderson: Video Unveiled," *TED Blog*, February 6, 2009, https://blog.ted.com/bill_gates_qa_w/.

151   **private residence in Manhattan**: Robert Frank, "Billionaires Try to Shrink World's Population, Report Says," *Wall Street Journal*, May 16, 2009, https://www.wsj.com /articles/BL-WHB-1322.

151   **negative impacts of population growth**: "About Us," Population Resource Center, https://web.archive.org/web/20080605202028/http://www.prcdc.org/about/.

151   **Gates reported in 2012**: Bill Gates, "2012 Annual Letter," *GatesNotes*, January 24, 2012, https://www.gatesnotes.com/About-Bill-Gates/2012-Annual-Letter.

152   **reduce the population of Nigeria**: A newer generation of billionaires, including Elon Musk (Tesla) and Jack Ma (Alibaba), has been vocal about their concerns about population growth. "The biggest issue in 20 years will be population collapse. Not explosion. Collapse," Musk noted in a public presentation in 2019. "I absolutely agree with that," Ma said. "The population problem is going to be facing huge challenge. 1.4 billion people in China sounds a lot, but I think next 20 years, we will see this thing will bring big trouble to China." Catherine Clifford, "Elon Musk and Jack Ma Agree: The Biggest Problem the World Will Face Is Population Collapse," CNBC, August 30, 2019, https://www.cnbc.com/2019/08/30/elon-musk-jack-ma-biggest -problem-world-will-face-is-population-drop.html.

152   **decades to EngenderHealth**: Jacob Levich, "Bill Gates and the Myth of Overpopulation," *Medium* (blog), April 26, 2019, https://medium.com/@jacob.levich/bill-gates -and-the-myth-of-overpopulation-ca3b1d89680.

152   **"facts are complicated"**: Alexis McGill Johnson, "I'm the Head of Planned Parenthood. We're Done Making Excuses for Our Founder," *New York Times*, April 17, 2021, https://www.nytimes.com/2021/04/17/opinion/planned-parenthood-margaret -sanger.html.

153   **Ford president Darren Walker**: Stephanie Beasley, "Top Global Foundations Mount Effort to Confront Legacies of Eugenics," Devex, October 1, 2021, https://www.devex .com/news/sponsored/top-global-foundations-mount-effort-to-confront-legacies -of-eugenics-101745.

153   **Rockefeller president Rajiv Shah**: "Statement by Dr. Rajiv J. Shah on the Anti-Eugenics Project's Dismantling Eugenics Convening," *Rockefeller Foundation* (blog), September 28, 2021, https://www.rockefellerfoundation.org/news/statement-by-dr -rajiv-j-shah-on-the-anti-eugenics-projects-dismantling-eugenics-convening/.

153   **"Eugenics is morally nauseating"**: Gates, *Moment of Lift*.

154   **"I have no interest in telling women"**: Gates, *Moment of Lift*.

154   **"indicators of contraceptive uptake"**: Leigh Senderowicz, "'I Was Obligated to Accept': A Qualitative Exploration of Contraceptive Coercion," *Social Science and Medicine* 239 (October 1, 2019): 112531, https://doi.org/10.1016/j.socscimed.2019.112531.

154   **"treatment for infertility"**: See also Matthew Connelly, *Fatal Misconception: The Struggle to Control World Population* (Cambridge, MA: Belknap Press of Harvard University Press, 2008).

155   **hardly begins to describe**: Gates, *Moment of Lift*.

155   **"change the conversation"**: Gates, *Moment of Lift*.

155   **upcoming summit in London**: Sabrina Tavernise, "Study Says Meeting Contraception Needs Could Cut Maternal Deaths by a Third," *New York Times*, July 9, 2012, https://www.nytimes.com/2012/07/10/health/meeting-contraception-needs-could -sink-maternal-death-rate.html.

155   **summit raised more than $2.5 billion**: Mark Tran, "Rich Countries Pledge $2.6bn for Family Planning in Global South," *Guardian*, July 11, 2012, https://www .theguardian.com/global-development/2012/jul/11/rich-countries-pledge-family -planning-women.

156 **69 poorest nations on earth**: "The transition to FP2030, Measurement Report 2021," FP2030, 2021, 7, https://fp2030.org/sites/default/files/Data-Hub/FP2030 _DataReport_v5.pdf.

156 **together pledging half**: "New Financial Commitments by Donors and Private Sector at the London Summit on Family Planning," London Summit on Family Planning, n.d., https://web.archive.org/web/20120912152550/http://www.london familyplanningsummit.co.uk/1530%20CommitmentSummary_Final_.pdf.

156 **"inheritance laws"**: Gates, *Moment of Lift*.

156 **"training them to steal"**: Gates, *Moment of Lift*.

156 **"policymakers, planners, or theologians"**: Gates, *Moment of Lift*.

156 **"play a second violin"**: Lisa Peters and Marlies Pilon, "What Happens When Bill and Melinda Gates Don't Focus on Software, but IUDs," *De Correspondent*, March 9, 2020, https://decorrespondent.nl/11010/wat-er-gebeurt-als-bill-en-melinda-gates-zich-niet -op-software-maar-spiraaltjes-storten/2436819793650-cd5e4602.

157 **FP2020's planning teams**: Win Brown et al., "Developing the '120 by 20' Goal for the Global FP2020 Initiative," *Studies in Family Planning* 45, no. 1 (March 2014): 73–84, doi:10.1111/j.1728-4465.2014.00377.x; Anne Hendrixson, "Population Control in the Troubled Present: The '120 by 20' Target and Implant Access Program," *Development and Change* 50, no. 3 (2019): 786–804, https://doi.org/10.1111/dech .12423.

157 **"London Olympics"**: Gates, *Moment of Lift*.

157 **"women's autonomy and agency"**: Petition available at https://reproductiverights.org /wp-content/uploads/2020/12/Civil-Society-Declaration_06_19_2012.pdf.

157 **gave a TED Talk**: Melinda Gates, "Change the Big Picture," Transcript, TEDx, April 12, 2012, https://www.gatesfoundation.org/ideas/speeches/2012/04/melinda-gates -tedxchange-the-big-picture.

158 **one-and-done implant**: David Bank, "Guaranteed Impact: Increasing Supplies and Cutting Prices for Contraceptives Without Spending a Dime," in Stanford University with ImpactAlpha, *Making Markets Work for the Poor*, Supplement, *Stanford Social Innovation Review* (Summer 2016): 17.

158 **coax Big Pharma**: Bank, "Guaranteed Impact," 18.

159 **new markets for Bayer and Merck**: Bank, "Guaranteed Impact," 18.

159 ***Killing the Black Body***: Dorothy Roberts, *Killing the Black Body: Race, Reproduction, and the Meaning of Liberty* (New York: Vintage Books, 1997).

159 **"its coercive deployment"**: Roberts, *Killing the Black Body*.

160 **"universal access to birth control"**: Gates, "Change the Big Picture."

160 **Natalie Revelle**: Bank, "Guaranteed Impact," 18.

161 **incentive to ramp up**: Bank, "Guaranteed Impact," 18.

161 **"also drives demand"**: Hendrixson, "Population Control in the Troubled Present," 797.

161 **"demand creation"**: Government of Malawi, "Malawi Costed Implementation Plan for Family Planning, 2016–2020," FP2030, September 2015, 19, https://fp2030.org /sites/default/files/Malawi-CIP-for-FP-2016-2020.pdf.

161 **"increasing and sustaining demand"**: "Pfizer's Sayana® Press Becomes First Inject- able Contraceptive in the United Kingdom Available for Administration by Self-

Injection," Pfizer, September 23, 2015, https://www.pfizer.com/news/press-release/press-release-detail/pfizer_s_sayana_press_becomes_first_injectable_contraceptive_in_the_united_kingdom_available_for_administration_by_self_injection.

161 **organizing their workloads around**: Senderowicz, "I Was Obligated to Accept."

162 **mobile clinic in Uganda**: Lisa Peters and Marlies Pilon, "On the Road with the Racing Doctors Who Want to Provide an Entire Country with Contraception," *De Correspondent*, March 5, 2020, https://decorrespondent.nl/11005/op-pad-met-de-racende-dokters-die-een-heel-land-van-anticonceptie-willen-voorzien/2435713154325-f40d79f1.

162 **her pain and bleeding immediately stopped**: This doesn't mean implants are dangerous. Virtually all medical interventions can have side effects. However, if the Gates Foundation is helping push implants in poor nations, is it not also ethically required to organize a clear and easy removal strategy? The Gates Foundation knows that implant removal is a problem—it has funded research on this issue—but it does not appear to have prioritized it alongside its goal of getting 120 million women on contraceptives. Megan Christofield and Maryjane Lacoste, "Accessible Contraceptive Implant Removal Services: An Essential Element of Quality Service Delivery and Scale-Up," *Global Health: Science and Practice* 4, no. 3 (September 28, 2016): 366–72, http://dx.doi.org/10.9745/GHSP-D-16-00096.

162 **that number had doubled**: "Uganda, FP2020 Core Indicator Summary Sheet, 2017," Track20, n.d., https://track20.org/download/pdf/2017%20FP2020%20CI%20Handouts/english/Uganda%202017%20FP2020%20CoreIndicators.pdf; "Uganda, FP2030 Indicator Summary Sheet: 2022 Measurement Report," Track20, n.d., https://track20.org/download/pdf/2022%20Country%20Briefs/English/Uganda%202022%20Indicator%20Summary%20Sheet.pdf.

162 **financially incentivized to push implants**: Peters and Pilon, "On the Road with the Racing Doctors Who Want to Provide an Entire Country with Contraception."

163 **reached only 60 million**: "Measurement," FP2020, n.d., http://progress.familyplanning2020.org/measurement.

163 **moved the goalpost**: "Gates Foundation, UNFPA Pledge US$3.1 Billion to Increase Access to Family Planning at Global Launch of FP2030 Partnership," Press Release, FP2030, November 18, 2021, https://fp2030.org/news/gates-foundation-unfpa-pledge-us31-billion-increase-access-family-planning-global-launch-fp2030.

163 **happy enough with the success**: "Launching FP2030," https://commitments.fp2030.org/launching-fp2030.

163 **"be in control of their own contraceptive care"**: Bill & Melinda Gates Foundation, FP2030 Commitment, August 1, 2018, https://fp2030.org/bill-and-melinda-gates-foundation.

163 **not historically supported abortion**: Adam Liptak, "In 6-to-3 Ruling, Supreme Court Ends Nearly 50 Years of Abortion Rights," *New York Times*, June 24, 2022, https://www.nytimes.com/2022/06/24/us/roe-wade-overturned-supreme-court.html.

163 **"the emotional and personal debate"**: Melinda Gates, "Reflections on My Recent Travels," *Impatient Optimists* (blog), June 2, 2014, https://web.archive.org/web/20140606215305/http://www.impatientoptimists.org/Posts/2014/06/Reflections-on-My-Trip-to-Toronto.

164 **massive foreign aid giving**: Luisa Blanchfield, "Abortion and Family Planning–Related Provisions in U.S. Foreign Assistance Law and Policy," Congressional Research Service, July 15, 2022, https://sgp.fas.org/crs/row/R41360.pdf.

164 **global gag rule**: "What Is the Global Gag Rule?," Planned Parenthood, n.d., https://www.plannedparenthoodaction.org/communities/planned-parenthood-global/end-global-gag-rule. As another example, the Tiahrt Amendments place rules on USAID's foreign aid funding to ensure it will be used for voluntary family planning efforts. This includes widespread prohibition of numerical targets (or quotas), incentives, bribes, gratuities, or financial rewards.

164 **President Biden rescinded**: Justin Goldberg, "Biden Administration Rescinds Global Gag Rule," Center for Reproductive Rights, February 1, 2021, https://reproductiverights.org/biden-administration-rescinds-global-gag-rule/.

164 **avoids a major hot-button issue**: "Country Support-FP2020 Partnership—FP2020 Momentum at the Midpoint 2015–2016," http://2015-2016progress.familyplanning 2020.org/page/fp2020-partnership/country-support. USAID spends more than half a billion dollars per year on family planning and reproductive health, and it describes itself as a "core partner" of FP2020 and FP2030; USAID, Family Planning and Reproductive Health Program Overview," n.d., https://web.archive.org/web/20210324212510/https://www.usaid.gov/sites/default/files/documents/FPRH-factsheet_OCT2020.pdf; "Partnerships and Projects," USAID, n.d., https://www.usaid.gov/global-health/health-areas/family-planning/partnerships-projects.

165 **the foundation has not endorsed it:** In early 2023, Senderowicz emailed me with an update that Gates had gotten back in touch with her about potentially working with her. The foundation has known about her work on contraceptive autonomy since as early as 2018.

CHAPTER 8: JOURNALISM

167 **Hood Canal**: Bank, *Breaking Windows*, 8.

167 **"Turbo Beaver" seaplane**: Bank, *Breaking Windows*, 8.

167 **a sumptuous dinner**: Bank, *Breaking Windows*, 16.

167 **Edstrom's daughter**: Edstrom and Eller, *Barbarians Led by Bill Gates*, 196.

168 **had a reputation:** Licea et al., "Insiders Say Bill Gates Was an Office Bully Who Pursued Sexual Affairs."

168 **editor John Dickinson**: Brit Hume, "PC Magazine Demonstrates a Classic Conflict of Interest," *Washington Post*, July 9, 1990, https://www.washingtonpost.com/archive/business/1990/07/09/pc-magazine-demonstrates-a-classic-conflict-of-interest/d6d563a1-bbc0-4639-874f-58a81442dfc8/.

168 **forced him to leave the magazine**: Howard Kurtz, "Columnist Severs PC Connection," *Washington Post*, July 7, 1992, https://www.washingtonpost.com/archive/lifestyle/1992/07/07/columnist-severs-pc-connection/1e955be9-264e-4e68-868e-c19a2d7eb059/.

168 **"every which way from Sunday"**: David Armstrong, "Ziff Happens," *Wired*, May 1, 1994, https://www.wired.com/1994/05/ziff/.

169 **Andrew Estrada**: Andrew Estrada, LinkedIn, n.d., https://www.linkedin.com/in/andrew-estrada28/. Note: In my early days reporting on the foundation, Estrada

provided some responses—often highly generalized, stock responses—to some questions by email. At one point, the foundation stopped responding to all questions.

170   **foundation's total spending on all media**: Note: Media Impact Funder's definition of media is broad and includes, for example, $850 million the Gates Foundation spent on "telecommunications infrastructure," like a $6 million grant to Marie Stopes International "to increase access and uptake of contraception for women and girls in Mali, Senegal, Burkina Faso, and Niger using innovative mobile technology to improve the quality of counseling and the effectiveness of referral systems." By contrast, Media Impact Funders doesn't include money that the Gates family spends outside of the foundation, like Melinda French Gates launching her own book imprint in 2021, Moment of Lift Books; Annie Goldsmith, "Melinda French Launches Women-Focused Book Imprint," *Town & Country*, October 7, 2021, https://www .townandcountrymag.com/society/money-and-power/a37896307/melinda-french -moment-of-lift-book-imprint/. Media Impact Funders, Foundation Maps for Media Funding, n.d., https://maps.foundationcenter.org/#/list/?subjects=all&popgroups=all &years=all&location=6295630&excludeLocation=0&geoScale=ADM0&layer=recip &boundingBox=-139.219,-31.354,135,66.513&gmOrgs=all&recipOrgs=all&tags =all&keywords=&pathwaysOrg=&pathwaysType=&acct=media&typesOfSupport =all&transactionTypes=all&amtRanges=all&minGrantAmt=0&maxGrantAmt=0 &gmTypes=all&minAssetsAmt=0&maxAssetsAmt=0&minGivingAmt=0&max GivingAmt=0&andOr=0&includeGov=1&custom=all&customArea=all&indica tor=&dataSource=oecd&chartType=trends&multiSubject=1&listType=gm&win dRoseAnd=undefined&zoom=2.

170   **the Alliance for Science**: Note: My analysis of Gates's giving $325 million to journalism did not include the money the foundation has given to the Alliance for Science or the New America Foundation because most of the work these groups do for Gates appears nonjournalistic in nature.

170   ***Washington Post* columnist Michael Gerson**: Michael Gerson, "A Shot at Hope," *Washington Post*, January 18, 2011, https://www.washingtonpost.com/amphtml/opinions /a-shot-at-hope/2011/01/17/ABYpLkD_story.html; Michael Gerson, "Bill Gates and 'the Last Ebola Epidemic,'" *Washington Post*, October 30, 2014, https://www.washing tonpost.com/opinions/michael-gerson-global-attention-on-disease-gives-bill-gates -his-moment/2014/10/30/54073af6-6064-11e4-9f3a-7e28799e0549_story.html; Michael Gerson, "Bill Gates and the Golden Age of Global Aid," *Washington Post*, September 28, 2015, https://www.washingtonpost.com/opinions/wiping-out-malaria -in-a-generation/2015/09/28/7e281310-6607-11e5-8325-a42b5a459b1e_story.html; Michael Gerson, "Bill Gates's New Pandemic Book Presents a Plea and a Plan," *Washington Post*, May 10, 2022, https://www.washingtonpost.com/opinions/2022/05/10 /bill-gates-covid-how-to-prevent-next-pandemic/; "Leadership: Board of Directors," The ONE Campaign, n.d., https://www.one.org/us/about/leadership/.

170   **the Poynter Institute for Media Studies**: Schwab, "Journalism's Gates Keepers."

171   **Center for Investigative Reporting**: "About Us," Reveal, n.d., http://revealnews.org /about-us/.

171   **partnership with ABC News**: Bill Carter, "Gates Foundation Backs ABC News Project," *New York Times*, October 6, 2010, https://archive.nytimes.com/mediadecoder

.blogs.nytimes.com/2010/10/06/gates-foundation-backs-abc-news-project/;
"Philanthropists Bill and Melinda Gates Tout Success of Global Health Initiatives,"
ABC News, https://web.archive.org/web/20091028172510/http://abcnews.go.com
/WN/GlobalHealth/.

171   **David Westin acknowledged**: Carter, "Gates Foundation Backs ABC News Project."

171   **Kate James**: Tom Paulson, "The Gates Foundation Conspiracy to Take Over the
      Media," *Humanosphere*, December 21, 2010, https://www.humanosphere.org/basics
      /2010/12/the-gates-foundation-conspiracy-to-take-over-the-media/.

172   **study on education**: Ho, "AP Analysis Shows How Bill Gates Influences Education
      Policy."

172   **a fourth layer**: In another, historical iteration, "the fourth estate" refers to a fourth
      entity in addition to the clergy, nobility, and commoners.

173   **investigation for *Huffington Post***: Robert Fortner and Alex Park, "Bill Gates Won't
      Save You from the Next Ebola," *HuffPost*, April 30, 2017, https://www.huffpost.com
      /entry/ebola-gates-foundation-public-health_n_5900a8c5e4b0026db1dd15e6.

174   **Fortner and Park**: Schwab, "Journalism's Gates Keepers."

174   **"neglected tropical diseases"**: Candid, "Gates Foundation Funds HuffPost Proj-
      ect to Fight Neglected Diseases," *Philanthropy News Digest*, November 27, 2016,
      https://philanthropynewsdigest.org/news/gates-foundation-funds-huffpost
      -project-to-fight-neglected-diseases; Gregory Beyer and Catharine Smith, "How
      You Can Help Stamp Out a Deadly Disease," *HuffPost*, November 22, 2016, https:
      //www.huffpost.com/entry/project-zero-neglected-tropical-diseases_n_582f10
      ebe4b099512f825994.

175   **doesn't mean Gates failed in its pushback**: As far as we can see, the Gates Founda-
      tion did not give additional funding to the *Huffington Post*. This is one of the most
      powerful levers Gates has, to stop funding an organization. Recipients of funding
      generally want to keep the money flowing, which means trying to please donors.

175   **reporting project for the Dutch news outlet**: Schwab, "Journalism's Gates Keepers."

175   **polio communications team**: Schwab, "Journalism's Gates Keepers."

176   *Columbia Journalism Review*: Schwab, "Journalism's Gates Keepers."

176   **"in-house media relations team"**: Most of the foundation's responses were given
      not to me but, rather, to the fact-checkers at *Columbia Journalism Review* just before
      publication. This isn't that different from Fortner and Park's experience, where the
      foundation sought to circumvent the normal editorial process, going around or
      above the journalist.

176   **"Bhekisisa's donor resources"**: Mia Malan, "The Balancing Act of Donor-Funded
      Journalism: A Case Study from South Africa," Global Investigative Journalism Net-
      work, February 14, 2018, https://gijn.org/2018/02/14/bhekisisa/; "What Is Bheki-
      sisa?," Bhekisisa, n.d., https://bhekisisa.org/what-is-bhekisisa/.

178   *Guardian*'s **global development beat**: "The Guardian Launches Global Develop-
      ment Website with Gates Foundation," *Guardian*, September 14, 2010, https://www
      .theguardian.com/gnm-press-office/guardian-launches-global-development-site.

178   **during his stint as a guest editor**: Bill Gates, "Why I Decided to Edit an Issue of TIME,"
      Time, January 4, 2018, https://time.com/5086870/bill-gates-guest-editor-time/.

178   **also played guest editor**: Bill Gates, "How I Became the Editor of WIRED (for

One Issue)," *GatesNotes*, November 12, 2013, https://www.gatesnotes.com/about -bill-gates/how-i-became-editor-of-wired; Bill Gates, "Bill Gates Signs Off as Guest Editor of The Verge," *The Verge*, February 27, 2015, https://www.theverge.com /2015/2/27/8118215/bill-gates-melinda-interview-life-in-2030; Gideon Lichfield, "Bill Gates Explains Why We Should All Be Optimists," *MIT Technology Review*, February 27, 2019, https://www.technologyreview.com/2019/02/27/1267/bill-gates -explains-why-we-should-all-be-optimists/; Bill Gates, "Japan Can Lead the World in Ending Infectious Diseases," *Asahi Shimbun*, May 9, 2016, https://web.archive .org/web/20160509232353/https://www.asahi.com/ajw/articles/AJ201605090001 .html; "The Epidemic You Don't Know About," *Times of India*, November 17, 2017, https://timesofindia.indiatimes.com/india/the-epidemic-you-dont-know-about /articleshow/61680295.cms; Clifton Leaf, "Why We Asked Bill Gates to Be Fortune's Guest Editor Today," *Fortune*, February 16, 2021, https://fortune.com/2021/02/16 /bill-gates-guest-editor-fortune-climate-change-new-book-how-to-avoid-a-climate -disaster/.

179   **its founder's positivism**: "Impatient Optimist," U.S. Trademark registration 5639253, Bill & Melinda Gates Foundation, October 12, 2017.

179   **take a victory lap**: Gates, "Why I Decided to Edit an Issue of TIME."

179   **$1.90 a day**: See, for example, Bill Gates's tweet from January 19, 2019, offering six graphs showing improvements in everything from poverty to child mortality: @Bill Gates, Twitter, https://twitter.com/BillGates/status/1086662632587907072?ref_src =twsrc%5Etfw%7Ctwcamp%5Etweetembed%7Ctwterm%5E10866626325879070 72%7Ctwgr%5E%7Ctwcon%5Es1_&ref_url=https://www.vox.com/future-perfect /2019/2/12/18215534/bill-gates-global-poverty-chart.

179   **three times higher:** Jason Hickel, "The True Extent of Global Poverty and Hunger: Questioning the Good News Narrative of the Millennium Development Goals," *Third World Quarterly* 37, no. 5 (May 3, 2016): 749–67, https://doi.org/10.1080/01436597 .2015.1109439.

180   **struggle to feed**: Yacob Abrehe Zereyesus and Lila Cardell, "Global Food Insecurity Grows in 2022 amid Backdrop of Higher Prices, Black Sea Conflict," USDA Economic Research Service, November 28, 2022, https://www.ers.usda.gov/amber -waves/2022/november/global-food-insecurity-grows-in-2022-amid-backdrop-of -higher-prices-black-sea-conflict/.

180   **"and not usually deemed newsworthy"**: Gates, "Why I Decided to Edit an Issue of TIME."

180   **Living Proof Project**: Note: In 2010, the foundation handed over the project to the Gates-funded ONE campaign; "Foundation Transitions the Living Proof Project to ONE," Bill & Melinda Gates Foundation, n.d., https://www.gatesfoundation .org/ideas/media-center/press-releases/2010/08/foundation-transitions-the-living -proof-project-to-one; "Bill Gates Urges More Spending on Health," *Sydney Morning Herald*, October 28, 2009, https://www.smh.com.au/world/bill-gates-urges-more -spending-on-health-20091028-hjhk.html.

180   **"reporting success stories"**: "What Is the Living Proof Project?," Bill & Melinda Gates Foundation, April 20, 2010, https://web.archive.org/web/20100420020651 /http://www.gatesfoundation.org/livingproofproject/Pages/what-is-living-proof

-project.aspx; "About," Living Proof Project, October 4, 2011, https://web.archive.org /web/20111004010529/http://one.org/livingproof/en/about/.

180   **largest all-time funder**: Solutions Journalism Network boasts myriad philanthropic funders, including the Ford, Hewlett, and Knight Foundations; "Major Funders," Solutions Journalism Network, n.d., https://www.solutionsjournalism.org/about /funders.

181   **"flawed, kind of one-sided view"**: David Bornstein, "A Journalist's Brief but Spectacular Take on Telling the Whole Story," *PBS NewsHour*, PBS, August 16, 2022, https://www.pbs.org/newshour/brief/420423/david-bornstein.

181   **"spread solutions journalism"**: "Democracy Initiative manager," job posting on Solutions Journalism Network, https://web.archive.org/web/20220414135304/https:// jobs.lever.co/solutionsjournalism/613ca01b-b480-46a4-94bf-3cdaf1f29777.

182   **Bridge International Academies**: Tina Rosenberg, "A By-the-E-Book Education, for $5 a Month," *New York Times*, May 22, 2013, https://archive.nytimes.com/opinionator .blogs.nytimes.com/2013/05/22/a-by-the-e-book-education-for-5-a-month/; Tina Rosenberg, "Liberia, Desperate to Educate, Turns to Charter Schools," *New York Times*, June 14, 2016, https://www.nytimes.com/2016/06/14/opinion/liberia -desperate-to-educate-turns-to-charter-schools.html.

182   **questionable teaching model**: Jason Beaubien, "Do For-Profit Schools Give Poor Kenyans a Real Choice?," NPR, November 12, 2013, https://www.npr.org/sections /parallels/2013/11/12/243730652/do-for-profit-schools-give-poor-kenyans-a-real -choice.

182   **Teachers receive little training**: Peg Tyre, "Can a Tech Start-Up Successfully Educate Children in Africa?," Pulitzer Center, June 27, 2017, https://pulitzercenter.org /stories/can-tech-start-successfully-educate-children-africa.

182   **self-published performance data**: Leonie Haimson, "NYC Public School Parents: NY Times and 'Solutions Journalism' Ignore Their Own Conflict of Interest Guidelines in Promoting Gates Investments in Privatization," *NYC Public School Parents* (blog), August 30, 2016, https://nycpublicschoolparents.blogspot.com/2016/08/ny -times-and-solutions-journalism.html.

182   **"Liberia's educational system"**: Rosenberg also did not mention that more than one hundred organizations, mostly based in Africa, had called on the World Bank to stop supporting Bridge. "It is alarming that charging poor people school fees—something that the global community has worked particularly hard to abolish over the last two decades due to their negative impact on the poor—is being promoted as a means of ending poverty," the sign-on letter noted. In March 2022, the World Bank did divest from Bridge Academies, now called NewGlobe schools. "'Just' $6 a Month? The World Bank Will Not End Poverty by Promoting Fee-Charging, For-Profit Schools in Kenya and Uganda," sign-on letter available at https://web.archive.org /web/20151231074556/http://globalinitiative-escr.org/wp-content/uploads/2015 /05/May-2015-Join-statement-reaction-to-WB-statement-on-Bridge-14.05.2015 .pdf; "Civil Society Groups Celebrate IFC's Divestment from Profit-Driven School Chain Bridge International Academies," Oxfam International, March 16, 2022, https: //www.oxfam.org/en/press-releases/civil-society-groups-celebrate-ifcs-divestment -profit-driven-school-chain-bridge.

183   **"regularly hypes controversial"**: Schwab, "Journalism's Gates Keepers."

183   **the news outlet finally issued corrections**: Tim Schwab, "The Conflict over Conflicts of Interest," *Columbia Journalism Review*, August 18, 2021, https://www.cjr.org /analysis/conflict-of-interests-new-york-times.php. Note: Many columns remain uncorrected. Rosenberg's columns about Bridge International, for example, include no financial disclosures. Rosenberg and Bornstein argue that SJN's ties are to the Gates Foundation, not to Bill Gates himself, so no disclosure is needed for projects personally funded by Gates.

183   **Teachers United**: "Seattle Times' Gates-Funded Education Lab Blog Experiment," *Deutsch29: Mercedes Schneider's Blog* (blog), August 25, 2014, see comments, https:// deutsch29.wordpress.com/2014/08/24/seattle-times-gates-funded-education-lab -blog-experiment/.

184   **Bornstein and Rosenberg**: Solutions Journalism Network, IRS 990 filing, 2020.

185   **also funds housing**: Pam Fessler, "In Seattle, a Move Across Town Could Be a Path out of Poverty," NPR, August 5, 2019, https://www.npr.org/2019/08/05/747610085 /in-seattle-a-move-across-town-could-be-a-path-out-of-poverty.

186   **"changing media landscape"**: Paulson, "The Gates Foundation Conspiracy to Take over the Media."

186   **Modi's dismal record**: Malaka Gharib, "Gates Foundation's Humanitarian Award to India's Modi Is Sparking Outrage," NPR, September 17, 2019, https://www.npr.org /sections/goatsandsoda/2019/09/17/761664492/gates-foundations-humanitarian -award-to-indias-modi-is-sparking-outrage.

187   **Center for Global Development**: Nurith Aizenman, "Gates Foundation Says World Not on Track to Meet Goal of Ending Poverty by 2030," NPR, September 17, 2019, https://www.npr.org/sections/goatsandsoda/2019/09/17/761548939/gates -foundation-says-world-not-on-track-to-meet-goal-of-ending-poverty-by-2030; Schwab, "Journalism's Gates Keepers."

187   **moral authority on poverty**: Ari Shapiro, "Bill Gates Addresses 'Tough Questions' on Poverty and Power," NPR, February 13, 2018, https://www.npr.org/sections /goatsandsoda/2018/02/13/585346426/bill-gates-addresses-tough-questions-on -poverty-and-power/.

188   **fan of the *Economist***: Bill Gates, "Where Can I Get Unbiased News?," *GatesNotes*, March 8, 2010, https://www.gatesnotes.com/where-can-i-get-unbiased-news.

188   **"Healthy Partnerships"**: Economist Intelligence Unit, "Solutions" and "Public Policy"; *Healthy Partnerships: How Governments Can Engage the Private Sector to Improve Health in Africa*, World Bank and International Finance Corporation, 2011, v, http: //graphics.eiu.com/upload/eb/Healthy-Partnerships_ExecSummary_StandAlone.pdf.

188   **Economist Intelligence Unit promotes**: Economist Intelligence Unit, "Solutions."

189   **examples where news outlets**: In some of these cases, Gates is funding noneditorial content, like advertising, though it sometimes looks and feels like journalism: "Human Capital and the Benefits, Explained," Vox, September 11, 2018, https:// www.vox.com/ad/17846116/human-capital-africa-education-world-population; FastCo Works, "Five Renowned Designers Illustrate Global Health Stories You Should Know About"; Candid, "Gates Foundation Funds HuffPost Project to Fight Neglected Diseases"; Paul Raeburn, "Do Industry Partnerships Undermine

Journalistic Credibility?," Undark, April 22, 2016, https://undark.org/2016/04/22/do-industry-partnerships-undermine-journalistic-credibility/; "The Chronicle of Higher Education and the Gates Foundation."

189   **American Public Media**: Mike Janssen, "Gates Funding Spurs Doubts over Pubmedia's Impartiality in Education Reporting," September 9, 2014, https://current.org/2014/09/gates-funding-spurs-doubts-over-pubmedias-impartiality-in-education-reporting/. In this case, Gates gave the news outlet the money as a grant, but it would have been hard to trace. It appears to have been awarded to Minnesota Public Radio, not American Public Media, and the grant description does not mention that it was used for a project called LearningCurve.

189   **$720,000 to the Slate Group**: Note: In late 2021, after receiving Gates's donation, Slate released a podcast favorably profiling my critical reporting on Gates. Again, it's not that Gates-funded newsrooms can never report critically on Gates, just that it is difficult to do and rare; Mary Harris, "How Did a Billionaire in Seattle Gain So Much Power Over Global Public Health," *Slate*, October 27, 2021, https://slate.com/technology/2021/10/bill-gates-foundation-covax-botched-global-vaccine-rollout.html.

189   *The Hidden Economics of Remarkable Women*: Laura Rosbrow-Telem, "What Melinda French Gates and Esther Duflo Think Women Need Right Now," *Foreign Policy* (blog), February 10, 2023, https://foreignpolicy.com/podcasts/hidden-economics-of-remarkable-women-hero/melinda-french-gates-esther-duflo/.

190   **"value journalistic independence"**: "In 10 Years: Philanthropy Funds Journalism," Philanthropy Northwest, March 8, 2016, https://philanthropynw.org/news/10-years-philanthropy-funds-journalism.

CHAPTER 9: EDUCATION

192   **"fear a monopoly"**: "Q&A with Ken Auletta," C-SPAN, October 29, 2009, 38:30, https://www.c-span.org/video/?289705–1/qa-ken-auletta.

192   **"why the government was completely wrong"**: Jurgensen, "In Bill Gates's Mind, a Life of Processing."

193   **"like an electrical plug"**: Michael Q. McShane, "Bill Gates at AEI on the Common Core," *American Enterprise Institute-AEI* (blog), March 14, 2014, https://www.aei.org/education/bill-gates-at-aei-on-the-common-core.

193   **"50 different plug"**: Valerie Strauss, "Bill Gates Calls on Teachers to Defend Common Core," *Washington Post*, March 14, 2014, https://www.washingtonpost.com/local/education/bill-gates-calls-on-teachers-to-defend-common-core/2014/03/14/395b130a-aafa-11e3-98f6-8e3c562f9996_story.html.

193   **marketplace of ideas**: Bill Gates, speech at the National Conference of State Legislatures, July 21, 2009, prepared remarks available through Web archive at https://web.archive.org/web/20090725061207/https://www.gatesfoundation.org/speeches-commentary/Pages/bill-gates-2009-conference-state-legislatures.aspx.

193   **civil rights issue**: Kevin Chappell, "One-on-One with Bill Gates: 'Why Aren't There Protests Every Day?,'" *Ebony*, October 2011, https://web.archive.org/web/20111104123826/http://www.ebonyjet.com/CurrentIssue/Oct2011_BillGates.aspx;

Alan Hughes, "Bill Gates Talks Innovation," *Black Enterprise* (blog), October 10, 2011, https://www.blackenterprise.com/bill-gates-talks-innovation/.

193   **newslike NBC program**: "Education Nation 2011: Summit," NBC News, February 12, 2014, https://www.nbcnews.com/feature/education-nation/education-nation-2011 -summit-n11681.

193   **The *Atlantic***: "The State of Education: Rebuilding a More Equitable System," *Atlantic*, October 27, 2022, https://www.theatlantic.com/live/state-of-edu-2021/; "Rebuilding the American Dream," *Atlantic*, 2017, https://www.theatlantic.com/sponsored/gates -foundation-2017/rebuilding-the-american-dream/1458/.

194   **spent sixty million dollars**: David M. Herszenhorn, "Billionaires Start $60 Million Schools Effort," *New York Times*, April 25, 2007, https://www.nytimes.com/2007/04/25 /education/25schools.html; Bill & Melinda Gates Foundation, "Strong American Schools Campaign Launches to Promote Education Reform in 2008 Presidential Election," April 25, 2007, https://web.archive.org/web/20070528182916/http://www.gatesfoundation .org/UnitedStates/Education/Announcements/Announce-070425a.htm.

194   **so ubiquitous**: Lyndsey Layton, "How Bill Gates Pulled Off the Swift Common Core Revolution," *Washington Post*, June 7, 2014, https://www.washingtonpost.com/politics /how-bill-gates-pulled-off-the-swift-common-core-revolution/2014/06/07/a830e32e -ec34-11e3-9f5c-9075d5508f0a_story.html; Matthew Bishop and Michael Green, "Billionaires Learn Giving Is Only a Start," *New York Times*, November 12, 2009, https://www.nytimes.com/2009/11/12/giving/12ESSAY.html. Note: Some of these revolving door characters got conflict-of-interest waivers that allowed them to work directly with Gates while in the federal government. See Stephanie Simon and Erin Mershon, "Gates Masters D.C.—and the World," Politico, February 4, 2014, https:// www.politico.com/story/2014/02/bill-gates-microsoft-policy-washington-103136.

194   **"tremendous distrust"**: Andrew Ross Sorkin, "So Bill Gates Has This Idea for a History Class . . . ," *New York Times*, September 5, 2014, https://www.nytimes .com/2014/09/07/magazine/so-bill-gates-has-this-idea-for-a-history-class.html; Caitlin Emma, "Exclusive: AFT Shuns Gates Funding—Success Academy Lawsuit Simmering—Defenders of the Common Core—Feds Grant California a Testing Pass," Politico, March 10, 2014, https://www.politico.com/tipsheets/morning-education /2014/03/exclusive-aft-shuns-gates-funding-success-academy-lawsuit-simmering -defenders-of-the-common-core-feds-grant-california-a-testing-pass-212543.

195   **diverse and widespread support**: Daniel Katz, "How to Spot a Fake Grassroots Educa-tion Reform Group," *Daniel Katz, Ph.D.* (blog), September 5, 2014, https://danielskatz .net/2014/09/05/how-to-spot-a-fake-grassroots-education-reform-group/.

195   **$11 million in grants**: "The Campaign for High School Equity Launch and Press Briefing," Campaign for High School Equity, June 19, 2007, https://web.archive .org/web/20070627101507/http://www.highschoolequity.org/ and https://web.archive .org/web/20071214220115/http://www.highschoolequity.org/about; Campaign for High School Equity, "Campaign for High School Equity Calls for ESEA That Ensures Success for All Students," PR Newswire, March 18, 2010, https://www.prnewswire .com/news-releases/campaign-for-high-school-equity-calls-for-esea-that-ensures -success-for-all-students-88403092.html.

195 **elevate its message**: Jessica E. Gross, employee post-travel disclosure form, U.S. House of Representatives Committee on Ethics, November 23, 2009; Kaitlyn Montan, employee post-travel disclosure form, U.S. House of Representatives Committee on Ethics, June 10, 2019. Note: In 2015, a Gates Foundation program officer, Danielle Gonzales, according to her profile on LinkedIn (https://www.linkedin.com/in /danielle-gonzales-0505/), left Gates to help run the Education and Society Program at Aspen, which is funded by the Gates Foundation. In the invitations it sends to members of Congress, Aspen trumpets its independence, noting, "Funding [for its work] is provided solely by grants from established foundations; no government, individual, foreign, corporate, or special interest money is accepted. The Network is supported by the Bill & Melinda Gates Foundation." Wendell Primes, employee post-travel disclosure form, U.S. House of Representatives Committee on Ethics, November 25, 2019.

195 **multipronged political campaign**: Layton, "How Bill Gates Pulled Off the Swift Common Core Revolution."

195 **challenging questions**: Layton's investigation into the foundation appeared in 2014— after both Warren Buffett and Melinda French Gates had stepped down from the *Washington Post*'s board, in 2011 and 2010, respectively. Would such a hard and high-profile investigation of Gates have been possible in 2010? "Warren Buffett to Retire from the Board of the Washington Post Company," Press Release, Graham Holdings Company, January 20, 2011, https://www.ghco.com/news-releases/news-release -details/warren-buffett-retire-board-washington-post-company/; "Melinda French Gates Leaves the Board of the Washington Post Company," Press Release, Graham Holdings Company, November 12, 2010, https://www.ghco.com/news-releases/news -release-details/melinda-french-gates-leaves-board-washington-post-company.

195 **A transcript**: My thanks to Mercedes Schneider for transcribing the video and posting it to her blog, found at https://deutsch29.wordpress.com/2014/06/21/transcript -of-gates-march-2014-washington-post-interview/.

198 **manufactures consent**: Sarah Reckhow and Megan Tompkins-Stange, "'Singing from the Same Hymnbook': Education Policy Advocacy at Gates and Broad," American Enterprise Institute, February 5, 2015, https://www.aei.org/wp-content/uploads /2015/01/Reckhow-Tompkins-Stange.pdf?x91208.

199 **"which states needed shoring up"**: Layton, "How Bill Gates Pulled Off the Swift Common Core Revolution."

199 **jettisoning them**: Layton, "How Bill Gates Pulled Off the Swift Common Core Revolution."

199 **rebranded them**: Peter Elkind, "How Business Got Schooled in the War over Common Core," *Fortune*, December 23, 2015, https://fortune.com/longform/common -core-standards/.

199 **Diane Ravitch**: Diane Ravitch, "Gates Foundation Funds 'Consumer Reports' for Common Core Resources," *Diane Ravitch's Blog*, August 15, 2014, https://dianeravitch .net/2014/08/15/gates-foundation-funds-consumer-reports-for-common-core -resources/.

200 **EdReports.org**: Caitlin Emma, "A 'Consumer Reports' for the Common Core— Another Louisiana Lawsuit Due in Court Today—New App Designed by Obama

Administration Targets Bullying," Politico, August 15, 2014, https://www.politico
.com/tipsheets/morning-education/2014/08/a-consumer-reports-for-the-common
-core-another-louisiana-lawsuit-due-in-court-today-new-app-designed-by-obama
-administration-targets-bullying-212543.

200 **"impose new and untested"**: Valerie Strauss, "Ravitch: Time for Congress to Investigate Bill Gates' Role in Common Core," *Washington Post*, June 9, 2014, https://
www.washingtonpost.com/news/answer-sheet/wp/2014/06/09/ravitch-time-for
-congress-to-investigate-bill-gates-role-in-common-core/.

200 **didn't actually do**: Valerie Strauss, "Why the Common Core Standards Failed—and
What It Means for School Reform," *Washington Post*, April 5, 2021, https://www
.washingtonpost.com/education/2021/04/05/common-core-failed-school-reform/;
Matt Barnum, "Nearly a Decade Later, Did the Common Core Work?," Chalkbeat,
April 29, 2019, https://www.chalkbeat.org/2019/4/29/21121004/nearly-a-decade
-later-did-the-common-core-work-new-research-offers-clues.

200 **failed to deliver results**: Valerie Strauss, "How Much Bill Gates's Disappointing
Small-Schools Effort Really Cost," *Washington Post*, November 30, 2021, https://www
.washingtonpost.com/news/answer-sheet/wp/2014/06/09/how-much-bill-gatess
-disappointing-small-schools-effort-really-cost/.

201 **"rounding error"**: Village Global, "Bill Gates on Startups, Investing and Solving the
World's Hardest Problems," 31:00.

201 **"starting to show"**: Village Global, "Bill Gates on Startups, Investing and Solving the
World's Hardest Problems," 34:00.

201 **around 13 percent**: Analysis of Gates Foundation grant records. Note: These analyses are not clear-cut because of the way the foundation codes its grants. For example,
the foundation codes most, but not all, of Gates's giving to Lakeside, the private
school the Gates children attended, not as related to "education" but, rather, as "community engagement." My analysis found $10.8 billion for projects that the Gates
Foundation's grant database codes as being related to education.

202 **"no reason to give up"**: Gates and Gates, "Why We Swing for the Fences."

202 **"rather odd"**: Wallace and Erickson, *Hard Drive*, 57.

202 **computerlike cognition**: *Inside Bill's Brain*, episode 2, at 22:55.

203 **"think weeks"**: Catherine Clifford, "Bill Gates Took Solo 'Think Weeks' in a Cabin
in the Woods—Why It's a Great Strategy," CNBC, July 28, 2019, https://www.cnbc
.com/2019/07/26/bill-gates-took-solo-think-weeks-in-a-cabin-in-the-woods.html;
Julian Hayes II, "In the 1980s, Bill Gates Would Escape to a Secret Cabin in the
Woods to Protect Himself from Burnout. Here's the Modern-Day, Easier Version of
His Approach," *Business Insider*, August 2, 2019, https://www.businessinsider.com
/bill-gates-took-think-weeks-the-1980s-launched-internet-explorer-2019-8.

203 **has given more than 100 million dollars**: Schwab, "Bill Gates Gives to the Rich
(Including Himself)."

203 **"It's chaos"**: *Inside Bill's Brain*, episode 2 at 2:00.

203 **"he literally thinks"**: "She Advocated for Women, Then Microsoft Pushed Her Off
Its Board—with Maria Klawe," *Big Technology Podcast*, July 8, 2021, 33:00, https://
podcasts.apple.com/us/podcast/she-advocated-for-women-then-microsoft-pushed
-her-off/id1522960417?i=1000528138094.

204 **"ignore the inequitable"**: Anthony Cody, *The Educator and the Oligarch: A Teacher Challenges the Gates Foundation* (New York: Garn Press, 2014).

205 **"wiggled around"**: Rich Karlgaard, "Talent Wars," *Forbes*, October 31, 2005, https://www.forbes.com/forbes/2005/1031/045.html?sh=5e9677c775dd.

205 **"Black and Latino"**: "K–12 Education," Bill & Melinda Gates Foundation," n.d., https://www.gatesfoundation.org/our-work/programs/us-program/k-12-education.

205 **"free time"**: Allison, "Transcript of a Video History Interview with Mr. William 'Bill' Gates."

206 **same rich educational experiences**: Loudenback, "Bill Gates' Kids May Not Inherit His Fortune, but He Is Setting Them Up for Success in Other Ways."

206 **This is from the PhD dissertation**: Allison Ragland, "Sustaining Black Captivity: A Critical Analysis of Corporate Philanthropic Discourse on Education" (PhD diss., Ohio State University, 2019), https://etd.ohiolink.edu/apexprod/rws_etd/send_file/send?accession=osu1555411670630373&disposition=inline.

207 **"bottom of the rich countries"**: "Bill Gates Interview on Oprah Farewell 2010.09.20."

207 **$575 million**: Tony Wan, "The Gates Foundation Spent $200M+ Trying to Improve Teacher Performance, and All It Got Was This Report," EdSurge, June 29, 2018, https://www.edsurge.com/news/2018-06-29-the-gates-foundation-spent-200m-trying-to-improve-teacher-performance-and-all-it-got-was-this-report; Brian M. Stecher et al., *Improving Teaching Effectiveness: Final Report: The Intensive Partnerships for Effective Teaching Through 2015–2016*, RAND Corporation, June 21, 2018, 333, https://www.rand.org/pubs/research_reports/RR2242.html.

207 **"most decisive factor"**: Gates, speech at the National Conference of State Legislatures.

208 **$100 million**: Marlene Sokol, "Sticker Shock: How Hillsborough County's Gates Grant Became a Budget Buster," *Tampa Bay Times*, December 15, 2015, https://www.tampabay.com/news/education/k12/sticker-shock-how-hillsborough-countys-gates-grant-became-a-budget-buster/2250988/.

208 **"system was encouraging"**: Bill Gates, "For Teachers, Shame Is No Solution," *New York Times*, February 22, 2012, https://www.nytimes.com/2012/02/23/opinion/for-teachers-shame-is-no-solution.html.

208 **another $50 million**: Sokol, "Sticker Shock"; Marlene Sokol, "Hillsborough Schools to Dismantle Gates-Funded System That Cost Millions to Develop," *Tampa Bay Times*, October 30, 2015, https://www.tampabay.com/news/education/k12/eakins-panel-will-help-hillsborough-schools-move-on-from-the-gates-grant/2251811/.

209 **name-and-shame exercise**: High school math teacher Gary Rubinstein found important contradictions in Gates's evaluation schema, noting that elementary school teachers who teach the same students both math and English often receive widely varying evaluation scores teaching these two subjects. "Looking through the data," Rubinstein wrote on his blog, "I noticed teachers, like a 5th grade teacher at P.S. 196 who scored 97 out of 100 in language arts and 2 out of 100 in math. This is with the same students in the same year! How can a teacher be so good and so bad at the same time? Any evaluation system in which this can happen is extremely flawed, of course, but I wanted to explore if this was a major outlier or if it was something quite common. I ran the numbers and the results shocked me (which is pretty hard to do). Here's what I learned . . . Out of 5,675 elementary school teachers, the average differ-

ence between the two scores was a whopping 22 points." Gary Rubinstein, "Analyz-ing Released NYC Value-Added Data Part 2," *TeachForUs* (blog), February 28, 2012, https://web.archive.org/web/20120305214412/https://garyrubinstein.teachforus.org /2012/02/28/analyzing-released-nyc-value-added-data-part-2/.

209   **committed suicide**: Ian Lovett, "Teacher's Death Exposes Tensions in Los Ange-les," *New York Times*, November 9, 2010, https://www.nytimes.com/2010/11/10 /education/10teacher.html.

209   **"not for sale!"**: Taylor Soper, "Teachers Protest in Downtown Seattle, Say Bill Gates Is Ruining Education," GeekWire, June 27, 2014, https://www.geekwire.com/2014 /teachers-protest-gates-foundation/; Jesse Hagopian, "Debating the Gates Foun-dation," *Socialist Worker*, March 13, 2012, https://socialistworker.org/2012/03/13 /debating-the-gates-foundation.

209   **"shaming poorly performing teachers"**: Gates, "For Teachers, Shame Is No Solution."

210   **preposterous good-cop routine**: Anthony Cody, "Teachers Face Good Cops or Bad Cops in Push for Evaluations," *EdWeek*, February 29, 2012, https://www.edweek .org/policy-politics/opinion-teachers-face-good-cops-or-bad-cops-in-push-for -evaluations/2012/02.

212   **or an exclamation point**: Stecher et al., *Improving Teaching Effectiveness*.

212   **Smiling, quiet, obedient**: "Better Connected, Future Vision," inBloom, video avail-able at https://vimeo.com/60661666.

212   **plumbing infrastructure**: Tricia Duryee, "Gates-Backed InBloom Winding Down After Non-Profit Faces Concerns over Privacy," video (at 53:40 and 56:00), Gee-kWire, April 21, 2014, https://www.geekwire.com/2014/gates-backed-inbloom -winding-non-profit-faces-concerns-privacy/. Note: The group changed its name from the Shared Learning Collaborative to inBloom early in its history. In 2011, Shared Learning Collaborative was incorporated in the state of Washington as a limited liability company. The same year, the Gates Foundation's annual tax filing reported that SLC was a "controlled entity," which, according to IRS rules, means Gates owned more than 50 percent of it. Documents from Gates and inBloom widely describe the project as a "non-profit." It's not clear that the project ever had 501c3 status. See "Shared Learning Collaborative Blossoms into 'inBloom Inc.,'" EdSurge, February 5, 2013, https://www.edsurge.com/news/2013-02-05-the-shared -learning-collaborative-gets-a-new-name-inbloom-inc; Query of Washington State Corporations and Charities Filing System; "Exempt Organizations Annual Report-ing Requirements—Form 990, Schedule R: 'Related Organization' and 'Controlled Entity' Reporting Differences," Internal Revenue Service, n.d., https://www.irs.gov /charities-non-profits/exempt-organizations-annual-reporting-requirements-form -990-schedule-r-related-organization-and-controlled-entity-reporting-differences.

213   **$4.35 billion**: Monica Bulger, Patrick McCormick, and Mikaela Pitcan, "The Legacy of InBloom," Data and Society, February 2, 2017, 11, https://datasociety.net/pubs/ecl /InBloom_feb_2017.pdf.

213   **helping states write**: Lyndsey Layton, "Common Standards for Nation's Schools a Longtime Goal," *Washington Post*, June 9, 2014, https://www.washingtonpost.com /local/education/common-standards-for-nations-schools-a-longtime-goal/2014/06 /09/cbe7e9ec-edb1-11e3-92b8-52344c12e8a1_story.html.

213   **"the database tracks"**: Stephanie Simon, "K–12 Student Database Jazzes Tech Startups, Spooks Parents," Reuters, March 3, 2013, https://web.archive.org/web /20130304030215/https://www.reuters.com/article/2013/03/03/us-education -database-idUSBRE92204W20130303.

214   **a major scandal involving data privacy:** Ruth McCambridge, "NY Parents Protest Foundation-Funded inBloom Educaiton Data Portal," *Non-Profit Quarterly,* May 2, 2013, https://nonprofitquarterly.org/ny-parents-protest-foundation-funded -inbloom-education-data-portal/.

214   **was shuttered upon news:** Jim Watterson, "News of the World: 10 Years Since Phone-Hacking Scandal Brought Down Tabloid," *Guardian,* July 10, 2021, https://www .theguardian.com/media/2021/jul/10/news-of-the-world-10-years-since-phone -hacking-scandal-brought-down-tabloid.

214   **Like dominoes:** Molly Hensley-Clancy, "How Rupert Murdoch Suffered a Rare Defeat in American Classrooms," BuzzFeed News, August 24, 2015, https://www .buzzfeednews.com/article/mollyhensleyclancy/how-rupert-murdoch-suffered-a -rare-defeat-in-american-classr; Natasha Singer, "inBloom Student Data Repository to Close," *New York Times,* April 21, 2014, https://archive.nytimes.com/bits.blogs .nytimes.com/2014/04/21/inbloom-student-data-repository-to-close/.

214   **independent appraisal:** Pivotal Ventures did not begin funding Data and Society until 2018, after the report on inBloom was published in 2017. Data and Society claims on its website that "We do not accept funding that would affect our ability to pursue work free of external interference, and we fiercely protect the independence of our researchers and fellows in their intellectual activities and individual funding relationships." "Data and Society Funder List," Data and Society Research Institute, n.d., https://datasociety.net/wp-content/uploads/2022/02/Funders-List-2021-Feb -2022.pdf; "About," Data and Society Research Institute, n.d., https://datasociety.net /about/.

214   **Any future U.S. edtech:"** Bulger, McCormick, and Pitcan, "The Legacy of InBloom."

215   **data collection:** "Report Offers Recommendations for How Systems Can Access and Use Postsecondary Outcomes Data to Support Students' Success," *Chiefs for Change* (blog), December 1, 2021, https://www.chiefsforchange.org/2021/12/01/report-offers -recommendations-for-how-systems-can-access-and-use-postsecondary-outcomes -data-to-support-students-success/. Note: Alongside the foundation's data collection efforts in education, it has a growing portfolio of projects aimed at what it calls "digital inclusion." This encompasses new digital banking systems and digital identification schemes aimed at promoting equity, such as bringing underrepresented communities onto a platform where they can more fully join the modern economy. In 2022, New York University's Center for Human Rights and Global Justice published a long report profiling the potential dangers of such efforts, specifically citing the Gates Foundation's key funding to groups working in this space, like G2Px, MOSIP, the Digital Impact Alliance, ID4D, ID4Africa, and the GSMA Foundation. "Proponents have cloaked this new paradigm in the language of human rights and inclusion," the report notes. "Like physical roads, national digital identification systems with biometric components (digital ID systems) are presented as the public infrastructure of the digital future. Yet these particular infrastructures have proven to

be dangerous, having been linked to severe and large-scale human rights violations in a range of countries around the world, affecting social, civil, and political rights. The benefits, meanwhile, remain ill-defined and poorly documented. Indeed, those who stand to benefit the most may not be those 'left behind,' but a small group of companies and security-minded governments." *Paving a Digital Road to Hell: A Primer on the Role of the World Bank and Global Networks in Promoting Digital ID*, Center for Human Rights and Global Justice, NYU School of Law, June 2022, https://chrgj.org/wp-content/uploads/2022/06/Report_Paving-a-Digital-Road-to-Hell.pdf.

215 **bankruptcy proceedings**: Natasha Singer, "Federal Regulators Seek to Stop Sale of Students' Data," *New York Times*, https://archive.nytimes.com/bits.blogs.nytimes.com/2014/05/23/federal-regulators-seek-to-stop-sale-of-students-data/.

216 **Amazon and Cisco**: Jeff Bryant and Velislava Hillman, "How Big Businesses Are Colonizing the Classroom," Progressive.org, February 16, 2022, https://progressive.org/api/content/45cc4ab4-89c7-11ec-80f6-12f1225286c6/.

216 **Out of these discussions**: Mercedes K. Schneider, *Common Core Dilemma: Who Owns Our Schools?* (New York: Teachers College Press, 2015), 20–22, 27.

216 **"comprehensive benchmarking"**: The foundation announced its first four grants for K–12 education in October 1999, with money going to Achieve, Partnership for Learning, Public Agenda, and West Seattle High School. The foundation's grant records show $350 million for projects explicitly described as for "common core" or "CCSS" (Common Core State Standards), but it is virtually certain that the real number is significantly higher. Jack Hassard, professor emeritus at Georgia State University, in 2014 estimated that Gates had spent $2.3 billion to advance Common Core. Jack Hassard, "Why Bill Gates Defends the Common Core," *Art of Teaching Science* (blog), March 15, 2014, https://jackhassard.org/why-bill-gates-defends-the-common-core/.

216 **Rex Tillerson**: Erin Kourkounis, "CEOs Tout Benefits of Common Core Standards," *Tampa Tribune*, October 28, 2013.

216 **"on the decline"**: Glenn Britt, "Investing in Innovation," *Forbes*, March 1, 2010, https://www.forbes.com/2010/03/01/science-technology-education-thought-leaders-britt.html?sh=60dc6d571eee.

217 **"regulatory capture"**: McShane, "Bill Gates at AEI on the Common Core."

217 **beef up**: "Is Bill Gates a Closet Liberal?," Salon, January 29, 1998, https://web.archive.org/web/20120607021236/https://www.salon.com/1998/01/29/feature_349/.

217 **paid low wages**: Daniel Costa, "STEM Labor Shortages? Microsoft Report Distorts Reality About Computing Occupations," Economic Policy Institute, November 19, 2012, https://www.epi.org/publication/pm195-stem-labor-shortages-microsoft-report-distorts/; Daniel Costa and Ron Hira, "H-1B Visas and Prevailing Wage Levels," Economic Policy Institute, May 4, 2020, https://www.epi.org/publication/h-1b-visas-and-prevailing-wage-levels/.

217 **"fought tooth and nail"**: Neil Krauss, "Support the Page Amendment, but Let's Not Pretend We Can Educate Ourselves out of Inequality," *MinnPost*, November 1, 2021, https://www.minnpost.com/community-voices/2021/11/support-the-page-amendment-but-lets-not-pretend-we-can-educate-ourselves-out-of-inequality/?hilite=neil+kraus.

218 **the "skills gap" narrative**: The foundation appears explicit about its research bias, noting, "We will support research, communications, and policy analysis efforts that highlight the importance of doubling the number of young people who earn a post-secondary credential." That is, Gates appears to fund research aimed at supporting its preformulated conclusion that the U.S. labor market requires a vastly better-educated workforce. Bill & Melinda Gates Foundation, *Postsecondary Success*, 2009, https://docs.gatesfoundation.org/documents/postsecondary-education-success -plan-brochure.pdf.

218 **"mission to help"**: Sara Rimer, "Gates Grants Aim to Help Low-Income Students Finish College," *New York Times*, December 9, 2008, https://www.nytimes.com/2008 /12/09/education/09gates.html; "Measuring Up 2008," National Center for Public Policy and Higher Education, 2008, 2, https://files.eric.ed.gov/fulltext/ED503494 .pdfhttps://web.archive.org/web/20090613023059/http://cew.georgetown.edu/mission .htmlhttps://web.archive.org/web/20201203174944/https://cew.georgetown.edu/about -us/https://web.archive.org/web/20201203165447/https://cew.georgetown.edu/about -us/faqs/https://cew.georgetown.edu/about-us/.

218 **"requiring at least a two-year"**: Jacques Steinberg, "More Employers to Require Some College, Report Says," *New York Times*, June 14, 2010, https://www.nytimes .com/2010/06/15/education/15degree.html.

218 **"about two-thirds"**: Anthony Carnevale, Nicole Smith, and Jeff Strohl, *Help Wanted: Projections of Jobs and Education Requirements Through 2018*, Center on Education and the Workforce at Georgetown University, June 2010, https://cewgeorgetown .wpenginepowered.com/wp-content/uploads/2014/12/fullreport.pdf.

218 **"point of numbness"**: Goldie Blumenstyk, "By 2020, They Said, 2 out of 3 Jobs Would Need More than a High-School Diploma. Were They Right?," *Chronicle of Higher Education*, January 22, 2020, https://www.chronicle.com/newsletter/the-edge /2020-01-22.

218 **high school equivalent**: U.S. Bureau of Labor Statistics, Employment Projections, Data, "Occupations That Need More Education for Entry Are Projected to Grow Faster than Average," Table 5.2: "Employment, Wages, and Projected Change in Employment by Typical Entry-Level Education," n.d., https://www.bls.gov/emp /tables/education-summary.htm.

219 **underemployed**: Federal Reserve Bank of New York, Economic Research, "Underemployment Rates for College Graduates," table, n.d., https://www.newyorkfed.org /research/college-labor-market/index.html#/underemployment.

219 **"the great equalizer"**: Bill & Melinda Gates Foundation, *Postsecondary Success*.

219 **"cradle to career"**: Bill & Melinda Gates Foundation, "Road Map Project," May 2013, https://docs.gatesfoundation.org/documents/BMGF_RoadmapProject_SIO_062413 _r4_onln.pdf.

219 **reverse-engineered**: Elkind, "How Business Got Schooled in the War over Common Core."

220 **"redesigning financial aid"**: Simon and Mershon, "Gates Masters D.C.—and the World."

220 **"labor-market success"**: Elizabeth Warren, "The College Transparency Act of 2017," May 15, 2017, https://www.warren.senate.gov/files/documents/2017_05_15_College

_Transparency_One_Pager.pdf. Note: This language is virtually indistinguishable from the foundation's own rhetoric from at least as far back as 2009: "Many colleges have little access to real-time knowledge if and when their students are beginning to drop out. Administrators have inconsistent access to data that ensure their programs are aligned with labor market demand. Students make critical choices about where to go to college and what to major in with little data about program quality or graduates' success. Without better data, educators, students, and policymakers lack the information they need to make good decisions that will support and reinforce a commitment to completion." Bill & Melinda Gates Foundation, *Postsecondary Success*.

220 **equity and justice**: Valerie Strauss, "Congress May Create Massive Program to Collect College Student Data," *Washington Post*, April 4, 2022, https://www .washingtonpost.com/education/2022/04/04/congress-student-data-collect-privacy/; Scott Jaschik, "House Approves College Transparency Act," *Inside Higher Ed*, February 7, 2022, https://www.insidehighered.com/news/2022/02/07/house-passes -college-transparency-act.

CHAPTER 10: WHITE MAN'S BURDEN

223 **paintings and photography**: National Portrait Gallery, *Portrait of Bill and Melinda Gates*, Object no. NPG.2010.83, https://www.si.edu/newsdesk/photos/bill-and-melinda -gates-portrait.

223 **Board of Regents**: Robin Pogrebin, "New Chairwoman Poised to Reform Smithsonian," *New York Times*, September 21, 2008, https://www.nytimes.com/2008/09/22 /arts/22muse.html; "Patty Stonesifer Elected Chair of Smithsonian Board of Regents," Smithsonian Institution, September 22, 2008, https://www.si.edu/newsdesk/releases /patty-stonesifer-elected-chair-smithsonian-board-regents. Note: Freedom of Information Act requests to the Smithsonian returned extremely heavily redacted documents that failed to delineate how much the National Portrait Gallery had paid for the Gateses' portrait or who had first proposed a portrait of them. The unredacted portions of the document do not cite Stonesifer as having any role in the decision. The National Portrait Gallery reports that the commission was decided upon in May 2008, a time when Stonesifer was on the Smithsonian's Board of Regents. She became the chair a few months later. Also notable: Even after she left her CEO position at the Gates Foundation, she remained a senior adviser there.

225 **"on a safari"**: Melinda Gates, "The Story of How Melinda Gates Met Bill Gates," Interview, Salesforce, December 1, 2016, https://www.youtube.com/watch?v =VqsFbzTcpdc.

225 **even their own wine expert**: Joss Kent (as told to Charlotte Metcalf), "Travel Safaris," *Spectator*, July 18, 2009, https://webcache.googleusercontent.com/search?q =cache:tx14f54M4J4J:https://reader.exacteditions.com/issues/5493/page/44&cd=3 &hl=en&ct=clnk&gl=us&client=firefox-b-1-d.

225 **"But it's really not at all trite"**: Gates, "The Story of How Melinda Gates Met Bill Gates," 2:50.

225 **"capitalistic societies"**: Melinda French Gates, Interview by Becky Quick, CNBC, April 24, 2019, https://www.youtube.com/watch?v=J9Xs5RF7qBk. Note: A 2021

survey by the Alliance for Democracies found that 44 percent of people, from 53 different countries, said they see the United States as a threat to their democracies. Some of the strongest sentiments about the United States came from the poorest nations. "Global Poll: Despite Grim Views of Democracies' Covid Response, People Around the World Want More Democracy," Press Release, Alliance of Democracies, 2021, n.d., https://www.allianceofdemocracies.org/initiatives/the-copenhagen -democracy-summit/dpi-2021.

225 **"That's really unsafe for the baby"**: "Administrator Samantha Power at Global Child Care Infrastructure Event," USAID, April 28, 2022, https://www.usaid.gov /news-information/press-releases/apr-28-2022-administrator-samantha-power -global-child-care-infrastructure-event.

226 **"This is the clearest illustration"**: Geneva Health Files (@filesgeneva), Twitter, April 29, 2022, https://twitter.com/FilesGeneva/status/1520154341264572416; Themrise Khan (@themrise), Twitter, April 30, 2022, https://twitter.com/themrise/status/1520 308825303179266.

226 **practice of hegemony**: Analysis of Gates Foundation's charitable grants based in part on World Bank classification of high-income countries. "World Bank Country and Lending Groups—World Bank Data Help Desk," n.d., https://datahelpdesk.worldbank .org/knowledgebase/articles/906519-world-bank-country-and-lending-groups.

227 **"phantom aid"**: "Phantom Aid: Money Allocated to Countries That Ends Up Funding INGOs," *Global Health Justice* (blog), n.d., https://depts.washington.edu /globalhealthjustice/category/phantom-aid/.

227 **McKinsey consultant**: John Aglionby, "EthioChicken: Ethiopia's Well-Hatched Idea," *Financial Times*, March 15, 2018; "Joseph Shields," LinkedIn, n.d., https://www .linkedin.com/in/joseph-shields-5338009/. Note: Gates's $12 million in donations to EthioChicken and its investor, Flow Equity, oddly, don't go to Ethiopia. They go to Mauritius, a renowned tax haven. The company did not respond to press inquiries.

227 **"very little knowledge"**: Peter Buffett, "The Charitable-Industrial Complex," *New York Times,* July 26, 2013, https://www.nytimes.com/2013/07/27/opinion/the-charitable -industrial-complex.html?_r=0.

228 **widespread dependence on Buffett's largesse**: Sean Cooper, "What Happens When a Buffett Buys Your Town?," *Tablet*, July 13, 2021, https://www.tabletmag.com /sections/news/articles/buffett-kingston-sean-cooper.

228 **"you want to fix governance"**: Gates, "Watch the Full Bill Gates Keynote," 30:52.

228 **"a third of the world"**: Gates, "Watch the Full Bill Gates Keynote," 31:30.

229 **"a robot that can go out"**: Gates, "Watch the Full Bill Gates Keynote," 3:10.

229 **McCoy identified**: McCoy et al., "The Bill & Melinda Gates Foundation's Grant-Making Programme for Global Health," 1645–53.

230 **the racism he experienced**: Daniel Kamanga, "I've Had Racism's Weight of Knee on My Neck; Will George Floyd's Death Give Me a Chance to Breath?," LinkedIn, June 5, 2020, https://web.archive.org/web/20220104010414/https://www.linkedin.com /pulse/ive-had-racisms-weight-knee-my-neck-george-floyds-death-kamanga/.

230 **accusations of racist behavior**: Das, Flitter, and Kulish, "A Culture of Fear at the Firm That Manages Bill Gates's Fortune."

230 **Lucica Ditiu**: Apoorva Mandavilli, "A Global Health Star Under Fire," *New York*

Times, September 12, 2020, https://www.nytimes.com/2020/09/12/health/ditiu-stoptb-united-nations.html.

230 **$2.5 million**: "United Nations Office for Project Services, Geneva," Bill & Melinda Gates Foundation, June 2021, https://www.gatesfoundation.org/about/committed-grants/2021/06/opp1216273.

230 **Erika Arthun**: "Members of the Board," Stop TB Partnership, n.d., https://www.stoptb.org/board/members-of-board.

231 **"lesson in Neocolonialism"**: Julia Feliz, "Response to Cornell SA Meeting," *Medium* (blog), October 25, 2019, https://medium.com/@jd.feliz/response-to-cornell-sa-meeting-69b7ca9e288e.

231 **A resolution**: Meghna Maharishi, "S.A. Passes Statement in Support of Julia Feliz as Some Fellows Push Back," *Cornell Daily Sun*, October 25, 2019, https://cornellsun.com/2019/10/25/s-a-passes-statement-in-support-of-julia-feliz-as-some-fellows-pushback/.

231 **"become champions for global development"**: "Homepage," Generation Africa Voices, n.d., https://www.generationafricavoices.org/.

231 **authentic African misery**: Generation Africa, storyteller profiles of Louis Lakor, Aisha Nabukeera, and Rachael Ouko, n.d., https://www.generationafricavoices.org/#glide-cohort.

232 **The Moth's board of directors**: The Moth, Board & Committees, n.d., http://themoth.org/board-committees; "International Women's Day: Stories of Redefining Motherhood," Gates Discovery Center, March 8, 2023, https://www.discovergates.org/international-womens-day-stories-of-redefining-motherhood/.

232 **hand in hand**: Diane Cardoso, "A Look at Global Stories of Women and Girls," The Moth, March 27, 2018, https://themoth.org/dispatches/a-look-at-global-stories.

232 **nearly 2,000 public op-eds**: "Locally Rooted, Globally Networked," New Voices Fellowship, https://web.archive.org/web/20220512094414/https://newvoicesfellows.aspeninstitute.org/

232 **holds a seat on its board**: "Our Board," Speak Up Africa, n.d., https://www.speakupafrica.org/our-board/. Note: The Gates Foundation reports making donations to a Speak Up Africa in New York and in Senegal. The foundation reports the two organizations share the same website. An email sent to Speak Up Africa, at its New York office, requesting information about its organizational structure, its most recent tax filing, and an interview did not get a response. Questions sent by email to Speak Up Africa in Senegal also did not get a response.

232 **Trump Building**: Speak Up Africa, IRS filing 990, 2015. Note: The group listed its address in 2015 as 40 Wall Street in New York, a building sometimes colloquially called the Trump Building (after Donald Trump); "40 Wall Street: New York, NY," The Trump Organization, n.d., https://www.trump.com/commercial-real-estate-portfolio/40-wall-street.

232 **high-tech sewage**: "The Gates Foundation's Approach Has Both Advantages and Limits," *Economist*, September 30, 2021, https://www.economist.com/international/2021/09/16/the-gates-foundations-approach-has-both-advantages-and-limits.

233 **only around 10 percent**: Bill & Melinda Gates Foundation, "DEI Progress Report," 2021, https://docs.gatesfoundation.org/documents/bill_and_melinda_gates_foundation

_2021_dei_progress_report.pdf; "U.S. Census Bureau QuickFacts: United States," n.d., https://www.census.gov/quickfacts/fact/table/US/PST045221.

233   **Zaidi has served**: "Anita Zaidi," Profile, Bill & Melinda Gates Foundation, March 16, 2022, https://web.archive.org/web/20220316055452/https://www.gatesfoundation.org/about/leadership/anita-zaidi.

233   **Project Syndicate**: "The Key to Development," Project Syndicate, June 30, 2021, https://www.project-syndicate.org/onpoint/gender-equality-the-key-to-sustainable-development-public-health-by-anita-zaidi-2021-06.

234   **"we look very carefully"**: Sana Syed, "A Conversation with Anita Zaidi—A Discussion of Global Child Health, Empowering Women and . . ." *Medium*, n.d., https://medium.com/@syedsana/a-conversation-with-anita-zaidi-a-discussion-of-global-child-health-af47699f070b.

234   **pediatrics department**: "Anita Zaidi," Profile.

234   **part-time faculty**: "Anita Zaidi," Faculty Profile, Aga Khan University, n.d., https://www.aku.edu/mcpk/faculty/pages/profile.aspx?ProfileID=295&Name=Anita Kaniz Mehdi Zaidi. Note: In 2022, Zaidi coauthored a study (funded by the Gates Foundation) in the *Lancet Global Health* reporting her affiliation as being with Aga Khan, not Gates. After I contacted the journal, it issued a correction, clarifying her employment at Gates. "Correction to Lancet Glob Health 2022; 10: E1289–97," *The Lancet Global Health* 10, no. 10 (October 1, 2022): e1394, https://doi.org/10.1016/S2214-109X(22)00385-0.

234   **$750,000 compensation**: The Aga Khan University, "Generous Gift from Alumni to Advance Paediatric Research," n.d., https://www.aku.edu/news/Pages/News_Details.aspx?nid=NEWS-002428; Bill & Melinda Gates Foundation, IRS 990 filing, 2021, Statement 10.

234   **founded and where she served**: "Our Profile," Vital Pakistan Trust, July 5, 2017, https://web.archive.org/web/20170705114023/http://www.vitalpakistantrust.org/about-us.php; "Board of Trustees," Vital Pakistan, June 13, 2022, https://web.archive.org/web/20220613170907/https://www.vitalpakistantrust.org/trustees.

234   **virtually all**: The Aga Khan University, "New MRI Technology to Power Insights into Newborn Health," n.d., https://www.aku.edu/news/Pages/News_Details.aspx?nid=NEWS-002526. Note: Vital Pakistan's financial audits report income of around forty million Pakistani rupees in 2016, thirty million in 2017, and seventy million in 2018, which would amount to around $1.3 million. The Gates Foundation reports more than $8 million in grants to Vital in 2016 and 2017, to be paid out over several years. If anything, Gates's reported funding would appear to exceed the sums reported in Vital's published audits.

236   **almost entirely scrubbed out**: "Our Profile," Vital Pakistan Trust. Note: In early 2023, I did a back-end search of Vital's website, and the only reference to her name I found was in a scientific study available for download.

236   **1,000 cases of paralytic polio**: "Reported Cases of Paralytic Polio, 2021," Our World in Data, n.d., https://ourworldindata.org/grapher/the-number-of-reported-paralytic-polio-cases.

236   **undernourished**: "Number of People Requiring Interventions for Neglected Tropical Diseases," Our World in Data, n.d., https://ourworldindata.org/grapher/number-of-people-requiring-interventions-for-neglected-tropical-diseases; "Number of

People Who Are Undernourished," Our World in Data, n.d., https://ourworldindata
.org/grapher/number-undernourished.

236 **children in Pakistan experience stunting**: "Saving Children from Stunting,"
UNICEF, n.d., https://www.unicef.org/pakistan/stories/saving-children-stunting.

237 **first-ever personal visit**: "Bill Gates Meets Prime Minister Imran Khan to Discuss
Progress Against Polio, Steps to Overcome Final Challenges to Eradication," Bill
& Melinda Gates Foundation, n.d., https://www.gatesfoundation.org/ideas/media
-center/press-releases/2022/02/bill-gates-meets-prime-minister-imran-khan-on
-polio-eradication-in-pakistan; "Bill Gates Make His First-Ever Visit to Pakistan;
Discusses Health Issues with Imran Khan," *Times of India*, February 17, 2022,
https://timesofindia.indiatimes.com/world/pakistan/bill-gates-make-his-first
-ever-visit-to-pakistan-discusses-health-issues-with-imran-khan/articleshow
/89641568.cms.

237 **"to ensure that every child"**: "Bill Gates Meets Prime Minister Imran Khan to Discuss Progress Against Polio, Steps to Overcome Final Challenges to Eradication."

237 **researchers published an essay**: Fyezah Jehan and Kheezran Ahmed, "When Will
Pakistan Stand on Two Legs? A Polio Story," *Speaking of Medicine and Health* (blog),
June 8, 2022, https://speakingofmedicine.plos.org/2022/06/08/when-will-pakistan
-stand-on-two-legs-a-polio-story/.

237 **"terror of poliovirus"**: Fyezah Jehan, Twitter, June 12, 2020 (https://twitter.com
/FyezahJehan/status/1271418835082543104), and February 18, 2022 (https://twitter
.com/fyezahjehan/status/1494512529116119042?s=12); "AKU Pneumonia Study
Published in the New England Journal of Medicine," Aga Khan University, July 2,
2020, https://www.aku.edu/news/Pages/News_Details.aspx?nid=NEWS-002240.

237 **universally recommend breastfeeding exclusively**: Amy Sarah Ginsburg et al., "Randomized Controlled Trial of Early, Small-Volume Formula Supplementation Among
Newborns: A Study Protocol," *PLOS ONE* 17, no. 2 (February 4, 2022): e0263129,
https://doi.org/10.1371/journal.pone.0263129.

237 **"no benefit and large potential for harm"**: Tanya Doherty et al., "Questioning
the Ethics of International Research on Formula Milk Supplementation in Low-
Income African Countries," *BMJ Global Health* 7, no. 5 (May 6, 2022): e009181,
doi:10.1136/bmjgh-2022–009181. See also reader comments to the article, available
at Ginsburg et al., "Randomized Controlled Trial of Early, Small-Volume Formula
Supplementation Among Newborns."

238 **silver bullet solutions**: John Cook, "These Bill Gates-Funded 'Super Bananas' Could
Have a Huge Impact on Global Health," GeekWire, June 16, 2014, https://www
.geekwire.com/2014/bill-gates-funded-super-bananas-huge-impact-global-health/;
Rachel Zimmerman, "Gates Fights Malnutrition with Cheese, Ketchup and Other
Fortified Food Items," *Wall Street Journal*, May 9, 2002, https://www.wsj.com/articles
/SB1020886090206568560. Arun Gupta and Navdeep Khaira, "Food for Thought:
Deficiencies," *Telegraph India*, October 21, 2021, https://www.telegraphindia.com
/opinion/food-for-thought-deficiencies/cid/1835254.

238 **quick-win intervention**: Jeremy D. Keenan et al., "Azithromycin to Reduce Childhood Mortality in Sub-Saharan Africa," *New England Journal of Medicine* 378, no. 17
(April 26, 2018): 1583–92, https://doi.org/10.1056/NEJMoa1715474.

238   **"dose sparing"**: Rodgers, "Pneumococcal Vaccine Update"; David Goldblatt et al., "Pneumococcal Conjugate Vaccine 13 Delivered as One Primary and One Booster Dose (1 + 1) Compared with Two Primary Doses and a Booster (2 + 1) in UK Infants: A Multicentre, Parallel Group Randomised Controlled Trial," *Lancet Infectious Diseases* 18, no. 2 (February 1, 2018): 171–79, http://dx.doi.org/10.1016/S1473-3099(17)30654-0; National Cancer Institute (NCI), "Comparing One or Two Doses of the Human Papillomavirus Vaccine for the Prevention of Human Papillomavirus Infection: ESCUDDO Study," Clinical trial registration (clinicaltrials.gov, September 22, 2022), https://clinicaltrials.gov/ct2/show/NCT03180034.

238   **plundered the tropics**: "Historical Study of LSHTM from Its Origins to 1960 Details Extent of Colonial Roots," London School of Hygiene and Tropical Medicine, August 11, 2022, https://www.lshtm.ac.uk/newsevents/news/2022/historical-study-lshtm-its-origins-1960-details-extent-colonial-roots.

241   **"paternalistic attitudes"**: Caesar A. Atuire and Olivia U. Rutazibwa, "An African Reading of the Covid-19 Pandemic and the Stakes of Decolonization," Yale Law School, July 29, 2021, https://law.yale.edu/yls-today/news/african-reading-covid-19-pandemic-and-stakes-decolonization.

241   **"narcissistic charity"**: Olusoji Adeyi, "Global Health, Narcissistic Charity, and Neo-Dependency," *Development Today*, December 31, 2021, https://www.development-today.com/archive/dt-2021/dt-9--2021/global-health-narcissistic-charity-and-neo-dependency.

241   **Manifest Destiny**: Tim Schwab, "The Gates Foundation Avoids a Reckoning on Race and Power," *Nation*, October 6, 2021, https://www.thenation.com/article/society/gates-foundation-colonialism/.

242   **losing control**: Muneera A Rasheed, "Navigating the Violent Process of Decolonisation in Global Health Research: A Guideline," *Lancet Global Health* 9, no. 12 (December 1, 2021): e1640–41, https://doi.org/10.1016/S2214-109X(21)00440-X.

CHAPTER 11: BLOAT

244   **lead to even more confusion**: Nat Levy, "Judge: Former Bill & Melinda Gates Tech Leader Entitled to $4.9M in Dispute with Foundation," GeekWire, October 9, 2018, https://www.geekwire.com/2018/judge-former-bill-melinda-gates-tech-leader-entitled-4-9m-damages-dispute-foundation/#:~:text=A%20King%20County%20judge%20has,as%20a%20%E2%80%9Cbroken%20promise.%E2%80%9D.

245   **appellate court**: Patrick Dorrian, "Gates Foundation Breached Contract of 'Chief Digital Officer,'" *Bloomberg Law*, November 17, 2020, https://news.bloomberglaw.com/daily-labor-report/gates-foundation-breached-contract-of-chief-digital-officer; John O'Brien, "Gates Foundation Successfully Argues Against $4.6M Verdict for Fired Employee, but Recalculation Ordered," *Legal Newsline*, November 19, 2020, https://legalnewsline.com/stories/565415071-gates-foundation-successfully-argues-against-4-6m-verdict-for-fired-employee-but-recalculation-ordered.

245   **"I'm very well grounded"**: "Bill Gates," Interview, *Playboy*, July 1994, https://web.archive.org/web/20100801071952/http://www.playboy.com/articles/bill-gates-playboy-interview/index.html?page=2.

246   **$1.65 billion**: Bill & Melinda Gates Foundation, Part I, Lines 25–26, IRS 990 filing, 2000.

246   **"spartan in structure"**: Greenfeld, "Giving Billions Isn't Easy."
246   **"limited set of issues"**: Cheryl Scott, "Announcements—Bill & Melinda Gates Founda-
      tion," n.d., https://web.archive.org/web/20070118220207/https://www.gatesfoundation
      .org/AboutUs/Announcements/Announce-070109.htm. Note: One source told me that
      Bill Gates penned an infamous internal memo at the foundation in the late 2000s,
      inveighing against the bloat and waste he saw happening—specifically excoriating
      the large sums of money spent on things like professional conferences, which could
      be better spent on programmatic work helping the poor. I wasn't able to get a copy
      of this memo, but writer Adam Fejerskov references what may be the same memo,
      offering a very different account: "Gates himself famously sent round a blistering
      memo with wording to the effect of 'Everything is screwed,' pointing to substantial
      changes and overruling earlier leadership decisions. What followed then was a state
      of paralysis, with programme officers afraid of acting, facing potential grave conse-
      quences if they did something considered wrong by Gates or foundation leadership."
      Fejerskov, *The Gates Foundation's Rise to Power*, 72.
246   **ballooned to 41**: Home page, Bill & Melinda Gates Foundation website, n.d., https://
      www.gatesfoundation.org/. Note: The foundation's website reports 1,736 employees
      through the end of 2021, while its IRS 990 form from 2021 reports 1,843.
246   **self-proclaimed experts-for-hire**: Bill & Melinda Gates Foundation, IRS 990 fil-
      ing, 2021. Note: In 2009, when asked by journalists how much it was spending on
      consultants, the foundation's chief financial officer suggested that the answer was
      unknowable: "The foundation's total spending on consulting also isn't immediately
      clear . . . because of the number and scope of the contracts, as well as the founda-
      tion's global footprint." Clay Holtzman, "Gates Foundation Spends Big on Con-
      sulting," *Puget Sound Business Journal*, June 14, 2009, https://www.bizjournals.com
      /seattle/stories/2009/06/15/story7.html.
247   **"It's fun work"**: Gates, "Watch the Full Bill Gates Keynote," Gates, 37:30.
247   **Trevor Mundel**: "Gates Foundation Names Dr. Trevor Mundel to Lead Global
      Health Program," Bill & Melinda Gates Foundation, September 2011, https://www
      .gatesfoundation.org/ideas/media-center/press-releases/2011/09/foundation-names
      -dr-trevor-mundel-to-lead-global-health-program.
248   **relatively modest**: Nathaniel Lee, "Warren Buffett Lives in a Modest House That's
      Worth .001% of His Total Wealth," *Business Insider*, November 10, 2020, https://
      www.businessinsider.com/warren-buffett-modest-home-bought-31500-looks
      -2017-6. Note: Buffett's home is much nicer and more expensive than the homes of
      most Americans, but it is modest relative to where the multibillionaire could live.
      Another problem with the Buffett-as-spendthrift narrative: he owns a private jet. See
      Theron Mohamed, "Warren Buffett Nicknamed His Private Jet 'The Indefensible'—
      Then Renamed It 'The Indispensable' After Realizing Its Value," *Markets Insider*,
      December 30, 2022, https://markets.businessinsider.com/news/stocks/warren
      -buffett-berkshire-hathaway-private-jet-plane-purchase-indefensible-indispensable
      -2021-10.
248   **Buffett also put additional rules**: Warren Buffett, Letter to Bill and Melinda
      Gates, posted on the website of Berkshire Hathaway, June 26, 2006, https://www
      .berkshirehathaway.com/donate/bmgfltr.pdf. Note: The actual language from Buffett:

"The value of my annual gift must be fully additive to the spending of at least 5% of the Foundation's net assets."

248 **Top recipients**: Analysis of Gates Foundation grants. Note: Tabulations combine all funding to subsidiaries as going to the parent project. As examples, Gates's giving to NIH includes all donations to different NIH offices and to the Foundation for the NIH; UNICEF includes gifts to the United States Fund for UNICEF; University of Washington includes donations to the University of Washington Foundation; PATH includes money to PATH, PATH Vaccine Solutions, PATH Drug Solutions, and PATH Shanghai Representative Office. Gates's giving to the World Bank includes donations to the International Bank for Reconstruction and Development (IBRD), the International Development Association (IDA), and the International Finance Corporation (IFC). This tabulation does not include all CGIAR institutes.

249 **K Street nonprofit development group**: Analysis of Gates Foundation grant records includes donations to Family Health International and FHI Solutions.

249 **spared no expense**: KPMG, "Bill & Melinda Gates Foundation, Consolidated Financial Statements, December 31, 2020 and 2019," April 26, 2021, 15, https://docs .gatesfoundation.org/documents/F_151002C-1B_Bill&MelindaGatesFoundation _FS.pdf; "Foundation Celebrates Groundbreaking for New Headquarters," Bill & Melinda Gates Foundation, n.d., https://www.gatesfoundation.org/ideas/media -center/press-releases/2008/07/foundation-celebrates-groundbreaking-for-new -headquarters.

249 **"I am furious"**: Bill Gates, "Yes, I Get Furious When Foreign Aid Is Wasted. But Britons Are Saving Lives . . . and Are Leading the World, Says Bill Gates," *Daily Mail Online*, March 17, 2013, https://www.dailymail.co.uk/debate/article-2294674/Bill -Gates-Yes-I-furious-foreign-aid-wasted-But-Britons-saving-lives—leading-world .html.

249 **saving a child's life**: David Wallace-Wells, "Bill Gates: 'We're in a Worse Place than I Expected,'" *New York Times*, September 13, 2022, https://www.nytimes.com/2022/09 /13/opinion/environment/bill-gates-climate-change-report.html.

249 **upward trend resumed**: Emily Glazer, Khadeeja Safdar, and Theo Francis, "Warren Buffett's Estate Planning Sends Charities Scrambling," *Wall Street Journal*, June 21, 2022, https://www.wsj.com/articles/warren-buffetts-estate-planning-bill-and-melinda -gates-foundation-sends-charities-scrambling-11655811074; Bill & Melinda Gates Foundation, Part VII, 2, IRS 990 Filings, 2014, 2015, 2016.

250 **"mission creep"**: Mark Suzman, "Warren Buffett's Generous Philanthropy," Bill & Melinda Gates Foundation, n.d., https://www.gatesfoundation.org/ideas/articles /warren-buffett-philanthropy.

250 **his money after death**: Buffett, Letter to Bill and Melinda Gates. Note: Buffett's actual wording was, "I am irrevocably committing to make annual gifts of Berkshire Hathaway 'B' shares throughout my lifetime for the benefit of BMG [Bill & Melinda Gates Foundation]. . . . BMG can rely on this pledge to immediately and permanently expand its activities. My doctor tells me that I am in excellent health, and I certainly feel that I am. If I should become incapacitated, however, and be unable to adminis- ter my affairs, I direct whoever is in charge of my affairs to honor the commitment I am making in this letter. Additionally, I will soon write a new will that will provide

for a continuance of this commitment—by distribution of the remaining earmarked shares or in some other manner—after my death."

250 **McKinsey consultants**: Glazer, Safdar, and Francis, "Warren Buffett's Estate Planning Sends Charities Scrambling."

251 **He abruptly stepped down**: Tim Schwab, "Warren Buffett Moves to Distance Himself from Bill Gates," *Nation*, June 25, 2021, https://www.thenation.com/article /society/warren-buffett-bill-gates/.

251 **after the deaths**: Lisa Stiffler, "Melinda French Gates Counters Bill Gates' Prediction That Their Foundation Will End in 25 Years," GeekWire, October 12, 2022, https:// www.geekwire.com/2022/melinda-french-gates-refutes-bill-gates-prediction-that -their-foundation-will-end-in-25-years/.

251 **massive savings account**: Glazer, Safdar, and Francis, "Warren Buffett's Estate Planning Sends Charities Scrambling."

252 **massive overhaul of teacher pay**: Sam Dillon, "Gates Urges School Budget Overhauls," *New York Times*, November 19, 2010, https://www.nytimes.com/2010/11/19 /us/19gates.html.

252 **fiduciary irresponsibility**: "Bill Gates: End-of-Life Care vs. Saving Teachers' Jobs," Interview by Walter Isaacson, June 8, 2010, Aspen Ideas Festival, YouTube, https:// www.youtube.com/watch?v=03MZG9vK0W8.

253 **"quite bleak"**: Robert A. Guth and Michael Corkery, "Gates Says Benefits Costs Hit Schools," *Wall Street Journal*, March 3, 2011, https://www.wsj.com/articles/SB10001 424052748704728004576176802077647470.

253 **which leave teachers overworked, under-resourced, and underpaid**: Agnes Walton and Nic Pollock, "Empty Classrooms, Abandoned Kids: Inside America's Great Teacher Resignation," *New York Times* opinion video, November 18, 2022, https:// www.nytimes.com/2022/11/18/opinion/teachers-quitting-education-crisis.html.

253 **unlimited vacation days**: Bill & Melinda Gates Foundation, "Participant & Candidate Travel & Expense Policy," Effective 9/28/2022, n.d., https://docs.gatesfoundation.org /Documents/Travel%20and%20Expense%20-%20Participant%20&%20Candidate .pdf; Benefits, Bill & Melinda Gates Foundation, n.d., https://www.gatesfoundation .org/about/careers/benefits.

253 **Parental leave**: Catherine Clifford, "Bill Gates' Foundation Says 52-Week Paid Leave Isn't Doable After All, but Will Give New Parents $20,000," CNBC, February 6, 2019, https://www.cnbc.com/2019/02/06/bill--melinda-gates-foundation-cancels-52 -week-paid-parental-leave.html.

253 **"work and personal life"**: Bill & Melinda Gates Foundation, "2013 Benefit Plan Summary," n.d., https://web.archive.org/web/20211201154022/https://docs .gatesfoundation.org/documents/benefits-summary-us.pdf.

254 **close to $1.5 million in total compensation**: Bill & Melinda Gates Foundation, Part VII, 2, and Statement 20, IRS 990, 2021.

254 **"research into condoms"**: Jeff Goodell, "Bill Gates: The Rolling Stone Interview," *Rolling Stone* (blog), March 13, 2014, https://www.rollingstone.com/culture/culture -news/bill-gates-the-rolling-stone-interview-111915/.

255 **nearly two billion dollars**: "Next-Gen Nuclear Plant and Jobs Are Coming to Wyoming," Energy.gov, November 16, 2021, https://www.energy.gov/ne/articles/next-gen

-nuclear-plant-and-jobs-are-coming-wyoming; Cooper, "Bill Gates: How the World Can Avoid a Climate Disaster," *60 Minutes*; Lisa Stiffler, "TerraPower Warns of 2-Year Minimum Delay for Launch of Demo Reactor Due to Russia-Ukraine War," GeekWire, December 19, 2022, https://www.geekwire.com/2022/bill-gates-backed-terrapower-warns-of-2-year-minimum-delay-for-launch-of-demo-reactor/; Catherine Clifford, "Bill Gates' TerraPower Aims to Build Its First Advanced Nuclear Reactor in a Coal Town in Wyoming," CNBC, November 17, 2021, https://www.cnbc.com/2021/11/17/bill-gates-terrapower-builds-its-first-nuclear-reactor-in-a-coal-town.html.

255   **ahead of the curve**: Edstrom and Eller, *Barbarians Led by Bill Gates*, 119–30 and 168–75; Kurt Eichenwald, "Microsoft's Lost Decade," *Vanity Fair*, August 2012, https://archive.vanityfair.com/article/2012/8/microsofts-lost-decade.

255   **"crush the competition"**: Edstrom and Eller, *Barbarians Led by Bill Gates*, 207.

255   **"too many fiefdoms"**: Edstrom and Eller, *Barbarians Led by Bill Gates*, 176.

256   **in-house development**: As one example, Gates's $500 million TB vaccine effort, Aeras, shuttered in 2018 after years of failing to develop a product. Gates MRI appears to have taken over vaccine development. "IAVI Acquires Aeras TB Vaccine Clinical Programs and Assets"; "Research Priorities," Bill & Melinda Gates Medical Research Institute.

256   **"performative layoffs"**: "Bill & Melinda Gates Foundation Reviews," Glassdoor, July 1, 2022, https://www.glassdoor.com/Reviews/Bill-and-Melinda-Gates-Foundation-Reviews-E9097.htm.

256   **"blind to the costs of this churn"**: "Bill & Melinda Gates Foundation Reviews," Glassdoor, May 29, 2022, https://www.glassdoor.com/Reviews/Bill-and-Melinda-Gates-Foundation-Reviews-E9097.htm.

256   *Vanity Fair*: Eichenwald, "Microsoft's Lost Decade."

257   **"Micro(soft) Managing"**: Rachel Schurman, "Micro(soft) Managing a 'Green Revolution' for Africa: The New Donor Culture and International Agricultural Development," *World Development* 112 (December 1, 2018): 180–92, https://doi.org/10.1016/j.worlddev.2018.08.003.

257   **rocking in his chair**: Rob Larson, *Bit Tyrants: The Political Economy of Silicon Valley* (Chicago: Haymarket Books, 2020), 570.

257   **"escalating face-off, almost a brawl"**: Gates, *Moment of Lift*, 205.

CHAPTER 12: SCIENCE

260   **minimizing the threats of climate change**: Joseph E. Stiglitz, "Are We Overreacting on Climate Change?," *New York Times*, July 16, 2020, https://www.nytimes.com/2020/07/16/books/review/bjorn-lomborg-false-alarm-joseph-stiglitz.html.

260   **social and economic benefits**: Bill Gates, "The Best Investment I've Ever Made," *Wall Street Journal*, January 16, 2019, https://www.wsj.com/articles/bill-gates-the-best-investment-ive-ever-made-11547683309.

260   **crystal clear**: "Measuring the Value of Health," Bill & Melinda Gates Foundation, January 23, 2019, https://www.gatesfoundation.org/ideas/articles/health-economist-global-health-financing.

260   **helped underwrite**: Analysis of Gates's giving to universities based on a review of the foundation's grant records. Analysis of Gates's underwriting scientific articles based

on Web of Science academic database. Note: It is difficult to follow all the money that flows from the foundation into scientific discourse because some unknown and potentially large portion of it appears to move through Gates's network of surrogates. For example, the Gates Foundation has donated more than $700 million to the Medicines for Malaria Venture, which appears to be more than half of the group's lifetime funding. MMV, in turn, has sponsored more than five hundred research articles, according to an analysis of Web of Science. "Medicines for Malaria Venture," Financial View, Financial Year to December 31, 2018, https://www.mmv.org/sites/default /files/uploads/docs/publications/2018/MMV_AR2018_Chapter8_.pdf.

261 **Keith Klugman**: Editorial Board, *Vaccine*, n.d., https://www.journals.elsevier.com /vaccine/journals.elsevier.com/vaccine/editorial-board; Editorial Board, *Journal of Global Antimicrobial Resistance*, n.d., https://www.journals.elsevier.com/journal -of-global-antimicrobial-resistance/journals.elsevier.com/journal-of-global -antimicrobial-resistance/editorial-board.

261 **funder, author, editor, and adviser**: A nonsystematic search turned up myriad examples of Gates Foundation staff sitting on editorial and advisory boards. Editorial Board, *American Journal of Clinical Nutrition*, https://web.archive.org/web /20190401111630/https://academic.oup.com/ajcn/pages/Editorial_Board; Editorial Board, *Journal of Adolescent Health*, https://www.journals.elsevier.com/journal-of -adolescent-health/editorial-board; Editorial Board, *Journal of Cost Effectiveness and Resource Allocation*, https://resource-allocation.biomedcentral.com/about/editorial -board; Editorial Board, *Clinical and Translational Science, Pharmacometrics & Systems Pharmacology*, https://ascpt.onlinelibrary.wiley.com/hub/journal/17528062 /editorial-board/editorial-leadership.

261 **network of influence**: "Members," Postsecondary Value Commission, April 24, 2019, https://postsecondaryvalue.org/members/; "Factsheet," Postsecondary Value Commission, https://www.postsecondaryvalue.org/wp-content/uploads/2020/02/Value -Commission-Factsheet.pdf; "Our Global Advisory Board: Leadership, Vision, Integrity," *WomenLift Health* (blog), n.d., https://www.womenlifthealth.org/global-advisory -board/; "Sponsors," *WomenLift Health* (blog), n.d., https://www.womenlifthealth.org /donors/.

261 **Eric Rubin**: Analysis of Web of Science academic database.

261 **governments should respond**: Bill Gates, "Responding to Covid-19—A Once-in-a-Century Pandemic?," *New England Journal of Medicine* 382, no. 18 (April 30, 2020): 1677–79, https://doi.org/10.1056/NEJMp2003762.

261 **Covid-19 testing or social distancing**: Robert Fortner, "How Bill Gates Underestimated the Pandemic He Predicted—and Got Away with It," *Medium* (blog), February 14, 2021, https://robertfortner-93061.medium.com/how-bill-gates-underestimated -the-pandemic-he-predicted-and-got-away-with-it-bef13c228a78.

261 **financial conflicts were "numerous"**: Schwab, "While the Poor Get Sick, Bill Gates Just Gets Richer"; Bill Gates, ICMJE Form for Disclosure of Potential Conflicts of Interest, *New England Journal of Medicine*, February 27, 2020, https://www.nejm .org/doi/suppl/10.1056/NEJMp2003762/suppl_file/nejmp2003762_disclosures .pdf.

262 **"Seattle micromanaged the methods"**: Melissa Barber, Twitter, September 20,

2021, https://web.archive.org/web/20210921144810/https://twitter.com/mellabarb/status/1440004465839456263.

263   **reluctant to bite the hand**: Sophie Harman, "The Bill and Melinda Gates Foundation and Legitimacy in Global Health Governance," *Global Governance* 22, no. 3 (2016): 350, https://www.jstor.org/stable/44860965.

263   **"the Bill chill"**: Harman, "The Bill and Melinda Gates Foundation and Legitimacy in Global Health Governance."

263   **how much influence the foundation had**: The foundation's influence does not appear to be always disclosed in alignment with ethical rules designed to bring transparency to science and to alert readers to potential bias in research. At times, the foundation's public disclosures verge on incomprehensible: a search of Web of Science, for example, turned up dozens of studies funded by the foundation and authored by Gates Foundation staff that nevertheless also reported to readers that the foundation had no role in the study.

264   **the funding effect**: Sheldon Krimsky and Tim Schwab, "Conflicts of Interest Among Committee Members in the National Academies' Genetically Engineered Crop Study," *PLOS ONE* 12, no. 2 (February 28, 2017): e0172317, https://doi.org/10.1371/journal.pone.0172317.

264   **From its first days of operation**: Anne-Emanuelle Birn, "Gates's Grandest Challenge: Transcending Technology as Public Health Ideology," *The Lancet* 366, no. 9484 (August 2005): 514–19, https://doi.org/10.1016/S0140-6736(05)66479-3.

265   **$800,000**: "State Staffing: State Employee Salaries," Washington State Fiscal Information, database queried February 12, 2023, https://fiscal.wa.gov/Staffing/Salaries.

265   **2015 book**: Jeremy N. Smith, *Epic Measures: One Doctor. Seven Billion Patients* (New York: HarperCollins, 2015).

266   **"progress relies on picking fights"**: Smith, *Epic Measures*. Note: Through a public records request to the University of Washington, I discovered that the IHME had spent more than ten thousand dollars to purchase copies of *Epic Measures* before it was published. Current and former staff whom I interviewed say copies of the book remained piled at the IHME offices for years, thrust into the arms of all visitors. Author Jeremy Smith told me that neither the IHME nor Gates had any financial or editorial role in the production of the book.

266   **"All that matters is being right"**: Smith, *Epic Measures*.

266   **six hundred million dollars**: Tim Schwab, "Playing Games with Public Health Data," *Nation*, December 14, 2020.

266   **"mind-blowing"**: W. Wayt Gibbs, "Bill Gates Views Good Data as Key to Global Health," *Scientific American*, August 1, 2016, https://www.scientificamerican.com/article/bill-gates-interview-good-data-key-to-global-health/.

267   **where to prioritize his spending**: Note: The Gates Foundation appears to have provided the large majority of the IHME's funding over the life of the organization. The institute advertises that its "core funding" comes from Gates but also boasts having a diversity of funders, like the NIH. Public records suggest NIH has only given the institute around $10 million; Institute for Health Metrics and Evaluation, Client Services Unit, n.d., https://web.archive.org/web/20230219010654/https://www.ihmeclientservices.org/.

267   **led to a falling-out**: Smith, *Epic Measures*.

267   **"manipulating the data"**: Christopher J. L. Murray, Alan D. Lopez, and Suwit
       Wibulpolprasert, "Monitoring Global Health: Time for New Solutions," *British Med-
       ical Journal* 329, no. 7474 (November 6, 2004): 1096–100.

267   **Ellison abandoned the project**: Javier C. Hernandez and Brittney L. Moraski, "Elli-
       son Pulls Plug on $115M Gift—News," *Harvard Crimson*, June 30, 2006, https://www
       .thecrimson.com/article/2006/6/30/ellison-pulls-plug-on-115-m/.

267   **pleasure-craft class of American aristocracy**: Tina Mankowski, "University of
       Washington Launches New Institute to Evaluate International Health Programs,"
       Bill & Melinda Gates Foundation, n.d., https://www.gatesfoundation.org/ideas
       /media-center/press-releases/2007/06/globalhealthpr070604.

267   **"he likes controversy"**: Gibbs, "Bill Gates Views Good Data as Key to Global
       Health."

268   **"a concentration of epistemic power"**: Mahajan reports that "Bill chill" is prevent-
       ing some would-be critics from blowing the whistle on the IHME. "We are receiv-
       ing millions of dollars for our polio campaign in Afghanistan and Pakistan from
       the Gates Foundation. We cannot jeopardize that campaign. Publicly criticizing the
       work of the IHME could potentially alienate the Gates Foundation," one UNICEF
       official, who asked for anonymity, admitted to Mahajan in a study she published
       in 2019. Manjari Mahajan, "The IHME in the Shifting Landscape of Global Health
       Metrics," *Global Policy* 10, no. S1 (January 28, 2019): 110–20, https://onlinelibrary
       .wiley.com/doi/full/10.1111/1758-5899.12605.

268   **"statistics that have not been vetted"**: The source told me that when the Gates
       Foundation's media director, Gabriella Stern, left the foundation to take charge of
       the WHO's media operations, she imported a Gatesian worldview that also sought
       to elevate the IHME's work.

269   **"democratizes information"**: Bill Gates, "The Brilliant Doctor Behind My Favorite
       Obscure Website," *GatesNotes*, n.d., https://www.gatesnotes.com/Epic-Measures;
       "Five Insights from the Global Burden of Disease Study 2019," Institute for Health
       Metrics and Evaluation, October 14, 2020, https://www.healthdata.org/research
       -article/five-insights-global-burden-disease-study-2019.

270   **Donald Trump**: "Donald Trump Warns of Up to 240,000 Coronavirus Deaths in
       US," *Financial Times*, April 1, 2020.

270   **openly lampooning the institute**: As an example, see the conversation between Ariel
       Karlinsky and Ilya Kashnitsky, January 18, 2022, https://twitter.com/ArielKarlinsky
       /status/1483480661482684422.

271   **plowing ahead**: Christopher Murray, "Op-Ed: My Research Team Makes Covid-19
       Death Projections. Here's Why Our Forecasts Often Change," *Los Angeles Times*,
       July 10, 2020, https://www.latimes.com/opinion/story/2020-07-10/covid-forecast
       -deaths-ihme-washington. Note: The IHME has always enjoyed unparalleled news
       media placement in part because, with Gates's funding, it has built a dedicated media
       office to promote its work, unusual among academic research bodies. The IHME
       even has a two-time Pulitzer finalist on staff, who, for a time, also had a position at
       the University of Southern California's Center for Health Journalism; Schwab, "The
       Conflict over Conflicts of Interest."

271 **criticism as a "black box"**: "IHME Global Public Goods," OPP1152504, Grant proposal narrative to the Gates Foundation, IHME, September 20, 2015.

271 **pushes back on allegations**: Schwab, "Playing Games with Public Health Data"; Institute for Health Metrics and Evaluation, Client Services Unit, n.d., https://web .archive.org/web/20230219010654/https://www.ihmeclientservices.org/.

272 **"fashionable to be public"**: When I first began investigating the IHME, sources cautioned me that though it is subject to public records requests as a public institution, I would have difficulty securing records. I did end up accessing hundreds of pages of documents, but the release of records from the University of Washington was pocked by hard-to-explain discrepancies. In one case, I requested a copy of an external evaluation of the IHME that I knew existed and that sources told me was unflattering. Even after I described the document in detail, the University of Washington insisted that no such record existed—that is, it could not find any record of the evaluation's existence. After I secured a copy of the evaluation through another source and showed it to the university, the school suddenly was able to locate its own internal copy. The evaluation, from 2012, broadly confirmed long-standing criticism, noting that the IHME is "not consistent in when and to whom it shares methods, data sources, authorship and [that] this is perceived as not being transparent" and that "the extensive resources of IHME relative to other institutions have created an unhealthy imbalance in the field." The evaluators called on the Gates Foundation, as the IHME's primary funder, to improve its accountability and transparency.

272 **institute's first temporary offices**: Schwab, "Playing Games with Public Health Data."

272 **"repurposing IHME staff on the fly"**: "Goalkeepers," Supplemental Narrative to Grant proposal narrative to the Gates Foundation, OPP1152504, IHME, March 29, 2018.

272 **"consultant advisor"**: "Tamer H. Farag," LinkedIn, n.d., https://www.linkedin.com /in/tamer-h-farag-2a596531; "IHME Global Public Goods."

273 **"exclusive academic control"**: American Association of University Professors, ed., *Recommended Principles to Guide Academy-Industry Relationships* (Washington, DC: American Association of University Professors, 2014).

273 **decrying billionaire industrialist**: Erica L. Green and Stephanie Saul, "What Charles Koch and Other Donors to George Mason University Got for Their Money," *New York Times*, May 5, 2018, https://www.nytimes.com/2018/05/05/us/koch-donors -george-mason.html; Ed Pilkington, "Koch Brothers Sought Say in Academic Hiring in Return for University Donation," *Guardian*, September 12, 2014, https://www .theguardian.com/world/2014/sep/12/koch-brothers-sought-say-academic-hiring -university-donation.

274 **dark-money strategy**: Sarah Larimer, "George Mason University Foundation Is Not Subject to Public Records Laws, Judge Rules," *Washington Post*, October 27, 2021, https://www.washingtonpost.com/news/grade-point/wp/2018/07/06/george-mason -university-foundation-is-not-a-public-body-judge-rules-in-records-case/.

274 **emblazoned across**: "William H. Gates Public Service Law Program," UW School of Law, July 13, 2022, https://www.law.uw.edu/careers/gates/; "About the Program," Mary Gates Scholarships, n.d., https://www.uwb.edu/financial-aid/scholarships /merit-scholarships/upcoming-opps/mary-gates-scholarships; "Mary Gates Hall,"

Undergraduate Academic Affairs (blog), n.d., https://www.washington.edu/uaa/about/mary-gates-hall/.

274   **highest governing board**: "About the Gates Family," *Give to the UW* (blog), n.d., https://www.washington.edu/giving/recognition/gates-volunteer-service-award/about-the-gates-family/.

276   **lucky to publish**: Schwab, "Playing Games with Public Health Data."

277   **new auditing process**: Schwab, "Playing Games with Public Health Data."

278   **one-hundred-thousand-dollar prize**: "'Activist Editor' Richard Horton of The Lancet Receives $100,000 Roux Prize for Lifetime Achievement in Population Health," Institute for Health Metrics and Evaluation, April 22, 2019, https://www.healthdata.org/news-release/%E2%80%98activist-editor%E2%80%99-richard-horton-lancet-receives-100000-roux-prize-lifetime-achievement.

CHAPTER 13: AGRICULTURE

280   **seed and agrochemical giant**: Bayer acquired Monsanto in 2018 and ended the use of the "Monsanto" name. To avoid confusion, and because my reporting focuses on Gates's work with Monsanto before the acquisition, I refer to the company throughout this chapter as "Monsanto." Jeff Daniels, "Germany's Bayer Closes $63 Billion Monsanto Takeover, Plans to Drop US Company's Name," CNBC, June 7, 2018, https://www.cnbc.com/2018/06/07/germanys-bayer-closes-monsanto-deal-plans-to-drop-us-companys-name.html.

280   **genetic traits**: William Neuman, "Rapid Rise in Seed Prices Draws U.S. Scrutiny," *New York Times*, March 12, 2010, https://www.nytimes.com/2010/03/12/business/12seed.html; Bart Elmore, "It Could Soon Be Harder to Find Produce Untouched by Chemicals," *Washington Post*, June 8, 2021, https://www.washingtonpost.com/outlook/2021/06/09/it-could-soon-be-harder-find-produce-untouched-by-chemicals/.

280   **don't grow GMOs**: Bill Chappell, "Bayer to Pay More than $10 Billion to Resolve Cancer Lawsuits over Weedkiller Roundup," NPR, June 24, 2020, https://www.npr.org/2020/06/24/882949098/bayer-to-pay-more-than-10-billion-to-resolve-roundup-cancer-lawsuits. Note: GMO (genetically modified organism) is imperfect shorthand, but I use it in this book as it is commonly used in public discourse. GMOs involve a variety of laboratory-based modifications like transgenesis, where a gene construct is moved from one organism into another.

281   **skyrocketed with the advent**: Danica Jefferies, "A Potentially Cancer-Causing Chemical Is Sprayed on Much of America's Farmland. Here Is Where It Is Used the Most," NBC News, October 28, 2022, https://www.nbcnews.com/data-graphics/toxic-herbicides-map-showing-high-use-state-rcna50052.

281   **technology agreements**: Monsanto v. U.S. Farmers, Center for Food Safety, 2005, https://www.centerforfoodsafety.org/files/cfsmonsantovsfarmerreport11305.pdf.

281   **"seed police"**: Donald L. Barlett and James B. Steele, "Monsanto's Harvest of Fear," *Vanity Fair*, April 2, 2008, https://www.vanityfair.com/news/2008/05/monsanto200805.

281   **library of documents**: University of California, San Francisco, Industry Documents Library, https://www.industrydocuments.ucsf.edu/results/#q=Monsanto&col=%5B%22bvhp%22%2C%22benzene%22%2C%22marketpr%22%2C%22nytepa%22%2C%2

2pfas%22%2C%22roundup%22%2C%22usrtk%22%2C%22sanjour%22%5D&h=%
7B%22hideDuplicates%22%3Atrue%2C%22hideFolders%22%3Atrue%7D&cache
=true&count=1615.

282 **caught up in this scandal**: Laura Krantz, "Harvard Professor Failed to Disclose Connection," *Boston Globe*, October 1, 2015, https://www.bostonglobe.com/metro/2015
/10/01/harvard-professor-failed-disclose-monsanto-connection-paper-touting
-gmos/lLJipJQmI5WKS6RAgQbnrN/story.html. Note: Juma, though he produced
a report very similar to what Monsanto had proposed he write, appeared to defend
the work as independent, telling the news media that his work was based on previous
research he published and that he took no money from Monsanto.

282 **after he died**: "Gates Foundation, Calestous Juma Bet on Huge Progress in African
Agriculture," Belfer Center for Science and International Affairs, January 22, 2015,
https://www.belfercenter.org/publication/gates-foundation-calestous-juma-bet
-huge-progress-african-agriculture; "Calestous Juma Fellowship," n.d., https://gcgh
.grandchallenges.org/challenge/calestous-juma-science-leadership-fellowship.

282 **no disclosures**: Calestous Juma, Public Comment to FDA, Docket No. FDA-2015-
N-3403, November 18, 2015, https://www.regulations.gov/comment/FDA-2015-N
-3403-0607.

282 **Monsanto executive Mark Edge**: "Altruism or PR? How Monsanto Plans to Snag
a Foothold in African Seed Markets," St. Louis Public Radio, December 14, 2016,
https://news.stlpublicradio.org/health-science-environment/2016-12-14/altruism
-or-pr-how-monsanto-plans-to-snag-a-foothold-in-african-seed-markets.

282 **"impose their preferences on Africa"**: Melissa Allison, "On Voters' Plates: Genetically Engineered Crops," *Seattle Times*, August 10, 2013, https://special.seattletimes
.com/o/html/businesstechnology/2021586574_gmooverviewxml.html.

283 **"a good choice"**: Bill Gates, Interview by Nilay Patel, The Verge, January 22, 2015,
4:30, n.d., https://www.youtube.com/watch?v=8RETFyDKcw0.

283 **$6.5 billion**: Of the foundation's grants coded as being primarily for "agricultural
development," the large majority of money went to organizations located outside
Africa, though most of this funding appears aimed at African agriculture. For example, Gates paid Harvard "to promote the benefits of science and technology for African
agriculture" and the Washington-D.C.-based World Resources Institute "to develop an
educational online resource on land and natural resource property rights in Africa."

283 **African-led**: The African continent is made up of a heterogeneous, diverse group of
nations and cannot be understood as one entity—in the same way that we would not
generally lump together Canada and Mexico as having a monolithic "North American" identity. Nevertheless, "Africa" is the framing the Gates Foundation often uses
in its work (which spans much of the continent), which is why the word appears in
places in this chapter.

283 **companies that have long eyed Africa**: Winnie Nanteza, "WEMA Achieves
Major Milestone in African Agriculture," Alliance for Science, May 29, 2018, https://
allianceforscience.org/blog/2018/05/wema-achieves-major-milestone-african
-agriculture/. Note: Gates has also put industry veterans like Monsanto alum Rob
Horsch and Enock Chikava into key director positions in the foundation's agricul-

tural work. See Horsch's and Chikava's LinkedIn profiles at https://www.linkedin
.com/in/rob-horsch/ and https://www.linkedin.com/in/enock-chikava-4881b7b1/.

284 **"better tools and knowledge"**: Bill Gates, "Growing Enough Food to Feed the
World," *GatesNotes*, January 19, 2012, https://www.gatesnotes.com/Growing-Enough
-Food-to-Feed-the-World.

284 **South Africa**: The industry trade group ISAAA provides the statistics on GMO
adoption, and its most recent, publicly available statistics, from 2019, report that
only around thirty countries (out of more than two hundred globally) today grow
GMOs. In many countries, this amounts to an extremely small acreage of non-
food GMO production—like a few hundred acres of cotton grown in Eswatini
and Ethiopia. Ninety percent of all GMOs grown worldwide come from only five
countries: Argentina, Brazil, Canada, India, and the United States. Virtually all of
this is soy, corn, canola, and cotton. (Of GMO products, India grows only cotton.)
"Brief 55, Executive Summary, Global Status of Commercialized Biotech/GM Crops
in 2019," ISAAA, 2019, 4, https://www.isaaa.org/resources/publications/briefs/55
/executivesummary/pdf/B55-ExecSum-English.pdf.

284 **helping to create, fund, and staff**: "AGRA Is Supporting the Government of Ethiopia in Designing Approaches to Attract Investments to Boost Wheat, Rice, Edible
Oilseed, and Animal Feed Value Chains," AGRA, n.d., https://agra.org/news/agra
-is-supporting-the-government-of-ethiopia-in-designing-approaches-to-attract
-investments-to-boost-wheat-rice-edible-oilseed-and-animal-feed-value-chains/.

284 **at least $27 million**: "Trust, Collaboration and Collective Learning: Synergos Expe-
rience in Namibia and Ethiopia," Synergos, 2016, 6, https://www.syngs.info/files
/trust-collaboration-collective-learning-in-namibia-and-ethiopia-synergos.pdf.

284 **Khalid Bomba**: "Origin & History," Ethiopian Agricultural Transformation Agency,
n.d., https://www.ata.gov.et/about-ata/origin-history-2/; "Khalid Bomba," LinkedIn,
n.d., https://www.linkedin.com/in/khalid-bomba-2a01352a/?originalSubdomain=it.

284 **"first official representative"**: "Foundation Appoints Ethiopia Representative," Bill
& Melinda Gates Foundation, n.d., https://www.gatesfoundation.org/ideas/media
-center/press-releases/2012/02/foundation-appoints-ethiopia-representative.

285 **revolving door**: LinkedIn shows multiple people having worked for both Gates and
the ATA. See, as examples, LinkedIn profiles for Ross Lescano Lipstein (https://www
.linkedin.com/in/ross-lescano-lipstein-a3a32015/) and Abeneazer Adam (https://
www.linkedin.com/in/abeneazer-adam-419859a5/?).

285 **agrochemical giant DuPont**: Joeva Rock and Alex Park, *Mapping Financial Flows of
Industrial Agriculture in Africa* (San Francisco: Thousand Currents, 2019).

285 **sixty-eight different policy reforms**: Rachel Percy, Ethel Sibanda, Daniel Ticehurst,
and Gareth Davies, *Mid-Term Evaluation of AGRA's 2017–2021 Strategy Implementation*, ITAD, January 27, 2020, 115–36, https://usrtk.org/wp-content/uploads/2021/02
/AGRA-MTE-report-final-27.01.20.pdf.

285 **"the normal timetable"**: "Policy and Advocacy," AGRA, n.d., https://agra.org/policy
-and-advocacy/.

285 **"concentrating power and profit"**: Million Belay and Bridget Mugambe, "Bill Gates
Should Stop Telling Africans What Kind of Agriculture Africans Need," *Scientific*

American, July 6, 2021, https://www.scientificamerican.com/article/bill-gates
-should-stop-telling-africans-what-kind-of-agriculture-africans-need1/.

286 **"harmed broader efforts"**: "Call to End Support for Green Revolution Programs
in Africa," Oakland Institute, September 8, 2021, https://www.oaklandinstitute.org
/call-end-support-green-revolution-programs-africa. Note: AGRA's target countries
have changed over time. As of September 2022, AGRA reported working in Burkina
Faso, Ethiopia, Ghana, Kenya, Malawi, Mali, Mozambique, Nigeria, Rwanda, Tanzania, and Uganda. In 2014, AGRA reported also working in Liberia, Niger, Senegal,
Sierra Leone, South Sudan, and Zambia—a total of seventeen different countries.
"Focus Countries," AGRA, n.d., https://agra.org/focus-countries/; AGRA, *Progress
Report, 2007–2014*, 2015, 4, https://agra.org/wp-content/uploads/2021/05/agra
-progress-report-2007-2014.pdf.

286 **"820 million people hungry"**: "Call to Revoke AGRA's Agnes Kalibata as Special Envoy
to 2021 UN Food Systems Summit," February 10, 2020, https://www.oaklandinstitute
.org/sites/oaklandinstitute.org/files/letter_antonio_guterresenglish.pdf.

287 **"humanitarian crisis"**: "Press Release: African Faith Communities Tell Gates Foundation, 'Big Farming Is No Solution for Africa,'" Southern African Faith Communities'
Institute, August 4, 2021, https://safcei.org/press-release-african-faith-communities
-tell-gates-foundation-big-farming-is-no-solution-for-africa/.

287 **two hundred million dollars**: Nina Shapiro, "Gates-Funded 'Green Revolution'
in Africa Has Failed, Critics Say," *Seattle Times*, September 8, 2022, https://www
.seattletimes.com/seattle-news/gates-funded-green-revolution-in-africa-has-failed
-critics-say. Note: The foundation appeared to announce a two-hundred-million-
dollar commitment in the *Seattle Times*, but it never appeared in its grant database.
As with many projects, it is likely that Gates has put more money into AGRA than
it reports, directing donations through surrogates, third parties, or unreported contracts.

287 **"fund the researchers"**: To Mayet's point, when Gates Foundation employee Prabhu
Pingali published a commentary about Gates's agricultural work in the *Proceedings
of the National Academies of Sciences*, he reported that "All the [peer] reviewers suggested are grantees of the Gates Foundation. It is hard to find reviewers who are
not grantees." Prabhu L. Pingali, "Green Revolution: Impacts, Limits, and the Path
Ahead," *Proceedings of the National Academy of Sciences* 109, no. 31 (July 31, 2012):
12302–8, https://doi.org/10.1073/pnas.0912953109.

288 **corporate partners**: "Our Partners," AGRA, n.d., https://agra.org/our-partners/;
"Microsoft Reaffirms Its Commitment to the Alliance for a Green Revolution in
Africa to Support Digital Transformation in Agriculture," New Center Middle East
& Africa, Microsoft, September 22, 2020, https://news.microsoft.com/en-xm/2020
/09/22/microsoft-reaffirms-its-commitment-to-the-alliance-for-a-green-revolution
-in-africa-to-support-digital-transformation-in-agriculture/.

288 **civil society groups**: "Our Partners—Civil Society and Farmer Organization Partners," AGRA, n.d., https://agra.org/our-partners/.

288 **Gary Toenniessen**: "African Farmer and World Agricultural Leader Announced
as President of the Alliance for a Green Revolution in Africa (AGRA)," Alliance
for a Green Revolution in Africa, November 22, 2007, https://web.archive.org

/web/20071122234420/http://www.agra-alliance.org/news/pr111407.html; "Gates, Rockefeller Foundation Turn to Feeding Africa," *Talk of the Nation*, NPR, September 13, 2006, https://www.npr.org/templates/story/story.php?storyId=6068582.

288 **at least $675 million**: Analysis of AGRA's IRS 990 filings and the Gates Foundation's charitable grant records.

288 **non-African**: AGRA, Board of Directors, Board and Staff, January 20, 2014, https://web.archive.org/web/20140120075220/http://www.agra.org/who-we-are/board--staff/board-of-directors.

288 **top brass**: "Our People," AGRA, n.d., https://agra.org/our-people. Note: AGRA is legally incorporated as a nonprofit organization in the United States, where it files an annual tax form with the IRS. It has also paid tens of thousands of dollars lobbying Congress, using the law firm bearing the name of Bill Gates's father, K&L Gates. Alliance for a Green Revolution in Africa, LD-2 Disclosure Form, Quarter 4, 2009, Lobbyist K&L Gates LLP, n.d., https://lda.senate.gov/filings/public/filing/007a9908-797c-4c95-83c7-891a2f422d54/print/.

288 **Internal policy documents**: Bill & Melinda Gates Foundation, Board Service Policy and Guidelines, n.d., https://docs.gatesfoundation.org/documents/board-service-policy.docx.

289 **"re-fashion its institutional identity"**: *AGRA Institutional Evaluation, Final Report*, DAI, February 15, 2016, xi, xiii, https://agra.org/wp-content/uploads/2021/05/AGRA-Institutional-Evaluation-2016_2.pdf. Note: The evaluation also cited "fatigue among staff caused by too frequent, top-down strategy refreshes"—a prominent complaint that staff and grantees have of the Gates Foundation, another indication of AGRA's pedigree as a Gates-based organization.

289 **"highly regarded political access"**: Percy et al., *Mid-Term Evaluation of AGRA's 2017–2021 Strategy Implementation*.

289 **spearheaded by**: "Bill & Melinda Gates, Rockefeller Foundations Form Alliance to Help Spur 'Green Revolution' in Africa," Bill & Melinda Gates Foundation, n.d., https://www.gatesfoundation.org/ideas/media-center/press-releases/2006/09/foundations-form-alliance-to-help-spur-green-revolution-in-africa.

289 **wave of suicides**: Daniel Zwerdling, "'Green Revolution' Trapping India's Farmers in Debt," *Morning Edition*, NPR, April 14, 2009, https://www.npr.org/2009/04/14/102944731/green-revolution-trapping-indias-farmers-in-debt; Salimah Shivji, "Burdened by Debt and Unable to Eke Out a Living, Many Farmers in India Turn to Suicide," CBC News, March 30, 2021, https://www.cbc.ca/news/world/india-farmers-suicide-1.5968086.

289 **"In the 1960s, there was this thing"**: Goodell, "Bill Gates: The Rolling Stone Interview."

290 **"New philanthropists"**: Mark Dowie, *American Foundations: An Investigative History* (Cambridge, MA: MIT Press, 2001), 105.

290 **"suggested socialism"**: Dowie, *American Foundations*, 117.

290 **same premise, approach**: "Bill & Melinda Gates, Rockefeller Foundations Form Alliance to Help Spur 'Green Revolution' in Africa." Note: AGRA takes pains to distance itself from GMOs, yet the group explicitly partners with the companies that sell GMOs. Sources I spoke with see AGRA as organizing its work to create

the enabling environment—promoting industrialized agriculture—to allow for the eventual introduction of GMOs.

291　**double yields and farmer income**: AGRA, *Progress Report, 2007–2014*, front matter; AGRA, *AGRA in 2008: Building on the New Momentum in African Agriculture*, 2009, 7, https://agra.org/wp-content/uploads/2021/05/agra-annual-report-2008.pdf.

291　**tens of millions more**: Percy et al., *Mid-Term Evaluation of AGRA's 2017–2021 Strategy Implementation*. Note: A full accounting of taxpayer dollars is difficult to construct because AGRA refused all press inquiries. Personal correspondence with European development agencies showed that German taxpayers had chipped in €25 million; the United Kingdom (IFAD) reports $9 million in funding for projects in partnership with AGRA, while UKAID did not respond to press inquiries. The Netherlands reports €15.2 million in funding for AGRA; Sweden (SIDA) reports $6.5 million to the "African Agribusiness Window of African Enterprise Challenge Fund (AECF) in 2012, when the fund was hosted by AGRA." Luxembourg reports providing $1,303,110; Canada (IDRC) reports CAD 7.4 million; Norway (NORAD) reports $300,000 in funding to AGRA; the other government bodies I contacted did not promptly respond to inquiries.

291　**subsidizing inputs**: Timothy A. Wise, "Failing Africa's Farmers: An Impact Assessment of the Alliance for a Green Revolution in Africa," Global Development and Environment Institute, Tufts University, Working Paper No. 20-01, July 2020, https://sites.tufts.edu/gdae/files/2020/07/20-01_Wise_FailureToYield.pdf.

291　**AGRA has created institutional ties**: Percy et al., *Mid-Term Evaluation of AGRA's 2017–2021 Strategy Implementation*. Note: AGRA describes itself as almost a McKinsey-style consultancy: "AGRA by design has attracted the largest collection of agricultural technical experts on the continent, with areas of specialization extending the full length of the value chain, from developing and delivering seeds, fertilizers, and agronomic best practices, to connecting farmers with markets." "Our People" and "Experts," AGRA, n.d., https://agra.org/our-people/.

292　**impossible for Wise**: Wise, "Failing Africa's Farmers."

292　**country-level case studies**: Rosa Luxemburg Foundation, *False Promises: The Alliance for a Green Revolution in Africa*, July 2020, https://www.rosalux.de/fileadmin/rls_uploads/pdfs/Studien/False_Promises_AGRA_en.pdf.

292　**Andrew Cox**: The Rockefeller Foundation's own published history of AGRA states that Rockefeller and Gates created the group and that African leaders were recruited only later: "After a meeting of the presidents and key vice presidents of the two foundations, the decision was made to establish a more comprehensive partnership for agricultural development in Africa that would build on current Rockefeller Foundation support for seeds, soils, and markets; expand to include work on extension, water resources, policy, and other interventions as necessary; and attract complementary financial commitments from national and international sources. AGRA was established in 2006 to implement this comprehensive funding program from Africa. During this startup phase, four program officers from the Rockefeller Foundation served as the corporate officers of AGRA while a permanent and predominantly African staff was being recruited."

293　**Al Jazeera**: "Revisiting the Gates Foundation's program to feed Africa," Al Jazeera,

The Take, March 11, 2022, 2:00, https://www.aljazeera.com/podcasts/2022/3/11/revisiting-the-gates-foundations-program-to-feed-africa.

293 **IRS requires nonprofit organizations**: "Public Disclosure and Availability of Exempt Organizations Returns and Applications: Public Disclosure Requirements in General," Internal Revenue Service, n.d., https://www.irs.gov/charities-non-profits/public-disclosure-and-availability-of-exempt-organizations-returns-and-applications-public-disclosure-requirements-in-general.

293 **"While there have always been detractors"**: Hailemariam Dessalegn, "A Food-Secure Africa Needs Contribution from All," *African Arguments* (blog), October 4, 2021, https://africanarguments.org/2021/10/a-food-secure-africa-needs-contribution-from-all/.

293 **"potentially damaging effects"**: "USAID and Congress: Stop Funding Industrial Agriculture in Africa," Community Alliance for Global Justice, August 30, 2022, https://cagj.org/2022/08/14064/; Ilhan Omar, Tom Malinowski, and Sara Jacobs, Letter to Representatives Hal Rogers and Barbara Lee, April 27, 2022, https://www.iatp.org/sites/default/files/2022-05/Quill%20-%20Letter%20%23L3613%20-%20AGRA%20appropriations%20letter%20-%20Version%20%231%20-%2004-26-2022%20%40%2011-20%20AM.pdf.

293 **German activists**: "Development Minister Schulze Questions the Gates Project," *Der Spiegel*, February 25, 2022, https://www.spiegel.de/wirtschaft/afrika-svenja-schulze-stellt-agrarprojekt-der-gates-stiftung-infrage-a-2042de13-6006-4339-907e-dc84ec321b24.

294 **wealthier, male farmers**: Randall Blair et al., "Partnership for Inclusive Agricultural Transformation in Africa, Final Evaluation," *Mathematica Policy Research Reports*, December 8, 2021, https://ideas.repec.org/p/mpr/mprres/a9b7d53d020844b0bd006dd372d4de14.html.

294 **as critics long predicted**: Timothy Wise, "Donors Must Rethink Africa's Flagging Green Revolution, New Evaluation Shows (Commentary)," *Mongabay Environmental News*, March 22, 2022, https://news.mongabay.com/2022/03/donors-must-rethink-africas-flagging-green-revolution-new-evaluation-shows-commentary/.

294 **largest private farmland owner**: Eric O'Keefe, "Farmer Bill," Land Report 100, *Land Report*, January 11, 2021, https://landreport.com/2021/01/farmer-bill/.

295 **Gates's large acreage of corn and soy**: Christopher Burbach, "Bill Gates' 20,000 Acres in Nebraska Help Make Him the Top Farmland Owner in the U.S.," *Lincoln Journal Star*, January 25, 2021, https://journalstar.com/agriculture/bill-gates-20–000-acres-in-nebraska-help-make-him-the-top-farmland-owner-in/article_ce5560f6-f14b-5a5a-86ae-f3fba47cf1f4.html.

295 **synthetic fertilizers**: Stefano Menegat, Alicia Ledo, and Reyes Tirado, "Greenhouse Gas Emissions from Global Production and Use of Nitrogen Synthetic Fertilisers in Agriculture," *Scientific Reports* 12, no. 1 (August 25, 2022): 14490, https://doi.org/10.1038/s41598-022-18773-w.

295 **allegations of profiteering**: Anne Maina, "Bold Action for Resilient Food Systems? End the Failing Green Revolution," *Nation* (blog), August 27, 2022, https://nation.africa/kenya/blogs-opinion/blogs/bold-action-for-resilient-food-systems-end-the-failing-green-revolution-3928148.

295 **Rodale Institute**: "About," Rodale Institute, n.d., https://rodaleinstitute.org/about/.

296 **offer degree programs**: "Agroecology Undergraduate Programs," North Carolina State University, n.d., https://agroecology.wordpress.ncsu.edu; "Agroecology," University of Wisconsin, n.d., https://agroecology.wisc.edu/.

296 **four hundred experts**: *Agriculture at a Crossroads—Global Report*, International Assessment of Agricultural Knowledge, Science and Technology for Development, 2009, 8, https://wedocs.unep.org/20.500.11822/8590.

296 **environmental or social costs**: *Agroecological and Other Innovative Approaches for Sustainable Agriculture and Food Systems That Enhance Food Security and Nutrition*, High-Level Panel of Experts on Food Security and Nutrition of the Committee on World Food Security, Rome, 2019, 17–18, https://www.fao.org/3/ca5602en/ca5602en.pdf.

296 **"As an environmentalist"**: Torie Bosch, "Leading Environmental Activist's Blunt Confession: I Was Completely Wrong to Oppose GMOs," *Slate*, January 3, 2013, https://slate.com/technology/2013/01/mark-lynas-environmentalist-who-opposed-gmos-admits-he-was-wrong.html.

296 **made a splash**: Michael Specter, "An Environmentalist's Conversion," *New Yorker*, January 7, 2013, https://www.newyorker.com/news/daily-comment/an-environmentalists-conversion; Bosch, "Leading Environmental Activist's Blunt Confession."

297 **quite coincidental**: Note: Web archives of the website of the Oxford Farming Conference show that in late 2012 and early 2013, the conference reported corporate sponsors like Bayer and Yara. See: https://web.archive.org/web/20120925023716/http://www.ofc.org.uk/patrons and https://web.archive.org/web/20130122033732/http://www.ofc.org.uk/patrons.

297 **leaked documents**: John Vidal and Hanna Gersmann, "Biotech Group Bids to Recruit High-Profile GM 'Ambassadors,'" *Guardian*, October 20, 2011, https://www.theguardian.com/environment/2011/oct/20/europabio-gm-ambassadors-europe.

297 **denied being**: "Draft Letter from EuropaBio to Potential GM Ambassadors," *Guardian*, October 20, 2011, https://www.theguardian.com/environment/interactive/2011/oct/20/gm-food.

297 **"Maybe in his mind"**: Will Storr, "Mark Lynas: Truth, Treachery and GM Food," *Observer*, March 9, 2013, https://www.theguardian.com/environment/2013/mar/09/mark-lynas-truth-treachery-gm.

297 **same talking point**: Robert Fraley, "Why Science Denialism Is Costing Us a Fortune," *Forbes*, February 18, 2016, https://www.forbes.com/sites/gmoanswers/2016/02/18/why-science-denialism-costing-fortune/.

297 **Gates praised**: Rogers, "Bill Gates, Time Traveler." Note: In 2021, the Cornell Alliance for Science transitioned from Cornell University to the Boyce Thompson Institute, where today it is known as the Alliance for Science; AJ Bouchie, "Sarah Evanega Joins BTI Faculty," Boyce Thompson Institute News, August 3, 2021, https://btiscience.org/explore-bti/news/post/sarah-evanega-joins-bti-faculty/.

298 **"Claims of consensus"**: Angelika Hilbeck et al., "No Scientific Consensus on GMO Safety," *Environmental Sciences Europe* 27, no. 4 (2015), https://enveurope.springeropen.com/articles/10.1186/s12302-014-0034-1. Note: A 2015 survey of members of the American Association for the Advancement of Science found that 88

percent of respondents believe that GMOs are safe, but, notably, 11 percent believe they are unsafe. This survey does not examine international scientific opinion, but rather American opinion. And it does not survey scientists with specific knowledge, training, or expertise related to GMOs. The findings do not therefore suggest the existence of an international, scientific consensus opinion as we have on climate change, for example. GMO promoters nevertheless point to this survey and other narrow evidence to claim the existence of a global scientific consensus. Cary Funk, "5 Key Findings on What Americans and Scientists Think About Science," *Pew Research Center* (blog), January 29, 2015, https://www.pewresearch.org/fact-tank/2015/01/29/5-key-findings-science/.

298   **"796 science champions"**: Joan Conrow, "Alliance for Science Expands Mission with $10 Million Reinvestment," Alliance for Science, n.d., https://allianceforscience.org/blog/2020/09/alliance-for-science-expands-mission-with-10-million-reinvestment/.

298   **Joeva Rock**: One of Cornell's first initiatives was to begin recruiting journalists, offering as much as $25,000 for reporting projects. "Cornell Alliance for Science Launches Global Ag Journalism Fellowship," Cornell Alliance for Science, June 10, 2015, https://web.archive.org/web/20150613005130/http://allianceforscience.cornell.edu/SJFellowship.

298   **"promoting GM seeds"**: Belay and Mugambe, "Bill Gates Should Stop Telling Africans What Kind of Agriculture Africans Need."

299   **"Every piece of bread"**: Ayenat Mersie, "Gates Foundation Pledges $7 Billion for Africa as Ukraine War Diverts Donor Cash," Reuters, November 18, 2022, https://www.reuters.com/world/africa/gates-foundation-pledges-7-billion-africa-ukraine-war-diverts-donor-cash-2022-11-17/; Mercy Kahenda, "There Is Nothing Harmful About GMO—Bill Gates," *Standard*, November 18, 2022, https://www.standardmedia.co.ke/health/health-science/article/2001461011/there-is-nothing-harmful-about-gmo-bill-gates.

299   **no GMO wheat in commercial production**: "What Are GMOS?," National Wheat Foundation, n.d., https://wheatfoundation.org/wheat-resources/gmos/.

300   **former Monsanto associate**: "Monsanto Failure," *New Scientist*, February 7, 2004, https://www.newscientist.com/article/mg18124330-700-monsanto-failure/.

300   **years of funding and promotion**: Bill Gates, "Building Better Bananas," *GatesNotes*, n.d., https://www.gatesnotes.com/Building-Better-Bananas.

300   **"ignorance and misinformation"**: Christopher Bendana, "Boosting Banana Nutrition for Ugandans," *Nature*, March 14, 2022, https://www.nature.com/articles/d41586-022-00749-5.

300   **"golden rice"**: "Nutritious Rice and Cassava Aim to Help Millions Fight Malnutrition," Bill & Melinda Gates Foundation, n.d., https://www.gatesfoundation.org/ideas/media-center/press-releases/2011/04/nutritious-rice-and-cassava-aim-to-help-millions-fight-malnutrition; Luis Ventura, "Four Ways That GMOs Can Save Lives," Alliance for Science, April 28, 2022, https://allianceforscience.org/blog/2022/04/four-ways-that-gmos-can-save-lives/.

300   **the Philippines**: Peter Rüegg, "For the First Time, Farmers in the Philippines Cultivated Golden Rice on a Larger Scale and Harvested Almost 70 Tons," Phys.org,

November 28, 2022, https://phys.org/news/2022-11-farmers-philippines-cultivated
-golden-rice.html; Talia Ogliore, "No Clear Path for Golden Rice to Reach Consumers," *The Source*, Washington University, February 7, 2020, https://source.wustl
.edu/2020/02/no-clear-path-for-golden-rice-to-reach-consumers/; Dominic Glover
and Glenn Davis Stone, "The Philippines Has Rated 'Golden Rice' Safe, but Farmers
Might Not Plant It," *The Conversation*, February 7, 2020, http://theconversation.com
/the-philippines-has-rated-golden-rice-safe-but-farmers-might-not-plant-it-129956.

301   **claimed benefits of GMOs**: Doug Gurian-Sherman, "Failure to Yield," Union of
Concerned Scientists, April 14, 2009, https://www.ucsusa.org/resources/failure
-yield-evaluating-performance-genetically-engineered-crops; Doug Gurian-
Sherman, "High and Dry," Union of Concerned Scientists, June 5, 2012, https://www
.ucsusa.org/resources/high-and-dry#ucs-report-downloads.

301   **"It's pretty incredible"**: "Bill Gates: GMOs Will End Starvation in Africa," Video,
Wall Street Journal, January 22, 2016, https://www.wsj.com/video/bill-gates-gmos
-will-end-starvation-in-africa/3085A8D1-BB58-4CAA-9394-E567033434A4.html.

301   **"singing 'Kumbaya'"**: Thalia Beaty, "Bill Gates: Technological Innovation Would
Help Solve Hunger," AP News, September 13, 2022, https://apnews.com/article
/russia-ukraine-science-technology-africa-e51baf120c03c206eceeb92f0634e87c
?utm_source=Twitter&utm_campaign=SocialFlow&utm_medium=AP.

302   **"a data-based vision"**: Bill Gates, "The Future of Progress," Goalkeepers, n.d., https://
www.gatesfoundation.org/goalkeepers/report/2022-report/. Note: When Gates says
"magic seeds," he seems to be talking about any new seed his foundation develops,
no matter the breeding technique, no matter if the seed is a GMO or a hybrid.

302   **"10 to 15 years"**: Wallace-Wells, "Bill Gates: 'We're in a Worse Place than I Expected.'"

302   **"behalf of Africa"**: Wallace-Wells, "Bill Gates: 'We're in a Worse Place than I Expected.'"

CHAPTER 14: INDIA

303   **where the government was failing**: "Gates Foundation Announces $100 Million
HIV/AIDS Prevention Effort in India," Bill & Melinda Gates Foundation, n.d.,
https://www.gatesfoundation.org/ideas/media-center/press-releases/2002/11/hivaids
-prevention-effort-in-india.

303   **"more needs to be done"**: Amy Waldman, "Gates Offers India $100 Million to Fight
AIDS," *New York Times*, November 12, 2002, https://www.nytimes.com/2002/11/12
/world/gates-offers-india-100-million-to-fight-aids.html.

304   **"deflected any suggestions"**: Waldman, "Gates Offers India $100 Million to Fight
AIDS."

304   **The Lancet**: "Philanthropist or Commercial Opportunist?," *The Lancet* 360, no.
9346 (November 23, 2002): 1617, https://www.thelancet.com/journals/lancet/article
/PIIS0140-6736(02)11593-5/fulltext.

304   **escalating conflict**: Jasmine N. M. Folz, "Free and Open Source Software in India:
Mobilising Technology for the National Good" (PhD diss., University of Manches-
ter, 2019), 55.

304   **"competing for government contracts"**: Kinsley, *Creative Capitalism*.

305   **for half of what the company pays**: Daisuke Wakabayashi, "Microsoft Backs Cricket
to Woo Indian Employees," Reuters, September 10, 2007, https://www.reuters.com

/article/us-microsoft-cricket-idUSN3040653220070910; Brian Dudley, "From Redmond to India, High Tech's Global Families," *Seattle Times*, August 8, 2004, https://www.seattletimes.com/business/from-redmond-to-india-high-techs-global-families.

305 **and its HIV/AIDS project, called Avahan**: "Avahan—The India AIDS Initiative," Bill & Melinda Gates Foundation, n.d., https://docs.gatesfoundation.org/documents/avahan_factsheet.pdf.

305 **Avahan's questionable legacy**: Manjari Mahajan, "Philanthropy and the Nation-State in Global Health: The Gates Foundation in India," *Global Public Health* 13, no. 10 (October 2018): 1357–68, https://pubmed.ncbi.nlm.nih.gov/29243555/.

305 *Forbes India* **reported**: Elizabeth Flock, "How Bill Gates Blew $258 Million in India's HIV Corridor," *Forbes India*, June 5, 2009, https://www.forbesindia.com/article/cross-border/how-bill-gates-blew-$258-million-in-indias-hiv-corridor/852/1.

305 **Ashok Alexander**: Bill & Melinda Gates Foundation, Part VIII, IRS 990 filing, 2007.

305 **"need the best talent"**: Mahajan, "Philanthropy and the Nation-State in Global Health."

306 **hiring technical specialists**: Flock, "How Bill Gates Blew $258 Million in India's HIV Corridor."

306 **"such execution focus"**: Mahajan, "Philanthropy and the Nation-State in Global Health."

307 **"Indian government is scaling"**: Bill Gates, "Why Our Foundation Invests in India," *HuffPost*, February 10, 2012, https://www.huffpost.com/entry/why-our-foundation-invest_b_1269014.

307 **hugely expensive**: In subsequent years, some research showed that the Indian government's efforts had actually been more effective than Gates's—and at a fraction of the cost. "While Avahan contributed to HIV prevention among high-risk communities in the highest prevalence states, the government's own programmes were more extensive, and by some accounts, helped turn the tide of the epidemic before Avahan's impacts could be realised," Mahajan reports, citing a number of studies. Mahajan, "Philanthropy and the Nation-State in Global Health."

308 **"unable to sustain"**: Flock, "How Bill Gates Blew $258 Million in India's HIV Corridor."

308 **"too resource-intensive"**: Mahajan, "Philanthropy and the Nation-State in Global Health."

308 **"branded condom"**: The foundation publicly boasted in 2009 of having given some $338 million to Avahan and working with more than one hundred NGOs, yet it does not clearly state where the money went. "Avahan—The India AIDS Initiative," Bill & Melinda Gates Foundation.

309 **independent research or scholarship**: "India," Bill & Melinda Gates Foundation, n.d., https://www.gatesfoundation.org/our-work/places/india; Michael Pickles et al., "Assessment of the Population-Level Effectiveness of the Avahan HIV-Prevention Programme in South India: A Preplanned, Causal-Pathway-Based Modelling Analysis," *Lancet Global Health* 1, no. 5 (November 1, 2013): e289–99, https://www.thelancet.com/journals/langlo/article/PIIS2214-109X(13)70083-4/fulltext.

309 **faulty projections**: Lalit Dandona, Vemu Lakshmi, Anil Kumar, and Rakhi Dandona, "Is the HIV Burden in India Being Overestimated?," *BMC Public Health* 6 (December

20, 2006): 308, https://www.ncbi.nlm.nih.gov/pmc/articles/PMC1774574/; Donald G. McNeil Jr., "U.N. to Say It Overstated H.I.V. Cases by Millions," *New York Times*, November 20, 2007, https://www.nytimes.com/2007/11/20/world/20aids.html.

309 **"technical support units"**: "Bihar" and "Uttar Pradesh," Bill & Melinda Gates Foundation, n.d., https://www.gatesfoundation.org/our-work/places/india/bihar and https://www.gatesfoundation.org/our-work/places/india/uttar-pradesh.

310 **"doctors be reskilled"**: "Interview with Gates Foundation CEO & India Country Office Director: 'We Don't Have an Agenda . . . We Work with the Govt,'" *Indian Express*, September 2, 2016, https://indianexpress.com/article/india/india-news -india/bill-and-melinda-gates-foundation-nachiket-sue-hiv-aids-avahan-nachiket -mor-3008992/.

310 **vague grant descriptions**: For example, one grant description is "to learn from and apply evidence generated by improved measurement systems and processes across the organization, contributing to increased impact and influence at scale." This tells us nothing about the destination of the money, whether it is used in India or elsewhere.

CARE has an office in India, but virtually all the foundation's grant funding is reported as going to its Atlanta office. Not only has CARE received hundreds of millions of dollars from Gates, but many Gates alums have gone on to work for the organization. The chief operating officer of CARE's India office previously spent a decade at the Gates Foundation, managing its relationship with the government of Bihar. Meanwhile, in CARE's home office in Atlanta, the CEO position was held by a former Gates Foundation executive from 2006 to 2015. "Debarshi Bhattacharya," CARE India, n.d., https://www.careindia.org/our-member/debarshi -bhattacharya/; Debarshi Bhattacharya, LinkedIn, n.d., https://www.linkedin.com /in/debarshi-bhattacharya-deb/?trk=org-employees&originalSubdomain=in; "Dr. Helene Gayle to Head CARE USA," Bill & Melinda Gates Foundation, n.d., https://www.gatesfoundation.org/ideas/media-center/press-releases/2005/12 /dr-helene-gayle-to-head-care-usa.

311 **"augment trust in the public health system"**: Homepage, CARE Bihar, n.d., 1:20, https://bihar.care.org/.

311 **government of Bihar**: Homepage, CARE Bihar, 5:30.

311 **hand off its programs**: "Uttar Pradesh," Bill & Melinda Gates Foundation.

314 **human papillomavirus**: The first reference to work on HPV in the foundation's grant records was a 2004 donation to Harvard—at which point, Merck's HPV vaccine, Gardasil, was already moving rapidly through clinical trials. Merck Sharp & Dohme LLC, "A Safety and Immunogenicity Study of Quadrivalent HPV (Types 6, 11, 16, 18) L1 Virus-Like Particle (VLP) Vaccine in Preadolescents and Adolescents (Base Study). A Long Term Immunogenicity, Safety, and Effectiveness Study of GARDA-SIL (Human Papillomavirus [Types 6, 11, 16, 18] Recombinant Vaccine) Among Adolescents Who Received GARDASIL at 9–18 Years of Age (Extension Study)," Clinical Trial Registration (clinicaltrials.gov, January 22, 2018), https://clinicaltrials .gov/ct2/show/NCT00092547.

314 **"women will die"**: "Bill Gates Explains the Importance of the HPV Vaccine to Women in Developing Countries," Gavi, n.d., https://www.gavi.org/bill-gates-explains -importance-hpv-vaccine-women-developing-countries.

314 **immunization technical advisory committees**: Alex Adjagba et al., "Supporting
Countries in Establishing and Strengthening NITAGs: Lessons Learned from 5 Years
of the SIVAC Initiative," *Vaccine* 33, no. 5 (January 29, 2015): 588–95, https://doi.org
/10.1016/j.vaccine.2014.12.026; Kamel Senouci et al., "The Supporting Independent
Immunization and Vaccine Advisory Committees (SIVAC) Initiative: A Country-
Driven, Multi-Partner Program to Support Evidence-Based Decision Making," *Vaccine* 28 (April 19, 2010): A26–30, https://doi.org/10.1016/j.vaccine.2010.02.028.

314 **"techno-managerial"**: Anubhuti Vishnoi, "Melinda Gates: Centre Shuts Health Mission Gate on Bill & Melinda Gates Foundation," *Economic Times*, February 9, 2017,
https://economictimes.indiatimes.com/news/politics-and-nation/centre-shuts
-gate-on-bill-melinda-gates-foundation/articleshow/57028697.cms?from=mdr;
Ministry of Health and Family Welfare, "Press Note," Press Information Bureau,
Government of India, February 8, 2017, https://pib.gov.in/newsite/PrintRelease.aspx
?relid=158277.

314 **Indian government defines**: Ministry of Health and Family Welfare, "Press Note."

315 **he had no knowledge**: Vishnoi, "Melinda Gates: Centre Shuts Health Mission Gate
on Bill & Melinda Gates Foundation." Note: When PHFI first launched, its website
shows that its governing board included myriad Gates employees and consultants. In
2006, Gates provided $15 million in seed money to launch the Public Health Founda-
tion of India (PHFI) "to contribute to the establishment of institutions of public health
in India." This money was pooled with government and private-sector funding. PHFI
then went on to host the "Immunization Technical Support Unit" with Gates's funding. "About Us, Governing Board," Public Health Foundation of India, n.d., https://
web.archive.org/web/20070203004624/http://www.phfi.org/about/gboard.html; "Our
Supporters," Public Health Foundation of India, July 19, 2017, https://phfi.org/our
-supporters/.

315 **born out of this problem**: "Our Supporters," Public Health Foundation of India.

316 **concerned about ethical issues**: Aarti Dhar, "PHFI Rejected HPV Vaccine Project Proposal," *Hindu*, February 17, 2011, https://www.thehindu.com/news/national
/PHFI-rejected-HPV-vaccine-project-proposal/article15448274.ece.

316 **international trial**: Sanjay Kumar and Declan Butler, "Calls in India for Legal Action
Against US Charity," *Nature*, September 9, 2013, https://www.nature.com/articles
/nature.2013.13700.

316 **medical ethicists and feminist groups**: Kaushik Sunder Rajan, *Pharmocracy: Value,
Politics, and Knowledge in Global Biomedicine* (Durham, NC: Duke University Press,
2017).

316 **basic preventative care**: "Memorandum on Concerns Around HPV Vaccines," to
Shri Ghulam Nabi Azad, Union Minister for Health and Family Welfare, Ministry of
Health and Family Welfare," Sama, October 1, 2009, https://samawomenshealth.in
/memorandum-on-concerns-around-hpv-vaccines/.

316 **"to preserve ethical standards"**: Marium Salwa and Tarek Abdullah Al-Munim,
"Ethical Issues Related to Human Papillomavirus Vaccination Programs: An Example from Bangladesh," *BMC Medical Ethics* 19, No. 39 (2018): 86.

317 **pneumonia vaccine**: Rodgers, "Creating a Life-Saving PCV Vaccine for Pneumonia
in India."

317 **funding the body that provides**: The expert committee Rodgers describes is the National Technical Advisory Group on Immunisation (NTAGI), whose secretariat was long housed at the adjacent, Gates-funded Immunization Technical Support Unit; see also Ministry of Health and Family Welfare, "Press Note."

317 **forthcoming about playing so many roles**: In late 2022, the news media even reported that the Gates Foundation intended to hire a board member of India's National Technical Advisory Group on Immunization to join the foundation's staff, Gagandeep Kang. Kang at that point had already established close institutional ties to the foundation, serving as one of a dozen members of its "Scientific Advisory Committee." "India's Ace Virologist Dr Gagandeep Kang to Join Gates Foundation as Director, Global Health," *Financial Express*, November 15, 2022, https://www.financialexpress.com/healthcare/indias-ace -virologist-dr-gagandeep-kang-to-join-gates-foundation-as-director-global-health /2815918/; "Scientific Advisory Committee," Bill & Melinda Gates Foundation, n.d., https://www.gatesfoundation.org/about/leadership/scientific-advisory-committee.

317 **no autopsies**: Pallava Bagla, "Indian Parliament Comes Down Hard on Cervical Cancer Trial," *Science*, September 9, 2013, https://www.science.org/content/article /indian-parliament-comes-down-hard-cervical-cancer-trial.

318 **"becomes politically impossible"**: Rajya Sabha Secretariat, "Alleged Irregularities in the Conduct of Studies Using Human Papilloma Virus (HPV) Vaccine by PATH in India," Report No. 72, Department of Health Research, Ministry of Health and Family Welfare, Related Parliamentary Standing Committee on Health and Family Welfare, August 2013, Parliament of India, New Delhi, 164.100.47.5/newcommittee /reports/EnglishCommittees/Committee on Health and Family Welfare/72.pdf.

318 **$54 billion endowment**: Schwab, "While the Poor Get Sick, Bill Gates Just Gets Richer"; and Schwab, "Bill Gates Gives to the Rich (Including Himself)."

318 **allegations of wrongdoing**: Kumar and Butler, "Calls in India for Legal Action Against US Charity"; McGoey, *No Such Thing as a Free Gift*.

319 **subsidiary of Gates**: This includes direct donations to PATH and related organizations like PATH Vaccine Solutions.

319 **Indian medical regulators**: Bagla, "Indian Parliament Comes Down Hard on Cervical Cancer Trial."

319 **new HPV vaccine**: "HPV Vaccination in South Asia: New Progress, Old Challenges" (editorial), *Lancet Oncology* 23, no. 10 (October 1, 2022): 1233, https:// pubmed.ncbi.nlm.nih.gov/36174615/; "Serum Institute of India launches the First Made-in-India qHPV Vaccine 'CERVAVAC,'" Serum Institute of India, January 24, 2023, https://www.seruminstitute.com/news_sii_cervavac_launch_240123.php.

320 **Foreign Contribution (Regulation) Act**: Vijaita Singh and Vidya Krishnan, "Gates Foundation on Centre's Radar," *Hindu*, February 9, 2016, https://www.thehindu.com /news/national/gates-foundation-on-centres-radar/article8215060.ece.

320 **stepping down from the bank**: Nachiket Mor, LinkedIn, n.d., https://www.linkedin .com/in/nachiketmor/details/experience/; Joel Rebello, "Nachiket Mor's 2nd Tenure on RBI Board Cut Short," *Economic Times*, October 1, 2018, https://m.economictimes .com/banking/nachiket-mors-2nd-tenure-on-rbi-board-cut-short/amp_article show/66022164.cms.

320 **did anything wrong**: "India, Nepal, and Sri Lanka," Ford Foundation, n.d., https://www.fordfoundation.org/our-work-around-the-world/india-nepal-and-sri-lanka/.

321 **place new restrictions**: Vidya Krishnan and Vijaita Singh, "PHFI Loses FCRA Licence for Lobbying," *Hindu*, April 19, 2017, https://www.thehindu.com/news/national/phfi-loses-fcra-licence-for-lobbying/article18149292.ece.

321 **These restrictions were lifted**: "FCRA Registration of MoC, PHFI Restored: Govt to Lok Sabha," *Indian Express*, February 8, 2022, https://indianexpress.com/article/india/fcra-registration-of-moc-phfi-restored-govt-to-lok-sabha-7763372/.

321 **Gates-funded PHFI**: Vishnoi, "Melinda Gates: Centre Shuts Health Mission Gate on Bill & Melinda Gates Foundation."

321 **human rights abuses in Kashmir**: "Has India's Kashmir Policy Under Modi Failed?," Al Jazeera, June 15, 2022, https://www.aljazeera.com/news/2022/6/15/has-india-kashmir-policy-under-modi-failed.

321 **condemned the Modi award**: Gharib, "Gates Foundation's Humanitarian Award to India's Modi Is Sparking Outrage."

321 **resigned in protest**: Sabah Hamid, "Why I Resigned from the Gates Foundation," *New York Times*, September 26, 2019, https://www.nytimes.com/2019/09/26/opinion/modi-gates-award.html.

323 **leading the G20**: "Strategy Consultant—SDGs & International Development Specialist," Job Posting, Flexing It, May 19, 2022, https://web.archive.org/web/20230215155230/https://www.flexingit.com/project/an-american-private-foundation/bdd003/.

CHAPTER 15: COVID-19

324 **University of Oxford's Jenner Institute**: David D. Kirkpatrick, "In Race for a Coronavirus Vaccine, an Oxford Group Leaps Ahead," *New York Times*, April 27, 2020, https://www.nytimes.com/2020/04/27/world/europe/coronavirus-vaccine-update-oxford.html.

324 **Adrian Hill**: Stephanie Baker, "Oxford's Covid-19 Vaccine Is the Coronavirus Front-Runner," Bloomberg, July 15, 2020, https://www.bloomberg.com/news/features/2020-07-15/oxford-s-covid-19-vaccine-is-the-coronavirus-front-runner.

324 **university's vaccine's enormous potential**: Kirkpatrick, "In Race for a Coronavirus Vaccine, an Oxford Group Leaps Ahead."

325 **Coalition for Epidemic Preparedness Innovations**: "Investment Overview, as of December 13, 2022," CEPI, https://100days.cepi.net/wp-content/uploads/2022/12/2022_12_13-CEPI-Investment-Overview.pdf; Katie Thomas and Megan Twohey, "How a Struggling Company Won $1.6 Billion to Make a Coronavirus Vaccine," *New York Times*, July 16, 2020, https://www.nytimes.com/2020/07/16/health/coronavirus-vaccine-novavax.html.

325 **four of its internal committees**: The Gates Foundation sits on the group's Governing Board, its Scientific Advisory Panel, and its Portfolio Strategy and Management Board—all of which have decision-making power in CEPI's "portfolio management process," according to an email from CEPI in 2022.

325 **"we know how to work with pharma"**: Twohey and Kulish, "Bill Gates, the Virus and the Quest to Vaccinate the World."

325 **"worried that drugmakers"**: Twohey and Kulish, "Bill Gates, the Virus and the Quest to Vaccinate the World."

326 **treat it as a necessary evil**: Richard Horton, "Offline: Bill Gates and the Fate of WHO," *The Lancet*, May 14, 2022, https://www.thelancet.com/journals/lancet/article /PIIS0140-6736(22)00874-1/fulltext?dgcid=raven_jbs_etoc_email.

327 **reporting that Bill Gates had "predicted"**: "Bill Gates Predicted Pandemic. Hear His Advice Now," CNN, June 26, 2020, https://edition.cnn.com/videos/health/2020 /06/26/bill-gates-virus-prediction-advice-town-hall-vpx.cnn; Joseph Guzman, "Bill Gates, Who Predicted the Pandemic, Names the Next Two Monster Disasters That Could Shake Our World," Text, *The Hill* (blog), February 11, 2021, https://thehill .com/changing-america/well-being/538426-bill-gates-who-predicted-the-pandemic -names-the-next-two-monster/.

327 **actually building factories**: Jennifer Calfas, "Bill Gates to Help Fund Coronavirus-Vaccine Development," *Wall Street Journal*, April 5, 2020, uncorrected version available at https://web.archive.org/web/20200405224915/https://www.wsj.com/articles /bill-gates-to-spend-billions-on-coronavirus-vaccine-development-11586124716; Isobel Asher Hamilton, "Bill Gates Is Helping Fund New Factories for 7 Potential Coronavirus Vaccines, Even Though It Will Waste Billions of Dollars," *Business Insider*, April 3, 2020, https://www.businessinsider.com/bill-gates-factories-7-different -vaccines-to-fight-coronavirus-2020-4.

327 **"need to team up"**: Jay Hancock, "They Pledged to Donate Rights to Their Covid Vaccine, Then Sold Them to Pharma," *Kaiser Health News*, August 25, 2020, https:// khn.org/news/rather-than-give-away-its-covid-vaccine-oxford-makes-a-deal-with -drugmaker/.

328 **Trevor Mundel**: Erin Banco, "How Bill Gates and His Partners Took Over the Global Covid Pandemic Response," Politico, September 14, 2022, https://www.politico.com /news/2022/09/14/global-covid-pandemic-response-bill-gates-partners-00053969.

328 **an open license**: Hancock, "They Pledged to Donate Rights to Their Covid Vaccine, Then Sold Them to Pharma."

328 **Oxford's Adrian Hill**: Kirkpatrick, "In Race for a Coronavirus Vaccine, an Oxford Group Leaps Ahead."

328 **helping companies speed up**: Rebecca Robbins et al., "Blunders Eroded U.S. Confidence in Early Vaccine Front-Runner," *New York Times*, December 8, 2020, https:// www.nytimes.com/2020/12/08/business/covid-vaccine-oxford-astrazeneca.html.

329 **trillions of dollars**: David M. Cutler and Lawrence H. Summers, "The Covid-19 Pandemic and the $16 Trillion Virus," *JAMA* 324, no. 15 (October 20, 2020): 1495–96, https://doi.org/10.1001/jama.2020.19759.

329 **"concentration of power"**: It's not clear, however, that the Oxford-AstraZeneca partnership should be seen as an example of Bill Gates single-handedly changing the direction of the pandemic response. Two Oxford scientists behind the Covid-19 vaccine had their own financial interests to consider, as their stakes in the spin-off company Vaccitech reportedly went on to make them extremely wealthy. Whatever role the foundation played, Oxford's decision shows us that the Gates Foundation was positioned to advise it—and that its advice was unambiguously organized around a patent-forward, Big Pharma model. Rupert Neate, "AstraZeneca Vaccine

Scientists Set for £22M Payday in New York Float," *Guardian*, April 7, 2021, https://www.theguardian.com/business/2021/apr/07/astrazeneca-vaccine-scientists-set-for-22m-payday-in-new-york-float.

329   **"the whole world is watching"**: Adele Peters, "Inside the Gates Foundation's Epic Fight Against Covid-19," Fast Company, December 14, 2020, https://www.fastcompany.com/90579390/inside-the-gates-foundations-epic-fight-against-covid-19.

329   **Jenner Institute**: "Funders & Partners," Jenner Institute, n.d., https://web.archive.org/web/20190517085723/https:/www.jenner.ac.uk/funders-partners.

329   **backing Oxford's vaccine**: "CEPI Expands Investment in Covid-19 Vaccine Development," CEPI, March 10, 2020, https://cepi.net/news_cepi/cepi-expands-investment-in-covid-19-vaccine-development/.

329   **up to $384 million**: "Oxford University Announces Landmark Partnership with AstraZeneca for the Development and Potential Large-Scale Distribution of Covid-19 Vaccine Candidate," University of Oxford, April 30, 2020, https://www.ox.ac.uk/news/2020-04-30-oxford-university-announces-landmark-partnership-astrazeneca-development-and; "Epidemic Response Group to Invest Up to $384 Mln in Novavax's Covid-19 Vaccine," Reuters, May 11, 2020, https://www.reuters.com/article/us-health-coronavirus-vaccines-cepi-idUKKBN22N2RP.

329   **"300 million doses"**: "AstraZeneca Takes Next Steps Towards Broad and Equitable Access to Oxford University's Covid-19 Vaccine," AstraZeneca, June 4, 2020, https://www.astrazeneca.com/media-centre/press-releases/2020/astrazeneca-takes-next-steps-towards-broad-and-equitable-access-to-oxford-universitys-covid-19-vaccine.html.

330   **"Phase Three data"**: Schwab, "While the Poor Get Sick, Bill Gates Just Gets Richer."

330   **"second-source agreements"**: Bill Gates, "These Breakthroughs Will Make 2021 Better than 2020," *GatesNotes*, December 22, 2020, https://www.gatesnotes.com/Year-in-Review-2020.

330   **a private company and the largest**: "About Us," Serum Institute of India.

331   **world's largest vaccine manufacturer**: "Up to 100 Million Covid-19 Vaccine Doses to Be Made Available for Low- and Middle-Income Countries as Early as 2021," Gavi, August 7, 2020, https://www.gavi.org/news/media-room/100-million-covid-19-vaccine-doses-available-low-and-middle-income-countries-2021; Gavi Staff, "New Collaboration Makes Further 100 Million Doses of Covid-19 Vaccine Available to Low- and Middle-Income Countries."

331   **"the financial risk"**: Gates, "These Breakthroughs Will Make 2021 Better than 2020."

331   **a dynamic duo**: Twohey and Kulish, "Bill Gates, the Virus and the Quest to Vaccinate the World."

331   **Serum drew criticism**: Helen Sullivan, "South Africa Paying More than Double EU Price for Oxford Vaccine," *Guardian*, January 22, 2021, https://www.theguardian.com/world/2021/jan/22/south-africa-paying-more-than-double-eu-price-for-oxford-astrazeneca-vaccine.

331   **Critics then cried foul**: Samanth Subramanian, "Why Is India, the World's Largest Vaccine Producer, Running Short of Vaccines?," Quartz, May 6, 2021, https://qz.com/2004650/why-does-india-have-a-covid-19-vaccine-shortage/.

331   **issued an export ban**: "Serum Institute of India Gets Nod to Export Covid-19 Vaccines

Under the COVAX Programme, Says Source," *Business Insider*, November 22, https://
www.businessinsider.in/science/health/news/serum-institute-of-india-gets-nod-to
-export-covid-19-vaccines-under-the-covax-programme-says-source/articleshow
/87852389.cms.

331 **Strive Masiyiwa**: "Indian Vaccine Maker Extends Freeze on Export of Covid Jabs,"
Financial Times, May 18, 2021, https://www.ft.com/content/63fbbb79-f657-4e6c
-b190-cffd0d630593.

331 **joined the board**: Schwab, "Will the Gates Foundation's Board Ever Hold Bill
Accountable?"

332 **reliable access to electricity to run freezers**: Jon Cohen, "AstraZeneca Lowers Efficacy Claim for Covid-19 Vaccine, a Bit, After Board's Rebuke," *Science*, March 25, 2021,
https://www.science.org/content/article/astrazeneca-lowers-efficacy-claim-covid-19
-vaccine-bit-after-boards-rebuke.

332 **poor nations began avoiding**: Francesco Guarascio, "Poorer Nations Shun Astra-
Zeneca Covid Vaccine—Document," Reuters, April 14, 2022, https://www.reuters
.com/business/healthcare-pharmaceuticals/poorer-nations-shun-astrazeneca-covid
-vaccine-document-2022-04-14/.

332 **sitting on an unused stockpile**: Angus Liu, "With 200M Unused Doses, AstraZeneca's Covid Vaccine Partner Serum Institute Halts Production," Fierce Pharma, April
22, 2022, https://www.fiercepharma.com/pharma/200m-unused-doses-astrazenecas
-covid-vaccine-partner-serum-institute-halts-production.

332 **"plagued by missteps"**: Cohen, "AstraZeneca Lowers Efficacy Claim for Covid-19
Vaccine, a Bit, After Board's Rebuke."

332 **saved more lives**: "Oxford Vaccine Saved Most Lives in Its First Year of Rollout,"
University of Oxford, July 15, 2022, https://www.ox.ac.uk/news/2022-07-15-oxford
-vaccine-saved-most-lives-its-first-year-rollout; "Global Vaccine Market Report: A
Shared Understanding for Equitable Access to Vaccines," World Health Organization,
2022, https://www.who.int/publications/m/item/global-vaccine-market-report-2022.

332 **big vaccine bet, Novavax**: Sarah Owermohle, Erin Banco, and Adam Cancryn, "'They
Rushed the Process': Vaccine Maker's Woes Hamper Global Inoculation Campaign,"
Politico, October 19, 2021, https://www.politico.com/news/2021/10/19/novavax
-vaccine-rush-process-global-campaign-516298; Carolyn Y. Johnson, "Maker of
Latest Experimental Vaccine Will Not Seek Authorization Until July at the Earliest,"
Washington Post, May 10, 2021, https://www.washingtonpost.com/health/2021/05
/10/novavax-coronavirus-vaccine/.

332 **another $400 million**: Thomas and Twohey, "How a Struggling Company Won $1.6
Billion to Make a Coronavirus Vaccine"; "Our Portfolio," CEPI, n.d., https://cepi.net
/research_dev/our-portfolio/.

332 **the green light from the FDA**: Rita Rubin, "Despite Its Fan Base, Newly Authorized
'Traditional' Novavax Covid-19 Vaccine Is Having Trouble Gaining a Foothold in
the US," *JAMA* 328, no. 11 (September 20, 2022): 1026–28, https://doi.org/10.1001
/jama.2022.13661; Rebecca Robbins and Carl Zimmer, "F.D.A. Authorizes Novavax's
Covid-19 Vaccine, a Latecomer," *New York Times*, July 13, 2022, https://www.nytimes
.com/2022/07/13/health/novavax-covid-vaccine-fda-authorization.html.

333 **pool money**: "COVAX Explained," Gavi, September 3, 2020, https://www.gavi.org /vaccineswork/covax-explained.

333 **delivering diagnostics and treatments**: "COVAX: The Vaccines Pillar of the Access to Covid-19 Tools (ACT) Accelerator, Structures and Principles," Gavi, November 9, 2020, https://www.who.int/publications/m/item/covax-the-vaccines-pillar-of-the -access-to-covid-19-tools-(act)-accelerator.

333 **described COVAX as a "Gates operation"**: Alexander Zaitchik, "How Bill Gates Impeded Global Access to Covid Vaccines," *New Republic*, April 12, 2021, https://newrepublic.com/article/162000/bill-gates-impeded-global-access-covid -vaccines.

333 **no public mandate**: Kai Kupferschmidt, "'Vaccine Nationalism' Threatens Global Plan to Distribute Covid-19 Shots Fairly," *Science*, July 28, 2020, https://www.science .org/content/article/vaccine-nationalism-threatens-global-plan-distribute-covid-19 -shots-fairly.

333 **Ecuador's then health minister**: Twohey and Kulish, "Bill Gates, the Virus and the Quest to Vaccinate the World."

334 **rich and the poor, the winners and losers**: Ashley Kirk, Finbarr Sheehy, and Cath Levett, "Canada and UK Among Countries with Most Vaccine Doses Ordered per Person," *Guardian*, January 29, 2021, https://www.theguardian.com/world/2021/jan/29 /canada-and-uk-among-countries-with-most-vaccine-doses-ordered-per-person.

334 **didn't alter the logic of the market**: Peters, "Inside the Gates Foundation's Epic Fight Against Covid-19."

334 **entirely without access**: Andrew Gregory, "Only 14% of Promised Covid Vaccine Doses Reach Poorest Nations," *Guardian*, October 21, 2021, https://www .theguardian.com/society/2021/oct/21/only-14-of-promised-covid-vaccine-doses -reach-poorest-nations.

334 **twice as many**: Maria Cheng and Lori Hinnant, "Rich Nations Dip into COVAX Supply While Poor Wait for Shots," AP News, August 14, 2021, https://apnews.com /article/joe-biden-middle-east-africa-europe-coronavirus-pandemic-5e57879c6cb2 2d96b942cbc973b9296c.

334 **the Associated Press reported**: Lori Hinnant and Maria Cheng, "Stalled at First Jab: Vaccine Shortages Hit Poor Countries," AP News, April 20, 2021, https://apnews .com/article/middle-east-coronavirus-pandemic-united-nations-b52bf58e35031e7 1a5ff85f7a59244f8; Maria Cheng and Aniruddha Ghosal, "Unwilling to Wait, Poorer Countries Seek Their Own Vaccines," AP News, April 20, 2021, https://apnews.com /article/business-honduras-coronavirus-vaccine-coronavirus-pandemic-central -america-16d7d06f031c89aaf37a4306747b9128.

334 **World Trade Organization**: Gabriel Scally, "The World Needs a Patent Waiver on Covid Vaccines. Why Is the UK Blocking It?," *Guardian*, April 18, 2021, https://www .theguardian.com/commentisfree/2021/apr/18/patent-waiver-covid-vaccines-uk -variants.

335 **"limited not because of IP rules"**: Bill Gates, "Bill Gates: How We Can Close the Vaccine Gap Much Faster Next Time," CNN, October 13, 2021, https://www.cnn .com/2021/10/13/opinions/closing-vaccine-gap-faster-bill-gates/index.html.

335 **"factory in India"**: "Covid-19: Bill Gates Hopeful World 'Completely Back to Nor-mal' by End of 2022—and Vaccine Sharing to Ramp Up," Video, Sky News, 2:45, April 25, 2021, https://news.sky.com/story/covid-19-bill-gates-hopeful-world-completely-back-to-normal-by-end-of-2022-and-vaccine-sharing-to-ramp-up-12285840.

335 **pandemic response effort was succeeding**: "Covid-19: Bill Gates Hopeful World 'Completely Back to Normal' by End of 2022," 8:15.

335 **"We have the facilities and equipment"**: Stephen Buranyi, "The World Is Desperate for More Covid Vaccines—Patents Shouldn't Get in the Way," *Guardian*, April 24, 2021, https://www.theguardian.com/commentisfree/2021/apr/24/covid-vaccines-patents-pharmaceutical-companies-secrecy.

335 **capable of producing vaccines**: Maria Cheng and Lori Hinnant, "Countries Urge Drug Companies to Share Vaccine Know-How," AP News, March 1, 2021, https://apnews.com/article/drug-companies-called-share-vaccine-info-22d92afbc3ea9ed519be007f8887bcf6; Sharon Lerner, "Factory Owners Around the World Stand Ready to Manufacture Covid-19 Vaccines," *The Intercept*, April 29, 2021, https://theintercept.com/2021/04/29/covid-vaccine-factory-production-ip/; Stephanie Nolen, "Here's Why Developing Countries Can Make mRNA Covid Vaccines," *New York Times,* October 22, 2021, https://www.nytimes.com/interactive/2021/10/22/science/developing-country-covid-vaccines.html.

335 **Human Rights Watch**: Human Rights Watch, "Experts Identify 100-Plus Firms to Make Covid-19 mRNA Vaccines," December 15, 2021, https://www.hrw.org/news/2021/12/15/experts-identify-100-plus-firms-make-covid-19-mrna-vaccines.

335 **"Any delay in ensuring"**: Joseph E. Stiglitz and Lori Wallach, "Preserving Intellec-tual Property Barriers to Covid-19 Vaccines Is Morally Wrong and Foolish," *Wash-ington Post*, April 26, 2021, https://www.washingtonpost.com/opinions/2021/04/26/preserving-intellectual-property-barriers-covid-19-vaccines-is-morally-wrong-foolish/.

336 **Chelsea Clinton**: Chelsea Clinton and Achal Prabhala, "The Vaccine Donations Aren't Enough," *Atlantic*, June 20, 2021, https://www.theatlantic.com/ideas/archive/2021/06/the-vaccine-donations-arent-enough-chelsea-clinton-achal-prabhala/619152/.

336 **"stupidest thing"**: Kai Kupferschmidt, "Bill Gates: 'That's the Dumbest Thing I've Ever Heard,'" *Die Zeit*, October 27, 2021, https://www.zeit.de/gesundheit/2021–10/bill-gates-corona-impfung-patente-patentrecht-stiftung-verteilung?utm_referrer=https%3A%2F%2Fwww.google.com%2F.

336 **sophisticated manufacturing**: Deep in the pandemic, Gates noted on CNN that "we're supporting the African efforts to build theirs [vaccine capacity] out by 2040," a much-belated effort. Gates, "How We Can Close the Vaccine Gap Much Faster Next Time."

336 **"narrow" waiver**: Kurt Schlosser, "Gates Foundation Reverses Position on COVID Vaccine Patent Protections After Mounting Pressure," GeekWire, May 7, 2021, https://www.geekwire.com/2021/gates-foundation-reverses-position-covid-vaccine-patent-protections-mounting-pressure/.

337 *New Republic*: Zaitchik, "How Bill Gates Impeded Global Access to Covid Vaccines."

338 **autopsies of the faceless COVAX**: Stephanie Nolen and Rebecca Robbins, "Covid

Vaccine Makers Kept $1.4 Billion in Prepayments for Canceled Shots for the World's Poor," *New York Times*, February 1, 2023, https://www.nytimes.com/2023/02/01 /health/covid-vaccines-covax-gavi-prepayments.html.

338 **failures of COVAX**: Rosa Furneaux, Olivia Goldhill, and Madlen Davies, "How COVAX Failed on Its Promise to Vaccinate the World," Bureau of Investigative Journalism, October 8, 2021, https://www.thebureauinvestigates.com/stories /2021-10-08/how-covax-failed-on-its-promise-to-vaccinate-the-world.

338 **lives-saved PR**: Oliver J. Watson et al., "Global Impact of the First Year of Covid-19 Vaccination: A Mathematical Modelling Study," *Lancet Infectious Diseases* 22, no. 9 (September 1, 2022): 1293–302, https://www.thelancet.com/journals/laninf/article /PIIS1473-3099(22)00320-6/fulltext; "Covid-19 Vaccines Have Saved 20 Million Lives So Far, Study Estimates," Gavi, n.d., https://www.gavi.org/vaccineswork/covid -19-vaccines-have-saved-20-million-lives-so-far-study-estimates; Storeng, Puyvallée, and Stein, "COVAX and the Rise of the 'Super Public Private Partnership' for Global Health."

339 **"crumbling vaccine system"**: Peters, "Inside the Gates Foundation's Epic Fight Against Covid-19." Note: The foundation's work on specific diseases and interventions theoretically can also have beneficial spillover effects that enhance public health more broadly. For example, some of the projects Gates supports on HIV/AIDS, polio, and tuberculosis have been reorganized to assist with outbreaks like Ebola and SARS-CoV-2 (Covid-19). However, these programs are often not designed for these cross-cutting purposes and thus offer limited benefits, with researchers describing them as parallel systems that don't always intersect with government-organized public health systems. Chikwe Ihekweazu, "Lessons from Nigeria's Adaptation of Global Health Initiatives During the Covid-19 Pandemic," *Emerging Infectious Diseases* 28, Suppl. 1 (December 2022): S299–301, https://www.ncbi.nlm.nih.gov/pmc /articles/PMC9745227/.

339 **success of Cuba**: Sam Meredith, "Why Cuba's Extraordinary Covid Vaccine Success Could Provide the Best Hope for Low-Income Countries," CNBC, January 13, 2022, https://www.cnbc.com/2022/01/13/why-cubas-extraordinary-covid-vaccine -success-could-provide-the-best-hope-for-the-global-south.html; Mary Beth Sheridan, "How Cuba Became a Pioneer in Covid-19 Vaccines for Kids," *Washington Post*, June 18, 2022, https://www.washingtonpost.com/world/2022/06/18/cuba -coronavirus-vaccine-abdala-soberana/.

339 **U.S. embargo**: Bill & Melinda Gates Foundation, "Sample Terms & Conditions, Project Support Grant Agreement," n.d., https://docs.gatesfoundation.org/documents /sample-terms-and-conditions.pdf.

340 **less expensive than other vaccines**: "Doctor on Developing Global Covid-19 Vaccine: 'We Got Zero Help from the U.S. Government,'" Yahoo! News, February 8, 2022, https://news.yahoo.com/covid-vaccines-policymakers-never-really-211439188 .html. Note: UNICEF's records show that Corbevax is the lowest-priced vaccine, at under two dollars per dose, compared to the Oxford-AstraZeneca-Serum vaccine, which sold, at its lowest price, for three dollars. Covid-19 Market Dashboard, UNICEF, n.d., https://www.unicef.org/supply/covid-19-market-dashboard.

340 **IndoVac**: "Indonesia's Bio Farma Ready to Produce IndoVac Covid-19 Vaccines,"

Bloomberg, September 11, 2022, https://www.bloomberg.com/press-releases/2022
-09-11/indonesia-s-bio-farma-ready-to-produce-indovac-covid-19-vaccines.

340 **Gates's top-pick vaccine manufacturer**: Thomas and Twohey, "How a Struggling Company Won $1.6 Billion to Make a Coronavirus Vaccine"; "Our Portfolio," CEPI.

340 **can be quickly scaled up**: Peter J. Hotez and Maria Elena Bottazzi, "A Covid Vaccine for All," *Scientific American*, December 30, 2021, https://www.scientificamerican .com/article/a-covid-vaccine-for-all/.

341 **"capacity building"**: During the pandemic, as poor nations and public health experts widely called for local and regional manufacturing of Covid-19 vaccines, the foundation began presenting itself as a champion of working with "developing country vaccine manufacturers," or DCVMs. "Over the past two decades, our foundation has given US$1 billion in support to DCVMs and related grantees and has worked with 19 DCVMS across 11 countries to bring 17 vaccines to market," the foundation boasted. "These collaborations have made a tremendous difference all over the world." The foundation, notably, does not name all 17 of these vaccines. And the few examples it gives of "developing country" partners include projects based in South Korea, a highly advanced economy. The foundation also points to its work with the Serum Institute of India, the largest vaccine manufacturer in the world and, arguably, part of Big Pharma. Zaidi, "Geographically Distributed Manufacturing Capacity Is Needed for Improved Global Health Security."

341 **notable about Peter Hotez**: "Gates Foundation Commits Nearly $70 Million to Help Fight Neglected Tropical Diseases," Bill & Melinda Gates Foundation, n.d., https://www.gatesfoundation.org/ideas/media-center/press-releases/2006/09/$70 -million-to-help-fight-neglected-tropical-diseases; "Albert B. Sabin Vaccine Institute Signs Agreement with GW Medical Center for Collaboration on $18 Million Bill & Melinda Gates Foundation Research Grant," Bill & Melinda Gates Foundation, n.d., https://www.gatesfoundation.org/ideas/media-center/press-releases/2000 /08/hookworm-vaccine-research.

341 **George Washington University**: "Albert B. Sabin Vaccine Institute Signs Agreement with GW Medical Center for Collaboration on $18 Million Bill & Melinda Gates Foundation Research Grant."

341 **"funding the diseases"**: Fratangelo, "How Gates Changes Global Public Health."

342 *Preventing the Next Pandemic*: Peter J. Hotez, *Preventing the Next Pandemic: Vaccine Diplomacy in a Time of Anti-Science* (Baltimore: Johns Hopkins University Press, 2021); Bill Gates, *How to Prevent the Next Pandemic* (New York: Alfred A. Knopf, 2022).

342 **"ten to the seven dollars"**: By this, Hotez means 10 to the seventh power, or $10,000,000 in this case, vs. 10 to the fifth power, which is $100,000.

343 **new malaria vaccine that the pharma giant GSK rolled out**: Abdi Latif Dahir, "Africans Welcome New Malaria Vaccine. But Is It a 'Game Changer'?," *New York Times*, October 7, 2021, https://www.nytimes.com/2021/10/07/world/africa /malaria-vaccine-africa.html; Amy Maxmen, "Scientists Hail Historic Malaria Vaccine Approval—but Point to Challenges Ahead," *Nature*, October 8, 2021, https://www.nature.com/articles/d41586-021-02755-5.

343 **publicly distanced itself**: Carmen Paun and Daniel Payne, "How the Gates Foundation Plans to Beat Malaria Without the Vaccine," Politico, August 4, 2022, https://www

.politico.com/newsletters/global-pulse/2022/07/07/moving-on-from-malaria -vaccine-00044349. Note: One caveat is that the Gates-funded Gavi put $155 million into the malaria vaccine's rollout, a decision the Gates Foundation publicly supported, as reported by Politico.

343 **college dropout**: Gates, "My Annual Letter: Vaccine Miracles."

343 **eradicate malaria**: "Malaria Forum," Bill & Melinda Gates Foundation, October 7, 2007, https://www.gatesfoundation.org/ideas/speeches/2007/10/melinda-french -gates-malaria-forum.

343 **"good vaccine for malaria"**: Moyers, "A Conversation with Bill Gates: Making a Healthier World for Children and Future Generations."

343 **forward-looking claims**: Nicholas Kristof, "A Conversation with Bill Gates," *New York Times*, January 24, 2009, https://www.nytimes.com/video/opinion/1231546145505/a -conversation-with-bill-gates.html.

344 **"involved in bed-nets"**: Andy Beckett, "Inside the Bill and Melinda Gates Foundation," *Guardian*, July 12, 2010, https://www.theguardian.com/world/2010/jul/12/bill -and-melinda-gates-foundation.

344 **Global Fund**: S. Bhatt et al., "The Effect of Malaria Control on *Plasmodium falciparum* in Africa Between 2000 and 2015," *Nature* 526, no. 7572 (October 2015): 207–11, https://doi.org/10.1038/nature15535; The Global Fund, Annex 1, *Results Report 2022*, September 7, 2022, https://www.theglobalfund.org/media/12261 /corporate_2022resultsreport_annex_en.pdf.

344 **progress against malaria has leveled off**: World Health Organization, *World Malaria Report 2020: 20 Years of Global Progress and Challenges*, 2020, vii.

344 **hundreds of thousands of deaths**: World Health Organization, *World Malaria Report 2020*, 18–20.

CONCLUSION

345 **"put the foundation's reputation"**: *Inside Bill's Brain*, episode 2 at 16:00 and 40:00.

345 **"March of Dimes posters"**: Donald G. McNeil Jr., "Gates Calls for a Final Push to Eradicate Polio," *New York Times*, January 31, 2011, https://www.nytimes.com/2011 /02/01/health/01polio.html.

345 **"the DPT"**: McGoey, *No Such Thing as a Free Gift*.

346 **Oliver Razum**: Robert Fortner, "Has the Billion Dollar Crusade to Eradicate Polio Come to an End?," *BMJ* 374, no. 1818 (July 29, 2021), https://www.bmj.com/content /374/bmj.n1818.

346 **"single thing I work on"**: Goodell, "Bill Gates: The Rolling Stone Interview."

346 **at the urging**: GPEI, "Historical Contributions 1988–2021," Global Polio Eradication Initiative, n.d., https://polioeradication.org/financing/donors/historical-contributions; William A. Muraskin, *Polio Eradication and Its Discontents: A Historian's Journey Through an International Public Health (Un)Civil War* (Hyderabad: Orient Blackswan, 2012), 1177; McGoey, *No Such Thing as a Free Gift*.

346 **pushed the WHO**: Fortner and Park, "Bill Gates Won't Save You from the Next Ebola."

347 **"We're orchestrating"**: "Bill Gates: 'We Can Eradicate Polio,'" BBC News, January 29, 2013, https://www.bbc.co.uk/news/av/health-21241946.

347 **were paralyzed in 2020**: Fortner, "Has the Billion Dollar Crusade to Eradicate Polio Come to an End?"

347 **man in New York**: "Why Has Polio Been Found in New York, London and Jerusalem?," CBS News, August 22, 2022, https://www.cbsnews.com/news/polio-in-new-york-london-jerusalem-reveals-rare-risk-of-oral-vaccine/.

347 **"goodies"**: Muraskin, *Polio Eradication and Its Discontents*.

348 **"No matter how much goodwill"**: Muraskin, *Polio Eradication and Its Discontents*.

351 **"surrendered by a donor"**: McGoey, *No Such Thing as a Free Gift*.

355 **give away the majority of their wealth**: "About the Giving Pledge," n.d., https://givingpledge.org/about.

355 **ten thousand workers**: Tiffany Ap, "Jeff Bezos's Plan to Give Away His Fortune Won't Help the 10,000 Workers Amazon Is Planning to Lay Off," Quartz, November 14, 2022, https://qz.com/jeff-bezos-philanthropy-amazon-layoffs-1849781304.

355 **no-strings-attached donations**: Tim Schwab, "Meet MacKenzie Scott, Our New Good Billionaire," *Nation*, July 9, 2021, https://www.thenation.com/article/economy/mackenzie-scott-billionaire-philanthropy/. Note: One of MacKenzie Scott's main philanthropic advisers, Tom Tierney, joined the Gates Foundation's board of trustees in 2021, which illustrates how small the world of Big Philanthropy is. Theodore Schleifer, "MacKenzie Scott, the Amazon Billionaire, Is Giving Away $1 Billion a Month to Charity," Vox, December 15, 2020, https://www.vox.com/recode/2020/12/15/22176710/mackenzie-scott-bezos-philanthropy-speed-four-billion; and "Tom Tierney," Bill & Melinda Gates Foundation, n.d., https://www.gatesfoundation.org/about/leadership/tom-tierney.

355 **Chuck Feeney**: "Chuck Feeney: The Billionaire Who Is Trying to Go Broke," *Forbes*, September 18, 2012, https://www.forbes.com/sites/stevenbertoni/2012/09/18/chuck-feeney-the-billionaire-who-is-trying-to-go-broke/?sh=3a9b8ea9291c.

355 **facing federal fraud charges**: Sam Reynolds, "Team Behind Sam Bankman-Fried's Charity FTX Future Fund Have Quit over Possible 'Deception or Dishonesty,'" *Fortune*, November 11, 2022, https://fortune.com/2022/11/11/team-behind-sam-bankman-fried-charity-ftx-future-fund-have-quit-over-possible-deception-or-dishonesty/; Zeke Faux, "A 30-Year-Old Crypto Billionaire Wants to Give His Fortune Away," Bloomberg, April 3, 2022, https://www.bloomberg.com/news/features/2022-04-03/sam-bankman-fried-ftx-s-crypto-billionaire-who-wants-to-give-his-fortune-away.

355 **teachers' pension plan in Ontario**: David Yaffe-Bellany, Matthew Goldstein, Lauren Hirsch, and Erin Griffith, "FTX Crypto Exchange Boss Says He Is Trying to Raise More Money," *New York Times*, November 10, 2022, https://www.nytimes.com/2022/11/10/technology/ftx-crypto-exchange.html.

355 **FTX Future Fund**: Reynolds, "Team Behind Sam Bankman-Fried's Charity FTX Future Fund Have Quit over Possible 'Deception or Dishonesty'"; Tracy Wang, "Sam Bankman-Fried's Crypto Empire 'Was Run by a Gang of Kids in the Bahamas,'" *Fortune*, November 11, 2022, https://fortune.com/2022/11/11/sam-bankman-fried-crypto-empire-ftx-alameda-run-gang-kids-bahamas-who-all-dated-each-other/.

356 **Bernie Sanders's proposal**: Thomas Kaplan, "Bernie Sanders Proposes a Wealth Tax: 'I Don't Think That Billionaires Should Exist,'" *New York Times*, September 24, 2019, https://www.nytimes.com/2019/09/24/us/politics/bernie-sanders-wealth-tax.html.

357 **"I think billionaires shouldn't exist"**: Mikaela Loach, Twitter, September 22, 2022, https://twitter.com/mikaelaloach/status/1572854129684541440?lang=en.

ACKNOWLEDGMENTS

Bill Gates has been a focus of my reporting since 2018, when I pitched an investigative reporting project on the Gates Foundation and won an Alicia Patterson reporting fellowship. Without that fellowship, I never would have undertaken my first investigation into the Gates Foundation—in 2019—and never would have written this book. Very likely, I wouldn't even be a writer. I owe the Alicia Patterson Foundation a huge debt of thanks.

I would not have received this fellowship if it were not for Linda Jue, who looked at my original pitch and told me she couldn't endorse such a weakly organized project. It was the kick in the pants I needed to refocus and refine my investigation. Linda also later introduced me to the *Nation*, where editor Don Guttenplan championed my reporting on Gates at a time when most news outlets would not consider putting a critical lens to the foundation.

I also thank Don for making an introduction to the Roam Agency, where my book agent, Roisin Davis, deftly negotiated a contract with Metropolitan Books, then oversaw the book's transition to Henry Holt. Roisin also took the time to provide thoughtful comments on my first draft. My first editor, Grigory Tovbis, was a great supporter and believer, and I was sorry to see him leave the project. I thank editor Tim Duggan and his colleagues at Henry Holt for gamely jumping on the train in motion and very effectively steering the project across the finish line.

Sachi McClendon, Paige Oamek, and Finley Muratova fact-checked the book, a herculean task that strengthened the work. Brian Mittendorf patiently answered my questions about the complexities of the IRS tax forms that private foundations file. Ray Madoff also went out of her way to help me understand taxation or point me in the right direction. James Love introduced me to several important sources and provided extensive background on intellectual property. Andrew Noymer provided me with an incisive overview of the Institute for Health Metrics and Evaluation—along with a list of sources to talk to—at a time when investigating something called "health metrics" seemed impossible. Rob Larson provided helpful, thoughtful answers to every question I had about economics. A number of others were especially generous with their time, either answering questions or giving feedback on parts of the book, including Anne Hendrixson, David McCoy, Monica Guerra, Nick Tampio, Manjari Mahajan, Lea Dougherty, and Tim Wise.

As for the actual writing of the book, there are many people I want to thank but cannot name. Many sources I spoke to for this book did so under the condition that they remain anonymous. My book would be greatly diminished without these whistleblowers who contacted me from every corner of the globe, all with some version of the same story: Bill Gates is not at all who he claims to be.

I also wish to thank the many other sources who generously took the time to speak to me—on the record—but whose names don't appear in this book. I reached out to hundreds of people in reporting this book, and tens of thousands of words were cut from my first draft. With those cuts went the voices of many sources.

Finally, I wish to thank the people who have provided moral support that got me to this point. This includes my parents, who have helped me in more ways than I probably know. I thank my brother for endless technical support. I thank Gigi and Som for their many acts of kindness, which allowed me to have some semblance of a writing career during the pandemic. I thank my longtime friend Shane Dillingham, who years ago on a bumpy car ride in Oaxaca hammered home the idea that I could become a writer if I wanted it, then remained a consistent supporter, generously giving feedback on several chapters of this book. The late Sheldon Krimsky collaborated with me early in my career and continued to be a source of important feedback and inspiration. The late

Todd Fisk went out of his way to support my early forays into writing, and he and his spouse, Inga, even helped build a website for me. John Claborn provided important feedback on several chapters, moral support, and high-level brainstorming throughout the production of this book. Writer Robert Fortner has, likewise, been a supportive colleague, offering perspective and patient explanations of the Gates Foundation's work on polio.

While there were many people who helped bring this book to life, it's also true that writing a book is an incredibly lonely task—and also a selfish one. Writing this book took time, attention, and energy away from the most important people in my life, and I have a debt to repay to my family for their endless patience, kindness, and diversions.

INDEX

ABOUT THE AUTHOR

TIM SCHWAB is an investigative journalist based in Washington, DC. His groundbreaking reporting on the Gates Foundation for the *Nation*, *Columbia Journalism Review*, and the *BMJ* has been honored with an Izzy Award and a Deadline Club Award. *The Bill Gates Problem* is his first book.